T0100363

Yunlin Su
Song Y. Yan

Principles of Compilers

A New Approach to Compilers
Including the Algebraic Method

Yunlin Su
Song Y. Yan

Principles of Compilers

A New Approach to Compilers Including the Algebraic Method

With 129 figures

 Springer

Authors
Prof. Yunlin Su
Head of Research Center of Information
Technology Universitas Ma Chung
Villa Puncak Tidar No-01 Malang
Java Timur, Indonesia
E-mail: su.yunlin@machung.ac.id

Prof. Song Y. Yan
Department of Mathematics
Massachusetts Institute of Technology
77 Massachusetts Avenue
Cambridge MA 02139, U.S.A.
E-mail: syan@math.mit.edu

ISBN 978-7-04-030577-7
Higher Education Press, Beijing

ISBN 978-3-642-20834-8   e-ISBN 978-3-642-02835-5
Springer Heidelberg Dordrecht London New York

Library of Congress Control Number: 2011926225

Printed on acid-free paper

Springer is part of Springer Science+Business Media (www.springer.com)

Preface

The compiler is one of the most important aspects of system software. When any computer user develops a computer program, one must use some programming language, rather than using a computer instruction set. This implies that there must be the compiler of the programming language that has been installed on the computer one uses, and otherwise the developed program cannot be run.

There are some differences between a compiler and programming language. Once language is designed, it must be kept unchanged (except when it contains a mistake that has to be corrected), while the techniques for implementing compilation might be changed over time. Hence people always explore the more efficient and more advanced new techniques to raise the quality of compilers.

The course similar to "The principles of Compilers" has become one of the most important courses in computer science within higher institutes. According to our knowledge, the development of compilation techniques evolves in two directions. One is towards the improvement of the compilation techniques for existing languages. Another is towards the research and development of the compilation techniques of new languages. These new languages include object-oriented languages, distributed languages, parallel languages, etc. This book introduces the newest knowledge in the field, and explores the compilation techniques suitable for the languages and computation. It associates the compilation of programming languages with the translation of natural languages in human brains so that the reader can easier understand the principles of compilers. Meanwhile, it introduces the algebraic method of compilation that belongs to formal technology.

This book consists of 16 chapters. Chapter 1, Introduction, outlines the process of compilation and associates the compilation of programming languages with the comprehension and generation of natural languages in human brains. Chapter 2 introduces the grammar and language. The generation of the language is based on the grammar and languages are the fundamentals of the compilation process. Chapter 3 introduces finite automata and regular languages, together with Chapter 4, it is devoted to lexical analysis, the first task of analysis stage. Chapter 3 may be regarded as the theoretical preparation of lexical analysis; while Chapter 4 is the concrete practice of lexical analysis. Chapters 5 – 7 commonly work together to discuss syntactical analysis. Chapter 5 introduces push-down automata that correspond to context-free grammars. Chapter 6 devotes to the discussion of context-free grammars and the context-free languages which they generate. Chapter 7 explores the second task of analytical stage — syntactical analysis. Following this is the semantic analysis. After the analytical stage finishes, the synthetic stage starts. The main task of the synthetic stage is to generate object code. Chapter 8 introduces and analyzes attribute grammars. Chapter 9 introduces a new compilation method — the formal method of compilation. Chapter 10 discusses the generation of the intermediate code. Chapter 11 expatiates the debugging and optimization techniques for compilers. Chapter 12 explicates the memory management that is related to compilation of programs. Chapter 13 is the destination of the compilation, the generation of object code. The chapter introduces the virtual machine MMIX that is proposed by D.E. Knuth in his book *The Art of Computer Programming*. This virtual machine is the mixture of features of 14 most popular machines in the current market, it has rich an instruction set, and makes object codes flexible. Chapters 14 and 15 expound the compilation techniques for object-oriented programming languages and parallel programming languages. Chapter 16 discusses issues for grid computing. Though grid computing has attracted one's attention there is no any language especially suitable for grid computing at the present. Hence, we just focus on its features, pointing out the issues which the compilation of the language should be tackled when the language exists.

We would like to express our sincere appreciation to Ms. Chen Hongying of Higher Education Press. Without her encouragement, help and patience, we could not finish the writing of this book. We also want to thank the authors whose contributions were referred to the book. A great part of the contents of the book is taken from them. We would like to acknowledge Tim Lammertink and Myrte de Vos for their kind help. Finally, we would like to express our gratitude to our family and students for their long-term support and understanding.

No doubt, there might be neglects or mistakes remaining in the book. We hope that the reader would be generous with your criticism.

Yunlin Su
Song Y. Yan
March 2011

Contents

Chapter 1   Introduction

Language allows us to know how octopuses make love and how to remove cherry stains and why Tad was heartbroken, and whether the Red Sox will win the World Series without great relief pitcher and how to build an atom bomb in your basement and how Catherine the Great died, among other things.

Steve Pinker

1.1 Language and Mankind

If you read the text above, you must be engaging in one of the mind's most enchanting process — the way one mind influences another through language. However, we put a precondition on it that you have to know English, otherwise the text has no influence at all to you. There are so many languages in the world that even no one can exactly tell how many there are. Therefore, there is the need of a bridge that connects different languages so that people can understand each other. The bridge is the translation. And the subject of the book is the translation between the formal language and the machine language, or compilation.

What is the compiler or the compilation program? Simply speaking, it is a program of which the function is to translate programs written in a programming language into machine codes that are to be run by the same kind of machine the codes belong to. In order to explain things behind this, we need to discuss it further.

Language is main means of human communication and the way in which most information is exchanged. By language, people link up each other, they express their attentions and feelings, and they describe matters or express their understanding [1]. It is one of the kinds of intelligence or the product of intelligence. However, in the long process of human evolution, there was a long period without language. Gradually, they invented oral language to meet the need of living. Therefore, oral language can be considered as the first breakthrough in language, it was also a breakthrough in human civilization. From oral language to written language, it underwent even longer time. The occurrence of written language represented a more significant breakthrough of human being in terms of languages. Human thinking and problem solving can be conceptualized as processes involving languages. Many, if not most or all, forms of thinking and problem solving are internal, that is, done in the absence of external stimuli. Abstraction of puzzles, for example, into verbal symbols provides a way to think about a solution. It is not difficult to imagine that without language the process of thinking cannot be completed, continued and deepened as if there is no language one simply cannot express his/her ideas to other. When one wants to reminisce, he/she is unable to describe the process that involves many objects and complicated plots. Written language is more powerful than oral language. It not only can link up people at the contemporary era, but also it can link up the present time and the ancient time so that people at the present time can also know things that took place in ancient period. By using written language, people not only can communicate with people in the vicinity, but also contact people at long distance. Especially with the modern communication tools, e.g., computer networks, televisions, and telephones, people may communicate with each other even quicker, more convenient and may make sure the security and secrecy of information. That means that written languages change the extent of time and space of communication of people.

The civilizations of the human being are divided into many branches. Each one is symbolized by different language. Each race or nation formed each own language due to the difference of living locations and evolution conditions. In history, there were several thousands languages. As time passed, many languages, especially the oral languages, that were used only by few people had extinguished. Until now there are still some languages that have only oral versions and have no corresponding written versions. Therefore, the languages that have real impacts and are used by the great throng of peoples are not too many. However, people who use these languages want to share the civilization; they want to cooperate with each other or to do business. Obviously, each language is so different from others that unless one has learnt it otherwise one has no way to understand, and vice versa. Hence, if two different language speakers want to converse with each other, they need a bridge to link them. It is the translation. Its task is to translate a language spoken by A to another language spoken by B and to translate the language spoken by B to a language spoken by A. It is not only necessary to translate the oral language (the translator of colloquial languages is a called interpreter) but also necessary, or even more important to translate the written languages including the works in social science, natural science, novels, etc. Without the translations, people speaking different languages cannot converse, communicate, and exchange their thinking or discoveries. In this sense, we may say that the world is small but the number of languages in the world is far too many.

Today as the rapid development of science and technology and the inevitable tendency of economy globalization happening in almost every country around the world, language translation including colloquial and literal, has become a heated profession. Take as an example for the colloquial translation or interpretation, it involves three persons, i.e., two, A and B. who want to converse with each other for some purpose, and one, C, who helps them with the thing. Suppose that A speaks the language X and B speaks the language Y. Obviously, in order for A and B understanding each other the task of C is to interpret the words of X spoken by A into language Y, meanwhile, he interprets the words of B spoken in Y spoken by B into language X. Therefore, C must be a bilingual in this circumstance. And this situation is shown in Fig. 1.1.

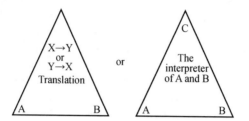

Fig. 1.1 Oral translation.

The role of C sometime needs to be done by two persons, say C or D, is in charge of the interpretation from X to Y or from Y to X.

While in the case of a literal translation, the translator mainly translates a foreign language into his native language for the native readers, or he translates his native language into foreign language to serve the foreign readers. No matter which case it is, the purpose is the same, i.e., to make the listener or reader understanding each other.

1.2 Language and Computer

It is well known that computer is one of the greatest inventions of mankind in the last century. It embodies the newest development of mankind's science and technology. Computer relies on its running to solve problems set by people while the running relies on the program that is composed of a sequence of the instructions in advance from the instruction set of the machine. The instruction set that is used to develop programs can be considered as the language of computer. It acts to follow the sequence of the instructions as if it speaks the language that consists of the sequence. This kind of language consists of the sequence of 0 s and 1 s.

Hence in order to make the computer running and working for peoples, one should develop the program with the purpose of solving intended problem. For doing so one needs to master the instruction set. We do not say that people cannot master the instruction set and develop programs by using it. However, it is really very tedious and cumbersome to "speak" the language to computer; especially it is too much for the common users of the computers. It is something like that one is required to understand the principles of the television and operate the existing components of the television if one wants to watch the television.

When the computer was just invented, there was not any other language to use for running the computer. The instruction set of computer was the unique language which people may use to develop programs. The historical period is called the period of manually programming. The instruction commonly contains the operation code that indicates the operation it performs, the addresses of the data which the operation performs as the control codes. At that time, only very few people were the designers or developers of the computers. For them to build the programs using the instruction set was not a problem though it also entailed them to work hard and spend lots of time. As computers became more and more popular, the users were no longer those who are very familiar with the principles inside the computers, they are just the real user, no different from the users of televisions. They want to freely use the computer to solve their varieties of problems. In this circumstance, no doubt, the machine language became their stumbling block in using computers [2]. In order to break away from the constraints of the machine language, from soon after the invention of computer, people had started searching the solution to the problem. The first step was to replace the operation codes of the instructions to the notations easily mnemonic, e.g., to use ADD to represent addition, SUB to represent subtract, MUL to represent multiplication, and DIV to represent division, or more simply, just to use $+$, $-$, $\times$, and $/$ (or $\div$) to represent the arithmetic operators. Then, they used symbolic addresses to take the place of real binary addresses, etc. Of course the language transformed in this way is no longer computer language, or original computer instruction set, although it basically corresponds to the computer instruction set, and they are completely equivalent. This was the first step that people broke away from computer language. Though it was a minor step, it was crucial. It indicates that people may not be confined by the computer instruction set, they may use more convenient language to develop programs for computers. This kind of languages is called assembly languages. Here the module given above was still suitable. As shown in Fig. 1.2, the left side of the bottom edge of the triangle represents any program written in assembly language which we call the source program, and the right side of the bottom edge is totally equivalent program written in a computer instruction set which was produced by the assembler on the top of the triangle and has the name of the object program or target program. And the assembler plays the role of the compiler of which the duty is to translate the source program into the executable object program written in machine language. Therefore, the assembler must also be executable on computer and by its operation it produces the object program as its output.

Hence the assembler is the early version of the compilers. As the language which source programs used was assembly language, it was only the

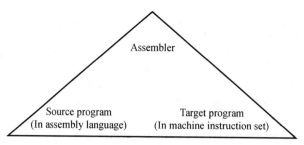

Fig. 1.2 Translation of computer assembly language.

simple adaptation of the machine instruction set (e.g., the operation code was the mnemonic code of the original one). Hence it is also called low-level language. Here the word low means that it is machine-oriented (low-level) and isn't mankind-oriented (high-level). Assembler is also a low-level form of the compilers as it hasn't used much the compilation principles which we used in the compilers for high-level programming languages.

After the success of assembly languages and their assemblers, people started the design of the mankind-oriented high-level programming languages. The common feature of these languages is that they broke away from the restriction of the computer instruction set. They adopted a subset of the commonly used language (in general it is English) and established the grammar to describe the statements or elements which people used to develop the programs. These languages are called procedure-oriented languages or simply procedural languages, or imperative languages. The earliest programming languages include FORTRAN (stands for FORmula TRANslation, it was first designed as early as 1954 [3]), ALGOL 60 [4], COBOL (stands for Common Business Oriented Language, it was first designed in 1959, and its success was strongly influenced by the United States Department of Defense). In terms of the occurrence of the programming languages, the 1960s was stormy. It was said that at that period over two thousand languages were developed, but only thirteen of them ever became significant either in terms of concept or usage. Among them, APL (stands for A Programming Language, developed by Dr. Kenneth Iverson at IBM [5]) is an interactive language. It devises a powerful yet compact notation for computation which incorporated many concepts from mathematics. PL/1 (stands for Programming Language/1) is suitable for scientific computation. With 1 in the name it probably intends to be number one in terms of its great deal of functionality. LISP (stands for List Processing, developed by McCarthy and his co-workers to design a conceptually simple language for handling symbolic expressions with its domain being artificial intelligence) [6]. PROLOG (stands for Programming for Logic) is another effort for use in artificial intelligence. SNOBOL (developed in the mid-1960s at Bell Telephone Laboratory [7]) is a language whose main strength is in processing string data. As the name SIMULA67 indicated that SIMULA was designed in 1967 and had simulation as its major application domain. And it was later refined in CLU, Euclid, and MODULA [8]. GPSS or SIMSCRIPT [9] provided the example that conventional programming languages can and have been augmented so that simulations can be easily described. The later development of the programming languages was the coming of the general-purpose language called ADA [10] in honor of Ada Augusta, Countess of Lovelace, the daughter of the famous poet Byron. She collaborated with Charles Babbage (1792 – 1871) who between 1820 and 1850 designed two machines for computation. One relied on the theory of finite difference and so he called it Difference Engine. The other embodied many of the principles of a modern digital computer and he called this Analytical Engine. Ada, as the collaborator of Charles Babbage, helped him with developing programs for the analytical engine. Therefore she has recently been recognized as the first programmer. The other language that later became very popular is C [11]. It initially was used for writing the kernel of the operating system UNIX.

Apart from few (if any) languages the languages aforementioned basically all are procedure-oriented languages. After the software crisis that took place in the late 1960s, the structured programming method was proposed, and it hastened parturition of Pascal (in honor of French mathematician Pascal, designed by Swiss computer scientist Niklaus Wirth [12]). Another methodology that was proposed to solve the software crisis is the object-oriented software design method, and it caused the production of the object-oriented languages. For example, based upon the C language, C++ was developed. Soon after it Java was also designed based upon C. In addition, SMALLTALK [13] is also of this kind.

As hardware unceasingly develops it also puts forward the new requirements to software. New computer architectures like distributed systems, parallel computer systems, computer networks, etc. all propose new requirements and challenges to computer programming. New languages that meet these needs sequentially come out.

No matter how the languages change, there is one thing unchanged that the source programs written in these languages must be compiled first before they become executable object programs on computers. That is to say that they obey the module as shown in Fig. 1.3.

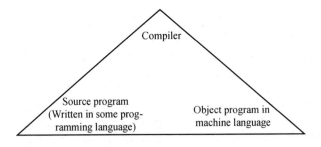

Fig. 1.3 A process of compilation.

In Fig. 1.3, the compiler should be written in machine language. Only by this way can it be executed on computer and translate the source programs into object programs. To write the compiler directly in machine language is not easy, and the work load is conceivably tremendous. Therefore, people thought of using high-level language instead. Then it is compiled by a simpler compiler written in machine language. By the two-run compilation process, the real executable compiler is realized, as shown in Fig. 1.4.

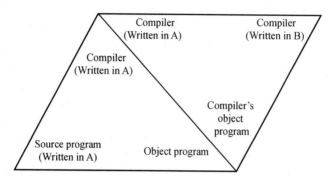

Fig. 1.4 Sequential compilation process.

There are two triangles in Fig. 1.4. At first the second triangle is put to run. After its run, it yields the compiler's object program which in turns to replace the compiler on the top of the first triangle executable. And via its run on computer it also yields the object program that corresponds to the source program. That is what we really need.

The module can be extended further. For example, one uses A language to write the source program, and the compiler is written in B. Obviously the compiler cannot be executed before it is compiled to the machine language. Now the compiler in B can be regarded as a source program. And its compiler is written in C. Once again, the C compiler is taken as a source program. It is compiled by a really executable compiler in machine language.

The sequence of programs works backward. The compiler in machine language first translates the C compiler into an executable compiler. Then by its turn it translates the compiler in B to machine language. Finally by its run it translates the source program into an executable object program.

The process can be extended to any levels. As long as the last level is executable, the backward process can continue to transform the former one to executable and in turn it transforms its former one again until the first level can be run. Then the whole compilation process ends.

In designing a programming language a number of criteria must be kept in mind in order to make the language welcome by users and qualified as a quality language.

1. A well-defined syntactic and semantic description of the programming language is essential

No matter what kind of description tool was used for the description, the goal should be that when a programmer uses the language to design his/her program, the description of the language, including syntactic and semantic, should provide explicit information to let him/her correctly work and just as he/she writes or talks in native language. If the description of the language cannot provide explicit, concise, and comprehensive information, then no one will be interested in using it as everyone must be afraid of meeting trouble in the design of the program. Therefore the well-defined syntactic and semantic description of the language is really, absolutely important.

In terms of use of the natural or native languages, including English and Chinese, they are all not perfect, they all have the problems of ambiguity or confusion. Nevertheless, as human has the higher ability in understanding language in comparison with computers, the problems which people were confronted with are less. However, as for the programming languages which people use to interact with computer, the situation is drastically different. In a programming language, even a minor bug or an ambiguity which people made in their program, the program may not be able to correctly run, or it reports mistakes. The bug of the programming languages sometimes was not easily found. When D. E. Knuth reported the "remaining trouble spots in ALGOL60" [14], it was 1967 after AGOL60 had been published for several years. Obviously, if people happen to use them, they must be wrong. From this example, one may know that it is not easy to realize the goal of well description. This is also why thousands of languages soon disappeared after the programming language storm took place in the 1960s [15]. Time like the great breakers that washed out the sands washed the programming languages that were not qualified in terms of the point.

2. Determinism of program structures

The determinism of program structures is intimately related to the explicit and comprehensive description of the language. With the determinism of the program structures, we mean that any programs in the language have deterministic levels or hierarchy, easily understand and this makes the design, debugging, and modifying easier to carry out. Therefore, the determinism of the structures is different from the description, but they complement each other.

3. Fast translation

This can also be said high efficiency of translation. When programmers design their programs, they must hope that the programs can be translated quickly. As Niklaus Wirth said that "A language that is simple to parse for the compiler is also simple to parse for the human programmer and that can only be an asset."

High efficiency is no doubt an important criterion for appraising the quality of programming languages. Starting from the early stage when people started using programming languages, they had concerned about the efficiency with which they designed programs. Therefore, a high efficiency has wider meaning than fast translation means. There are several implications of the high efficiency.

1) The high efficiency of the execution of programs.

Initially, when talking about high efficiency, almost no exception, it meant the efficiency of the execution of the programs. And this entails the quality of the compiler that compiles the source programs to object programs with the high efficiency of the execution. Therefore, it may involve the design of the optimal compiler, the efficient register allocation, as well as the mechanism design for supporting the running of programs. Though the efficiency of the execution of programs is intimately related to the design of the language, the quality of the compilation by the compiler decidedly affects the efficiency of the execution of the programs.

2) The efficiency of the compilation.

Probably, this point is just consistent with what Wirth expressed. The large-scale productive program means that they frequently run. Hence the saving of even only few minutes is still crucial if the great number of running is taken into account for every day. This is why it becomes an issue which people are concerned with. The issue is related to the quality of the compiler. The other kind of the program is also related to the quality of the compiler. It is the compiler that is in charge of the compilation of student programs or programs used for teaching. Typically, the programs written by students will not be used for production. They were the results of their learning. Only the correctness is concerned. Therefore, we just need to make the compiler working efficiently to compile the program to point out the errors (if any) in the program. Therefore, in this situation the important thing is still the fast translation of the compiler, rather than that compiler can produce the object program with high execution efficiency and optimization.

3) The efficiency of the writing, debugging, and running of the programs.

In terms of the efficiency, the third aspect is that of writing, debugging and running of programs. For example, if we use a language to solve some problems, it turned out that the time spent by the programmer on designing, coding, debugging, modifying, and running of the program was the least and the energy spent by the programmer was also the least. If this really happened it would be most welcome by the programmer or the user of the language. In the practical sense, this is the real standard that measures the efficiency of some language in solving problems on the computer. When using a language to solve problems, one should pursue the efficiency rather than the traditional one which are considered the efficiency of compilation only.

4. Reliability

The so-called reliability means that features should be designed in such a way that syntactic and logical errors are both discouraged and easily discovered. Comments both enhance the comprehensiveness and play a role for the reader of the program to check the correctness of the program. Hence any designer of the language should provide the facility in the language he/she designs. Programmer when designing a program should also make use of the facility to enhance the reliability of the program.

5. Machine independent

High-level programming language is intended to use in a variety of machines, of course, one of its goals is the ability to move the programs from a machine to a machine.

6. Generality

The idea of generality is that all features should be composed of different aspects of a few basic concepts. That also means that related concepts should be unified into a single framework as the class does in the object-oriented language.

7. Extensibility

The reason for taking this as a desirable feature is that translators are usually forced to choose one representation for all objects of a given type and this can be very inefficient. Programming language should allow the extension of itself via simple, natural and elegant mechanism.

Almost every language provides the definition mechanism of subroutine or subprogram. In developing large programs, a great part of the tasks for the programmer can be regarded as the extension of the language as he/she has to make a decision i.e. in order to solve the problem, how should he/she utilize the primitive characteristics to simulate the data structures of the problem. Hence, from the view point of the concept, it is equal to extend the original language to include the structures simulated. Moreover, the hardware environment that has rapidly developed and changed recently also requires the change of software to meet them, especially the parallel computer systems, clusters, distributed computer systems, etc., all require the programming languages that are suitable to them. In the book later we will discuss the computer architecture for explicitly parallel instruction computing (EPIC). It is the extension of the very long instruction word (VLIW). These developments in hardware all require the new programming languages that are suitable their compilers.

8. Provability

It will be desirable that when a program is developed, there is also a mechanism to carry out the verification of the program. Is there a formal definition of all features of the language? If it is so, this will permit formal verification of programs. However, the cost of the process of formal verification is very high, either unaided or aided by machine, and requires a high-level mathematical sophistication. It seems that as though this goal may never be completely achieved, it continues to be worth striving for.

9. Consistency with commonly used notations

People usually get used to some notations. If they are changed in a newly designed language, people must feel inconvenient and hard to accept the new notations. For example, the operator + that is predefined to work on integers, reals, and mixed integers, and real arguments, may be extended by the programmer to work on complex numbers and matrices, etc. But if it is replaced by other notations, people will not be happy to use it.

These nine criteria are the guidelines for creating a successful programming language design. However, people discover that the best designed language unnecessarily satisfies all the guidelines. The "go to" statement is such an example. In the early created languages, almost no exception, all set up the statement to realize the transfer of the control.

In order for programs not only able to be executed sequentially, but also able to transfer, the initial motivation of setting "go to" statement was not wrong. However, in practice, the misuse of the "go to" statement may really cause problems. This was why Edgar Dijkstra published the famous letter, accusing that the "go to" statement is harmful. He proposed that the "go to" statement should be removed from the programming language. His opinion initiated a long-term debate on whether the "go to" statement should be removed or not. Later in 1974, D. E. Knuth [16] made a thoughtful argument to end the debate. He pointed out that though the "go to" statement is a statement which is easily misused, banishing it from the language repertoire seems like a too severe form of surgery. From the debate, an idea of programming methodology gradually became explicit, it was the structured programming. PASCAL was the representative of the structural programming languages. Then MODULA, C and ADA were also the products under the effect of the methodology.

The so-called software crisis reflected the serious problems in the development of software, e.g., the quality of the software couldn't be guaranteed. There were too many bugs hiding in the code and the development life period was always suspended. It forced people to search for the solution. Then another approach was proposed. It is the object-oriented programming. The languages that correspond to this method are object-oriented programming languages, as we have mentioned, SMALLTALK, C++, and JAVA belong to the category.

The occurrences of network environment, distributed environment and parallel computers have put forward the new thinking of parallel and distributed programming. Definitely, these require the languages for doing so.

1.3 Compilation of Programming Languages

From the discussion above, we have known that the programs written in high-level programming languages need to be compiled before they can run or executed on computer. Therefore, to write programs is something like that the communications between two persons need a third person to translate. In the process, people are concerned about the efficiency — the execution of programs. In practice, the focuses or goals may be varied. If the goals are different, the result may also be different. For example, in the course of compilers, in view of the nature of the course, we are naturally concerned about the compilers. The goals of compilers may be followings:

1. To develop the compiler as small as possible

According to the energy saving principle, of course we will take it as our goal to produce a compiler as small as possible. In other words, it is all right as long as it can handle basic tasks of compilation. Such a compiler, however, may not be complete, as it may not be able to handle sophisticate situations. The possible case that corresponds to the situation may be the subset of the language. It just considers the basic elements of the language, rather than the whole language. This kind of compilers may be taken as the project of students with the purpose of providing training practice to students. For training students to master the basic skills of the compilers, this kind of compilers may play well but in practical applications they are far from complete and unqualified to fulfill the practical task of compilation.

2. To create a compiler that possesses the better ability of diagnosis and recovery from failures

A compiler should be able to discover the errors within the source programs written by the users, not only static errors, but also dynamic errors. After the error is found, it should also determine the source of the error, sequentially it presents the hint for correction. Only such kind of compilers can be considered as user-friendly. It is also very helpful for users to guarantee the correctness of the programs. However, it does not guarantee that the object programs produced must be efficient. This kind of compilers is suitable for the teaching environment as its ability of compilation and hinting is instructive for students. It belongs to the so-called dirty compiler category. It can also be used as the preliminary compiler, after which the clean or optimized compiler may work again on the source programs and produce the optimized object programs with high efficiency.

3. To produce the compiler that will compile flexible and efficient object programs

Based upon producing correct object programs from source programs, the compiler requires that the object programs have higher efficiency. Therefore, apart from the compilation, the compiler also implements the optimization of object programs.

If we pay attention to the process by which the object programs are yielded or to the final product — object programs, the possible goals can be as follows.

1) The time spent by the compiler to translate the source program is the least. If this is the goal, we must require that the speed of compilation of the source program and confirmation of correctness of the source program is fastest, and it uses the fastest speed again to generate the object program. As for the efficiency of the object program, it is not its business and out of its consideration.

2) The object program which the compiler generates is most efficient. It is contrast to the first one as its focus is the efficiency of the object program rather than the speed or efficiency of the compilation.

3) The size of the object program which the compiler generates should be smaller. Notice that 2) was concerned about the time efficiency, here it is concerned about the space efficiency. Therefore, the two are not equivalent. Of course, in general, the shorter the program is, the faster it runs. However, it is not always like this. For example, the program may be short, but it contains lots of loops, then it may be time-consuming. Hence the goal here is pursued mainly from the space which the object program occupies. If the memory space of the computer is limited, it may consider this as the goal.

From the discussion above, we can see that the goals of writing compilers may be a variety, and it is impossible to require that the compilers written by different groups of people or written for different purposes simultaneously meet all the same requirements. As for developing other systems, we can only realize the compromise of the different goals. Now we focus on the compiler and the compilation process. For the compiler, as its specific goal is to translate programs written in some language into the target language of a kind of computers, the compiler is used to establish the correspondence between the two sides — the source language and the computer. In other words, for a programming language and a kind of computers, there needs a compiler for the language that runs on the computer. If there are m programming languages and n computer systems, according to the correspondence between the language and computer given above, we need to develop $m \times n$ compilers. Of course, this is not the case that we look for as it implies a tremendous work load. In order to reduce the work load, the approach we take is to find out in the compiler which part is computer-related and which part is computer independent. For those computers independent parts, we make them shared by all compilers. Only for those computer related, we direct at the different computer to design the corresponding parts of the compiler separately. Just out of the reason, the compiler we developed is not written directly in the computer instruction set as only in this way, instead it can be unrelated to the specific computer. The works that need to relate to the specific computer should be suspended as late as possible (for example, let it happen when the compiler is really working for compilation, rather than when it was developed). By the effort, the number of the compilers for m languages and n computers may be reduced from $m \times n$ to $m + n$. Here we just briefly introduce the idea, we will expound it in details later in the book.

Further we will explain the working principles of the compilers. We begin our discussion with general languages. When we study a language, no matter it is native language or foreign language, the first we should study is the words, i.e., the individual words to stand things. It includes the spelling, the writing, the pronunciation, etc. Then we study the grammar with which the individual words may be linked together to form a meaningful sentence with correct grammar. As for the compiler, its working process contains two phases, the analysis phase and the synthetic phase. The analytical phase includes two parts again: lexical analysis and syntactic analysis. Lexical analysis starts from the input of the source program. The input of the source program is considered as the input of the character stream. The lexical analysis has to differentiate the words in sentences, they include identifiers, constants, key words, variable names, operators, punctuation symbols, etc. At the time, it has also to check the correctness of the spelling or writing of the words. Only when they all are correct, may the next analysis, i.e., the syntactic analysis be called on. And in order for syntactic analysis easier to work, all the characters in the input form should be transformed into the intermediate code form. In this aspect, it is somehow similar to the product of language understanding in mind. The question now is that in order for the neural system in our brain to process the utterances, what representations result in memory when listeners understand utterances or texts? What, for example, would be stored in memory when you hear "The kid is on the bed"? Research has suggested that the meaning representation begins with basic units called propositions [17, 18]. Propositions are the main ideas of utterance. They are a kind of the intermediate code form easy to process and produce the understanding. For "The kid is on the bed", the main idea is that something is on something else. When one reads the utterance, he/she will extracts the proposition on and understand the relationship which it expresses between the kid and the bed. Often propositions are written like this: On (kid, bed). Many utterances contain more than one position. Consider "The dog watches the kid playing on the ground board". We have as the first component proposition On (kid, ground board). From that, we build up

```
Playing (kid, On (kid, ground board))
```

Finally we get to

```
Watch (dog, Playing (kid, On (kid, ground board)))
```

The intermediate code form makes every language unit having the same format which we call token. They are linked together to represent the original sentence.

The syntactic analysis takes the token sequence as input, then it analyzes each sentence based upon the grammar of the programming language. If after this, it did not find any error in the program (sentence sequence),it further transforms the source program into the intermediate code representation again so that the sequential synthetic phase may work on the representation and transform it into the target program. Hence the working process may be shown in Fig. 1.5.

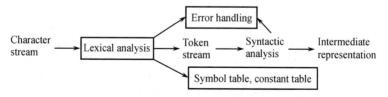

Fig. 1.5 Working process of syntactic analysis.

The symbol table of Fig. 1.5 represents the structure in which for each identifier a record is contained. As for the constant table, it represents the structure in which for each constant a record is contained. In the symbol table, apart from the identifier and the address that allocates to it (but it is not the real memory address, it is only a relative address), it also contains the segments for its various attributes. This kind of the data structure may accelerate the searching of the record of every identifier, and it can also accelerate the store of the identifier into the record or the retrieval of the identifier from it. Upon the lexical analysis in working, when it meets an identifier for the first time, if the lexical analysis confirms that it is an identifier, it is called the definition occurrence of the identifier. Then the later occurrence is called the application occurrence. As the definition occurrence appears, the compiler puts it to the symbol table, and allocates an address to it according to the order it occurred, the allocated address is also stored in the table. Meanwhile, based on the definition or declaration for it made by the source program, the relative attributes are also put into the table. On the application occurrence, the identifier is transformed to intermediate form according to the record obtained from the definition occurrence, and it is also needed to check whether the attributes implied in the application occurrence are consistent with that of the definition occurrence. If they are not consistent, the lexical analysis will consider that there is an error there.

The constant table is similar to the symbol table. For a constant, lexical analysis first needs to transform each character that represents the digit (If the constant represents a signed integer, it may contains a symbol + or −. If it is a real or a float number, it may also contains +, −, decimal point, and exponential symbol.) into corresponding numeric value. In the process, it is also required to check whether it is correct or not. After the correctness is confirmed then the constant is put in the constant table, and the address is assigned to it as well as its attributes are put into the table.

For more concrete details of the symbol table and constant table, we will further explain them later in the book.

The error handling may be carried out in both lexical analysis phase and syntactic analysis phase, even in the later synthetic stage (including semantic analysis). Actually, usually the lexical analysis and syntactic analysis may handle the majority of the errors detected by the compiler. The errors that can be found by lexical analysis include such errors as that the input characters cannot be linked to form any symbol of the language; while the errors that usually can be found by the syntactic analysis include such errors as that the token stream violates the grammar rules or structural rules of the language. During the semantic stage, the compiler intends to detect the following construction: it is correct in syntactic structure, but it simply has no meaning in the operation concerned. For example, we want to perform the additional operations of two identifiers, but one identifier may be the name of an array while the other is the name of a procedure. The error handling should not stop the working of the compiler after it discovers an error so that it can continue the compilation and continue to find out more errors (if any). Definitely, the user prefers knowing more errors in his/her program to only knowing an error.

We have outlined the analytical stage in the preceding part. As we mentioned before, for the complete compilation process, after the analytical stage has been finished, the next stage will be synthetic stage, the tasks of which may be divided into the generation of the intermediate code, the optimization of the code and the generation of code. Fig. 1.6 shows the process.

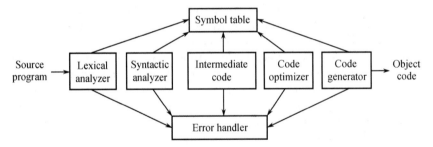

Fig. 1.6 Working process of compiler.

The intermediate code may be considered as a program of abstract machine. This intermediate code should be easy to generate, at the same time it should also be easy to translate to the object code.

The intermediate code may have several forms. A more popular one is the form of three addresses in which the program is expressed as the sequence of instructions and each at most has three operands as shown in the following expression:

$$id_1 := id_2 + id_3$$

or

$$id_1 \leftarrow (+id_2, id_3).$$

The intermediate code forms also have several properties. At first, apart from assignment (i.e., the value of right-hand side is assigned to left-hand side), each three-address instruction has at most one operator. Therefore, when the instruction is formed, the compiler must decide the order of operation, for example, the multiplication or division should be performed before addition or subtract. Second, the compiler should generate a temporal name for storing the value which each instruction calculates. Third, some three-address instruction may have the operands less than three. As for more details about the generation of the intermediate code we will introduce later in the book.

The code optimization stage intends to improve the intermediate code in order to produce the machine code that may run faster. The optimization may be divided into local optimization and global optimization. The local optimization in general is simpler, for example, some instructions are combined into one instruction so that the number of instructions in the program reduces. The global optimization involves the modification of the algorithm of the program. The amount of the code optimization implemented by different compilers may vary remarkably; the time consumed may be different too. For example, in comparison to other compilers some optimized compiler may spend most time on optimization. However, there are also some other compilers that only briefly perform optimization, they may also remarkably reduce the running time of the object code while the compilation time was not so much.

The task of the object generation stage is simply to generate the object code. Usually the object codes consists of the assembly code or the relocatable machine codes. For every variable which the source program uses, memory unit for storing is needed. Then each intermediate instruction is translated into the machine instructions that equally perform the same task. Thus the machine code is yielded. However, there is also a key task for code generation, that is the allocation of registers to variables as the allocation may speed up the operation of the computer.

1.4 Number of Passes of Compiler

Before we start our discussion, we have to introduce the term scanning or pass first. Scanning means the whole process of reading or passing the source program from very beginning to its end. Obviously, in order to implement the compilation of the source program it is absolutely necessary to scan the program once from its beginning to its end. Without doing so for the whole program, how can the compiler collect all information of the program? Hence for any compiler, scanning the source program at least once is the must. If the scanning of the program can be done backward and forward repeatedly, one pass is enough. We do not allow to do so as we want a thing to be regular.

For a certain compiler one pass is enough for it to implement the compilation of the source programs. For those languages in which the definition occurrence of the identifiers precedes the applied occurrences of the identifiers it is the case, while for others it may need more than two passes.

In practice, there are many ways that arrange various stages of the compiler into one pass (in one pass it may involve a stage or a number of stages of the compiler. In reverse, a number of stages that are consecutive may be put into one pass, of course they may also be put into separate passes.) Usually one pass exclusively assigned for a stage (e.g., the lexical stage or syntactic stage) has its advantages, as in this way the tasks of the compiler may be assigned to different groups or different individuals. This is consistent with the principle of software engineering. It is also feasible that a number of stages are combined in one pass, for example, one pass may be composed of the lexical analysis, syntactic analysis, semantic analysis and intermediate code generation. If it is the case, then the token stream formed by lexical analysis may be directly translated into the intermediate code and the activities of these stages within the pass may be carried out interlacingly. We may consider the syntactical analysis as one that assumes main responsibility, it intends to find out the grammar structure of the tokens which have been seen. It gets the next token by calling the lexical analysis. As the grammar structure of the token stream was found, the syntactic analysis calls the intermediate code generator to perform the semantic analysis and generate the intermediate code.

To divide compiler stages into a number of passes is beneficial to the division of the compilation work. However, it does not mean that the more the pass number is, the better. A reasonable idea is to have less pass number — the less, the better, as it must take time to read and write the intermediate file. On the other hand, however, if many stages were put into one pass, it is likely to store the whole program in the memory as one stage may need the information obtained in other stage. In this case the compiler may require much larger memory space than it really needs. Therefore it causes serious problem for the memory space. To put a number of stages into one pass can also cause other problems. For example, the interface between the lexical analysis and the syntactic analysis may be confined to a token, and then it is equal to set up a bottleneck for their running. On the other hand, it is usually very difficult to perform code generation before the intermediate code is completely generated.

Therefore, it is not necessarily efficient to put some stages into one pass, and it would be rather better to put them in different scans. If we adopt the so-called post patching-up technique, however, it is feasible to put the intermediate code and the target code generation together. By means of assembler, the so-called post patching-up technique is as follows. Suppose that we have an assembler with two passes. The first pass is aimed at discovering all the identifiers that represent memory units, and when the identifier is found, its memory address is derived. Then in the second pass, the memory address will replace the identifier. In summary, to make compiler with fewer numbers of passes is proper as it will avoid multiple times of the input and output of intermediate files. However, if some works are really necessary to be divided into different passes, it will be no good at all to grudgingly combine them together as this will cause unnecessary problems or difficulties.

1.5 An Example of Compilation of a Statement

In this section, we will illustrate the working principles of the compiler by the compilation of a statement.

Example Suppose that the capital is a, and it is stored in the bank with compound interest rate r. How much will be the amount of the sum of the capital and the interest? Write a program that computes the amount. Suppose the time period is n.

So we denote a as the sum of the capital and interest and initialize it as 1. Then the formula that computes the amount is as follows:

$$a := (1+r)^n \times a$$

The corresponding program that computes the amount is as follows:

$$\text{var } n : \text{int},$$
$$a, r : \text{real},$$
$$a := 1,$$

i.e.,

$$a := (1+r) \uparrow n \times a.$$

The compilation of the statement begins with the input of the character stream that constitutes the program. Then the lexical analysis works first. It transforms the characters into tokens. It confirms that var, int, real all are key words of the language, and n, a, r are identifiers. The identifier n has the attribute of integer while a, r have the attribute of real number. There is also a constant 1 that is integer. By this assumption, the symbol table and constant table are shown in Tables 1.1 and 1.2.

Table 1.1 Symbol table

Symbol name	Intermediate code	Attribute
n	id_1	int
a	id_2	real
r	id_3	real

Table 1.2 Constant table

Constant value	Intermediate code
1	c

With symbol table, we can draw the process of the compilation of the statement according to the compilation process given in Fig. 1.6. Since there is no error in the program we omit the error handling part.

In Fig. 1.7, for the sake of simplicity, we use EXP in place of the exponent operation id1↑ n.

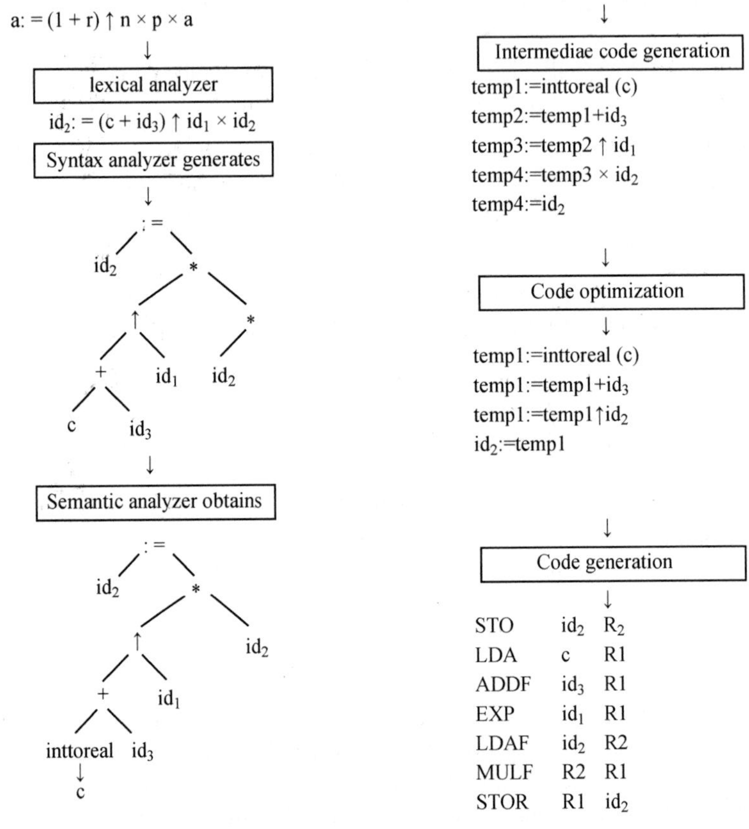

Fig. 1.7 An example of compilation process of source program.

In the practical computer, in general, the exponential instruction is not directly provided, but usually it provides the macro-instruction of the exponential computation. In the intermediate code generation, we have used 5 assignment instructions. In the code generation, the number is not changed and the number of instruction used is not reduced. However, the number of the temporal memory units is reduced from 4 to 1. Therefore, the optimization of the programs can be either the decrease of the number of instructions or the number of memory units used, or both.

1.6 Organization of the Book

As a monograph on compiler principles, our intention is to bring the reader to the front of the field, including the principles of the compilers for distributed and parallel programming as well as the ideas of compilation for grid computing. So far, the authors found that many books on compilers seldom dealt with these topics though more and more computer systems were designed with these principles. And the books on compilers left a gap between the need and the reality. That makes the students who studied compiler principles have no idea about how should the two kinds of languages be handled with compilation. To teach the students with obsolete materials is no good at all for them, no matter how these materials are disguised as useful things. In addition we intend to use the concise and explicit language as possible as we can to cover the necessary knowledge of compilers. In our introduction, we also encourage the reader to exert his/her creative thinking to supplement the details of the compilation. As the title of the book indicates, it just provides the principles instead of details. In this way, we provide the broader way to the reader to enhance himself/herself.

Chapter 2 focuses on grammars and languages. Starting from Chapter 2, at the beginning of each chapter, we first introduce the motivation of studying the chapter. In this way, we want the reader having the purpose of the study in mind. Therefore, he/she will not be blind when the study starts. Both grammars and languages are the fundamentals of the programming as the design of any programming language is based upon them. The syntactic analysis stage is carried out by contrasting to the grammar of the language.

Chapter 3 expounds the finite state automata (or briefly finite automata, FA) and regular expressions. The automata theory which we discuss is the design tool of the compiler. It is an essential tool of the lexical analysis. The compiler design has become a rather mature branch of computer science, rather than ad hoc or contrived one. It is done under the guideline of the theory for finite automata.

Chapter 4 discusses the lexical analysis. The lexical analysis is intimately related to the topics of Chapter 3.

Chapter 5 further introduces the pushdown automata (PDA) that is the extension of the finite state automata. We introduce two kinds of pushdown automata with acceptance by final state and empty stack. We also describe the properties of the pushdown automata.

Chapter 6 focuses on the context-free grammars, i.e., Type 2 grammars. We explore the characteristics of these grammars as well as their relations with pushdown automata. This is the preparation for discussion on syntactic analysis.

Chapter 7 is with the subject of syntactic analysis. It may be seen as one of the kernels of compilers. We deeply discuss the top-down syntactic analysis and bottom-up syntactic analysis techniques. Both techniques are still in use and dominate over the syntactic analysis domain. For the top-down syntactic analysis, we first introduce the LL(1) analytic technique, including definition of LL(1) grammars, properties of LL(1) grammars, and decision of whether a given grammar is or not an LL(1) grammar. If it is not an LL(1) grammar, it may be feasible to transform it into LL(1). We also provide the may of the transformation Finally, we introduce the implementation of the LL(1) syntactic analysis. Sequentially, we devote almost the same pages to discuss the LR(1) of bottom-up syntactic analysis in which we explain LR(0), SLR(1), LALR(1), and LR(1) one by one. Then the implementation of the technique is also given.

Chapter 8 deals with the attribute grammars and their analysis. This is the supplement of the analysis for the context-free grammars. The programming languages mainly contain the characteristics of the context-free grammars but they also contain small part that is not context-free. The attribute grammars direct at the analysis of the part.

Chapter 9 introduces an algebraic method for compiler design. This chapter may be seen as one of the high lights of the book. As far as we know, there are very rare books on compilers that contain the content. We do so because we believe that the algebraic method is not only useful for the design, it will also be popular in the future.

Chapter 10 discusses the generation of the intermediate code. In this chapter, we introduce some kinds of the intermediate languages that are commonly used.

Chapter 11 deals with the issues on debugging and optimization. In this chapter, a variety of ways for checking errors are discussed. The aim is simply for eliminating these errors before the program is translated to the object program. As for optimization, we provide the approaches to local optimization and global optimization.

Chapter 12 deals with the issues on storage management. As some books pointed out that the storage management does not belong to the category of compilers, it should belong to that of operating systems. It is the operating system that is in charge of the management of the storage. On the other hand, no compiler is not concerned about the allocation of its symbol table, its constant table, its object code as well as its source program, etc. Therefore, in this way it is very natural that we have to discuss the issues on the storage management.

Chapter 13 is the final issues on the compilers of procedural languages, and the generation of the object code. The unique feature of the chapter is that we adopt the MMIX machine as the target machine. In our point of view, it is better to use a pseudo machine like MMIX than any specific machine as MMIX is claimed to be the representative of the machines in the 21st century while any specific machine will definitely be obsolete in the next few years.

Chapters 14 – 16, under the titles of compilation of object-oriented languages, compilation of parallel languages, and compilation of grid computing, discuss the issues regarding the compilation of these new kinds of languages or computing. These are frontiers of compilers. If any new book or monograph on the field does not involve on these topics, it is hard to regard really as the book on the field any more, or it can only be regarded as an obsolete book on the field. However, as these fields are still growing, not mature at all, we can only introduce the state of the art of current level.

Problems

Problem 1.1 For the compilation of programming languages, why are the two phases — analysis and synthesis necessary? For the translation of natural languages, what phase do you consider important?

Problem 1.2 From the design of programs, expound the necessity of languages for thinking.

Problem 1.3 According to your understanding of the text, analyze and compare the pros and cons of single-pass and multi-pass scanning technique.

References

[1]   Pinker S (1994) The language instinct: How the mind creates language. Morrow, New York.

[2]   Ritchie DM et al (1978) The C programming language. Bell Syst Tech J, 57, 6, 1991–2020.

[3]   Backus JW et al (1957) The FORTRAN automatic coding system. Proc Western Jt Comp Conf AIEE (now IEEE) Los Angles.

[4]   Naur P (ed) (1963) Revised report on the algorithmic language ALGOL 60. Comm ACM 6(1): 1–17.

[5]   Iverson K (1962) A programming language. Wiley, New York.

[6]   McCarthy J et al (1965) LISP 1.5 programmer's manual, 2nd edn. MIT Press, Cambridge.

[7]   Farber DJ et al (1964) SNOBOL, a string manipulation language. JACM, 11(1): 21–30.

[8]   Wirth N (1977) MODULA, a language for modular programming. Softw Prac Exp. 7: 3–35.

[9]   Kiviat P et al (1969) The SIMSCRIPT II programming language. Prentice Hall. Englewood Cliffs.

[10] Wirth N (1971) The programming language pascal. Acta Inf, 1(1): 35–63.

[11] Knuth DE (1964) The remaining trouble spots in ALGOL 60. Comm ACM, 7(5): 273–283.

[12] Sammet J (1969) Programming Languages: History and fundamentals. Prentice Hall, Englewood Cliffs.

[13] Goldberg et al (1980) Smalltalk-80: The language and its implementation. Addison-Wesley, Boston.

[14] Horowitz E (1983) Fundamentals of programming languages. Springer, Berlin.

[15]   United States Department of Defense (1980) The Ada Language Reference Manual, Washington D. C.

[16]   Knuth DE (1974) Structured programming with GOTO statement. Comp Surveys, 6(4): 261 – 301.

[17]   Clark HH, Clark EV (1977) Psychology and language; An introduction to psycholinguistics. Harcourt Brace Jovanovich, New York.

[18]   Kintsch W (1974) The representation of meaning in memory. Hillsdale, Erlbaum.

Chapter 2   Grammars and Languages

*To explain how children acquire meanings, we charac-
terized children as scientists whose hypotheses are constrained by innate principles. We can use the same anal-
ogy to describe how children acquire the rules by which
units of meaning are combined into larger units — in
other words, grammar.*

Richard J. Gerrig, Philip G. Zimbardo

2.1 Motivation of the Chapter

From the development of the mankind language, the language itself was created first without the establishment of the grammar. As the knowledge of
mankind enriched and developed, the grammar was created to help the study
of the language and to make the language normalized. As any native language
is very complicate and the grammar was founded after the language, no matter what language is, not any grammar can totally describe the phenomena
of the language. In addition, there exist ambiguities in the native languages.
For the human being, in general, these phenomena of ambiguities can be
handled by human themselves. For computers, however, it is hard for them
to accept and even to understand ambiguity. Programming languages are different from native languages in that the generation of the language is almost
at the same time. The the purpose of the grammar is to help the users of the
language to avoid any ambiguity and to express the meaning correctly. The
program should be correctly written in order to be run on computer with
correct results. Therefore, the research on compilers should be started with
the discussion on the relation between grammars and languages.

2.2 Preliminary Knowledge

Definition 2.1   Character. Commonly used Latin alphabet, Arabic numerals, punctuation symbols, arithmetic operators, Greek alphabet, etc. all are characters. For character, as for the point in geometry, we do not further define it. We suppose that it is well known common sense. In the following or in the future, we just use the lower case to denote the character while the Latin alphabet is used for character list.

Definition 2.2 Alphabet. The finite set of the characters. In general, if the Latin alphabet is taken as the alphabet, then the upper case is used for the purpose. For example, we have A = {a, b, c, 1, 2}.

Definition 2.3 Character String. Any string that consists of 0 or more characters is called a string. The string that consists of 0 character is called an empty string. It is denoted as "ε". It indicates that there is no any character in the string. If A is defined as an alphabet as aforementioned, then a, 1, 1a, abc, 1ba,..., all are the character strings over A or briefly strings. Usually strings are denoted as Greek letters as α, β etc.

Definition 2.4 The operations on strings. Given A = {a, b, c, 1, 2}, the strings over A are determined. There are three kinds of the operations over the strings.

    1) Concatenation or juxtaposition. For example, a and 1 are strings, then a1 and 1a are concatenation or juxtaposition of them. In general, if α and β are strings, then $\alpha\beta$ and $\beta\alpha$ are strings too.

    2) Disjunction or selecting one operation. If α and β are strings, $\alpha \mid \beta$ represents that selecting one from the two, the result is still a string. Obviously, the operation satisfies the commutative law, i.e., $\alpha \mid \beta = \beta \mid \alpha$.

    3) Closure. Given a string α, we can define the closure operation as follows.

$$\begin{aligned} \alpha^* &= \varepsilon \mid \alpha \mid \alpha\alpha \mid \alpha\alpha\alpha \mid \ldots \\ &= \varepsilon \mid \alpha^1 \mid \alpha^2 \mid \alpha^3 \mid \ldots. \end{aligned} \tag{2.1}$$

This is also called the Kleene closure. We can also define positive closure as follows,

$$\begin{aligned} \alpha^+ &= \alpha \mid \alpha\alpha \mid \alpha\alpha\alpha \mid \ldots \\ &= \alpha \mid \alpha^2 \mid \alpha^3 \mid \ldots. \end{aligned} \tag{2.2}$$

The introduction of closure operations makes it possible that finite number of strings or even a string may become the infinite number of strings. For a finite set of strings A = {α, β, γ}, it may be regarded as A = ($\alpha \mid \beta \mid \gamma$), hence

$$\begin{aligned} A^* &= \varepsilon \mid A \mid A^2 \mid A^3 \mid \ldots \\ &= \varepsilon \mid (\alpha \mid \beta \mid \gamma) \mid (\alpha \mid \beta \mid \gamma)(\alpha \mid \beta \mid \gamma) \mid (\alpha \mid \beta \mid \gamma)(\alpha \mid \beta \mid \gamma)(\alpha \mid \beta \mid \gamma) \mid \ldots. \end{aligned} \tag{2.3}$$

Similarly, we can also define

$$A^+ = A \mid A^2 \mid A^3 \mid \ldots$$
$$= (\alpha \mid \beta \mid \gamma) \mid (\alpha \mid \beta \mid \gamma)(\alpha \mid \beta \mid \gamma) \mid (\alpha \mid \beta \mid \gamma)(\alpha \mid \beta \mid \gamma)(\alpha \mid \beta \mid \gamma) \mid \ldots .$$

$$(2.4)$$

From Eqs $(2.1)-(2.4)$, we may get

$$\alpha^* = \varepsilon \mid \alpha^+ \tag{2.5}$$
$$A^* = \varepsilon \mid A^+. \tag{2.6}$$

We need to point out the difference between empty string ε and empty set $\varnothing$. Empty string is a string without any character inside while empty set is a set without any element. The two things share a fact that both contain nothing. But they are different as one has no character in it and another has no element (it may be characters or something else). For set, we may also define its closure.

Definition 2.5 The closure of set. Let $A = \{a, b, c\}$ be a set. The closure operation of set A is defined as

$$A^* = \varepsilon \cup A \cup AA \cup AAA \cup \ldots$$
$$= \varepsilon \cup A \cup A^2 \cup A^3 \cup \ldots \tag{2.7}$$

Similarly, we have

$$A^+ = A \cup A^2 \cup A^3 \cup \ldots \tag{2.8}$$

What we get in this way is still a set, but it can be regarded as string too, the set of strings.

Definition 2.6 Regular expression. Given a set, e.g., $A = \{a, b, c\}$. The regular expression over A is defined as:

1) The element in A is regular expression.

2) If p, q are regular expressions, then after the following operation the result is still a regular expression:

(1) concatenation, i.e., pq, pp, and qq;

(2) disjunction, i.e., p | q or q | p;

(3) closure, i.e., p* or q*.

3) Return to 2), start from the regular expressions obtained by 1) or 2), repeatedly perform the operations in 2), what we get all are regular expressions.

2.3 Grammar

Definition 2.7 Formal grammar. According to linguist Noam Chomsky [1], a grammar is a quadruple $G = (V_N, V_T, P, S)$, where

- V_N is a set of nonterminals. In general, we denote them as upper case letters (e.g., A, B, C). The so-called nonterminal means that it may appear at the left hand side of the productions to be explained soon, and it may derive the terminals or nonterminals at the right hand side of productions.
- V_T is a set of terminals. In general, we use lower case letters to denote the element of the terminal set (e.g., a, b, c, etc.) The so-called terminal means that there is no thing that can be derived from it, and it cannot appear alone on the left hand side of productions. Here we have $V_N \cup V_T = \varnothing$, that is that they are disjunctive, or they have no common element.
- S is a start or distinguished symbol, $S \in V_N$.
- P is a set of productions (or rules). The production is as following

$$\alpha \to \beta, \tag{2.9}$$

where α is called the left part of the production while β is called the right part, and

$$\alpha \in (V_N \cup V_T)^+,$$
$$\beta \in (V_N \cup V_T)^*.$$

That means that α is a nonempty string that consists of terminals and nonterminals, while β is a string that also consists of terminals and nonterminals but it may be empty.

Notice that the left part of productions cannot consist of terminals alone as we have mentioned that terminal cannot be used for derivation.

Definition 2.8 Derivation. Given a grammar $G = (V_N, V_T, P, S)$, a derivation means the following step:

If

$$\alpha \to uwTvx \tag{2.10}$$

is a production in P, where u, w, v, x $\in (V_N \cup V_T)^*$, and

$$T \to y \cup z \tag{2.11}$$

is another production in P, then T in Eq. (2.10) may be replaced by the right part of Eq. (2.11) and Eq. (2.10) now becomes

$$\alpha \to uw(y \cup z)vx. \tag{2.12}$$

This is a derivation step in G.

For a grammar, derivation is the only kind of operations. In general, the first derivation starts with the production of which the left part is the start symbol. Then the nonterminal within the right part of the production is replaced by the right part of the production of which the left part is the nonterminal. It is just like we did from Eqs. (2.10) and (2.11) to get Eq. (2.12). The process will continue until finally there is no any nonterminal again in the string obtained.

Definition 2.9 Rightmost derivation. In the productions of the grammar, if in the right part of the production to be used for derivation, there are more than one nonterminals, then the derivation is carried out for the rightmost nonterminal. If all the derivations are carried out with the rule, then it is called rightmost derivation.

Definition 2.10 Leftmost derivation. In the productions of the grammar, if in the right part of the production to be used for derivation, there are more than one nonterminals, then the derivation is carried out for the leftmost nonterminal. If all the derivations are carried out with the rule, then it is called leftmost derivation.

Definition 2.11 Grammar hierarchy. Chomsky divides the grammars into four types — Type 0, Type 1, Type 2, and Type 3.

We now explain these grammars separately.

Definition 2.12 Type 0 grammars. Within the grammar $G = (V_N, V_T, P, S)$ for the productions with the form $\alpha \to \beta$, where $\alpha = \phi A \psi$, where ϕ and ψ are arbitrary strings in $(V_N \cup V_T)^*$ (empty string is allowable) and A is the start symbol S or other nonterminal; $\beta = \xi \omega \varnothing, \xi, \omega, \varnothing \in (V_N \cup V_T)^*$ (that means that all of them may be empty). Apart from these descriptions, there is no any restriction again. This type of grammar is called of Type 0.

If we define that the length of a string be the number of terminals and nonterminals, and denote $| \alpha |$ as the length of α. Then the definition of Type 0 means that there is no restriction on the lengths of α and β.

Type 0 grammar is the most general form of grammars. It is also called phrase structure grammar.

Example 2.1 A Type 0 grammar is as follows.

$$
\begin{cases}
\text{S} \to \text{ABSCD}, \\
\text{BA} \to \text{AB}, \\
\text{DC} \to \text{CD}, \\
\text{A} \to \text{aA}, \\
\text{B} \to \text{bB}, \\
\text{C} \to \text{cC}, \\
\text{D} \to \text{Dd}, \\
\text{BSC} \to \text{BC}, \\
\text{A} \to \varepsilon, \\
\text{B} \to \varepsilon, \\
\text{C} \to \varepsilon, \\
\text{D} \to \varepsilon, \\
\text{S} \to \varepsilon.
\end{cases} \tag{2.13}
$$

In these productions, the only one that shrinks is BSC $\to$ BC, for it we have $| \alpha | > | \beta |$. Apart from this one (excluding those that have empty right parts), they have $\mid \alpha \mid \leqslant \mid \beta \mid$. It is not a shrink grammar. As it has both $\mid \alpha \mid \leqslant \mid \beta \mid$ and $\mid \alpha \mid > \mid \beta \mid$, it is Type 0.

Definition 2.13 Type 1 grammar. In the grammar $G = (V_N, V_T, P, S)$ for the productions with the form $\alpha \to \beta$ in P, if we always have $\mid \alpha \mid \leqslant \mid \beta \mid$, unless $\mid \beta \mid = 0$, then the grammar is called Type 1 grammar. Type 1 grammar is also called context-sensitive grammar (CSG).

Example 2.2 The following grammar $G = (V_N, V_T, P, S)$ is a context-sensitive grammar, where $V_N = \{S, A, B, C, D, E, F\}$, $V_T = \{a, b, c\}$.

The production set P consists of the following productions:

$$\begin{cases} S \to ABCS, \\ S \to F, \\ CA \to AC, \\ BA \to AB, \\ CB \to BC, \\ CF \to Fc, \\ CF \to Ec, \\ BE \to Eb, \\ BE \to Db, \\ AD \to Da, \\ D \to \varepsilon. \end{cases} \tag{2.14}$$

Definition 2.14 Type 2 grammar. In the grammar $G = (V_N, V_T, P, S)$ for the productions with the form $\alpha \to \beta$ in P, if they always have $\mid \alpha \mid = 1$, that is, the left part of every production consists of one nonterminal only, then the grammar is called Type 2 grammar. It is also called context- free grammar (CFG).

Example 2.3 The following grammar $G = (V_N, V_T, P, S)$ is Type 2 grammar, where $V_N = \{S, A, B, C, D\}$, $V_T = \{a, b, c, d, e\}$. And production set P consists of the following productions.

$$\begin{cases} S \to DCD, \\ D \to B, \\ D \to AD, \\ A \to b, \\ A \to c, \\ B \to d, \\ B \to a, \\ C \to \varepsilon. \end{cases} \tag{2.15}$$

Definition 2.15 Type 3 grammar. In the grammar $G = (V_N, V_T, P, S)$, for the productions with form $\alpha \to \beta$ in P, they have only two forms, i.e.,

$$A \to aB \tag{2.16}$$

or

$$A \rightarrow b.$$

It may be as

$$A \rightarrow Ba \tag{2.17}$$

or

$$A \rightarrow b.$$

where A, B are nonterminals while a, b are terminals. This kind of grammars is called Type 3 grammar. It is also called regular grammar (RG) or linear grammar (LG). Depending on the right part of the production whether the nonterminal appears on the left or on the right it is called the left linear grammar or the right linear grammar. Therefore, correspondingly Eq. (2.16) is called the right linear and Eq. (2.17) is called left linear.

2.4 Language

We define a language before we establish the relation between the grammar and the language generated by the grammar.

Definition 2.16 Language. The any set of strings over a finite alphabet Σ, i.e., the any subset of Σ^* is called the language.

Simply speaking language is the set of strings. Hence, Σ^*, ϕ, and Σ all are languages since the language is only a set of special kinds (the set of strings). For any finite language we can determine the language by enumerating its elements. For example, {abc, xyz, e, u} is a language over set {a, b, ..., z}. We are interested, however, in infinite languages. In general, in infinite languages cannot be determined by enumerating. Before we present the features between grammars and languages, we like to further explore the languages.

At first we make some supplement about the operations of strings.

Definition 2.17 Reversal of the string. Given a string w, the reversal of w, denoted as w^R is a string generated from w via changing the order of the characters in w so that the first in the original left to right order becomes the last, and the second one becomes the second from the end, etc. For example, $(\text{alphabet})^R = \text{tebahpla}$. By using mathematical induction method with the length of the string, the reversal of the string may be formally defined:

1) If the length of w is zero, then $w = w^R = \varepsilon$; if the length of w is 1, i.e., w is a character, say, a, then $w^R = a^R = a = w$.

2) Suppose that the reversal of a string with length n has been defined, and w is a string with length n+1, let for $a \in \Sigma$, $w = ua$ and $| u | = n$, then $w^R = au^R$. Since for the string u with length n, we have defined its reversal, it means that u^R has been defined, w^R is defined.

We will make use of the definition to illustrate how mathematical induction proof depends on the definition. We will prove that for arbitrary w and u, $(wu)^R = u^R w^R$.

For example, $(\text{textbook})^R = (\text{book})^R (\text{text})^R = \text{koobtxet}$. We now prove this via mathematical induction over the length of u.

The basic step

For $\mid u \mid = 0$, $u = \varepsilon$, and $(wu)^R = (w\varepsilon)^R = w^R = \varepsilon^R w^R = \varepsilon^R w^R = u^R w^R$.

Induction hypothesis

If $\mid u \mid \leqslant n$, then $(wu)^R = u^R w^R$.

Induction proof

Suppose that $\mid u \mid = n + 1$, and there exists some $a \in \Sigma$ and $x \in \Sigma^*$ so that $u = xa$, and $\mid x \mid = n$, then

$$
\begin{aligned}
(wu)^R &= (w(xa))^R && \text{for } u = xa \\
&= ((wx)a)^R && \text{for the concatenation is associative} \\
&= a(wx)^R && \text{from the definition of reversal of } (wx)a \\
&= ax^R w^R && \text{from the induction hypothesis} \\
&= (xa)^R w^R && \text{from the definition of reversal of } xa \\
&= u^R w^R && \text{since } u = xa \qquad\qquad (2.18)
\end{aligned}
$$

Now we extend our study from individual strings to the finite sets or infinite sets of strings.

We mentioned above that Σ^*, ϕ, and Σ are languages. As a language is only a special kind of set, for a finite language it is feasible to determine it via enumerating its elements — strings. For example, as we have seen that {school, car, is, of, y, z} is a language over {a, b, ... , z}. But for a general language, the enumeration method is no longer feasible to describe or determine a language as most of the languages are infinite. The languages that can be considered is {0, 01, 011, 0111, ...}, {w $\mid$ w $\in \{0,1\}^*$ and in w, the number of 0's and the number of 1's are equal} and {w $\mid$ w $\in \Sigma^*$, w = w^R}. The last language is called the palindrome. It is the same to read it forward from the left and backward from the right. From now on we will describe our language as

$$L = \{w \mid w \in \Sigma^*, w \text{ has some properties}\} \qquad\qquad (2.19)$$

It is the same as the general form with which we describe the infinite set.

If Σ is infinite, then definitely Σ^* is infinite too. But whether it is numerablely infinite or not? It is not hard to see, it is numerablely infinite. In order to prove the point, it is necessary to establish the one to one correspondence between integer set N and Σ^*. In order to construct an one to one bimapping f: $N \leftrightarrow \Sigma^*$, at first it needs to determine the order of the finite alphabet, e.g., $\Sigma = \{a_1, a_2, \ldots, a_n\}$, where, $a_1, \ldots, a_n$ are totally different. Then we enumerate the elements of Σ^* by the following method:

1) For each $k \geqslant 0$, the enumeration of all the strings with length k precedes that of the strings with length $k + 1$.

2) For the n^k strings with length k, the enumeration is done according to the lexical order, i.e., suppose for some m, $0 \leqslant m \leqslant k - 1$, $a_{i1}, \ldots, a_{ik}$ precedes $a_{j1}, \ldots, a_{jk}$, if for $i = 1, \ldots, m, i_1 = j_1$, then $i_{m+1} < j_{m+1}$.

For example, if $\Sigma = \{0, 1\}$, then the order of elements of Σ^* is as follows:

$$\varepsilon, 0, 1, 00, 01, 10, 11, 000, 001, 010, 011, \ldots. \tag{2.20}$$

If Σ is the Latin alphabet, then one may use $\Sigma = \{a_1, a_2, \ldots, a_{26}\}$ to denote $\{a, b, \ldots, z\}$.

The order of the strings with the same length will be the lexical order in the common dictionary. This order is different from the order that the long strings precede the shorter ones.

As language is a set (the set of strings), the operations union, intersection, and difference may be carried out on languages. When from the context one may understand that Σ is a special finite alphabet, then we may use $\overline{A}$ to denote the complement of A, in place of rather long notation $\Sigma^* - A$.

Some operations only make sense for languages. At first, consider the connection of languages. If L_1 and L_2 are two languages over the alphabet Σ, then the connection of them is $L = L_1 \circ L_2$ or briefly $L = L_1 L_2$, where,

$$L = \{w \mid w \in \Sigma^*, W = xy, \text{where } x \in L_1, y \in L_2\}. \tag{2.21}$$

For example, if $\Sigma = \{a, b\}$, $L_1 = \{w \mid w \in \Sigma^*$, w contains even number of a's$\}$ and $L_2 = \{w \mid w$ starts with a and the rest is all b's$\}$, then $L_1 \circ L_2 = \{w \mid w$ contains odd number of a and the number of b's is uncertain$\}$.

The other operation of languages is Kleene closure, e.g., L^*, where L is a language.

L^* is the set of the connections of L itself, including that of zero L. The connection of zero L is ε, the connection of one L is itself, hence

$$L^* = \{w \mid w \in \Sigma^*, \ w = w_1 w_2 \ldots w_k, k \geqslant 0, \ w_1, \ldots, w_k \in L\}. \tag{2.22}$$

For example, if $L = \{ab, b, baa\}$, then $bbaaabbbbaaabb \in L^*$ as $bbaaabbb-baaabb = b \circ baa \circ ab \circ b \circ baa \circ b \circ b$, and here b, baa, and ab belong to the strings of L.

Notice here that there are two concepts. On one hand, for any finite alphabet Σ, we use Σ^* to denote all the strings over Σ. On the other hand, we use L^* to represent the Kleene closure of language L. The two notations are exactly the same.

It is true. If we let $L = \Sigma$ and apply the definition above, then Σ^* represents the set of all strings w's. that means that there exists $k \geqslant 0$, and $w_1, \ldots, w_k \in \Sigma$ so that $w = w_1 \ldots w_k$. As w_i is the language over Σ, hence, according to the definition, Σ^* is the set of strings (language) over Σ.

Example 2.4 Prove that $\phi^* = \{\varepsilon\}$.

Based on the definition above, let $L = \phi$, then for $k \geqslant 0$, and $w_1, \ldots, w_k \in L$, the only possible connection is $k = 0$ and it is ε. Hence the only element of L^* is ε.

Example 2.5 Prove that if L is such a language that $L = \{w \mid w \in \{a, b\}^+$, and in w the number of a's and the number of b's are different$\}$, then $L^+ \subseteq \{a, b\}^+$.

We now prove it. At first, notice that for any languages L_1, L_2, if $L_1 \subseteq L_2$, then $L_1^* \subseteq L_2^*$. This can be obtained from the definition of closure. Furthermore, as $\{a, b\} \subseteq L$, and a and b are the strings with different numbers of a and b. So $\{a, b\} \subseteq L$, but from the definition, $L \subseteq \{a, b\}^*$. Therefore, $L^* \subseteq \{\{a, b\}^+\}^* = \{a, b\}^+$. We now can denote L^+ as LL^* and

$$L^+ = \{w \mid w \in \Sigma^*, \text{ and } \exists\, w_1 \ldots w_k \in L, \text{ and } k \geqslant 1 \text{ so that } w_1 \circ w_2 \circ \ldots \circ w_k\}$$
(2.23)

L^+ can be regarded as the closure of L under the connection operation. Hence L^+ is a minimal language that consists of L and the connections of all elements of L. It means that if there are some languages that hold the same elements, then L^+ is the smallest one among them.

2.5 Language Generated by a Grammar

In Section 2.2, we defined grammar and pointed out that the only operation for grammar is the derivation. The purpose of the derivation is to generate the string that is composed of terminals. All the strings that are derived from the grammar form the language. It is the language generated or accepted by the grammar. In this section, we will exemplify a few languages generated by their corresponding grammars [2].

Example 2.6 Consider the language generated by the grammar given in Example 2.1.

$$\begin{cases} S \rightarrow ABSCD, \\ BA \rightarrow AB, \\ DC \rightarrow CD, \\ A \rightarrow aA, \\ B \rightarrow bB, \\ C \rightarrow cC, \\ D \rightarrow dD, \\ BSC \rightarrow BC, \\ A \rightarrow \varepsilon, \\ B \rightarrow \varepsilon, \\ C \rightarrow \varepsilon, \\ D \rightarrow \varepsilon, \\ S \rightarrow \varepsilon. \end{cases} \qquad (2.24)$$

At first, we have

$$S \rightarrow ABSCD \rightarrow ABCD \rightarrow \varepsilon\,\varepsilon\,\varepsilon\,\varepsilon \rightarrow \varepsilon.$$

Hence we have $\varepsilon \in L(G)$, where $L(G)$ means the language L generated by the grammar G. Furthermore, $S \to ABSCD \to ABCD \to aABCD \to aA \to a$. So $a \in L(G)$. Similarly, we may get b, c, $d \in L(G)$. In addition,

$$S \to ABSCD \to ABABSCDCD$$
$$\to ABABCDCD$$
$$\to AABBCCDD$$
$$\to \ldots$$
$$\to a^m b^n c^p d^q.$$

Finally by mathematic induction proof, we may get $L(G) = \{a^m b^n c^p d^q \mid m, n, p, q \geqslant 0\}$.

Example 2.7 Consider the language generated by the grammar given in Example 2.2.

$$\begin{cases} S \to ABCS, \\ S \to F, \\ CA \to AC, \\ BA \to AB, \\ CB \to BC, \\ CF \to Fc, \\ CF \to Ec, \\ BE \to Eb, \\ BE \to Db, \\ AD \to Da, \\ D \to \varepsilon. \end{cases} \tag{2.25}$$

It is easy to find out that

$$S \to ABCS \to ABCABCS \to \ldots \to (ABC)^n F.$$

Making use the several last parts of productions, let see

$$S \to ABCABCF \to ABACBCF \to ABABCCF \to AABBCCF \to$$
$$AABBCFc \to AABBEcc \to AABEbcc \to AADbbcc \to$$
$$ADabbcc \to Daabbcc \to aabbcc.$$

In the process the three productions are important for obtaining the form we desire to have. These productions are

$$CA \to AC,$$
$$BA \to AB,$$
$$CB \to BC.$$

With these productions we have the following derivations

$$S \rightarrow ABCABCABCF \rightarrow ABACBCABCF \rightarrow ABABCCABCF \rightarrow$$
$$ABABCACBCF \rightarrow ABABACCBCF \rightarrow ABABACBCCF \rightarrow$$
$$ABABABCCCF \rightarrow AAABBBCCCF.$$

Therefore, by repeatedly using these productions, we may derive $S \rightarrow A^n B^n C^n$. Sequentially, by using the later productions, we may conclude that the grammar generates the strings with form $a^n b^n c^n (n \geqslant 1)$. The only way to remove the nonterminals from the strings is to follow the process shown above. Since all the strings generated by the grammar have the same form $a^n b^n c^n$, $n \geqslant 1$, thereby the language generated is

$$L(G) = \{a^n b^n c^n \mid n \geqslant 1\}.$$

Example 2.8   Consider the language generated by the grammar given in Example 2.3.

$$\begin{cases} S \rightarrow DCD, \\ D \rightarrow B, \\ D \rightarrow AD, \\ A \rightarrow b, \\ A \rightarrow c, \\ B \rightarrow d, \\ B \rightarrow a, \\ C \rightarrow e. \end{cases} \tag{2.26}$$

At first we have

$$S \rightarrow DCD \rightarrow BCB.$$

As B has two productions that takes it as left part, $B \rightarrow d$ and $B \rightarrow a$, or $B \rightarrow (d \mid a)$ and $C \rightarrow e$, hence we have $S \rightarrow (d \mid a) e (d \mid a)$ and $(d \mid a) e (d \mid a) \in L(G)$. On the other hand, $S \rightarrow DCD \rightarrow ADCAD \rightarrow AADCAAD \rightarrow \cdots \rightarrow A^m DCA^n D \rightarrow A^m BCA^n B$, hence $S \rightarrow (b \mid c)^m (d \mid a) e (b \mid c)^n (d \mid a)$. So the language generated by the grammar is $L(G) = (b \mid c)^m (d \mid a) e (b \mid c)^n (d \mid a) \mid m, n \geqslant 0)$.

Example 2.9   Consider the grammar $G = (V_n, V_T, P, S)$, where $V_N = \{S, A\}$, $V_T = \{a, b\}$.

The production set P consists of

$$\begin{cases} S \rightarrow aS, \\ S \rightarrow \varepsilon, \\ S \rightarrow bA, \\ A \rightarrow bS, \\ A \rightarrow aA. \end{cases} \tag{2.27}$$

For the grammar, the language generated by it is simple. It is the so-called regular language as the grammar is the regular grammar. At first, it generates ε and a, hence these two belong to the language it generates, ε, a ∈ L(G). From S → bA → bbS → bbε → bb, we also have bb ∈ L(G). Then we do the derivations S → aS → aaS → ... → a^mS → a^mbA → a^mbbS → ... → a^m(bb)^{n}S. So the language generated by the grammar has the following form

$$a^m, a^m(bb)^n, a^m(bb)^n a^p(bb)^q, \ldots, a^m(bb)^l \ldots a^r, a^m(bb)^l \ldots a^p(bb)^{qm}. \quad (2.28)$$

In order to discuss the properties of the languages generated by grammars, we need to introduce the concept of Turing machine. Thereby the next section will devote to it.

2.6 Turing Machine

Before we formally discuss the concept of Turing machines, it is necessary to introduce the founder of the theory — Alan M. Turing (1912 – 1954). Turing is an excellent mathematician and philosopher. As a boy, he was fascinated by chemistry, performing a variety of experiments, and by machinery. In 1931 he won a scholarship to King's College, Cambridge. After completing his dissertation which included a rediscovery of the central limit theorem, a famous theorem in statistics, he was elected a fellow of his college. In 1935 he was fascinated with the decision problem posed by the great German mathematician David Helbert. The problem asked whether there is a general method that can be applied to any assertion to determine whether the assertion is true. In 1936 he published the paper entitled "On Computable Numbers, with an *Application to the Entscheidungsproblem* (problem of decidability) on Proceedings London Mathematical Society, vol. 42, 1936. It was in the paper that he proposed the very general computation model, now widely known as the Turing machine. During World War II he joined the Foreign Office, to lead the successful effort in Bletchley Park (then the British Government's Cryptography School in Milton Keynes) to crack the German "Enigma" cipher, which Nazi Germany used to communicate with the U-boats in the North Atlantic. In this undertaking his contribution to the breaking of the code of Enigma, played an important role in winning the war. After the war Turing worked on the development of early computers. He was interested in the ability of machines to think, proposing that if a computer could not be distinguished from a person based on written replies to questions, it should be considered to be "thinking". He was also interested in biology, having written on morphogenesis, the development of form in organism. In 1954 Turing committed suicide by taking cyanide, without leaving a clear explanation. The Association for Computing Machinery [3] in the U.S.A. created the Turing Award in 1966, to commemorate Turing's original contribution.

As we mentioned above, the Turing machine is the most general model of a computing machine. Basically, a Turing machine consists of a control unit, the soul of the machine, which at any step is in one of finitely many different states, together with a tape divided into cells and which has a boundary in the left hand side (the restriction can be lifted so that it can be like the right side too, but by the removal of the restriction does not change the computation power of the Turing machine) but stretches infinitely in the right hand side. Turing machine has read and write capabilities on the tape as the control unit moves back and forth along this tape, changing states depending on the tape symbol read. At first, the input message should be written on the tape, then the control unit reads the leftmost message, the Turing machine starts its running in this way, it may move forth and back on the tape, as well as change the symbols on the tape, until considers that its running comes to the end.

Definition 2.18 Turing machine. A Turing machine is a heptatuple $M = (K, \Gamma, \Sigma, \delta, S, b, H)$.

K — the finite set of the states.

Γ — the alphabet, the symbols of the tape, including blank symbol b, $K \cap \Gamma = \phi$.

Σ — the subset of Γ, not including b. It is the set of input.

δ — the transfer function, a mapping from $(K - H) \times \Gamma$ to $K \times \Gamma \times \{L, R\}$, where, L represents left (it stands for the left move of the write/read head of the tape) while R represents right (it stands for the right move of the write/read head of the tape). Hence δ represents the next state function, for example:

(1) for $\forall q \in K - H$, if $\delta(q, a) = (p, R)$, it represents that the current state of the Turing machine is q, with input a, it will have p as the next state and the tape head will move right for one cell;

(2) for $\forall q \in K - H$, if $\delta(q, a) = (p.c, L)$, similarly, it represents that the next state will be p, and the input symbol a will be changed to c, and the tape head will move left for one cell.

S — $\in K$, the initial state of the Turing machine.

b — the blank symbol on the tape. Notice that the input symbols do not contain b.

H — $\subseteq K$, the set of final states. It means that the number of final states may be more than one.

We may use $\alpha_1 q \alpha_2$ to denote an instantaneous description (ID) of the Turing machine, where $q (q \in K)$ is the current state of M, α_1, α_2 are strings in Γ. α_1 means the string from the left boundary of the tape until the symbol under the tape head, and α_2 means the string from the right of the tape head till the first blank symbol on the right side of tape (notice that in α_1 and α_2 there may be the blank symbol b). The ID represents that the Turing machine now is under control of state q, and the tape head is going to scan the leftmost symbol in α_2. If $\alpha_2 = \varepsilon$, then it represents that the tape head is scanning a blank symbol.

More exactly speaking, suppose that $\alpha_1 = x_1 x_2 \ldots x_{i-1}$, $\alpha_2 = x_i \ldots x_n$, then $x_1 x_2 \ldots x_{i-1} q x_i \ldots x_n$ is the current ID, and suppose that there is

$$\delta(q, x_i) = (p, y, L) \tag{2.29}$$

in the mapping from $(K - H) \times \Gamma$ to $K \times \Gamma \times \{L, R\}$. It indicates that the next state is p, and y will be written on where x_i is located. Meanwhile the tape head is moved to left for one cell. In addition if $i - 1 = n$, then x_i is taken as b, if $i = 1$, as tape is on the left boundary and tape head cannot move left again, there will be no the next ID. If $i > 1$, then we may use the following expression to represent the ID:

$$x_1 x_2 \ldots x_{i-1} q x_i \ldots x_n \vdash x_1 x_2 \ldots x_{i-2} p x_{i-1} y x_{i+1} \ldots x_n. \tag{2.30}$$

If $y x_{i+1} \ldots x_n$ is only a blank string, then it may be deleted. It indicates that the machine stops running, but according to the definition, only when the machine enters one of final states then can the computation normally finishes, otherwise, the finish can only be regarded as abnormal stop.

$\delta(q, x_i)$ may take another form, i.e.,

$$\delta(q, x_i) = (p, y, R). \tag{2.31}$$

As Eq. (2.29), the next state is p, y will be written on where x_i is located, but this time the tape head will move right for one cell. In this circumstance, we use the following expression to represent the ID:

$$x_1 x_2 \ldots x_{i-1} q x_i x_{i+1} \ldots x_n \vdash x_1 x_2 \ldots x_{i-1} y p x_{i+1} \ldots x_n. \tag{2.32}$$

Notice that in this circumstance if $i - 1 = n$, then string $x_{i+1} \ldots x_n$ is a blank string, then the next state is facing a blank.

Fig. 2.1 shows the visual model of the Turing machine.

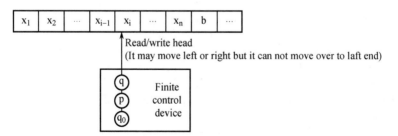

Fig. 2.1 Turing machine model.

If two IDs are related via $\vdash_M$, then we say that the second ID is yielded from the movement of the first ID. If the ID is produced from the finite number (including zero) of movements of the other ID, then we say that they are related via $\vdash_M$, and we denote it $\vdash_M^*$. When no confusion will happen, either $\vdash_M$ or $\vdash_M^*$ may be simplified as $\vdash$ or $\vdash^*$.

Example 2.10 Consider the following Turing machine, it has

$$K = \{q_0, q_1, q_2, q_3, q_4\},$$
$$\Gamma = \{0, 1, x, y, b\},$$
$$\Sigma = \{0, 1\},$$
$$H = \{q_4\}.$$

The transition function δ is defined as follows.

States \ Symbols	0	1	x	y	b
q_0	(q_1, x, R)	—	—	(q_1, y, R)	—
q_1	$(q_1, 0, R)$	(q_2, y, L)	—	(q_1, y, L)	—
q_2	$(q_2, 0, L)$	—	(q_0, x, R)	(q_2, y, L)	—
q_3	—	—	—	(q_3, y, R)	(q_4, b, R)
q_4	—	—	—	—	—

At the beginning, let the tape contain $0^n 1^n$, following it being the infinite number of b's, i.e., blanks. Take $0^2 1^2$ as an example, according to the definition of δ, we have the following computation:

$$q_0 0011 \vdash \rightarrow x q_1 011 \vdash \rightarrow x 0 q_1 11 \vdash \rightarrow x q_2 0 y 1 \vdash \rightarrow q_2 x 0 y 1 \vdash \rightarrow$$
$$x q_0 0 y 1 \vdash \rightarrow x x q_1 y 1 \vdash \rightarrow x x y q_1 1 \vdash \rightarrow x x q_2 y y \vdash \rightarrow x q_2 x y y \vdash \rightarrow$$
$$x x q_0 y y \vdash \rightarrow x x y q_3 y \vdash \rightarrow x x y y q_3 \vdash \rightarrow x x y y b q_4 \quad\quad (2.33)$$

The computation process above, i.e., machine M repeatedly substitutes x for the leftmost 0, and move right to find the leftmost 1, then substitute it with y. Then move left again to find the rightmost x, move one more cell to find the leftmost 0. In this way, it forms a cycle. It then repeats the cycle until M cannot find any 1 left. When M found that there is no any 0 left and there is no any 1 left either, in this circumstance, it means that the number of 0's and the number of 1's are equal. Then the string is accepted by M. Otherwise if the number of 0's is more than that of 1's or vice versa, then M does not accept.

The computation process commences with q_0, its role is to start the whole process. This is its unique role. After it found the leftmost 0, it changes the state to q_1 making the computation entering to the cycle above. Meanwhile, the 0 is replaced by x, and it moves right to continue the searching of the corresponding 1. Therefore, the role of q_1 is to move right to continue the search, passing 0's and y's to look for the leftmost 1. When it has found the 1, its role also finished, and now it is the turn of q_2. The role of q_2 is to move left for searching for x. When it found x, it suddenly changes to

q_0. Under the state q_0, M moves right, looks for the leftmost 0 and begins the other cycle. When M moves right to look for 1 under the state q_1, if it meets b or x before it meets 1, that means that the numbers of 0's and 1's are not consistent. Hence the string is rejected. As for state q_3, it is the state that replaces q_0 when it found y on the tape (notice that y is not an input symbol, the same as x, they are temporal symbols introduced during the computation). The q_3 is used for scanning y and checking whether there is 1 left or not. If there is no 1 left, that means that b follows y, then q_3 is changed to q_4, and the computation comes to the end, and the input string is acceptable. Otherwise the computation cannot finish, or the input string cannot be accepted. Therefore, state q_4 is the final state.

Example 2.11 Consider a Turing machine $M = (K, \Gamma, \Sigma, \delta, q_0, b, \{q_2\})$, where

$$K = \{q_0, q_1, q_2\},$$
$$\Gamma = \{u, a, b\}, \qquad \text{(u is the left boundary symbol of the tape)}$$
$$\Sigma = \{a\},$$
$$H = \{q_2\}.$$

The transition function δ is defined as follows:

$$\delta(q_0, u) = (q_0, R),$$
$$\delta(q_0, a) = (q_1, b),$$
$$\delta(q_0, b) = (q_2, b),$$
$$\delta(q_1, a) = (q_0, a),$$
$$\delta(q_1, b) = (q_0, R).$$

In this machine, when M starts with state q_0 if it encounters the left boundary symbol u of the tape, it does not change u but continues to move right for one cell. When it encounters an a, the state is changed to q_1. Meanwhile, input a is removed and the cell becomes b. When q_1 meets b it is turned to q_0 and moves right. If q_1 meets a, it is also turned to q_0 but the tape head does not move.

In order to more explicitly investigate the moves of the Turing machine, assume that there are three a's on the tape. The operations are shown in Fig. 2.2.

So far, the Turing machine enters the final state q_2, the whole computation process terminates. As we can see that the work of the Turing machine is to delete the a's on the input tape. No matter how many a's there are on the tape, it can delete all of them, but one per time.

Example 2.12 Consider the following Turing machine,

$$M = (K, \Gamma, \Sigma, \delta, q_0, b, \{q_1\}),$$

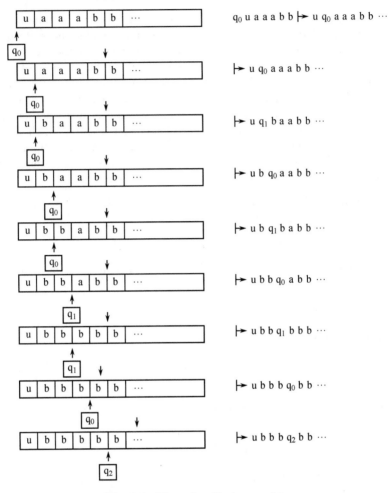

q_0 u a a a b b $\vdash$ u q_0 a a a b b ⋯

$\vdash$ u q_0 a a a b b ⋯

$\vdash$ u q_1 b a a b b ⋯

$\vdash$ u b q_0 a a b b ⋯

$\vdash$ u b q_1 b a b b ⋯

$\vdash$ u b b q_0 a b b ⋯

$\vdash$ u b b q_1 b b b ⋯

$\vdash$ u b b b q_0 b b ⋯

$\vdash$ u b b b q_2 b b ⋯

Fig. 2.2 The other Turing machine.

where

$$K = \{q_0, q_1\},$$
$$\Gamma = \{u, a, b\}, \qquad \text{(u stands for the left boundary symbol)}$$
$$\Sigma = \{a\},$$
$$H = \{q_1\}.$$

The transition function δ is defined by the following expressions:

$$\delta(q_0, a) = (q_0, L),$$
$$\delta(q_0, b) = (q_1, b),$$
$$\delta(q_0, u) = (q_0, R).$$

In order to observe the operations of the Turing machine more explicitly, we do the same as we did above. We also assume that the input on the tape is the string uaaabb.... We have

$$q_0\text{uaaabb} \vdash \rightarrow \text{u}q_0\text{aaabb} \vdash \rightarrow q_0\text{uaaabb} \vdash \rightarrow \text{u}q_0\text{aaabb} \vdash \rightarrow$$
$$q_0\text{uaaabb} \vdash \rightarrow \text{u}q_0\text{aaabb} \vdash \rightarrow q_0\text{uaaabb}. \tag{2.34}$$

Therefore, in this circumstance the Turing machine only moves forward and backward between the left boundary and the first non blank character a. It cannot move to the blank character where it enters the final state. However, if the input string is ubabb..., that means that the blank character follows the left boundary symbol, then we have

$$q_0\text{ubabb} \vdash \rightarrow \text{u}q_0\text{babb} \vdash \rightarrow \text{u}q_1\text{babb}. \tag{2.35}$$

By moving only for one cell, it has encountered the blank character and it immediately enters the final state.

We have given the definition of the Turing machine and three examples of the machine. From these we may see that Turing machine carries the computation directing at the input on the input tape until it enters the final state. The input that leads the Turing machine enters the final state is regarded as the statement of the language the machine recognized or accepted. Therefore, we can now define the language which the Turing machine recognizes or accepts [4].

Definition 2.19 The language accepted or recognized by the Turing machine L(M). The set of those words in Σ^* that cause M to enter a final state when M starts its operation with state q_0 and the tape head of M is initially located at the leftmost cell. Formally, the language accepted by $M = (K, \Gamma, \Sigma, \delta, q_0, b, H)$ is

$$\{w \mid w \in \Sigma^* \wedge q_0 w \vdash \rightarrow \alpha_1 p \alpha_2 \wedge p \in H \wedge \alpha_1, \alpha_2 \in \Gamma^*\}.$$

According to the definition, it is not hard to see that the three examples of Turing machine above recognize their respective languages. The first Turing machine recognizes $\{0^n 1^n \mid n \geqslant 1\}$. The language which the second Turing machine recognizes is $\{a^n \mid n \geqslant 0\}$. The third Turing machine recognizes language $\{b\}$. From these examples, we can also see that given a Turing machine that recognizes language L, without loss of generality, we can assume that whenever the input is accepted, the machine enters a final state and it no longer moves. There is another possibility, however, that for the character or statement which it does not recognize, it never stops. The third example belongs to the case.

Definition 2.20 Recursive language. Let $M = (K, \Gamma, \Sigma, \delta, b, q_0, H)$ be a Turing machine, where $H = \{y, n\}$ consists of two discriminable final states y (stands for yes) and n (stands for no). Any terminating instantaneous description with the final state y is said to be a configuration accepted, while the terminating instantaneous description with final state n is said to be a configuration rejected. We say that M accepts input $w \in (\Sigma - \{u, b\})^*$, that is, within w there is no any blank or left boundary symbol and $q_0 w$ yields an acceptable configuration. And we say that M rejects the input w if $q_0 w$ yields a configuration with n as the final state.

Let $\Sigma_0 \subseteq \Sigma - \{u, b\}$ be a finite alphabet, Σ_0 is called input alphabet of the Turing machine M. By fixing Σ_0 as the subset of $\Sigma - \{u, b\}$, we allow that during its computation M may use additional symbols of Γ apart from the characters within the input alphabet. We say that a language $L \subseteq \Sigma_0^*$ is decidable by M, if for any sentence w (i.e., the string) of the language L, M will accepts it, while for any $w \sim\in L$, M will rejects it.

If there exists a Turing machine that decides L, then a language L is said to be recursive.

Definition 2.21 Recursive function. Let $M = (K, \Gamma, \Sigma, \delta, b, q_0, H)$ be a Turing machine, $\Sigma_0 \subseteq \Sigma - \{u, b\}$ is a finite alphabet, and $w \in \Sigma_0^*$ is the input of M. Suppose that M terminates upon input w and we have $uq_0 bw \overset{*}{\longmapsto} uhby$ ($h \in H, y \in \Sigma_0^*$), then we say that y is the output of M upon input w and we denote it M(w). Notice that only when for input w the machine M comes to its end state, then the M(w) makes sense. In this case, M terminates with the configuration y, where $y \in \Sigma_0^*$.

Now we say that a function f is recursive if there exists a Turing machine M that computes f.

For the two definitions above, one uses the Turing machine to describe a language, while another uses the Turing machine to describe a function. Therefore, naturally we may imagine that the Turing machine is an algorithm that correctly and reliably implements some computational task. Thereby we introduce a new definition.

Definition 2.22 Recursively enumerable [5] language. Let $M = (K, \Gamma, \Sigma, \delta, b, q_0, H)$ be a Turing machine, $\Sigma_0 \subseteq \Sigma - \{u, b\}$ be a finite alphabet, and let $L \subseteq \Sigma^*$ be a language. We say that M semi-decides language L, if for any string $w \in \Sigma_0^*$ the following fact holds: $w \in L$ if and only if M terminates when it computes on input w. A language is said to be recursively enumerable if and only if there exists a Turing machine M that semi-decides L.

Before we present the important conclusion of the language which a grammar generates we need to present another concept.

Definition 2.23 Nondeterministic Turing machine. A nondeterministic Turing machine, as its deterministic peer, is a heptatuple $M = (K, \Gamma, \Sigma, \Delta, b, q_0, H)$, where K, Γ, Σ have the same meaning as in its corresponding peer, q_0 is also the same as in the original one. The difference happens on Δ and δ: Δ is not a function like δ that uniquely maps $(K - H) \times \Sigma$ to $K \times (\Sigma \cup \{L, R\})$, instead, it maps to a subset of $K \times (\Sigma \cup \{L, R\})$. That means that for an element of $(K - H) \times \Sigma$ there are arbitrary numbers of elements from $K \times (\Sigma \cup \{L, R\})$ that can be its mappings. Now the configuration and the relations $\underset{M}{\longmapsto}$ and $\underset{M}{\overset{*}{\longmapsto}}$ are defined naturally, but they are not necessarily unique. That means that a configuration may have arbitrary numbers of the configurations in the next step.

Definition 2.24 The language which the nondeterministic Turing machine semi-decides. Let $M = (K, \Gamma, \Sigma, \Delta, b, q_0, H)$ be a nondeterministic Turing machine. We say that M accepts an input $w \in (\Sigma - \{u, b\})^*$ if $uq_0bw \underset{M}{\overset{*}{\longmapsto}} uvhas$, where $h \in H, a \in \Sigma, v, s \in \Sigma^*$. Notice that a nondeterministic Turing machine accepts an input as long as for the input at least there exists a computation of M that terminates although there may be many non-terminable computations. We say that M semi-decides a language $L \subseteq (\Sigma - \{u, b\})^*$, if for any $w \in (\Sigma - \{u, b\})^*$, the following condition holds: $w \in L$ if and only if M accepts w.

The definition talks about semi-deciding, we may further define a Turing machine deciding a language, or deciding a function, although it is more subtle.

Definition 2.25 The language which a nondeterministic Turing machine decides. Let $M = (K, \Gamma, \Sigma, \Delta, b, q_0, \{y, n\})$ be a nondeterministic Turing machine, where $y, n \in K$, we say that M decides a language $L \subseteq (\Sigma - \{u, b\})^*$ if for all $w \in (\Sigma - \{u, b\})^*$ the following conditions hold:

1) Depending on M and w, there exists a natural number N such that in N steps, there exists no configuration C of M that satisfies $uq_0bw \underset{M}{\overset{*}{\longmapsto}} C$ (C stands for the instantaneous description (ID) mentioned above).

2) $w \in L$ if and only if $uq_0bw \underset{M}{\overset{*}{\longmapsto}} uvyas$, where $v, s \in \Sigma^*, a \in \Sigma$.

The definition reflects the difficulty which the nondeterministic Turing machine meets when it carries out the computation. At first for a nondeterministic Turing machine that decides a language, we require that all its computation terminate. Thereby we assume that after N steps there will be no computation going on, hence N is the upper bound that relates the machine and the input. Secondly, for machine M that decides a language, we only require that among all the possible computations, there will be at least one that terminates with accepting the input, here y stands for the terminate state (yes). Other computations will terminate with the reject state (n). This is an extremely unusual, anti-symmetric and anti-perceivable convention. Similarly, we have the following definition.

Definition 2.26 A function which a nondeterministic Turing machine computes. We say that a nondeterministic Turing machine $M = (K, \Gamma, \Sigma, \Delta, b, q_0, H)$ computes a function f: $(\Sigma - \{u, b\})^* \rightarrow (\Sigma - \{u, b\})^*$, if for all $w \in (\Sigma - \{u, b\})^*$ the following two conditions hold:

1) Depending on M and w, there exists a natural number N such that after N steps there exists no configuration C of M that satisfies $uq_0bw \xrightarrow[M]{N} C$. C has the same meaning as in Definition 2.25.

2) $uq_0bw \vdash_M^* uvhas$, where $v, s \in \Sigma^*$, $a \in \Sigma$ if and only if $va=ub$ and $v = f(w)$.

For a nondeterministic Turing machine that computes a function, we require that the results of all the possible computations be consistent, otherwise we cannot determine which one is correct. In deciding or semi-deciding a language, we solve this problem via the assumption that the positive result predominates.

Now we present the important conclusion on the language generated by a grammar.

Theorem 2.1 A language is generated by a grammar if and only if it is recursively enumerable.

Before the proof of the Theorem 2.1 is given, we need to extend the concept of the Turing machine, introducing the concept of multitape Turing machine.

Definition 2.27 The k tape Turing machine. Suppose that $k \geqslant 1$ is an integer.

The k tape Turing machine $M = (K, \Gamma, \Sigma, \delta, b, q_0, H)$ is almost the same as the ordinary Turing machine, where the meanings of $K, \Gamma, \Sigma, q_0, H$ are exactly the same as in the definition of ordinary Turing machine. However, now for the δ, as the transition function, it is the mapping from $(K - H) \times \Sigma^k$ to $K \times (\Sigma - \{L, R\})^k$. In other words, given each state q and input symbols $(a_1, \ldots, a_k)$ on k tapes, then there will be $\delta(q, (a_1, \ldots, a_k)) = (p, (b_1, \ldots, b_k))$, where p stands for the next state of state q, and b_j is that on jth tape the result of the operation of M in place of a_j. Naturally, for some $j \leqslant k$, if $a_j=u$ then the tape head on the tape j will move right, that means that the operation is R.

From the definition we know that for any integer $k \geqslant 1$, a k tape Turing machine is a Turing machine with k tapes and corresponding heads for each tape and its control unit deals with the information on each tape. The computation is performed with the input on all the k tapes. Therefore, the configuration of the Turing machine must contain all the information on these tapes.

Definition 2.28 The configuration of the k tape Turing machine. Let $M = (K, \Gamma, \Sigma, \delta, b, q_0, H)$ be an k tape Turing machine. The configuration of M is an element of

$$K \times (u\Sigma^* \times (\Sigma(\Sigma - \{b\}) \cup \{e\}))^k$$

where $e \in \Sigma$, that is, a configuration identifies the state, the contents of the tapes and the positions of the tape heads, e represents the possible changes that happens on the tail of the tape.

Having these we now prove Theorem 2.1.

Proof   Necessity. By necessity if the language is generated by the grammar G, it must be recursively enumerable. That also means that there will be a Turing machine that accepts it. Let $G = (V_n, V_t, P, S)$ be a grammar. We will design a Turing machine that semi-decides the language generated by G. In fact, M is not deterministic, but in the theory of the Turing machine, the following facts have been established that it is feasible to transform the non-deterministic Turing machine into deterministic Turing machine, and both the Turing machines semi-decide the same language.

The Turing machine which we construct is a 3 tapes Turing machine. The first tape contains the input denoted by w and the content keeps unchanged. On the second tape, M intends to reconstruct the derivations of G that starts from S and carries out on input w. Hence, M starts with writing S on the second tape, then according to the production M replaces S with the right side of the production of which the left side is S. The sequential step is to replace the nonterminal on the tape with the right side of the production of which the nonterminal occupies the left side. Every step is just the repeat of the process until w occurs on the tape. However, since it is a nondeterministic Turing machine, every step starts with nondeterministic transformation, and it has to guess among $|P|$ productions, $|P|$ means the number of the productions. In every step, we have to choose which production is used. Suppose that the production selected is $u \rightarrow v$, where $u \in (V_n \cup V_t)^+$, $v \in (V_n \cup V_t)^*$. Then M scans the contents on the second tape from left to right, looking for the nonterminal on the tape. If it found one, it replaces the nonterminal with the right side of the production of which it stands on the left side. The meaning of the nondeterministic is that we do not know in advance which productions should be used for a number of the productions that all have the same nonterminals stand on the left side. If the process did not generate w on the tape, that means that the intention of generating w on the tape fails. And the derivation should start again with other inputs. If finally w occurs on the second tape after several derivation steps, then we say that w is accepted by M. In this case, we have proven that w is really generated by a Turing machine and the language is recursively enumerable.

By the way, the third tape is used for storing the productions of the grammar G. When the Turing machine scans the content of second tape and found a nonterminal, it has to check the third tape to find the production of which the nonterminal occurs on the left side.

Sufficency   The task of the proof is to define a grammar from the Turing machine that accepts the language, so that the grammar also accepts the language. Assume that $M = (K, \Gamma, \Sigma, \delta, b, q_0, H)$ is a Turing machine. According to the definition of Turing machine, of course, K and Γ are disjoint. Both of them do not contain the new terminate symbol $\uparrow$. For convenience, we further assume that if M terminates, then it always terminates on the configuration uhb, i.e., it terminates after it deletes the contents of the tape. As we have mentioned that any Turing machine that semi-decides a language can be transformed into the equivalent Turing machine that satisfies the same condition. We need to define a grammar that generates the language $L \subseteq (\Sigma - \{u, b\})^*$ which M semi-decides. It is $G = (V_n, \Sigma - \{u, b\}, P, S)$. Now we need to specify the components of G.

The V_n of nonterminal symbol set of G consists of all the states of K, including the start symbol S (the initial state q_0 may be used as S), in addition, the left boundary symbol u, the blank symbol and the terminate token $\uparrow$. Perceivably, the derivations of G will simulate the backward computation of M. We will simulate the computation through the initial configuration. Consider the string uvaqw $\uparrow$. Then the productions of G are the actions that simulate M backwardly. For each $q \in K$, and each $a \in \Sigma$, depending on $\delta(q,a)$ there are following rules:

1) If for some $p \in K$ and $b \in \Sigma$, $\delta(q, a) = (p, b)$, then in G there will be production bp $\rightarrow$ aq.

2) If for some $p \in K$, $\delta(q, a) = (p, R)$, then the corresponding production in G will be: for all $c \in \Sigma$, acp$\rightarrow$aqc and abq$\rightarrow$aq$\uparrow$ (this rule reverses the extension of the tape to right via a blank symbol).

3) If for some $p \in K$ and $a \neq b \in \Sigma$, $\delta(q, a) == (p, L)$, then G will have the corresponding production pa$\rightarrow$aq.

4) If for some $p \in K$, $\delta(q, b) = (p, L)$, then for all $c \in \Sigma$, G will have the corresponding production pab$\rightarrow$aqc and p$\uparrow$$\rightarrow$bp$\uparrow$. This rule is for deleting the excessive blanks reversely.

We have to point out here that many books on the field usually assert the equivalence of the transition function and the production, just through the transformation from the former to the later. They did not indicate the difference between these two things. Actually, however, in grammar, the complete derivation should be that in the final string there will be no any nonterminal, i.e., no element of K. In the string, there are only the symbols of Σ, otherwise the derivation is called the dirty derivation.

The productions obtained from function δ, however, are unavoidably containing the nonterminal symbol in K. Therefore, in order to define completely G, it is necessary to contain extra productions that are used for deleting the nonterminals. Hence, we stipulate that G also contains the productions used to the transformation of the start of the computation (the termination of the derivation) and the termination of the computation (the start of the derivation). The production

$$S \rightarrow \text{ubh } \uparrow$$

forces that an cceptable computation will precisely finish the derivation at the termination place. In addition, the production

$$\text{ubs} \rightarrow \varepsilon$$

will delete the last part of the left side of the input, and $\uparrow \rightarrow \varepsilon$ will delete the termination token, making only the input string left.

The following assertion makes more precise the idea that grammar G backwardly simulates the computation of M.

Assertion For two arbitrary configurations of M, $u_1q_1a_1w_1$ and $u_2q_2a_2w_2$, there will be $u_1q_1a_1w_1 \longmapsto u_2q_2a_2w_2$ if and only if $u_2q_2a_2w_2 \uparrow \xrightarrow[G]{} u_1q_1a_1w_1 \uparrow$.

The proof of the assertion is omitted here. We just point out that the proof is a case analysis of the properties of the actions of M. We now almost come to the end of the proof of the theorem. We need to prove that for all $w \in (\Sigma - \{u, b\})^*$, M terminates upon w if and only if $w \in L(G)$; but $w \in L(G)$ if and only if

$$S \xrightarrow[G]{} ubh \uparrow \xrightarrow[G]{*} ubsw \uparrow \xrightarrow[G]{} w \uparrow \xrightarrow[G]{} w$$

Since $S \rightarrow ubh \uparrow$ is a production that involves S, and the productions $ubs \rightarrow e$ and $\uparrow \rightarrow e$ are the productions that allow to delete the state and the termination token. Through the assertion above, $ubh \uparrow \xrightarrow[G]{*} ubSw \uparrow$ if and only if $uq_0bw \xrightarrow[M]{*} uhb$, and this happens if and only if M terminates upon w.

Now the proof of the sufficency aspect of the theorem is completed. The proof of theorem is also completed.

However, in the proof we used the idea of multitape Turing machine. We need to show the relation between single tape Turing machine and multitape Turing machine to make our proof reliable in terms of its base. We have the following theorem.

Theorem 2.2 If a language L is accepted by a multitape Turing machine, it is accepted by a single tape Turing machine.

Proof Let L be accepted by M_1, a multitape Turing machine with k tapes. We can construct M_2, a single tape Turing machine with 2k tracks (for this concept, we will explain it later). Half these tracks simulate the tapes of M_1, and other half of the tracks each holds only a single marker that indicates where the head for the corresponding tape of M is presently located. The finite control of M_2 stores the state of M_1, along with a count of the number of head markers to the right of M_2's tape head.

To simulate a move of M_1, M_2 must visit the k head markers so that M_2 knows where are the tape heads of M_1. It must remember how many head markers are to its left at all time. After visiting each head marker and storing the scanned symbol in a component of its finite control, M_2 knows what tape symbols (the input of M_1) are being scanned by each of M_1 heads. M_2 also knows the current state of M_1, which it stores in M_2's own finite control. Thus M_2 knows how will M_1 move. M_2 revisits each of the head markers on its tape changes the symbol in the track representing the corresponding tapes of M_1, and moves the head marker left or right if necessary. Finally, M_2 changes the state of M_1 as recorded in its own finite control. Until now, M_2 has been simulated one move of M_1.

We select as M_2's accepting states all those states that record M_1's state as one of the accepting states of M_1. Thus whenever the simulated M_1 accepts, M_2 also accepts. Otherwise M_2 does not accept.

Now we turn to the concept of track which we mentioned above. We can imagine that the tape of the Turing machine is divided into k tracks, for $k \geqslant 1$ being integer. In this way, the tape can be considered as k tuples, one component for each track. A 3-track Turing Machine is shown in Fig. 2.3.

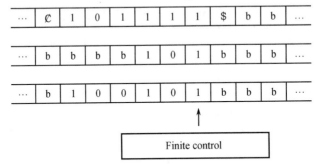

Fig. 2.3   A 3-track Turing machine.

From the design of the multi track Turing machine, we can see that the Turing machine with k-tracks is not much different from a Turing machine with k tapes. Actually in the theorem we just proved above, we used the same idea. We also have the following definition.

Definition 2.29   The Turing machine with two-way infinite tape. A Turing machine with a two-way infinite tape is denoted by $M = (K, \Gamma, \Sigma, \delta, b, q_0, H)$ as in the original model. As the name implies that the tape is infinite both to the left and to the right. The way we denote an ID of such a Turing machine is the same as for the one-way (to the right) infinite Turing machine. We imagine, however, that there is an infinity of blank cells both to the left and right of the current nonblank portion of the tape.

The relation $\underset{M}{\longmapsto}$, which relates two ID's if the ID on the right is obtained from the one on the left by a single move, is defined as follows. The original model with the exception that if $\delta(q, X) = (p, Y, L)$, then $qX\alpha \underset{M}{\longmapsto} pbY\alpha$ (in the original model, for this situation, no move could be made). And if $\delta(q, X) = (p, b, R)$, then $qX\alpha \longmapsto p\alpha$ (in the original model, the b would appear to the left of p).

The initial ID is qw. While there is a left end tape in the original model, there is no left end of the tape for the Turing machine to "fall off". So it can proceed left as far as it wishes. The trick behind the construction is to use two tracks on the semi-infinite tape. The upper track represents the cells of the original Turing machine that are at or to the right of the initial portion. The lower track represents the positions left of the initial position, but in reverse order. The exact arrangement can be as shown in Fig. 2.4.

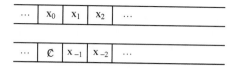

Fig. 2.4 A semi-infinite tape can simulate a two-way infinite tape.

In Fig. 2.5, the two-way infinite tape has been transformed into one-way 2-track infinite tape. The first cell of the tape holds the symbol $\mathcal{C}$ in the lower track, indicating that it is the leftmost cell and the following symbols are the adjacent left symbols from right to left. The finite control of the Turing machine tells whether it would scan a symbol appearing on the upper track (corresponding to the original right-side of the two-way infinite tape) or the lower track (corresponding to the original left-side of the two-way infinite tape).

We now give a formal construction of $M_1 = (K_1, \Gamma_1, \Sigma_1, \delta_1, b, q_1, H_1)$. The states K_1 are all objects of the form $[q, U]$ or $[q, D]$, where $q \in K_1$, and the symbol q_1 is in K_1 too. The second component will indicate whether M_1 will work on the upper (U stands for upper) or lower (D stands lower) track. The tape symbols in Γ_1 are all objects of the form $[X, Y]$, where X and $Y \in \Gamma$. In addition, Y may be $\mathcal{C}$, a symbol not in Γ. Σ_1 consists of all symbols $[a, b]$, where a is in Σ. H_1 is $\{[q, U], [q, D] \mid q$ is in $H\}$. it should be evident that M_1 can simulate M in the sense that while M moves to the right of the initial position of its input head, M_1 works on the upper track. While M moves to the left of its tape head position, M_1 works on its lower track, moving in the direction opposite to the direction in which M moves. The input symbols of M_1 are input symbols of M on the upper track with a blank on the lower track. Such a symbol can be identified with the corresponding input symbol of M. b is identified with $[b, b]$.

We summarize the idea and omit the formal proof with the following theorem.

Theorem 2.3 Language L is recognized by a Turing machine with a two-way infinite tape if and only if it is recognized by a Turing machine with a one-way infinite tape.

We now almost come to the end of the discussion of the Turing machine. In the discussion, we introduced the original concept of the Turing machine that is one tape and deterministic, and then sequentially we modified or extended it to nondeterministic and multitape Turing machine, including extended it from one-way infinite tape to two-way infinite tape. However, finally we found that all these extensions or modifications do not change or extend the functions of the original Turing machine. Therefore, it also means that the basic fact is Theorem 2.1 that a language is generated by a grammar if and only if it is recursively enumerable, if and only if it is accepted by a Turing machine. In this way, the Turing machine can be used in the syntactic analysis. This is the reason why we like to introduce the concept of Turing machine in the book compilation-oriented. The following result is also important for us. Based on the Turing machine, we can identify grammar with more useful computational model.

Definition 2.30 The grammar computation function. Let $G = (V_N, V_T, P, S)$ be A grammar, and let f: $\Sigma^* \to \Sigma^*$ be a function. We say that G computes F if for all w's and v's $\in \Sigma^*$, the following expressions holds:

$$SwS \xrightarrow[G]{*} v$$

if and only if v = f(w). That is, the string that consists of input w with a start symbol of G in both sides of w would generate a string of Σ^* under G, and it is just the correct value v of the f(w).

Function f: $\Sigma^* \to \Sigma^*$ is called grammatically computable [6, 7] if and only if there exists a grammar G that computes it. Similar to Theorem 2.1, we have the following theorem.

Theorem 2.4 A function f: $\Sigma^* \to \Sigma^*$ is recursive if and only if it is grammatically computable.

2.7 Issues Concerning Grammars and Languages

In this chapter, we have discussed several issues concerning grammars and languages. We now summarize them as follows:

1) Given a grammar, derive the language generated by the grammar.

If one wants to solve the problem, it must use the productions of the grammar exhaustively to derive all possible statements of the grammar. As it is impossible to do the exhaustive derivations, the feasible solution is to use the mathematical induction. After deriving the necessary statements as the basic ones and making the hypothetical one, one uses the mathematical induction method to prove the general one — the language generated by the grammar.

2) Given a language, search for a grammar that generates it.

This problem is the inverse problem of 1). If the problem above may be solved with the derivations from the production given, then this problem is to establish the grammar through the language, i.e., to establish the production set of the grammar. Obviously, it is a difficult problem.

3) Given a grammar and a sentence (statement), decide whether the statement is generated by the grammar.

The problem may have different layers. If the grammar given is the grammar of words, then the statements of the grammar are the words. The problem reduces to decide whether the word can be derived from the productions of the grammar. More specifically, to decide whether the word belongs to the vocabulary of the grammar.

If the grammar given is the grammar of statements or sentences, then the statement or sentence given is a string of words. Hence the problem is transformed into deciding whether the statement can be generated by the grammar.

A grammar that defines the words may define many words in its vocabulary. That means that the number of words may be very large. In this case, in order to decide whether a word belongs to the grammar or not, the grammar may need to make much effort to obtain the decision.

Similarly, a grammar that defines the statement may define many legal statements. The grammar of the programming language is exactly the case, as it can generate lots of legal programs. Therefore, the other task of the compilation is to decide whether the statement (the program) belongs to the language generated by the grammar. This is the topic of the syntax analysis. Both lexical analysis and syntax analysis are the major topics of the compilers, and are the major topics of the book.

4) Given two grammars, analyze whether the two are equivalent or not, i.e., whether the languages they generate are the same or not.

As for the investigation of the problem, there are two methods. One is, to analyze the grammars themselves, to see whether they are equal. However, this can be very difficult. It is hard to perceive the equality or the difference of the grammars. Therefore, in general this is not a feasible solution. The second one seems more practical. We derive both the languages from both the grammars. After we generate the languages, we may compare them to see whether they are equal or not. Although this is not an easy thing either, it can be carried out.

Centering on each one of these issues, the research methods may be different. In the book, we will concentrate on each one as more as possible. Of course, the concerning problems are not limited to these. The issues that are worth investigating include the relation between languages and the Turing machines, the simplification of the grammars, etc. But for the goals of the book we are not concerned very much about these issues and we will not discuss them.

Problems

Problem 2.1 Prove that any grammar can be transformed into an equivalent grammar that has the form uAv → uwv of production rule, where $A \in V_N$ and $u, v, w \in (V_N \cup V_T)^*$.

Problem 2.2 Prove Theorem 2.1. For the only if direction, given a grammar, how to construct a Turing machine so that when it has input w, it outputs a string $u\Sigma^*$ such that $SwS \xrightarrow[G]{*} u$, if such a string u exists. For if direction, use a proof that is similar to the proof of Theorem 2.1 but with forward (rather than backward) direction.

Problem 2.3 Design and completely write a Turing machine that scans towards right until it found two consecutive 0's. The set of characters on the tape is $\{0, 1, b, u\}$, and the input set is $\{0, 1\}$.

Problem 2.4 Find out the grammars that generate the following languages:

1) $\{ww \mid w \in \{a, b\}^*\}$;
2) $\{(x^2) \uparrow n \mid n \geqslant 0\}$;
3) $\{(a^n) \uparrow 2 \mid n \geqslant 0\}$;
4) $\{a^i \mid I \text{ is not a prime}\}$.

Problem 2.5 Under what condition, the kleene closure of a language L is equal to its positive closure?

References

[1] Chomsky N (1956) Three models for the description of language. IRE Trans Inf Theory 2(3): 113–124.

[2] Hopcroft J E, Ullman J D (1969) Formal languages and theit relation to Automata, Addison-Wesley, Reading, Mass.

[3] Hopcroft J E, Ullman J D (2007) Introduction to Automata Theory, Languages and Computation. Addison-Wesley, Reading, Mass.

[4] Knuth D E Trabb Pardo L (1977) Early development of programming languages. In Dekker M (ed) Encyclopedia of computer science and technology 7. Marcel Dekker, New York.

[5] Ledgard H f (1971) Ten mini-languages; a study of topical issues in programming languages. Computing Surveys 3(3): 115–146.

[6] Simon M (1999) Automata theory. World Scientific, Singapore.

[7] Simovici D A, Tenney R L (1999) Theory of formal languages with applications, World Scientific, Singapore.

Chapter 3 Finite State Automata and Regular Languages

Aspects of automata theory are essential tools in a variety of new disciplines, ...

John E. Hopcroft, Rajeev Motwani
and Jeffrey D. Ullman

3.1 Motivations of the Chapter

One of the most important functions of a computer is to recognize specified patterns. For example, a text-editing software often needs to replace a string of symbols with another string of symbols, whereas a compiler system must scan the symbols of a program to locate a certain key-word. In fact, the fastest string search algorithm is based on pattern recognition, which is in turn, based on automata theory.

Automata theory and formal languages are the most fundamental topics in all subjects of modern computer science, especially in e.g., compiler constructions, artificial intelligence, computability and complexity theory. This chapter, together with the later chapter on push-down automata and Turing machines, provide a theoretical foundation for compiler construction in particular and for modern computer science in general.

3.2 Languages, Grammars and Automata

In this section, we shall provide an account of some basic concepts of languages, grammars and automata, which are fundamental to finite automata in this chapter and the push-down automata in a later next Chapter 5.

Definition 3.1 An alphabet Σ is a finite set of symbols. A word or a string over an alphabet Σ is a finite sequence of symbols from Σ. An empty word (or string), denoted by λ, is the sequence consisting of no symbols. The length of a word w, denoted by $|w|$, is the number of symbols in w.

Example 3.1 Let $\Sigma = \{a, b, c\}$. Then $\omega_1 = acb$ and $\omega_2 = aababc$ are two words over Σ, and $|w_1| = 3$ and $|w_2| = 6$. Let $w = \lambda$, then $|w| = 0$. Suppose $\omega = ab$, then $\lambda ab = ab\lambda = ab$.

Definition 3.2 Let Σ be an alphabet, and λ the empty word containing no symbols. Then Σ^* is defined to be the set of words obtained by concatenating zero or more symbols from Σ. If the set does not contain λ, then we denote it by Σ^+. That is,

$$\Sigma^+ = \Sigma^* - \{\lambda\}. \tag{3.1}$$

A language over an alphabet Σ is a subset of Σ^*.

Example 3.2 Let $\Sigma = \{a, b\}$. Then

$$\Sigma^* = \{\lambda, a, b, aa, ab, ba, bb, aaa, aab, aba, baa, abb, bab, bba, bbb, \ldots\},$$
$$\Sigma^+ = \{a, b, aa, ab, ba, bb, aaa, aab, aba, baa, abb, bab, bba, bbb, \ldots\}.$$

The sets L_1 and L_2 given by

$$L_1 = \{a, b, aa, bb, aaaba\},$$
$$L_2 = \{a^n b^n : n \in \mathbb{N}\}$$

are all languages over Σ, where $\mathbb{N}$ denotes the set of positive integers ($\mathbb{Z}^+$ is also used to represent the set of positive integers).

Definition 3.3 Let ω_1 and ω_2 be two words, and L_1, L_2 and L be sets of words.

1) The concatenation of two words is formed by juxtaposing the symbols that form the words.

2) The concatenation of L_1 and L_2, denoted by $L_1 L_2$, is the set of all words formed by concatenating a word from L_1 and a word from L_2. That is,

$$L_1 L_2 = \{\omega_1 \omega_2 : \omega_1 \in L_1, \omega_2 \in L_2\}. \tag{3.2}$$

3) Powers of L are defined by the concatenation of L with itself the appropriate number of times, e.g.,

(1) $L^0 = \lambda$;
(2) $L^1 = L$;
(3) $L^2 = LL$;
(4) $L^3 = LLL$;
(5) $L^k = \underbrace{LL \cdots L}_{k \text{ times}}$.

4) The complement of a language L, denoted by $\overline{L}$ is defined by

$$\overline{L} = \Sigma^* - L. \tag{3.3}$$

Example 3.3 The following are some examples of concatenation of two words, two sets of words, and powers of a set of words:

1) If ω_1 = abc and ω_2 = aabab, then $\omega_1\omega_2$ = abcaabab.

2) If L_1 = {a, aba, cab, λ} and L_2 = {ca, cb}, then

$$L_1 L_2 = \{aca, acb, abaca, abacb, cabca, cabcb, ca, cb\}.$$

3) If L = {a, b}, then

(1) $L^0 = \lambda$;

(2) $L^1 = \{a, b\}$;

(3) $L^2 = LL = \{aa, ab, ba, bb\}$;

(4) $L^3 = LLL = \{aaa, aab, aba, abb, baa, bab, bba, bbb\}$.

Definition 3.4 Let L be a set of words. Then L^*, the Kleene closure of L, is defined by

$$L^* = L_0 \cup L_1 \cup L_2 \cup \cdots = \bigcup_{i=0}^{\infty} L^i \tag{3.4}$$

and L^+, the positive closure of L is defined by

$$L^+ = L_1 \cup L_2 \cup L_2 \cup \cdots = \bigcup_{i=1}^{\infty} L^i. \tag{3.5}$$

Example 3.4 If $\Sigma = \{0, 1\}$ and L = {0, 10}, then L^* consists of the empty word λ and all the words that can be formed using 0 and 10 with the property that every 1 is followed by a 0.

Definition 3.5 A grammar G is defined as a quadruple

$$G = (V, T, S, P), \tag{3.6}$$

where

V is a finite set of objects called variables;

T is a finite set of objects called terminal symbols;

$S \in V$ is a special symbol called start variables;

P is a finite set of productions.

Definition 3.6 Let G = (V, T, S, P) be a grammar. Then the set

$$L(G) = \{w \in T^* : S \overset{*}{\Longrightarrow} w\} \tag{3.7}$$

is the language generated by G, where $S \overset{*}{\Longrightarrow} w$ represents an unspecified number of derivations (including zero, if not including zero, we then use $S \overset{+}{\Longrightarrow} w$) that can be taken from S to w.

Example 3.5 Find the grammar that generates the language

$$L(G) = \{a^n b^n : n \in \mathbb{N}\}.$$

Both grammar G_1 defined by

$$G_1 = (\{S\}, \{a, b\}, S, P_1)$$

with P_1 consisting of the productions

$$S \to aSb,$$
$$S \to \lambda,$$

and grammar G_2 defined by

$$G_2 = (\{S, A\}, \{a, b\}, S, P_2),$$

with P_2 consisting of the productions

$$S \to aAb|\lambda,$$
$$A \to aAb|\lambda$$

will generate the language $L = \{a^n b^n : n \in \mathbb{N}\}$.

Automata are abstract (mathematical) machines, that can read information from input and write information to output. This input/output process is controlled by its finite state control unit (see Fig. 3.1). An automaton can be thought as a model of algorithm, or a compiler of a language, or even a general computer. In artificial intelligence, for example, automata are employed to model both behavioral situations and intelligent systems, including game playing, human intelligence, machine learning, nervous system activity, and robotic motion systems.

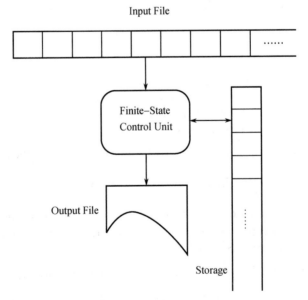

Fig. 3.1 A general automaton.

An automaton whose output is limited to a simple answer "yes" or "no" is called a (decision) problem solver or a language accepter. On an input with a string, the accepter either accepts (recognises) the string or rejects it. A more general automaton, capable of producing strings of symbols as output, is called a function transducer.

There are essentially two different types of automata: deterministic automata and nondeterministic automata. In deterministic automata, each move is uniquely determined by the current internal state, the current input symbol and the information currently in the temporary storage. On the other hand, in nondeterministic automata, we cannot predict the exact future behaviour of a automaton, but only a set of possible actions. One of the very important objectives of this chapter and the next chapter is actually to study the relationship between deterministic and nondeterministic automata of various types (e.g., finite automata, push-down automata, and more generally, Turing machines).

3.3 Deterministic Finite Automata

Finite-state automata or finite automata for short, are the simplest automata (see Fig. 3.2). In this and the subsequent sections, we shall study the basic concepts and results of finite automata (both deterministic and nondeterministic), and the properties of regular languages, with an emphasis on the relationship between finite automata and regular languages.

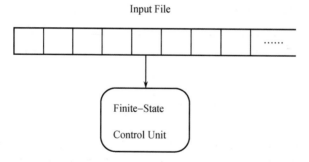

Fig. 3.2 Finite automaton.

Definition 3.7 A deterministic finite automaton (DFA), denoted by M, is a quintuple algebraic system (more specifically, a semigroup):

$$M = (Q, \Sigma, \delta, q_0, F), \tag{3.8}$$

where

    Q is a finite set of internal states;
    Σ is the input alphabet;
    $q_0 \in Q$ is the initial state;
    $F \subseteq Q$ is the set of final states, or accepting states;

δ is the state transition function

$$\delta : Q \times \Sigma \to Q. \tag{3.9}$$

Remark: The above DFA is defined without output; we can, of course, define it with additional output as follows:

$$M = (Q, \Sigma, U, \delta, \sigma, q_0, F),$$

where
U is the output alphabet;
σ is the output function

$$\sigma : Q \times \Sigma \to U. \tag{3.10}$$

Example 3.6 Let M be a DFA defined by

$$M = (Q, \Sigma, \delta, q_0, F)$$
$$= (\{A, B, C\}, \{0, 1\}, \delta, A, \{B\}),$$

where the transition function δ is given by the following formulas:

$$\delta(A, 0) = A \qquad \delta(A, 1) = B$$
$$\delta(B, 0) = C \qquad \delta(B, 1) = B$$
$$\delta(C, 0) = C \qquad \delta(C, 1) = C$$

or alternatively by the following table, called a transition table:

	0	1
Ⓐ	A	B
Ⓑ	C	B
Ⓒ	C	C

Initial state: A   Final state: B

Then the DFA can be represented by a directed graph shown in Fig. 3.3, where the initial state A has a starting right arrow, and the final state B has been double circled.

The machine defined above can read a given finite input tape containing a word and either accepts the word or rejects it. The word is accepted if after reading the tape, the machine is in any one of the accepting states.

Example 3.7 Consider the machine defined in Example 3.6. Suppose now that the machine reads the word 00011. Then the following are the actions of the machine as it reads 00011:

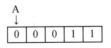

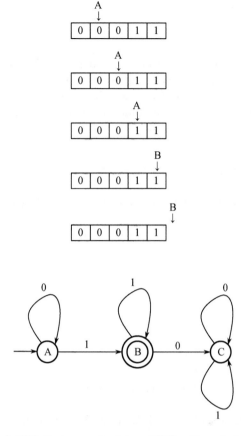

Fig. 3.3 A DFA that accepts strings $0^m 1^n$ with $m \geqslant 0$ and $n \geqslant 1$.

Since the machine is in the final state B after having read the input word, then the word 00011 is accepted by this machine. However, the machine cannot accept the word 000110, because

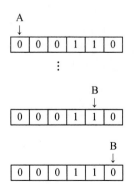

That is, the machine does not stop at the final state B after having read the word 000110. In fact, it stopped at the state C which is not a final state.

There are several other ways to describe actions of an automaton. One very useful way can described as follows (for the same automaton defined above and the same word 00011):

It is plain to verify that the automaton described in Fig. 3.3 can accept the following words:

$$0,$$
$$1,$$
$$01,$$
$$001,$$
$$011,$$
$$0000011,$$
$$00111111111,$$
$$\cdots,$$
$$0^m 1^n, \text{ with } m \geqslant 0 \text{ and } n \geqslant 1.$$

In set notation, the set of words L that can be accepted by the DFA is

$$L = \{0^m 1^n : m \geqslant 0, n \geqslant 1\}.$$

Example 3.8   Fig. 3.4 shows another example of a DFA, M, which has two

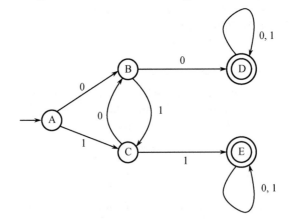

Fig. 3.4 A DFA that accepts strings with two consecutive 0's or 1's.

final states D and E. The DFA, M is defined by

$$M = (Q, \Sigma, \delta, q_0, F)$$
$$= (\{A, B, C, D, E\}, \{0, 1\}, \delta, A, \{D, E\}),$$

where the transition function is given by the following transition table:

	0	1
Ⓐ	B	C
Ⓑ	D	C
Ⓒ	B	E
Ⓓ	D	D
Ⓔ	E	E

Initial state: A   Final states: D and E

It is clear that the following strings can be accepted by this DFA:

00,
11,
0011110,
01001111000,
110111101001010,
10101010101010100,
0101010101010101011.

But the followings strings cannot be accepted by this DFA:

01,
10,
010101010101010101,
0101010101010101010,
1010101010101010101.

An automaton is finite in the sense that there are only finite states within the automaton. For example, in the automaton in Fig. 3.3, there are only three states: A, B and C. A finite automaton is deterministic in the sense that for a given state and a given input, the next state of the automaton is completely determined. For example, again in the automaton in Fig. 3.3, given state A and input 0, the next state can only be A.

3.4 Nondeterministic Finite Automata

In contrast to deterministic automata, nondeterminism allows a machine to select arbitrarily from several possible responses to a given situation, including the possibility of selecting from several initial states. If one of the various responses to a word leaves the machine in an accepting state, then the word is said to be accepted. In this subsection, we study non-deterministic finite automata.

Definition 3.8   A Non-deterministic finite automaton (NFA), M, is a quin-tuple algebraic system:

$$M = (Q, \Sigma, \delta, S, F), \tag{3.11}$$

where

Q is a finite set of states;

Σ is the input alphabet;

$S \subseteq Q$ is the set of initial states, usually $S = \{q_0\}$ as DFA, but it may be the case that it contains more than one state;

$F \subseteq Q$ is the set of final states;

the transition function is defined by

$$\delta : Q \times (\Sigma \cup \lambda) \to 2^Q, \tag{3.12}$$

where 2^Q is the set of all subsets of Q.

Example 3.9   Let M be the non-deterministic finite automaton defined by

$$M = (Q, \Sigma, \delta, S, F)$$
$$= (\{A, B, C, D, E\}, \{0, 1\}, \delta, \{A, B\}, \{E\}),$$

where δ is given by

$$\delta(A, 0) = \{A, C\}, \qquad \delta(A, 1) = A,$$
$$\delta(B, 0) = B, \qquad \delta(B, 1) = \{B, D\},$$
$$\delta(C, 0) = E, \qquad \delta(C, 1) = \lambda,$$
$$\delta(D, 0) = \lambda, \qquad \delta(C, 1) = E,$$
$$\delta(E, 0) = E, \qquad \delta(D, 1) = E.$$

Then the NFA can be represented by the directed graph in Fig. 3.5, or alternatively, by the following transition table:

	0	1
Ⓐ	{A, C}	A
Ⓑ	B	{B, D}
Ⓒ	E	λ
Ⓓ	λ	E
Ⓔ	E	E

Initial state: A   Final state: E

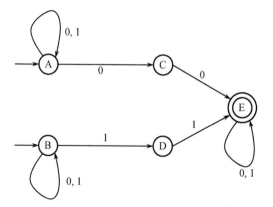

Fig. 3.5 A NFA that accepts strings with two consecutive 0's or 1's.

3.5 Regular Expressions

We have seen that finite-state automata can be used as language recognisers (or accepters). But what sets can be recognised (or accepted) by these machines? In this and the next a few sections, we shall answer this question by showing that the sets which can be recognised by finite-state automata are regular sets.

Definition 3.9 Let Σ be an alphabet. The regular expressions over Σ are defined recursively as follows:

1) $\varnothing$ is a regular expression;
2) λ (empty string) is a regular expression;
3) x is a regular expression if $x \in \Sigma$;
4) $r_1 \cup r_2$ is a regular expression if r_1 and r_2 are regular expressions;
5) $r_1 r_2$ is a regular expression if r_1 and r_2 are regular expressions;
6) r^* is a regular expression if r is a regular expression.

Each regular expression represents a set specifically by the following rules:

1) $\varnothing$ represents the empty set, i.e., the set with no string;
2) λ represents the set $\{\lambda\}$ containing the empty string;
3) x represents the set $\{x\}$ containing the string with one symbol x;
4) $r_1 \cup r_2$ represents the union of the sets represented by r_1 and r_2;
5) $r_1 r_2$ represents the concatenation of the sets represented by r_1 and r_2;
6) r^* represents the Kleene closure of the set represented by r.

Definition 3.10 The language generated by a regular expression, denoted by $L(r)$, is defined recursively as follows:

1) $L(\varnothing) = \varnothing$;
2) $L(\lambda) = \lambda$;
3) $L(r) = \{r\}$, if $r \in \Sigma$;
4) $L(r_1 \cup r_2) = L(r_1) \cup L(r_2)$;

5) $L(r_1 r_2) = L(r_1) \otimes L(r_2)$;
6) $L(r^*) = (L(r))^*$.

So it is natural now to give a definition for regular languages:

Definition 3.11 The regular languages are defined recursively as follows:
1) $\varnothing$ is a regular language;
2) $\{\lambda\}$ is a regular language;
3) $\{x\}$ is a regular language if $x \in \Sigma$;
4) $L_1 \cup L_2$ is a regular language if L_1 and L_2 are regular languages;
5) $L_1 L_2$ is a regular language if L_1 and L_2 are regular languages;
6) L^* is a regular language if L is a regular language.

Thus, regular expressions are a shorthand way of describing regular languages.

Example 3.10 Let $\Sigma = \{a, b\}$. Then the following regular expressions represent the indicated sets of strings:
1) a : represents the set $\{a\}$;
2) a^* : represents the set $\{a\}^* = \{\lambda, a, \ aa, \ aaa, \cdots\}$;
3) b : represents the set $\{b\}$;
4) ab : represents the set $\{a\}\{b\} = \{ab\}$;
5) $a \cup b$: represents the set $\{a\} \cup \{b\} = \{a, b\}$;
6) $(ab)^*$: represents the set $\{ab\}^* = \{\lambda, \ ab, \ abab, \ ababab, \cdots\}$;
7) $a^* \cup (ab)^*$: represents the set

$$\{a\} \cup \{ab\}^* = \{\lambda, a, aa, aaa, \cdots, ab, abab, ababab, \cdots\};$$

8) a^*b : represents the set $\{a\}^*\{b\} = \{b, \ ab, \ aab, \ aaab, \cdots\}$;
9) $b(ab)^*$: represents the set $\{b\}\{ab\}^* = \{b, \ bab, \ babab, \cdots\}$;
10) $a^*b(ab)^*$: represents the set of all strings that begin with any number (possibly 0) of a, followed by a single b, followed by any number (possibly 0) of pair ab.

Example 3.11 Let $\Sigma = \{a, b\}$. By definition, $\varnothing$ and λ are regular sets. In view of the previous example, the following sets are also regular:
1) $\{a\}$;
2) $\{\lambda, \ a, \ aa, \ aaa, \cdots\}$;
3) $\{b\}$;
4) $\{a, b\}$;
5) $\{\lambda, \ ab, \ abab, \ ababab, \cdots\}$;
6) $\{b, \ ab, \ aab, \ aaab, \cdots\}$.

3.6 Regular Grammar

The second way of describing regular languages is by means of a certain grammar, the regular grammar.

Definition 3.12 A grammar $G = (V, T, S, P)$ is said to be right-linear if all productions are of the form

$$A \rightarrow xB, \qquad (3.13)$$
$$A \rightarrow x,$$

where $A, B \in V$ and $x \in T^*$.

A grammar $G = (V, T, S, P)$ is said to be left-linear if all productions are of the form

$$A \rightarrow Bx, \qquad (3.14)$$
$$A \rightarrow x.$$

A regular grammar is one that is either right-linear or left-linear.

Example 3.12 The grammar $G_1 = (\{S\}, \{a, b\}, S, P_1)$, with P_1 given by

$$S \rightarrow abS,$$
$$S \rightarrow a$$

is right-linear, whereas the grammar $G_2 = (\{S, S_1, S_2\}, \{a, b\}, S, P_2)$, with P_2 given by

$$S \rightarrow S_1 ab,$$
$$S_1 \rightarrow S_1 ab,$$
$$S_1 \rightarrow S_2,$$
$$S_2 \rightarrow a$$

is left-linear. Both G_1 and G_2 are regular grammars.

By G_1, we can have the following derivations:

$$S \Longrightarrow abS$$
$$\Longrightarrow aba$$
$$S \Longrightarrow abS$$
$$\Longrightarrow ababS$$
$$\Longrightarrow ababa$$
$$\Longrightarrow (ab)^2 a$$
$$S \overset{*}{\Longrightarrow} ababS$$
$$\Longrightarrow abababS$$
$$\Longrightarrow abababa$$
$$\Longrightarrow (ab)^3 a$$
$$\vdots$$
$$\Longrightarrow (ab)^n a, \text{ for } n \geqslant 1.$$

The regular language L, denoted by $L(G_1)$, generated by the regular grammar G_1 is thus

$$L(G_1) = \{(ab)^n a : \text{ for } n \geqslant 1\}.$$

Similarly, by G_2, we have

$$
\begin{aligned}
S &\Longrightarrow S_1 ab \\
&\Longrightarrow S_2 ab \\
&\Longrightarrow aab \\
S &\Longrightarrow S_1 ab \\
&\Longrightarrow S_1 abab \\
&\Longrightarrow S_2 abab \\
&\Longrightarrow aabab \\
&\Longrightarrow a(ab)^2 \\
S &\overset{*}{\Longrightarrow} S_1 abab \\
&\Longrightarrow S_1 ababab \\
&\Longrightarrow S_2 ababab \\
&\Longrightarrow aababab \\
&\Longrightarrow a(ab)^3 \\
&\;\;\vdots \\
&\Longrightarrow a(ab)^n, \text{ for } n \geqslant 1.
\end{aligned}
$$

The regular language L, denoted by $L(G_2)$, generated by the regular grammar G_2 is thus

$$L(G_2) = \{a(ab)^n : \text{for } n \geqslant 1\}.$$

Theorem 3.1 Let $G = (V, T, S, P)$ be a regular grammar (either right-linear or left-linear). Then $L(G)$ is a regular language.

Theorem 3.2 A language L is regular if and only if there exists a regular grammar (either left-linear or right-linear) G, such that $L = L(G)$.

Thus, regular languages and regular grammars are, in fact, equivalent concepts. From a regular language, we can get it's regular grammar. From a regular grammar, we can also generate it's regular languages.

3.7 Kleene's and Moore's Theorems

The third way to describe regular languages is by finite automata (FA). In 1956, Stephen Kleene proved that regular sets are the sets that are accepted by a finite automaton. Consequently, this result is called the Kleene's Theorem.

Theorem 3.3 (Kleene's Theorem) A language L over an alphabet Σ is regular if and only if it is acceptable (recognisable) by a finite automaton FA, $M = (Q, \Sigma, \delta, q_0, F)$.

The proof of the only if part of the theorem involves showing that
1) $\varnothing$ is accepted by a finite automata;
2) $\{\lambda\}$ is accepted by a finite automata;
3) For each $x \in \Sigma$, x is accepted by a finite automata;
4) AB is accepted by a finite automata if both A and B are;
5) $A \cup B$ is accepted by a finite automata if both A and B are;
6) A^* is accepted by a finite automata if A is.
The proof of the *if* part of the theorem can be done by induction on the number of states in a finite automaton FA that accepts L.

The Kleene's theorem is one of the central results in automata theory. It outlines the limitations as well as the capabilities of finite automata, because there are certainly many languages that are not regular, and hence not accepted by finite automata.

Finally, we introduce another important result about regular sets, the equivalence theorem, discovered by E. F. Moore in 1956:

Theorem 3.4 (Moore's Theorem) There exists an algorithm to determine whether or not two given regular sets over Σ are equivalent.

The Moore's theorem is one of the results of decidability for regular languages. There are some more decidability results for regular languages. However, we do not study them here due to the limitation of space.

3.8 Pumping Theorems and Closure Properties for L_{REG}

As we have seen, a language L is regular if and only if there exists a finite automata (FA) to accept it; if no FA can accept it, it is then not a regular language. Our next result will provide another technique showing languages nonregular.

Theorem 3.5 (Pumping Theorem for Regular Languages) Let L be a regular language. There exists a positive integer N (depending on L) such that for any $x \in L$ and $|x| \geqslant n$, there exist strings u, v and w, satisfying the following conditions:

$$x = uvw, \tag{3.15}$$
$$|v| > 0, \tag{3.16}$$
$$|uv| \leqslant N, \tag{3.17}$$
$$uv^i w \in L, \forall i \geqslant 0. \tag{3.18}$$

The number N is called the pumping number for the regular language L.

This theorem describes a property that is common to all regular languages. So we can use it to show that a language is nonregular if we can show that the property fails to hold for the language.

Example 3.13   Use the pumping theorem to show that

$$L = \{a^n b^n : n \in \mathbb{Z}^+\}$$

is not a regular language.

Suppose that

$$L = \{a^n b^n : n \in \mathbb{Z}^+\} = \underbrace{aa \cdots a}_{n \text{ times}} \underbrace{bb \cdots b}_{n \text{ times}}$$

is regular and let N be the pumping number for L. We must show that no matter what N is, we may find x with $|x| \geqslant N$, that produces a contradiction. Let $x = a^N b^N$. According to Theorem 3.5, there are strings u, v, and w, such that Eqs. (3.15)–(3.18) in the theorem hold. From Eqs. (3.15) and (3.16) we can see that $uv = a^k$ for some k. So from Eq. (3.17) we have $v = a^j$ form for some $j > 0$. Then Eq. (3.18) says that $uv^m w \in L, \forall m \geqslant a$. But

$$
\begin{aligned}
uv^m w &= (uv)v^{m-1}w \\
&= a^k(a^j)^{m-1}a^{N-k}b^N \\
&= a^{N+j(m-1)}b^N \qquad (w = 0^{N-k}b^N, \text{since } uv = a^k) \\
&= a^{N+t}b^N. \qquad (\text{let } t = j(m-1) \text{ when } m > 1)
\end{aligned}
$$

Clearly, there are t more consecutive a's than there are consecutive b's in x. Since this string is not in the form $a^n b^n$, then it is not regular.

Finally we present some closure properties for regular languages.

Theorem 3.6   The family of regular languages is closed under the operations union, intersection, difference, concatenation, right-quotient, complementation, and star-closure. That is,

$$L_1 \text{ and } L_2 \text{ are regular} \implies L_1 \cup L_2, L_1 \cap L_2, L_1 - L_2, L_1 L_2, \overline{L_1}, L_1^* \text{ are regular.}$$
$$(3.19)$$

3.9   Applications of Finite Automata

One of the applications of automata theory in computer science is compiler construction. For instance, a compiler must be able to recognize which strings of symbols in the source program should be considered as representations of single objects, such as variables, names, numerical constants, and reserved words. This pattern-recognition task is handled by the lexical analyzer within the compiler. The design of lexical analysers depends more or less on automata theory. In fact, a lexical analyzer is a finite automaton.

Example 3.14 Suppose that we wish to design a lexical analyzer for identifiers; an identifier is defined to be a letter followed by any number of letters or digits, i.e.,

$$\text{identifier} = \{\{\text{letter}\}\{\text{letter}, \text{digit}\}^*\}.$$

It is easy to see that the DFA in Fig. 3.6 will accept the above defined identifier. The corresponding transition table for the DFA is given as follows:

state/symbol	letter	digit
Ⓐ	B	C
Ⓑ	B	B
Ⓒ	C	C

Initial state: A   Final state: B

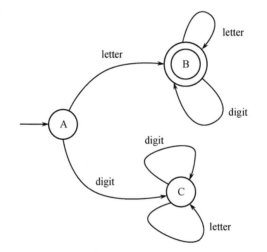

Fig. 3.6 DFA that accepts identifier.

For example, all the elements in set S_1 are acceptable identifiers by the DFA, whereas all the elements in set S_2 are unacceptable identifiers:

$$S_1 = \{C, A21, x2w101, s13579\},$$
$$S_2 = \{87, 2add, 7w101\}.$$

Example 3.15 Suppose that we now want to design a lexical analyzer for real numbers; a real number can be either in decimal form (e.g., 45, 79) or in exponential form (e.g., 34. 0E-9). The DFA described in Fig. 3.7 will accept the real numbers just defined. The corresponding transition table for the DFA is given as follows:

State/symbol	Digit	·	E	+	−
①	2				
②	2	3	5		
③	4				
④	4		5		
⑤	7			6	6
⑥	7		5		
⑦	7				

Initial state: 1   Final state: 4 and 7

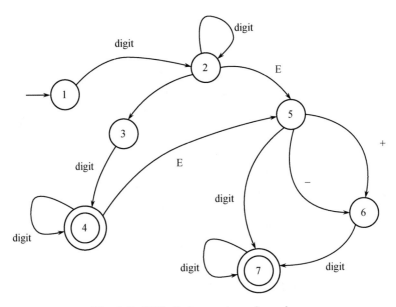

Fig. 3.7 DFA that accepts real numbers.

For example, all elements in the set

$$S = \{54.3, 54.3E7, 54.3E + 7, 54.3E - 7, 54E7, 54E + 7, 54E - 7\}$$

are acceptable real numbers by the DFA defined above.

3.10 Variants of Finite Automata

In this section, we shall provide a brief introduction to some variants of finite-state automata, including stochastic automata, fuzzy automata, Petri nets, connectionist machines, and cellular automata. These automata are the natural extensions of the classical finite automata (particularly nondeterministic finite automata) and are very useful in certain areas of computer science.

Stochastic Automata

Intelligent behavior is very often characterised by a lack of deterministic predictability. Given the same input, an intelligent being (e.g., a robot's brain) might appear to act in varying ways. The apparent uncertainty in behavior requires models that reflect that uncertainty. One way of achieving such a model is through the use of probability. Stochastic automata are types of probabilistic automata, which are, in fact, very similar to nondeterministic automata (NFA) discussed in the previous sections.

Definition 3.13   A stochastic automaton, M, is a six-tuple:

$$M = (Q, \Sigma, V, \delta, q_0, F), \tag{3.20}$$

where

1) Q is a finite set of states;
2) $q_0 \in Q$ is the initial state;
3) $F \subseteq Q$ is the set of final states or accepting states, denoted by a double circle;
4) Σ is a finite set of inputs or instructions;
5) V is the valuation space $[0, 1]$;
6) δ is transition function

$$\delta : Q \times \Sigma \times Q \to V. \tag{3.21}$$

It is required that for any fixed non-final state q and any fixed instruction a

$$\sum_{q' \in Q} \delta(q, a, q') = 1. \tag{3.22}$$

This requirement allows us to interpret

$$\delta(q, a, q') = x \tag{3.23}$$

as meaning that x is the probability of the machine going from state q to state q' utilising the instruction a and the sum of the probability must be 1.

Example 3.16   Let $M = (Q, \Sigma, V, \delta, q_0, F)$ be a stochastic automaton with

$\Sigma = \{a, b\}$

$Q = \{A, B, C\}$	$q_0 = A$	$F = C$
$\delta(A, a, A) = 0.7$	$\delta(B, a, A) = 1$	$\delta(C, a, C) = 1$
$\delta(A, a, C) = 0.1$	$\delta(B, b, B) = 0.6$	$\delta(C, b, C) = 1$
$\delta(A, a, B) = 0.2$	$\delta(B, b, C) = 0.4$	
$\delta(A, b, B) = 0.9$		
$\delta(A, b, C) = 0.1$		

where $\sum\limits_{q' \in Q} \delta(q, a, q') = 1$. This stochastic automaton can be diagrammatically shown in Fig. 3.8. Suppose that we now wish to calculate the probability that the automaton will go to state C from A given instructions a and b:

$$
\begin{aligned}
\delta'(A, ab, C\} &= \sum_{q \in Q} \delta(A, a, q) \cdot \delta(q, b, C) \\
&= \delta(A, a, A) \cdot \delta(A, b, C) + \delta(A, a, B) \cdot \delta(B, b, C) + \\
&\quad\ \delta(A, a, C) \cdot \delta(C, b, C) \\
&= 0.7 \times 0.1 + 0.2 \times 0.4 + 0.1 \times 1 \\
&= 0.25.
\end{aligned}
$$

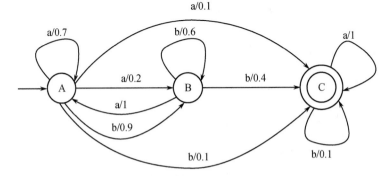

Fig. 3.8   A stochastic automaton.

Fuzzy Automata

In stochastic automata, the uncertainty was modelled by probability. We now introduce another similar automata in which the uncertainty was modelled by fuzziness, rather than by probability. A fuzzy automaton is again similar to a nondeterministic automaton in that several destination states may be entered simultaneously; however, it is also similar to a stochastic automaton in that there is a measure of the degree to which the automaton transitions between states, that measure being between 0 and 1.

Definition 3.14   A fuzzy automaton, M, is a six-tuple

$$
M = (Q, \Sigma, V, \delta, q_0, F), \tag{3.24}
$$

where

    Q is a finite set of states;

    $q_0 \in Q$ is the initial state;

    Σ is a finite set of inputs or instructions;

    $F \subseteq Q$ is the set of final states or accepting states, denoted by a double circle;

V is the valuation space $[0, 1]$;

δ is transition function:

$$\delta : Q \times \Sigma \times Q \to V. \qquad (3.25)$$

Example 3.17 Let $M = (Q, \Sigma, V, \delta, q_0, F)$ be a fuzzy automaton with

$$\Sigma = \{a, b\}$$
$$Q = \{A, B, C\} \qquad q_0 = A \qquad\qquad F = C$$
$$\delta(A, a, A) = 0.8 \qquad \delta(B, a, C) = 0.9 \qquad \delta(C, b, B) = 0.4$$
$$\delta(A, a, B) = 0.7$$
$$\delta(A, a, C) = 0.5$$
$$\delta(A, b, C) = 0.4$$

Then M can be graphically described in Fig. 3.9. Note that a fuzzy automata is not necessarily stochastic, say, e.g., $\sum_{q' \in Q} \delta(C, b, q') = 0.4 \neq 1$. Suppose that now we also wish to calculate the certainty that the automaton will go to state C from A given instructions a and b:

$$
\begin{aligned}
\delta'(A, ab, C\} &= \bigvee_{q \in Q} [\delta(A, a, q) \wedge \delta(q, b, C)] \\
&= [\delta(A, a, A) \wedge \delta(A, b, C)] \vee [\delta(A, a, B) \wedge \delta(B, b, C)] \vee \\
&\quad\; [\delta(A, a, C) \wedge \delta(C, b, C)] \\
&= (0.8 \wedge 0.4) \vee (0.7 \wedge 0.4) \vee (0.5 \wedge 0.7) \\
&= 0.4 \vee 0.4 \vee 0.5 \\
&= 0.5.
\end{aligned}
$$

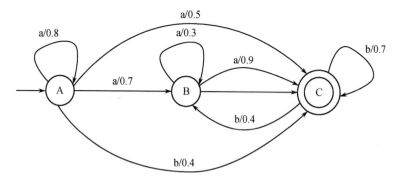

Fig. 3.9 A fuzzy automaton.

Note that "$\wedge$" (resp. "$\vee$") means that the minimum (resp. maximum) is being taken over all the possible states.

Fuzzy automata are an important tool for modelling uncertainty in artificial intelligence, particularly in fuzzy logic based expert systems.

Cellular Automata

Cellular automata, also known as tessellation structures, and iterative circuit computers, is a model of parallel computation. The basic ideas for cellular automata are due to John von Neumann (1903–1957), who introduced them, probably not because of interest in them, but rather as vehicles to study the feasibility of designing automata to reproduce themselves. This is why we call cellular automata self-reproducing automata. We shall only give a very brief introduction to this powerful automata.

Consider a two-dimensional lattice of cells extending indefinitely in all directions (see Fig. 3.10). Suppose that each cell (e.g., A) is a finite automaton that can assume any one of the n states, $q_1, q_2, \cdots, q_n$. All cells are identical in their structure, but at any given time they may be in different states. At each time step, every machine assumes a state which is determined by the states of its four neighboring cells B, C, D, E and of itself at the preceding time step. One of the possible states is a "quiescent" one and if a given cell and its four neighbours are in this quiescent state at time t then the given cell remains in the same state at time t + 1. If all cells in the array arrive at the quiescent state at the same instant, no further changes of state are possible. In the following, we shall present a formal definition for a simple linear cellular automaton:

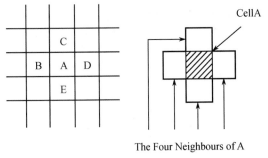

The Four Neighbours of A

(a)   (b)

Fig. 3.10 Two-dimensional lattice of cells.

Definition 3.15   A bi-infinite linear cellular automaton, M, is a 5-tuple algebraic system defined by

$$M = (\mathbb{Z}, \Sigma, q, N, \delta), \tag{3.26}$$

where

$\mathbb{Z} = \{\cdots, -i, \cdots, 0, \cdots, i, \cdots\}$ is the set of cells; $i \in \mathbb{Z}$ is the location of the cell i.

$\Sigma = \{0, 1, 2, \cdots, k-1\}$ is a finite non-empty set of (cell-)states; At each step of the computation, each cell is in a particular state.

$N = (a_1, \cdots, a_r)$ is the neighborhood; it is a strictly increasing sequence of signed integers for some $r \geqslant 1$, giving the addresses of the neighbours related to each cell. This means that the neighbours of cell i are indexed by $i + a_1, \cdots, i + a_r$. We call $r = |N|$ the size of the neighborhood. Cells are simultaneously changing their states at each time step according to the states of their neighbours.

δ is the local transition function defined by

$$\delta : \Sigma^{|N|} \to \Sigma. \tag{3.27}$$

If at a given step the neighbours of a cell are respectively in states $p_1, \cdots, p_r$, then at the next step the state of the cell will be $\delta(p_1, \cdots, p_r)$.

$q \in \Sigma$ is the distinguished quiescent state, which satisfies the condition $\delta(q, \cdots, q) = q$.

We remark, in conclusion, that a cellular automaton is, in a way, a neural network except that the atomic cells have the power of an arbitrary finite-state automaton but are, on the other hand, restricted to be identical to each other. In fact, cellular automata can be simulated by a particular neural network defined as follows: A bi-infinite neural network is a 5-tuple algebraic system:

$$M = (\mathbb{Z}, \Sigma, W, B, \delta_i) \tag{3.28}$$

where

1) $\mathbb{Z} = \{\cdots, -i, \cdots, 0, \cdots, i, \cdots\}$ is the set of neurons. of the cell i;
2) $\Sigma = \{0, 1, 2, \cdots, k-1\}$ is a finite non-empty set of (neuron-) states;
3) $W = (w_{ij})_{i,j} \in \mathbb{Z}, w_{ij} \in \mathbb{R}$ is the bi-infinite connection matrix, satisfying

$$\forall x = (x_i)_{i \in \mathbb{Z}} \in \Sigma^{\mathbb{Z}}$$

and

$$\forall i \in \mathbb{Z} \Rightarrow \sum_j w_{ij} x_j \tag{3.29}$$

is convergent;

4) $B \in \mathbb{R}^{\mathbb{Z}}$ is the threshold vector;
5) δ_i is the activation function of neuron i, defined by

$$\delta_i : \mathbb{R} \to \Sigma. \tag{3.30}$$

We refer interested readers to Refs. [4] and [5] for more information about cellular automata and neural-like cellular automata.

Problems

Problem 3.1 Find the grammar that generates the language

$$L(G) = \{a^n b^{n+1} : n \in \mathbb{N}\}.$$

Find the language generated by the grammar with productions:

$$S \to Aa$$
$$A \to B$$
$$B \to Aa.$$

Problem 3.2　Use the pumping theorem to show that

$$L = \{a^i b^j : i \neq j, i, j \in \mathbb{Z}^+\}$$

and

$$L = \{x \in \{0, 1\}^* : x \text{ contains equal numbers of 0's and 1's}\}$$

are not regular languages.

Problem 3.3　Let L_1 and L_2 are regular languages. Show that L_1/L_2 and $L_1 \ominus L_2$ are regular, where L_1/L_2 and $L_1 \ominus L_2$ are defined as follows:

$$L_1/L_2 = \{x : xy \in L_1 \text{ for some } y \in L_2\}$$
$$L_1 \ominus L_2 = \{x : x \in L_1 \text{ or } x \in L_2, \text{but } x \text{ is not in both } L_1 \text{ and } L_2\}.$$

Problem 3.4　Pattern Matching: On UNIX operating system, we can e.g., use the following command

$$\text{rm } {}^*\text{sy}^*$$

to remove all the files with letters sy in the middle of their names; for example, files with names ysy011, 100sypaper, and 01syreport will be removed. Design an automaton for an operating system, that can accept all the patterns of the form:

$$\{\{\text{letter, digit}\}^* \{\text{letter, digit}\}^*\}.$$

For example, the patterns 123abd, doc311, d1f22 are all accepted by the automaton.

References

[1]　Yan S Y (1988) Introduction to formal languages and machine computation, World Scientific, New Jersey. (The materials in this chapter are mainly based on this book of the second author.)

[2]　Hopcraft J E, Motwani R, Ullman J D (2006) Introduction to automata theory, languages and computation, 3rd edn. Addison-Wesley, Reading, Mass. (A general reference in finite automata and regular languages.)

Chapter 4   Lexical Analysis

> *Our review of the underlying cognitive mechanisms in-*
> *volved in word recognition has covered a wide range of*
> *topics — from the contextual effects phases, to logogens,*
> *to connectionism, to lexical decision task (LDT).*
>
> *Lexicaldecision task is a priming task in which a subject*
> *is shown a related word and asked to evaluate quickly*
> *whether a second string of letters makes a legal word*
> *or not.*
>
> *Robert L. Solso*

4.1 Motivation of the Chapter

According to the cognitive science, the understanding of the language by mankind starts with the word recognition. Without the phase, the understanding of language cannot take place at all. Similarly, as the first phase of a compiler, the main task of the lexical analyzer is to read the input characters of the source program, group them into lexemes, and produce as output of a sequence of tokens for each lexeme in the source program. However, before we discuss the lexical analyzer further, we would like to discuss the language understanding in terms of intelligence first. We want to explore why we need the lexical analysis in language understanding.

Among the various intelligences that human being possesses, language ability no doubt is a very important one which people use to communicate each other, to express minds and feelings, to keep the past, present, and future things for oneself or for others. If the oral language is said also an ability which other high-level animals possess, the written language ability certainly is a unique characteristic of mankind.

From the perspective of intelligence, how does the human being produce language and understand language? From the research and discovery of cognitive scientists we know that the baby starts learning language from grasping the words or vocabulary [1]. Only when one grasps enough words, can he/she understand the real things in his/her surroundings. Some estimates (Baddele,

1990) showed that the number of words a person knows shall be about 20000 to 40000 and the recognition memory would be many times of that number. With these words in mind, a person is able to know the meaning of the string of words if he/she also knows the arrangement of these words. Therefore to understand a language starts from understanding of words. Language is composed of sentences and each sentence is the string of words arranged according to some existing rules. For written language, the hierarchy of a sentence is lexeme → word or morphology → phrase → sentence. As for the sentence expressed via sound the hierarchy is phoneme → syllable → sound words → sound sentence. Among them each layer has to be bound by the grammar rules. Therefore, according to the modern linguists, to understand a language involves five layers: phonetic analysis, lexical analysis, syntactic analysis, semantic analysis and pragmatical analysis. Phonetic analysis means that according to the phoneme rules the independent phonemes are separated one by one from the speech sound stream. Then according to phoneme morphological rules, the syllable and its corresponding lexeme or words are found one by one. As for the analysis of the sentence of written language, the phonetic analysis is not necessary, because the lexical analysis is done via the reading in order for one to understand the meaning. When a person reads a language which he/she is familiar with, the understanding layers are what we mentioned above, excluding the layer of phonetic analysis. When one wants to understand oral language, the phonetic analysis must be included. Therefore, the phonetic analysis is the essential basis for understanding oral language.

Take English as an example. In English, there are approximately 45 different phonemes. For example, when you hear some one saying "right" and "light", if you are English native speaker, you will not have any difficulty in discerning between phonemes r and l. But if the native language of the speaker is Japanese, then it is likely that he/she could not pronounce them clearly. Since in Chinese there are many words that have the same pronunciation, the same situation is likely to happen. Only when the analysis is carried out for the whole context, may the discerning of these words be possible.

The lexical analysis, therefore, is an essential step for language understanding, as well as for the compilation because it is also taken as the basis of understanding programs. This is why we have the chapter, and we also regard it as the commencement step of the compilation.

4.2 Lexical Analyzer

Talking about the role of the lexical analyzer, we first should talk about the role of the compiler since the lexical analyzer is part of it. The role of the compiler is to compile or to translate a kind of languages into another, usually into a language executable on computer. In other words, it compiles or translates a program written in a human-oriented language into a machine code that is machine-oriented. As the implementer of the first phase of compilation, the role of the lexical analyzer is to read the input characters (the composition of the program) and produce the output as a sequence of tokens that the syntactical analyzer (parser) uses for the syntax analysis [2].

No matter whether the program is inputted into memory via the input of characters through key board one by one, or via the file that is stored in the memory in advance, the source program is present in form of the character stream.

Suppose that we have a simple C program as follows:

```
/* c program — 1 */
main( )
{
printf ("c program — 1\n");
}
```

Suppose that the length of words of memory is 32 bits (4 bytes). Then the initial input form of the program is as follows:

/	*		C
	p	r	o
g	r	a	m
—	1		*
/		m	a
i	n	(	
	)		{
p	r	i	n
t	f	(	"
c		p	r
o	g	r	a
m	—	1	\
n	"	)	;
	}		

4.2.1 Role of Lexical Analyzer

The main task of the lexical analyzer is to read these characters one by one from the buffer, then group them into tokens according to different situations [3]. These tokens will be encoded. In this way, the original character string now becomes the token string or token stream, providing the input to the syntax analyzer. Later we will see how the lexical analyzer works on the input above, to form the token string from it.

Apart from the main task that transforms the input character stream into a token string, the lexical analyzer may also perform certain secondary tasks at the user interface [4]. Such task is to strip out from the source program comments and white space in the form of blank, tab, and newline characters. Another task is to correlate error messages from the compiler with the source program. For example, the lexical analyzer may keep track of the number of newline seen, so that a line number can be associated with an error message. In some cases, the lexical analyzer is in charge of making a copy of the source program with the error messages marked in it. If the source language supports some macro-preprocessor function, these preprocessor functions may also be implemented as the lexical analysis [5] takes place.

For some compilers, they may divide the lexical analyzer into two phases, the first is called scanning and the second lexical analysis. The scanner is in charge of the simple task while the lexical analyzer is really doing the more complex operations.

Now we return to our example above. The lexical analyzer reads the input characters one by one. Then according to the regulation of lexical grammar of C language, the character stream is grouped into different tokens and so, it becomes the stream of tokens. In C language, the tokens can be key words, they are usually reserved for specific uses, not allowing to be used for the identifiers; then identifiers, integers, real numbers, a notation of single character, comments, and character string (user uses for printing), etc [6]. The lexical analyzer starts its work with reading the first word of the input. It reads the " / " , it knows that this is not a letter, rather it is an operator. However, here it should not have expression, so it continues its reading to the second character to see if it is "*" or not. If it is not "*", then it confirms that it is wrong. Otherwise it knows that the combination of "/" and "*" forms the identification of the start of comment line, and all the character string before the identification of the end of comment line — the combination of "*" and "/" is the comment. Regarding this, we have the definition that states that

```
#define is-comment-starter(chch) ((ch)(ch)=="/" "*")
```

and

```
#define is-comment-stopper(chch) ((ch)(ch)=="*" "/")
```

These two regulations specify the starter and the stopper of a comment, "/" "*"and "*" "/". Comment is written for programmers who wrote the program for other in order to provide some information or memorandum to them. Hence the comment need not to provide to the compiler. But when the compiler prints the list of the program, it is necessary to print the comment as it occurs in the original form. Therefore, the comments should be stored in a specific place where they occur in the original order. Hence the comment area needs to store the contents of the comments; in addition, it should also retain the places or addresses where they are located in order for them to "go home". In the current programming languages, the comments may occur at any place. So in a program there may be many comments.

As we have mentioned above that the main task of the lexical analyzer is to group the input character string, it needs also to decide the end of the input, and to discern the layout characters [7]. Therefore, in the lexical grammar that is used by the lexical analyzer for reference of doing its job, there is also the need to define the upper case, the lower case, etc. In the following, we list part of it for the demonstration.

```
#define is-end-of-input(ch)    ((ch)==" \ 0")
#define is-layout(ch) (!is-end-of-input (ch)&&(ch)<=")
```

where the first one defines the identification of the end of input while the second defines the layout symbol.

```
#define is-uc-letter(ch)  ("A"<=(ch)&&(ch)<="Z")
#define is-lc-letter(ch)  ("a"<=(ch)&&(ch)<="z")
#define is-letter(ch)  (is-uc-letter(ch)||is-lc-letter(ch))
#define is-digit(ch)  ("0"<=(ch)&&(ch)<="9")
#define is-letter-or-digit(ch)  (is-letter(ch)||is-digit(ch))
```

These are the definitions of letters and digits. The first one defines the upper case of the letters and the second defines the lower case; the third one defines the upper case or lower case; the fourth defines digits; and the last one defines letters or digits.

```
#define is-underscore(ch) ((ch)=="_")
#define is-operator(ch) (strchr(+-×÷),(ch))!=0)
#define is-separator(ch)  (strchr(";( ){ }",(ch))!=0)
```

These are the definitions of underscore, arithmetic operators and separators. In addition, there are the definitions of the relation operators. The six relation operators are $<, <=, =, <>, >, >=$ and the followings are their definitions:

```
#define is-relop-LT  ((ch)=="<")
#define is-relop-LE  ((ch)(ch)=="<" "=")
#define is-relop-EQ  ((ch)=="=")
#define is-relop-NE  ((ch)(ch)=="<" ">")
#define is-relop-GT  ((ch)==">")
#define is-relop-GE  ((ch)(ch)==">" "=")
```

The lexical analyzer needs to discern such the tokens as key words (or reserved words), identifiers, relation operators, comments, etc. Every programming language has the dictionary used for the reserved words that are the words used in the statements. In the dictionary, it also contains the codes of these words in machine. When the lexical analyzer found a reserved word in the input, it checks the correctness of the word (the spelling, the existence) from the dictionary. If it can find the same word from the dictionary, the correctness is satisfied. Then from the place of the word in the dictionary, the code used in the machine for the word is also found. The code will take place of the word in the intermediate form of the program. One of the advantages of the intermediate form is that for every identifier as well as the reserved word, they all have the same length and have identity bits to show their attributes. Otherwise they have different lengths and will take time to handle. Let us have a look at the dictionary of C language. It contains the following words (this is not exhaustive):

auto	break	case	char	const	continue
default	do	double	else	enum	extern
float	for	goto	if	in	long
register	return	short	signed	sizeof	static
struct	switch	typedef	union	unsigned	void
volatile	while				

Apart from these reserved words, there are also other data type declaration words, main(), opt, #include, #define, #line, #error, #pragma etc that need to be discerned. Notice that the dictionary must be complete that it contains all the legal words used in the C language as the statement names and so on. Otherwise if some are missing when the lexical analyzer found its appearance in the program, it will not recognize it and will consider it as an error. Notice that the list above is not the real list occurring in machine as in machine, each one should also have its code. The sorting of these words are not very necessary as it does not contain many words and so its searching will not be consuming. Even by sequential searching method, the efficiency is still acceptable.

4.2.2   Identifier analysis

We have known from previous discussion that any identifier is a string that must start with a letter and followed by any number (but in the concrete implementation, the number shall be limited) of letters, digits, and underscores. It can be seen as a regular expression. We can describe the identifiers of C language by

[a-z A-Z _] [a-z A-Z _ 0-9]*

Then the grammar that generates the regular expressions may be written as follows:

letter→a|b|...|z|A|B|...|Z|_
    digit→0|1|...|9

```
id→[a-z A-Z _]A
A→[a-z A-Z _ 0-9]A
A→ ε
```

Notice, that the "A" as the nonterminal is not the "A" as the letter. And the regular expression can also be written as

```
letter_(letter_|digit)*
```

Having the expression, we can check the correctness of the identifier via contrasting it with the expression to see if the identifier coincides in the structure. But as we have mentioned that in practice, the identifier is somewhat different from the expression that the number of components of the identifier is limited. Hence when the lexical analyzer scanned the string of the identifier it must count the number of the components. When the length of the practical identifier exceeds the limit then either it cuts it off (then it needs to check the uniqueness of the identifier) or declares that an error occurs, the identifier is too long.

After checking the correctness of each identifier, it is stored in the table specially used for the identifiers. It is called the symbol table in which the identifiers are stored and each is assigned an address for storing its value. The identifier is also replaced by its intermediate code. In general the lexical analyzer encodes the identifiers according to the order that they occur in the program. For example, the first identifier may be encoded as I1 (where I stands for an identifier) and correspondingly the second one is encoded as I2, etc. Usually, the identity bits occupy two bits of the words. For example, we use λ to denote the identity, and respectively, we use $\lambda = 00$ to represent reserved words, $\lambda = 01$ to represent identifiers, $\lambda = 10$ to represent integers and $\lambda = 11$ to represent real constants, other bits in the word represent the number of the identifiers or the address in the memory that stores the value of the item.

In the lexical analysis of the identifiers, there is an important task, i.e., to decide the declaration of the identifier. For most programming languages, there is such requirement, that is, the declaration of the identifier (it is called the definition occurrence of the identifier) should precede the occurrence of it in the program (it is called the application occurrence). Therefore, the principle is called the definition occurrence precedes the application occurrence. The principle implies that for an identifier there needs a declaration only, otherwise it will commit the error of repeated definition. It does not allow twice definitions with the two having different types. It is not allowed to use an identifier without definition. If these regulations are violated, then the lexical analyzer will handle it as an error case.

4.2.3 Handling of Constants

The handling of constants is more complicate than that of identifiers.

As for identifier, integers and real numbers may also be expressed as the regular expression. For example, in general text books on compilers, they usually expressed the real numbers as follows:

(+|-|)digit*.digit digit*(e(+|-|)digit digit*|)

The expression indicates that a real number may or may not contain sign symbol (+ or −). Following the symbol (if any) is zero or many digits, then a decimal point follows. After the decimal point, it must have at least one digit. If the number contains the exponent part, it should start with a letter e (implies the exponent) then a sign symbol follows again, or it is absent, then at least one digit follows.

If an unary postfix operator ? is introduced to mean "zero or one occurrence". That is, r? is equivalent to r|ε, or put another way, $L(r?) = L(r) \cup \{\varepsilon\}$. Then another expression

digit(.digit)?(E[+-]?digits)?

is given [8].

These two expressions want to express the same thing, real numbers. We cannot say that they are not correct. In terms of the structure of real numbers, they are absolutely right. But on the other hand, if we consider some restrictions of real numbers, they do not conclude them in the expression. We know that in the expression of real numbers, the leading zeros should not be allowed. It is also required that the zeros tail be eliminated. But as digit represents any digit from 0, 1, ..., 9, that means in both the expressions above, the leading zeros and zeros tail are included.

Apart from the two minor bugs, the two expressions above are basically correct. Therefore, we may define a grammar that generates the regular expression.

```
N→+R|
    -R|
    digit R |
    .P
R→digit R|
    .P
P→digit L|
    digit
L→digit L|
    e A|
    digit
A→+ M|
    -M|
```

```
     digit M|
        digit
M→digit M|
        digit
```

The productions above really generates the regular expression of real numbers but may include the leading zeros and zeros tail. The lexical analyzer may base on the grammar to handle real numbers [9]. The handling method is to group the digits that represent integer or real numbers together to form digit string, then translate the number into the binary number and put it in the constant number table [10]. The order of handling is also according to the order by which these constants occur. That is, after the first number had been handled in this way and store in the constant table, when the second number occurs, at first it is checked to see whether it has occurred or not in the table. If it has existed in the table, then it does not need to store in the constant table again. Otherwise it will be handled as the first number and put into the constant table.

As for the identifier, however, constant numbers have also the properties that are not regular. In any programming language, as the restriction of the capacity of the memory, in general, one integer can only occupy one word of the memory (32 bits or 64 bits), and one real number occupies the double or two times of the integer number. Therefore, when doing spelling and transformation of the constant number, the size or the value of the number will be checked. When the length or the size of the number exceeds the restriction, the lexical analyzer will report the error.

In order to present a legal expression of the real number without the leading zeros or the tail zeros, we want to modify the expression. We introduce the new terminal digit1 to represent [1..9], the original digit still represents [0..9]. Then the modified regular expression of real numbers now becomes following:

$$(+|-|)(0|\text{digit1 digit}^*).(0|\text{digit1}|\text{digit1 digit}|\text{digit}$$
$$\text{digit1}^*)(e(+|-|)\text{digitdigit1})?$$

The reader may check which kinds of real numbers are included in the expression.

4.2.4 Structure of Lexical Analyzer

So far, we have analyzed the works of lexical analysis on handling comments, reserved words, identifiers and constants. By these, we have seen the role of the lexical analyzer. Sequentially, we introduce the structure of the lexical analyzer.

The basic task of the lexical analyzer is that given a set S that specifies the tokens, and the place p in the input stream, then the lexical analyzer decides which regular expression in S matches the input segment starting from p, and decides the role of the segment in the program.

According to the task of the lexical analyzer, the analyzer can be constructed manually or automatically by computer. Both are done based on the tokens designated by the regular expression [11]. Here we mainly explain the structure of the manually generated lexical analyzer. Fig. 4.1 demonstrates the heading file of the lexical analyzer lex.h that defines 7 kinds of tokens: comment lines, identifiers, reserved words, constants, tokens with single character, ERRONEOUS token, and EOF token. The so-called token with single character means operators such as $+$, $-$, $\times$ (or $*$), $\div$ (or $/$), separators such as ; , ..., (,), {, }, etc. Fig. 4.1 shows the form of Token-types with the extending field. The field records the starting position of the token in the input, it also contains the definition of constants-like.

```
/* Define class constants;0-255 reserved for ASCII characters; */
        #define EOF            256
        #define comment        257
        #define constant       258
        #define reserved word  259
        #define identifier     260
        #define ERRONEOUS      261
        typedef struct {
              char * file-name;
              int line-number;
              int char-number;
            } position-in-file;
        typedef struct  {
              int class;
              char *repr;
              position-in-file pos;
            } token-type;
        extern token-type token;
        extern void start-lex (void);
        extern void get-next-token (void);
```

Fig. 4.1 Heading file lex.h of manually generated lexical analyzer.

The main program of the lexical analyzer consists of the following parts: the declaration of local data that manages input files; the declaration of global variables Token; the routine start-lex( ) that starts the lexical analyzer; and get-next-token( ). The get-next-token(0) is used to scan the input stream, and get the next token and put the data into Token table. Fig. 4.2 shows the data and commencement of the lexical analyzer.

The main program of the lexical analyzer repeatedly invokes subroutine get-next-token( ). The get-next-token( ) and its subprogram check the current input character to see what kind of token it belongs to, then it prints the

```
#include "input.h"          /* for get-input( ) */
#include  "lex.h"
/*private */
static char *input;
static int dot;             /* dot position in input */
static int input-char       /* character at dot position */
#define next-char( )        ( input-char=input[++dot])
/* public */
Token-type Token;
void start-lex (void) {
  input=get-input( );
  dot=0;input-char=input[dot];
  }
```

Fig. 4.2 Data and commencement part of manually generated lexical analyzer.

information found from the Token. When an EOF is recognized and handled, the loop ends. Fig. 4.3 shows the main program of the lexical analyzer.

```
#include "lex."            /* for start-lex (h), get-next-token ( )*/
int main( ) {
start.lex( );
  do {
     get-next-token( );
     switch(Token.class) {
     case COMMENT; printf("comment"), store-comment( ); break;
     case CONSTANT; printf("constant"), handle-constant( ); break;
     case IDENTIFIER; printf("identifier"), handle-identifier( ), break;
     case RESERVED WORD; printf (" reserved word"), handle-reserved
           word( ); break;
     case ERRONEOUS; printf("erroneous"), handle-erroneous( ); break;
     case EOF; printf("end-of-file pseudo-token"); handle-eof( ); break;
     default; printf("operator or separator"); single-token( ); break;
     }
     printf (": %s \n", Token.repr);
  } while (Token.class != EOF);
  return 0;
}
```

Fig. 4.3 Main program of manually generated lexical analyzer.

We do not introduce the details of work of get-next-token( ). After jump out from comment and layout character, get-next-token( ) records the position of the token, and the position is stored in the Token-pos field. Sequentially, the get-next-token( ) separates the first character of the token based on the current input stored in input-char. There are five cases: letter, digit, operator/separator, erroneous, and EOF.

What we talked about handling mainly includes two aspects. On the one hand, we represent the source program in the intermediate language form;

on the other hand, we construct a variety of tables from information in the input. For reserved words, as we have mentioned before, there is no need to construct table, there is a dictionary stored inside the compiler already. Each reserved word has been encoded with fixed code. Hence for the reserved word, the only thing which we need to do with its occurrence in the source program is to replace it with its code, then we got its intermediate form. For the identifier, it is different story. At first, we need to group the components into one token, then according to the order of occurrence by which it occurs in the source program, it is assigned a number with the token sign. There is one more thing for it, i.e., the assignment of address in memory that is used for storing its value. As for constants, it contains integers and real numbers (floating point numbers) and they are separately stored in different areas. Therefore, the areas which the lexical analyzer uses include [12]:

- DR[i] retains the reserved word dictionary, i is the index;
- SA[j] source program area, j is the address;
- IA[k] Intermediate language area, it corresponds to the source program area, but it has represented every component with its intermediate form.

Suppose that we stipulate that reserved words, identifiers, and constants have the following identity code:

	λ	(identity)
reserved word	0	reserved word i $\rightarrow$ the index of the reserved word in dictionary
identifier	1	identifier id $\rightarrow$ the address of the id in LT table
integer	2	constant ct_1 $\rightarrow$ the address of ct_1 in CT1 table
real constant	3	constant ct_2 $\rightarrow$ the address of ct_2 in CT2 table

The handling method for reserved words is, at first the components of the reserved word are grouped together to form a word, then check the word contrasting the words in the dictionary to see whether it matches one of them or not. If it matches, then take the code of the word in the dictionary and the code is the intermediate form of the word and put it into the intermediate language area that corresponds to the source program area. On the other hand, if it does not match any word in the dictionary, that means that the word does not belong to reserved word, it is an error. So an erroneous message should be issued to the programmer about the word.

The handling method for identifiers is, like for the reserved words, at first the components of the identifier are grouped into a token, then against the existing identifier table (IT), the token is checked to see whether it has existed or not [13]. Only the first identifier can meet the situation that the IT table is empty. If the identifier is not equal to any that already exists in the IT table, that means that this is a newly defined identifier, hence it should be put into IT table and in the intermediate language area, then the representation shown above will take place of the original identifier so that every identifier now has the same length with the same identity. If the identifier has already existed in the IT table, then it does not need to put in the table, the only thing needed to do is to put its intermediate code into the IA area. Fig. 4.4 shows this correspondence.

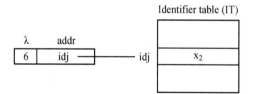

Fig. 4.4 Intermediate form of the identifier versus the IT table.

When handling the constants, the first step is also to group the components of it. But there is one thing that differs from that of identifiers. That is, the constant should be converted from decimal one to binary one as the value in machine. The handling process for integers is the same for real numbers. But the real numbers will occupy double words as many as the integers do. Since for integers, each occupies one word length, then the real number will occupy two word length. Fig. 4.5 shows the difference [14].

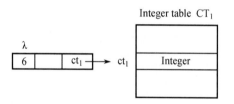

(a) Integer constants

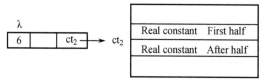

(b) Real constants

Fig. 4.5 Constant representation and constant table.

As for the handling of identifiers, after the constant is grouped, it has to be checked against the constant table to see if the table contains the constant already. If it does then it is not necessary to put the constant into the table again. But if it does not occur in the table, then it is stored in the table sequentially and the address which the constant stores in is taken as the intermediate representation that occurs in the intermediate language area. If it has already existed in the constant table, it does not need to be put into the table. Only the corresponding address needs to be put into intermediate language area to replace the original occurrence in the source program.

In the following a simple program in C and its corresponding intermediate language form are given. We will make it more directly perceived through the senses as much as possible so that the reader will be able to understand the working process of the lexical analysis [15]. Fig. 4.6 shows the process via the contrast of the source program with its intermediate peer.

```
#include <stdio.h>
main ( ){
        int x=1,total=0,y;
        while (x<=10) {
            y=x*x;
            printf ("% d\n", y);
            total+=1;
            ++x;
        }
        printf ("Total is %d\n", total);
        return 0;
}
```

(a) C language source program

0 The internal code of #	1 The internal repr of y	0 The internal code of "	0 The internal code of printf
0 The internal code of include	0 The internal code of ;	4 The internal code of %d	0 The internal code of (
0 The internal code of <	0 The internal code of prinef	4 The internal code of \n	0 The internal code of "
0 The internal code of stdio.h	0 The internal code of (	0 The internal code of "	1 The character string total
0 The internal code of >	0 The internal addr of x	0 The internal code of ,	4 The character string is
0 The internal code of main( )	0 The internal code of <=	1 The internal code of y	4 The character string %d
0 The internal code of {	2 The internal addr of 10	0 The internal code of)	4 The character string /n
0 The internal code of int	0 The internal code of)	0 The internal code of ;	0 The internal code of "
1 The internal repr of x	0 The internal code of {	1 The internal repr of total	0 The internal code of ,
0 The internal code of =	1 The internal addr of y	0 The internal code of +=	1 The internal code of toral
2 The internal address of 1	0 The internal code of =	1 The internal addr of y	0 The internal code of)
0 The internal code of ,	1 The internal repr of x	0 The internal code of ;	0 The internal code of ;
1 The internal repr of total	0 The internal addre of *	0 The internal code of ++	0 The internal code of return
0 The internal code of =	0 The internal code of ;	1 The internal repr of x	2 The internal addr of 0
2 The internal addr of 0	0 The internal code of printf	0 The internal code of ;	0 The internal code of ;
0 The internal code of ,	0 The internal code of (	0 The internal code of }	0 The internal code of }

(b) The intermediate language representation of the source program

Fig. 4.6 Source programs versus intermediate language representation.

Remark in Fig. 4.6 above, the code 4 has exceeded the extent of two bits. But it is only for the purpose of explanation. In practice we may need to use more bits as the identity bits.

The lex works in the following manner: At first the source program is written by lex as lex.1, then it is compiled by the compiler of lex to produce lex.yy.c in C language. The program lex.yy.c involves transformation map that is constructed from regular expression of lex.1 and the standard subroutines that recognize lexicons. The transformation map is the state transformation obtained from each configuration definition state of the right part of production. For example in S→ABC, it may have the following configuration states:

$$S \rightarrow \cdot ABC,$$
$$S \rightarrow A \cdot BC,$$
$$S \rightarrow AB \cdot C,$$
$$S \rightarrow ABC \cdot$$

These configurations should be considered along with other configurations obtained from other productions. For example, If there is another production that has A as its left part,

$$A \rightarrow B\beta$$

where β is a string consisting of terminals and nonterminals, then

$$S \rightarrow \cdot ABC$$
$$A \rightarrow \cdot B\beta$$

should be taken as a basic term, or considered as a state. Consequently, from

$$S \rightarrow \cdot ABC$$

to

$$S \rightarrow A \cdot BC$$

is a state transformation. For all the productions of a grammar, we have to write down all the state transformations. In the syntactical analysis later, we will discuss the state transformation in more details. In lex.1 the transformation map is represented in table where the actions associated with regular expressions are represented as code in C, they are directly moved to lex.yy.c. Finally, lex.yy.c is compiled into object program a.out. And it is just the lexical analyzer that transforms the input strings into token sequence.

The process above is shown in Fig. 4.7.

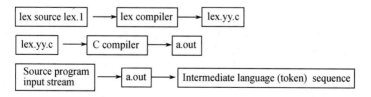

Fig. 4.7 Lexical analyzer based on regular expressions constructed by lex.

In order for the reader understand the lex.1 deeper, we list the skeleton of it as shown in Fig. 4.8. It contains three parts: the first part is the definitions of rules, the second part is the regular expressions and code segment, and the third part is the code in C language. It is also the one directly moved to lex.yy.c mentioned above.

```
% {
    #include  "lex.h"
    Token-type  Token;
    int line-number=1;              /* declaration part */
% }
    whitespace  [\t]
    letter     [a-z, A-Z]
    digit      [0-9]                /* definition of terminals */
    underscore      "_"
    letter-or-digit     ({letter} | {digit})
    underscored-tail    ({underscore}{letter-or-digit}+)
    identifier          ({letter}{letter-or-digit}*{underscored-tail}*)
    operator     [+ −×\]
    separator    [; , ( ) { }]
% %
{digit}+      {return INTEGER}
{identifier}    {return IDENTIFIER}
{operator} | {separator}      {return yytext(0);}  /* definition of regular
                                                       expression */
# [ * # \ n]* #        {/* neglect comment */}
{whitespace}     {/* neglect space*/}
\n line-number++; linefeed, line-number increases
-  {return ERRONOUS}
% %
void start-lex(void){ }
void get-next-token(void)   {
  Token.class=yytext( );
  if (Token.class==0)    {
    Token.class=EOF; Token.repr="<EOF>";return;
    }
  Token.pos.line-number=line-number;
  strcpy(Token.repr=(char*)malloc(strlen(yytext)+1),yytext);
  }
    int yywrap (void) {return 1;}
```

Fig. 4.8 The skeleton of lex that automatically generates lexical analyzer.

In lex, the comment is neglected. This is different from practice. In practice, the comments are kept for use in printing the list of the source program.

In addition, prominently, it does not contain the handling of reserved words as the reserved words cannot be handled as regular expressions.

Now look at the lex itself. For input, lex produces the file in C called lex.yy.c. The file contains a routine yylex. Routine int yylex (void) contains an inner loop.When the routine is invoked, it begins spelling the characters in input file according to regular expressions in the second part. For each recognized token the related C code is executed and the following handling is carried out. The representation form of the token can be found from array char yytext [ ]. When C language code executes the statement with numeric return value, the return value is just the value of the token. It represents that they are the values of corresponding tokens. After the relative handling is finished, the inner loop yylex ends. The class operator/separator is single char token and it is the first character of array yytext [ ] (hence it is yytext [0]).

The third part is the C language code that is truly executable. The lexical analyzer generated by lex does not need to initiate and the routine start.lex( ) is empty. The routine let-next-token( ) starts with invoking yylex( ). This invocation jumps over the comments and format symbols until it found the real token. Then it returns the value of the token class and carries out the corresponding process for the token class. When it detects the end of input, routine yylex( ) returns 0. The malloc( ) statement in this part is used to allocate space for array yytext [ ] as the space will store the result which the execution of get-next-token( ) obtains, that is, to store the token obtained in the space allocated while routine yywrap( ) is used to aid the processing of the end of file.

4.3 Output of Lexical Analyzer

In the last section, we have mentioned that after the analysis of the lexical analyzer, the source program input is transformed into the program in intermediate language and stored in intermediate language area. These identifiers, constants, and reserved words with arbitrary lengths all are replaced by tokens with fixed lengths and with different signs. At first the reserved words will be replaced by the corresponding code in the reserved word dictionary. Secondly, the identifier is replaced by an integer, following the sign bit (for example $\lambda = 1$). Meanwhile, however, in using token to take place of the identifier, a table is needed for storing the identifiers for check. As the amount of identifiers in a program varies, in general, it is more than that of constants, hence how to build the table of identifiers is a problem that causes special concern of the compiler.

The symbol table (identifier table) may be seen as the extended record array indexed by the character string (rather than the number) and the character string is just the identifier. The relative record contains the relative information collected for the identifier. The structure of the symbol table may be represented as follows:

```
struct   identifier  {
     char  a[int];
     int ptr;
}
```

Therefore, the basic interface of the symbol table module consists of a function identity: function identity (identifier name).

It returns the pointer that points to the record of the identifier, i.e., the machine code of the identifier. The pointer points to the address which stores the information of the identifier. After this no matter how many times which the character string is called, they always return the value. When we receive the information that relates to the identifier, we keep the information in the corresponding store unit.

In the compiler of C language, the symbol table module may contain the following information:

(1) The real character strings used for printing the source program and object program.

(2) Macro definition. A macro definition is to take the definition of identifiers as a macro, an instruction similar to a subroutine, and it takes some character string as a value.

(3) Definition of a series of types, variables, and function.

(4) Definition of a series of structures, common body names.

(5) Definition of a series of structures, field selection symbols of common bodies.

A simple method to implement the symbol table is the linear table, that is, when the declaration of some identifier is met in the declaration part of programs, then the identifier is registered in the symbol table, along with the address for storing its value, it looks like (identifier, value). The manner for implementing symbol tables is comparatively simple, as searching an item needed can be done by linear search. If the size of the table is not big, the efficiency is not a problem either. However, if the program is large and the symbol table is very big, then the data structure may be unsuitable due to its inefficiency. Instead the hash function may be the best substitution. Hash function is a mapping from name space N to address space A [16], namely, Hash $N \rightarrow A$. In general, $|N| \geqslant |A|$. In other words, given an identifier id, Hash (id) is a value in A and it is the address for storing id. When the identifier is to be accessed again, the function Hash (id) is computed first. When the value results then the address is found. Since $|N| \geqslant |A|$, however, it is likely that two different id_1 and id_2 compute $\mathrm{Hash}(id_1) = \mathrm{Hash}(id_2)$. When the thing happens, it is called conflict. Obviously conflict is not desirable. In order to resolve conflict, two methods are available. One is to chain the identifiers with the same hash value so that in the chain all the identifiers possess the same hash value. As such identifiers are not many, searching the desirable item from the chain is not difficult. Another method is called rehash. When the conflict occurs, then another hash function Rehash is invoked to recomputed the address assigned to the identifier. When the identifier is to be accessed, Hash and Rehash need to be computed again.

Hence the key problem is how to design a better hash function that causes conflicts as few as possible, this is not a simple problem. If a hash function causes many conflicts, it is definitely not a good Hash function. McKenzie, Harries and Bell proposed following Hash function based on the analysis of several widely used Hash functions in 1990. After using it in practice, it showed that it has good performance, where two parameters N and k are used, and their best values are N = 1 008 and $k = 613$. In addition, c_i is the ASCII value of ith character of identifier, n is the length of the identifier.

$$h_0 = 0$$
$$h_i = k \times h_{i-1} + c_i, \quad 1 \leqslant i \leqslant n$$
$$H = BITS(h_n, 30) \bmod N$$

Function BITS (h, m) produces rightmost m digits of integer h. Hence in the computation above, we take 30 digits of the rightmost. If we take k as 4, and N as 1 403, then the speed of the iterative algorithm is fastest as multiplying by 4 is simply left shift twice. But if the value of k is too small, then similar identifiers will be aggregated. In contrast, if the value of N is big, the opportunity that conflict occurs is smaller but the amount of storage occupied will correspondingly increase. The investigation shows that when k is 613 and N is 1 008, then we get 610 as the length hash value, 812 as the width hash value, and 1005 as height hash value.

4.4 Error Handling

Errors which lexical analyzer discovers may be grouped into the following classes as we described above:
  1) wrong spellings of the reserved words.
  2) Identifier errors.
  3) number errors.
  4) punctuation errors.
  There are two attitudes towards errors:
  One is strictly following the rules (the grammar) to treat errors, once an error is found, then the error report is issued immediately to user or programmer and the error type and position are also reported as one can as possible. In general case, however, to provide such an information is not easy. The common lexical analyzer can only report the possible error type, it is very difficult for it to locate the specific location of the error.
  Another treatment manner is more tolerant or more human nature, namely, when the error is found, the lexical analyzer manages to correct the error itself, rather than to issue immediately a report to user or programmer. The aim is to save the time of user or programmer and to improve efficiency.
  For example, if the error takes place in the spelling of the reserved word, if it is discovered that the wrong reserved word differs from the correct one only in one letter, then the lexical analyzer will regard it as correct and correct the wrong letter.
  If the error takes place in the input of the identifier, and it is determined that it is not another identifier, then the same treatment may be taken.

If for reserved words, identifiers or numbers, the errors are caused by excess in typing or mistyping. For example for a number if it contains two decimal points, then obviously the correction can be done by eliminating one decimal point, but which one should be deleted needs to be decided.

If the error is caused by missing of character, it also needs to decide what character should be added to make it correct.

If the error is caused by that the application occurrence precedes the definition occurrence, then a definition occurrence should be added before the application occurrence. But if for one item there are two definitions, and they are inconsistent, then one of them should be deleted. Nevertheless which one should be reserved needs to carefully decided.

Comparatively speaking, the types of errors in the lexical analysis are not many and their handlings are rather simple. Most of the errors are caused by mistyping of one or more characters, missing or excess in typing, or misspelling, etc. The key points should be put on these classes. It is unnecessary to attend to every and each aspect of the matter.

Problems

Problem 4.1 Write a program using the language which you are familiar with that recognizes the real numbers and identifiers.

Problem 4.2 Some one gives the regular expression of real numbers as

$$(+|-|) \ \text{digit}^*.\text{digit digit}^*(e(+|-|)\text{digit digit}^*|)$$

Explain what problem will the regular expression cause? If the problem is to avoid, how should it be written?

Problem 4.3 Write a complete input scanner.

Problem 4.4 Suppose that your symbol table can admit $10-100$ identifiers while sometimes you need to handle 100 000 000 identifiers with proper efficiency. Hence allocating a hash table with the size of admitting 100 000 000 is not consistent with the requirement of the problem. Design a suitable hash table algorithm to solve the problem.

References

[1] McCullough WS, Pitts W (1943) A logical calculus of the ideas immanent in nervous activity, Bull. Math. Biophysics 5: 115–133.

[2] Lesk ME Lex-a lexical analyzer generator, Computing Science Tech Report, 39, Bell Laboratories, Murray Hill, N J. It also appears in Vol.2 of the Unix Programming's Manual, Bell Laboratories with the same title but with E.Schmidt as coauthor. Murray Hill, N J. http://dinosaur.compil- ertool.net/lex/index.html.

[3]   Kleene SC Representation of events innerve nets and finite automata. In: Shannon CE, McCarthy J (eds) Automata studies, 34, pp. 3–40.

[4]   http://www.cs.princeton.edu/~appel/modern/java/JLex. Accessed 12 Oct 2009.

[5]   Hopcroft JE, Motwani R, Ulman JD (2006) Introduction to automata theory, languages and computation. Addison-Wesley, Boston.

[6]   Huffman DA (1954) The synthesis of sequential machines. J Franklin Inst. 257, pp 3–4, 161, 190, 275–303.

[7]   http://jflex.de/. Accessed 19 Nov 2009.

[8]   Aho AV, Corasick MJ (1975) Efficient string matching, an aid to bibliographic search. Comm ACM, 18(6): 333–340.

[9]   Free software Foundation. http://www.gnu.org/software/flex/. Accessed 19 Nov 2009.

[10] Aho AV (1990) Algorithms for finding patterns in strings. In Laeuwen J van (ed) Handbook of theretical computer science. MIT Press, Cambridge.

[11] Shannon C, McCarthy J (eds) (1956) Automata Studies. Princeton Univ Press, NJ.

[12] Thompson K (1968) Regular expression search algorithm. Comm ACM 11 (6): 419–422.

[13] McNaughton R, Yamada H (1960) Regular expressions and state graph for automata, Ire Trans. On Electronic Computers EC-9:1: 38–47.

[14] Moore EF, Gedanken experiments on sequential machines, in [15], pp. 129–153.

[15] Knuth DE, Morris JH, Pratt WR (1997) Fast Pattern matching in strings, SIAM J. Computing 6:2: 323–350.

[16] McKenzie BJ, Harries R (1990) Bell TC. Selecting a hashing algorithm. Software — Practice and Experience, 20(2): 672–689.

Chapter 5   Push-Down Automata and Context-Free Languages

Context-free grammars have played a central role in compiler technology since the 1960s .... There is an automaton-like notation, called the "pushdown automaton", that also describes all and only the context-free languages.

John E. Hopcroft, Rajeev Motwani and Jeffrey D. Ullman

5.1 Motivation of the Chapter

Push-down automata (PDA) form the most important class of automata between finite automata and Turing machines. As can be seen from the previous chapter, deterministic finite automata (DFA) cannot accept even very simple languages such as

$$\{x^n y^n \mid n \in \mathbb{N}\},$$

but fortunately, there exists a more powerful machine, push-down automata, which can accept it. Just as DFA and nondeterministic finite automata (NFA), there are also two types of push-down automata: deterministic push-down automata (DPDA) and non-deterministic push-down automata (NPDA). The languages which can be accepted by PDA are called context-free languages (CFL), denoted by L_{CF}. Diagrammatically, a PDA is a finite state automaton (see Fig. 5.1), with memories (push-down stacks). In this chapter, we shall study PDA and their associated languages, context-free languages L_{CF}. For the sake of completeness of the automata theory and formal languages, We shall also study Turing machines and their associated languages.

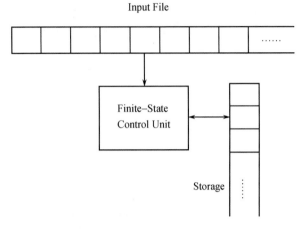

Fig. 5.1 Push-down automata.

5.2 Push-Down Automata

We first give a formal definition of the NPDA.

Definition 5.1 A non-deterministic push-down automata (NPDA) is defined by

$$M = (Q, \Sigma, \Gamma, \delta, q_0, z, F), \tag{5.1}$$

where

Q is a finite set of internal states;

Σ is a finite set called the input alphabet;

Γ is a finite set of symbols called the stack alphabet;

δ is the transition function, which is defined as

$$\delta : Q \times (\Sigma \cup \{\lambda\} \times \Gamma \to \text{ finite subsets of } Q \times \Gamma^*; \tag{5.2}$$

$z \in \Gamma$ is the stack initial symbol;

$q_0 \in Q$ is the initial state;

$F \subseteq Q$ is the set of final states.

Example 5.1 Let an NPDA, M, be $M = (Q, \Sigma, \Gamma, \delta, q_0, z, F)$ with

$$Q = \{q_0, q_1, q_2, q_3\},$$
$$\Sigma = \{a, b\},$$
$$\Gamma = \{0, 1\},$$
$$z = 0,$$
$$F = q_3,$$

and

$$\delta(q_0, a, 0) = \{(q_1, 10), (q_3, \lambda)\},$$
$$\delta(q_0, \lambda, 0) = \{(q_3, \lambda)\},$$
$$\delta(q_1, a, 1) = \{(q_1, 11)\},$$
$$\delta(q_1, b, 1) = \{(q_2, \lambda)\},$$
$$\delta(q_2, b, 1) = \{(q_2, \lambda)\},$$
$$\delta(q_2, \lambda, 0) = \{(q_3, \lambda)\}.$$

Then the automaton accepts the language

$$L = L(M) = \{a^n b^n : n \in \mathbb{N}\} \cup \{a\}.$$

A deterministic push-down automaton (DPDA) is an automaton that never has a choice in its move:

Definition 5.2 A push-down automata (PDA) is said to be deterministic, if it is an automaton, $M = (Q, \Sigma, \Gamma, \delta, q_0, z, F)$, as in Definition 5.1, subject to the following two restrictions: for every $q \in Q, a \in \Sigma \cup \{\lambda\}$ and $b \in \Gamma$,
(1) $\delta(q, a, b)$ contains at most one element;
(2) if $\delta(q, \lambda, b)$ is not empty, then $\delta(q, c, b)$ must be empty for every $c \in \Sigma$.

5.3 Context-Free Languages (L_{CF})

This section establishes the relationship between push-down automata and context-free languages. We first discuss context-free grammars and context-free languages.

Definition 5.3 A grammar $G = (V, T, S, P)$ is said to be context-free if all productions have the form

$$A \to x, \tag{5.3}$$

where $A \in V$, and $x \in (V \cup T)^*$.
A language L is said to be context-free if there is a context-free grammar G such that $L = L(G)$.

Example 5.2 The grammar $G(V, T, S, P)$, with productions

$$S \to abB,$$
$$A \to aaBb,$$
$$B \to bbAa,$$
$$A \to \lambda$$

is context-free. Some typical derivations in this grammar are:

$$S \Longrightarrow abB$$
$$\Longrightarrow abbbAa$$
$$\Longrightarrow abbba$$

$$S \Longrightarrow abB$$
$$\Longrightarrow abbbAa$$
$$\Longrightarrow abbbaaBba$$
$$\Longrightarrow abbbaabbAaba$$
$$\Longrightarrow abbbaabbaba$$

$$S \overset{*}{\Longrightarrow} abbbaabbAaba$$
$$\Longrightarrow abbbaabbaaBbaba$$
$$\Longrightarrow abbbaabbaabbAababa$$
$$\Longrightarrow abbbaabbaabbababa$$
$$\Longrightarrow ab(bbaa)^2 bba(ba)^2$$

$$S \overset{*}{\Longrightarrow} abbbaabbaabbAababa$$
$$\Longrightarrow abbbaabbaabbaaBbababa$$
$$\Longrightarrow abbbaabbaabbaabbAabababa$$
$$\Longrightarrow ab(bbaa)^3 bba(ba)^3$$

$$\vdots$$

$$S \Longrightarrow ab(bbaa)^n bba(ba)^n, \text{ for } n \geqslant 0.$$

Thus, the language generated by this grammar is

$$L(G) = \{ab(bbaa)^n bba(ba)^n : n \geqslant 0\}.$$

Remark: Every regular grammar is a context-free grammar, so a regular language is a context-free language. For example, we know that

$$L = \{a^n b^n : n \geqslant 0\}$$

is not a regular language, but this language can be generated by the grammar $G = (\{S\}, \{a, b\}, S, P)$ with P given by $S \rightarrow aSb$ and $S \rightarrow \lambda$, which is apparently a context-free grammar. So, the family of context-free languages is the superset of the family of regular languages, whereas the family of regular languages is the proper subset of the family of context-free languages.

We call a string $x \in (V \cup T)^*$ a sentential form of G if there is a derivation $S \overset{*}{\Longrightarrow} x$ in G. But notice that there may be several variables in a sentential form, in such a case, we have a choice of order to replace the variables. A derivation is said to be leftmost if in each step the leftmost variable in the sentential form is replaced. If in each step the rightmost variable is replaced, then we called the derivation rightmost.

Example 5.3 Let $G = (\{S, A\}, \{a, b\}, S, P)$ with P given by

$$
\begin{array}{ll}
\text{(i)} & S \to AA, \\
\text{(ii)} & A \to AAA, \\
\text{(iii)} & A \to bA, \\
\text{(iv)} & A \to Ab, \\
\text{(v)} & A \to a.
\end{array}
$$

Then we have the following three distinct derivations for string $L(G) =$ ababaa :

$$
\begin{array}{lll}
S \xRightarrow{i} AA & S \xRightarrow{i} AA & S \xRightarrow{i} AA \\
\xRightarrow{v} aA & \xRightarrow{v} Aa & \xRightarrow{v} aA \\
\xRightarrow{ii} aAAA & \xRightarrow{ii} AAAa & \xRightarrow{ii} aAAA \\
\xRightarrow{iii} abAAA & \xRightarrow{iii} AAbAa & \xRightarrow{v} aAAa \\
\xRightarrow{v} abaAA & \xRightarrow{v} AAbaa & \xRightarrow{iii} abAAa \\
\xRightarrow{iii} ababAA & \xRightarrow{iii} AbAbaa & \xRightarrow{iii} abAbAa \\
\xRightarrow{v} ababaA & \xRightarrow{v} Ababaa & \xRightarrow{v} ababAa \\
\xRightarrow{v} ababaa & \xRightarrow{v} ababaa & \xRightarrow{v} ababaa \\
\text{Derivation(1)} & \text{Derivation(2)} & \text{Derivation(3)}
\end{array}
$$

It is clear that derivation (1) is left-most, (2) is right-most, whereas (3) is neither.

5.4 Pumping Theorems for Context-Free Languages

Theorem 5.1 (Pumping Theorem for Context-free Languages)
Let L be a context-free language. There exists a positive integer $N \in \mathbb{Z}^+$ (depending on L) such that for any $z \in L$ and $|z| \geqslant N$, there exist strings u, v, w, x and y satisfying the following conditions:

$$z = uvwxy, \tag{5.4}$$

$$|v| + |x| > N, \tag{5.5}$$

$$uv^i wx^i y \in L, \quad \forall i \geqslant 0. \tag{5.6}$$

The number N is called pumping number for the context-free language L.

Like its counter-part for regular languages, the pumping theorem for context-free languages provides a tool for demonstrating that languages are not context-free.

5.5 Push-Down Automata and Context-Free Languages

Now we investigate the relationship between push-down automata and context-free languages.

Theorem 5.2 A Language L is context-free if and only if it is acceptable (recognisable) by some PDA. A Language L is deterministic context-free if and only if it is acceptable (recognisable) by some DPDA.

Remark: It is interesting to note that nondeterminism does not add more computing power to deterministic finite automata (DFAs). That is, DFAs and NFAs accept exactly the same languages. In contrast, this is not the case for push-down automata (PDA). There are languages that can be accepted by NPDA but that cannot be accepted by DPDA. So the class of deterministic context-free languages forms a proper subclass of the class of context-free languages. Since the languages of logic, mathematics and programming (with some exceptions) are readily described by context-free grammars, push-down automata provide an appropriate mechanism for parsing sentences in programming languages.

Finally we present some closure/nonclosure properties for context-free languages.

Theorem 5.3 The family of context-free languages is closed under the operations union, concatenation, and star-closure. That is

$$L_1 \text{ and } L_2 \text{ are context-free } \implies L_1 \cup L_2, L_1 L_2, L_1^* \text{ are context-free.} \quad (5.7)$$

Theorem 5.4 The family of context-free languages is not closed under intersection and complementation. That is

$$L_1 \text{ and } L_2 \text{ are context-free } \not\implies L_1 \cap L_2, \overline{L_1} \text{ are not context-free.} \quad (5.8)$$

Theorem 5.5 Let L_1 be a context-free language and L_2 be a regular language. Then $L_1 \cup L_2$ is context-free, but not necessarily regular. That is, the family of context-free languages is closed under regular intersection.

5.6 Applications of Context-Free Languages

Context-free grammars and languages have important applications in programming language definition and compiler construction. The most popular language definition method, Backus-Naur Form (BNF), after John Backus, who invented the method and Peter Naur, who refined it for the programming language ALGOL, directly corresponds to context-free grammar. In fact, many parts of a ALGOL-like or Pascal-like programming languages are susceptible to definition by restricted forms of context-free grammars.

Example 5.4 The following grammar (context-free grammar, but using BNF notation) defines a language of even, non-negative integers.

$$
\begin{array}{lll}
\langle\text{even-integer}\rangle & ::= & \langle\text{even-digit}\rangle \mid \langle\text{integer}\rangle\langle\text{even-digit}\rangle \\
\langle\text{integer}\rangle & ::= & \langle\text{digit}\rangle \mid \langle\text{digit}\rangle\langle\text{integer}\rangle \\
\langle\text{digit}\rangle & ::= & \langle\text{even-digit}\rangle \mid \langle\text{odd-digit}\rangle \\
\langle\text{even-digit}\rangle & ::= & 0 \mid 2 \mid 4 \mid 6 \mid 8 \\
\langle\text{odd-digit}\rangle & ::= & 1 \mid 3 \mid 5 \mid 7 \mid 9
\end{array}
$$

With this grammar, we can easily generate the even integers, and show their parse trees, which are useful in syntax analysis and code generation in compiler construction.

5.7 Turing Machines

As we have seen, finite automata (FA) can recognise regular languages (L_{REG}), but not non-regular languages, such as $L = \{a^n b^n \mid n \in \mathbb{N}\}$, which is known to be context-free language. PDA, however, can recognise all the context-free languages L_{CF} generated by context-free grammars G_{CF}. There are languages, however, say for example, context-sensitive languages L_{CS}, such as $L = \{a^n b^n c^n \mid n \in \mathbb{N}\}$, that cannot be generated by context-free grammars. Fortunately, there are other machines, called Linear Bounded Automata (LBA), more powerful than push-down automata, that can recognise all the languages generated by context-sensitive grammars G_{CS}. However, LBA cannot recognise all languages generated by phrase-structure grammars G_{PS}. To avoid the limitations of the above mentioned three special types of automata, a Turing Machine (TM), named after the British mathematician Alan Turing is used. Turing machines can recognise all the languages generated by phrase-structure grammars, called the recursively enumerable languages L_{RE}, that includes, of course, all the regular languages, context-free languages and context-sensitive languages. In addition, Turing machines can also model all the computations that can be performed on any computing machine. In this section, we shall study Turing machines and their associated languages L_{RE}.

A standard Turing machine (see Fig. 5.2) has the following features:
1) The Turing machine has a tape that is unbounded in both directions.
2) The Turing machine is deterministic.
3) There are no special input and output files.

Definition 5.4 A Turing Machine (TM) is defined by

$$M = (Q, \Sigma, \Gamma, \delta, q_0, \Box, F) \tag{5.9}$$

where

Q is a finite set of internal states;

Σ is a finite set of symbols called the input alphabet, we assume that $\Sigma \subseteq \Gamma - \{\Box\}$;

Γ is a finite set of symbols called the tape alphabet;

δ is the transition function, which is defined as

$$\delta : Q \times \Gamma \to Q \times \Gamma \times \{L, R\}; \tag{5.10}$$

$\Box \in \Gamma$ is a special symbol called the blank;

$q_0 \in Q$ is the initial state;

$F \subseteq Q$ is the set of final states.

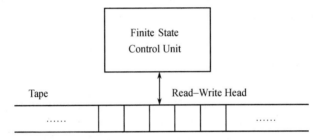

Fig. 5.2 Standard Turing Machine.

5.8 Turing Machines as Language Accepters

A Turing machine can be viewed as an accepter in the following sense. A string w is written on the tape, with blanks filling out the unused portions. The machine is started in the initial state q_0 with the read-write head positioned on the leftmost symbol of w. If, after a sequence of moves, the Turing machine enters a final state and halts, then w is considered to be accepted by the Turing machine. We shall provide a precise definition for the above descriptions and present some examples of how Turing machines accept strings that can not be accepted by a DFA or PDA.

Definition 5.5 Let $M = (Q, \Sigma, \Gamma, \delta, q_0, \Box, F)$ be a Turing machine. Then the languages that can be accepted by M are defined by

$$L(M) = \{w \in \Sigma^* : q_0 w \overset{*}{\vdash} w_1 q_f w_2, \text{ for } q_f \in F, \text{and } w_1, w_2 \in \Gamma^*\}. \tag{5.11}$$

Example 5.5 Let $\Sigma = \{a, b\}$. Design a Turing machine that accepts the language

$$L = \{a^n b^n : n \geqslant 1\}.$$

As we have seen from the preceding section that this language is a context-free language and can be accepted by a push-down automata. In this example, we shall see that this language can be accepted by a Turing machine as well. Let q_0 be the initial state, and suppose that we use the x's to replace a' and y's to replace b'. Then we can design the transitions as follows (see Fig. 5.3):

$$\delta(q_0, a) = (q_1, x, R),$$
$$\delta(q_1, a) = (q_1, a, R),$$
$$\delta(q_1, y) = (q_1, y, R),$$
$$\delta(q_1, b) = (q_2, y, L),$$
$$\delta(q_2, y) = (q_2, y, L),$$
$$\delta(q_2, a) = (q_2, a, L),$$
$$\delta(q_2, x) = (q_0, x, R),$$
$$\delta(q_0, y) = (q_3, y, R),$$
$$\delta(q_3, y) = (q_3, y, R),$$
$$\delta(q_3, \square) = (q_4, \square, R).$$

So finally, the designed Turing machine is as follows:

$$M = (Q, \Sigma, \Gamma, \delta, q_0, \square, F)$$
$$= (\{q_0, q_1, q_2, q_3, q_4\}, \{a, b\}, \{a, b, x, y, \square\}\delta, q_0, \square, \{q_4\}).$$

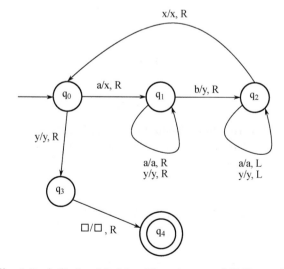

Fig. 5.3 A Turing Machine That Accepts $\{a^n b^n | n \geqslant 1\}$.

For a particular input aaabbb, we have the following successive instantaneous descriptions (IDs) of the designed Turing machine:

$$q_0aaabbb \vdash xq_1aabbb$$
$$\vdash xaq_1abbb$$
$$\vdash xaaq_1bbb$$
$$\vdash xaq_2aybb$$
$$\vdash xq_2aaybb$$
$$\vdash q_2xaaybb$$
$$\vdash xq_0aaybb$$
$$\vdash xxq_1aybb$$
$$\vdash xxaq_1ybb$$
$$\vdash xxayq_1bb$$
$$\vdash xxaq_2yyb$$
$$\vdash xxq_2ayyb$$
$$\vdash xq_2xayyb$$
$$\vdash xxq_0ayyb$$
$$\vdash xxxq_1yyb$$
$$\vdash xxxyq_1yb$$
$$\vdash xxxyyq_1b$$
$$\vdash xxxyq_2yy$$
$$\vdash xxxq_2yyy$$
$$\vdash xxq_2xyyy$$
$$\vdash xxxq_0yyy$$
$$\vdash xxxyq_3yy$$
$$\vdash xxxyyq_3y$$
$$\vdash xxxyyyq_3\square$$
$$\vdash xxxyyy\square q_4\square$$

At this point the Turing machine halts in a final state, so the string aaabbb is accepted by the Turing machine. The above successive instantaneous descriptions can also be showed diagrammatically as follows:

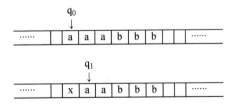

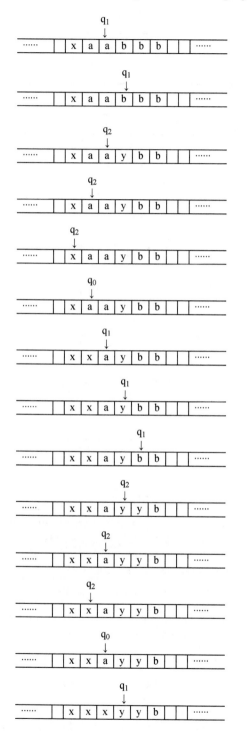

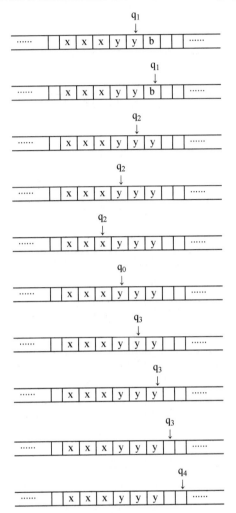

Remark: The above example shows that Turing machines can accept languages that can be accepted by push-down automata. It is, of course the case that Turing machines can accept languages that can be accepted by finite automata. For example, the following regular language

$$L_{REG} = \{w \in \{a, b\}^* : w \text{ contains the substring aba}\}.$$

can be accepted by both Turing machines and finite automata; Fig. 5.4 gives a Turing machine and a finite automaton that accept the above language.

Example 5.6   Design a Turing machine that accepts the language

$$L = \{a^n b^n c^n : n \geqslant 1\}.$$

As we already know that this language is not a context-free language, thus it cannot be accepted by a push-down automata. In this example, we shall show

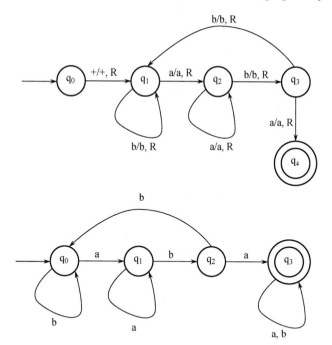

Fig. 5.4 A TM and a DFA that accept the language $\{a, b\}^*\{aba\}\{a, b\}^*$.

that it is possible to design a Turing machine that accepts this language.

$$\delta(q_0, a) = (q_1, x, R),$$
$$\delta(q_1, a) = (q_1, a, R),$$
$$\delta(q_1, y) = (q_1, y, R),$$
$$\delta(q_1, b) = (q_2, y, L),$$
$$\delta(q_2, y) = (q_2, y, L),$$
$$\delta(q_2, a) = (q_2, a, L),$$
$$\delta(q_2, x) = (q_0, x, R),$$
$$\delta(q_0, y) = (q_3, y, R),$$
$$\delta(q_3, y) = (q_3, y, R),$$
$$\delta(q_3, \square) = (q_4, \square, R).$$

We design the Turing as follows:

$$M = (Q, \Sigma, \Gamma, \delta, q_0, \square, F),$$

where

$$Q = \{q_0, q_1, q_2, q_3, q_4, q_5\},$$
$$\Sigma = \{a, b, c\},$$
$$\Gamma = \{a, b, cx, y, z, \square\},$$
$$F = \{q_4\},$$
$$\delta : Q \times \Gamma \to Q \times \Gamma \times \{L, R\} \text{ is defined by}$$

$$\delta(q_0, a) = (q_1, x, R),$$
$$\delta(q_1, a) = (q_1, a, R),$$
$$\delta(q_1, y) = (q_1, y, R),$$
$$\delta(q_1, b) = (q_2, y, R),$$
$$\delta(q_2, z) = (q_2, z, R),$$
$$\delta(q_2, b) = (q_2, b, R),$$
$$\delta(q_2, c) = (q_3, z, L),$$
$$\delta(q_3, a) = (q_3, a, L),$$
$$\delta(q_3, b) = (q_3, b, L),$$
$$\delta(q_3, y) = (q_3, y, L),$$
$$\delta(q_3, z) = (q_3, z, L),$$
$$\delta(q_3, x) = (q_0, xR),$$
$$\delta(q_0, y) = (q_4, y, R),$$
$$\delta(q_4, \square) = (q_5, \square, R).$$

For the particular input aabbcc, we have the following successive instantaneous descriptions of the designed Turing machine:

$$
\begin{aligned}
q_0 \text{aabbcc} &\vdash x q_1 \text{abbcc} \\
&\vdash x a q_1 \text{bbcc} \\
&\vdash x a y q_2 \text{bcc} \\
&\vdash x a y b q_2 \text{cc} \\
&\vdash x a y q_3 \text{bzc} \\
&\vdash x a q_3 \text{ybzc} \\
&\vdash x q_3 \text{aybzc} \\
&\vdash q_3 \text{xaybzc} \\
&\vdash x q_0 \text{aybzc} \\
&\vdash x x q_1 \text{ybzc} \\
&\vdash x x y g_1 \text{bzc} \\
&\vdash x x y y q_2 \text{zc}
\end{aligned}
$$

$$\vdash xxyyzq_2c$$
$$\vdash xxyyq_3zz$$
$$\vdash xxyq_3yzz$$
$$\vdash xxq_3yyzz$$
$$\vdash xq_3xyyzz$$
$$\vdash xxq_0yyzz$$
$$\vdash xxyq_4yzz$$
$$\vdash xxyyq_4zz$$
$$\vdash xxyyzq_4z$$
$$\vdash xxyyzzq_4\square$$
$$\vdash xxyyzz\square q_4\square$$

Fig. 5.5 gives a Turing machine that accepts $\{a^n b^n c^n : n \geqslant 1\}$.

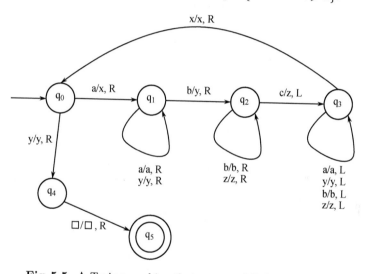

Fig. 5.5 A Turing machine that accepts $\{a^n b^n c^n : n \geqslant 1\}$.

Theorem 5.6 The class of Turing-acceptable languages properly includes the classes of regular languages and context-free languages.

5.9 Equivalence of Various Turing Machines

We could, of course, list many more different types of Turing machines. However, all the different types of Turing machines have the same power. This establishes the following important result about the equivalence of the various Turing machines.

Theorem 5.7   A Language L is accepted by a multitape, or multidimensional, or nondeterministic, or probabilistic Turing Machine, if and only if it is accepted by a standard Turing machine.

We now establish another important result for Turing machines.

Let $\Sigma = \{a, b, c\}$. We said the set $S = \Sigma^+$ is countable if we can find an enumeration procedure that produces its elements in some order, e.g., dictionary order.

Theorem 5.8   The set of all Turing Machines, although infinite, is countable.

Theorem 5.9   Let S be an infinite countable set. Then its power set 2^S is not countable.

5.10   Recursively Enumerable Languages (L_{RE})

In this section, we shall study languages associated with Turing machines.

Definition 5.6   A language L over an input alphabet Σ is said to be recursively enumerable, denoted by L_{RE}, if there exists a Turing machine that accepts it. Recursively enumerable languages are also called Turing acceptable languages, or Turing recognisable languages.

Definition 5.7   A language L over an input alphabet Σ is said to be recursive, denoted by L_{REC}, if there exists a Turing machine that accepts L, and that halts on every input $w \in \Sigma^+$. Recursive languages are also called Turing decidable languages, or recursively decidable languages; we shall discuss the concept "decidable" in Chapter 7.

The term "recursive" comes from the theory of recursive functions. It is clear that a recursive language is also a recursively enumerable, but on the other hand, a recursively enumerable language is not necessarily recursive. That is:

Theorem 5.10   There exists a recursively enumerable language that is not recursive. That is

$$L_{REC} \subset L_{RE}. \tag{5.12}$$

From a Turing machine point of view, both recursively enumerable languages and recursive languages are Turing acceptable; the only difference between the two types of languages is that recursive languages will halt on every input $w \in \Sigma^+$; whereas recursively enumerable languages may not halt on every input $w \in \Sigma^+$, that is, they may fall into an infinite loop on some input $w \in \Sigma^+$.

We list in the following some important properties about recursive and recursively enumerable languages:

Theorem 5.11 A language L is recursive if and only if both L and its complement $\overline{L}$ are recursively enumerable.

Theorem 5.12 There is a recursively enumerable language L whose complement $\overline{L}$ is not recursively enumerable.

Interestingly, recursively enumerable languages are not the highest languages; there exist languages that cannot be accepted by any Turing machine:

Theorem 5.13 For any nonempty alphabet Σ, there exist languages over Σ that are not recursively enumerable.

There is yet another approach to studying Turing acceptable languages, namely, the grammatical approach:

Definition 5.8 A grammar $G = (V, T, S, P)$ is called a phrase-structure grammar or a unrestricted grammar if all productions have the form

$$x \rightarrow y, \tag{5.13}$$

where $x \in (V \cup T)^{+}$, and $y \in (V \cup T)^{*}$.

Definition 5.9 Any language generated by an unrestricted grammar is recursively enumerable.

Theorem 5.14 For every recursively enumerable language L, there is an unrestricted grammar G, such that $L = L(G)$.

5.11 Context-Sensitive Languages (L$_{CS}$)

The context-sensitive grammar represents an intermediate step between context-free grammars and unrestricted grammars. No restrictions are placed on the left-hand side of a production, but the length of the right-hand side is required to be at least as long as the left.

Definition 5.10 A phrase-structure grammar $G = (V, T, S, P)$ is called a context-sensitive grammar, denoted by G_{rmCS}, if all productions have the form

$$x \rightarrow y, \tag{5.14}$$

where $x, y \in (V \cup T)^{+}$, and length $(x) \leqslant$ length (y) (or briefly as $|x| \leqslant |y|$).

A language L is called a context-sensitive language, denoted by L_{CSL}, if there exists a context-sensitive grammar G, such that $L = L(G)$ or $L = L(G) \cup \lambda$.

Example 5.7 Design a context-sensitive grammar to generate the context-sensitive language

$$L = \{a^{n}b^{n}c^{n} : n > 0\}.$$

We can construct the grammar $G(V, T, S, P)$ with the following productions:

$$
\begin{array}{ll}
\text{(i)} & S \to abc \\
\text{(ii)} & S \to aAbc \\
\text{(iii)} & A \to abC \\
\text{(iv)} & A \to aAbC \\
\text{(v)} & Cb \to bC \\
\text{(vi)} & Cc \to cc.
\end{array}
$$

By Definition 5.10, it is context-sensitive. Some typical derivations in this grammar are:

$$
S \stackrel{(i)}{\Longrightarrow} abc
$$

Derivation (1)

$$
\begin{aligned}
S &\stackrel{(ii)}{\Longrightarrow} aAbc \\
&\stackrel{(iii)}{\Longrightarrow} aabCbc \\
&\stackrel{(v)}{\Longrightarrow} aabbCc \\
&\stackrel{(vi)}{\Longrightarrow} aabbcc
\end{aligned}
$$

Derivation (2)

$$
\begin{aligned}
S &\stackrel{(ii)}{\Longrightarrow} aAbc \\
&\stackrel{(iv)}{\Longrightarrow} aaAbCbc \\
&\stackrel{(iii)}{\Longrightarrow} aaabCbCbc \\
&\stackrel{(v)}{\Longrightarrow} aaabbCCbc \\
&\stackrel{(v)}{\Longrightarrow} aaabbCbCc \\
&\stackrel{(v)}{\Longrightarrow} aaabbbCCc \\
&\stackrel{(vi)}{\Longrightarrow} aaabbbCcc \\
&\stackrel{(vi)}{\Longrightarrow} aaabbbccc
\end{aligned}
$$

Derivation (3)

We have examined several variants of the standard Turing machines that do not alter the set of languages accepted by the machines. Restricting the amount of available tape for computation decreases the capabilities of a Turing machine computation. A linear bounded automata is a restricted Turing machine in which the amount of available tape is determined by the length of the input string. The input alphabet contains two symbols "⟨" and "⟩", that designate the left and right boundaries of the tape.

Definition 5.11   A linear bounded automaton (LBA) is an algebraic structure

$$
M = (Q, \Sigma, \Gamma, \delta, q_0, \langle, \rangle, F), \tag{5.15}
$$

where $Q, \Sigma, \Gamma, \delta, q_0$, and F are the same as for a nondeterministic Turing machine. The symbols $\langle$ and $\rangle$ are distinguished elements of Γ.

Theorem 5.15   For every context-sensitive language L, denoted by L_{CS}, not including λ, there is some LBA, M, that accepts L_{CS}. That is, $L_{CS} = L(M)$.

Theorem 5.16   If a language L is accepted by some LBA, M, then there exists a context-sensitive grammar G that accepts L. That is $L = L(G)$.

Theorem 5.17 Every context-sensitive language L is recursive. That is, $\forall L_{CS} \in L_{REC}$.

Theorem 5.18 There exists a recursive language that is not context-sensitive. That is, $L_{CS} \subset L_{REC}$.

5.12 Hierarchy of Machines, Grammars and Languages

In this section, we shall study the Chomsky hierarchy of formal languages and their generating grammars and their corresponding machines.

5.12.1 Hierarchy of Machines

All the classes (families) of machines we have studied so far are finite (state) machines, but some of the machines have exactly the same power (here by the same power, we mean they accept exactly the same language), whilst some of the machines have more power than others. For example, deterministic finite automata (DFA) have the same power as nondeterministic finite automata (NFA); nondeterministic push-down automata (NPDA) have more power than deterministic push-down automata (DPDA); push-down automata (PDA) with two push-down stores have more power than the push-down automata (PDA) with only one push-down store; but push-down automata (PDA) with more than two push-down stores have the same power as push-down automata with two push-down stores. Interestingly enough, push-down automata with two or more push-down stores have the same power as Turing machines; All different types of Turing machines (such as deterministic, nondeterministic, probabilistic, multitape and multidimensional, etc.) have the same power. However, restricting the amount of available tape for computation decreases the capabilities of a Turing machine; linear bounded automata is such a type of restricted Turing machines in which the amount of available tape is determined by the length of the input string. The relation between the various classes of finite machines over the same alphabet Σ can be summarized as follows:

Deterministic Finite Automata (DFA)

$\Updownarrow$

Nondeterministic Finite Automata (NFA)

$\cap$

Deterministic Push-Down Automata (DPDA)

$\cap$

Nondeterministic Push-Down Automata (NPDA)

$\cap$

Linear-Bounded Automata (LBA)

$\cap$

Deterministic Push-Down Automata (DPDA)
with two push-down stores

$\updownarrow$

Nondeterministic Push-Down Automata (NPDA)
with two push-down stores

$\updownarrow$

Deterministic Turing Machines (DTM)

$\updownarrow$

Nondeterministic Turing Machines (NTM)

$\updownarrow$

Probabilistic Turing Machines (PTM)

$\updownarrow$

Multitape Turing Machines

$\updownarrow$

Multidimensional Turing Machines

So, there are essentially four main classes of machines: finite automata (FA), push-down automata (PDA), linear-bounded automata (LBA) and Turing ma-chines (TM). The hierarchy of these classes of machines can be described as follows:

Finite Automata (FA)

$\cap$

Push-Down Automata (PDA)

$\cap$

Linear-Bounded Automata (LBA)

$\cap$

Turing Machines (TM)

5.12.2 Hierarchy of Grammars and Languages

Now we move on to the study of the Chomsky hierarchy of formal grammars and their generating languages. First let us recall that two grammars are called equivalent if they generate the same language.

Definition 5.12   A generative grammar $G = (V, T, S, P)$ is said to be of type i if it satisfies the corresponding restrictions in the following list:

Type 0: No restrictions. That is, every production in P is just in the general form $x \rightarrow y$, where $x \in (V \cup T)^+$ and $y \in (V \cup T)^*$. Type 0 grammars are often called unrestricted grammars, or phrase-structure grammars, denoted by G_{PS}. The languages generated by Type 0 grammars are called Type 0 languages, or recursively enumerable languages, denoted by L_{RE}.

Type 1: Every production in P has the form $x \rightarrow y$, where $x, y \in (V \cup T)^+$, and $|x| \leqslant |y|$. Type 1 grammars are also called context-sensitive grammars, denoted by G_{CS}. The languages generated by Type 1 grammars are called Type 1 languages, or context-sensitive languages, denoted by L_{CS}.

Type 2: Every production in P has the form $A \rightarrow x$, where $A \in V$, and $x \in (V \cup T)^*$. Type 2 grammars are also called context-free grammars, denoted by G_{CF}. The languages generated by Type 2 grammars are called Type 2 languages, or context-free languages, denoted by L_{CF}.

Type 3: Every production in P has the form either $A \rightarrow Bx$ and $A \rightarrow x$, or $A \rightarrow xB$ and $A \rightarrow x$, where $A, B \in V$, and $x \in T^*$. Type 3 grammars are called regular grammars, denoted by G_{REG}. The languages generated by Type 3 grammars are called Type 3 languages, or regular languages, denoted by L_{REG}.

We have, in fact, already studied all the above listed grammars and their generating languages in the previous sections of this chapter. What we are interested in here is the hierarchy of the grammars and their corresponding languages, which may be described as follows:

$$Type\ 0\ Grammars\ (G_{PS}) \quad \Leftrightarrow \quad Type\ 0\ Languages\ (L_{RE})$$
$$\cap \qquad\qquad\qquad\qquad\qquad \cap$$
$$Type\ 1\ Grammars\ (G_{CS}) \quad \Leftrightarrow \quad Type\ 1\ Languages\ (L_{CS})$$
$$\cap \qquad\qquad\qquad\qquad\qquad \cap$$
$$Type\ 2\ Grammars\ (G_{CF}) \quad \Leftrightarrow \quad Type\ 2\ Languages\ (L_{CF})$$
$$\cap \qquad\qquad\qquad\qquad\qquad \cap$$
$$Type\ 3\ Grammars\ (G_{REG}) \quad \Leftrightarrow \quad Type\ 3\ Languages\ (L_{REG})$$

5.13   Relations Among Machines, Languages and Grammars

We have already seen that languages and grammars are actually equivalent concepts; on one hand, given a language, we can find the grammar which generates the language; on the other hand, given a grammar, we can find the set of languages generated by the given grammar. Remarkably enough, languages also have a one-to-one correspondence with the various machines. Fig. 5.6 shows the hierarchical relationships between various formal languages and their accepting machines. That is, regular languages (L_{REG}) generated by regular grammars (G_{REG}) are acceptable by finite-state automata (FA), context-free languages (L_{CF}) generated by context-free grammars (G_{CF}) are acceptable by push-down automata (P_{DA}), context-sensitive languages (L_{CS}) generated by context-sensitive grammars (G_{CS}) are acceptable by linear bounded automata (L_{BA}), and recursively enumerable languages (L_{RE}) generated by phrase-structure grammars (G_{PS}) are acceptable by Turing machines. Thus, we finally arrive at the hierarchical relations between various languages, grammars and machines as follows:

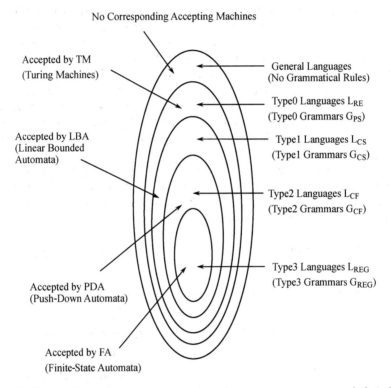

Fig. 5.6 Hierarchical relations among various languages, grammars and their Machines.

Grammars	G_{REG}	$\subset$	G_{CF}	$\subset$	G_{CS}	$\subset$	G_{RE}
	$\updownarrow$		$\updownarrow$		$\updownarrow$		$\updownarrow$
Languages	L_{REG}	$\subset$	L_{CF}	$\subset$	L_{CS}	$\subset$	L_{RE}
	$\updownarrow$		$\updownarrow$		$\updownarrow$		$\updownarrow$
Machines	FA	$\subset$	PDA	$\subset$	LBA	$\subset$	TM

Literally, the relationships between the various grammars, languages and machines can also be summarized as follows:

Grammars	Languages	Accepting Machines
Type 0 grammars (or phrase-structure grammars, unrestricted grammars)	Recursively enumerable languages	Turing Machines
Type 1 grammars (or context-sensitive grammars, monotonic grammars)	Context-sensitive languages	Linear-bounded automata
Type 2 grammars (or context-free grammars)	Context-free languages	Push-down automata
Type 3 grammars (or regular grammars, linear grammars)	Regular languages	Finite automata

If we wish to include some other (small) language families such as deterministic context-free languages and recursive languages, we will then arrive at an extended hierarchy as shown in Fig. 5.7.

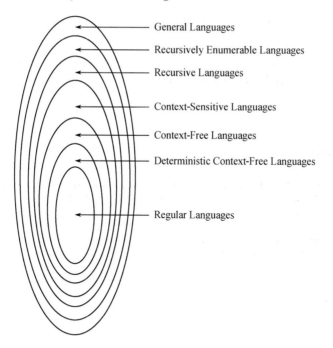

General Languages

Recursively Enumerable Languages

Recursive Languages

Context-Sensitive Languages

Context-Free Languages

Deterministic Context-Free Languages

Regular Languages

Fig. 5.7 Extended hierarchy of formal languages.

Problems

Problem 5.1   Use the above pumping theorem to show that

$$L = \{a^n b^n c^n : n \geqslant 0\}$$

is not a context-free language.

Problem 5.2   Show that the family of context-free languages is not closed under the operation difference in general, but it is closed under regular difference, that is,

$$L_1 \text{ is regular are } L_2 \text{ is context-free} \implies L_1 - L_2 \text{ is context-free.}$$

Problem 5.3   Show that the Turing machine constructed in Example 5.5 cannot accept the language $L = \{a^n b^m : m \geqslant 1, n > m\}$.

Problem 5.4   Construct Turing machines that accept the languages $L_1 = \{a^n b^{2n} : n \geqslant 1\}$ and $L_2 = \{a^{2^n} : n \geqslant 1\}$ over $\Sigma = \{a, b\}$.

Problem 5.5   Construct a Turing machine that accepts the language

$$L = \{a^k b^m c^n : k, m, n > 0, k = m \text{ or } k = n \text{ or } m = n\}$$

over $\Sigma = \{a, b, c\}$.

Problem 5.6   Find a context-sensitive grammar for the languages $L_1 = \{a^n b^n a^{2n} : n > 0\}$ and $L_2 = \{a^n b^m c^n d^m : n, m > 0\}$.

References

[1]   Yan S Y (1988) Introduction to formal languages and machine computation, World Scientific, New Jersey. (The materials in this chapter are mainly based on this book of the second author.)

[2]   Hopcraft J E, Motwani R, Ullman J D (2006) Introduction to automata theory, languages and computation, 3rd end. Addison-Wesley, Reading, Mass. (A general reference in push-down automata and context-free languages.)

Chapter 6 Context-Free Grammars

Language is a process of free creation, its law and principles are fixed, but the manner in which the principles of generation are used is free and infinitely varied. Even the interpretation and use of words involves a process of free creation.

Noam Chomsky

6.1 Motivation of the Chapter

In the compilation of source programs, the second phase of the process is the syntactical analysis. Based on the lexical analysis, the syntactical analysis checks the correctness of the source programs in terms of the grammar of the language used. And it is well-known that most of the properties of the programming languages are context-free. Therefore, naturally if we want to check whether a program is correct or not in terms of syntax, we should check if the syntax of the program is consistent with context-free, at least for most of it. In order to do so, the basis is to know about the context-free grammars. This chapter and Chapter 5 together form the preparation of the syntactical analysis.

The context-free grammars generate the context-free languages, and the context-free languages were initially introduced to provide a model of natural languages. Hence they are very important for understanding natural language. Later the investigation of programming languages will show that they are equally important in the area of programming language. We can even say that the importance of programming languages is even more vital than natural languages. Because in common conversation between people, it is not so strictly obeying the rules of the context-free grammar so that the counterpart of the conversation may still understand the meaning or intention of the speaker. But for computer, it is not the case. Even a minor mistake in program will affect the understanding of the compiler, so that it will not be able to correctly compile the program and the program will not be executable. After all, at the present time, the computer is not as intelligent as human.

Therefore, in one word, the motivation of the chapter is, together with the last chapter, to provide sufficient knowledge for the next chapter — syntax analysis. The three chapters provide the core knowledge for the whole course.

6.2 Context-Free Grammars

In Chapter 2, we have briefly introduced context-free grammar, i.e., Type-2 grammar. In this chapter, we will concentrate on the investigation of this type of grammars, especially the aspects related to syntactical analysis. For the sake of completeness, we will mention other types of grammars too in the beginning of our discussion.

We refer to symbols V_N and V_T as nonterminal alphabet and terminal alphabet respectively, we denote $V = V_N \cup V_T$, and they satisfies that $V_N \cap V_T = \varnothing$. We refer to the symbols in V_N and V_T as nonterminal symbols (or simply nonterminals) and terminal symbols (or simply terminals). Then we have the following definition:

Definition 6.1 Let $G = (V_N, V_T, S, P)$ where S is the distinguished or start symbol of the grammar, and P is the set of productions. The production has the form of $\alpha \to \beta$, we denote $\pi = \alpha \to \beta \in P$. We say that it is generative if α (a string) contains at least one nonterminal symbol, and it is analytic if β contains at least one such symbol. It is clear that π is a generative production if and only if its reverse π^{-1}, or $\beta \to \alpha$ is analytic.

Example 6.1 The productions in the following grammar

$$G = (\{X, Y, Z\}, \{x, y\}, X, \{xxX \to xyXYx, XxY \to \varepsilon, Z \to yyx\})$$

are classified as follows:

$$
\begin{aligned}
&\pi_0: xxX \to xyXYx \quad &&\text{analytic and generayive} \\
&\pi_1: XxY \to \varepsilon \quad &&\text{generative} \\
&\pi_2: Z \to yyx \quad &&\text{generative}
\end{aligned}
$$

Definition 6.2 A grammar G is generative if all its productions are generative. G is analytic if all its productions are analytic.

If G is a generative grammar, then the language generated by G relative to its terminal alphabet

$$L_G(G \mid V_T) = \{\alpha \in V_T^* \mid S \overset{*}{\underset{G}{\Rightarrow}} \alpha\} \tag{6.1}$$

will be referred to the language generated by G. To simplify the notation, we just denote $L(G) = \{\alpha \in V_T \mid S \overset{*}{\underset{G}{\Rightarrow}} \alpha\}$. If G is an analytic grammar, then the language recognized by G relative to its terminal alphabet

$$L_G(G \mid V_T) = \{\alpha \in V_T \mid \alpha \overset{*}{\underset{G}{\Rightarrow}} S\} \tag{6.2}$$

will be referred to the language recognized by G.

If there is no risk of confusion, we may denote both the language generated by a generative grammar G, or the language recognized by an analytic grammar G, by L(G). From now on, we just focus predominantly on generative grammars. They are classified according to the form of their productions. The term grammar will be used for generative grammar in order to simplify the exposition.

Definition 6.3 A derivation $\alpha_0 \overset{G}{\Longrightarrow} \alpha_1 \overset{G}{\Longrightarrow} \ldots \overset{G}{\Longrightarrow} \alpha_n$ in a generative grammar $G = (V_N, V_T, S, P)$ is complete if $\alpha \in V_T^*$.

If $S \overset{*}{\underset{G}{\Longrightarrow}} \alpha$, we refer to α as a sentential form of G.

Clearly, every word in L(G) is a sentential form of G that contains no nonterminal symbols.

Definition 6.4 Let V_N, V_T be two disjoint alphabets. A production $\alpha \to \beta$ is

1) a context-free production on V_N, V_t if α consists of one nonterminal symbol A and $\beta \in (V_N \cup V_T)^*$;

2) a context-sensitive production if $\alpha = \alpha' A \alpha''$ and $\beta = \alpha' \gamma \alpha''$ where $A \in V_T$, $\alpha', \alpha'', \gamma \in (V_N \cup V_T)^*$ and $\gamma \neq \varepsilon$.

Example 6.2 Let $V_N = \{X, Y, Z\}$ and $V_T = \{x, y\}$. The following productions are of context-free over V_N and V_T:

$$\pi_0 : \ X \to xyXYx,$$
$$\pi_1 : \ Y \to \varepsilon,$$
$$\pi_2 : \ Z \to yyx$$

while the production π_3: xYXy→xyXZXy is context-sensitive. Note that π_3 involves replacing y by yXZ when Y is surrounded by x at left and Xy at the right, that is, Y occurs in the context of x and Xy. This is why it is called context-sensitive. Context-free productions of the form $X \to \varepsilon$ are called null productions or erasure productions. The effect of $X \to \varepsilon$ is to erase the symbol X.

A grammar without erasure production is said to be ε-free.

The classes of generative grammars that correspond to the restriction on productions described in Definition 6.4 are introduced next. This classification is due to Noam Chomsky and it is called Chomsky hierarchy.

Definition 6.5[1] Let $G = (V_N, V_T, S, P)$ be a grammar.

1) Every grammar is a grammar of Type 0. That means that Type 0 grammar is most common one. There is no any restriction over it.

2) G is Type 1 (or, context-sensitive) if its productions contain context-sensitive one with the possible exception of a production $S \to \varepsilon$; If P contains $S \to \varepsilon$, then S does not occur in the right part of any production of G.

3) G is Type 2 (or, context-free) if all its productions are context-free.

4) G is Type 3 (or, regular) if every production has the form $X \to uY$ or $X \to u$, where $X, Y \in V_N$ and $u \in V_T^*$.

In addition, we shall say that G is a length-increasing grammar if all its productions length-increasing (due to $| \alpha | \leqslant | \beta |$ in $\alpha \to \beta$) with the possible exception of a production $S \to \varepsilon$.

It is clear that every grammar of Type 3 is also of Type 2, every grammar of Type 2 is also of Type 1, and every grammar of Type 1 is also of Type 0 and every context-sensitive grammar is also length-increasing.

For Type 3 grammars, productions may include those of the form $X \to Y$, or $X \to \varepsilon$.

If $G = (V_N, V_T, S, P)$ is a grammar, then we use upper case of letters with or without subscripts, to denote single nonterminals, lower case of letters in the alphabet (u, v, w, x, y, z) to denote words in V_T^*, and lower case of Greek letters to denote words in $(V_N \cup V_T)^*$. With this convention, the language generated by G is given by

$$L(G) = (u \in V_T^* \mid S \underset{G}{\overset{*}{\Longrightarrow}} u). \tag{6.3}$$

Definition 6.6   Let Γ be a class of grammars. A language L is a Γ-language if there is a grammar G in Γ such that $L(G) = L$.

For example, L is a context-free language if there exists a context-free grammar G such that $L = L(G)$. Similarly, K is a length-increasing language if there is a grammar G_1 such as that $K = L(G_1)$, etc. We denote by L_i the class of languages generated by grammars of type i for $0 \leqslant i \leqslant 3$. Clearly, we have $L_3 \subseteq L_2 \subseteq L_1$ and $L_1 \subseteq L_0$. Actually, they are

$$L_3 \subseteq L_2 \subseteq L_1 \subseteq L_0. \tag{6.4}$$

As with the grammars, the corresponding classes of language L_i are referred to as the Chomsky hierarchy. All the inclusions can be shown to be strict. Also, it is clear that every language in L_1 is length-increasing. Actually, we shall prove that L_1 coincides with the class of length-increasing languages.

Example 6.3   The language generated by the context-free grammar

$$G = (\{S\}, \{a, b\}, S, \{S \to \varepsilon, S \to aSb\})$$

is $\{a^n b^n \mid n \in N\}$.

We now prove it by induction on $n \geqslant 0$ that $a^n b^n \in L(G)$ for every $n \in N$.

The case $n = 0$ follows from the existence of the production $\pi_0 \colon S \to \varepsilon$ in G. Suppose now that $a^n b^n \in L(G)$, so $S \underset{G}{\overset{*}{\Longrightarrow}} a^n b^n$. Using the production $S \to aSb$ we obtain the derivation

$$S \underset{G}{\overset{*}{\Longrightarrow}} aSb \underset{G}{\overset{*}{\Longrightarrow}} \cdots \underset{G}{\overset{*}{\Longrightarrow}} aa^n b^n b = a^{n=1} b^{n+1}$$

that shows that $a^{n+1} b^{n+1} \in L(G)$.

Conversely, we prove by induction on the length $m \geqslant 1$ of the derivation $S \overset{*}{\underset{G}{\Longrightarrow}} u$ that u has the form $u = a^n b^n$ for some $n \in \mathbb{N}$.

If $m = 1$, $S \overset{*}{\underset{G}{\Longrightarrow}} u$ implies $x = \varepsilon$ since $S \to \varepsilon$ is the single production that erases S. Therefore, $x = a^n b^n$ for $n = 0$.

Suppose that the statement holds for derivation of length m and let $S \overset{*}{\underset{G}{\Longrightarrow}} u$ be a derivation of length $m+1$. If we write the step of this derivation explicitly we have

$$S \overset{*}{\underset{G}{\Longrightarrow}} aSb \overset{*}{\underset{G}{\Longrightarrow}} u,$$

so $u = avb$ where $S \overset{*}{\underset{G}{\Longrightarrow}} v$ is a derivation of length m. By the induction hypothesis, $y = a^n b^n$ for some $n \in \mathbb{N}$, so $u = a^{n+1} b^{n+1}$, that concludes our argument.

Example 6.4 Consider the length-increasing grammar

$$G = (\{S, X, Y\}, \{a, b.c\}, s, P),$$

where P consists of the following productions:

$$
\begin{aligned}
&\pi_0 : S \to abc, &&\pi_1 : S \to aXbc, \\
&\pi_2 : Xb \to bX, &&\pi_3 : Xc \to Ybcc, \\
&\pi_4 : bY \to Yb, &&\pi_5 : aY \to aaX, \\
&\pi_6 : aY \to aa.
\end{aligned}
$$

We claim that $L(G) = \{a^n b^n c^n \mid n \in P\}$.

We have the induction basis $abc \in L(G)$ that corresponds to $n = 1$. For $a^n b^n c^n$ where $n > 1$, the symbol Y must be generated starting from S, and the first production applied is $S \to aXbc$.

Note that for every $i \geqslant 1$ we have $a^i Xb^i c^i \overset{*}{\Longrightarrow} a^{i+1} Xb^{i+1} c^{i+1}$. Actually, we have

$$
\begin{aligned}
a^i Xb^i c^i &\overset{1}{\underset{\pi_2}{\Longrightarrow}} a^i b^i Xc^i \\
&\overset{1}{\underset{\pi_3}{\Longrightarrow}} a^i b^i Ybc^{i+1} \\
&\overset{1}{\underset{\pi_4}{\Longrightarrow}} a^i Yb^{i+1} c^{i+1} \\
&\overset{1}{\underset{\pi_5}{\Longrightarrow}} a^{i+1} Xb^{i+1} c^{i+1}.
\end{aligned}
\tag{6.5}
$$

We claim that a word α contains the infix aY (which allows us to apply the production π_5) and $S \overset{*}{\Longrightarrow} \alpha$ if and only if α has the form $\alpha = a^i Yb^{i=1} c^{i+1}$ for some $i \geqslant 1$. An easy argument by induction on $i \geqslant 1$ shows that if $\alpha = a^i Yb^{i+1} c^{i+1}$, then $S \overset{*}{\Longrightarrow} \alpha$. We need to prove only the inverse implication. This can be done by strong induction on the length $n \geqslant 3$ of the derivation $S \overset{*}{\Longrightarrow} \alpha$.

The shortest derivation that allows us to generate the word containing the infix aY is

$$S \Longrightarrow aXbc \Longrightarrow abXc \Longrightarrow abYbcc \Longrightarrow aYb^2c^2, \qquad (6.6)$$

and this word has the prescribed form. Suppose now that for derivation shorter than n the condition is satisfied, and let $S \overset{*}{\underset{G}{\Longrightarrow}} \alpha$ be a derivation of length n such that α contains the infix aY. By the induction hypothesis the previous word in this derivation that contains the infix aY has the form $\alpha' = a^jYb^{j+1}c^{j+1}$. To proceed from α' we must apply the production π_5 and replace y by X. Thus we have

$$S \overset{*}{\underset{G}{\Longrightarrow}} a^jYb^{j+1}c^{j+1} \underset{G}{\Longrightarrow} a^{j+1}Xb^{j+1}c^{j+1}. \qquad (6.7)$$

Next, the symbol x must be shifted to the right using the production π_2, transform itself into an Y (when in touch with the c$\bar{\text{s}}$) and Y must be shifted to the left to create the infix aY. This can happen only through the application of the productions π_3 and π_4 as follows:

$$A^{j+1}Xb^{j+1}c^{j+1} \overset{j+1}{\underset{\pi_2}{\Longrightarrow}} a^{j+1}b^{j+1}Xc^{j+1}$$

$$\overset{1}{\underset{\pi_3}{\Longrightarrow}} a^{j+1}b^{j+1}Ybc^{j+2}$$

$$\overset{1}{\underset{\pi_4}{\Longrightarrow}} a^{j+1}Yb^{j+2}c^{j+2}. \qquad (6.8)$$

That proves that α has the desired form. Therefore, all the words in the language L(G) has the form $a^nb^nc^n$.

Although this grammar is not context-sensitive (only productions π_0, π_1, π_5, and π_6 are context-sensitive), we will exhibit a context-sensitive grammar for this language. Moreover, we will show that this language is not context-free. So it will serve to show that $L_2 \subseteq L_1$.

Now we turn our attention to real programming language.

Example 6.5 Suppose that E stands for expression, T stands for term, F stands for factor, then the following productions will generate the arithmetic expressions that consist of $+, -, \times, /$.

$$E \to E + T,$$
$$E \to E - T,$$
$$E \to T,$$
$$T \to T \times F,$$
$$T \to T/F,$$
$$T \to F,$$
$$F \to (E),$$
$$F \to a \mid b \mid c.$$

The language which the grammar recognizes is all the arithmetic expressions that consist of operators $+$, $-$, $\times$ and $/$ and three variables a, b, and c. That means that all the arithmetic expressions can be derived from these productions step by step. For example, the arithmetic expression

$$(a \times b + b \times c + c \times a)/(a + b + c)$$

may be derived from the productions above step by step

$$
\begin{aligned}
E &\to T \\
&\to T/F \\
&\to F/F \\
&\to (E)/F \\
&\to (E + T)/F \\
&\to (E + T + T)/F \\
&\to (T + T + T)/F \\
&\to (T \times F + T + T)/F \\
&\to (F \times F + T + T)/F \\
&\to (a \times F + T + T)/F \\
&\to (a \times b + T \times F + T)/F \\
&\to (a \times b + F \times F + T)/F \\
&\to (a \times b + b \times F + T)/F \\
&\to (a \times b + b \times c + T)/F \\
&\to (a \times b + b \times c + F)/F \\
&\to (a \times b + b \times c + c \times a)/F \\
&\to (a \times b + b \times c + c \times a)/(E) \\
&\to (a \times b + b \times c + c \times a)/(E + T) \\
&\to (a \times b + b \times c + c \times a)/(E + T + T) \\
&\to (a \times b + b \times c + c \times a)/(T + T + T) \\
&\to (a \times b + b \times c + c \times a)/(F + T + T) \\
&\to (a \times b + b \times c + c \times a)/(a + T + T) \\
&\to (a \times b + b \times c + c \times a)/(a + F + T) \\
&\to (a \times b + b \times c + c \times a)/(a + b + T) \\
&\to (a \times b + b \times c + c \times a)/(a + b + F) \\
&\to (a \times b + b \times c + c \times a)/(a + b + c).
\end{aligned}
$$

Therefore, we may claim that $(a \times b + b \times c + c \times a)/(a + b + c)$ is a sentence which the grammar aforementioned recognizes.

In the derivation above, the reader may find out that in each step or each derivation, only one nonterminal was replaced or only one action was done. And the step always changes the leftmost nonterminal either by a new nonterminal or by a terminal. The derivation done in this manner is called leftmost derivation. On the other hand, if the derivation always changes the rightmost nonterminal, then the derivation is called rightmost derivation. The so-called change nonterminal, actually it replaces the nonterminal with the right part of the production of which the left part is the nonterminal.

Using derivation tree may make the derivation more directly perceived through the sense. Corresponding to the derivation given above, we draw the derivation tree as shown in Fig. 6.1.

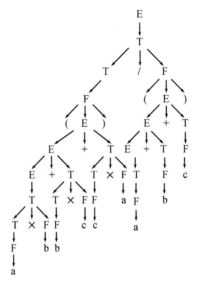

Fig. 6.1 Derivation Tree.

The derivation tree may be formally described as follows:

Let $G = (V_N, V_T, S, P)$ be a context-free grammar. The derivation tree of a sentence of G is as follows:

1) Every vertex has a label that is a symbol in $V_N \cup V_T \cup \varepsilon$.

2) The label of the root is S.

3) If a vertex is an inner vertex and its label is A, then $A \in V_N$. In other words, All the inner vertices of the tree are of nonterminals.

4) If a vertex n has label A and vertices $n_1, n_2, \ldots, n_k$ are the subnodes of n from left to right, and their labels are $X_1, X_2, \ldots, X_k$ respectively. Then

$$A \to X_1 X_2 \ldots X_k \qquad (6.9)$$

must be a production of P.

5) If a vertex n has the label ε, then n must be a leaf, and it is the only child of its parent node.

6) All the leaf nodes of the tree from left to right form the sentence.

In the formal description of the derivation tree, we did not involve leftmost derivation. Actually, the derivation tree may also be constructed through the rightmost derivation. The key is whether the leftmost derivation tree is the same as the rightmost derivation tree? It may also be asked whether the leftmost derivation and rightmost derivation of a sentence are the same? as derivation completely corresponds to derivation tree.

Definition 6.7 [2]   Grammar $G = (V_N, V_T, S, P)$ is called non-ambiguous if for all the sentences which it recognizes each only has one derivation tree.

There exists ambiguous grammar. The following is an example of ambiguous grammar.

Example 6.6   The production set P of grammar $G = (V_N, V_T, S, P)$ consists of the following productions:

$$E \rightarrow E + T,$$
$$E \rightarrow T,$$
$$T \rightarrow T \times F,$$
$$T \rightarrow F,$$
$$F \rightarrow (E),$$
$$F \rightarrow a \mid b \mid c.$$

For example, sentence (expression) $a \times b + b \times c + c \times a$ has two different derivation trees as shown in Fig. 6.2.

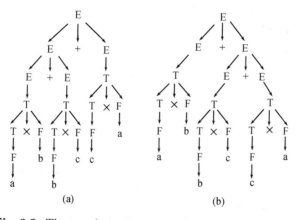

Fig. 6.2   The two derivation trees of $a \times b + b \times c + c \times a$.

For two derivation trees, it looks like that their derivations are the same.

$$E \rightarrow E + E$$
$$\rightarrow E + E + E$$
$$\rightarrow T + E + E$$

$$\rightarrow T \times F + E + E$$
$$\rightarrow F \times F + E + E$$
$$\rightarrow a \times F + E + E$$
$$\rightarrow a \times b + E + E$$
$$\rightarrow a \times b + T + E$$
$$\rightarrow a \times b + T \times F + E$$
$$\rightarrow a \times b + F \times F + E$$
$$\rightarrow a \times b + b \times F + E$$
$$\rightarrow a \times b + b \times c + E$$
$$\rightarrow a \times b + b \times c + T$$
$$\rightarrow a \times b + b \times c + T \times F$$
$$\rightarrow a \times b + b \times c + F \times F$$
$$\rightarrow a \times b + b \times c + c \times F$$
$$\rightarrow a \times b + b \times c + c \times a.$$

Actually, the two derivations are different in that in the right side $E + E$ one is to replace the first E to get $E + E + E$ while the another is to replace the second E to get $E + E + E$. Strictly speaking, they are $(E + E) + E$ and $E + (E + E)$. Since with an expression $a \times b + b \times c + c \times a$, there are two derivation trees, i.e., the leftmost derivation tree and the rightmost derivation tree. They are different. So this is an ambiguous grammar.

Given a grammar, how to decide whether it is ambiguous or not. We now present a sufficient condition for it.

Theorem 6.1 In a grammar, if in its productions, there is one that there are more than two occurrences of a nonterminal that consecutively appear while on the left of the production, it is the nonterminal too. Then the grammar must be ambiguous.

Proof Without losing generality, suppose that the production is as follows:

$$A \rightarrow AA.\ldots$$

It is easy to imagine that using the leftmost and rightmost derivation to the same production, we must get different derivation trees. Therefore, that this is an ambiguous grammar is proved.

Directly perceiving through the sense, the derivation tree of an ambiguous must have the following form: its two same subtrees may either appear on the left subtree or appear on the right subtree of the whole tree. And these two positions are adjacent.

6.3 Characteristics of Context-Free Grammars

In this section we discuss several elementary characteristics of context-free grammars. We first introduce two normal forms for context-free grammars, then we discuss other characteristics that are useful for syntactic analysis.

Definition 6.8   The normal form for a kind of grammars means that for this kind of grammars, all the productions of them may have the same expression form. For example, for regular grammars, left linear expression, or right linear expression is the normal form of these grammars.

Definition 6.9   A context-free grammar $G = (V_N, V_T, S, P)$ is in the Chomsky normal form (CNF), if all the productions of it are either of the form $X \to YZ$ or of the form $X \to a$, where $X, Y, Z \in V_N$, and $a \in V_T$.

If G is in Chomsky normal form, then G is ε-free, so $\varepsilon \notin L(G)$.

Theorem 6.2   Given any context-free grammar $G = (V_N, V_T, S, P)$ such that $\varepsilon \notin L(G)$, then there is an equivalent grammar in the Chomsky normal form.

Proof   As we mentioned above, we can assume that G is ε-free grammar. We can also assume that there is no production $X \to Y$. And every production that contains a terminal symbol is of the form $X \to a$. The productions of G have either the form $X \to a$ or the form $X \to X_{11}X_{12}...X_{1k}$ with $k \geqslant 2$.

Productions of the form $X \to a$ or $X \to X_{i1}X_{i2}$ already conform to Chomsky normal form, if $\pi\colon X \to X_{i1}X_{i2} \ldots X_{ik}$ is a production of P with $k \geqslant 3$, then we can introduce $k - 2$ new nonterminals $Z_1, Z_2, \ldots, Z_{k-2}$ and the productions

$$X \to X_{i1}Z_1, Z_1 \to X_{i2}Z_2, \ldots, Z_{k-2} \to X_{i(k-1)}X_{1k}. \qquad (6.10)$$

Now we define grammar $G' = (V_N \cup V_N', V_T, S, P'')$ where V_N' consists of all symbols $Z_j (j = 1, \ldots, k - 2)$ and P' consists of all the original productions with the forms $X \to a$ or $X \to X_{i1}X_{i2}$, and of productions obtained from productions of P having the form $X \to X_{i1}...X_{ik}$ with $k \geqslant 3$. By applying the method we used above, it is easy to see that G' is equivalent to G and G' is in the Chomsky normal form.

Example 6.7   Let $G = (\{S_1, S_2, S_3\}, \{a, b\}, S_1, P)$ be the context-free grammar with P consisting of the following productions:

$$
\begin{array}{lll}
S_1 \to aS_3, & S_1 \to bS_2, & S_2 \to a, \\
S_2 \to aS_1, & S_2 \to bS_1S_1, & S_3 \to b, \\
S_3 \to bS_1, & S_3 \to aS_3S_3.
\end{array}
$$

By introducing the new nonterminal symbols X_a, X_b, Z_1, Z_2 and transforming the original productions to the following productions, we obtain a grammar in the Chomsky normal form:

$$
\begin{array}{lll}
S_1 \to X_a S_3, & S_1 \to X_b S_2, & S_2 \to a, \\
S_2 \to X_a S_1, & S_2 \to X_b Z_1, & Z_1 \to S_1 S_1, \\
S_3 \to b, & S_3 \to X_b S_1, & S_3 \to X_a Z_2, \\
Z_2 \to S_2 S_2, & X_a \to a, & X_b \to b
\end{array}
$$

Obviously the grammar that has nonterminal symbols S_1, S_2, S_3, Z_1, Z_2, terminal symbols a and b, and the productions above is a context-free grammar and is in the Chomsky normal form. It is also equivalent to grammar G given.

Using the Chomsky normal form we can prove an important decidability result for the class of Type 2. The result relates the length of a word to the length of derivation.

Lemma 6.1 [3]   Let $G = (V_N, V_T, S, P)$ be a context-free grammar in the Chomsky normal form. Then if $S \xRightarrow[\alpha]{*} x$ we have $|\alpha| \leqslant 2 |x| - 1$.

Proof   The proof is slightly stronger than the statement stated in the lemma, namely, if $X \xRightarrow[\alpha]{*} x$ for some $X \in V_N$, then $|\alpha| \leqslant 2 |x| - 1$.

We prove the lemma by induction on $n = |x| \geqslant 1$. If $n = 1$, we have $x = a$ for $a \in V_T$ and the derivation $X \xRightarrow[\alpha]{*} x$ consists in the application of production $\pi \colon X \to a$. Therefore, for $|\alpha| = 1$, the inequality holds.

Suppose that the statement holds for words of length less than n, and let $x \in L(G)$ be a word such that $|x| = n$, where $n > 1$. Let the first production applied be $X \to YZ$. Then we can write $x = uv$, there $Y \xRightarrow[\beta]{*} u$, and $Z \xRightarrow[\gamma]{*} v$, and we have $|\alpha| = |\beta| + |\gamma| + 1$, because the productions used in the last two derivations are exactly the ones used in $X \xRightarrow[\alpha]{*} x$. Applying the inductive hypothesis we obtain

$$
\begin{aligned}
|\alpha| = |\beta| + |\gamma| + 1 &\leqslant 2 |u| - 1 + 2 |v| - 1 + 1 = 2(|u| + |v|) - 1 \\
&= 2 |x| - 1.
\end{aligned} \tag{6.11}
$$

Theorem 6.3   There is an algorithm to determine for a context-free grammar $G = (V_N, V_T, S, P)$ and a word $x \in V_T^*$ whether or not $x \in L(G)$.

Proof   Before we start our proof, we have to mention the following facts: At first, for every context-free grammar G, there is a context-free, ε-free grammar G' such that $L(G') = L(G) - \{\varepsilon\}$. Furthermore, if G is a context-free grammar, then there is an equivalent context-free grammar G' such that one of the following cases occurs:

1) if $\varepsilon \notin L(G)$, then G is ε-free.
2) if $\varepsilon \in L(G)$, then G' contains a unique erasure production $S' \to \varepsilon$ where S' is the start symbol of G', and S' does not occur in any right part of any production of G'.

Having these facts, we may construct a grammar G' equivalent to G such that one of the following two cases occurs:

1) If $\varepsilon \notin L(G)$, G' is ε-free.

2) If $\varepsilon \in L(G)$, G' contains a unique erasure production $S' \to \varepsilon$, where S' is the start symbol of G', and S' does not occur in any right part of any production of G'.

If $x = \varepsilon$, then $x \in L(G)$ if and only if $S \to \varepsilon$ is a production in G'. Suppose that $x \ne \varepsilon$. Let G_1 be a context-free grammar in the Chomsky normal form such that $L(G_1) = L(G') - \{\varepsilon\}$. We have $x \in L(G_1)$ if and only if $x \in L(G)$. By Lemma 6.1, if $S \xrightarrow{*}_{\alpha} x$, then $\mid \alpha \mid \leqslant 2 \mid x \mid -1$, so by listing all derivations of length at most $2 \mid x \mid -1$ we can decide if $x \in L(G)$.

Definition 6.10 A context-free grammar $G = (V_N, V_T, S, P)$ is in the Greibach normal form if all its productions are of the form $X \to a\alpha$, where $X \in V_N$, $a \in V_T$, and $\alpha \in V_N^*$.

If G is in the Greibach normal form, then G is ε-free, so $\varepsilon \notin L(G)$.

Every ε-free context-free grammar has an equivalent grammar in the Greibach normal form. In the following discussion we will prove the fact. But in order to do so we have to introduce some more preliminary knowledge.

Definition 6.11 Left-recursive symbol. Let $G = (V_N, V_T, S, P)$ be a context-free grammar. A nonterminal symbol X is left-recursive (right-recursive) if there exists a derivation $X \xrightarrow{+}_{G} X\alpha (X \xrightarrow{+}_{G} \alpha X)$ for some $\alpha \in (V_N \cup V_T)^*$.

The concept of the left-recursive symbol is important in compiler design.

A context-free grammar G is immediately left-recursive (or immediately right-recursive) if it contains a production $X \to X\alpha (X \to \alpha X)$.

G is left-recursive (right-recursive) if it contains a left-recursive nonterminal (right-recursive nonterminal) [4].

Lemma 6.2 Let $G = (V_N, V_T, S, P)$ be a context-free grammar, and let X,Y be two nonterminal symbols. Suppose that $X \to \alpha Y\beta \in P$ and let

$$Y \to \gamma_1, \ldots, Y \to \gamma_n$$

be the list of all productions in P whose left part is Y. Then G is equivalent to the grammar $G'' = (V_N, V_T, S, P')$, where

$$P' = (P - \{X \to \alpha Y\beta\} \cup \{X \to \alpha\gamma_i\beta \mid 1 \leqslant i \leqslant n\}.$$

Proof Obviously we have $L(G') \subseteq L(G)$. Indeed if a production $X \to \alpha\gamma_i\beta$ $(1 \leqslant i \leqslant n)$ is used in a derivation step

$$\gamma'X\gamma'' \xRightarrow{}_{G} \gamma'\alpha\gamma_i\gamma'',$$

then we can write in G:

$$\gamma'X\gamma'' \xRightarrow{}_{G} \gamma'\alpha Y\beta\gamma'' \Longrightarrow \gamma'\alpha\gamma_i\beta\gamma''. \qquad (6.12)$$

To prove the converse inclusion, $L(G) \subseteq L(G')$, we prove by induction on n, the length of a derivation $u \xrightarrow{*}_{G} \omega$, that we have $u \xrightarrow{*}_{G} \omega$ where $u \in (V_N \cup V_T)^*$

and $\omega \in V_T^*$. For n = 1, the statement of the lemma is immediate. Suppose that this statement holds for derivation of length less than n and let $u \overset{n}{\underset{G}{\Rightarrow}} \omega$. If the production $X \to \alpha Y \beta$ is not used in this derivation, then we obviously have $u \overset{*}{\underset{G}{\Rightarrow}} \omega$. Otherwise this derivation can be written as

$$u \overset{*}{\underset{G}{\Rightarrow}} \omega' X \omega'' \Longrightarrow \omega' \alpha Y \beta \omega'' \overset{*}{\underset{G}{\Rightarrow}} \omega. \tag{6.13}$$

Thus, ω can be written as a product, $\omega = u' u_\alpha u_Y u_\beta u''$, where $\omega' \overset{*}{\underset{G}{\Rightarrow}} u'$, $\alpha \overset{*}{\underset{G}{\Rightarrow}} u_\alpha$, $Y \overset{*}{\underset{G}{\Rightarrow}} u_Y$, $\beta \overset{*}{\underset{G}{\Rightarrow}} u_\beta$, $\omega'' \overset{*}{\underset{G}{\Rightarrow}} u''$ are derivations that are shorter than n. By the inductive hypothesis, we have the derivations

$$\omega' \overset{*}{\underset{G}{\Rightarrow}} u', \quad \alpha \overset{*}{\underset{G}{\Rightarrow}} u_\alpha,$$

$$\beta \overset{*}{\underset{G}{\Rightarrow}} u', \quad \omega'' \overset{*}{\underset{G}{\Rightarrow}} u''.$$

Also, the existence of the derivation $Y \overset{*}{\underset{G}{\Rightarrow}} u_Y$ entails the existence of a derivation $\gamma_i \overset{*}{\underset{g}{\Rightarrow}} u_Y$. By the inductive hypothesis, we obtain the derivation $\gamma_i \overset{*}{\underset{G}{\Rightarrow}} u_Y$. Thus we obtain the derivation $u = \omega' \alpha X \beta \omega'' \overset{*}{\underset{G}{\Rightarrow}} \omega' \alpha \gamma_i \beta \omega'' = \omega$.

By taking u=S, we obtain the desired conclusion.

The following theorem indicates that it is possible to eliminate immediate left-recursiveness in context-free grammars.

Theorem 6.4   Let $G = (V_N, V_T, S, P)$ be a context-free grammar that contains no erasure productions. Denote by P_X the set of productions in P having X as their left part. If $X \in V_N$ is a left-recursive symbol, the set P_X consists of two classes of productions.

1) the productions of P_X whose right parts begin with X:

$$X \to X\alpha_1, \ldots, X \to X\alpha_k,$$

where $\alpha_i \neq \varepsilon$ for $1 \leqslant i \leqslant k$.

2) The remaining productions in P_X:

$$X \to \beta_1, \ldots, X \to \beta_1,$$

where no β_j begins with X, $1 \leqslant j \leqslant l$.

Let Y be a new nonterminal symbol, and let $G'' = (V_N \cup \{Y\}, V_T, S, P')$ be the context-free grammar whose set of productions is given by

$$P' = (P - P_X) \cup \{X \to \beta_j Y, X \to \beta_j \mid 1 \leqslant j \leqslant l\} \cup$$
$$\{Y \to \alpha_i Y, Y \to \alpha_i \mid 1 \leqslant i \leqslant k\}. \tag{6.14}$$

The grammar G' and G are equivalent.

Proof Note that we replace the productions that make X a left-recursive symbol by productions that make the new symbol Y a right recursive symbol. Also, since $\alpha_j \neq \varepsilon$ for $1 \leqslant j \leqslant k$, Y is not left-recursive.

Let $u \in L(G)$ and let

$$S \underset{G,\text{left}}{\Longrightarrow} \gamma_1 \underset{G,\text{left}}{\Longrightarrow} \dots \underset{G,\text{left}}{\Longrightarrow} \gamma_n = u \tag{6.15}$$

be a leftmost derivation of u. If X does not occur in the derivation, then the same derivation can occur in G', and we have $x \in L(G')$. Otherwise, suppose that $X \underset{G,\text{left}}{\overset{*}{\Longrightarrow}} \omega$ is a derivation that allows us to generate an infix ω of x from X and is part of previous derivation. The last derivation necessarily has the form

$$X \underset{G,\text{left}}{\Longrightarrow} X\alpha_{i1} \underset{G,\text{left}}{\Longrightarrow} X\alpha_{i2}\alpha_{i1} \Longrightarrow \dots$$
$$\underset{G,\text{left}}{\Longrightarrow} X\alpha_{il}\dots\alpha_{i2}\alpha_{i1} \underset{G,\text{left}}{\Longrightarrow} \beta_j\alpha_{il}\dots\alpha_{i2}\alpha_{i1}. \tag{6.16}$$

The word $\beta_j\alpha_{il}\dots\alpha_{i2}\alpha_{i1}$ can also be derived in G' from X using the derivation

$$X \underset{G,\text{right}}{\Longrightarrow} \beta_j Y \underset{G,\text{right}}{\Longrightarrow} \beta_j\alpha_{il}Y \underset{G,\text{right}}{\Longrightarrow} \dots$$
$$\underset{G,\text{right}}{\Longrightarrow} \beta_j\alpha_{il}\dots\alpha_{i2}Y \underset{G,\text{right}}{\Longrightarrow} \beta_j\alpha_{il}\dots\alpha_{i2}\alpha_{i1}. \tag{6.17}$$

Thus, every leftmost derivation $S \underset{G,\text{left}}{\overset{*}{\Longrightarrow}} x$ corresponds to a rightmost derivation

$$S \underset{G,\text{right}}{\overset{*}{\Longrightarrow}} x, \text{ so } L(G) \subseteq L(G'). \tag{6.18}$$

The reverse implication can be argued in a completely similar manner, so we have $L(G) = L(G')$.

For an ε-free context-free grammar, it can have two normal forms — Chomsky normal form and Greibach normal form. We may ask how are the two normal forms related? The following lemma answers the question.

Lemma 6.3 Let $G = (\{X_1, \dots, X_n\}, V_T, X_1, P)$ be a context-free grammar in the Chomsky normal form. There exists an equivalent grammar $G' = (V_N, V_T, X_1, P')$ that satisfies the following conditions:

1) $\{X_1, \dots, X_n\} \subseteq V_N$.

2) The productions that have X_i as their left parts have the form $X_i \to a\alpha$ or $X_i \to X_j\alpha \in P'$, where $a \in V_T$, $\alpha \in (V_N)^*$ and $i < j$.

3) If $Y \in V_N - \{X_1, \dots, X_n\}$, then for every production $Y \to \gamma \in P'$, $\gamma \neq \varepsilon$, all symbols in γ except the first symbol are nonterminals, and the first symbol of γ belongs to $\{X_1, \dots, X_n\} \cup V_T$.

With a constructive proof, we will start with the productions in the form $X_i \to X_jX_l$ and $X_i \to a$, then we gradually transform them into the form $X \to a\alpha$ where $a \in V_T$ and $\alpha \in (V_N)^*$.

In the Chomsky normal form the productions of the context-free grammar are of the form $X_i \to X_jX_k$ and $X_i \to a$, where $a \in V_T$.

Proof   At first we sort the productions $X_i \rightarrow X_j X_k$ so that they occur in such order that the nonterminal in left parts with smaller index comes first. Meanwhile, the index of the nonterminal in left part should be less than that of the first nontermianl in right part. Those productions satisfying the requirement is said having increasing order. Those productions that do not satisfy the requirement must have the form $X_l \rightarrow X_m X_n$ where $l > m$. If $l = m$, it must be left-recursive. For the first step, we transform the later productions into the increasing order. This is not difficult to do. For example, if we have $X_3 \rightarrow X_1 X_4$, but previously we must have productions with left part being X_1 and are in increasing order. Let say that $X_1 \rightarrow X_2 X_i$, $X_2 \rightarrow X_3 X_1$, then by replacing the nonterminal X_1 in right part, we may get $X_3 \rightarrow X_1 X_4 \rightarrow X_2 X_i X_4 \rightarrow X_3 X_1 X_i X_4$. This is a left recursive production. Using the method of eliminating left recursive symbol we may get the production without left recursive symbol.

Suppose that k is a number such that $0 \leqslant k \leqslant n$. Starting with $k = 0$, we consider an inductive process such that modifies the productions of the form $X_i \rightarrow X_j \alpha$, where $0 \leqslant i < k$ to produce an equivalent grammar G_k with the property that for any productions in G_k of the form $X_i \rightarrow X_j \alpha$, where $0 \leqslant i < k$, we have $i < j$.

For $k = 0$, we have nothing to do, since there are no productions $X_i \rightarrow X_j \alpha$ with $i < 0$. Suppose that we have built the grammar G_k, that is, for every production $X_i \rightarrow X_j \alpha$ (with $0 \leqslant i < k$ we have $i < j$). Let $X_k \rightarrow X_j \alpha$ be a production such that $j \leqslant k$. As we mentioned above that there must be the productions with X_j being left part and being in increasing order, then we may replace X_j by the right part of the production and by this way the indices of the nonterminals in right parts will be increased until the indices of nonterminals at both parts are the same, that is, X_k becomes left recursive symbol. We will be able to eliminate the left recursion. On the other hand, if $X_j \rightarrow \gamma_1, \ldots, X_j \rightarrow \gamma_m$ are the productions that have X_j in their left part, we can replace $X_k \rightarrow X_j \alpha$ by $X_k \rightarrow \gamma_1 \alpha, \ldots, X_k \rightarrow \gamma_m \alpha$. In this case, it is only one step to Greibach normal form.

By the inductive hypothesis, if $X_k \rightarrow X_l \beta$ is one of these new productions with $k > l$. By repeating the operation that replacing X_l with the nonterminal occurring at the first position of right part of production that has X_l as left part at most $k - 1$ times, we obtain productions of the form $X_k \rightarrow X_p$ with $k \leqslant p$. Once again, if we have $k = p$, left recursion happens and we will eliminate it by the method mentioned above. Otherwise, the productions that have X_k in their left parts are of the form $X_k \rightarrow \beta$ such that β does not begin with X_k. By introducing a new symbol Y_k and replacing these productions by productions of the form $X_k \rightarrow \beta Y_k$, $X_k \rightarrow \beta$, $Y_k \rightarrow \alpha Y_k$, and $Y_k \rightarrow \alpha$ with $\alpha, \beta \neq \varepsilon$, it is clear that these productions obtained satisfy the requirements of the lemma.

Theorem 6.5   For every ε-free context-free grammar G, there is an equivalent grammar in the Greibach normal form.

Proof   Without losing generality, we can assume that G is in the Chomsky normal form and has the form $G = (\{X_1, \ldots, X_n\}, V_T, X_1, P)$. By applying Lemma 6.3 we obtain a context free grammar $G' = (V_N, V_T, X_1, P')$ that is equivalent to G such that

1) $\{X_1, \ldots, X_n\} \subseteq V_N$;

2) the productions that have X_i as their left parts have the form $X_i \to a\alpha$ or $X_i \to X_j\alpha \in P$, where $a \in V_T$, $\alpha \in (V_N)^*$ and $i < j$;

3) if $Y \in V_N - \{X_1, \ldots, X_n\}$, then for every production $X \to \gamma \in P'$, $\gamma \neq \varepsilon$, all symbols in γ except the first symbol are nonterminals, and the first symbol of γ belongs to $\{X_1, \ldots, X_n\} \cup V_T$.

Note that the productions that rewrite the symbol X_n are necessarily of the form $X_n \to a\alpha$, where a is a terminal symbol and α contains only nonterminal symbols. The right part of a production of the form $X_n \to \ldots$ begins with a terminal symbol or with X_n.

Then the X_n in all productions $X_{n-1} \to X_n$ will be replaced by the right part of the productions $X_n \to \ldots$.

Thus, all productions $X_{n-1} \to \ldots$ have the form $X_{n-1} \to a\gamma$, where $\gamma \in (V_N)^*$. This process is repeated for $X_{n-2}, \ldots, X_1$.

Finally, since the first symbol of γ in $Y \to \gamma$ is a terminal or a symbol X_i, an application of Lemma 6.2 allows us to replace the productions $Y \to X_i \ldots$ with the productions whose right part begins with a terminal, thereby obtaining a grammar in the Greibach normal form equivalent to the initial grammar.

Based on the theorem we may design an algorithm that transforms a context-free grammar in the Chomsky normal form into equivalent grammar in the Greibach normal form.

Algorithm T (transformation of a context-free grammar in Chomsky normal form into an equivalent grammar in the Greibach normal form)

Input: A context-free grammar in the Chomsky normal form with the production set P that consists of the productions in the form $X_i \to X_k X_l$ and $X_i \to a$.

Output: All the productions wil have the form $X_i \to a\alpha$, where $a \in V_T$ and $\alpha \in (V_n)^*$, V_n consists of the original $\{X_1, \ldots, X_n\}$ plus the additional norterminals used in the transformation.

T1 (sorting the productions)   For all the productions in form of $X_i \to X_k X_l$, they will occur in increasing order. On one hand the indices of the nonterminals in left parts of the productions occur in increasing order; on the other hand, for each production, we have $k > i$. If a production $X_j \to X_u X_v$ has $j > u$, then by using the productins with $X_u, X_{u+1}, \ldots$ as left parts, we may transform the production given into the form $X_j \to X_j \ldots$. then left recursion happens with the production.

Meanwhile, starting from X_1, if we have $X_1 \to X_2 \ldots$ and $X_2 \to a$, by replacing X_2 in the right part of the first production, we obtain $X_1 \to a\alpha$, where α is a string of nonterminals. Then the production obtained and $X_2 \to a$ are in the Greibach normal form.

T2 (eliminating left recursion)   In the step T1, we get the production of the form $X_j \to X_j\gamma$ where $\gamma \in (V_n)^*$. Since we have two forms of the productions $X_j \to X_j\gamma$ and $X_j \to a$, by replacing the X_j at the right part of the first production with a of the right part of the second production, we obtain $X_j \to a\gamma$ and this is a production in the Greibach normal form. In general, when we encounter a production with left recursive symbol

$$X \to X\gamma,$$
$$X \to a. \tag{6.19}$$

We may transform the first production into

$$X \to aY,$$
$$Y \to \gamma Y \mid \varepsilon. \tag{6.20}$$

Then the left recursion of the production is eliminated.

T3 (Transforming the productions into Greibach normal form)   For all the productions with the index of nonterminal at left part being less than that of the first nonterminal at right part of production, we replace the nonterminal with the terminal that occurs in the productions with the specific nonterminal as the left part, and we do this from higher indecies to lower indices, then we get the productions in the following form

$$X_i \to a\gamma(a \in V_T, \gamma \in (\{X_1, X_2, \ldots, X_n\} \cup \{Y_1, Y_2, \ldots, Y_m\})^* \tag{6.21}$$

and now $V_N = \{X_1, X_2, \ldots, X_n, Y_1, \ldots, Y_m\}$ where $B_j(1 \leqslant j \leqslant m)$ are newly introduced nonterminals that occur in the following productions:

$$Y_j \to b_l(b_l \in V_T),$$
$$Y_j \to b_l\alpha(\alpha \in V_N^*). \tag{6.22}$$

Now no matter whether the productions with X_i as left parts or with Y_j as left parts, they all are in Greibach normal form.

Example 6.8   Let $G = (\{X_1, X_2, X_3\}, \{a, b\}, X_1, P)$ be a context-free grammar whose set of productions is

$$P = \{X_1 \to X_2X_3, X_2 \to X_1X_2, X_2 \to a, X_3 \to X_1X_3, X_3 \to b\}. \tag{6.23}$$

By inspection we may see that G is in Chomsky normal form. Note that X_1 is a left recursive symbol as we have

$$X_1 \underset{G}{\Longrightarrow} X_2X_3 \underset{G}{\Longrightarrow} X_1X_2X_3. \tag{6.24}$$

Also, X_2 is left-recursive due to

$$X_2 \underset{G}{\Longrightarrow} X_1X_2 \underset{G}{\Longrightarrow} X_2X_3X_2. \tag{6.25}$$

We replace the production $X_2 \to X_1X_2$ with $X_2 \to X_2X_3X_2$. At this point, the set of productions that have X_2 as their left part is

$$X_2 \to X_2X_3X_2, \quad X_2 \to a. \tag{6.26}$$

Then to eliminate the left-recursiveness of X_2 we introduce a new nonterminal symbol Y_1 and replace the productions $X_2 \rightarrow X_2X_3X_2$ and $X_2 \rightarrow a$ with

$$X_2 \rightarrow aY_1, \quad X_2 \rightarrow a, \quad Y_1 \rightarrow X_3X_2Y_1, \quad Y_1 \rightarrow X_3X_2.$$

The current set of productions is

$$X_1 \rightarrow X_2X_3, \quad X_2 \rightarrow aY_1, \quad X_2 \rightarrow a, \quad Y_1 \rightarrow X_3X_2Y_1,$$
$$Y_1 \rightarrow X_3X_2, \quad X_3 \rightarrow X_1X_3, \quad X_3 \rightarrow b.$$

Now we use $X_3 \rightarrow aY_1X_3X_3$ and $X_3 \rightarrow aX_3X_3$ to replace the X_3 occurring as the first symbol at the right parts of productions above, as well as using $X_2 \rightarrow aY_1$ and $X_2 \rightarrow a$ to replace X_2 occurring as the first symbol at the right part of productions above. Finally we obtain the set of productuins

$$X_1 \rightarrow aY_1X_3, \quad X_1 \rightarrow aX_3, \quad X_2 \rightarrow aY_1,$$
$$X_2 \rightarrow a, \quad X_3 \rightarrow aY_1X_3X_3, \quad X_3 \rightarrow aX_3X_3,$$
$$X_3 \rightarrow b, \quad Y_1 \rightarrow aY_1X_3X_3X_2Y_1, \quad Y_1 \rightarrow aX_3X_3X_2Y_1,$$
$$Y_1 \rightarrow bX_2Y_1, \quad Y_1 \rightarrow aY_1X_3X_3X_2, \quad Y_1 \rightarrow aX_3X_3X_2,$$
$$Y_1 \rightarrow bX_2$$

of the grammar $G' = (\{X_1, X_2, X_3, Y_1\}, \{a, b\}, X_1, P')$ and P' consists of the set we finally got above.

Example 6.9 Let $G = (\{A, B, C\}, \{a, b\}, A, P)$ is a context-free grammar with the following set of productions:

$$A \rightarrow BC, \quad B \rightarrow CA \mid b, \quad C \rightarrow AB \mid a.$$

Transform the productions into the Greibach normal form.

According to the algorithm given above, we sort the productions according to the indices of nonterminals. We assign A as X_1, B as X_2 and C as X_3, then the productions become

$$X_1 \rightarrow X_2X_3, \quad X_2 \rightarrow X_3X_1 \mid b, \quad X_3 \rightarrow X_1X_2 \mid a.$$

Now the third production is not in increasing order in terms of the indices of the nonterminals at left part and right part. We need to change it. By substituting X_1 with $X_1 \rightarrow X_2X_3$ and X_2 with $X_2 \rightarrow X_3X_1$, we have

$$X_3 \rightarrow X_1X_2 \rightarrow X_2X_3X_2 \rightarrow X_3X_1X_3X_2.$$

Obviously it is a left-recursive production. Apart from this one, we also have two other productions with respect to X_3, they are

$$X_3 \rightarrow bX_3X_2, \quad X_3 \rightarrow a.$$

They are in the Greibach normal form already.

Now the problem is to eliminate the left-recursion. Using the two later productions and introducing a new nonterminal symbol Y, we obtain

$$X_3 \to bX_3X_2Y, \quad X_3 \to aY, \qquad X_3 \to bX_3X_2, \quad X_3 \to a;$$
$$Y \to X_1X_3X_2, \qquad Y \to X_1X_3X_2Y.$$

The productions with respect to Y are not in the Greibach normal form yet. But at first we handle X_2, we have

$$X_2 \to bX_3X_2YX_1, \quad X_2 \to bX_3X_2X_1, \quad X_2 \to aYX_1,$$
$$X_2 \to aX_1, \qquad X_2 \to b.$$

Using these productions, we may transform the production with respect to X_1 into the Greibach form as follows:

$$X_1 \to bX_3X_2YX_1X_3, \quad X_1 \to bX_3X_2X_1X_3, \quad X_1 \to aYX_1X_3,$$
$$X_1 \to aX_1X_3, \qquad X_1 \to bX_3.$$

Now we may transform productions with respect to Y, and we obtain

$$Y \to bX_3X_2YX_1X_3X_3X_2, \quad Y \to bX_3X_2X_1X_3X_3X_2,$$
$$Y \to aYX_1X_3X_3X_2, \quad Y \to aX_1X_3X_3X_2,$$
$$Y \to bX_3X_3X_2, \quad Y \to bX_3X_2YX_1X_3X_3X_2Y,$$
$$Y \to bX_3X_2X_1X_3X_3X_2Y, \quad Y \to aYX_1X_3X_3X_2Y,$$
$$Y \to aX_1X_3X_3X_2Y, \quad Y \to bX_3X_3X_2Y.$$

Up to now, we have obtained a context-free grammar that is equivalent to grammar G and its productions are in the Greibach normal form. We denote it as $G' = (\{A, B, C, D\}, \{a, b\}, A, P')$ where P' is the following set of productions:

$$A \to bCBDAC, A \to bCBAC, A \to aDAC, A \to aAC, A \to bC;$$
$$B \to bCBDA, B \to bCBA, B \to aDA, B \to aA, B \to b;$$
$$C \to bCBD, C \to bCB, C \to aD, C \to a;$$
$$D \to bCBDACCBD, D \to bCBACCBD, D \to bCCBD;$$
$$D \to aDACCBD, D \to aACCBD, D \to bCBDACCB;$$
$$D \to bCBACCB, D \to bCCB, D \to aDACCB, D \to aACCB.$$

After the discussion of the two normal forms of context-free grammars, we will discuss several related results whose main applications is to show certain languages do not belong to context-free languages. This is very important to syntactical analysis. If we get the conclusion it means that the language is not programming language. Our discussion is almost parallel to the discussion of regular languages. As in the case of regular languages, these results are traditionally named pumping lemmas. But in the last chapters we have used theorems to refer them. We feel that it is indeed more suitable to refer them as theorems. For our discussion, we need to identify subsequence of symbols of words that occur in certain positions. We identify a subset M of $\mathbf{N}$ (integers) as a marking set. As no further assumptions are made about this set below, the results hold for all marking sets.

Definition 6.12 [5] Let A be an alphabet, and let $\omega = a_{i0}, \ldots, a_{i|\omega|-1}$ be a word in A^*. The set of marked occurrences in ω is the set $\{0, \ldots, |\omega| - 1\} \cap M$, and the M-weight of ω is the number $|\omega|_M = |\{0, \ldots, |\omega| - 1\} \cap M|$.

If the marking set is clear from the context, we may denote $\|\omega\|_M$ simply by $\|\omega\|$.

Theorem 6.6 (Pumping lemma of Ogden) Let G be a context-free grammar, and let M be a marking set. There exists a number $n_G \in N$ such that if $\omega \in L(G)$ and $\|\omega\|_M \geqslant n_G$, then we can write $\omega = xyzut$ such that $\|y\|_M \geqslant 1$ or $\|u\|_N \geqslant 1$, $\|yzu\|_M \leqslant n_G$ and $xy^nzu^nt \in L(G)$ for all n.

Proof Let $G = (V_N, V_T, S, P)$, and let $L(G) = \max\{|\alpha| \| S \to \alpha \in P\}$. We can assume that $L(G) \geqslant 2$, since otherwise $L(G) \in V_T^* \cup \{\varepsilon\}$. We define the number $n_G = L(G)^{|M|+1}$, and suppose that $\omega \in L(G)$ such that $\|\omega\|_M \geqslant n_G$.

Let T be a derivation tree of a derivation $S \overset{*}{\underset{G}{\Rightarrow}} \omega$. Suppose that an internal node v of T is labeled by the nonterminal symbol X and that word $(T_{[v]}) = s$. Then the weight of v is defined as $\text{weight}(v) = \|s\|_M$. Clearly, we have $\text{weight}(v) = \Sigma\{\text{weight}(v') \mid v' \in \text{CHILDREN}(v)\}$.

Let V be the set of vertices of T. Define the function h: $V \to N$ by 0
    if $v \in \text{LEAVES}(T)$
$h(v) = \{1 + \max\{h(v') \mid v' \in \text{CHILDREN}(v)\}$
    if $|\{v' \mid v' \in \text{CHILDREN}(v), \text{weight}(v') > 0\}| > 1$
$\max\{h(v') \mid v' \in \text{CHILDREN}(v)\}$, otherwise for every $v \in V$.

Let v be an internal node of T. If $h(v) == h(v_1)$, where $v_1 \in \text{CHILDREN}(v)$, then the third case of above definition applies. In this case, there is almost one child of v that has positive weight (namely, the node v_1), hence $\text{weight}(v) = \text{weight}(v_1)$.

Conversely, suppose that v has a child v_1 such that $\text{weight}(v) = \text{weight}(v_1)$. Since we have $\text{weight}(v) = \Sigma\{\text{weight}(v') \mid v' \in \text{CHILDREN}(v)\}$, it follows that every other child of v has a zero weight. Therefore, $\text{weight}(v) = \text{weight}(v')$, by the definition of h. This allows us to conclude that, for an internal node v, there exists a child v' of v such that $h(v) = h(v')$ if and only if a child v' exists such that $\text{weight}(v) = \text{weight}(v')$.

Now we want to prove that for each node v of T we have $\text{weight}(v) \leqslant L(G)^{h(v)}$. The proof is carried out by induction on $\text{height}(v)$.

If $\text{height}(v) = 0$, v is a leaf, $h(v) = 0$ and $\text{weight}(v) \leqslant 1$, so $\text{weight}(v) \leqslant L(G)^{h(v)}$.

Suppose that the inequality holds, vertices of height less than n, and let v be a vertex of height n. Then the following two cases may occur:

1) If $h(v) = h(v_1)$, where $v_1 \in$ CHILDREN(v), then weight(v) = weight$(v_1) \leqslant L(G)^{h(v_1)}$ by the inductive hypothesis. Thus weight(v) $\leqslant L(G)^{h(v)}$.

2) If $h(v) > h(v_1)$ for every $v_1 \in$ CHILDREN(v), then $h(v) = 1 + \max\{h(v_1) \mid v_1 \in$ CHILDREN(v)$\}$, and v has more than one child with positive weight. Let $v_{i0}, \ldots, v_{ik-1}$ be the set of all such children of v, where $k > 1$. Note that we have $k \leqslant L(G)$ by the definition of derivation trees. Therefore,

$$\text{weight}(v) = \text{weight}(v_{i0}) + \ldots + \text{weight}(v_{ik-1})$$
$$\leqslant L(G)^{h(i0)} + \ldots + L(G)^{h(vik-1)} \text{ (by the inductive hypothesis)}$$
$$\leqslant L(G) \cdot L(G)^{\max\{h(vi0),\ldots,h(vik-1)\}}$$
$$= L(G)^{1++\max\{h(vi0),\ldots,h(vik-1)\}}$$
$$= L(G)^{h(v)} \tag{6.27}$$

Since $\|\omega\|_M$ equals the weight of the root v_{root} of the tree T and $\|\omega\|_M \geqslant n_G$ it follows that $L(G)^{|A_n|+1} = n_G \leqslant \text{weight}(v_{root}) \leqslant L(G)^{h(v_{root})}$. Thus, $h(v_{root}) \geqslant |A_n| + 1$. Consequently, y contains a branch B such that each node in B with $h(v) > 0$ has a child v' such that $h(v) = 1 + h(v')$. Then there is a sequence of nodes $(v_0, v_1, \ldots)$ along B such that

$$h(v_0) = |A_N| + 1, h(v_1) = |A_N|, \ldots, h(v_i) = |A_N| - (i-1), \ldots$$

since there are more than $|A_N|$ nodes in this sequence, there must be two nodes v_i and v_j with $i < j$, that are labeled with the same nonterminal symbol X (see Fig. 6.3). Let z be the word over V_T given by $z = \text{word}(T_{vj})$. Then word(T_{vj}) includes z, and so, it must have the form yzu for some $y, u \in V_T^*$. Further yzu is an infix of ω, so $\omega = xyzut$ for some $x, t \in V_T^*$ and there are the derivations in G:

$$S \underset{\omega_0}{\overset{*}{\Longrightarrow}} xXt, \quad X \underset{\omega_1}{\overset{*}{\Longrightarrow}} yXu, \quad X \underset{\omega_2}{\overset{*}{\Longrightarrow}} z. \tag{6.28}$$

By repeated applications of the second derivation, we obtain:

$$S \underset{\omega_0}{\overset{*}{\Longrightarrow}} xXt \underset{\omega_1}{\overset{*}{\Longrightarrow}} xyXut \underset{\omega_1}{\overset{*}{\Longrightarrow}} xy^2Xu^2t \underset{\omega_1}{\overset{*}{\Longrightarrow}} \ldots \underset{\omega_1}{\overset{*}{\Longrightarrow}} xy^nXu^nt \underset{\omega_2}{\overset{*}{\Longrightarrow}} xy^nzu^nt, \tag{6.29}$$

so $xy^nzu^nt \in L(G)$ for $n \in \mathbb{N}$.

Since $h(v_i) > h(v_j)$, we must have $\|yzu\|_M > \|z\|_M$, so either $\|y\|_M \geqslant 1$, or $\|u\|_M \geqslant 1$. Also, since $h(v_i) \leqslant |A_N| + 1$, it follows that $\|yzu\|_M \leqslant L(G)^{|An|+1} = n_G$.

This argument of pumping theorem brings the next statement that tells us something about certain phrases of words in the language generated by the grammar.

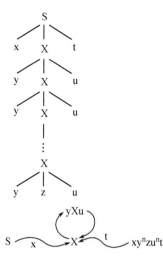

Fig. 6.3 Derivation Tree T.

Corollary 6.1   For every context-free grammar G and marking set M, there exists a number n_G such that if $\omega \in L(G)$ and $\|\omega\|_M \geqslant n_G$, then ω can be written as $\omega = xyzut$ such that $\|y\|_M \geqslant 1$, $\|u\|_M \geqslant 1$, $\|yzu\|_M \leqslant n_G$ and $y^i zu \in \mathrm{PHRASE}(\omega_i, G)$ where $\omega_i = xy^i zu^i t \in L(G)$ for every $i \in N$.

Proof   The proof can be found from the proof of the theorem above.

There is another version of pumping theorem. It corresponds to the case when the marking set M coincides with N.

Theorem 6.7   (Pumping lemma of Bar-hillel, Perles, and Shamir)   Let G be a context-free grammar. There exists a number $n_G \in N$ such that if $\omega \in L(G)$ and $|\omega| \geqslant n_G$, then we can write $\omega = xyzut$ such that $|y| \geqslant 1$ or $|u| \geqslant 1$, $|yzu| \leqslant n_G$ and $xy^n zu^n t \in L(G)$ for all $n \in N$.

Proof   If $M = N$ then $\|\omega\|_M = |\omega|$, then the argument in the proof of Ogden lemma holds for current situation.

Example 6.10   Let $A = \{a, b, c\}$, and let $L = \{a^n b^n c^n \mid n \in N\}$. The language L is not context-free.

We prove the fact by using pumping theorem of Bar-Hillel, Perles and Shamir. Suppose that L were a context-free language. Then there is $n_G \in N$ satisfying the property stated in lemma of Bar-Hillel et al. Let $\omega = a^{n_G} b^{n_G} c^{n_G}$. Clearly $|\omega| = 3n_G > n_G$, so $\omega = xyzut$ for some x, y, z, u, t such that $|y| \geqslant 1$ or $|u| \geqslant 1$, $|yzu| \leqslant n_G$ and $xy^n zu^n t \in L(G)$ for all $n \in N$.

Note that neither y nor u may contain more than one type of symbols. Indeed, if y contained both a's and b's, then we could write $y = y^i a...ab...by^n$ since

$$xy^2 zu^2 t = xy'a...ab...by''y'a...ab...by'' zu^2 t. \qquad (6.30)$$

Now we obtain a contradiction, since no b symbol may precede a symbol in any word of $L(G)$. A similar argument holds for u. Thus, each y and u may contain only one kind of symbols. Consequently pumping y and u would violate the condition $n_a(\omega) = n_b(\omega) = n_c(\omega)$ satisfied by all words of $\omega \in L(G)$. This shows that $L(G)$ does not satisfy the condition of Theorem 6.7, hence $L(G)$ is not context-free.

The Ogden lemma can also be used to prove the fact. Suppose that n_G be a number whose existence is guaranteed by this theorem. We also assume that we mark all positions that contain b in the word $a^{n_G} b^{n_G} c^{n_G}$. Clearly $|\omega| = 3n_G > n_G$, so $\omega = xyzut$ such that $\|y\|_M \geqslant 1$ or $\|u\|_M \geqslant 1$, $\|yzu\|_M \leqslant n_G$ and $xy^n zu^n t \in L(G)$ for every $n \in N$. Then at least one of y and z must contain a and b. Moreover, by the same argument as above, they may consist only of one type of symbols so they must both must be infixes of b^{n_G}. Thus pumping y and u increases the number of b's that violates the condition $n_a(\omega) = n_b(\omega) = n_c(\omega)$.

The following is another example that shows that Ogden lemma is more powerful as it can be used to disprove that the language is context-free while another lemma cannot.

Example 6.11   Consider the language $L = \{a^n b^n c^j \mid 0 \leqslant j \leqslant n\}$. We shall prove that this language is not context-free. Note that here, L satisfies the condition of Bar-Hillel et al lemma, hence it cannot be used to prove the fact of this example. Let $\omega = a^n b^n c^j$ for some $n \geqslant n_g$, and let $j < n_G$. By choosing $y = a^p$ and $u = b^{p\omega}$ with $p \geqslant 1$ we can write $\omega = xyzut$ such that $|y| \geqslant 1$ or $|u| \geqslant 1$, $|yzu| \leqslant n_G$ and $xy^n zu^n t \in L(G)$ for all $n \in N$, since the pumping will increase the number of a's and b's without violating the definition of the language.

To prove that L is not context-free, we use the reduction ad absurdum. Assume that L is a context-free language, and let n_G be the number defined in the Ogden lemma. Let $\omega = a^{n_G} b^{n_G} c^j$ for some $j < n_G$ and mark all positions that contain c. Since $|\omega| = 2n_G + j > n_G$, it follows that $\omega = xyzut$ such that $\|y\|_M \geqslant 1$ or $\|u\|_M \geqslant 1$, $\|yzu\|_M \leqslant n_G$ and $xy^n zu^n t \in L(G)$ for all $n \in N$. Note that y and u must be infixes of a^{n_G}, b^{n_G} or C^j. Since only positions that contain c's are marked, at least one of these words must contain c's that are marked, so at least one of them is in infix of c^j. Note that if they were both infixes of c^j, then by pumping, we could obtain a word in $L(G)$ such that the number of c's would exceed the numbers of a's or b's. If y is an infix of b^{n_G}, the pumping will increase the number of b's while the number of a's will remain constant and thus the definition of L would be violated. A similar contradiction occurs when y is an infix of a^{n_G}.

There are more characteristics of context-free grammars and languages. For example, we know that the class of context-free languages is closed with respect to union, product, and Kleene closure. Now we explore other closure (and no closure) characteristics of the class of languages with respect to other operations.

Theorem 6.8 The class of context-free languages is not closed with respect to intersection.

Proof Consider the context-free grammars

$$G_1 = (\{S, X, Y\}, \{a, b, c\}, S, \{S \rightarrow XY, X \rightarrow aXb, X \rightarrow \varepsilon, Y \rightarrow cY, Y \rightarrow \varepsilon\}),$$
$$G_2 = (\{S, X, Y\}, \{a, b, c\}, S, \{S \rightarrow XY, X \rightarrow aX, X \rightarrow \varepsilon, Y \rightarrow bYc, Y \rightarrow \varepsilon\}).$$

It is easy to see that

$$L_1 = L(G_1) = \{a^n b^n c^m \mid n, m \in N\},$$
$$L_2 = L(G_2) = \{a^n b^m c^m \mid n, m \in N\}.$$

Therefore, both $L_1 = \{a^n b^n c^m \mid n, m \in N\}$ and $L_2 = \{a^n b^m c^m \mid n, m \in N\}$ are context-free languages. But since $L_1 \cap L_2 = \{a^n b^n c^n \mid n \in N\}$, $L_1 \cap L_2$ does not belong to context-free.

Corollary 6.2 The class of context-free languages is not closed with respect to complement.

Proof We prove it via reduction ad absurdum again. Suppose that the class is closed with respect to complement. Since the class of context-free languages is closed with respect to union, and intersection can be expressed through union and complement ($\sim A \cap \sim B =\sim (A \cup B)$). Therefore this would imply that the class is closed with respect to intersection.

Theorem 6.9 If L is a context-free language and R is a regular language, then $L \cap R$ is a context-free language.

Proof Without losing generality, we may assume that both L and R are languages over the same alphabet V_T. Initially, we also assume that neither L nor R contain the null word.

Suppose that $L = L(G)$ where $G = (V_N, V_T, S_1, P)$ is a ε-free context-free grammar, and $R = L(M)$, where M is a deterministic finite automaton $M = (Q, V_T, \delta, q_0, F)$. Define the context-free grammar $G' = (V'_N, V_T, S', P')$ as follows. The nonterminal alphabet V'_N consists of the new initial symbol S' together with $(\mid V_N \mid + \mid V_T \mid) \mid Q \mid^2$ new symbols of the form $s^{qq'}$ for every symbol $s \in V_N \cup V_T$ and every pair of states (q, q') of the automaton M. The set P' consists of the following productions: $S \rightarrow S^{q_0 q}$ for every final state q of M.

$X^{qq'} \rightarrow s_0^{qq_1} s_1^{q_1 q_2} \ldots s_{n-1}^{q_{n-1} q'}$ for every production $X \rightarrow s_0 s_1 \ldots s_{n-1}$ in P and every sequence of states $(q_1, \ldots, q_{n-1})$.

$A^{qq'} \rightarrow a$ for every terminal symbol a of G such that $\delta(q, a) = q'$ in M. We claim that if $s^{qq'} \xRightarrow[G']{n} x$ for some $x \in V_T^*$, then $\delta^*(q, x) = q'$ in M and that, if $s \in V_N \cup V_T$, then $s \xRightarrow[G]{*} x$. The argument is proved by induction on $n \geqslant 1$.

If $n = 1$, we have $s = x = a$ for some $a \in V_T$ and $\delta(q, a) = q'$ and the claim is clearly satisfied.

Suppose that the claim holds for derivations of length less than n, and let $S^{qq'} \underset{G'}{\overset{n}{\Longrightarrow}} x$ be a derivation of length n. If we write the first step of this derivation explicitly, we obtain

$$S^{qq'} \underset{G'}{\Longrightarrow} s_0^{qq_1} s_1^{q_1 q_2} \ldots s_{n-1}^{q_{n-1} q'} \underset{G'}{\overset{*}{\Longrightarrow}} x. \tag{6.31}$$

Therefore, we have the production $s \to s_0 s_1 \ldots s_{n-1}$ in P. And we can write x as $x = x_0 x_1 \ldots x_{n-1}$, such that we have the derivations

$$s_0^{qq_1} \underset{G}{\overset{*}{\Longrightarrow}} x_0,$$

$$s_1^{q_1 q_2} \underset{G}{\overset{*}{\Longrightarrow}} x_1,$$

$$\vdots$$

$$s_{i-1}^{q_{i-1} q_i} \underset{G}{\overset{*}{\Longrightarrow}} x_{i-1},$$

$$\vdots$$

$$s_{n-1}^{q_{n-1} q_n} \underset{G}{\overset{*}{\Longrightarrow}} x_{n-1}. \tag{6.32}$$

That are all shorter than n. By the inductive hypothesis we have

$$\delta^*(q, x_0) = q_1, \delta^*(q_1, x_1) = q_2, \ldots, \delta^*(q_{n-1}, x_{n-1}) = q', \tag{6.33}$$

so $\delta^*(q, x_0, \ldots, x_{n-1}) = \delta^*(q, x) = q'$. Also, if s_i is a nonterminal, then $s_i \underset{G}{\overset{*}{\Longrightarrow}} x_i$; otherwise, if $s_i \in V_T$, we have $s_i = x_i$, so $s_i \underset{G}{\overset{*}{\Longrightarrow}} x_i$ for $0 \leqslant i \leqslant n - 1$. This allows us to construct the derivation

$$s \underset{G}{\Longrightarrow} s_0, \ldots, s_{n-1} \underset{G}{\overset{*}{\Longrightarrow}} x_0 \ldots x_{n-1} \tag{6.34}$$

which justifies our claim.

Now we prove the theorem by showing that $L(G') = L \cap R$. Suppose that $x \in L(G')$. We have the derivation $S' \underset{G'}{\Longrightarrow} S^{q_0 q} \underset{G'}{\overset{*}{\Longrightarrow}} x$. By the previous claim, this implies both $S \underset{G}{\overset{*}{\Longrightarrow}} x$ and $\delta^*(q_0, x) = q$. Thus $x \in L \cap R$.

Conversely, suppose that $x = a_0 a_1 \ldots a_{n-1} \in L \cap R$, We have the derivation $S \underset{G}{\overset{*}{\Longrightarrow}} x$, so in G' we can write

$$S' \underset{G'}{\Longrightarrow} S^{q_0 q} \underset{G'}{\Longrightarrow} a_0^{q_0 q_1} a_1^{q_1 q_2} \ldots a_{n-1}^{q_{n-1} q} \tag{6.35}$$

for some final state q and any states $q_1, \ldots, q_{n-1}$. We can select these intermediate states such that $\delta(q_i, a_i) = q_{i+1}$ for $0 \leqslant i \leqslant n-2$ and $\delta(q_{n-1}, a_{n-1}) = q$.

Therefore, there are the following productions in P':

$$a_0^{q_0 q_1} \to a_0, a_1^{q_1 q_2} \to a_1, \ldots, a_{n-1}^{q_{n-1} q'} \to a_{n-1}, \tag{6.36}$$

This implies the existence of the derivation $S' \overset{*}{\underset{G}{\Longrightarrow}} a_0 a_1 \ldots a_{n-1}$.

If $\varepsilon \in R$ or $\varepsilon \in L$ we consider the regular language $R' = R - \{\varepsilon\}$ and the context-free language $L' = L - \{\varepsilon\}$. By the previous argument we can construct an ε-free context-free grammar G' such that $L(G') = L' \cap R'$. If $\varepsilon \notin L \cap R$, then $L \cap R = L' \cap R'$ and this shows that $L \cap R$ is context-free. If $\varepsilon \in L \cap R$, we have $L \cap R = (L' \cap R') \cup \{\varepsilon\}$, then starting from $G' = (V'_n, V_T, S', P')$ we construct the context-free grammar:

$$G'' = (V'_n \cup \{S''\}, V_T, S'', P \cup \{S'' \to S', S'' \to \varepsilon\}) \tag{6.37}$$

and we have $L \cap R = L(G'')$.

Theorem 6.10 Let s: $A^* \to B^*$ be a substitution. If $s(a)$ is a context-free language for every $a \in A$ and $L \subseteq A^*$ is a context-free language, then $s(L)$ is a context-free language.

Proof Suppose that $L = L(G)$, where $G = (V_N, A, S, P)$ is a context-free grammar, and let $s(a)$ is generated by the context-free grammar $G_a = (V_N^a, B, S_a P)$ for $a \in A$. We may assume that the set of nonterminal symbols A_N^a is pairwise disjoint. Let P' be the set of productions from P as follows. In each production of P replace every letter $a \in A$ by the nonterminal S_a. We claim that the language $s(L)$ is generated by the grammar

$$G' = (V_N \cup \cup_{a \in A} V_N^a, B, S, P' \cup \cup_{a \in A} P_a). \tag{6.38}$$

Let $y \in s(L)$. There exists a word $x = a_{i0} a_{i1} \ldots a_{in-1} \in L$ such that $y \in s(x)$. This means that $y = y_0 y_1 \ldots y_{n-1}$, where $y_k \in s(a_{ik}) = L(G_{aik})$ for $0 \leqslant k \leqslant n-1$. Thus we have the derivation $S_{aik} \overset{*}{\underset{G_{aik}}{\Longrightarrow}} y_k$ for $0 \leqslant k \leqslant n-1$, and the same derivation can be done in G'. Consequently we obtain the derivation

$$S \overset{*}{\underset{G'}{\Longrightarrow}} S_{ai0} \ldots S_{ain-1} \overset{*}{\underset{G'}{\Longrightarrow}} y_0 \ldots y_{n-1} = y \tag{6.39}$$

that implies $y \in L(G')$, so $s(L) \subseteq L(G')$.

Conversely, if $y \in L(G')$ then any derivation $S \overset{*}{\underset{G'}{\Longrightarrow}} y$ is the form of Equation (6.38).

In the argument above we have $S_{aik} \overset{*}{\underset{G_{aik}}{\Longrightarrow}} y_k$ for $0 \leqslant k \leqslant n-1$, we can write $y = y_0 \ldots y_{n-1}$, and $y_k \in L(G_{aik}) = s(a_{ik})$ for $0 \leqslant k \leqslant n-1$. This implies $y = y_0 \ldots y_{n-1} \in s(a_{i0}) \ldots s(a_{in-1}) = s(x) \in S(L)$, so $L(G') \subseteq s(L)$.

Since $s(L) = L(G'')$, it follows that $s(L)$ is context-free language.

Corollary 6.3 If h: $A^* \to B^*$ is a morphism and $L \subseteq A^*$ is a context-free language, then $h(L)$ is a context-free language.

Proof The statement follows immediately from Theorem 6.10 since morphism may be regarded as special case of substitutions.

Theorem 6.11 The class of context-free languages is closed with respect to inverse morphic images. In other words, if h: $B^* \to A^*$ is a morphism, and $L \subseteq A^*$ is a context-free language, then $h^{-1}(L)$ is a context-free language.

Proof   Suppose that $B = \{b_0, b_1, \ldots, b_{m-1}\}$ and that $h(b_i) = x_i$ for $0 \leqslant i \leqslant m-1$. Let $B' = \{b'_0, \ldots, b'_{m-1}\}$, and let s be the substitution given by $s(a) = B'^* a B'^*$ for $a \in A$. Consider the finite language $H = \{b'_i x_i \mid 0 \leqslant i \leqslant m-1\}$ and the mapping g: $P(A^*) \rightarrow P((A \cup B')^*)$ given by $g(L) = s(L) \cap H^*$.

Define the morphisms $h_1: (A \cup B')^* \rightarrow (\{c\} \cup B)^*$ and $h_2: (\{c\} \cup B)^* \rightarrow B^*$ by $h_1(a) = c$ for $a \in A$, $h_1(b') = b$ for all $b' \in B$, and $h_2(c) = \varepsilon$, $h_2(b) = b$ for $b \in B$. We claim that for every language $L \in P(A)$ such that $\varepsilon \notin L$, $h^{-1}(L) = g(h_2(h_1(L)))$ and hence, by three applications of Corollary 6.3, $h^{-1}(L)$ is context-free. This follows from the following equivalent statements:

1) $U = b_{i0} b_{i1} \ldots b_{ik-1} \in h^{-1}(L)$.
2) $h(u) = x_{i0} x_{i1} \ldots x_{ik-1} \in L$.
3) $b'_{i0} x_{i0} \ldots b'_{ik-1} x_{ik-1} \in g(L)$.
4) $h_1(b'_{i0} x_{i0} \ldots b'_{il-1} x_{ik-1}) = b_{i0} c \ldots c \ldots b_{ik-1} c \ldots c \in h_1(g(L))$.
5) $h_2(b_{i0} c \ldots c \ldots b_{ik-1} c \ldots c) = b_{i0} \ldots b_{ik-1} = u \in h_2(h_1(g(L)))$.

If $\varepsilon \in L$, the language $L - \{\varepsilon\}$ is context-free, so $h^{-1}(L - \{\varepsilon\})$ is also context-free. Note that $h^{-1}(L) = h^{-1}(L - \{\varepsilon\}) \cup h^{-1}(\{\varepsilon\})$ and that $h^{-1}(\{\varepsilon\}) = \{a \in A \mid h(a) = \varepsilon\}^*$. Since $h^{-1}(\{\varepsilon\})$ is regular, it follows that $h^{-1}(L)$ is context-free.

Definition 6.13   A transducer is a 6-tuple $J = (A, Q, B, \theta, q_0, F)$, where A is the input alphabet, B is the output alphabet, Q is a finite set called the set of states, θ is a finite relation, $\theta \in Q \times A^* \times B^* \times Q$, called the transition relation, q_0 is the initial state of the transducer, and F is the set of final states, where $F \subseteq Q$. The set Q is disjoint from $A \cup B$. A graph of transducer J is shown in Fig. 6.4.

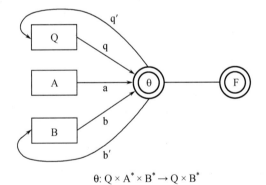

$$\theta: Q \times A^* \times B^* \rightarrow Q \times B^*$$

Fig. 6.4   Graph of the transducer J.

If $(q, x, y, q') \in \theta$, then applying the input word x to the transducer J in state Q results in the output word y and place J into the state q', usually called the next state of J. The activity of J begins in the state q_0.

Note that θ may contain several quadruples having q, x as their first two components, and thus J is a nondeterministic device. Also, θ may contain a quadruple of the form (q, ε, y, q'), sometimes called a null transition, that means that J may produce an output word y without consuming an input symbol.

In summary, a transducer $J = (A, Q, B, \theta, q_0, F)$ is
- ε-free if $(q, x, y, q') \in \theta$ implies $y \neq \varepsilon$;
- k-bounded if $(q, x, y, q') \in \theta$ implies $\mid x \mid \leqslant k$ and $\mid y \mid \leqslant k$;
- k-output if $(q, x, y, q') \in \theta$ implies $\mid y \mid = k$.

Transducer can be represented by labeled directed multigraphs. Let $/$ be a symbol such that $\notin A \cup B$. The graph of a transducer $J = (A, Q, B, \theta, q_0)$ is the labeled directed multigraph $G(J) = (G, A^*/B^*, m)$ where $G = (Q, E, s, d)$ is a directed multigraph whose set of vertices is the set Q of states of J and whose set of edges E contains an edge e with $s(e) = q, d(e) = q'$, and $m(e) = x/y$ for every quadruple $(q, x, y, q') \in \theta$. The following convention introduced for automata, the initial state q_0 is denoted by an incoming arrow, and the final states are circled.

Example 6.12 Let $Q = \{q_0, q_1, q_2, q_3\}$, $A = \{a, b\}$, and $B = \{0, 1\}$. If θ is the relation

$$\theta = \{(q_0, ab, 0, q_1), (q_1, bb, 01, q_3), (q_0, ba, 00, q_2), (q_2, aa, 011, q_3),$$
$$(q_3, \varepsilon, 100, q_0), (q_2, aa, 0011, q_1)\}$$
$$F = \{q_3\},$$

then the graph of the transducer $J = (A, Q, B, \theta, q_0, F)$ is given in Fig. 6.5.

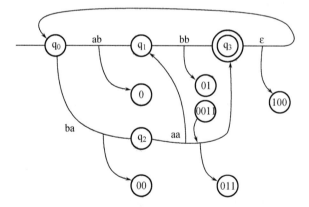

Fig. 6.5 Graph of the transducer $J = (A, Q, B, \Theta, q_0, F)$.

Theorem 6.12 Let $J = (A, Q, B, \theta, q_0, F)$ be a transducer. If $L \subseteq A^*$ is a context-free language, then $J(L)$ is a context-free language over B.

Proof We know that If $J = (A, Q, B, \theta, q_0, F)$ is a transducer, then there exists an alphabet C, a morphism h: $C^* \to A^*$, a morphism g: $C^* \to B^*$ and a regular language $R \subseteq C^*$ such that for every language $L \subseteq A^*$ we have $J(L) = g(h^{-1}(L) \cap R)$. Since the class of context-free language is closed with respect to inverse morphic images, intersection with regular languages, and morphic images, it follows that $J(L)$ is a context-free language.

There are the closure characteristics of context-free languages with respect to quotients with regular languages as the following theorem states.

Theorem 6.13 [6]   If L is a context-free language and R is a regular language, then LR^{-1} and $R^{-1}L$ are both context-free languages.

Proof   Let A be an alphabet, and let c be a symbol such that $c \notin A$. Define the morphism h: $(A \cup \{c\})^* \to A^*$ by $h(a) = a$ for $a \in A$ and $h(c) = \varepsilon$ Then by Theorems 6.9 and 6.6, the language $h^{-1}(L) \cap A^*cR$ is context-free. Note that $\omega \in h^{-1}(L) \cap A^*cR$ if and only if $\omega = ucv$ where $uv \in L$ and $v \in R$ which is equivalent to $u \in LR^{-1}$. Now consider the transducer J whose graph in Fig. 6.5. J will process a word $\omega = ucv$ with $u, v \in A^*$ as follows: all symbols in A are sent to the output intact until c is read. From that point on, the transducer produces only the null word at its output. Under the previous assumptions, $J(\omega) = u$.

The following statements are equivalent:
1) $u \in LR^{-1}$.
2) $uv \in L$ for some $v \in R$.
3) $ucv \in h^{-1}(L) \cap A^*cR$.
4) $u = J(h^{-1}(L) \cap A^*cR)$.

Thus, $LR^{-1} = J(h^{-1}(L) \cap A^*cR)$ which means that LR^{-1} belongs to context-free language. The second part of the theorem follows from the following relation:

$$R^{-1}L = (L^r(R^r)^{-1})^r, \qquad (6.40)$$

where r is the operation of reversal.

Problems

Problem 6.1   Assume that G is a context-free language with ε-free. Prove that for the derivation tree of each sentence of L(G), there are at most $2|\omega| - 1$ nodes where $|\omega|$ is the length of sentence ω.

Problem 6.2   Consider a context-free grammar

$$G = (\{S, X, Y\}, \{a, b\}, S, \{S \to XY, X \to aX, X \to \varepsilon, Y \to bY, Y \to \varepsilon\}).$$

1) Prove that L(G) is a regular language.
2) Prove that for a sentence $\alpha \in L(G)$, though $S \overset{*}{\underset{G}{\Longrightarrow}} \alpha$, There is no the leftmost derivation.

Problem 6.3   A sentence $\alpha \in A^*$ is said to be palindrome if $\alpha = \alpha^R$ where R means reverse, that means that reading α from left to right is the same as reading it from right to left. Suppose that $L_{A,pal}$ is a language consisting of all the palindromes over A. Prove that $L_{A,pal}$ and $A^* - L_{a,pal}$ are not regular context-free languages.

Problem 6.4   For the following context-free grammars, find their equivalent context-free grammars in Chomsky normal form.

1) $G = (\{S\}, \{a, b\}, \{S \to a, S \to aS, S \to aSbS\})$.

2) $G = (\{S, X, Y\}, \{a, b\}, S, \{S \rightarrow XYb, S \rightarrow ab, X \rightarrow SYS, X \rightarrow ba, Y \rightarrow XSX, Y \rightarrow b\})$.

3) $G = (\{S\}, \{+, \times, (,), a\}, S, \{S \rightarrow S + S, S \rightarrow S \times S, S \rightarrow a, S \rightarrow (S)\})$.

Problem 6.5 Find the equivalent grammars in Greibach normal form of the grammars in last Problem.

Problem 6.6 Prove that for a context-free grammar with ε-free G there exists an equivalent grammar G' in which the productions have the form $X \rightarrow a$ or $X \rightarrow abb$ where a and b are terminals, and α is a sentence form that contains nonterninals.

Problem 6.7 Argue whether each context-free language with ε-free L can be generated by the context-free grammar with productions in the forms $X \rightarrow YZU$ and $X \rightarrow a$, where X, Y, and U are nonterminals and a is a terminal.

Problem 6.8 A grammar G is said to be operator grammar if it has the property (among other essential requirements) that no production of which the right side is or has two adjacent nonterminals. Show that every context-free grammar can be converted into an operator grammar. Hint: First transform the grammar into Gribach normal form.

Problem 6.9 Show that every context-free grammar G can be converted into an operator grammar in which each production is of one of the following form

$$A \rightarrow aBcC \quad A \rightarrow aBb \quad A \rightarrow aB \quad A \rightarrow a.$$

If ε is in the language, then $S \rightarrow \varepsilon$ is also a production.

Problem 6.10 Consider a context-free grammar

$$G = (\{S\}, \{a\}, S, \{S \rightarrow a^pS, S \rightarrow a^qS, S \rightarrow \varepsilon\}).$$

1) Show that G is an ambiguous grammar, and $L(G) = \{a^p\}^*\{a^q\}^*$.
2) Construct a non-ambiguous grammar that is equivalent to G.

Problem 6.11 Prove that

$$L = \{a^mb^mc^nd^n | m, n \in N\} \cup \{a^mb^nc^nd^m | m, n \in N\}$$

is inherently ambiguous.

References

[1]   Chomsky N, Schützenberger MP (1963) The algebraic theory of context-free languages. In: Braffort P, Hischberg D (eds) Computer programming and formal systems. North-Holland, Amsterdam.

[2]   Hopcroft JE, Ulman JD (1979) Introduction to automata theory, languages and computation. Addison-Wesley, Reading, Mass.

[3] Kozen DC (1997) Automata and computability. Automata and computability. Springer, New York.

[4] Greibach SA (1965) A note on code set and context-free languages. Mathematical Linguistics and Automatic Translation 15, Harvard University, Computation Lab Rept.

[5] Aho AV, Sethi R, Ullman JD (2003) Compilers: Principles, techniques and tools. Pearson Education, London.

[6] Simovici, Dan A, Tenny Richard L (1999) Theory of formal languages with applications. World Scientific, New York.

Chapter 7　Syntax Analysis

> *The next level in the linguistic hierarchy is that of syntax, or the rules that govern the combination of morphemes in phrases and sentences. In recent years the principles underlying syntax have been extended to include how information can be transformed from one to another.*
>
> Robert L. Solso

7.1　Motivation of the Chapter

The syntax analysis is the essential step for the compilation of programs written in programming languages. In order to produce the object programs executable on the computer, the source program has to be analyzed with respect to its correctness, the correctness of the lexicon, syntax and semantics. And in general, the construction of the compiler puts the first two, i.e., the analysis of the lexicon and analysis of the syntax into a phase — the analysis phase. In the two analyses, obviously the syntax analysis is more important than the lexical analysis though it is the base of the former. In comparison with the lexical analysis, the syntax analysis has more issues to explore. In the development history of compilers many researchers and software engineers had devoted lots of their times to design methods for the syntax analysis. The syntax analysis had been regarded as the key to the success of compilers, and it was also regarded as the most arduous task in the construction of compilers. Now in the field of the syntax analysis there are many successful techniques that are widely used in the construction of compilers, especially in the design of the syntax analysis, we should introduce and discuss them in the book that devotes to the principles of compilers. The aim of this chapter is to explain the role of the syntax analysis and to introduce the important techniques used in the syntax analysis, and to compare these techniques in terms of their efficiency and easiness, etc. We also want to point out that though the main ideas of the methods introduced here come from the existing references we have also made our improvements to make them even more understandable or more efficient. We do not only channel other results. In the following discussion, we will point out the role of the syntax analysis, and explore the procedure of the analysis, and discuss a number of issues involving in the syntax analysis. When we explain the methods we will provide examples to show the practice. Sometimes we also provide algorithms to make the methods more operable and more precise.

7.2   Role of Syntax Analysis in Compilers

The syntax analyzer, or parser as many called it, takes the output of the lexical analyzer as input. In order to produce the object code that is executable on computers, it has to verify the correctness of the source program, or to point out the errors commonly occurring in the source programs and recover from these errors if possible. Therefore, the role of the syntax analyzer has duality. On one hand, it is responsible for reporting any syntax error in an intelligible fashion. In this aspect, it should also be able to recover from the errors and continue processing the remainder of its input.On the other hand, if it verifies that the source program is correct in terms of the syntax structure, its task is to transform the source program into the intermediate code so that in further step it can be used to produce the object code. In this aspect, there are a number of techniques that were invented to handle the problem. However, after all, both two aspects are based on referring the grammar, or more specifically, on referring the production of the grammar. If some part of the source program violates the regulation set by the production, it issues the error report and tries to recover from the error; otherwise it confirms the correctness of this part of the source program and continues with generating the intermediate code or other relevant things. There are three general types of the syntax analyzers, or parsers for grammars. Universal parsing methods, such as Cocke-Younger-Kasami algorithm [1] and Earley's algorithm [2] of orient their works to any grammar. These methods, however, are too inefficient to use in producing compilers. The methods commonly used in compilers are classified as either top-down or bottom-up. As their names indicate, top-down parsers build parse trees from the top (root) to the bottom (leaves) while bottom-up parses build parse trees from the leaves and work up to the root. In both cases, the input to the parser is scanned from left to right, one symbol at a time.

In the sense of the formal grammars we have discussed above, the languages which are recognized and most of the programming languages basically are context-free. Therefore, the source programs written by users can be considered as sentences of the context-free grammar if they are correctly written. In other words, they are the strings which the grammar accepts. When discussing the strings which the grammar accepts, we had mentioned two approaches—the leftmost derivation and rightmost derivation. The two approaches just correspond to top-down and bottom-up respectively. At the moment, we just leave the topic and consider the nature of syntactic errors and general strategies for error recovery.

Syntax Error Handling

If a compiler can only process correct programs, it will not be useful. Since many programmers cannot make their programs immediately correct in the first time they wrote them. In this case, the compiler has nothing to do in facing this kind of programs with errors. Therefore, a good compiler should assist the programmer in identifying and locating errors. Specially, as we now discuss the syntax analysis, we are concerned about the errors that occur in syntax. We require that the compiler should be able to detect the syntactic errors. It turned out that much of the error detection and recovery in a compiler is centered around the syntax analysis phase. One reason for this is that many errors are syntactic in nature or are exposed. When the stream of tokens comes from the lexical analyzer, they may disobey the grammatical rules for defining the programming language, such as an arithmetic expression with unbalanced parentheses. Another reason is the precision of modern parsing method. The compiler can detect the existence of syntactic errors in programs very efficiently.

Accurately detecting the presence of semantic and logical errors at compiling time is more difficult. However, in this chapter we just focus on the syntactical error handling.

The syntactical error handling has the following goals:

- It reports the existence of errors clearly and precisely.
- It recovers from each error quickly so that it can continue to detect subsequent errors.
- It will not remarkably slow down the processing of correct programs.

Obviously, if the detection of errors and recovery from errors are very difficult, the realization of these goals is a great challenge. Fortunately, in reality, it is not the case. Common errors are simple and a relatively straightforward error-handling is enough. However, in some cases the detection of an error is long behind the position where the error occurs, and the precise nature of the error may also be difficult to detect. Therefore, in these cases people cannot expect highly that the error handler precisely reports the positions of errors. The reports can only be taken as references. In difficult cases, the error handler may have to guess what the programmer had in mind when he wrote the program.

Several parsing methods such as the LL and LR (they will be discussed soon in this chapter) detect an error as soon as possible. More precisely they detect an occurring error as soon as they see a prefix of the input that is not a prefix of any legal string in the language.

A common punctuation error is to use a comma in place of the semicolon in the argument list of a function declaration, or vice versa. Others are to leave out a mandatory semicolon at the end of a line and to put in an extraneous semicolon at the end of a line before the word else. Perhaps the reason why semicolon errors are so common is that the use of semicolons varies from one language to another. Hence, in order to avoid such errors, the programmer should refer to the manual of the programming language for the regulation.

How should an error handler report the presence of an error? A common strategy which many compilers adopt is to print the offending line with a pointer to the position where an error is detected. However, if there is a reasonable likelihood of what the error actually is, an informative understandable diagnostic message may be included, for example, "semicolon missing at this position".

After the errors are detected, the next step is to recover from these errors. From the view point of program writers, they want the error handler to provide the accurate information so that they can easily correct the program according to the message given. But the error handler does not always have the strength to do so. There are a number of different strategies that an error handler may adopt to recover a syntactic error. Here, we list the following strategies:

- Panic mode.
  With the strategy, when an error is discovered, the parser discards the input symbol at a time until one of a designated set of the synchronizing token is found. The synchronizing tokens are usually delimiters, such as semicolon or end, whose role in the source program is clear. The compiler designer must select the synchronizing tokens proper for the source language. One of the disadvantages of this strategy is that it often skips a considerable amount of input without checking for any possible errors. However its advantage is clear that it is simple. And, unlike some other methods to be considered later, it is guaranteed not to go into an infinite loop.

- Phrase-level recovery.
  With the strategy, when an error is discovered, the parser may perform the local correction on the remaining input. That is, it may replace a prefix of the remaining input by a string that allows the parser to continue (otherwise the parser cannot do again). The choice of the local correction is up to the compiler designer. However commonly the typical local correction is to replace a comma by a semicolon, or to delete a seemingly extraneous semicolon, or to insert a missing semicolon. For this strategy, it has the danger that improper correction may lead the program into infinite loops. Hence we must be very careful to choose the replacements. This can be regarded as the drawback of the strategy, and the other drawback is that the actual error is likely to occur before the point of detection.

- Error productions.
  If we have a good idea of the common errors that might be encountered, we can augment the grammar for the language in hands with productions that will generate erroneous constructs. This is the idea of the strategy. We use the grammar augmented by these error productions to construct our syntactical analyzer. If an error for production is used by the analyzer,

we can generate appropriate error diagnostics to indicate the erroneous construct that has been recognized in input.

- Global correction.
  This strategy is global-oriented. It will be nice if in processing an incorrect input string we just make there are as few changes as possible. There are algorithms for choosing a minimal sequence of changes to obtain a globally correct program. Given an incorrect input string x and program G, these algorithms will find a parse tree for a related string y, such that the number of insertions, deletions, and changes of tokens for transforming x into y is as small as possible. It sounds that, the idea is very good. However, so far, it is only of theoretical interest as in general its implementation is costly in terms of time and space.

7.3 Methods of Syntax Analysis

The aim of the syntax analysis is to verify the correctness of programs in terms of the syntax of the programming language. That means that we want to know whether we can derive the source program or not from the distinguished nonterminal symbol using productions. If at the end of these derivations, we really get the source program, we can say that the source program is really correct in terms of the syntax of the language. And the process is from the root of the parsing tree toward the leaves of the tree, hence it is called the top-down analysis. The other way starts from the source program, i.e., the leaves of the parsing tree. Some leaves can be combined together to form the right part of a production, and then to replace them by the parent of these strings. Gradually, the process is going up to climb up the tree towards the root. If at the end the process reduces to the root of the parsing tree, it also means that the root matches the leaves or the source program. Therefore, this is called the bottom-up analysis. In the analysis process, in order to ensure the efficiency, we want to avoid the backtracking of the passed path. That means that we want the process keeping going in one direction, rather than going back and forth in two directions LL(1) and LR(1) were developed from the idea. Specifically, LL(1) is originated from the top-down approach while LR(1) is originated from bottom-up approach. The first "L" in LL(1) stands for scanning the input from left to right, the second "L" stands for producing leftmost derivation, and the "1" in parenthesis stands for using one input symbol of look ahead at each step to make parsing action decision. As for LR(1), the first "L" has the same meaning as in LL(1), while "R" stands for constructing a rightmost derivation in reverse, and the "1" in the parenthesis stands for the number of input symbol of look ahead that is used in making parsing decisions. Sometimes "1" is omitted, and the default value is still 1. We discuss the two approaches, separately, as follows.

The top-down syntax analysis can be considered as an attempt to find a leftmost derivation for an input string or a legitimate source program. Equivalently, it can be viewed as an attempt to construct a parsing tree for the input starting from the root (distinguished symbol, for programming language, it usually is PROGRAM) and creating the leaves of the parsing tree in preorder. Top-down syntax analysis starts from the distinguished symbol of the grammar, works down and right towards the right end of a production, step by step, gradually creates the parsing tree with the input string (the source program) being the leaves. In the whole process, any backtracking step is not allowed so that the process of creating the parsing tree completely deterministic. Meanwhile, it should also be uniquely deterministic.

In order to realize the requirement above, how should we do? Obviously the requirement should be that in every step, the creation of the parsing tree has only one way out. For example, suppose that we have the following production set of a program and the input is baabb.

$$S \rightarrow bA \mid aB,$$
$$A \rightarrow bSS \mid aS \mid a,$$
$$B \rightarrow aBB \mid bS \mid b.$$

The top-down analysis for checking the correctness of input string that starts with distinguished symbol S should only have one way to go, i.e., S→bA rather than

S→aB, as the input starts with b. So the initial form of the parsing tree is

Following the subparsing tree, the creation of the parsing tree should go on with the derivation of A. Now there are three productions that take A as left part, they are

$$A \rightarrow bAA.$$
$$A \rightarrow aS,$$
$$A \rightarrow a.$$

Referring to the second character b of the input string, it is clear that we should only use the production A→aS. Though A→a also has a at the right part, it will end the derivation while the parsing tree does not match the input string.

From our discussion, we know that starting the creation of the parsing tree at the beginning, distinguished symbol, and derivation which we use must be uniquely determined. If the production with the distinguished symbol being the left part has only one, say

$$S \rightarrow aAb,$$

but then there are two productions with A being left part and they are

$$A \to aB, \quad A \to aC.$$

In this case in order to continue the creation of the parsing tree, should we use A→aB or A→aC? Since both have a as the first character, without knowing the following one we have no idea about which one is the right choice. In order to solve the problem we need to introduce the concept of FIRST(α) that will differentiate productions each other according to their FIRST().

Definition 7.1 [2]   Let A → α be a production of a context-free grammar G. We define FIRST(A → α) = {a | a is the first terminal symbol occurring in α from left to right, or starting from

$$A \to \alpha,$$
$$A \xRightarrow[G]{+} a\}.$$

Example 7.1   In the following set of productions

$$E \to EAE \mid (E) \mid -E \mid id \mid \varepsilon,$$
$$A \to + \mid - \mid \times \mid / \mid \uparrow .$$

The FIRST() of each production is as follows:

$$FIRST(E \to EAE) = \{+, -, \times, /, \uparrow \},$$
$$FIRST(E \to (E)) = \{(\},$$
$$FIRST(E \to -E) = \{ - \},$$
$$FIRST(E \to id) = \{id\}.$$

The occurrence of E → ε challenges the concept of FIRST() that makes FIRST() cannot distinguish totally productions each other. As FIRST(X → ε) = {ε} cannot help, we need to consider the changes caused by the occurrence of the ε production.

For example, in the following set of productions:

$$P \to XY,$$
$$P \to YU,$$
$$X \to aX,$$
$$X \to \varepsilon,$$
$$Y \to c,$$
$$Y \to bY,$$
$$U \to c.$$

Now we consider FIRST(P → XY) first. Since we have X → aX, we immediately have a $\in$ FIRST(P → XY), but apart from a, there are more

in FIRST(P → XY). Since X → ε, we have P → XY → Y → c or
P → XY → Y → bY. Therefore, we have

$$FIRST(P → XY) = \{a, b, c\}.$$

Similarly, we have

$$FIRST(P → YU) = \{b, c\}.$$

In order to decide which production should be used among two or more productions, we need to consider another concept called FOLLOW(). It stands for follower set.

Definition 7.2 Given a grammar G. For the nonterminal symbol A, FOLLOW(A) = {x | x ∈ V_T and x may occur immediately after A in the productions of G}.

According to the definition, we point out that:
1) For the distinguished symbol S, we stipulate that FOLLOW(S) = {$ | $ is the end token located at the right end of input string}.
2) If A → αBβ is a production of G, then FOLLOW(B) = {x | x ∈ FIRST(β) but x ≠ ε} Here, FIRST(β) may have a number of cases. β stands for a string of terminals and nonterminals. If its first character is terminal then it is in FIRST(β). If it is a nonterminal then we have to see the FIRST() of production with the nonterminal being its left part. In this case, if the nonterminal occurs as left part of more than one production, then the FIRST() may have more than one element.
3) If there is a production A → αB or A → αBβ, where for β, FIRST (β) contains ε (that is β $\overset{*}{\Longrightarrow}$ ε), then FOLLOW (β) belongs to FELLOW (A).

Example 7.2 Given the set of productions of the grammar G as follows:

$$S → XY,$$
$$X → PQ,$$
$$X → YU,$$
$$P → pP,$$
$$P → ε,$$
$$Q → qQ,$$
$$Q → d,$$
$$Y → yY,$$
$$Y → e,$$
$$U → uU,$$
$$U → f.$$

The FIRST()'s and FOLLOW()'s of these productions are as follows.

$$\text{FIRST}(S \to XY) = \{p, \varepsilon, y, e\},$$
$$\text{FIRST}(X \to PQ) = \{p, \varepsilon, q\},$$
$$\text{FIRST}(X \to YU) = \{y, e\},$$
$$\text{FIRST}(P \to pP) = \{p\},$$
$$\text{FIRST}(P \to \varepsilon) = \{\varepsilon\},$$
$$\text{FIRST}(Q \to qQ) = \{q\},$$
$$\text{FIRST}(Q \to d) = \{d\},$$
$$\text{FIRST}(Y \to yY) = \{y\},$$
$$\text{FIRST}(Y \to e) = \{e\},$$
$$\text{FIRST}(U \to uU) = \{u\},$$
$$\text{FIRST}(U \to f) = \{f\},$$
$$\text{FOLLOW}(S) = \{\$\},$$
$$\text{FOLLOW}(Y) = \{u, f, \$\},$$
$$\text{FOLLOW}(X) = \text{FOLLOW}(Q) = \{y, e\},$$
$$\text{FOLLOW}(P) = \text{FIRST}(Q) = \{q, d\}.$$

The thing that really distinguishes one production from other is the combination of FIRST() and FOLLOW(), so it is in order to combine them. We have the following definiton.

Definition 7.3 Let G be a grammar and A be one of its nonterminals, and $A \to \alpha$ be one of its productions, then the derivation symbol set (abbreviated as of DS) of $A \to \alpha$ is defined as

$$\text{DS}(A \to \alpha) = \{a \mid a \in \text{FIRST}(A \to \alpha) \text{ or if } \alpha \overset{*}{\Longrightarrow} a, \text{ then } a \in \text{FOLLOW}(A)\}.$$

Therefore, in the example above, we have

$$\text{DS}(S \to XY) = \{p, y, e, q, \},$$
$$\text{DS}(X \to PQ) = \{p, q, d\},$$
$$\text{DS}(X \to YU) = \{y, e\},$$
$$\text{DS}(P \to pP) = \{p\},$$
$$\text{DS}(P \to \varepsilon) = \{q, d\},$$
$$\text{DS}(Y \to yY) = \{y\},$$
$$\text{DS}(Y \to e) = \{e\},$$
$$\text{DS}(Q \to qQ) = \{q\},$$
$$\text{DS}(Q \to d) = \{d\},$$
$$\text{DS}(U \to uU) = \{u\},$$
$$\text{DS}(U \to f) = \{f\}.$$

Now we can see that the productions with the same left part all have different derivation sets, hence it will be deterministic which production should be used in the derivation process.

However, there is a case that will causes the derivations unable to proceed. We mean the situation of left recursion, for example, in

$$A \rightarrow A\alpha,$$
$$A \rightarrow a,$$

the first production belongs to the case. From the angle of the derivation it will form

$$A \rightarrow A\alpha \rightarrow A\alpha\alpha \rightarrow \ldots \rightarrow A\alpha\alpha\ldots\alpha.$$

This derivation repeats to have A occurring as the first symbol of right part so that the derivation cannot have a breakthrough. In addition, from the angle of the derivation set, we have

$$DS(A \rightarrow A\alpha) = \{a\},$$
$$DS(A \rightarrow a) = \{a\}.$$

The two derivation sets are totally equal. In this case, if the derivation involves the decision of using which production with A as the left part, no decision can be made, and the derivation cannot be carried out. Therefore, in order to break the impediment, the left recursion should be eliminated. The following approach can eliminate the left recursions.

Lemma   The left recursion of nonterminal A in production $A \rightarrow A\alpha$ can be eliminated if there is another production that also has A as its left part: $A \rightarrow \beta$, where α and β are sequences of terminals and nonterminals that do not start with A. This is done by rewriting the productions for A in the following manner:

$$A \rightarrow \beta B,$$
$$B \rightarrow \alpha B \mid \varepsilon.$$

The proof of the lemma is not difficult. We do not give the formal proof. We just mention that every string that is derived from the original productions can also be derived from the later productions. For example, the form of the strings that is derived from the former productions is $\beta\alpha^*$. By using the later productions, we have $A \rightarrow \beta B \rightarrow \beta\alpha B \rightarrow \ldots \rightarrow \beta\alpha\ldots\alpha B \rightarrow \beta\alpha^*$. In reverse, every sting that is derived from later productions can also be derived from the former productions. For example, the form of the strings that is derived from the later productions is $\beta\alpha^*$. Then in the former productions we have $A \rightarrow A\alpha \rightarrow A\alpha\alpha \rightarrow A\alpha\alpha\ldots\alpha \Longrightarrow A\alpha^*$.

In final step, we replace A with β and get $\beta\alpha^*$. That means that the two sets of sentences which two grammars generate are equal.

In general, no matter how many left recursive productions there are, we can eliminate immediate left recursion from them by using the following technique. First, we group the productions with left recursion of nonterminal A as

$$A \to A\alpha_1 \mid A\alpha_2 \mid \ldots \mid A\alpha_m \mid \beta_1 \mid \beta_2 \mid \ldots \mid \beta_n,$$

where no β_i begins with an A. Then, we replace the A-productions (the left recursive ones) by

$$A \to \beta_1 A' \mid \beta_2 A' \mid \ldots \mid \beta_n A',$$
$$A' \to \alpha_1 A' \mid \alpha_2 A' \mid \ldots \mid \alpha_m A'.$$

The nonterminal A generates the same strings as before but is no longer left recursive. This procedure eliminates all immediate left recursion from the A and A' productions (provided that no α_i is ε). But it does not eliminate the left recursion involving derivations of two or more steps. For example, consider the productions

$$S \to Ab \mid a,$$
$$A \to Ac \mid Sd \mid \varepsilon.$$

In these productions, there are two kinds of left recursions. $A \to Ac$ is the kind we have seen above while the nonterminal S is left recursive because $S \to Ab \to Sdb$. It is a left recursion involving derivations of two steps.

The process of the eliminating left recursion can be formally represented as an algorithm as follows. It will systematically eliminate left recursion from a grammar. It is guaranteed to work if the grammar has no cycles (derivations of the form $A \Longrightarrow +A$) or ε-productions (productions of the form $A \to \varepsilon$)

Algorithm 7.1 Eliminating left recursion.

Input: Grammar G with productions being of left recursion but with no cycles or ε-productions.

Output: An equivalent grammar with no left recursion.

Algorithm steps:

Step 1 Arrange the nonterminals in some order so that the productions are divided into two parts, in one part there is no left recursion while in the other part there are left recursions. We now list these productions with the increasing order of the indices of the nonterminals, e.g.,

$$A_i \to A_i\alpha_1 \mid A_i\alpha_2 \mid \ldots \mid A_i\alpha_m \quad \text{and} \quad A_i \to \beta_1 \mid \beta_2 \mid \ldots \mid \beta_n,$$
$$A_j \to A_j\rho_1 \mid A_j\rho_2 \mid \ldots \mid A_j\rho_k \quad \text{and} \quad A_j \to \tau_1 \mid \tau_2 \mid \ldots \mid \tau_l \quad (\text{where } j > i).$$

Step 2 for $u := i$ to v do begin (assume that i is the lowest index of nonterminal with the left recursion and v is the greatest one) replace each production of the form $A_i \to A_i\alpha_1 \mid A_i\alpha_2 \mid \ldots$ by the productions $A_i \to (\beta_1 \mid \ldots \mid \beta_n)B$, $A_i \to \beta_1 \mid \ldots \mid \beta_n$ and newly established productions

$$B_i \to \alpha_1 \mid \ldots \mid \alpha_m, \qquad B_i \to (\alpha_1 \mid \ldots \mid \alpha_m)B_i,$$

where B_i is a new nonterminal:

    end

But the algorithm is just eliminating the immediate left recursion productions. If there is also the indirect left recursion, we can transform it into the immediate left recursion one. The approach is similar to what we did in transforming productions to the Greibach normal form from the Chomsky normal form, that is for the production of the form $A_u \rightarrow A_v A_t$ where $u > v$, we replace A_v with the right part of the production with A_v as a left part to increase the index, and iteratively doing so if needed (at most we need to do $u - v$ times) until the right part also has A_u as the first element. In this case, the immediate left recursion is formed.

The reason for the procedure above works is that after a number of iterations, any production of the form $A_u \rightarrow A_v \ldots$ where $v < u$, must become $A_u \rightarrow A_x \ldots$. There are two possibilities here, either $u = x$ and immediate left recursion takes place, we can eliminate the immediate left recursion by the algorithm above; or $x > u$. In this case, nothing happens.

Therefore, in order to eliminate the immediate left recursion for the A_i-productions actually we performed the same procedure when we transform the Chomsky normal form to the Greibach normal form.

There is another thing that impedes the execution of derivation with production uniquely decided. We mean ambiguity. A grammar that produces more than one parse tree for some sentence is said to be ambiguous. In other words, an ambiguous grammar is one that produces more than one leftmost or rightmost derivation for the same sentence. When ambiguity happens for the derivation we will not be able to decide which derivation we should take for realizing our aim. For certain types of parsers, like top-down analysis which we discuss right now, it is desirable that the grammar be made unambiguous, for if it is not, we cannot uniquely determine which derivation or parse tree to select for a sentence. However there is exception. For some applications we shall also consider methods whereby we can use certain ambiguous grammars, together with disambiguating rules that "throw away" undesirable parse trees, leaving us with only one tree for each sentence. We will not discuss the case.

In order for us to have uniquely determination of the derivation, we need to rewrite the originally ambiguous grammar to eliminate the ambiguity. Fortunately, some ambiguous grammar is related to left recursion. The grammar is ambiguous while it is also left recursion grammar. In this case when the left recursion is eliminated, the ambiguity problem is solved. Of course this is ideal case. Others are not so lucky. But they are also able to rewrite to eliminate the ambiguity. As an example, we can eliminate the ambiguity from the following "dangling-else" grammar:

    stmt→if expr then stmt
        | if expr then stmt else stmt
        | other

Here "other" stands for any other statement. This is an ambiguous grammar as for some sentences they have two parse trees. But it is not difficult to rewrite it so that it becomes unambiguous one.

Now we introduce the concept of LL(1) grammar.

Definition 7.4 In a grammar G, if for any nonterminal that occurs as left part of more than two productions their derivation sets are disjoint, then the grammar G is called LL(1) grammar.

The determination of LL(1) grammar.

Now that we have known what is LL(1) grammar, and that in order to deterministically carry out top-down derivation we must adopt LL(1) method to make sure that all the productions with the same specific nonterminal as the left parts have disjoint derivation sets. If it is the case, then the derivation process can be proceeded deterministically from beginning until the end. If the condition is not satisfied, however, does it mean that the LL(1) method can not be used? The answer is not yet deterministic. We still have chance if the grammar can be transformed into LL(1) one. Otherwise, many grammars are stopped outside the door of LL(1) and LL(1) will not be attractive. But only some grammars can be transformed into LL(1) one. For others they really can not be analyzed by LL(1) method.

Now the problem is how to transform the grammar that is known to be non-LL(1) into LL(1). We see the following example.

Example 7.3 Given a grammar that describes programs as follows:
  PROGRAM→begin DECLIST comma STATELIST end,
  DECLIST→d semi DECLIST,
  DECLIST→d,
  STATELIST→s semi STATELIST,
  STATELIST→s.
Decide whether it is LL(1) or not? If it is not, is it possible to transform it into LL(1) one?

Solution We just need to check the derivation sets for DECLIST and STATEMENT as only these two nonterminals each has two derivation sets. We look at DECLIST first.
  DS(DECLIST→d semi DECLIST)={d}
  DS(DECLIST→d)={d}
So the two have completely equal derivation sets. The grammar is not LL(1) one. Notice the difference of the two productions. For the former one the terminal d is followed by semi while for the later it is followed by an empty. It implies that in right part of PROGRAM it will be followed by comma. Therefore what is needed is only to introduce a nonterminal. We then have
  PROGRAM→begin DECLIST comma STATELIST end,
  DECLIST→d X,
  X→semi DECLIST,
  X→ ε.

Now we only need to check the derivation sets of X:

DS(X→semi DECLIST)={semi},

DS(X→ ε)={comma}.

We still have to handle STATELIST. Similarly, we obtain

STATELIST→s Y,

Y→semi STATELIST,

Y→ ε.

The two derivation sets for Y are disjoint. In the end, we transform the original grammar into LL(1) one. The method we used is called left factoring. Left factoring is a grammar transformation that is useful for producing a grammar suitable for predictive parsing. The basic idea is that when it is not clear which of two alternative productions to use to expand a nonterminal A, we may be able to rewrite the A-production to defer the decision until we have seen enough of the input to make the right choice.

For example, suppose that we have the two productions

stmt→if expr then stmt else stmt

| if expr then stmt

On seeing the input token if, we cannot immediately tell which production to choose to expand stmt, in general, if $A \to \alpha\beta_1 \mid \alpha\beta_2$ are two A-productions, and the input begins with a nonempty string derived from α, we do not know whether to expend A to $\alpha\beta_1$ or $\alpha\beta_2$. However, we may defer the decision by expending A to $\alpha A'$. Then, after seeing the input derived from α, we expend A' to β_1 or β_2. That is, left-factored, the original productions become

$$A \to \alpha A',$$
$$A' \to \beta_1 \mid \beta_2.$$

Algorithm 7.2   Left factoring grammar.

Input: A grammar G is given.

Output: An equivalent left-factored grammar.

Algorithm steps: For each nonterminal A find the longest prefix α common to two or more of its alternatives. If $\alpha \neq \varepsilon$, i.e., there is a nontrivial common prefix, replace all the A productions

$$A \to \alpha\beta_1 \mid \alpha\beta_2 \mid \ldots \mid \alpha\beta_n \mid \gamma,$$

where, γ represents all alternatives that do not begin with α by

$$A \to \alpha A' \mid \gamma,$$
$$A' \to \beta_1 \mid \beta_2 \mid \ldots \mid \beta_n.$$

Here A' is a new nonterminal. Repeatedly apply this transformation until no two alternatives for a nonterminal have a common prefix. Then the original grammar G is left factored.

Left factoring really can help us with some grammars. However, it is not a panacea. For some grammars, it does not work at all. Now consider another example:

$$P \rightarrow Qx,$$
$$P \rightarrow Ry,$$
$$Q \rightarrow sQm,$$
$$Q \rightarrow q,$$
$$R \rightarrow sRn,$$
$$R \rightarrow r.$$

In this example, the derivation sets of both alternatives of P contain s, so the grammar is not LL(1) grammar. We use left factoring method to transform it. We replace P productions with followings:

$$P \rightarrow sQmx,$$
$$P \rightarrow qx,$$
$$P \rightarrow sRny,$$
$$P \rightarrow Rny.$$

Now there are derivation sets that are still intersected, so we need to do the left factoring. We get

$$P \rightarrow qx,$$
$$P \rightarrow ry,$$
$$P \rightarrow sP_1,$$
$$P_1 \rightarrow Qmx,$$
$$P_1 \rightarrow Rny.$$

Now the first three derivation sets are disjoint. But the last two P_1 productions become the situation similar to that of P productions before. We then handle them as we did for P productions. This time we get

$$P_1 \rightarrow qmx,$$
$$P_1 \rightarrow qmx,$$
$$P_1 \rightarrow sRnny,$$
$$P_1 \rightarrow rny.$$

The derivation set of the first P_1 and that of the third one are intersected again. Once again we use left factoring to deal with. We get

$$P_1 \rightarrow qmx,$$
$$P_1 \rightarrow my,$$
$$P_1 \rightarrow sP_2,$$

$$P_2 \rightarrow Qmmx,$$
$$P_2 \rightarrow Rnny.$$

Now the situations of P_2 are similar to both of P_1 and P, even they have longer right parts. Obviously the process can not end. Therefore our attempt to transform any grammars by left factoring is destined to fail.

Previously, we have discussed the indirect left recursion, now we once again to discuss it and present a concrete example:

$$S \rightarrow RT,$$
$$R \rightarrow TU,$$
$$T \rightarrow SW,$$
$$U \rightarrow VT,$$
$$W \rightarrow RU.$$

Notice that the production set is not complete. Here we start from S and make the derivations $S \rightarrow RT \rightarrow TUT \rightarrow SWVSW$. Then the left recursion on S occurs. Therefore we can always try to transform any indirect left recursion into direct left recursion. The following shows the fact. Consider the following grammar

$$S \rightarrow Aa \mid b,$$
$$A \rightarrow Ac \mid Sd \mid \varepsilon.$$

At first we transform it to be

$$S \rightarrow Sda \mid b,$$
$$A \rightarrow Ac \mid Aad \mid bd \mid \varepsilon.$$

Then transform again to get

$$S \rightarrow bS',$$
$$S' \rightarrow daS' \mid \varepsilon,$$
$$A \rightarrow bdA' \mid \varepsilon,$$
$$A' \rightarrow cA' \mid adA' \mid \varepsilon.$$

The example shows that there is the so-called inherited left recursion grammar for which all the productions with the same nonterminal as their left parts contain common terminals in theirs derivation symbol sets. We are unable to eliminate the left recursion for this kind of grammar. There is also some grammar that looks vey simple, but it is not LL(1) grammar and cannot be transformed to be LL(1) grammar.

The language which a LL(1) grammar generates is called LL(1) language. Now we have seen that a non left recursion grammar can or cannot be transformed to LL(1) grammar that is equivalent to itself. It is the same to say that a grammar can or cannot be transformed so that both generate the same language.

A problem comes up that does the algorithm exist that is able to determine whether a given language is of LL(1) or not? The answer to the question is no. This kind of problems is called undecidable or unsolvable. Theoretically, it has been proven that this kind of algorithm does not exist. At least, there is no such algorithm that is applied to any case.

7.4 LL(1) Syntactical Analysis Method

After we explained the LL(1) grammars and LL(1) languages, we now introduce the LL(1) syntactical analysis method. It belongs to the top-down syntactical method.

In order to perform the LL(1) syntactical analysis, at first we have to determine whether the given grammar is of LL(1). The specific process is as follows:

1) Check if the grammar contains left recursion. If it does, the left recursion should be eliminated. If it cannot be eliminated then the process ends, the syntactical analysis fails.

2) If the grammar does not contain left recursion or the left recursion is eliminated then the next step is to check whether the derivation sets of the productions with the same left part disjoint. If they disjoint, then the LL(1) syntactical analysis can be immediately carried out. However, if they do not disjoint, then they need to be transformed through extracting common factors or other methods. If the transformation fails, the syntactical analysis also ends with failure.

When the two steps above succeed, the top-down syntactical analysis of the compiler may really start. Now associating with Example 6.1 we introduce the syntactical analysis process.

The productions of the grammar after transforming to LL(1) grammar are as follows:

PROGRAM → begin DECLIST comma STATELIST end,

DECLIST → dX,

X → semi DECLIST,

X → ε,

STATELIST → sY,

Y → semi STATELIST,

Y → ε.

Sequentially, the derivation set of each production is evaluated. We have

DS(PROGRAM→begin DECLIST comma STATELIST end)={begin},

```
DS(DECLIST→dX)={d},
DS(X→semi DECLIST)={semi},
DS(X→ ε)={comma},
DS(Y→semi STATELIST)={semi},
DS(Y→ ε)={end}.
```

Using these derivation sets, we construct the LL(1) syntactical analysis table as shown in Table 7.1.

Table 7.1 LL(1) syntactical analysis table

Nonterminal	Input symbol(terminal)					
	begin	d	semi	comma	s	end
PROGRAM	PROGRAM →begin					
DECLIST		DECLIST→d				
X			X→semi	X→ ε		
STATELIST					STATELIST →s	
Y			Y→semi			Y→ ε

Note: suppose that the input sentence is begin d semi d semi d comma s semi s end.

We store the table in memory, meanwhile, the input is also stored in memory. Notice that productions with X and Y as the left part have the same derivation set and both consist of single element semi. But since the two occur at different times the whole derivation can be deterministically carried out without any difficulty (see Fig. 7.1).

begin d semi d semi d comma s semi s end

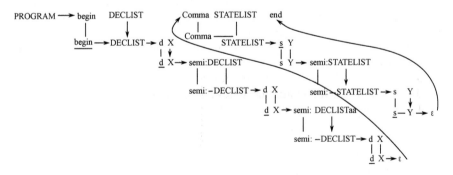

Fig. 7.1 Syntax analysis process.

At first begin is scanned. As in the analysis table the record is PROGRAM →begin..., we check the productions and found that at the right part of production PROGRAM→ really starts with begin. Following begin is DECLIST. Referring to the input sentence, the second character is d. We look up the analysis table, the record that corresponds to d is DECLIST→d, so we need to go to check the production with DECLIST as left part. This can be considered as going to subprogram. We see that the production with DECLIST as left part has d X as its right part. Therefore we advance to the production with X as left part. Meanwhile, we contrast it with input semi. The record under column semi is X→semi.... Then we advance to the second term of the right part that corresponds to input d. So far the derivation is still working on the position DECLIST. Therefore when input advances to another semi, its record is X→semi DECLIST. We then go to processing the production with DECLIST as left part. This time (the second time that we met semi) d is the first term of the right part. And we are working on the position X. We go forward in the input string, we meet comma and the record is X→ ε. That means that we have passed through DECLIST in production PROGRAM→begin DECLIST comma STATELIST end. Therefore we go to element comma. It does not correspond to any production but requires that we go to the production with STATELIST as left part as its right part starts with s and in the input s just follows comma. We check the production with STATELIST as left part, it is STATELIST→s Y. So we go to the production with Y as left part and semi as the first term of the right part. We found that it is Y→semi STATELIST. Then we go to the production STATELIST→s Y. But this time semi does not follow s again, rather end follows s as the production Y→ ε takes place. It also proclaims the success of the analysis. The success means that the input is the legal program of the language in terms of the syntax.

Now we use an algorithm to describe the process of LL(1) syntactical analysis. We call the algorithm LL(1) syntactical analysis algorithm, and is abbreviated to LA.

Algorithm 7.3 (Algorithm LA).

Input. It takes as input all the productions that have been transformed to LL(1) productions, and the syntactical analysis table for DS of each production (as shown by Table 7.1) and input sentence (program).

Output. If the analysis determines the legality of the input program, it reports success, otherwise it reports failure.

The steps of the algorithm are follows:

LA1 (begin). Take the first element of the input program and check the syntactical analysis table to see if the record of the table for this step matches the input element or not. The first production to be checked should be the one with the start symbol of the grammar as its left part and the record in the row corresponding to the start symbol should match the first element of the input program.

LA2 (advance the derivation). In the production that takes the start symbol as the left part, we check the right part of it to see if the record in the analysis table matches the input symbol. If they do, then advance the analysis to the next symbol at right. However, if on the production the next symbol is not a terminal, then it means that it needs to derive further from the nonterminal until a production with a terminal as the first element of its right part, or if in the process we meet a production with ε as its right part, then we need to see the followers of the nonterminal that occurs as left part of the production. The reason for doing so is that the elements of DS consist of two kinds. One is the first terminal which the nonterminal may derive from the production with it as the left part, either the first terminal occurs as the first symbol on the right part of the production, or the first symbol is not a terminal rather it is a nonterminal, but the derivation from the nontermianal will yield the first terminal aforementioned as the first symbol. The other is the follower symbol that comes from when a production in discussion has ε as the right part, then DS element of this nontermianl is the first symbol of the nonterminal following the nonterminal, or if it also derives an ε, then it is the first symbol of the nonterminal following the nonterminal or the follower symbol of it and so on. When the first item of the right part of the production is not a terminal, we have to go to LA3.

LA3 (branch and return). On the production with the start symbol as left part, the process advances on the right part one symbol after another symbol. For terminal symbol (as a comma in the last example) we just need to check if the input matches the same symbol on the production. If it is a nontermianl then we will go to a subprogram that handles the nonterminal as we will derive its DS that corresponds to the input program. In this process if once again we meet a nontermianl we will go to another subprogram. In this way, the subprograms are embedded. Therefore, when returning from a subprogram, we need to return to where the subprogram was invoked. If it returns to the main program that for the first time it goes to the subprogram of the nonterminal, then it advances to the next symbol on the right of the nonterminal in the production with a start symbol as the left part. Finally we come to matching the final symbol of the input with a final symbol of right part of the production with a start symbol as left part. When the process smoothly proceeds without any inconsistency, then the algorithm reports success and also means that the input program is legal in terms of syntax.

Actually, the algorithm above can also be used to construct parsing tree as long as the transformed LL(1) productions are taken as parsing tree with start symbol as the root of the tree and nonterminals as the inner vertices. Now we still take the input above as our example to draw the parsing tree that is shown in Fig. 7.2.

Thus the leaves of the tree are linked to become

begin d semi d semi d comma s semi s end

Here, we invoke X→semi DECLIST twice and invoke X→ ε once, also we invoke Y→semi STATELIST once and Y→ ε once. We go to DECLIST from X→semi DECLIST after matching the first semi, and when we handle DE-CLIST, we get DECLIST→d X. Then we go to subprogram X and from X we got d and semi DECLIST. So we go to DECLIST twice. We obtain

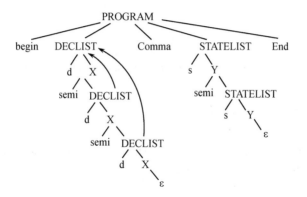

Fig. 7.2 parsing tree.

DECLIST→d X

    →d semi DECLIST   (we invoke X→semi DECLIST for
                                                    the first time)

    →d semi d X

    →d semi d semi DECLIST (X→semi DECLST is invoked for
                                                    the second time)

    →d semi d semi d X

    →d semi d semi d   (X→ ε is invoked once)

Similarly,

STATELIST→s Y

    →s semi STATELST   (we invoke Y→semi STATELIST for
                                                   the first time)

    →s semi s Y

    →s semi s   (Y→ ε is invoked once)

By making use the idea of regarding nonterminal as subprogram, the process of top-down syntactical analysis can be seen clearly.

We consider another example that is on arithmetic expressions. After transformation the productions become of LL(1):

$$E \rightarrow TE',$$
$$E' \rightarrow +TE',$$
$$E' \rightarrow \varepsilon,$$
$$T \rightarrow FT',$$
$$T \rightarrow *FT',$$
$$T \rightarrow \varepsilon,$$

$$F \rightarrow (E),$$
$$F \rightarrow id.$$

At first, we need to evaluate the Derivation Set (DS) of each production. They are

$$DS(E \rightarrow TE') = \{(, id\},$$
$$DS(E' \rightarrow +TE') = \{+\},$$
$$DS(E' \rightarrow \varepsilon) = \{\$\}, \qquad (\$ \text{ is the end sign of input string})$$
$$DS(T \rightarrow FT') = \{(, id\},$$
$$DS(T' \rightarrow *FT') = \{*\},$$
$$DS(T' \rightarrow \varepsilon) = \{+,), \$\},$$
$$DS(F \rightarrow (E)) = \{(\},$$
$$DS(F \rightarrow id) = \{id\}.$$

We now construct the syntactical analysis table (see Table 7.2). This time we add symbol $\sqrt{}$ to indicate that it is also a follower symbol.

Table 7.2 LL(1) syntactical analysis table

Nonterminal	Input symbol					
	id	+	*	(	)	$
E	E→TE′			E→TE′	$\sqrt{}$	$\sqrt{}$
E′		E′→+TE′			E′→ε	E′→ε
T	T→FT′	$\sqrt{}$		T→FT′	$\sqrt{}$	$\sqrt{}$
T′		T′→ε	T′→*FT		T′→ε	T′→ε
F	F→id	$\sqrt{}$	$\sqrt{}$	F→(E)	$\sqrt{}$	$\sqrt{}$

Now we consider the LL(1) syntactical analysis of the input sentence $(id + id * id) * id$. According to the algorithm given above, the analysis starts with the production with the start symbol as left part. As there is only one production of this kind, that is $E \rightarrow TE'$, referring to input string $(id...,$ we go to production $T \rightarrow FT'$, then we go further to $F \rightarrow (E)$. Both these two branch to subprogram. From production $F \rightarrow (E)$, since the input is $(id +$, we advance to $(TE'$, from T we turn to the production of T as left part $T \rightarrow FT'$. From F, we get id as we have $F \rightarrow id$. The id is consistent with the input id. From F, we advance to the second item T′. However, in order to match the input, T′ can only derive ε, so actually we leave subprogram of T and return to the next item E′. The production with E′ as left part has $+TE'$ as right part. This time the T will provide id again via $T \rightarrow FT'$. After F provides id via $F \rightarrow id$, then $T' \rightarrow *FT'$. Then $E' \rightarrow \varepsilon$. So now we have $(id + id * id)$. We advance to next symbol in the production. The symbol is T′ as the original production is $T \rightarrow FT'$. $T' \rightarrow *FT$. The first symbol * matches the input, the next one F has $F \rightarrow id$, Therefore we have $(id + id * id) * id$. The following T′ and E′ are removed via $T' \rightarrow \varepsilon$ and $E' \rightarrow \varepsilon$. If we write down the whole derivation we have the following process:

$$
\begin{aligned}
E &\to TE' \\
&\to FT'E' \\
&\to (E)T'E' \\
&\to (TE')T'E' \\
&\to (FT'E')T'E' \\
&\to (idT'E')T'E' \\
&\to (id\varepsilon E')T'E' \\
&\to (id + TE')T'E' \\
&\to (id + FT'E'')T'E' \\
&\to (id + id * FT'E')T'E' \\
&\to (id + id * idT'E')T'E' \\
&\to (id + id * id\varepsilon E')T'E' \\
&\to (id + id * id\varepsilon)T'E' \\
&\to (id + id * id) * FT'E' \\
&\to (id + id * id) * idT'E' \\
&\to (id + id * id) * id.
\end{aligned}
$$

It seems that the process of derivations is very tedious. Actually, it is done in this way within the computer. Here we follow the principle of the leftmost derivation. The reader may contrast the derivation with the Fig. 7.3 to more clearly understand the process of LL(1) syntactical analysis.

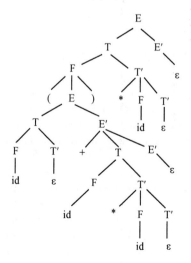

Fig. 7.3 The parsing tree of $((id + id * id) * id)$.

In terms of subprogram invocations, they are shown in Fig. 7.4.

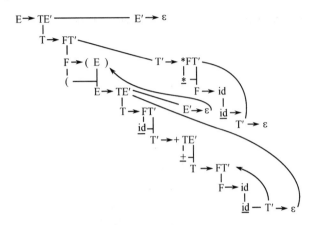
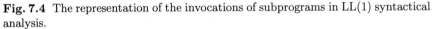

Fig. 7.4 The representation of the invocations of subprograms in LL(1) syntactical analysis.

Notice that in the figure, the arrows downward represent the invocation while the upward ones represent return to the caller who invokes the subprogram. From the discussion above, we can see that via the contrasts between the DS element and the input that occurs at the left of the DS symbol, the analysis is deterministic. It does not need backtracking. It is very important for the parsing methods as only by this way it can be efficient. Whether a syntactical analysis method can be accepted to apply or not mainly depends on the criterion – efficiency. According to this in the following we introduce another method — bottom-up method, or its representation, LR(1) syntactical analysis method.

7.5 Bottom-Up Syntactical Analysis Method

In the last section, we discussed top-down syntactical analysis method, especially LL(1) syntactical analysis method. The main idea of the method is that starting from the start symbol of the grammar, the analysis carries out the derivations from top to down without backtracking. This process continues until it derivates the input program. If the result of the derivations is consistent with the input, then the analysis reports success, and it means that the input is legal in terms of the syntax. Otherwise it reports failure and the input is illegal.

The solution to the problem usually is not unique [5]. Now that it can be top-down we naturally think of bottom-up instead. At least it can be tentative. In this section, we will discuss the bottom-up syntactical analysis method.

In contrast to the top-down method, bottom-up method starts from the input program, that is that it starts from terminal symbol, rather than from nonterminal. We regard the input elements as the leaves of the parsing tree. Then we climb the tree through shift-reduction operations. The aim of shift operations is to combine the leaves that belong to the same parents while the reduction operations are for reducing the leaves to their parents. By this way, the analysis "climbs" the parsing tree until the input reduces to the root of the tree, i.e., the start symbol of the grammar. Similar to LL(1) method, if the analysis successfully finishes, it reports success, and it means that the input program is legal in terms of syntax; otherwise it reports failure and the input is illegal.

In order to reduce a number of terminal symbols to their parents and then to reduce nonterminal symbols to the start symbol, or more generally to reduce the string of nonterminals and terminals to the start symbol, the reduction operations are essential. Before we discuss the details of reduction operation, we introduce the concept of handle first.

We introduce the concept of handle both informally and formally. At first, informally, a "handle" of a string is a substring that matches the right side of a production, and whose reduction to the nonterminal on the left part of production represents one step along the reverse of the rightmost derivation. In many cases the leftmost substring β that matches the right part of some production $A \rightarrow \beta$ is not a handle, because a reduction by the production $A \rightarrow \beta$ yields a string that cannot be reduced to the start symbol.

Then formally, we have

Definition 7.5 If S is the start symbol of a context-free grammar G, and we have a rightmost derivation

$$S \overset{*}{\Longrightarrow} \alpha A \omega \Longrightarrow \alpha \beta \omega,$$

then $A \rightarrow \beta$ in the position following α is a handle of $\alpha\beta\omega$. Note that the string ω to the right of handle contains only terminal symbols.

We say a handle rather than the handle because the grammar could be ambiguous with more than one rightmost derivation of $\alpha\beta\omega$.

Example 7.4 Suppose that G is a context-free grammar with the following productions:

$$S' \rightarrow aS,$$
$$S \rightarrow As \mid A,$$
$$A \rightarrow bSc \mid bc.$$

There are rightmost derivations for it as follows:

$$S' \rightarrow aS \rightarrow aAs \rightarrow abScs \rightarrow abbSccs.$$

Here abbSccs is a right-sentential form, and bSc is a handle as by production $A \rightarrow bSc$ it can be reduced to A.

From the definition, we can see that handle is very important to a reduction because only through handle the reduction may be carried out [5].

Therefore, in order to perform the bottom-up syntactical analysis, and make sure that no backtracks is needed, then it must be assured that in any sentential forms all the handles are uniquely determined.

Therefore, reductions are key operations for the bottom-up syntactical analysis. While branching from a handle to another handle, however, it needs to depend on another operation – shift operation.

Definition 7.6   Given a context-free grammar that is defined by a set of productions P. Suppose that γ is any right sentential form, then after the process that performs the rightmost reduction to γ, the moving a handle position to another nearest handle position that is obtained by relying on that handle to do the reduction operation is called shift operation.

It can be said that the shift operation is the preparation for the reduction operation. Only when the shift operations are done, the reduction operations can be carried out continuously until finally the process finishes with a start symbol as the result. In order to proceed in our discussion, we need the concepts of equivalence and equivalent classes.

Definition 7.7   Given a set S and a relation R defined between elements of S. R is said:

1) Reflexive. It means that for $\forall a \in S$, aRa.
2) Symmetric. It means that for $\forall a, b, aRb \Longrightarrow bRa$.
3) Transitive. It means that for $\forall a, b, c \in S, aRb, bRc \Longrightarrow aRc$.

Definition 7.8   Given a set S and a relation R defined between elements of S, R is said to be equivalent relation, if it is reflexive, symmetric and transitive.

Definition 7.7 given a set S and a relation R defined between elements of S, the relation R causes partitioning S into groups such that

1) All the elements in the same group are equivalent.
2) The elements that belong to different groups are not equivalent.
3) Any element of S must be in and only in one group.

The group of this kind is called equivalent class. As the elements in each group are equivalent, we can choose anyone to be the representative of the group. Then the number of equivalent groups is equal to the number of the representatives of the groups.

Now we return to the productions of the grammar and consider its configuration set (this concept will be discussed soon). Given the productions of context- free grammar G as follows:

$$S' \to Sc,$$
$$S \to SA \mid A,$$
$$A \to aSb \mid ab.$$

In order for our discussion below we number the productions from 1 to 5 (there are five productions now), and for every position of the right part of the production, that is the positions between two symbols and position before the first symbol and after the last symbol in right part we add tokens to them. These are called configurations. Our token contains two numbers. The first one denotes the number of the production, and the second denotes the order of the position from left to right in the right part of the production. The positions are numbered from 0. So now we have the productions with numbered configurations:

1) $S' \rightarrow_{(1,0)} S_{(1,1)} c_{(1,2)}$;
2) $S \rightarrow_{(2,0)} S_{(2,1)} A_{(2,2)}$;
3) $S \rightarrow_{(3,0)} A_{(3,1)}$;
4) $A \rightarrow_{(4,0)} a_{(4,1)} S_{(4,2)} b_{(4,3)}$;
5) $A \rightarrow_{(5,0)} a_{(5,1)} b_{(5,2)}$.

Therefore, for grammar G its configuration set consists of $\{(1,0),(1,1), (1,2),(2,0),(2,1),(2,2),(3,0),(3,1),(4,0),(4,1),(4,2),(5,0),(5,1),(5,2)\}$.

In the set, we define relation R as follows: (1, 0) faces S, we define it to be equivalent to configurations where are on the leftmost of right part of productions with S as the left part. Sequentially if the configuration faces another nonterminal, then it will be equivalent to the configurations where are on the leftmost of the right part of the production with this nonterminal as left part. The equivalence will be transitive in this way until no configuration faces a nonterminal again or all the configurations that should be taken into account in this way have been exhausted. So we have the following equivalent relations. We use $\sim$ to denote R, and have

$$(1,\,0) \sim (2,\,0) \sim (3,\,0) \sim (4,\,0) \sim (5,\,0).$$

Meanwhile, we use numbers to denote these equivalent classes with starting from the least positive integer 1.

Notice that the equivalent classes here are not exactly same as the traditional equivalent classes in that a configuration may belong to more than one equivalent class. This is also the subtle point of the configuration equivalence. However, in order to proceed the bottom-up syntactical analysis, this is necessary. For example, according to the principle above, for (2, 1), as it faces nonterminal A, we have

$$(2,\,1) \sim (4,\,0), \qquad (2,\,1) \sim (5,\,0).$$

On the other hand, since $(1,0) \sim (2,0)$, both face S, so their next configurations are equivalent too, so $(2,1) \sim (1,1)$, hence we have

$$(1,\,1) \sim (2,\,1) \sim (4,\,0) \sim (5,\,0).$$

Now we see that both (4, 0) and (5, 0) belong to two equivalent classes. We define shift function f to represent the numbering of classes. The f takes the configuration and the character as arguments, and the next configuration or its equivalent class as the value. We start with the configuration (1, 0), as there is no input character yet, we take — to represent the empty character, so

$$f((1, 0), -) = \{(1, 0), (2, 0), (3, 0), (4, 0), (5, 0)\} = 1,$$
$$f(1, S) = \{(1, 1), (2, 1)\} = 2f((2, 1), -) = \{(4, 0), (5, 0)\},$$

so

$$\{(1, 1), (2, 2), (4, 0), (5, 0)\} = 2.$$

Subsequently, we define

$$f(2, c) = \{(1, 2)\} = 3,$$
$$f(2, A) = \{(2, 3)\} = 4,$$
$$f(1, A) = \{(3, 1)\} = 5,$$
$$f(1, a) = \{(4, 1), (5, 1)\} = 6,$$

but $(4, 1)$ faces S. According to the equivalent relation, we have

$$(4, 1) \sim (2, 0) \sim (3, 0) \sim (4, 0) \sim (5, 0) \sim (5, 1),$$

so

$$\{(4, 1), (2, 0), (3, 0), (4, 0), (5, 0), (5, 1)\} = 6,$$
$$f(6, s) = \{(4, 2), (2, 1)\} = 7,$$
$$f(7, b) = \{(4, 3)\} = 8,$$
$$f(6, b) = \{(5, 2)\} = 9.$$

These class numbers are considered as state numbers. By this way, configurations and states establish the correspondence. We find that different configurations may have the same state number as they belong to the same equivalent class, while a configuration may have more than one state number. We then have the following productions with states in corresponding configurations:

$$S' \rightarrow_1 S_2 c_3,$$
$$S \rightarrow_{1, 6} S_{2, 7} A_4,$$
$$S \rightarrow_{1, 6} A_5,$$
$$A \rightarrow_{1, 2, 6} a_6 S_7 b_8,$$
$$A \rightarrow_{1, 2, 6} a_6 b_9.$$

By the way, there is a need to supplement that for

$$A \rightarrow \varepsilon.$$

Since the right part has no symbol, there is only a position on it, it corresponds to a state.

Having the states, we can have more understanding on the reduce-shift operations of the bottom-up syntactical analysis method. On the right sentential form if a position corresponds to the internal position of the right part of some production, then it will need moving right to the terminal or nonterminal symbol adjacent to it. The current state will change to the state that corresponds to the next position. This is why in this circumstance a shift operation is needed. When it is on the last position of a production it needs to reduce the right part string into the nonterminal on the left part of the production. And by this way the whole process likes climbing up the tree until it comes to the top of the tree, the start symbol of the grammar.

In this process one needs to know that in terms of the current production in use, there is no symbol beside the symbol on the right side. However, when the reduction operation is done, then the position corresponds to the right side of the nonterminal that is a left part of some production. And the nonterminal must occur in the right part of other production. And in the production it must have an adjacent symbol on its right. Or if it is the left part of ε production, it must have the follower symbol. And the follower symbol must be obtained from a production that the nonterminal occurs as an element of the right part of the production. The terminal following it is the follower of it, or the element of FS of its adjacent nonterminal is the follower of it. Otherwise the sentence must be wrong. Therefore, handle is nothing but a right part of a production that can be used for reduction. If the productions are given according to the order given above, then the bottom-up syntactical analysis can be carried out from the bottom up to the top. If this process finishes with the start symbol of the grammar, it reports success and the input sentence is confirmed to be a correct sentence of the grammar.

7.6 LR(1) Syntactical Analysis Method

After we have explained the idea of the bottom-up syntactical method, we start introducing a specific method and widely use it. We mean the LR(1) method.

As we have mentioned previously that LR(1) means a method that scans the input left to right and producing rightmost derivation through looking ahead one symbol on the input while LR(0) means that it need not using look ahead symbol.

7.6.1 LR(0) Syntactical Analysis

The LR(0) syntactical analysis precisely determines the prefix property of the deterministic context-free language. A language L is said to have prefix property if at any time prefix of the sentence w of L must not be in L. This property of LR(0) assures that a sentence of the language can be reduced to the start symbol as any prefix of it cannot be reduced to the start symbol. Actually, the prefix property is not a strict limitation as so long an end token is introduced into any deterministic context-free language, then the language is transformed into one with the prefix property, because any sentence is a legal sentence of the language L only when it contains the end token. As any prefix of the sentence cannot contain the end token, it cannot be a legal sentence of L.

Directly perceiving through the sense, if there is a rightmost derivation

$$S \overset{*}{\Longrightarrow} \delta Aw \Longrightarrow \delta \alpha \beta w$$

and $\delta \alpha = \gamma$, and in each case, δAw really is the right sentential form for γw. In this case, we may perform bottom-up syntactical analysis of a symbol string x of $L(G)$, and it has a right sentential form of G. When we carry out a series of reduce-shift operations, we may reach the start symbol of G without backtracking. In this way, we have the rightmost derivation of x.

More explicitly speaking, as we saw in the grammar given above, it has 9 states. Apart from states $3, 4, 5, 8$, and 9 that are respectively the final state of productions $1, 2, 3, 4$, and 5, the remaining states are only used for shift operations, while $3, 4, 5, 8$, and 9 are used for reductions. They are responsible for the reduction of each production separately and each reduction operation will reduce input string that matches the right part of the production to the nonterminal in left part of the production. For example, both 4 and 5 reduce the right part sequence to the nonterminal in left part. State 4 and state 5 reduce the right parts of strings of productions 2 and 3 to nonterminal S, while states 8 and 9 reduce the right part strings of production 4 and 5 to nonterminal A.

Just because of the property that the grammar has, there is no need to look ahead any symbol, the analysis can be deterministically carried out, hence this is a LR(0) grammar.

In the description above, the states that are responsible for shift operations do not involve in reduce operations and vice versa. This case is called shift-reduce conflict-free. However, generally speaking, shift-reduce conflict is likely to happen in common grammars. For example, suppose that we have

$$N) \ T \to_{(N, 0)} i_{(N, 1)},$$
$$N+1) \ T \to_{(N+1, 0)} i_{(N+1, 1)} E_{(N+1, 2)}.$$

Suppose that $(N, 0)$ and $(N+1, 0)$ are numbered m, then

$$f(m, i) = m + 1 = (N, 1) = (N+1, 1) = \{(N, 1), (N+1, 1)\}.$$

Now there is shift-reduce conflict with the state $m+1$. This can be seen from the production N) and N+1). In the production N), the state $m+1$ requires to reduce the input string to nonterminal T according to production N), that is to say, to reduce the input string that is coincident with the right part of the production N) to the left part of the production N). On the other hand, according to the production N + 1), the state m+1 is an internal state that should do shift operation. It should shift to the state that corresponds to the configuration $(N + 1, 2)$. The state number of $(N + 1, 2)$ will be assigned from the equivalent configurations. This is an obvious shift-reduce conflict.

We consider another example of LR(0) grammar. Let grammar G be a context-free grammar with the following productions:

$$1) \; S' \to S\$;$$
$$2) \; S \to T;$$
$$3) \; S \to S + T;$$
$$4) \; T \to (S);$$
$$5) \; T \to i.$$

We establish the configurations with these productions:

$$1) \; S' \to_{(1, 0)} S_{(1, 1)}\$_{(1, 2)};$$
$$2) \; S \to_{(2, 0)} T_{(2, 1)};$$
$$3) \; S \to_{(3, 0)} S_{(3, 1)} +_{(3, 2)} T_{(3, 3)};$$
$$4) \; T \to_{(4, 0)} (_{(4, 1)}S_{(4, 2)})_{(4, 3)};$$
$$5) \; T \to_{(5, 0)} i_{(5, 1)}.$$

At first we have equivalent configuration group $\{(1, 0), (2, 0), (3, 0), (4, 0), (5, 0)\}$, and we denote it 1. Then

$$f(1, S) = 2 = \{(1, 1), (3, 1)\},$$
$$f(2, \$) = 3 = \{(1, 2)\},$$
$$f(1, T) = 4 = \{(2, 1)\} = f(7, T),$$
$$f(2, +) = 5 = \{(3, 2), (4, 0), (5, 0)\},$$
$$f(5, T) = 6 = \{(3, 3)\},$$
$$f(1, () = f(5, () = 7 = \{(4, 1), (2, 0), (3, 0), (4, 0), (5, 0)\},$$
$$f(7, S) = 8 = \{(3, 1), (4, 2)\},$$
$$f(8,)) = 9 = \{(4, 3)\},$$
$$f(7, i) = f(1, i) = 10 = \{(5, 1)\}.$$

So we have the productions with states attaching to configurations as follows:

$$S' \to_1 S_2 \$_3,$$
$$S \to_{1, 7} T_4,$$

$$S \rightarrow_{1,7} S_{2,8} +_5 T_6,$$
$$T \rightarrow_{1,5,7} (_7 S_8)_9,$$
$$T \rightarrow_{1,5,7} i_{10}.$$

By the productions with states attaching to configurations, we can establish a shift-reduce table that corresponds to the grammar. Table 7.3 is an essential tool for the LR syntactical method.

Table 7.3 LR(0) syntactical analysis table

State	Symbol								
	i	+	(	)	$	S'	S	T	⊥
1	S_{10}		S_7			halt	S_2	S_4	
2		S_5			S_3				
3	R_1	R_1	R_1	R_1	R_1	R_1	R_1	R_1	R_1
4									R_2
5	S_{10}		S_7					S_6	
6									R_3
7	S_{10}		S_7					S_8	
8		S_5		S_9					
9									R_4
10									R_5

Note: ⊥ on the table denotes the end mark of the input.

On the table, the items starting with S denote shift action while the items starting with R denote reduce action, so S_i means shifting to the state i. But i after R, R_i means reduction according to the production number i. For example, R_1 means the reduction according to production number one, i.e. the first production. Reduction means that the current string on input will be replaced by the nonterminal of left part of the production. Actually, the state 1 cannot encounter symbol S'. However, we put item halt on the place to indicate that it is the successful finish situation. The empty place on the table represents the impossible situation. If the state in the input string meets the symbol with the empty item on the table that means that an error case occurs and the analyzer should report failure.

For LR(0) syntactical analysis as we have mentioned that the states in charge of doing shift operation and that in charge of doing reduction are separated, the items on the rows of states have different characteristics. That means that they each contains only one operation, either shift or reduction. In this circumstance, of course, the analysis is simple.

We must point out, however, only very few grammars are of LR(0). For example, the grammar that contains production like $A \rightarrow \varepsilon$ cannot be of LR(0) as if the production is contained in the production set, the state $A \rightarrow_n$ must be in conflict with the same state in $P \rightarrow \alpha A \beta$. By the former production no matter what symbol is coming, including β, a reduction operation should be carried out. However, by the later production, if a β comes, the state should shift to a new state that corresponds to the configuration after β, hence a shift-reduce conflict occurs.

Apart from shift-reduce conflict, it is also likely to have reduce-reduce conflict. This is such a case that there are two productions like

$$T \rightarrow i,$$
$$V \rightarrow i,$$

and it happens that they both have the same state corresponding to two configurations

$$T \rightarrow_n i,$$
$$V \rightarrow_n i.$$

That means that the initial configurations of two productions have the same state. Consequently, the two configurations after i have the same state too, as $f(n, i)$ has only one value. But how to do the reduction? Should we reduce to T or to V? We are in conflict now. And this is reduce-reduce conflict.

Shift-reduce conflict and reduce-reduce conflict are commonly seen cases.

7.6.2 SLR(1) Syntactical Analysis

In the last section, we point out that LR(0) method is too weak to be practical. It is because it does not need to look ahead any input symbol, it can make a decision by checking the state only. However, in practice, it is very rare to have such a case. As the improvement of LR(0), the first step is to generate SLR(1) grammar. The S in SLR(1) means simple. So it is a simple LR(1) syntactical analysis. In this analysis, relatively simple shift-reduce conflict is allowed. When the case occurs, it can be resolved by looking ahead one symbol. Concretely speaking, for a production with a nonterminal A as the left part, for some state in it, if the lookahead symbol of it does not belong to the follower symbol of A, then reduce operation on the symbol (or symbol string) in front of the state cannot use the production. Instead, a shift in operation should be carried out with the lookahead symbol as the input.

We show an example of SLR(1) grammar:

$$S \rightarrow real\ IDLIST,$$
$$IDLIST \rightarrow IDLIST, ID,$$
$$IDLIST \rightarrow ID,$$
$$ID \rightarrow A \mid B \mid C \mid D.$$

We omit the details of establishing states and directly assign the states to the configurations. We get the productions with states attaching to corresponding configurations:

$$S \rightarrow_1 real_2 IDLIST_3,$$
$$IDLIST \rightarrow_2 IDLIST_{3,4} ID_5,$$
$$IDLIST \rightarrow_2 ID_6,$$
$$ID \rightarrow_{2,4} A \mid B \mid C \mid D_7.$$

With these productions with states attached, we may obtain the corresponding syntactical analysis table (see Table 7.4).

In this table, we may see that on line of the state 3, there are two different items. One is S4 that corresponds to input ",", that means that on the state 3, if the input is a comma the state will shift to the state 4. The another item corresponds to input end mark $\perp$, this time it will do reduce operation to reduce the previous string to the left part of the production 1, that is the start symbol S. This is the first time that we see that there are two different actions-shift and reduce-on the same line. This is a shift-reduce conflict. The conflict can be resolved easily by looking ahead one symbol.

Table 7.4 SLR(1) syntactical analysis table

State	Symbol						
	S	IDLIST	ID	real	,	A, B, C, D	$\perp$
1	halt			S2			
2		S3	S6			S7	
3					S4		R1
4			S5			S7	
5				R2	R2	R2	R2
6				R3	R3	R3	R3
7				R4	R4	R4	R4

We have an easy explanation about the insertion of "halt". Imagine that we have another production

$$S' \rightarrow S$$

and we add the state to its configurations, so we have

$$S' \rightarrow_1 S_{halt} \perp.$$

This is why we put a halt on the intersect column S and row state 1.

SLR(1) goes forward a step in comparison with LR(0), and it may resolve the shift-reduce conflict by distinguishing whether the looking ahead symbol belongs to the follower of some nonterminal or not. However, the power of SLR(1) is limited. Therefore, we need to seek for more powerful method. Our solution is LALR(1) syntactical analysis method. "LA" here means look ahead. That means that it resolves the conflicts by more carefully looking ahead input symbols.

7.6.3 LALR(1) Syntactical Analysis

Since the limitation of SLR(1), it has lower practicality. Therefore, people considered how to improve it in order to have a better analytical method. LALR(1) is a step toward the aim.

At first we analyze what made SLR(1) less practicality. We have seen that while looking ahead one input symbol, SLR(1) did not care much its context, especially the past context. In more general cases, only considering the past context then can one symbol be determined whether it is legal follower or not.

We now consider and analyze the following example.

Example 7.5 Suppose that the grammar G is given with the following productions:

$$1) \; S \to T \text{ else } F;$$
$$2) \; T \to E;$$
$$3) \; T \to i;$$
$$4) \; F \to E;$$
$$5) \; E \to E + i;$$
$$6) \; E \to i.$$

In order to explain the problem more explicitly, we analyze the grammar step by step again. We start from the configuration $(1, 0)$. By equivalence relation of configurations, and the transitivity of the relation, we have

$$(1,\, 0) \sim (2,\, 0) \sim (3,\, 0) \sim (5,\, 0) \sim (6,\, 0).$$

We assign the equivalent configuration group the initial state 1. We have

$$f((1,\, 0),\, -) = 1 = \{(2,\, 0), (3,\, 0), (5,\, 0), (6,\, 0)\},$$
$$f(1,\, T) = \{(1,\, 1)\} = 2,$$
$$f(2,\, \text{else}) = 3 = \{(4,\, 0), (5,\, 0), (6,\, 0)\},$$
$$f(3,\, F) = 4 = \{(1,\, 3)\},$$
$$f(1,\, E) = 5 = \{(2,\, 1), (5,\, 1)\},$$
$$f(1,\, i) = 6 = \{(6,\, 1), (3,\, 1)\},$$
$$f(3,\, E) = 7 = \{(4,\, 1), (5,\, 1)\},$$
$$f(6,\, ;) = 8 = \{(3,\, 2)\},$$
$$f(5,\, +) = f(7,\, +) = 9 = \{(5,\, 2)\},$$
$$f(9,\, i) = 10 = \{(5,\, 3)\},$$
$$f(4,\, ;) = 11 = \{(1,\, 4)\},$$
$$f(5,\, ;) = 12 = \{(2,\, 2)\}.$$

From here, we get the following productions with states attached:

1) $S \rightarrow_1 T_2 \text{ else}_3 F_4; 11;$

2) $T \rightarrow_1 E_5; 12;$

3) $T \rightarrow_1 i_6; 8;$

4) $F \rightarrow_3 E_7;$

5) $E \rightarrow_{1,3} E_{5,7} +_9 i_{10};$

6) $E \rightarrow_{1,3} i_6.$

Consequently, we may establish the analysis table as shown in Table 7.5:

Table 7.5 LALR(1) syntactical analysis table

State	Symbol								
	S	T	F	E	else	;	+	i	$\perp$
1	Halt	S_2		S_5				S_6	
2					S_3				
3			S_4	S_7				S_6	
4						S_{11}			
5					R_2		S_9		
6					R_6	S_8/R_6	R_6		
7					R_4				
8					R_3				
9								S_{10}	
10					R_5	R_5	R_5		
11									R_1
12									R_2

Notice that on the table above, a shift-reduce conflict occurs on the line state 6. The conflict is caused by i on the right part of the production 3 and the i on the right part of the production 6. According to the production 6, the state before i (1 and 3) comes from different ways. If it comes from the nonterminal T in production 1, when the i is followed by ;, it should be reduced to E and reduce action should be taken. However, the state is 3, it comes from the state after else on the production 1. In this case, the follower of i on the production 6 is the follower of E. Then from the production 4, the follower of E is the follower of F. Hence it is ;. Therefore according to the production 6, when the look ahead symbol that follows i is ;, the action that should be done is shift. It should shift to the state 8. This is where the conflict comes from.

Now in order to solve the conflict, the past context should be taken into account. On the productions 5 and 6, the state 1 comes from state 1 before T on the first production while state 3 comes from configuration after "else". Therefore, if we assign single state to the configuration that following i then conflict must occurs. And this is where the problem is. After we found the problem, we know how to overcome it. The problem will be immediately resolved as long as we add one more state to differentiate the two sources of the state 6. The resulting result is as follows:

1) $S \to_1 T_2$ else $_3F_4$; $_{11}$;
2) $T \to_1 E_5$; $_{12}$;
3) $T \to_1 i_6$; $_8$;
4) $F \to_3 E_7$;
5) $E \to_{1,3} E_{5,7} +_9 i_{10}$;
6) $E \to_{1,3} i_{6,13}$.

Now we will have a new syntactical analysis table (see Table 7.6) in place of the above one and this one solves the shift-reduce conflict.

This table can be used to analyze the LALR(1) grammar. With the method, if shift-reduce conflict takes place, we try to distinguish the past context of a configuration. The conflict of this kind usually can be resolved.

Table 7.6 LALR(1) syntactical analytical table that solves the conflict

State	Symbol								
	S	T	F	E	else	;	+	i	⊥
1	Halt	S_2		S_5				S_6	
2					S_3				
3			S_4	S_7				S_{12}	
4						S_{11}			
5					R_2		S_9		
6					R_6	S_8	R_6		
7						R_4	S_9		
8					R_3				
9								S_{10}	
10					R_5	R_5	R_5		
11									R_1
12									R_2
13					R_6				R_6

7.6.4 LR(1) Syntactical Analysis

We have mentioned that the LR(0) syntactical analysis method can only be suitable to such a grammar that each state on its productions either is for shift action or is for reduce action. It did not need to consider the lookahead symbol. Once the look ahead symbol needs to be considered, it is no longer suitable. Then we need a stronger method. And SLR(1) lends itself to the situation. In SLR(1), we allow such a case that a state either carries out a shift action or a reduce action according to different lookahead symbols. The fact reflects on the table that on the same line (corresponding to a state) with different columns, it may have shift and reduce items on them. The practicability of this one, however, is also limited as in most cases, the situation is more complicated that even for the same row and the same column, depending on the past context it has different tackling methods, either doing shift action or doing reduce action. Therefore, it needs to split a state to two states, one for the shift action and another one for reduce action. In some cases, even one state is split to more states. In the example of last section, we just did so. And it is the LALR(1) syntactical analysis method.

Now we want to say again that the power of LALR(1) is still limited. For more complicated grammars, it fails to work. If it is the case, we have to try a stronger method, it is the common LR(1) syntactical analysis method.

The LR(1) syntactical analysis method is different from LR(0), SLR(1), and LALR(1) in that it has much more number of states while the last three ones have basically the same state numbers. Their sizes of the syntactical analysis tables are also almost the same. For LALR(1), the size of states is slightly more than SLR(1) as some states in SLR(1) will be split into two states. The number of states of LR(1), however, will increase remarkably as for one configuration it will become a state depending on one input, hence the number of states will be much more than the number of configurations.

In the following, we will introduce another version of the analytical method while we introduce the general LR(1) syntactical analysis method. The method makes our state transitions like an automaton. Consider the grammar with following productions (see Example 7.6).

Example 7.6   A grammar is given via the following productions:

$$1) \text{ S} \to \text{A};$$
$$2) \text{ S} \to \text{xb};$$
$$3) \text{ A} \to \text{aAb};$$
$$4) \text{ A} \to \text{B};$$
$$5) \text{ B} \to \text{x}.$$

At first we add a production $S' \to S$ so that the determination of state is consistent with our original practice. This is called the incremental grammar of the original grammar. Now we have:

$$1) \text{ S}' \to \cdot \text{S}\{\bot\};$$
$$2) \text{ S} \to \cdot \text{A}\{\bot\};$$
$$3) \text{ S} \to \cdot \text{xb}\{\bot\};$$
$$4) \text{ A} \to \cdot \text{aAb}\{\bot\};$$
$$5) \text{ A} \to \cdot \text{B}\{\bot\};$$
$$6) \text{ B} \to \cdot \text{x}\{\bot\}.$$

Where inside { } is the following symbol. It is the end mark following the input string. • indicates configuration. It is similar to what we used (m, n) before. From the point, as different inputs come, we will have different states. Then what we get is similar to the previous automaton.

We establish all the states first and it is shown as follows:

$$S' \to_0 S_1,$$
$$S \to_0 A_2,$$
$$S \to_0 x_3 b_4,$$
$$A \to_{0,5} a_{13,5} A_{7,8} b_{9,10},$$
$$A \to_{0,5} B_{611},$$
$$B \to_{0,5} x_{3,12}.$$

By this we can draw an LR(1) automaton as shown in Fig. 7.5:

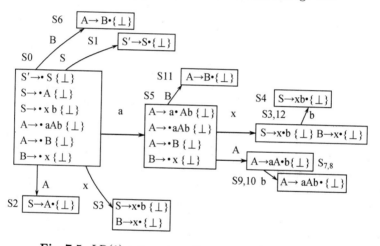

Fig. 7.5 LR(1) automaton of grammar of example 7.6.

We can see that all the cores of LR(1) states correspond to the states of SLR(1). The reason for the situation is that the cores are determined by the symbols which other states allow to shift in. Therefore, if we do not consider the lookahead symbols, the core is a LR(0) state. If the state is transformed then new LR(1) state is generated while its core is still the LR(0) state. Therefore, LR(1) states are the result of the split of LR(0) states.

The source of power of LR(1) comes from the split of states. Just depending on the split, the problems which SLR(1) or LALR(1) cannot solve can be solved satisfactorily by LR(1) method. Of course not all problems are solvable by LR(1).

It is not that every such split is necessary. Contrasting with Fig. 7.5 we can see that states 6 and state 2 can be combined together to form a new single state $S_{2,6}$ as they each consists of a configuration only. Through further analysis, we can find that more states can be combined. After such a combination we get the LALR(1) automaton as shown in Fig. 7.6.

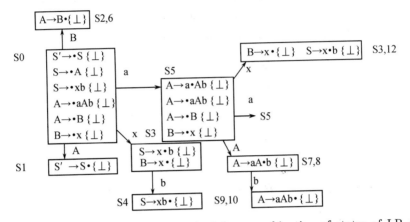

Fig. 7.6   LALR (1) automaton obtained from combination of states of LR (1) automaton of Fig. 7.5.

In Figs. 7.5 and 7.6, those states that • that locates at the rightmost position of the production is for reduce action while other states are for shift actions. The symbols beside the arrows outsides productions are the input symbols.

From the introduction above we know that the number of states for LR (1) is much more than that of LALR (1) though it is not obvious in the example above. In the practical programming languages, the amount of states used by LR (1) syntactical analysis will be several levels higher than that used by corresponding LALR(1) syntactical analysis. Here is the statistics given by reference: A SLR (1) syntactical analysis table of a programming language after compression spent a number of KB of the memory on the average, while LR(1) table needed a number of MB of the memory. When we construct such table the memory we need probably is several tens times of the amount. Fortes Galvez implemented a different realization of LR (1) in 1992. It slightly reduced the size of LR (1) syntactical analysis table. On the other hand, most of the programming languages just need the LALR (1) syntactical analysis table, so we do not need to worry about the size of LR (1) table as we rarely use it.

After considering LR (1) we naturally want to know what about LR (k) syntactical analysis for k ⩾ 2, is it more powerful than LR(1)? [7] The studies affirm that LR(k) (k ⩾ 2) syntactical analysis is slightly more powerful than LR(1) indeed, but it is at the expense of bigger size of the analysis table. People originally thought that when a grammar was not of LR (1), can it be analyzed via LR (2)? However, it turned out that the probability for it being of LR(2) is very low. The conclusion no doubt is depressing as it is not like that when LR(0) cannot solve the problem, we use SLR(1) to solve it instead, or further use LALR(1) before we use LR(1). When LR (1) fails to work, probably LR(2) does not work either. Therefore, theoretically LR(2) has some significance, but it is never used so far.

We now illustrate the practical procedure of syntactical analysis via LALR (1). We consider the grammar above:

$$S' \rightarrow S,$$
$$S \rightarrow A,$$
$$S \rightarrow xb,$$
$$A \rightarrow aAb,$$
$$A \rightarrow B,$$
$$B \rightarrow x,$$

and suppose that the input string is aaaaxbbbb. At first, we construct the productions with states attached. They are as follows:

$$S' \rightarrow_0 S_1,$$
$$S \rightarrow_0 A_2,$$
$$S \rightarrow_0 x_3 b_4.$$
$$A \rightarrow_{0,5} a_{13,5} A_{8,7} b_{10,9},$$
$$A \rightarrow_{0,5} B_{6,11},$$
$$B \rightarrow_{0,5} x_{3,12}.$$

With these productions and states, we may construct the syntactical analysis table as shown in Table 7.7.

Table 7.7 LR(1) syntactical analysis table

State	Symbol							
	S'	S	A	B	x	a	b	$\perp$
0	Halt	S_1	S_2	S_6	S_3			
1								R_1
2								R_2
3							S_4	R_6
4								R_3
5			S_7	S_{11}	S_{12}			
6								R_5
7							S_9	
8							S_{10}	
9								R_4
10								R_4
11								R_5
12								R_6
13			S_8					

Before we really start the practical analysis with input string, we should notice that the analysis needs two stacks, one for symbols and another one for states. Besides, the handles of terminals and nonterminals are different in that for terminals, we simply put them to the input stack, change or do not change the state. But for nonterminals, while we put it into the symbol stack, sometimes we will change the symbol as well as the state. Therefore, in some books, they differentiate the handles as "goto" and "action".

Initially, two stacks are empty, but in the state stack, we put 0 to indicate the empty situation while in the input symbol stack, we keep it empty.

Input Symbol Stack	State Stack
	0

Then a comes, we have

Input Symbol Stack	State Stack
	5
a	0

The second a comes

Input Symbol Stack	State Stack
a	5
a	0

Until four a's all were put in the stack, the state stack does not change.

Input Symbol Stack	State Stack
a	5
a	0
a	
a	

Then x enters the input stack, according to the analysis table, the state 5 changes to the state 10.

Input Symbol Stack   State Stack

x
a
a
a
a

12
0

The state 12 is for reduce, it makes x to reduce to B, and the state returns to 5.

Now in input stack, from top to down, we have Baaaa, and in the state stack, also from top to down, we have 5 0. The state 5 meets symbol B it shifts to the state 11. Therefore, we have the following situation.

Input Symbol Stack   State Stack

B
a
a
a
a

11
0

Under the state 11, B is reduced to A and the state 11 is removed and we have 5 and 0 in the state stack.

Input Symbol Stack   State Stack

A
a
a
a
a

5
0

The state 5 meets A, it shifts to the state 7, so the situation changes again as follows.

Input Symbol Stack

State Stack

| A |
| a |
| a |
| a |
| a |

| 7 |
| 0 |

Under the state 7, b comes and enters the input stack, the state 7 shifts to the state 9 and the situation becomes as follows.

Input Symbol Stack

State Stack

| b |
| A |
| a |
| a |
| a |
| a |

| 9 |
| 0 |

Now in the input stack, from top to down what we see is bAa, it is not anything but the right part of the production with A as the left part. Since the state is 9, it will reduce the three symbols to A. The situation becomes as follows.

Input Symbol Stack

State Stack

| A |
| a |
| a |
| a |

| 5 |
| 0 |

The state 5 meets A and shifts to 7. Hence we have the following situation.

Input Symbol Stack   State Stack

A
a
a
a

7
0

As the second b enters the input stack, once again we have bAa from top
to down and the state changes to 9. It reduces the three symbols to A. The
situation will repeat again twice more until at the end.

Input Symbol Stack   State Stack

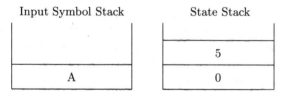

This time the three symbols bAa will be reduced to A and in the state stack
only the state 0 remains.

Input Symbol Stack   State Stack

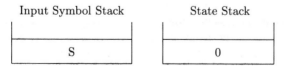

However, according to the analysis table, when the input stack is empty, the
state 5 is actually state 0, and when the state 0 meets the symbol A it shifts
to the state 2. The state 2 is for reduce. It reduces A to S and the state
becomes the state 0 again.

Input Symbol Stack   State Stack

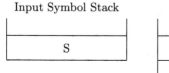

Then we have a shift action to change the situation to as follows.

Input Symbol Stack   State Stack

S

1
0

Now the state 1 reduces S to S′ and the state becomes 0. So finally we have the following situation.

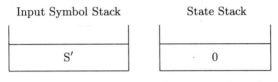

| Input Symbol Stack | State Stack |

It declares the success of the analysis. It also means that the input string is the sentence of the grammar.

7.6.5 Comparison Between LL(1) Syntactical Analysis Method and LR(1) Syntactical Analysis Method

It is not an easy thing to compare two completely different methods, especially compiler developers each has different favor. In Chinese, there is a proverb that says that the benevolent sees benevolence and the wise sees wisdom. That means that different people have different views. Either they prefer one of these methods, or they select other methods (they select from top-down analysis or bottom-up analysis). There are many debates indeed between these two methods. Therefore, here we can only have a brief comparison.

At first, from the start of the syntactical analysis, we should say that LR(1) is superior in the aspect as it need not to do any check before it starts an analysis. The LL(1) analysis is different from LR(1). It has to check whether the grammar is qualified to use the LL(1) analysis method or not. It checks whether the grammar contains the left recursion or not and whether the DS's of productions with the same left part intersect or not. If there exist such problems, then the LL(1) method cannot be used immediately until they are resolved. Since LR(1) has no these troubles, it can be used immediately to rather wider category of grammars and languages. Furthermore, usually there is no need for the transformation of the grammar. Therefore, theoretically LR(1) method is more superior than LL(1).

The following example[8] shows, however, that in some cases, the LR (1) method also requires the transformation of the grammar. Suppose that the grammar G_1 is given with the following productions:

$$S \rightarrow COC|CLC,$$
$$COC \rightarrow orb\ EC\ stick\ SC\ stick\ SC\ crb,$$
$$EC \rightarrow u\ semi\ EC|u,$$
$$CLC \rightarrow PLU\ semi\ SC|PLU,$$
$$PLU \rightarrow lab\ PLU|u,$$

where COC stands for a conditional clause, CLC stands for a closed clause, orb stands for an open round bracket, EC stands for an enquiry clause, SC stands for a sequential clause, crb stands for a closed round bracket, semi stands for a semicolon, u stands for an unit, PLU stands for a possibly labeled unit.

The problem comes from the fact that the unit in the conditional clause cannot have label while the unit in the sequential clause of the closed clause may have label. This language is LL(1) if the rules of the closed clause and conditional clause are combined together (two productions of SC must be transformed, otherwise their DS's must intersect). The grammar obtained after transformation is denoted with different notation, and we have grammar G_2 as follows:

$$S \rightarrow orb\ T,$$
$$T \rightarrow lab\ V|u\ W,$$
$$V \rightarrow lab\ V|u\ X,$$
$$W \rightarrow crb|semi\ T|stick\ SC\ stick\ SC\ crb,$$
$$X \rightarrow\ semi\ V|crb,$$
$$SC \rightarrow PLU\ Y,$$
$$Y \rightarrow semi\ PLU\ Y|z,$$
$$PLU \rightarrow lab\ PLU|u.$$

However, it can be proven that the original grammar G1 is not of LR(1). This is because when the string

$$(\ u$$

is read and the look ahead symbol is semi, there is no way to determine whether one should use the production of PLU to reduce it to PLU or use the first production of EC to shift to a new state. Thus we will have a shift-reduce conflict that cannot be solved.

This example and the examples from ALGOL 68 and other languages show that if a grammar can be of LL(1) only through manual transformation, then that it can be of LR(1) must also be processed beforehand. That means that what we said before that LR(1) does not require the transformation of grammar is not completely true. It also means that the theoretical superiority of LR(1) (i.e., its generality) over LL(1) is not significant in practice.

Furthermore, the comparison between these two in terms of the sizes of syntactical analysis tables and the time taken results in totally different conclusion: The experience showed that the elements of LL syntactical analysis that can be stored in single word may reduce the size of the typical LL (1) syntactical analysis table down to about 4K words. But if we use the LR (1) syntactical analysis table which we described in the text the size is about 50K words. However, such a comparison is not fair as in most of the cases, we did not use the general LR (1) syntactical analysis, we use LALR(1) syntactical analysis instead that is more forthright. In addition, the amount can be decreased up to 90% via optimization. Nevertheless, in terms of the size of syntactical analysis, LL(1) is better than LR(1) indeed[9].

Now we analyze the two from recovery from errors. We have mentioned that LL(1) method is deterministic. Through the DS, we know whether every step of derivation is correct or not. Suppose that on some step, a lookahead symbol of a nonterminal does not belong to the DS of the production with the nontermianl as left part, then we immediately detect that there is something wrong in the input string. In LL(1) syntactical analysis the method for recovery from errors is rather simple. It only needs to plan the shortest way out, from the remaining input deleting the symbols until discovering that some symbol s may be accepted by the path. Then following the path to find out the symbol that can be accepted. That is the method for recovery from errors. This method is called allowable set of recovery from errors. On the other hand, however, in LR(1) syntactical analysis method, the procedure for recovery from errors is rather difficult. This is because most of the message which one collects in the method possess the nature of postulation. There is a method that proceeds as follows: when an error takes place, then the states must be moved out from the stack, the operation will continue until a state that allows the nonterminal to shift into another state. The next step is to shift in the dummy element. Finally, it jumps over the input symbols until a new symbol which the new state can accept. From the procedure that is just described, one may see that the procedure for recovery from errors of LR (1) is more difficult indeed.

Cohen and Roth (1978) analyzed the longest, shortest and average times which LL(1) and SLR(1) spent on the sentence analysis, the statistics showed that LL(1) was 50% faster than SLR (1) did.

After we compared the two methods in terms of transformation processing, the size of the syntactical analysis table and recovery from errors, we like the reader to be aware that the two methods each has its strong points. Therefore, whether one adopts LL(1) method or LR(1) method will totally depends on one's preference. If some one insists that comparison should have a result, then the result of one being superior over other is only relative one, rather than an absolute one.

We also like to point out their commonalities after we discuss their differences. The two methods both are suitable for embedding actions into syntax in order to do some works of the compilation process. Later we will introduce how to implement this point in LL(1) syntactical analysis. As for how to implement this LR(1) syntactical analysis, as these actions usually are related to reduce actions, hence they will be related to the final states of productions. Therefore, if one needs to have actions but not being in the end of productions, then one needs to introduce pseudo rules. In summary, in practice, which method one should select usually depends on which one will result in the generator of the better syntactical analysis program. Sometimes rather than to let the two methods compete with each other it would be better to let them cooperate together. That means to combine them to carry out the analysis process. For example, the C compiler on PDP-11 adopts recursively descending method, i.e., the top-down syntactical analysis method to handle most of the expressions, while for some other expressions, it uses the simple bottom-up method (the operator precedence method.)

Problems

Problem 7.1 Show that every LL(1) grammar is an LR(1) grammar.

Problem 7.2 Show that the family of grammar G_n defined by

$$S \to A_i b_i, \qquad 1 \leqslant i \leqslant n,$$

$$A_i \to a_j A_i | a_j, \qquad 1 \leqslant i, j \leqslant n \text{ but } j \neq i.$$

1) Show that G_n has $2n^2 - n$ productions and $2^n + n^2 + n$ sets of LR(0) items. What does this result say about how big an LR parser can get in comparison to the size of the grammar.

2) Is G_n SLR(1)?

3) Is G_n LALR(1)?

Problem 7.3 Give an algorithm for detecting unreachable entries in the LR parsing table.

Problem 7.4 Given a Chomsky normal form grammar G, show how to add productions for single insertion, deletion, and mutation errors to the grammar so that the enlarged grammar generates all possible token strings.

Problem 7.5 A context-free grammar is said to be q grammar if and only if it has the following properties:

1) The right part of every production either begins with a terminal or it is empty.

2) For every nonterminal that occurs in more than one production, the derivation sets of these productions are disjoint.

Show that:

1) Any q grammar is of LL(1).

2) Any s grammar is also q grammar. The so-called s grammar is that: (1) Every right part of the production begin with a terminal. (2) If a nonterminal occurs in the left part of productions for one than once, then the right parts of these productions all begin with different terminals.

3) Any LL(1) grammar can be converted to a q grammar.

Problem 7.6 Show that no LR(1) grammar can be ambiguous.

References

[1] Grune D, Jacobs CJH (1990) Parsing Technique: A Practical Guide, Ellis Horwood, New York.

[2] Sippu S, Soisalon-Soinenan E (1989/1990) Parsing Theory, vol. II LL(k) Parsing and LR(k) Parsing. Springer, Berlin.

[3] Robin Hunter (1988) Compilers: their design and construction using Pascal. Cambridge University Press, Cambridge.

[4] Aho A V, Ullman J D (1973) the theory of parsing, translation, and compiling, vol. II: Compiling. Prentice-Hall, Englewood Cliffs, New Jersey.

[5] Chen Huowang, Qian Jiahua, Sun Yongqiang (1980) Compiler principles. Defense Industry Press, Beijing.

[6] Jin Chengzhi (1981) Compilers: The principles and implementation. Higher Education Press, Beijing.

[7] Aho A V, Ullman J D (1972) The theory of parsing, translation and compiling, vol. I: Parsing,. Prentice-Hall, Englewood Cliffs, New Jersey.

[8] Grune D, Bal H E, Jacobs C J (2007) Modern compiler design. Addison-Wiley, Reading, MA.

[9] Chapman NP (1987) LR Parsing: Theory and Practice. Cambridge University Press, Cambridge.

Chapter 8 Attribute Grammars and Analysis

What attributes should a good manager possess?

Longman Dictionary of Contemporary English

8.1 Motivation of the Chapter

In the Chapter 7, we concentrated on the discussion of parsing methods, i.e. the top-down and bottom-up syntactical methods, especially LL(1) and LR(1) syntactical analysis methods. From the discussion, we can see that in order to carry out LL(1) or LR(1) syntactical analysis there is a need for the premise that the grammar to be analyzed is a context-free one, otherwise both methods do not work. In other words, in order to analyze a programming language through the top-down or bottom-up method, the language must be guaranteed to be context-free. Therefore, we need to explore the description or definition of the programming language. Before any programming language is designed, the designers must take into account the requirements from two sides. One is the requirements of the programmers who would use the language to develop programs. Because they want the language explicit, distinct, authoritative, and unambiguous; meanwhile, it should be easy to read and easy to use. Another one is the requirements of the developers of the language compiler, they want the structure of programs in the language easy to implement, or the development of the compiler also easy.

Besides the two aspects mentioned above, there is another consideration that should also be taken into account — the requirement from the proof of the correctness of programs. Therefore the designers of the programming language select the method of formalization definition to fully describe syntax and semantics of the language. The first attempt of the formalization definition language was ALGOL 60 report [1]. The most part of the grammar was described via the context-free grammar. They could not do the syntax and semantics of the rest of the language by using the context-free grammar. Hence the only way was to use English to describe them. Moreover, there were lots of problems of ambiguities, even it was unavoidable for the revised report (Naur, 1963; [2]).

The formalization definition technique for programming languages developed continuingly in the following years, the ALGOL W report (Bauer, Becker, Graham, and Satterthwaitek, 1968) attempted to put some type information into formalization part of the syntax. The revised report of ALGOL 68 (van Wijngaarden et al., 1975) defined the whole syntax of the language by using two level grammar (it is called W grammar after the name of the inventor). Their works once again authenticated that any programming language cannot be completely generated by context-free grammars because according to the definition context-free grammar can only contain finite number of productions. By these productions there is no way to describe the non-context-free features of the language. Hence the attribute grammars lend themselves to overcome the problem.

8.2   Attribute Grammar

The attribute grammar has been used in the definition of syntaxes of many languages. To translate programs written in any programming language, a compiler may need to keep track of many quantities besides the code generated for the program. For example, the compiler may need to know the type of identifier, the location of the first instruction in the target code, or the number of the instructions generated. Therefore we talk abstractly about attributes associated with the constitute of the program. By attribute, we mean any quantity, e.g., a type, a string, a memory location, or whatsoever. However, in the context of the chapter, we mainly mean the attributes that the context-free grammar cannot describe. Since attribute grammar is constructed based on the context-free grammar, it can handle the computation that is required by the context processing, and then explain the syntax analysis of the context-free grammar. As the illustration, we use the context-free grammar to define part of Pascal language. Then we extend the grammar, defining the non-context-free aspects of the language using the attribute grammar (The definition of this part of Pascal is given here according to the work of Watt (1977) and McGettrick (1980)) [3].

At first we point out which attributes are not of context-free. For example, we construct the parsing tree of the input sentence via the top-down method. In the parsing tree, the leaves represent the terminals. But they are just the terminals only, they do not contain other characteristics of the terminals, i.e., the attributes. As the leaf of the abstract syntax tree (AST), the terminal may have its initial attribute, e.g., an identifier that represents an integer has the type attribute "integer", but it has no the value yet. Its value will be provided by the input of the program and this is not defined in the grammar that belongs to the context-free. A token that represents an identifier has its initial attribute value "identifier", but has no the address value and numerical value stored in the location yet. They are also provided by later input and not defined by the context-free grammar, all of which will be done by the attribute grammar.

The lexical analysis and parsing analysis work together to complete the analytical process of the context-free part of source programs. Analytic features may be local ones or in the embedded form. As for other cases, for example, to check the number of the formal parameters in the entry of routine, to see if it is consistent with the number which the declaration stipulates, is not of context-free.

In order to check the imperative context-free conditions and collect information of a specific language to handle the semantics, we need to handle the context. In some sense, the attribute grammar is a supplement of the context-free grammar that directs its intention at semantic analysis. In a compiler that purely deals with the compilation of programs, the context-free process is divided into two phases. At first, it checks all the relations of the context in the language. Only when the check is passed, then can the input be regarded as correct. Second, it collects other informations called the attributes. These informations are stored in the nodes of the abstract syntax tree. The context handling is done via checking all the context relations and evaluating all the attributes of the nodes.

Therefore, in simple words, the computation required by the context processing may be described in the syntactical analysis of the context-free grammar, and generates the attribute grammar. In order to meet the need, the context-free grammar is extended along two directions: one is the data, and another is the evaluation.

For each grammar symbol, no matter whether it is terminal or nonterminal, it is stipulated to have null or more attributes. Each attribute has its name and type called formal attribute. The formal attribute will be realized as a real attribute consistent with the formal type of specific value. The attributes are used for keeping the semantic information of the specific nodes. Therefore, all the nodes that correspond to the same grammar symbol S have the same formal attribute, but their real values — the real attributes are not the same.

For every production rule like $A \rightarrow M_1 M_2 \ldots M_n$, there is a series of relative computation rules — the attribute computation. They stipulate how to compute the attribute of A according to the attributes of the attributes M_i $(1 \leqslant i \leqslant n)$ at the right part. These computation rules check the context conditions and issue warning and error message in case some sort of errors occurs. They are related to production rules, rather than associated with nonterminals. This is because the computation rule is related to the attributes of the member M_i, while the member M_i is determined by production rules.

The attributes of every grammar symbol are categorized as a synthetic attribute and an inherited attribute. If a variable occurs twice or more times in a production, then each occurrence has the same attribute values. Then information may be transmitted from the start symbol to the sentence or program generated. The attribute used in this way is called inherited attribute. Of course, it may be worked in the reverse way, i.e., the attribute value is transmitted from where it is obtained in the sentence to the start symbol, and the attributes of this kind are called synthetic. At the beginning, only terminal symbol have the synthetic attribute. The values of synthetic attribute are directly obtained from the program text. Synthetic attribute of a child node may be accessed by the computation rules of the parent node, and further computation is allowed to take place on the parent node. Notice that the computation can only be carried out when all values which the computation depends on are determined. The computation on parent node not only becomes the synthetic attribute on the node but also the inherited attributes of its children.

Now we add the attributes to the productions of the context-free grammar [4], where the upwards arrow denotes the synthetic attribute while the downwards arrow denotes the inherited attribute.

```
<PROGRAM>::=program <name>↑NAME
            (<PROGRAM PARAMETERS>)
            <BLOCK>↓STANDARDENV↓{ }↓{ }
```

The uppercase letters following the arrows represent the attribute variables. From the representation, we see that NAME has the synthetic attribute as its value and is obtained from the lexical analysis. STANDARDENV has inherited attribute as its value and is obtained from the set of standard identifiers and their implications.

There are two more inherited attributes that belong to block. They are empty at the moment. They are any formal parameters and any global labels. We now supplement it as follows:

```
<BLOCK>↓GLOB↓FORM↓GLOBLAB ::=<LABEL DECLARATION>↑LOCLAB
        <CONSTANT DEFINITION>↓GLOB↓FORM↑NEWLOC1
        <TYPE DEFINITION> ↓GLOB↓NEWLOC1↑NEWLOC2
        <VARIABLE DECLARATION>↓GLOB↓NEWLOC2↑NEWLOC3
        <PROCEDURE and FUNCTION DECLARARION>↓GLOB↓NEWLOC3↑LABELS↑
NEWLOC
        <STATEMENT PART>↓ENV↓LABELS↑STMLAB
```

Now we expatiate these attributes. GLOB, FORM, and GLOBLAB represent respectively global variables, formal parameters, and global labels. These global attributes belong to inherited attributes. The local labels that belong to <LABEL DECLARATION> obtain their values from the program and they are synthetic attributes. The global properties and formal parameters of <CONSTANT DEFINITION> belong to inherited attributes while its NEWLOC1 represents new local constants. Their values are obtained from the program and they are also synthetic attributes. As we mentioned above that synthetic attributes not only can be the synthetic attributes of the parent node, but also become the inherited attributes of its children nodes. This is shown in our explanation above. NEWLOC1 originally was a synthetic attribute in <CONSTANT DEFINITION>, but it becomes the inherited attribute in <TYPE DEFINITION>.

NEWLOC2 and NEWLOC3 have the same transformation.

Besides, they have to obey the following rules:

1) In order to form ENV, all the identifiers that are in GLOB but not in NEWLOC should be added to NEWLOC.

2) In order to form LABELS, all the labels that are in GLOBLAB but not in LOCLAB should be added to LOCLAB.

3) STMLAB (i.e., the labels of statements) is the subset of LABELS.

The attributes of productions defined in this way may make sure that the definition occurrences of the local identifiers always precede their applied occurrences, and local constants (rather than local variables) may occur in type definition, etc., Furthermore we have

```
<STATEMENT PART>↓ENV↓LABELS↑STMLAB
::=<COMPOUND STATEMENT>↓ENV↓LABELS↑STMLAB
<COMPOUND STATEMENT> ↓ENV↓LABELS↑STMLAB
::=begin
      <STATEMENT>↓ENV↓LABELS↑STMLAB
        { ;<STATEMENT>↓ENV↓LABELS↑STMLABi}
   end
```

where the part inside { } may have null or multiple occurrences. And STMLABi are disjoint. STMLAB is the union of STMLABi.

```
<STATEMENT PART>↓ENV↓LABELS↑STMLAB
   ::=<COMPOUND STATEMENT>↓ENV↓LABELS↑STMLAB
<COMPOUND STATEMENT>↓ENV↓LABELS↑STMLAB
   ::= begin
      <STATEMENT>↓ENV↓LABELS↑STMLAB
      { ;<STATEMENT>↓ENV↓LABELS↑STMLABi}
      end
```

where the items inside { } may occur null or multiple times. And STMLABi all are disjoint. STAMLAB is their union.

```
<STATEMENT>↓ENV↓LABELS↑STMLAB
   ::=<NOLABEL STATEMENT>↓ENV↓LABELS↑STMLAB
      |<LABEL>↑LABEL:<NOLABEL STATEMENT>↓ENV↓ LABELS↑STMLAB
```

where STMLAB=LABELS∪STMLAB.

```
<NOLABEL STATEMENT>↓ENV↓LABELS↑STMLAB
   ::=<SIMPLE STATEMENT>↓ENV↓LABELS↑STMLAB
      |<STRUCTURED STATEMENT>↓ENV↓LABELS↑STMLAB
<SIMPLE STATEMENT>↓ENV↓LABELS↑STMLAB
   ::=<ASSIGNMENT STATEMENT>↓ENV
      |<PROCEDURE STATEMENT>↓ENV
```

```
|<GOTO STATEMENT> ↓LABELS
|<NULL STATEMENT>
```

Notice that the simple statement (unless goto statement) cannot contain any label. As for goto statement, label is a part of the statement.

```
<STRUCTURED STATEMENT>↓ENV↓LABELS↑STMLAB
  ::=<COMPOUND STATEMENT> ↓ENV↓LABELS↑STMLAB
    |<CONDITIONAL SATATEMENT>↓ENV↓LABELS↑STMLAB
    |<REPEAT STATEMENT> ↓ENV↓LABELS↑STMLAB
    |<WITH STATEMENT>↓ENV↓LABELS↑STMLAB
<ASSIGNMENT STATEMENT>↓ENV::= <VARIABLE>↓ENV↑TYPE1
                          :=<EXPRESSION>↓ENV↑TYPE2
```

where TYPE1 is the type of the variable in ENV. TYPE1 and TYPE2 are assignment compatible.

It is needed to point out that the categorizing attribute as synthetic and inherited is not logically necessary, but it is very helpful. And this categorization is essential part of the theory of attribute grammars.

In summary, the attribute grammar is based on the context-free grammar for defining the attributes of terminals and nonterminals. Then in turn it describes the non-context-free features of the language. In fact, any 0 type language may be described by the attribute grammar. Therefore, the attribute grammar is functionally powerful. Programming language may be seen as the context-free language with additional a number of non-context-free constraints. This implies that the attribute grammar can handle them well, and the technique that generates efficient analytical program from proper attribute grammar has been developed. Moreover the technique has very good readability, hence the attribute grammar can deal with the programming language well. Therefore, as the supplement of the context-free grammar, the attribute grammar meets both the requirements of programmers for the definition of syntax and semantics of the language [5], and the requirements of compiler writers for the implementation of the language.

8.3 Dependence Graph and Evaluation of Attributes

In the last section, we mentioned that for every production rule like A → $M_1M_2...M_n$ there is a series evaluation rules (i.e., attribute evaluation rules) for evaluating every attribute. And this is intimately related to dependency graph. The dependency graph is used for the description of evaluation rules. Therefore, it is needed to define the dependency graph first.

Definition 8.1 Dependency graph. In the parsing tree that corresponds to production rule A → $M_1M_2...M_n$, if the attribute b of a node depends on attribute c, then on the node the semantic rule evaluation for b must be carried out after the evaluation for c. In a parsing tree, the inter dependency relation between the synthetic attribute and inherited attribute may be described via the directed graph. This directed graph is called dependency graph.

Fig. 8.1 shows a simple and yet practical attribute grammar rule. It presents the constant definition declaration via nonterminals Defined-identifier and Expression.

```
Constant-definition(INH old symbol table, SYN new symbol table)
→"CONST" defined-identifier=Expression";"
ATTRIBUTE RULES:
    SET Expression.symbol table To
        Constant-definition.old symbol table;
    SET constant-definition.new symbol table To
      Update symbol table (
          Constant-definition.old table;
          Defined-identifier.name;
          Check type of constant-definition (Expression.Type)
          Expression.Value
      );
      Defined-identifier (SYN name)→...
      Expression (INH symbol table, SYN type, SYN value)→...
```

Fig. 8.1 A simple attribute rule in the constant definition [6].

In the declaration of the constant definition, there are two nonterminals Defined-identifier and Expression. The attribute grammar creates two nodes with two attributes for the grammar rule. The two attributes are an old symbol table and a new symbol table. The first one is an inherited attribute that represents the symbol table before the constant table was applied; the second one is a synthetic attribute that represents the symbol table after the identifier is inserted. The values of these two attributes are obtained through attribute evaluation rules. The first evaluation rule assigns the inherited attribute symbol table of Expression to the inherited attribute Constant-definition.old symbol table, hence the evaluation rule of Expression may refer it to determine the synthetic values of Expression type and Value. The symbol names in the grammar can be used as the identifiers in the evaluation rules. Identifier Expression represents arbitrary node created for the rule Expression. The attributes of that node may be accessed just as that they are the segments of a record. The second evaluation rule creates a new symbol table and identifies it as the Constant-definition.new symbol table. It is done via the calling function Update symbol table(). This function occurs in somewhere else with the following declaration:

```
FUNCTION Update symbol table (
    Symbol table, Name, Type, Value )
```

```
Returning a symbol table;
```

The number of actual parameters of the Update symbol table in Fig. 8.1 should be the same as that of formal parameters here. The symbol table is replaced by the old symbol table. The name is replaced by the Defined-identifier name. The type is replaced by the Expression type. Value is replaced by Expression value.

The rule dependency [7] of Constant-definition in Fig. 8.1 is shown in Fig. 8.2.

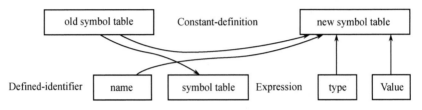

Fig. 8.2 Rule dependency of constant definition in Fig. 8.1.

There are two more points that need to explain about Fig. 8.1. At first, in the function Update symbol table, the nonterminal Defined-identifier, not only the identifier, is used. This is because the two are significantly different. The occurrence of an identifier definition, i.e., the identifier only presents one piece of information, that is its name, while another occurrence of identifier application, i.e., the Defined-identifier presents many other information besides its name, such as range information, type, categories (they are constants, variables, parameters, segments, selectors, etc), values, distributed information, etc. Secondly, in the function Update symbol table, Checked type of constant, definition (Expression.type), not only the Expression.type is used. This is because the execution of context check of constant type requires calling functions, rather than directly using values. And the check is necessary. If the check succeeds, it will return the initial Expression type that is also what we need. Otherwise it will issue error information, and the routine will return a special value Erroneous-type.

Besides, it is also needed to distinguish the difference between the data stream and dependency relation. In Fig. 8.2, the arrows represent the data stream, rather than the dependency relation. If the data stream flows from variable a to variable b, then b depends on a. The data dependency sometimes is denoted in pairs. For example, (a, b) implies that b depends on a. It also implies that "data flow from a to b", or "a is the precondition of b". Simply speaking, the attribute dependency graph actually contains arrow heads of the data stream.

Now we add the secondary attributes of Expression to constant definition of Fig. 8.1, as shown in Fig. 8.3. In this way, we create the complete data flow for the constant definition.

```
Expression (INH symbol table, SYN type, SYN Value)→
  Number
  ATTRIBUTE RULES:
    SET Expression, type To Number, type;
    SET Expression, Value To Number, Value;
```

Fig. 8.3 Secondary attribute grammar of Expression.

If CONST Pi = 3.141 592 65 is added, then the result is shown in Fig. 8.4. Usually, the semantics of expression depends on the contents of the symbol table while the symbol table is provided in advance. Therefore, we say that the symbol table is an inherited attribute of Expression. The semantics of a number, however, is independent to symbol table, hence this is the reason why there is no arrow from the number to the symbol table.

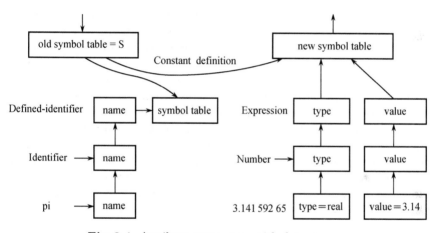

Fig. 8.4 Attribute syntax tree with data stream.

We have mentioned previously that the attribute grammar involves evaluation of the attributes, it provides a series of relative evaluation rules — attribute evaluation rules. For example, the evaluation of the production rule A→BCD requires that at the end of output the attribute value is assigned. Before the general method of the attribute evaluation is given, we discuss the procedure of the attribute evaluation of the production. In Fig. 8.5, four nodes A, B, C, and D are given. Each node has the inherited attribute (INH) and the synthetic attribute (SYN) respectively locating on both sides of the node. The arrow of output has two directions, the upwards points to the synthetic attribute of A, the downwards points to the inherited attributes of B, C, and D. Consequently the evaluation rule depends on the parent node of A, then via passing the attribute value of A it provides information downwards. It also depends on the children nodes of A, i.e., B, C, and D. Then via assigning the value to their synthetic attribute it provides the value upwards.

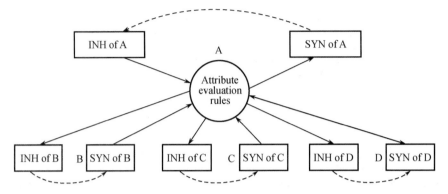

Fig. 8.5 A data stream in nodes with attributes.

From Fig. 8.5 it may be seen that the direction of the data stream is flowing from the inherited attribute of A to the synthetic attribute of A, the same
rules apply to nodes B, C, and D. Hence under their respective evaluation
rules, the data stream flows from each inherited attribute to the synthetic
attribute. Meanwhile, the evaluation rules of A cause the data stream also
flowing from the synthetic attribute to the inherited attribute of B, the same
as for C and D. The same rule also works for node A. Therefore, the data
stream also flows from the synthetic attribute of A to its inherited attribute.
The data stream is not shown on the Figure. Generally speaking, the inherited attribute may be regarded as an input parameter while the synthetic
attribute may be regarded as the output parameter. There is time order on
input and output. In general, input should precede output. But there is also
some exception, some synthetic attributes may acquire values before inherited
attributes [8].

The following is the general method for the attribute evaluation:

1) Create corresponding abstract syntax tree.

2) Construct attribute dependency graph.

3) Allocate space for attributes of each node of the tree.

4) Fill the attributes of terminals of the tree with the values acquired
from representation of terminals.

5) Topologically sorts out the nodes of the dependency graph. Then according to the order execute the evaluation rules to assign values to attributes,
until no more new value may be assigned. And make sure that only where
there is one attribute value may be used then can it be used, and each attribute can only get one value each time.

For the attribute syntax tree of Fig. 8.4, we may perform the evaluation
according to the evaluation method specified above. The order of the attribute
evaluation may be determined according to the direction of the data stream.
The attribute syntax tree obtained after the attribute evaluation is shown in
Fig. 8.6.

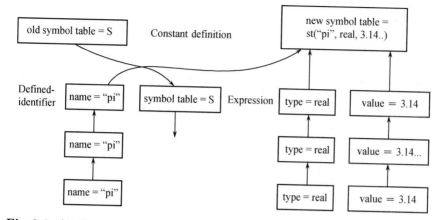

Fig. 8.6 Attribute syntax tree of Fig. 8.4 obtained after the attribute evaluation.

The simple attribute evaluation method only allows the value assignments in the following form:

```
attribute₁=func₁(attribute₁,₁, attribute₁,₂,...)
attribute₂=func₂(attribute₂,₁, attribute₂,₂,...)
      ......
```

More complex attribute evaluation allows that in the rule part some features of the practical programming language are used. For example, the statements if, while, case, etc., and local variables are called local attributes.

A simple and the most general method that realizes the attribute evaluation is only to realize the data stream machine. The method that realizes the data stream machine is: access all the nodes of the data stream graph, finish all possible assignment in each node. Repeat the procedure until all the synthetic attributes of the root have obtained values. Only when all the attributes which an assignment needs have had values then can the assignment be carried out. This method is called dynamic attribute evaluation as the order which the evaluation depends on is determined on run time of the compiler.

8.3.1   Dynamic Attribute Evaluation

The role of the attribute grammar is that it can transmit from any place of the parsing tree to places with a controllable mode. In order to show the attribute evaluation method, we illustrate it via a simple attribute grammar. It actually is a dynamic attribute evaluation. For example, it may be used to compute the code of letters in ASCII (American Standard Code for Information Interchange) or in EBCDIC (Extended Binary-Coded Decimal

Interchange Code) [9].

In order for readers to understand the two codes, we briefly introduce them here. Table 8.1 is the list of ASCII.

Table 8.1 ASCII

Decimal code	Character	Decimal code	Character	Decimal code	Character
0	NUL	37	%	74	J
1	SOH	38	&	75	K
2	STX	39	'	76	L
3	ETX	40	(	77	M
4	EOT	41	)	78	N
5	ENQ	42	*	79	O
6	ACK	43	+	80	P
7	BEL	44	,	81	Q
8	BS	45	–	82	R
9	HT	46	.	83	S
10	LF	47	/	84	T
11	VT	48	0	85	U
12	FF	49	1	86	V
13	CR	50	2	87	W
14	SO	51	3	88	X
15	SI	52	4	89	Y
16	DLE	53	5	90	Z
17	DC1	54	6	91	[
18	DC2	55	5	92	\
19	DC3	56	8	93	]
20	DC4	57	9	94	↑
21	NAK	58	:	95	←
22	SYN	59	;	96	`
23	ETB	60	<	97	a
24	CAN	61	=	98	b
25	EM	62	>	99	c
26	SUB	63	?	100	d
27	ESC	64	@	101	e
28	FS	65	A	102	f
29	GS	66	B	103	g
30	RS	67	C	104	h
31	US	68	D	105	i
32	SP	69	E	106	j
33	!	70	F	107	k
34	"	71	G	108	l
35	#	72	H	109	m
36	$	73	I	110	n

Continued

Decimal code	Character	Decimal code	Character	Decimal code	Character
111	o	117	u	123	{
112	p	118	v	124	|
113	q	119	w	125	}
114	r	120	x	126	~
115	s	121	y	127	DEL
116	t	122	z		

For EBCDIC, we do not list the specific codes in details, but we show its format. EBCDIC consists of eight bits too, and the eight bits are divided into two zones. The first four bits constitute the zone, and the last four bits constitute the digit. Both zone and digit constitute the code of characters in EBCDIC.

```
8   4   2   1          8   4   2   1
+---+---+---+---+      +---+---+---+---+
| 0 | 0 | 1 | 1 |      | 0 | 1 | 0 | 1 |
+---+---+---+---+      +---+---+---+---+
      zone                  digit
```

The digits shown on the top represent the weight of each bit. Fig. 8.7 below presents the grammar of ASCII and EBCDIC.

```
Code→↑Digit-Seq↓Base-Tag
Digit-Seq→↑Digit-Seq Digit | Digit
Digit→Digit-Token
Digit-Token→0 | 1 | 2 | 3 | 4 | 5 | 6 | 7 | 8 | 9
Base-Tag→ 'A' | 'E'
```

Fig. 8.7 A context-free grammar of ASCII and EBCDIC.

The grammar defines the grammar of ASCII and EBCDIC as well as the attributes of the elements. In the last production, A stands for ASCII while E stands for EBCDIC. If the Base-Tag A following the series of digits, then this is a code of character in ASCII. If E following the series of digits, then it is a code of character in EBCDIC. The key point here is that the evaluation of the code of character depends on the Base-Tag (A and E). But for the sake of simplicity, we omit the details, instead we just use the real Digit-Seq value.

Fig. 8.8 shows more concrete attribute grammar of ASCII and EBCDIC.

From Fig. 8.8 it is easy to draw the dependency graph of Code, Digit-Seq, Digit and Base-Tag. But we omit it as it mainly involves the issues of implementations rather than the principles.

In order to implement the data stream by the method specified above, we must visit all the nodes on the dependency graph. Usually when visiting these nodes one should avoid the infinite loop. There is a simple way to avoid loop,

```
Code(SYN Value)→
    ↑Digit-Seq↓Base-Tag
    ATTRIBUTE RULES
      SET Digit-Seq.Base To Base-Tag.Base ;
      SET Code.Value To Digit-Seq.Value;
Digit-Seq( INH Base.SYN Value)→
    ↑Digit.Seq[1]*↑Digit
    ATTRIBUTE RULES
    SET Digit-Seq[1].Base To Digit-Seq.Base;
    SET Digit.Base To Digit.Seq.Base;
    SET Digit-Seq.Value To Digit-Seq.Value;
    |Digit
    ATTRIBUTE RULES
    SET Digit.Base To Digit-Seq.Base;
    SET Digit-Seq.Value To Digit.Value;
Digit(INH Base,SYN Value)→
  Digit-Token
    ATTRIBUTE RULES
      SET Digit.Value  To Checked Digit Value(
      Value-of (Digit-Token,repr[0]-Value,of ('0',
        Base
        );
Base-Tag(SYN Base)→
   'A'
    ATTRIBUTE RULES
      SET Base-Tag.Base To ASCII;
      'E'
    ATTRIBUTE RULES
      SET Base-Tag. Base To EBCDIC;
```

Fig. 8.8 The Attribute grammar of ASCII and EBCDIC

Note: Digit-Seq[1] above may be regarded as the parent node of Digit-Seq, to distinguish it from Digit-Seq.

that is, to link these nodes to the parsing tree to visit them, since parsing tree has no loop. Then recursively traveling all nodes in the parsing tree may automatically visit all the nodes on the dependency graph. On every node, we complete all the assignments according to the evaluation rules as much as possible, then travel children nodes, and attempt to do the assignments again according to the rules when returning from them. The assignments before traversing are to transmit inherited attributes downwards while assignments after traveling are to acquire synthetic attributes and transmit them upwards.

8.3.2 Loop Handling

Since in the attribute evaluation, starting from some node, then the evaluation will traverse children of the node, sequentially it maybe returns to the node. In this case the loop will occur. If the loop continues infinitely, our work will be affected by the undesirable thing. Therefore, we must prevent the loop from happening. In order to do so it is necessary to detect the existence of the loop. The work may be done through both a dynamic loop detection and a static loop detection.

In the dynamic loop detection the loop is detected during the attribute evaluation of a practical parsing tree when the loop exists in the parsing tree. The static loop detection deduces whether the parsing tree can generate a loop or not from attribute grammar itself. What it detects is all the parsing trees the grammar generates. Therefore, if the dynamic loop detection does not find any loop in the specific parsing tree, then we consider that the specific parsing tree has no loops. If the static loop detection has not found any loop in the detection of an attribute grammar, then we consider that all the parsing trees which the grammar generates have no loops. Therefore, the static loop detection is more valuable than the dynamic loop detection but also more difficult.

Now we further analyze these two detection methods.

For the dynamic loop detection, there is a slightly rough method that checks the number of rings. If the parsing tree has m attributes, but we found that it contains more than m rings, then we can confirm that the parsing tree contains loops, because if the parsing tree has no loops, then each ring may evaluate at most one attribute. Therefore, if the evaluation proceeded after m runs, all the evaluation should finish. If it did not stop, it means that it must contain loop.

For the static loop detection, we need to seek for the reasons that the loop exists from the production rules. Obviously, a loop cannot be generated from the dependency graph of a production rule R, because the attribute evaluation rule may assign values to an attribution set (including the inherited attributes of R's children nodes and synthetic attributes of R) and what it used is another attribute set (including the synthetic attributes of R's children nodes and inherited attributes of R). If the two sets disjoint, then they have no common elements, so they cannot form a loop. In a parsing tree if there exists an attribute dependency loop, then the data stream must leave the original node, traverse around some part of the tree, and then back to the node. Perhaps the process may move in a roundabout way until it returns to the original attribute node. For example, it departs from an inherited attribute of the node N, goes down to the tree below N, at the bottom it travels to a subtree twice, and travels to another subtree once, then it goes up to a synthetic attribute of N, then continues to go to the rest of the tree, where it passes through the left brother node of N, and then passes through the right brother node of N, finally returns to node N, reaches an inherited attribute of N. If the inherited attribute is the same as that it left from, the dependency loop forms.

In an attribute dependency graph, for a node, there may be two dependencies, that are dependency from the inherited attribute to the synthetic attribute and from the synthetic attribute to the inherited attribute. The former one is called the IS (Inherited-synthetic) dependency and the later is called the SI (Synthetic-Inherited) dependency. The IS-SI graph may be used to detect the existence of loops as the loops satisfy the transitive relation, hence they may be used for the detection of the existence of loops. Through ring, the detection of loops is possible.

8.4 L Attribute Grammas and S Attribute Grammars

The research on attribute grammars is mainly caused by the need for specifying the non-context-free features of programming languages. It involves evaluation rules. On the implementation of these evaluation rules is also the objects of our research because some special features of the evaluation rules are likely to bring some conveniences or advantages. On the section, we will discuss L attributes and S attributes, and they are just what we talk about.

Definition 8.2 A class of syntax-directed definitions is called L attributed definitions, if their attributes can always be evaluated in the depth-first search order. L here stands for left, because attribute information appears to flow from left to right. Therefore, on the way of traversing the parsing tree from left to right, the attribute evaluation may be done [10].

A syntax-directed definition is L attributed if each inherited attribute of X_j, $1 \leqslant j \leqslant n$, on the right side of $A \rightarrow X_1 X_2 \ldots X_n$, depends only on:

1) the attributes of the symbols X_1, X_2, $\ldots$, X_{j-1} to the left of X_j in the production;

2) the inherited attribute of A.

Hence the feature of L attributes is that the inherited attribute of a subnode of a nonterminal N depends only the synthetic attributes of left subnodes of the production and the inherited attributes of A itself. That means that the data dependency graph of any production has no the data stream arrow from a subnode to itself or to its left subnode.

Many programming languages are of L attributed as their intrinsic data flow from left to right is helpful for programmers to read and to understand programs. For example, the dependency graph of Constant-definition, where there is no data stream from Expression to Defined-identifier (from right to left). But the example of ASCII and EBCDIC is not L attribute grammar as there is a data stream from right to left in it.

Fig. 8.9 shows part of analytical tree of L attribute grammar.

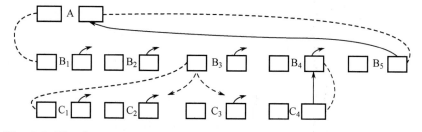

Fig. 8.9 The data stream in part of analytical tree of an L attribute grammar.

In the figure above, every node has two boxes, one in each side. The left one represents the inherited attribute while right one represents the synthetic attribute. The name of the node is in between. The node A has five subnodes B_1, B_2, B_3, B_4, and B_5, while C_1, C_2, C_3, and C_4 are subnodes of B_3. The upwards arrow represents the synthetic attribute data stream of the subnode, they all point to right or the synthetic attributes of the parent node. When the attribute evaluation starts functioning on a node, all the inherited attributes of the node have been acquired, and these attributes may be transferred to any its subnodes that need them. On the figure, they are shown via dotted lines with arrows.

Suppose that the attribute evaluation is functioning on the node C_3, there are only two attribute sets that participate in the function:

- All the attributes of nodes that are on the path from the top to the node that is processed. That are C_3, B_3, and A.
- The synthetic attributes of left sibling nodes of those nodes. That are C_1, C_2, B_1, and B_2.

The right sibling of C_3, B_3 and A did not participate in as their synthetic attributes do not function.

On the figure one thing is hided. That is that the inherited attributes remain in node where they belong to. Their values are transferred along the path from top to the node that is processed (for example, the constant definition that was described before). This structure is just provided by a top-down analysis.

The attribute evaluation in L attribute grammar may be conveniently contained in the top-down analysis. And applying top-down analysis also entails some tricks to complete the evaluation. The key problem is that the inherited attributes must be transferred from a parent node to subnodes. On the other hand, in the bottom-up analysis, only when all the subnodes have been processed, then may thing on the parent node be defined and created. Therefore, when any inherited attribute is needed, there is no place yet to transfer it down.

The bottom-up analysis program, however, has a stack to shift in terminals and to reduce nonterminals. We establish the correspondence between the stack and the attribute stack. The attribute stack may keep attributes of the stack element on the same order of elements. In this way, it will be alright as long as inherited attributes can be put on the stack in advance. But in order to put the inherited tributes into the tack, some code for doing so must be executed. In the bottom-up analysis, the code may only be executed in the end of the production to be selected, i.e., when all corresponding entries have been recognized and the reduction is to be done. But now we want to do it in the midst of the production, we require that

$$A{\to}B\{C; \text{inh-attr}:=f(B.\text{syn.attr});C\}$$

where the part in the brackets is the actions we need to execute, the assignment of inherited attribute to C. In order to do so, we introduce ε-production:

$$A{\to}B \text{ A-actional } C$$
$$A\text{-actional} \to \varepsilon\{C.\text{inh-attr}:=f(B.\text{syn-attr});\}$$

Now the code in A-actional is at the end of a production to be selected, and it will be executed when the right part of A.actional$\to \varepsilon$ is reduced. This is feasible. But the grammar is no longer of LALR(1) as the introduction of ε into the grammar is harmful to the bottom-up syntactical analysis. Only when the entry A$\to$B. C is the only entry in the state set that can the analysis program function and determine this entry, and execute the segment of codes. Moreover, it also ensures that the parent node is A, and the analysis program knew that it would need to create the parent node.

There are other approaches that attribute grammars carry out the bottom-up analysis. One of them is to use such an attribute stack: It takes the position of only synthetic attribute as that of only inherited attribute of the next node. In this case, there is no need to execute any code.

Definition 8.3 An attribute grammar is called S-attribute grammar, if all the attributes in it are synthesized and there is no inherited attribute.

Since synthetic attributes are transferred from the bottom to the top, it is easy to carry out the bottom-up analysis. The synthetic attributes of every subnode are put into the stack, and then the code at the end of production to be selected functions. Its parent node pops it out from the stack, processes it and replaces the attributes with the synthetic attributes of the parent node.

An L attribute grammar can be easily transformed to the S attribute grammar, but the transformation does not enhance the readability of the method. The basic method of the transformation is to suspend the evaluation that cannot be carried out now until when they can be done. In addition, the more particular thing is any evaluation that needs inherited attribute will be replaced by data structure that defines the evaluation and creates all the synthetic attributes. The data structure will act as a synthetic attribute, and will be transferred upwards to the level where the missing inherited attribute may be used. It will be used as the synthetic attribute of a constant or a node to carry out the evaluation required. By this way, any L attribute grammar can be transformed to the S attribute grammar.

Fig. 8.10 shows the attribute value stream of the abstract syntax tree to summary the L attribute grammars and S attribute grammars.

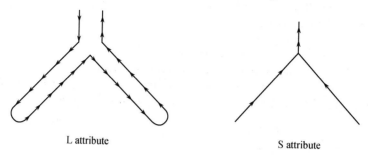

L attribute   S attribute

Fig. 8.10 L attribute and S attribute.

From the figure, we can see that in L attribute grammars the attribute values flow down along a branch then flow up again along the next branch. But in S attribute grammars the attribute values only flow along one direction, down to up.

We now finish the discussion of attribute grammars. They are the useful supplement of context-free grammars. Especially when we handle the nonterminals, obviously we need them to help the compilation process.

Problems

Problem 8.1 Let synthesized attribute val give the value of the binary number generated by S in the following grammar. For example, on input 110.011, S.val = 6.375

$$S \to L.L|L,$$
$$L \to LB|B,$$
$$B \to 0|1.$$

1) Use synthesized attributes to determine S.val.

2) Determine S.val with a syntax-directed definition in which the only synthesized attribute of B is c, giving the contribution of the bit generated by B to the final value. For example, the contribution of the first and last bits in 110.011 to the value 6.375 is 4 and 0.125, respectively.

Problem 8.2 Suppose that we have an L-attributed definition whose underlying grammar is either LL(1), or one for which we can resolve ambiguities and construct a predictive parser. Show that we may keep inherited and synthesized attributes on the parser stack of a top-down parser driven by the predictive parsing table.

Problem 8.3 For each following item, point out whether it belongs to a nonterminal or a production rule of a nonterminal.

1) Inherited attribute.

2) Synthesized attribute.

3) Attribute evaluation rule.

4) Dependence graph.

5) IS-SI graph.

6) The nodes of abstract parser tree.

7) The subnode pointers of the abstract parser tree.

Problem 8.4 Consider the following attribute grammar, construct the IS-SI graph of A, and point out the loop contained in the grammar.

$$S(SYN\ S) \rightarrow$$

$$A(i_1, s_1)$$

ATTRIBUTE RULES:

SET i_1 TO s_1 ;

SET s TO s_1;

$A(INH\ i_1,\ SYN\ s_1) \rightarrow$

$A(i_2, s_2)$ 'a'

ATTRIBUTE RULES:

SET i_2 TO s_1;

SET s_1 TO s_2 ;

|

$B(i_2, s_2)$

ATTRIBUTE RULES:

SET i_2 TO s_1;

SET s_1 TO s_2 ;

$B(INH\ I,\ SYN\ s) \rightarrow$

'b'

ATTRIBUTE RULES; SET s TO c;

Problem 8.5 Given the following attributes of the nonterminals

$$S(INH\ i_1, i_2,\ SYN\ s_1, s_2) \rightarrow$$

T U

ATTRIBUTE RULES:

SET T.i TO $f_1(S.i_1, U.s)$;

SET U.i TO $f_2(S.i_2)$;

SET $S.s_1$ TO $f_3(T.s)$;

SET S.s) TO $f_4(U.s)$;

Draw its complete dependence graph.

References

[1] Irons ET (1961) A syntax directed compiler for Algol 60. Comm ACM, 4(1): 51–55.

[2] Knuth DE (1968) Semantics of context-free languages. Mathmatical Systems Theory 2(2): 127–145. Etrata 5(1): 95–96.

[3] Reps TW (1984) Generating Language-Based Environments. MIT Press, Cambridge.

[4] Lewis PM, Rosenktrantz DJ, Stearns RE (1974) Attributed translations. J Computer and System Sciences, 9(3): 279–307.

[5] Mayoh BH (1981) Attribute grammars and mathematical semantics. SiAM J Computing 10(3): 503–518.

[6] Kennedy K, Ramanathan J (1979) A deterministic attribute grammar evaluator based on dynamic sequencing. TOPLAS 1(1): 142–160.

[7] Engelfrief J (1984) Attribute evaluation methods. Lorho pp 103–138.

[8] Cohen R, Harry E (1979) Automatic generation of near-optimal linear-time translators for non-circular attribute grammars. Sixth ACM Symposium on Principles of Programming Languages, pp 121–134.

[9] Kastens U (1980) Ordered attribute grammars. Acta Informatica, 13(3): 229–256.

[10] Bochmann GV (1976) Semantics evaluation from left to right. Comm ACM, 19(2): 55–62.

Chapter 9 Algebraic Method of Compiler Design

We must not lose sight of the ultimate goal, that of the construction of programming language implementations which are known to be correct by virtue of quality of the logical reasoning which has been devoted to them. Of course, such an implementation will still need to be comprehensively tested before delivery; but it will immediately pass all the tests, and then continue to work correctly for the benefit of programmers forever after.

C.A.R. Hoare

Setting up equations is like translating from one language into another.

G. Polya

9.1 Motivation of the Chapter

This chapter will be independent of the last several chapters. It will introduce a grand new method for the design of compilers of the procedure oriented programming languages. The method is based on that these languages satisfy the algebraic laws. The new practical strategy is to reduce any source program to a canonical form through a series algebraic transformations. And the canonical form precisely specifies the features of the object machine. The outstanding character of the method is that the correctness of the compiler is ensured by that of each algebra transformation, while the correctness of these transformations is proven by more basic laws.

The aims of introduceing new methods in compiler design are as follows. At first, we want to widen the thinking train of readers. When they study the methods of compiler design, especially when they are engaged in the design of a compiler, they know that apart from the methods we introduce before, there are many different ones. Furthermore, we want to show the frontier of the field, especially the effort of associating correctness with the translation process. No doubt, the correctness is essential for any software [1]. Without it, software has no any value. The assertion is absolute right for compilers. This is why since 1960s a large number of approaches have been suggested to tackle the problem of compiler correctness. But we cannot include all the approaches in this book. We choose the current method because it has some advantages over other existing methods. It also benefits from the view described by others: the compilation process is completely characterized within a uniform framework of a procedural language whose semantics is given by algebraic laws. We will refer to this language as a reasoning language. The source language is a subset of this language. But we also supplement additional specification operators such as constructions to model assumptions and assertions. By doing so the approach develops the compiler while it provides the proof of correctness of the compiler. As long as the algebraic transformations are correct, then the compiler derived from these transformations in the canonical form is also correct. Finally, we want to emphasize the importance of the formal method to the reader. Denotational, algebraic and axiomatic methods all belong to category of formal methods. Many researchers are working on the methods and accomplish high achievements. Therefore, the reader is encouraged to make an effort on this aspect. One thing should be pointed out that the chapter emphasizes the algebraic approach to compilation [2], rather than the translation between particular pairs of languages. It only involves the code generation phase of the compiler, instead of the entire development process of the compiler. Therefore though this chapter is independent of the last chapters, it has intimate relation with the following chapters, intermediate code generation and object code generation.

9.2 Source Language

We first introduce the source language that is a subset of the reasoning language. We need to describe it because our goal is to translate the programs written in the source language to the object language. The language can be considered as an extension of the guarded command language proposed by E.W. Dijkstra with procedures and general recursions.

The operators of the source programming language are listed in Fig. 9.1, in which we use x to stand for an arbitrary program variable, e for an expression, b for a Boolean expression, p and q for program and X for a program identifier.

We make explanation about these operators.

- skip   When the operator is executed, it produces no change for the program and terminates successfully.
- x := e   The assignment starts with the evaluation of the expression e. Its value is then assigned to x. For the sake of simplicity, we assume that the evaluation of e always works without failure. So the assignment always

skip	do nothing
x:=e	assignment
p;q	sequential composition
p⊓q	nondeterminism (demonic)
p◁b▷q	conditional: if b then p else q
b*p	iteration: while b do p
dec x·p	(static) declaration of variable x for use in p
proc X≅p·q	procedure X with body p and scope q
μX·p	recursive program X with body p

Fig. 9.1 The Operators of source language.

terminates.

- p; q   The program p; q runs as usual sequential composition does, that is, if the execution of p successfully terminates, then the execution of q follows that of p.

- p ⊓ q   The program p ⊓ q runs either like p or like q. This nondeterminism is called demonic. Because if p or q fails *, p ⊓ q fails. At least in principle, this is not better than the situation where p ⊓ q always fails because it cannot be relied at all.

- p ◁ b ▷ q   This is a conditional statement. Its execution starts with the evaluation of the boolean expression b. If b holds, then p is executed, otherwise q is executed.

- b * p   This is an iteration statement that stands for a loop. It starts with the evaluation of boolean expression b. If it holds p is executed and this is followed by the same iteration until b does not hold again. If b does not hold from the beginning, the statement just behaves like skip. Although iteration is a special case of the recursion, it is convenient to name it as an independent operation.

  Note: We consider that a program fails if it diverges (or aborts), the operator ⊥ has the same meaning.

- dec x · p   This is a declaration that declares the variable x for use in the program p (the scope of the declaration). Here there is a difference from common practice that we do not enforce that a variable be declared before it is used. Undeclared (or global) variable can be considered as playing the role of input and output commands: the initial values of these variables are taken as the input to the program and their final values as the output yielded by the program. Our intention is to simplify the dealing of type information.

- proc X ≅ p · q   It introduces a non-recursive procedure with name X and body p. The program q following the symbol × is the scope of the procedure. Occurrences of X in q are interpreted as the calling of procedure X. We separate procedures from the recursion with the intention of reducing complexity.

- μ X · p   This is a recursive program. It has the name X and the body p. Similar to proc X ≅ p · q above, occurrences of X in p are interpreted as recursive calls of X.

It needs to point out that the source language allows arbitrary nesting of variable and procedure declarations, as well as recursive definitions. For the purpose of generality, we avoid defining the syntax of expressions. We use uop and bop as operators of source language to stand for arbitrary unary and binary operators, respectively. According to the practical situation, we assume that the target machine has instructions that directly implement these operators.

The source language is embedded in a specification space that includes the constructions presented in Fig. 9.2. As in Fig. 9.1, x stands for an arbitrary program variable, b for boolean expression, and p and q for programs (or specification).

$\perp$	abort
$\top$	miracle
p u q	nondeterminism (angle)
$b_\perp$	assertion: if b then skip else $\perp$
$b^\top$	assumption: if b then skip else $\top$
$b \rightarrow p$	guarded command: if b then p else $\top$
$x:\in b$	generalized assignment: assign a value to x that makes b true. if not possible, $x:\in b$ acts as $\top$
var x	declaration of variable x with undetermined (dynamic) scope
end x	end the previous (dynamic) scope of x introduced by
a var	

Fig. 9.2   Specification space.

The following is the explanation of these operators.

- Abort ($\perp$)   It has the most possible undefined behaviors: it may fail to terminate, or it may terminate with any result out of expectation. Following Hoare[1, 2], we identify abort with all programs that might diverge before doing action visible to its environment. The motivation for the decision is that, in principle, any program allowing continuously to diverge may be considered as the programming error, as one can never rely on it. Later we will point out that most of the operators of the reasoning language are strict: they abort when any of their arguments abort. For example, true*skip is a divergent program as it is equivalent to the recursive program $\mu X \cdot X$. We can regard abort as a construction of source language. But we believe that no any programmer will use $\perp$ intentionally. Rather it usually arises as a consequence of undesirable computation such as non-terminating recursion.

- Miracle ($\top$)   It is the other extreme: It has the most possible defined behavior and can serve any purpose. But it is only a theoretical concept to be useful for reasoning. Obviously, it cannot be implemented; otherwise we would not need to write programs—we just let $\top$ do for us.

- Program p ⊔ q   It behaves either as p or as q. But unlike ⊓, this choice is so-called angle in that the most suitable program for a given situation is the one that is chosen. Therefore, p ⊔ q fails only when both p and q fail, and it acts as miracle then.

- Assertion $b_\perp$ The intentional use of $b_\perp$ is to model an assertion. It acts as skip if b holds at the place where the assertion is placed; otherwise it fails and it behaves like abort.

- Assumption $b^\top$ This is to model an assumption. It can be regarded as a miraculous test: it leaves the state unchanged, behaving like skip; otherwise it behaves like miracle.

- Guarded command b → p   Under the notation if b holds it impels the execution of p; Otherwise it behaves like miracle. It implies that a guard has not much difference from an assumption of the given condition.

- Program X: ∈ b   It is a generalized or nondeterministic assignment. Its effect is to assign to x an arbitrary value that makes the condition b hold. It is also suggested that when such a value does not exist the assignment acts like miracle. Therefore, the nondeterminism in this case may be regarded as angel. The main reason for such design is that we use nondeterminism to abstract the way by which control state is encoded in the target machine. Under the situation, the condition b describes the set of the next possible states and x represents the machine components, e.g. registers. If there is no such value of x that makes b true, the machine behaves like ⊤ that can serve any purpose, as we mentioned above. Our main aim is to save the compiler designers from dealing with states not satisfying b. Of course, there is alternative choice that considers the assignment failing when there is no value of x that makes b hold. The choice in this case would be demonic. There are applications where both interpretations are useful. Hence the two must be considered as reasonable.

- var x and end x   These two notations seem to be unnecessary redundancy. The operator dec is the usual construct available in most programming languages for introducing local variables with a lexical (or static) scope semantics.

Nevertheless, for reasoning purpose it is useful to have independent constructs to introduce a variable and to end its scope. From the point of view of operation, one can think of var x as pushing the current value of x into an implicit stack and end x as popping out the value from the stack, and the popped value is assigned to x. If the stack was empty, this value is arbitrary. So var x introduces x with a dynamic scope semantics, this scope extends up to the next end x is executed or up to the end of the static scope of x, whichever happens first.

Furthermore, while the source language allows only single assignment, the specification language allows multiple assignments of the form

$$x_1, \ldots, x_n := e_1, \ldots, e_n$$

Of course, multiple assignment is implementable and could also be considered as a source operator. But in this chapter we just use it for reasoning. Although some of the above constructs are not strictly necessary, as some of them can be defined in terms of others, each one represents a helpful concept both for specification and for reasoning.

We will use the algebraic laws to present the semantics of the specification (reasoning) language. Most of the laws are expressed as equations of the form p = q. Informally the equation means that p and q have the same behavior: for an arbitrary initial state s, p terminates if and only if q does, and the final state produced by p starting in s is the same as the one produced by q. The programs p and q may consume different amount of resources (for example, memory) and run at different speeds; But what the equation really means is that an external observer (who is unable to see the internal states) cannot distinguish between them. Therefore, we can replace p with q or vice versa in any context.

It is also possible to attach a boolean condition to a law, meaning that the law is guaranteed to hold only if the condition yields a true value. Furthermore, the laws can be inequations (rather than equations). These use the refinement relation informally. For the purpose of illustration, a few algebraic laws are given below. They describe the fact that $\subseteq$ is a lattice ordering (If the reader is interested in knowing more about lattice theory, he/she is encouraged to refer to modern algebraic books). For all programs p, q and r we have

$$p \subseteq \top, \qquad \text{(miracle is the top of the lattice)}$$

$$\bot \subseteq p, \qquad \text{(abort is the bottom)}$$

$$(r \subseteq p \wedge r \subseteq q) \equiv r \subseteq (p \sqcap q), \qquad (\sqcap \text{ is the greatest lower bound})$$

$$(p \subseteq r) \wedge (q \subseteq r) \equiv (p u q) \subseteq r. \qquad (u \text{ is the least upper bound})$$

An additional and extremely important fact about the refinement relation is that all the operators of the reasoning language are monotonic with respect to it. This means that if q refines p, then the replacement of p with q in any context leads to a refinement of the entire context. More formally, for an arbitrary context F:

$$p \subseteq q \Rightarrow F(p) \subseteq F(q).$$

After introducing the operators of source language and specification language, we may sequentially present an overview of the approach to compilation. But first we need to define the machine used as the target of our compiler. The target machine is very simple. It consists of four components:

P	a sequential register (program counter)
A	a general purpose register (accumulator)
M	a store for variables (RAM)
m	a store for instructions (ROM)

We need to emphasize that the essential feature of our approach to compilation is the embedding of the target language within the reasoning language. We represent the machine components as program variables and design the instructions as assignment that update the machine state. We define the instructions of our simple machine as follows:

$$load(n) \Leftrightarrow (\text{def as}) \quad A, P := M[n], P + 1.$$

(As we mentioned above, we use multiple assignment here, A is assigned to M[n], meanwhile, in doing so, the program counter is increased by one.)

$$store(n) \Leftrightarrow (\text{def as}) \quad M, \ P := (M \odot \{n \rightarrow A\}), P + 1.$$

We use value A to update the memory at position n, the program counter is increased by one.

$$bop - A(n) \Leftrightarrow (\text{def as}) \quad A, P := (A \ bop \ M[n]), \ P + 1.$$

The value in A and value in memory at position n execute a binary operation and the result is kept in A, the program counter is increased by one.

$$uop - A \Leftrightarrow (\text{def as}) \quad A, \ P := (uop \ A), P + 1.$$

The value in A executes an unary operation and the result is still kept in A, the program counter is increased by one.

$$jump(k) \Leftrightarrow (\text{def as}) \quad P := k.$$

The content of the program counter is assigned to k, so the next instruction to be executed will be at position k,

$$cjump(k) \Leftrightarrow (\text{def as}) \quad P := (P + 1 \lhd A \rhd k).$$

If the value in A holds, the next instruction to be executed is at position P+1, that means that the machine will execute consecutively, otherwise it will jump to execute instruction at position k.

Where we use map overriding ($\odot$) to update M at position n with the value of A. Of course we may use a more conventional notation M[n]:= A as well. But we do not use it because it is not suitable for reasoning since M[n] is not really a variable. Especially we will need to define operators like non-freeness and substitution that regard two variables as different if they are syntactically different; but M[e] and M[f] will be the same if e and f evaluate to the same value even if they are syntactically different.

Recall that we mentioned that we do not deal with type information. But in this context we assume that P is an integer variable, and that M is an array variable. The conditional assignment that defines cjump is just an abbreviation of the conditional

$$(P := P + 1) \lhd A \rhd (P := k).$$

A similar strategy can be adopted to model the components and instructions of other target machines.

The normal form for describing the behavior of our simple machine that executes a stored program is an iterated execution of instructions taken from the memory m at location P:

$$dec \ P, A \cdot P := s; (s \leqslant P < f) * m[P]; (P = f)_\perp,$$

where s is the intended start address and f is the finish address of the code to be executed. The requirement to start at the right instruction is expressed by the initial assignment $P := s$, and the requirement to terminate at the right place is expressed by the final assertion $(P = f)_\perp$. The iteration program $(s \leqslant P < f) * m[P]$ means that while the value of P is in between s and f, then the execution of m[P] is realized.

The design of a compiler in this approach is a constructive proof that every one, however deeply structured, can be improved by some programs in this normal form. The process is split into three main phases: elimination of control; simplification (or decomposition) of expressions and data refinement (or the change of data representation).

In order to illustrate these phases, and the compilation process in general, we present some examples. The main theorem that states the correctness of the compiler for this simple machine will be given in the end of this chapter.

Example 9.1   (A simple assignment)   At first we consider the compilation of an assignment of the form
$$x := y,$$
where both x and y are variables. That we consider so simple example is because we want to explain the entire process following all the steps. One of the tasks involved in the translation process is the elimination of nested expressions. The expected outcome of this phase is a program in which each assignment will eventually give rise to one of the patterns used to define the machine instructions. Then, by definition, the actual instruction names can be introduced in place of these patterns. Note that the above assignment does not correspond to any of the machine instructions defined above: all the instructions are defined in terms of the machine registers.

The assignment above is translated to
$$\text{dec } A \cdot A := y; \ x := A,$$
where A, as illustrated above, is the general purpose register of our simple machine. And the assignment will be translated to two instructions: a load instruction and a store instruction. It can be easily observed that the two sequential assignments behave exactly the same as $x := y$. That A is a local variable means that its scope ends after the two assignments are executed, hence its final value cannot be observed after that point.

But the transformed program still operates on abstract global variables with symbolic names, whereas the target program operates only on the concrete memory M. From the compiler's symbol table, say Ψ, an injection maps each variable onto distinct memory address, and we define a data refinement Ψ^+ that maps each program variable x onto the corresponding machine location, so the value of x is held as $M[\Psi x]^*$. The purpose of the data refinement is to substitute $M[\Psi x]$ for x throughout the program. When this data refinement is performed on our simple program it becomes
$$\text{dec } A \cdot A := M[\Psi y],$$
$$M := M \odot \{\Psi x \rightarrow A\}.$$
Among three phases which we mentioned above, that are, expression simplification, data refinement and control elimination, we have introduced the first two, only control elimination remains. The task is to reduce the nested control structure of the source program to a single flat iteration, like that of the target program. This may be done by introducing a control state variable to schedule the selection and sequencing of actions. In the case of our simple

target machine, a single pointer P indicates the location in memory of the next instruction. Then our program becomes

$$\text{dec } P, A \cdot P := s;$$
$$(s \leqslant P < s + 2) * [(P = s) \rightarrow load(\Psi y), \square(P = s + 1) \rightarrow$$
$$store(\Psi x)];$$
$$(P = s + 2)_\perp.$$

Now the whole expression is the program, we get that indicates that these instructions must be loaded into the memory m at positions s and s+1, completing the overall process. Note that the product of the compilation process is just a program in the same language (the normal form) from which we can easily obtain the sequence of generated instructions of the target language.

Note: Ψx is the address of x in the memory M, whereas $M[\Psi x]$ represents the memory cell (location) that holds this value.

Example 9.2 (A simple conditional statement)   Consider the following conditional statement that assigns x or y to z depending on whether the bop relation holds or not between x and y:

$$(z := x) \lhd x \text{ bop } y \rhd (z := y).$$

The conditional statement may express a maximum (or minimum) finding program in which case bop would stand for $\leqslant$ (or $\geqslant$). But we would prefer sticking to the notation of the source language where bop stands for arbitrary binary operators. We might derive the normal form of the statement as we did for the assignment statement step by step. But it is very similar to the first one, we just omit the details and directly present the normal form of it:

$$\text{dec } P, A \cdot P := s; (s \leqslant P < s + 8),$$
$$(P = s) \rightarrow load(\Psi_x),$$
$$\square(P = s + 1) \rightarrow A \text{ bop } M[\Psi_y],$$
$$\square(P = s + 2) \rightarrow cjump(s + 6),$$
$$\square(P = s + 3) \rightarrow load(\Psi_x),$$
$$\square(P = s + 4) \rightarrow store(\Psi_z),$$
$$\square(P = s + 5) \rightarrow jump(s + 8),$$
$$\square(P = s + 6) \rightarrow load(\Psi_y),$$
$$\square(P = s + 7) \rightarrow store(\Psi_z),$$
$$(P = s + 8)_\perp.$$

After the first instruction $((P = s) \rightarrow load(\Psi x))$ is executed, the value of x is kept in general purpose register A, so the second instruction performs bop operation between x and y and A holds the result (x bop y). If this value is false, then a jump occurs and the final two instructions are executed, then

the value of y is assigned to z, otherwise the instruction below the cjump
instruction until instruction $P = s + 5$ are executed and in this case the value
of x is assigned to z. The main feature of this approach to the compilation
is that while the compiler is designed the correctness of the compiler is also
proven. We now want to know how is it realized. From the basic algebraic
laws of the language there several theorems will be needed to carry out the
expounding and proving of the correctness of the compilation process. Now we
first study one of the main theorems, the so-called theorem of the compilation
process that expounds the correctness of that process.

Theorem 9.1   (compilation process) Let p be an arbitrary source program.
Given a constant s and a symbol table Ψ that maps each global variable of p
to the address of the memory M allocated to hold its value, there is a constant
f and a sequence of machine instructions held in m between locations s and
f such that
$$\Psi_\omega^*(p) \subseteq \text{dec } P, A \cdot P := s; (s \leqslant P < f) * m[P]; (P = f)_\perp,$$
where Ψ^* is a function (built from the symbol table Ψ) that performs the
necessary change of the data representation: from the abstract data space of
the source program to the concrete state of the machine represented by the
memory M.

Note that Ψ^* plays an essential role in the correctness statement above:
it would not make any sense to compare the program p with its normal form
directly, since they operate on different data spaces. While p operates on the
program variables x, y, ..., z its normal form operates on the concrete store
M. At the current moment we do not give the proof of the theorem, it will
be given in the end of the chapter.

9.3   Algebraic Foundation and Reasoning Language

In this section at first we will briefly describe a theoretical basis for the
kind of the refinement algebra we will be using. Then we will introduce the
reasoning language based on the refinement algebra. The source language we
use is a subset of the reasoning language. Meanwhile, in this section we will
give examples of the refinement calculi based on these ideas and address the
problem of the data refinement. We will also link our approach to compilation
to the more general task of deriving programs from specifications. Therefore,
the contents of this section are crucial to the approach to compilation which
we study.

9.3.1   Algebra Fundamentals

At first we introduce the concept of the partial order.

Definition 9.1   A pair $(S, \sqsubseteq)$ is called a partial order where S is a set and $\sqsubseteq$ is a binary relation (the partial ordering) on S satisfying the following axioms, for all x, y, z $\in$ S:

$$x \sqsubseteq x, \qquad \text{(reflexivity)}$$
$$(x \sqsubseteq y) \wedge (y \sqsubseteq z) \Rightarrow (x \sqsubseteq z), \qquad \text{(transitivity)}$$
$$(x \sqsubseteq y) \wedge (y \sqsubseteq x) \Rightarrow (x = y). \qquad \text{(antisymmetry)}$$

Definition 9.2   A pair $(S, \sqsubseteq)$ is called a total order, if $(s, \sqsubseteq)$ is a partial order and for each pair of elements in S, they all are comparable: $(x \sqsubseteq y) \vee (y \sqsubseteq x)$. For the sake of simplicity, we will abbreviate $(S, \sqsubseteq)$ to S. Wherever the misunderstanding may happen whether it stands for partial order or total order, we will make it clear.

Definition 9.3   Given a subset T of S (partial or total order), we say that $x \in S$ is an upper bound for T if $y \sqsubseteq x$ for $\forall y \in T$. x is the least upper bound of T if it is both an upper bound for T and whenever y is another upper bound for T then $x \sqsubseteq y$.

Definition 9.4   Given a subset T of S (partial or total order), we say that $x \in S$ is a lower bound for T if $x \sqsubseteq y$ for $\forall y \in T$. x is greatest lower bound of T if x is a lower bound and whenever y is another lower bound for T then $y \sqsubseteq x$.

An element $\perp$ is a least element or bottom of S if $\perp \sqsubseteq x$ for $\forall x \in S$. $\top$ is a greatest element or top of S if $x \sqsubseteq \top$ for $\forall x \in S$.

Definition 9.5   Given set S and T with T partially ordered by $\sqsubseteq_T$, the set $S \rightarrow T$ of functions from S to T is said to be partially ordered by $\sqsubseteq_T$ defined by

$$f \sqsubseteq g \Leftrightarrow (\text{def as}) \; f(x) \sqsubseteq_T g(x) \text{ for } \forall x \in S.$$

In addition, if S is partially ordered by $\sqsubseteq_S$, then f: $S \rightarrow T$ is said to be monotonic if

$$x \sqsubseteq_S y \Rightarrow f(x) \sqsubseteq_T f(y) \text{ for } \forall x, y \in S.$$

We denote by $\{S \rightarrow T\}$ the set of monotonic functions from S to T. If S is discrete (that is, $x \sqsubseteq_S y$ holds if and only if $x = y$), then $S \rightarrow T$ and $\{S \rightarrow T\}$ are identical.

Definition 9.6   Given a partially ordered set S, it is said to be a complete lattice if it contains greatest lower bounds and least upper bounds for $\forall$ T, $U \sqsubseteq S$, where T, U are the subsets of S. Geometrically the greatest lower bound is the meet of two sets while the lower upper bound is the join of two sets. A consequence is that every complete lattice has a bottom and a top element. There are two additional well-known properties of complete lattices. They are:

1) Any finite totally ordered set is a complete lattice.

2) If S is a partially ordered set and T is a complete lattice, then $\{S \to T\}$ is a complete lattice.

The boolean set $\{true, false\}$ is a simple example of a complete lattice when it is ordered by the implication relation. The least upper bound $\lor$ and the greatest lower bound $\land$ have their usual interpretations as disjunction and conjunction, respectively. The bottom element is false and the top element is true. This is actually a complete distributive lattice, since for $\forall$ a, b, c $\in$ $\{false, true\}$:

$$a \land (b \lor c) = (a \land b) \lor (a \land c),$$
$$a \lor (b \land c) = (a \lor b) \land (a \lor c).$$

In lattice theory, the above two properties are actually equivalent. The lattice under consideration has yet another property that it is a boolean lattice, since it has a complement (negation) element for every element. In the following discussion we will refer to this kind of lattices as Bool.

Now we divert to the lattice of predicates. We consider programs first. As all knows that programs usually operate on a state space formed from a set of variables. We use State to stand for the set of all possible states partially ordered by the equality relation. Therefore it is a discrete partial order. In practice we need a way to describe particular sets of states, for example, to specify the set of initial states of programs, as well as the set of final states. This can be described by boolean-valued functions (or predicates) on the state space. As State is a partial order, and Bool is a complete lattice, $\{State \to Bool\}$ is also a complete lattice. Furthermore, as State is discrete, $\{State \to Bool\}$ and State $\to$ Bool are identical. Then we will refer to it as the Predicate lattice. The Least upper bound a $\lor$ b is the disjunction of the predicates a or b, and the greatest lower bound a $\land$ b is their conjunction predicate a and b. The bottom element false describes the empty set of states and the top element true describes the set of all possible states. The concrete definitions are as follows:

$$(a \lor b) \Leftrightarrow (def \ as) \ \lambda x \cdot a(x) \lor b(x),$$
$$(a \land b) \Leftrightarrow (def \ as) \ \lambda x \cdot a(x) \land b(x),$$
$$true \Leftrightarrow (def \ as) \ \lambda x \cdot true,$$
$$false \Leftrightarrow (def \ as) \ \lambda x \cdot false,$$

Where we introduce the notation $\lambda x \cdot t$ that stands for a lambda abstraction (anonymous function) with the parameter x and body t. In the above definition, x ranges over State. The lattice ordering is the implication on predicates that is defined by pointwise extension in the usual way:

$$a \Rightarrow b \Leftrightarrow (def \ as) \forall x \cdot a(x) \Rightarrow b(x).$$

We use the notation $\forall$ x p $\to$ q (read as for all x, if p then q) to stand for the universal qualification in the predicate calculus. In particular, p can be omitted when it is equivalent to true, as in the above definition.

In this notation, it is hard to express the operations which we defined before, but with some restrictions, we still can express them as follows:

$p \sqsubseteq q \Leftrightarrow (\text{def as})\lambda x \cdot p(x) \Rightarrow q(x),$

$p \sqcap q \Leftrightarrow (\text{def as})\lambda x \cdot (p(x) \vee q(x) \vee \perp).$

The order of execution of the right hand side is that $p(x)$ is executed first if it can be executed, if it fails then $q(x)$ is executed, otherwise the result is demon.

$puq \Leftrightarrow (\text{def as})\lambda x \cdot (p(x) \vee q(x) \vee \top)$

Similarly, the order of execution of the right hand side is also from the leftmost to rightmost.

We now introduce another lattice that provides a theoretical basis for Dijkstra's view of programs as predicate transformers (functions from predicates to predicates)[3].

Definition 9.7 The notation

$wp(p, a) = c$

means that if the program p is executed in an initial state satisfying its weakest precondition c, it will eventually terminate in a state satisfying the postcondition a.

In the definition, as the name suggests, the weakest precondition c describes the largest possible set of initial states that ensures that execution of p will terminate in a state satisfying a. It should be clear that the focus is on total rather than on partial correctness in the style of Hoare Logic [4]. This means that the aim is not only to satisfy a on the even termination of p, but also to ensure that p will always terminate when it is executed in any state determined by c.

Definition 9.8 The predicate transformer lattice (PredTran) is the set of all monotonic functions from one predicate lattice to another {Predicate→ Predicate}. The result of the applying program (predicate transformer) p to predicate a, denoted $p(a)$, is equivalent to Dijkstra's $wp(p, a)$.

Clearly, PredTran is a complete lattice and therefore it contains arbitrary least upper bounds (u) and greatest lower bounds ($\sqcap$): $\sqcup$ is interpreted as anglic nondeterminism and $\sqcap$ as demonic nondeterminism. The top element is miracle ($\top$); it establishes every postcondition. The bottom element is abort ($\perp$), the predicate transformer does not establish any postcondition. We now define $\top$ and $\perp$ as follows:

$\top \Leftrightarrow (\text{def as})\lambda a \cdot true,$

$\perp \Leftrightarrow (\text{def as})\lambda a \cdot false.$

According to Dijkstra's view any program constructs can be defined as predicate transformers. As example we define skip (the identity predicate transformer), assignment and sequential composition:

$skip \Leftrightarrow (\text{def as})\lambda a \cdot a,$

$x := e \Leftrightarrow (\text{def as})\lambda a \cdot a[x \leftarrow e],$

p; q $\Leftrightarrow$ (def as)λa · p(q(a)),

where a[x ← e] denotes the result of the substituting e for every occurrence of x in a. Furthermore Dijkstra [5] has suggested five healthiness conditions which every construct of a programming language must satisfy. They are defined below (we assume that implicit qualification over a and b stands for predicate and over p stands for program).

1) p(false) = false,   law of excluded miracle

2) If a $\Rightarrow$ b then p(a) $\Rightarrow$ p(b),   monotonicity

3) p(a) $\wedge$ p(b) = p(a $\wedge$ b),   conjunctivity

4) p(a) $\vee$ p(b) = p(a $\vee$ b),   disjunctivity

5) p($\exists$i| i $\geqslant$ 0 · a$_i$) = $\exists$i : i $\geqslant$: p(a$_i$),   continuity

for all sequence of predicates

$$a_0, a_1, \ldots, \text{such that } a_i \Rightarrow a_{i+1} \text{ for } \forall i \geqslant 0.$$

The last property is equivalent to requiring that nondeterminism be bounded. The notation $\exists$ x p; q stands for an existential quantification and is read as: there exists an x such that p and q hold. The healthiness conditions have been pointed out that they do not always hold. For example, the fourth property is satisfied only by deterministic programs. It is easy to exemplify a failure of disjunctivity by taking suitable values for p, a, and b:

$$p = (x := 2 \sqcap p := 3),$$
$$a = (x = 2),$$
$$b = (x = 3).$$

Let us now calculate the value of p(a):

p(a) = x := 2(x = 2) $\wedge$ x := 3(x = 2)   {predicate transformer definition of $\wedge$}

  = true $\wedge$ false   {predicate transformer definition of Assignment}

  = false   {true $\wedge$ $\wedge$false = false}.

Similarly, one can show that p(b) = false, and consequently, that p(a) $\vee$p(b) = false. It is also trivial to show that p(a $\vee$ b) = true. Therefore, we conclude that the fourth property does not hold in general for nondeterministic programs. Instead, the implication

p(a) $\vee$ p(b) $\Rightarrow$ p(a $\overset{\prime}{\vee}$ b)

does hold. The complete lattice PredTran includes predicate transformers useful for the specification purpose; they are not implementable in general. Among above properties, only monotonicity is satisfied by all the predicate transformers in PredTran: $\top$ trivially breaks the law of the excluded miracle. The fact that greatest lower bounds over arbitrary sets are allowed implies that the assumption of bounded nondeterminism (and therefore continuity) is not satisfied; and angelic nondeterminism violates the property of conjunctivity. Failure of conjunctivity can also be illustrated by a similar example to that used to show failure of disjunctivity. Let p, a, and b be as follows:

$$p = (x := 2 \sqcup x := 3),$$
$$a = (x := 2),$$
$$b = (x := 3).$$

It is easy to show that, in this particular case, $p(a) \wedge p(b) = \text{true}$ whereas $p(a \wedge b) = \text{false}$.

Nevertheless, the healthiness conditions are still fundamentally important. They are the criteria for distinguishing the implementable from the non-implementable in a general space of specifications.

Based on the weakest preconditions, people proposed and developed refinement calculi. This calculi aim at formalizing the well established stepwise refinement method for the systematic construction of programs from high-level specifications. In essence, all the refinement calculi extend a given procedural language (in particular, Dijkstra's guarded command language) with additional features for specifications. For example, let [a, c] be a specification construct used to describe a program that will terminate in a state satisfying c if it executes in a state satisfying a. This can be viewed as a predicate transformer in just the same way as other operators of the language. It can be defined as

$$[a, c] \Leftrightarrow (\text{def as}) \lambda b \cdot a \wedge (c \Rightarrow b).$$

Thus the extended language is a specification language, and programs appear as a subclass of specifications. Programming is then viewed as constructing a sequence of specifications; the initial specification is in a high-level of abstraction (usually not implementable) and the final specification is in the executable program. The derivation process is to gradually transform specifications into programs. The intermediate steps of the derivation will normally contain a mixture of specification and program constructs; but these are formal objects too, since specifications and programs are embedded in the same semantic framework.

Derivation requires the notion of the refinement relation between specifications. The precise definition of the refinement relation is the ordering on the lattice of predicate transformers described above. Two mathematical properties of this ordering are of the fundamental importance to model stepwise refinement. The first one is that in order to allow a given specification to be replaced by a refinement of it in an arbitrary context, the monotonicity of the language operators with respect to this ordering is necessary; this property is also known as compositionality.

The second one is transitivity. As the derivation process normally entails a large number of steps, it is necessary to ensure that the final product of the derivation (that is, the program) satisfies the original specification.

The additional tools required in the process are rules for introducing programming constructs from given specifications. For example, the following rules illustrate the introduction of skip and sequential composition:

$$[a, c] \sqsubseteq skip \text{ if } a \Rightarrow c,$$
$$[a, c] \sqsubseteq [a, b]; [b, c].$$

There are also rules for manipulating specifications [6]; for example, weakening the precondition of a given specification or strengthening its postcondition (or both) lead to a specification that refines the original one:

$$[a_1, c_1] \sqsubseteq [a_2, c_2] \text{ if } a_1 \Rightarrow a_2 \wedge c_2 \Rightarrow c_1.$$

The discussion above describes how to transform an abstract specification into a program by progressively introducing control structures; this is known as algorithmic or control refinement. But this is only part of the process to obtain an implementation. Specifications are usually stated in terms of mathematical data types like sets and relations, and these are not normally available in procedural programming languages. Therefore, the complementary step to control refinement is the transformation of the abstract data types into concrete types such as arrays, and records which can be efficiently implemented. This task is called data refinement.

The basic idea of data refinement is the use of an abstraction function to determine the abstract state which a given concrete state represents; in addition, the set of concrete states may be constrained by an invariant relation. It was first introduced by Hoare[7]. Then many approaches have been suggested that build on these ideas. The more recent approaches use a single relation to capture both the abstraction function and the invariant, thus relaxing the assumption that the abstract state is functionally dependent on the concrete state.

In connection with the refinement calculi, data refinement is characterized as a special case of algorithmic refinement between blocks. A block of the form

$$dec \ x : Tx \cdot p$$

is used to represent the abstract program p operating on the variables x with type[①] Tx.

Similarly

$$dec \ x' : Tx' \cdot p'$$

represents the concrete program p' that operates on the variables x' with the type Tx'. The data refinement is captured by the inequation

$$(dec \ x : Tx \cdot p) \sqsubseteq (dec \ x' : Tx' \cdot p').$$

The general aim is to construct the concrete block by replacing the abstract local variables with the concrete ones, in such a way that the overall effect of the abstract block is preserved. In particular, p' is constructed with the same structure as p in the sense that each command in p' is the translation of a corresponding command in p, according to a uniform rule.

An essential ingredient to this strategy is an abstract invariant I that links the abstract variables x to the concrete variables x'. This is called the coupling invariant. The need for this invariant is that a direct comparison of the programs operating on data space is not possible. For example, in the

---

[①] Our language is untyped, and types are considered here only for the present discussion.

design of the compiler this invariant would establish the relationship between the data space of the source program and that of the target program. As exemplified in the previous section, the concrete representation of a variable y in the memory M of our simple target machine is denoted by $M[\Psi\ y]$, where Ψ is a symbol table that maps identifiers to their respective addresses in M. For a list of global variables $y_1, \ldots, y_n$ representing the states of the source program, the relevant coupling invariant would be

$$y_1 = M[\Psi y_1] \wedge \ldots \wedge y_n = M[\Psi y_n].$$

In this approach to the data refinement, a new relation between programs is defined to express that program p'(operating on variables x') is a data refinement of the program p (operating on variables x) under coupling invariant I. This is written $p \leqslant_{I,x,x'} p$ ' and is formally defined by

$$p \ \leqslant_{I,x,x'} p' \Leftrightarrow (\text{def as}) \ (\exists \ x \ \cdot I \wedge p(a)) \Rightarrow p'(\exists \ x \cdot I \wedge a)$$

for $\forall$ a not containing x' (considering programs as predicate transformers).

Broadly, the antecedent requires that the initial values of the concrete variables couple to some set of abstract values for which the abstract program will succeed in establishing postcondition a; the consequent requires that the concrete program yields new concrete values that also couple to an acceptable abstract state.

To illustrate a simple example of the data refinement, consider the coupling invariant, given the relation above that relates the data space of the source program to that of the target program. We can show that the program

x := y

is data refined by the program

$$M := M \odot \{\psi_x \to M[\psi_y]\}.$$

Note that this captures the desired intention: the effect of the latter program is to update the memory at position ψ_x (the address of x) with $M[\psi_y]$, the value stored in the memory cell with address ψ_y (the address of y). More generally, we can prove that an arbitrary source program operating on the source variables is data refined by the corresponding target program which operates on M.

This definition is chosen for two main reasons. The first is that it guarantees the characteristics of the data refinement given above, that is

if $(p \leqslant_{I,x,x'} p')$ then $(\text{dec } x : Tx \cdot p) \subseteq (\text{dec } x' : Tx' \cdot p')$.

The second reason is that it distributes through the program constructors, thus allowing data refinement to be carried out piecewise. For example, the distribution through sequential composition is given by

if $(p \leqslant_{I,x,x'} p')$ and $(q \leqslant_{I,x,x'} q')$ then $(p; q) \leqslant_{I,x,x'} (p'; q')$.

But we can also adopt another approach to avoid the need of the defining data refinement relation. The use of the algorithmic refinement relation can not only characterize the data refinement, but also carry out the calculations. The basic idea is to introduce an encoding program, say ψ that computes abstract states from concrete states and a decoding program, say Φ that computes concrete states from abstract states. Then, for a given abstract program p, the task is to find a concrete program p' such that

$\psi; p; \Phi \subseteq p'$.

With the aid of specification features, it is possible to give a very high-level definition for ψ and Φ. Using the same convention adopted above that x stands for the abstract variable, x′ for the concrete variable and I for the coupling invariant, ψ is defined by

$\psi \Leftrightarrow$ (def as) var x; x :$\in^\perp$ I; endx′.

The meaning of the expression is that it introduces the abstract variable x and assigns its value such that the invariant is satisfied, and then removes the concrete variable from the data space. The use of $\perp$ as an annotation in the above generalized assignment command means that it aborts if I cannot be established. Similarly we have the definition of Φ:

$\Phi \Leftrightarrow$ (def as) var x′; x′ :$\in^\perp$ I; end x.

This one introduces the concrete variable x′ and assigns its value such that the invariant is satisfied, and removes the abstract variable from the data space. But the generalized assignment command result in a miracle in this case if I cannot be established.

It needs to point out that these two kinds of generalized assignment commands are introduced only for the purpose of the present discussion, henceforth we will still use the previous notation x: $\in$ b, instead of x: $\in^\top$ b, as they are the same by definition.

Note that having separate commands to introduce and end the scope of variables is an essential feature to define the encoding and decoding programs: the first introduces x and ends the scope of x′; the second introduces x′ and ends the scope of x.

In this approach, the data refinement can also be performed piecewise, as we can prove the distributivity properties such as

$\psi; (p; q); \Phi \subseteq (\psi; p; \Phi) : (\psi; q; \Phi)$

that illustrates that both algorithmic and data refinement can be carried out within the framework of one common relation.

We have mentioned previously that the task of compilation is the program refinement. In the sense, we can establish some connection between our point of view of compiler design and the more general task of deriving programs from specifications [8]. Henceforth we will refer to deriving programs simply as derivation. In both cases, a programming language is extended with specification features, so that a uniform framework is built and the interface between programs and specifications (when expressed in terms of distinct formalisms) is avoided.

In a derivation, the idea is to start with an arbitrary specification and end with a program formed solely from constructs that can be executed by computer. In our case, the initial object is an arbitrary source program and the final product is its normal form. But the tools used for achieving the goals in both cases are identical in nature: transformations leading to refinement in the sense already discussed.

Derivation entails two main tasks: the control and data refinement. We also split the design of the compiler into these two main phases. However, while in a derivation control refinement is concerned with progressively introducing control structure in the specification, we do the reverse process. We reduce the nested control structure of a source program to the single flat iteration of the normal form program. Regarding the data refinement, the general idea is the same both in a derivation process and in a designing compiler: to replace abstract data types with concrete representations. In particular, we use the idea of encoding and decoding programs. As discussed before, this avoids the need to defining a separate relation to carry out data refinement. An encoding program retrieves the abstract space of the source program from the concrete state representing the memory of the machine. Conversely, a decoding program maps the abstract space to the concrete machine state. In the following section, we will formally define the pair formed by an encoding and the respective decoding program as a simulation. It satisfies the distributivity properties illustrated above, allowing the data refinement to be carried out piecewise. But it should be pointed out too, that there are some differences between designing a compiler in this way and the more general task of deriving programs from specifications. For example, we are not interested in capturing requirements in general, and therefore, our language does not include the construct to serve this purpose. In our language, the closest to a specification statement which we have is the generalized assignment command. We abstract it from the way where the control state is encoded in a particular target machine. Another difference is that we are mostly concerned with the program transformation. We need a wide range of laws relating the operators of the language. The set of these laws must be complete in that it should allow us to reduce an arbitrary program to normal form. Therefore, the frame we use is better characterized as a refinement algebra, rather than as a calculus.

9.3.2 Reasoning Language

In this section, we give meaning to our specification (reasoning) language in terms of equations and inequations (laws) relating operators of the language. Usually we present the laws as self-evident axioms, normally preceded by an informal (operational) justification. Moreover, it is not our aim to describe a complete set of laws in the logical sense. Nevertheless, they are complete in that they will allow us to reduce an arbitrary source program to a normal form.

Most of the algebraic laws are expressed as equations of the form $p = q$. It means that p and q have the same behavior: the program p and q may possibly consume a different amount of resources (for example, memory) and run at different speeds, but regarding the task they perform is impossible to distinguish between them. Therefore, we can replace p with q (and vice versa) in any context. It is also possible to attach a boolean condition to a law, meaning that the law is guaranteed to hold only if the condition evaluates to be true. Furthermore, the laws can be inequation (rather than equation) expressing refinement.

It is possible to select a small subset of our language and define the additional operators in terms of the more basic ones. But this is not our concern here. What we emphasize is the algebraic laws that will be used in the process of designing a compiler. However, we do illustrate how a few operators can be defined from others. In particular, iteration is defined as a special case of the recursion and all the laws about the iteration are proven. They deserve such special attention because of their role in the proof of the normal form reduction theorems.

Another concern is the correctness of the laws of the basic operators. To achieve this we need to link the algebraic semantics of the language with a suitable mathematical model in which the basic operators can be defined and their laws verified. In the end of this section, we will further discuss this issue and argue that the existence of nontrivial models for reasoning language shows that in some sense the reasoning language and its algebraic laws are consistent.

As we have explained before both the programming and specification operators of the reasoning language have the same status in that they can be viewed as predicate transformers. In this uniform framework, there is no need to distinguish between programs and specifications. We will refer to both of them as "programs". Another remark is that programs have both a syntactic and a semantic existence. On one hand, we perform syntactic operations on them, such as substitution. On the other hand, the algebraic laws relating language operators express semantic properties. Strictly speaking, we should distinguish between these two natures of programs. But it is not convenient to do so and it will be clear from the context which view we are taking.

1. Concepts and Notation

1) Name conventions

For the purpose of the convenience of the following discussion, we define some conventions as regards the names used to denote program terms:

X, Y, Z	variables denoting programs
p, q, r	arbitrary but given programs
x, y, z	list of variables
a, b, c	boolean expressions
e, f, g	list of expressions

We also use subscripts in addition to the above conventions. For example, $b_0, b_1, \ldots$ stand for boolean expressions (also referred to as conditions). We use comma for list concatenation: x, y stands for the concatenation of lists x and y. Further conventions are explained when necessary.

2) Precedence rules

In order to clarify the priority order and to reduce the number of brackets around program terms, we define the following precedence rules. Operators with the same precedence appear on the same line. As usual, we will assume that brackets bind tighter than any operator. Procedures will be discussed separately later.

uop	unary operators	binds tightest
bop	binary operators	
,	list concatenation	
:∈ and :=	(generalized) assignment	
→	guarded command	
*	iteration	
;	sequential composition	
⊔ and ⊓	nondeterminism (angelic and demonic)	
◁ ▷	conditional	
μ	recursion	
dec	block with local declarations	binds loosest

3) Free and bound identifiers

An occurrence of a variable x in a program p is bound (or local) if it is in the scope of a static declaration of x in p, and free (or global) otherwise. For example, x is bound in dec x·x := y, but free in x := y. Notice that the command for the dynamic declaration is not binders for variables. For example, x is free in var x as well as in end x. A list of variables is free in p if each variable in the list is not bound in p.

In the case of program identifiers, we say that an occurrence of x is free in a program p if it is not in the scope of any program (with name x) defined in p, and bound otherwise.

4) Substitution

For variables x and y,

$$P[x \leftarrow y]$$

denotes the result of the substituting y for every occurrence of x in P. It is possible for x to be in the scope of (static) declarations of variables with the same name as y. In this case, a systematic renaming of local variables of P occurs in order to avoid variable capture. This is usually referred to as safe substitution. If x and y are (equal-length) lists of variables, the substitution is positional. In this case, no variable may appear more than once in the list.

Similarly,

$$f[x \leftarrow e]$$

denotes the substitution of the list of expressions e for the (equal-length) list of variables x in the list of expressions f.

We also allow the substitution of programs for program identifiers:

$$p[X \leftarrow q].$$

This avoids capture of any free identifiers of q by renaming local declarations in p, as discussed above. For conciseness, we will sometimes avoid writing substitutions of the latter kind by making (free) occurrences of X explicit, as in F(X). Then the substitution of q for X in this case is written F(q). In any case, we assume that no capture of free identifiers occur.

5) Laws, declarations, lemmas, theorems and proofs

Each of the laws described in the following sections is given a number and a name suggestive of its use. For example,

$$(; -\text{skip unit})$$

is the name associated with the law that says that skip is the unit of sequential composition. Every reference to a law comprises both its name and its number. Each of the definition, lemmas and theorems are also given a number and a name for further references.

Some of the laws could be alternatively described as lemmas or theorems, as they are provable to more basic ones. Most of the derived laws are presented with their proofs, but in any case we always make it clear whether a given law can be derived. Our proofs are confined to reasoning with conditional (in) equations. The proof strategy is to start with one of the sides and try to reach the other side by a series of algebraic transformations. Each step is annotated with one or more references to laws, definitions, lemmas, or theorems.

Each proof is essentially a program transformation activity. We assume that the program being transformed is (syntactically) valid to start with. Then the application of most of the laws will always produce valid programs. Nevertheless, some of the laws (e.g., Laws 9.2, 9.42, and 9.47) contain free variables on their left hand sides (LHS) that do not appear on their right hand sides (RHS). Therefore, the reverse (right to left) application of these equations requires the user to provide an explicit instantiation (binding) of these free variables; in these circumstances, one must take care to avoid transforming a valid program into one that is not even syntactically well-formed. One advantage of mechanizing the transformation is that one can ensure that this problem will not arise. In our case, this is actually simplified by the fact that we do not deal with context information like types. Even undeclared variables can be introduced during the transformations; these variables are considered to be global.

2. Skip, Abort and Miracle

The skip command has no effect and always terminates successfully.

The abort command, denoted by $\perp$, is the most unpredictable of all programs. It may fail to terminate, or it may terminate with any result whatsoever. Thus $\perp$ represents the behavior, of a broken machine, or a program that has run wild. We identify abort with all programs that might diverge before doing any action visible to its environment. The motivation for this choice is that, in principle, a program that is continuously allowed to diverge can be considered a programming error, since one cannot rely on it at all. This is formalized in part 6 of this section where we state that every program is a refinement of $\bot$. For example, the replacement $\bot$ with an assignment such as x := 1 is an improvement in the sense we have already discussed: while the behavior of the former is totally arbitrary, the later always terminate with an expected result.

The miracle command, denoted by $\top$, is the other extreme: it can be used to serve any purpose and more formally, it refines every program. But it is infeasible in that it cannot be implemented, otherwise we would not need to write programs — $\top$ would do anything for us. We use $\top$ just for reasoning needed to imagine an ideal result.

3. Sequential composition

From this part, we start introducing the laws and others which we mentioned at the beginning of the section. The program p; q denotes the usual sequential composition of programs p and q. If the execution of p terminates successfully then the execution of q follows that of p.

Since the execution of skip always terminates and leaves everything unchanged, to precede or follow a program p by skip does not change the effect of p. In other words, skip is both the left and right units of the sequential composition.

Law 9.1   (skip; p)= p= (p; skip)   (; -skip unit)

We state that the execution of a program p after the termination of $\bot$ cannot redeem the situation, because $\bot$ cannot be relied on to terminate. More precisely, $\bot$ is a left zero of the sequential composition.

Law 9.2 $\bot; p = \bot$ (; -$\bot$ left zero)

To precede a program p by $\top$ results in a miracle; $\top$ is a left zero of the sequential composition.

Law 9.3 $\top; p = \top$ (; -$\top$ left zero)

The sequential composition is associative.

Law 9.4   (p; q); r = p; (q; r)   (; assoc)

4. Demonic nondeterminism

The program $p \sqcap q$ denotes the demonic choice of programs p and q; either p or q is selected, the choice being totally arbitrary. The abort command already allows completely arbitrary behavior, so an offer of further choice makes no difference to it.

Law 9.5 $p \sqcap \bot = \bot$ ($\sqcap$-$\bot$ zero)

On the other hand, the miracle command offers no choice at all.

Law 9.6 $p \sqcap \top = p$ ($\sqcap$-$\top$ unit)

When the two alternatives are the same program, the choice becomes vacuous - -⊓ is idempotent.

Law 9.7 $p \sqcap p = p$ (⊓ idemp)

The order in which a choice is offered is immaterial ⊓ is commutative.

Law 9.8 $p \sqcap q = q \sqcap p$ (⊓ comm)

Demonic choice is associative.

Law 9.9 $(p \sqcap q) \sqcap r = p \sqcap (q \sqcap r)$ (⊓ assoc)

5. Angelic nondeterminism

The angelic choice of two programs p and q is denoted by $p \sqcup q$. Informally, it is a program that may act like p or q, whichever is more suitable in a given context.

As we have mentioned above, ⊥ is totally unpredictable, and therefore the least suitable program for all purpose.

Law 9.10 $\bot \sqcup p = p$ (⊔-⊥ unit)

On the other hand, ⊤ suits any situation.

Law 9.11 $\top \sqcup p = p$ (⊔-⊤ zero).

Like ⊓, angelic choice ⊔ is idempotent, commutative and associative.

Law 9.12 $p \sqcup p = p$ (⊔ idemp)

Law 9.13 $p \sqcup q = q \sqcup p$ (⊔ comm)

Law 9.14 $(p \sqcup q) \sqcup r = p \sqcup (q \sqcup r)$ (⊔ assoc)

6. Ordering Relation

Here we define the ordering relation ⊑ on programs: $p \sqsubseteq q$ holds whenever the program q is at least as deterministic as p or, alternatively, whenever q offers only a subset of the choices offered by p. In this case, q is at least as predictable as p. This coincides with the meaning we adopt for refinement. Thus $p \sqsubseteq q$ can be read as "p is refined by q".

We define ⊑ in terms of ⊓. Informally, if the demonic choice of p and q always yields p, one can be sure that p is worse than q in all situations.

Definition 9.9 (The ordering relation) $p \sqsubseteq q \Leftrightarrow (\text{def as})(p \sqcap q) = p$

In the final section, we prove that this ordering coincides with the ordering on the lattice of predicate transformers described in the beginning of this chapter. Alternatively, the ordering relation could have been defined in terms of ⊔.

Law 9.15 $p \sqsubseteq q \equiv (p \sqcup q) = p$ (⊑-⊔)

From Definition 9.9 and the laws of $\sqcap$, we conclude that $\sqsubseteq$ is a partial ordering on programs.

Law 9.16 $p \sqsubseteq p$ ($\sqsubseteq$ reflexivity)

Law 9.17 $(p \sqsubseteq q) \wedge (q \sqsubseteq p) \Rightarrow (p = q)$ ($\sqsubseteq$ antisymmetry)

Law 9.18 $(p \sqsubseteq q) \wedge (q \sqsubseteq r) \Rightarrow (p \sqsubseteq r)$ ($\sqsubseteq$ transitivity)

Moreover $\sqsubseteq$ is a lattice ordering. The bottom and top elements are $\perp$ and $\top$, respectively; the meet (greatest lower bound) and join (least upper bound) operators are $\sqcap$ and $\sqcup$, in this order. These are also consequences of the definition of $\sqsubseteq$ and the laws of $\sqcap$ and $\sqcup$.

Law 9.19 $\perp \sqsubseteq p$ ($\sqsubseteq$-$\perp$ bottom)

Law 9.20 $p \sqsubseteq \top$ ($\sqsubseteq$-$\top$ top)

Law 9.21 $(r \sqsubseteq p \wedge r \sqsubseteq q) \equiv r \sqsubseteq (p \sqcap q)$ ($\sqsubseteq$ -$\sqcap$ glb)

Law 9.22 $(p \sqsubseteq r) \wedge (q \sqsubseteq r) \equiv (p \sqcup q) \sqsubseteq r$ ($\sqsubseteq$-$\sqcup$ lub)

In order to be able to use the algebraic laws to transform subcomponents of compound programs, it is crucial that $p \sqsubseteq q$ imply that $F(p) \sqsubseteq F(q)$, for all contexts F (functions from programs to programs). This is equivalent to saying that F (and consequently, all the operators of our language) must be monotonic with respect to $\sqsubseteq$. Then we have the law as follows.

Law 9.23 If $p \sqsubseteq q$, then
   1) $(p \sqcap r) \sqsubseteq (q \sqcap r)$ ($\sqcap$ monotonic)
   2) $(r; p) \sqsubseteq (r; q)$ and $(p; r) \sqsubseteq (q; r)$ (; monotonic)

We will not state monotonicity laws explicitly for the remaining operators of our language.

7. Unbounded Nondeterminism

Here we generalize the operators $\sqcap$ and $\sqcup$ to take an arbitrary set of programs, say p, as argument. $\sqcup$ p denotes the least upper bound of p; its definition is given below.

Definition 9.10 (least upper bound) $(\sqcup p \sqsubseteq p) \equiv (\forall X | X \in p \cdot X \sqsubseteq p)$.

The above definition states that p refines the least upper bound of the set p if and only if, for $\forall\, X \in p$, p refines X.

The greatest lower bound of p, denoted by $\sqcap$ p, is defined in a similar way.

Definition 9.11 (Greatest lower bound) $(p \sqsubseteq \sqcap p) \equiv (\forall X | X \in p \cdot p \sqsubseteq X)$.

Let $\sqcup$ be the set of all programs, and $\o/$ be empty set. Then we have
$$\sqcup\, \o/ = \perp = \sqcap\, U\o/$$
$$\sqcap\, \o/ = \top = \sqcup\, U.$$

From the above we can easily show that sequential composition does not distribute rightward through the least upper bound or the greatest lower bound in general, since we have

$$\bot; \sqcap \varnothing = \bot \neq \sqcap \varnothing$$
$$\top; \sqcup \varnothing = \top \neq \sqcup \varnothing.$$

The rightward distribution of sequential composition through these operators is used below to define Dijkstra's healthiness conditions. However, the leftward distribution is valid in general, and can be verified by considering programs as predicate transformers. In the following, the notation $\{X| \; b \cdot F(X)\}$ should be read as: the set of elements $F(X)$ for $\forall \; X$ in the range specified by b.

Law 9.24

    1) $\sqcup \; p; p = \sqcup \{X|X \in p \cdot (X; p)\}$ (; -$\sqcup$ left dist)

    2) $\sqcap \; p; p = \sqcap \{X|X \in p \cdot (X; p)\}$ (; -$\sqcap$ left dist)

It is also possible to verify that the lattice of programs (considered as predicate transformers) is distributive.

Law 9.25

    1) $(\sqcup \; p) \sqcap p = \sqcup \{X|X \in p \cdot (X \sqcap p)\}$ ($\sqcap$-$\sqcup$ dist)

    2) $(\sqcap \; p) \sqcup p = \sqcap \{X|X \in p \cdot (X \sqcup p)\}$ ($\sqcup$-$\sqcap$ dist)

As discussed before, among all predicate transformers Dijkstra singles out the implementable ones by certain healthiness conditions. Here we formulate these conditions as equations relating operators of our language.

    1) $p; \bot = \bot$ p is non-miraculous

    2) $p; \sqcap p = \sqcap \{X|X \in p \cdot (p; X)\}$ p is conjuctive

         for all (non-empty) sets of programs p

    3) $p; \sqcup p = \sqcup \{X|X \in p \cdot (p; X)\}$ p is disjunctive

         for all (non-empty) sets of programs p

    4) $p; \sqcup \{i|i \geqslant 0 \cdot q_i\} = \sqcup \{i|i \geqslant 0 \cdot p_i; q_i\}$ p is continuous

         provided $q_i \sqsubseteq q_{i+1}$ for all $i \geqslant 0$

We say that a program p is universally conjunctive if the second equation above holds for all sets of programs p (possibly empty). Similarly, if the third equation holds for all p, we say that p is universally disjunctive.

8. Recursion

Let X stand for the name of the recursive program we wish to construct, and let $F(X)$ define the intended behavior of the program, for a given context F. If F is defined solely in terms of the notations introduced already, it follows by structural induction that F is monotonic:

$$p \sqsubseteq q \Rightarrow F(p) \sqsubseteq F(q).$$

Actually, this will remain true for the commands that will be introduced later, since they are all monotonic.

The following two properties [6], say that $\mu X \cdot F(X)$ is a solution to the equation $X = F(X)$; furthermore, it is the least solution.

Law 9.26 $\mu X \cdot F(X) = F(\mu X \cdot F(X))$ (μ fixed point)

Law 9.27 $F(Y) \sqsubseteq Y \Rightarrow \mu X \cdot F(X) \sqsubseteq Y$ (μ least fixed point)

9. Approximate Inverse

Let F and G be functions on programs such that for all programs X and Y

$$F(X) = Y \equiv X = G(Y).$$

Then G is the inverse of F, and vice versa. Therefore, $G(F(X)) = X = F(G(X))$, for all X. It is well-known, however, that a function has an inverse if and only if it is bijective. As the set of bijective functions is relatively small this makes the notion of inverse rather limited. The standard approach is to generalize the notion of inverse functions as follows.

Definition 9.12 (Approximate inverse)   Let F and F^{-1} be functions on programs such that, for all X and Y

$$F(X) \sqsubseteq Y \equiv X \sqsubseteq F^{-1}(Y)$$

Then we call F the weakest inverse of F^{-1}, and F^{-1} the strongest inverse of F. The pair (F, F^{-1}) is called the Galois connection.

The left and right weakest inverses of the sequential composition are defined together with a calculus of the program development. Broadly speaking, the aim is to decompose a task (specification) r into two subtasks p and q, such that

$$r \sqsubseteq p; q.$$

The method allows one to calculate the weakest specification that must be satisfied by one of the components p and q when the other one is known and then gets the problem totally solved. For example, one can calculate the weakest specification of p from q and r. It is denoted by $q \setminus r$ and satisfies $r \sqsubseteq (q \setminus r); q$. This is called the weakest prespecification. Dually, r/p is the weakest specification of the component q satisfying $r \sqsubseteq p; (r/p)$. It is named the weakest postspecification.

The strongest inverse of language constructs is less commonly used. This is because perhaps they exist only for operators that are universally disjunctive. Article [8] have suggested a method to reason about recursion based on the notion of the strongest inverse which they call weak-op-inverse. We list some of the properties of strongest inverses as follows.

Before presenting the properties of strongest inverses, we review two basic definitions. F is universally conjunctive if for all sets (possibly empty) p,

$$F(\sqcap p) = \sqcap \{X \mid X \in p \cdot F(X)\}.$$

Similarly, F is universally disjunctive if for all sets (possibly empty) p,

$$F(\sqcup p) = \sqcup \{X \mid X \in p \cdot F(X)\}.$$

Theorem 9.2   (Strongest inverses)

1) If F^{-1} exists then F and F^{-1} are monotonic.
2) F^{-1} is unique if it exists.
3) If F^{-1} exists then for all programs X,
   $$F(F^{-1}(X)) \sqsubseteq X \sqsubseteq F^{-1}(F(X)).$$
4) F exists if and only if F is universally disjunctive; in this case, it is defined by
   $$F^{-1}(Y) \Leftrightarrow (\text{def as}) \sqcup \{X \mid F(X) \sqsubseteq Y \cdot X\}.$$
5) F^{-1} is universally conjunctive if it exists.

The following lemma shows that sequential composition has a strongest inverse in its first argument. This allows a concise proof (will be given later in this chapter) of an important property about composition of the iteration command.

Lemma 9.1   (Strongest inverse of ;)   Let
$$F(X) \Leftrightarrow (\text{def as})(X; p).$$
Then F has a strongest inverse which we denote by
$$F^{-1}(X) \Leftrightarrow (\text{def as})X; \sqcup p.$$
Furthermore, for all X,
$$(X; \sqcup p); p \sqsubseteq p.$$
From law 9.24 (; -$\sqcup$ left dist) it follows that F is disjunctive. Consequently, from Theorem 9.2 4), it has a strongest inverse. The inequation follows from Theorem 9.2 3).

10. Simulation

Here we consider the inverse of programs themselves. An inverse of the program S is a program T that satisfies
$$S; T = \text{skip} = T; S.$$
That means that running S followed by T and T followed by S are the same as not running any program at all, since skip has no effect whatsoever.

The inversion of programs has been previously discussed by Dijkstra and Gries. A More formal approach to program inversion is given in [9]. It defines proof rules for inverting programs written in Dijkstra's language. A common feature of these works is the use of the notion of the exact inverse given above. But it seemed that this notion of inverse is rather limited, hence we adopt a weaker definition of the program inversion.

Definition 9.13   (Simulation)   Let S and S^{-1} be programs such that
$$(S; S^{-1}) \sqsubseteq \text{skip} \sqsubseteq (S^{-1}; S).$$
Then the pair (S, S^{-1}) is called a simulation, S^{-1} is the strongest inverse of S, whereas S is the weakest inverse of S^{-1}.

A very simple example of simulations is the pair $(\bot, \top)$ since
$$(\bot; \top) = \bot \sqsubseteq \text{skip} \sqsubseteq \top = (\top; \bot).$$
For further examples of simulations one might see them later.

Simulations are useful for calculation in general. When carrying out program transformation, it is not seldom to meet situations where a program followed by its inverse (that is $S; S^{-1}$ or $S^{-1}; S$) appears as a subterm of the program being transformed. Thus, from the definition of simulations, it is possible to eliminate the subterm of the above form by replacing them with skip (of course, this is only valid for the inequational reasoning). This will be illustrated in many proofs in the next two sections where we give further examples of simulations.

But the most valuable uses for the concept of simulations are for data refinement. This was discussed in some detail in the previous section where we introduced the concepts of encoding and decoding programs that form a simulation pair. The distributivity properties of simulations given below are particularly useful to prove the correctness of the change of the data representation phase of the compilation process, where the abstract space of the source program is replaced by the concrete state of the target machine. The appropriate encoding and decoding programs will be defined when the need arises.

Now we present some of the properties of simulations.

Theorem 9.3 (Simulation) Let S be a program. The following properties hold:

1) S^{-1} is unique if it exists.
2) S^{-1} exists if and only if S is universally disjunctive.
3) S^{-1} is universally conjunctive if it exists.

We define the following abbreviations.

Definition 9.14 (Simulation functions)   Let $\{ S, S^{-1}\}$ be a simulation. We use S and S^{-1} themselves as functions defined by
$$S(X) \Leftrightarrow (\text{def as})S; X; S^{-1},$$
$$S^{-1}(X) \Leftrightarrow (\text{def as})S^{-1}; X; S.$$

The next theorem shows that the concepts of simulations and appropriate inverse are closely related.

Theorem 9.4 (Lift of simulation)
Let S and S^{-1} be simulation functions as defined above. Then S^{-1} is the strongest inverse of S. Furthermore from Theorem 9.2 we have
$$S(S^{-1}(X)) \sqsubseteq X \sqsubseteq S^{-1}(S(X)).$$

The following theorem shows how simulation functions distribute through all the language operators introduced so far, with possible improvement in the distributed result.

Theorem 9.5 (Distributivity of simulation functions)

1) $S(\bot) = \bot$;
2) $S(\top) \sqsubseteq \top$;
3) $S(\text{skip}) \sqsubseteq \text{skip}$;

4) $S(X; Y) \sqsubseteq S(X); S(Y)$;

5) $S(\sqcap p) \sqsubseteq \sqcap \{X \mid X \in p \cdot S(X)\}$;

6) $S(\sqcup p) = \sqcup \{X \mid X \in p \cdot S(X)\}$;

7) $S(\mu X \cdot F(X)) \sqsubseteq \mu X \cdot S(F(S^{-1}(X)))$.

11. Assumption and assertion

The assumption of a condition b, designated as $b^\top$, can be regarded as a miraculous test: it leaves the state unchanged (behaving like skip) if b is true; otherwise it behaves like $\top$. The assertion of b, designated as $b_\perp$, also behaves like skip when b is true; otherwise it fails, behaving like $\perp$.

We assume that the evaluation of an expression always yields a result. Clearly, for boolean expressions this is either true or false. While this decision considerably simplifies our algebraic system, it is worth pointing out that there are no theoretical limitations that prevent one from dealing with undefined expressions.

The intended purpose of assumptions and assertions is to give preconditions and postconditions, respectively, the status of programs. For example,

$$a^\top; p; b_\perp$$

is used to express the fact that the assumption of a is an obligation placed on the environment of the program p. If the environment fails to provide a state satisfying a, $a^\top$ behaves like miracle; this saves the programmer from dealing with state not satisfying a, since no program can implement $\top$. On the other hand, an assertion is an obligation placed on the program itself. If p fails to make b true on its completion, it ends up behaving like abort.

The first three laws formally state the assumption and the assertion of a true condition are equivalent to skip, that the assumption of a false condition leads to miracle, and that the assertion of a false condition leads to abort.

Law 9.28 $\text{true}^\top = \text{true}_\perp = \text{skip}$ ($b^\perp$, $b_\perp$true cond)

Law 9.29 $\text{false}^\top = \top$ ($b^\top$ false cond)

Law 9.30 $\text{false}_\perp = \perp$ ($b_\perp$ false cond)

Two consecutive assumptions can be combined, giving rise to an assumption of the conjunction of the original condition; this obviously means that if any of the condition is not satisfied, the result will be miraculous. An analogous law holds for assertions.

Law 9.31 $(a^\top; b^\top) = (a \wedge b)^\top = (a^\top \sqcup b^\top)$ ($b^\top$ conjunction)

Law 9.32 $(a_\perp; b_\perp) = (a \wedge b)_\perp = (a_\perp \sqcap b_\perp)$ ($b_\perp$ conjunction)

The assumption of the disjunction of two conditions will behave like a miracle if and only if none of the conditions are satisfied. There is a similar law for assertions.

Law 9.33 $(a \vee b)^\top = (a^\top \sqcap b^\top)$ ($b^\top$ disjunction)

Law 9.34 $(a \lor b)_\perp = (a_\perp \sqcup b_\perp)$ ($b_\perp$ disjunction)

It does not matter if a choice is made before or after an assumption (or an assertion) is executed.

Law 9.35 $b^\top; (p \sqcap q) = (b^\top; p) \sqcap (b^\top; q)$ ($b^\top$-$\sqcap$ dist)

Law 9.36 $b_\perp; (p \sqcap q) = (b_\perp; p) \sqcap (b_\perp; q)$ ($b_\perp$-$\sqcap$ dist)

The next law states that $(b_\perp, b^\top)$ is a simulation.

Law 9.37 $(b_\perp; b^\top) = b_\perp \sqsubseteq skip \sqsubseteq b^\top = (b^\top; b_\perp)$ ($b_\perp$-$b^\top$ simulation).

An assumption commutes with an arbitrary program p in the following sense.

Law 9.38 If the free variable of b are not assigned by p,
$$(p; b^\top) \sqsubseteq (b^\top; p) \quad (b^\top; p \text{ commute})$$

The inequality occurs when b is false and p is $\perp$, in which case the left-hand side reduces to $\perp$ whereas the right-hand side reduces to $\top$.

12. Guarded command

The standard notation $b \to p$ stands for a guarded command. If the guard b is true, the whole command behaves like p; otherwise it behaves like $\top$. This suggests that a guard have the same effect as an assumption of the given condition, that allows us to define a guarded command as follows:

Definition 9.15 (Guarded command)
$$b \to p \Leftrightarrow (\text{def as})b^\top; p$$

The laws of guarded commands can therefore be proven from the above definition and the laws of sequential composition and assumptions.

Law 9.39 $(\text{true} \to p) = p$ ($\to$ true guard)

Law 9.40 $(\text{false} \to p) = \top$ ($\to$ false guard)

Guards can be unnested by taking their conjunction.

Law 9.41 $a \to (b \to p) = (a \land b) \to p$ ($\to$ guard conjunction)

Guard distributes over $\sqcap$.

Law 9.42 $b \to (p \sqcap q) = (b \to p) \sqcap (b \to q)$ (guard -$\sqcap$ dist)

The demonic choice of guarded commands can be written as a single guarded command by taking the disjunction of their guards. This is easily derived from the last two laws.

Law 9.43 $(a \to p \sqcap b \to q) = (a \lor b) \to (a \to p \sqcap b \to q)$ ($\to$ guard disjunction 1)

Proof

$$RHS = (a \lor b) \to (a \to p) \sqcap (a \lor b) \to (b \to p) \quad \{Law\ 9.42\ (guard\ \text{-}\sqcap\ dist)\}$$
$$= (a \lor b) \to (a \to p \sqcap b \to q) \quad \{Law\ 9.41\ (\to guard\ conjunction)\}$$
$$= LHS$$

When p and q above are the same program, we have the following laws.

Law 9.44 $(a \to p \sqcap b \to p) = (a \lor b) \to p$ $(\to guard\ disjunction\ 2)$

Surprisingly, perhaps this is not a consequence of the previous one.
Sequential composition distributes leftward through guarded commands.

Law 9.45 $(b \to p);\ q = b \to (p;\ q)$ $(;\ \text{-}\to left\ dist)$

13. Guarded Command Set

Our main use of guarded commands is to model the possible actions of deterministic executing mechanism. The fact that the mechanism can perform one of the n actions, according to its current state, can be modeled by a program fragment of the form

$$b_1 \to action_1 \sqcap \ldots \sqcap b_n \to action_n$$

provided that $b_1, .., b_n$ are pairwise disjoint. Instead of mentioning this disjointness condition explicitly, we will write the above as

$$b_1 \to action_1 \square \ldots \square b_n \to action_n$$

and will call it as the guarded command set. Strictly speaking, $\square$ is not a new operator of our language. It is just syntactic sugar to improve conciseness and readability. Any theorem that uses $\square$ can be readily restated in terms of $\sqcap$ with the associated disjointness condition. As an example we have the following law.

If a guarded command set has the same guard as a command in this set, then the guarded set behaves the same as the command with this guard.

Law 9.46 $a \to (a \to p\ \square\ b \to q) = a \to p$ $(\square\ elim)$

Proof   The proof relies on the (implicit) assumption that a and b are disjoint (or $a \land b =$ false).

$$LHS = a \to (a \to p \sqcap b \to q)$$
$$= (a \to (a \to p)) \sqcap (a \to (b \to q)) \quad \{Law\ 9.42\ (guard\text{-}\sqcap\ dist)\}$$
$$= (a \to p) \sqcap (false \to q) \quad \{Law\ 9.41\ (\to guard\ conjunction)$$
$$\text{and}\ a \land b = false\}\}$$
$$= a \to p \quad \{Law\ 9.40\ (\to false\ guard)\ and\ Law\ 9.6\ (\text{-}\sqcap\ unit).$$

Other laws and theorems involving $\square$ will be discussed if need be.

14. Conditional

A conditional command has the general syntax $p \lhd b \rhd q$ that is concise form of the more usual notation

If b then p else q

It can also be defined in terms of more basic operators.

Definition 9.16   (Conditional)

$(p \lhd b \rhd q) \Leftrightarrow (\text{def as})(b \rightarrow p \; \square \; \neg b \rightarrow q).$

The most basic property of a conditional is that its left branch is executed if the condition holds initially; otherwise its right branch is executed.

Law 9.47 $(a \wedge b)^\top ; (p \lhd b \vee c \rhd q) = (a \wedge b)^\top ; p$ ($\lhd \; \rhd$ true cond)

Law 9.48 $(a \wedge \neg b)^\top ; (p \lhd b \wedge c \rhd q) = (a \wedge \neg b)^\top ; p$ ($\lhd \; \rhd$ false cond)

The left branch of a conditional can always be preceded by an assumption of the condition. Similarly, to precede the right branch by an assumption of the negation of the condition has no effect.

Law 9.49 $(b^\top ; p) \lhd b \rhd q = (p \lhd b \rhd q) = p \lhd b \rhd (\neg \; b^\top ; q)$ ($\lhd \; \rhd$ void $b^\top$)

If the two branches are the same program, the conditional can be eliminated.

Law 9.50 $p \lhd b \rhd p = p$ ($\lhd \; \rhd$ idemp)

Guard distributes through the conditional.

Law 9.51 $a \rightarrow (p \lhd b \rhd q) = (a \rightarrow p) \lhd b \rhd (a \rightarrow q)$ (guard- $\lhd \; \rhd$ dist)

Sequential composition distributes leftward through the conditional.

Law 9.52 $(p \lhd b \rhd q); r = (p; r) \lhd b \rhd (q; r)$ (; - $\lhd \; \rhd$ left dist)

The following two laws allow the elimination of nested conditionals in certain cases.

Law 9.53 $p \lhd b \rhd (p \lhd c \rhd q) = p \lhd b \vee c \rhd q$ ($\lhd \; \rhd$ cond disjunction)

Law 9.54 $(p \lhd b \rhd q) \lhd c \rhd q = p \lhd b \wedge c \rhd q$ ($\lhd \; \rhd$ cond conjunction)

We have considered assumptions and assertions as primitive commands and have defined guarded commands and conditionals in terms of them. The following equations show that an alternative could be to consider the conditional as a constructor and regard assumptions, assertions and guarded commands as special cases. These are stated as laws because they are not necessary in our proofs.

$b_\perp = \text{skip} \lhd b \rhd \perp,$

$b^\top = \text{skip} \lhd b \rhd \top,$

$b \rightarrow p = p \lhd b \rhd \top.$

15. Assignment

The command $x := e$ stands for a multiple assignment where x is a list of distinct variables, and e is an equal-length list of expressions. The components of e are evaluated and simultaneously assigned to the corresponding (same position) components of x. For example,

$$x, y := y, x$$

swaps the values of x and y.

We have mentioned that the evaluation of an expression always yields a result, so the assignment will always terminate. Furthermore, the validity of most of the laws relies on the fact that expression evaluation does not change the value of any variable; that is, no side-effect is generated.

Obviously, the assignment of the value of a variable to itself does not change any thing.

Law 9.55   (x:= x) = skip   (:= skip)

In fact, such a vacuous assignment can be added to any other assignment without changing its effect.

Law 9.56   (x, y := e, y) = (x := e)   (:= identity)

The list of variables and expressions may be subjected to the same permutation without changing the effect of the assignment.

Law 9.57   (x, y, z:= e, f, g) = (y, x, z:= f, e, g)   (:= sym)

The sequential composition of two assignments to the same variable is easily combined to a single assignment.

Law 9.58   (x := e; x := f) = (x := f [x ← e])   (:= combination)

Recall that f[x ← e] denotes the substitution of e for every occurrence of x in f.

If the value of a variable is known, the occurrence of this variable in an expression can be replaced with that value.

Law 9.59   (x = e)→(y := f) = (x = e) → (y := f [x←e])   (: = substitution)

Assignment is universally conjunctive.

Law 9.60   x := e; ⊓ p= ⊓ {X| X∈ p · (x := e; X)}   (:= -⊓ right dist)

Assignment distributes rightward through a conditional, replacing occurrences of the assigned variables in the condition by the corresponding expressions.

Law 9.61   x := e; (p◁ b ▷ q) = (x := e; p) ◁b [x←e]▷ (x := e : q)   (:= -◁ ▷ right dist)

Similarly, assignment commutes with an assertion in the following sense.

Law 9.62   (x := e; b⊥) = (b[x←e])⊥ ; x := e   (:= -b⊥ commutation)

16. Generalized Assignment

The notation x: ∈b stands for a generalized or a nondeterministic assignment command. Whenever possible, x is assigned an arbitrary value that makes the condition b hold. But if no such value exists, the assignment behaves like $\top$.

Law 9.63 $(\text{x} :\in \text{false}) = \top$ $(: \in \text{false cond})$

On the other hand, a true condition imposes no constrains on the final value of x. In this case, the generalized assignment might even leave everything unchanged, behaving like skip.

Law 9.64 $(\text{x}: \in \text{true}) \sqsubseteq \text{skip}$ $(: \in \text{true cond})$

To follow a generalized assignment by an assumption of the same condition has no effect. If the assignment establishes the condition, the assumption behaves like skip; otherwise, the assignment itself (and consequently, its composition with the assumption) behaves like $\top$.

Law 9.65 $\text{x}: \in \text{b}; \text{b}^\top = \text{x}: \in \text{b}$ $(: \in \text{void b}^\top)$

A similar law holds for assertions.

Law 9.66 $\text{x}: \in \text{b} ; \text{b}_\perp = \text{x}: \in \text{b}$ $(: \in \text{void b}_\perp)$

A generalized assignment is refined by an assumption of the same condition. The reason is that the final values of variables of the assignment might be arbitrary, whereas the assumption does not change the value of any variable. Actually, an assumption can be regarded as a generalized assignment to an empty list of variables.

Law 9.67 $(\text{x}: \in \text{b}) \sqsubseteq \text{b}^\top$ $(: \in \text{refined by b}^\top)$

Generalized assignment distributes rightward through the conditional, provided that the following condition is observed.

Law 9.68 If x does not occur in b,
$$\text{X} :\in \text{a}; (\text{p} \vartriangleleft \text{b} \vartriangleright \text{q}) = (\text{x} :\in \text{a}; \text{p}) \vartriangleleft \text{b} \vartriangleright (\text{x} :\in \text{a}; \text{q})$$
$$(; \in - \vartriangleleft \vartriangleright \text{right dist})$$

In general, an assignment cannot be expressed in terms of a generalized assignment only. For example, there is no generalized assignment that corresponds to the assignment x := x+1. The reason is that we have not introduced the notation to allow the condition of a generalized assignment of the form x: ∈b to refer back to the initial value of x. But x := e can always be written as a generalized assignment whenever the expression e does not mention x.

Law 9.69 If e does not mention x,
$$\text{x} : \in (\text{x} = \text{e}) = \text{x} := \text{e}   (:\in - := \text{conversion}).$$

If x and y are to be assigned arbitrary values (in sequence) to make a given condition hold, we can reduce the nondeterminism by ensuring that the same (arbitrary) value is assigned to both x and y.

Law 9.70 If b does not mention y,

(x: ∈b; y: ∈b[x←y]) ⊑ (x: ∈b; y:= x)   (: ∈ refined by :=)

We can commute the order of execution of assignment and an arbitrary program p, provided that no interference occurs with the global variables.

Law 9.71 If no free variables of b nor x is assigned by p,
    (p; x: ∈b) ⊑ (x: ∈b; p)   (x: ∈b; p commute)

The inequality occurs when p is ⊥ and assignment results in ⊤.

17. Iteration

We use b*p to denote the iteration command. It is a concise form of more conventional syntax,
    while b do p
Iteration can be defined as a special case of the recursion.

Definition 9.17 (Iteration)
    $b*p \Leftrightarrow$ (def as)$\mu X \cdot ((p; X) \lhd b \rhd skip)$

As iteration is a derived operator in our language, we are able to prove (rather than just postulate) some of its properties. This illustrates the modularity provided by the algebraic laws in developing more elaborate transformation strategies from the basic ones. These strategies are largely used in the next two sections, substantially simplifying the proof of normal form the reduction.

If the condition b does not hold initially, the iteration b*p behaves like skip; otherwise it behaves like p followed by the whole iteration.

Law 9.72 $(a \wedge \neg b)^\top ; b*p = (a \wedge \neg b)^\top$ (* elim)

Proof

> LHS $= (a \wedge \neg b)^\top ; (p; b*p) \lhd b \rhd skip$
>
> > {Definition 9.17 (Iteration) and Law 9.26 (μ fixed point)}
>
> $= (a \wedge \neg b)^\top$
>
> > {Law 9.63 ($\lhd \rhd$ false cond) and Law 9.1 (; -skip unit)}
>
> = RHS.

Law 9.73 $a^\top ; (a \vee b)*p = a^\top ; p; (a \vee b)*p$ (* unfold)

Proof

> LHS$= a^\top ; ((p; (a \vee b)*p) \lhd (a \vee b) \rhd skip)$ {Definition 9.10
>
> > (Iteration) and Law 9.26 (μ fixed point)}
>
> $= a^\top ; ((p; (a \vee b)*p)$ { Law 9.47 ($\lhd \rhd$ true cond)}
>
> = RHS

A recurrent step in our proof is to unfold an iteration and simplify the unfolded body when this is a guarded command set.

Law 9.74 Let $R = (a \rightarrow p \,\square\, b \rightarrow q)$. Then
$$a^\top; (a \vee b)^*R = a^\top; p\ ; (a \vee b)^*R \qquad (\text{*-}\square \text{ unfold})$$

Proof The formula follows immediately from Law 9.73 (*unfold) and Law 9.46 ($\square$ elim).

A guarded command set within an iteration can be eliminated if the condition of the Iteration allows only one of the guards to hold.

Law 9.75 Let $R = (a \rightarrow p \square\, b \rightarrow q)$. Then $a^*R = a^*p \qquad (\text{*-}\square \text{ elim})$

Proof

LHS$= a^* (a \rightarrow p \,\square\, b \rightarrow q)$
$= \mu X \cdot ((a^\top; (a \rightarrow p \,\square\, b \rightarrow q); X) \triangleleft a \triangleright skip)$ {Definition 9.10
                                 (Iteration) and Law 9.49 ($\triangleleft \ \triangleright$ void $b^\top$)}
$= \mu X \cdot ((a^\top; p; X) \triangleleft a \triangleright skip)$ {Law 9.46 ($\square$ elim)}
$= a^*p$ {Law 9.49 ($\triangleleft \ \triangleright$ void $b^\top$) and Definition 9.10 (Iteration)}
$=$ RHS.

The following allows the replacement of a guarded command inside an iteration.

Law 9.76 Let $R = (a \rightarrow p \,\square\, b \rightarrow q)$. If $r; (a \vee b) * R \sqsubseteq p; (a \vee b) * R$, then
$(a \vee b) * (a \rightarrow r \,\square\, b \rightarrow q) \sqsubseteq (a \vee b) * R$ (* replace guard command)

Proof This time, the proof starts from right hand side.

RHS$= (a \vee b) * (a \rightarrow p \,\square\, b \rightarrow q)$
$= ((a \rightarrow p \square\, b \rightarrow q); (a \vee b) * ((a \rightarrow p \square b \rightarrow q) * R)) \triangleleft a \vee b \triangleright skip$
              {Definition 9.10 (Iteration) and Law 9.26 (μ fixed point)}
$= (a \rightarrow (p; (a \rightarrow p \square\, b \rightarrow q) \,\square\, b \rightarrow (q; (a \rightarrow p \,\square\, b \rightarrow q)) \triangleleft a \vee b \triangleright skip))$
              {Law 9.24 (; -$\sqcap$ left dist)}
$\sqsupseteq (a \rightarrow (r; (a \rightarrow p \square\, b \rightarrow q)) \,\square\, b \rightarrow (q; (a \rightarrow p \,\square\, b \rightarrow q))) \triangleleft a \vee b \triangleright skip$
              {Assumption}
$= ((a \rightarrow r \,\square\, b \rightarrow q); (a \rightarrow p \,\square\, b \rightarrow q)) \triangleleft a \vee b \triangleright skip$
              {Law 9.24 (; $\sqcap$ left dist)}
$= (a \vee b) * (a \rightarrow r \,\square\, b \rightarrow q)$ {Law 9.27 (μ least fixed point)}.

The following law establishes the connection between tail-recursion and iteration. Its proof illustrates the use of approximate inverses of programming constructs.

Law 9.77 $(b * p); q = \mu X \cdot ((p; X) \triangleleft b \triangleright q)$ (* -μ tail recursion)

Proof The proof is carried out in two directions: LHS $\sqsupseteq$ RHS and RHS $\sqsupseteq$ LHS. At first, we establish LHS $\sqsupseteq$ RHS.

(b * p); q

$\quad = ((\text{p: } b * p)\lhd b \rhd \text{skip}); q$ {Definition 9.10 (Iteration) and
Law 9.26 (μ fixed point)}

$\quad = (p; ((b * p); q)\lhd b \rhd q$ {Law 9.62 (; - $\lhd \rhd$ left dist) and
Law 9.1 (; - skip unit)}

$\quad \sqsupseteq \mu X\cdot((p; X)\lhd b \rhd q) = \text{RHS}$ {Law 9.26 (μ least fixed point)}.

RHS= $(\mu X\cdot((p; X)\lhd b \rhd q))$

$\quad = (p; (\mu X\cdot(p; X)\lhd b \rhd q))\lhd b \rhd q$

$\quad \sqsupseteq (p; (\mu X\cdot(p; X)\lhd b \rhd q)); q); q)\lhd b \rhd q$

$\qquad$ {From Lemma 9.1 (strongest inverse of ;) we have (RHS; $\sqcup$ q);
$\qquad\qquad q \sqsubseteq$ RHS}

$\sqsupseteq((p; ((\mu X\cdot((p; X)\lhd b \rhd q); \sqcup q)\lhd b \rhd\text{skip}); q$

$\qquad$ {Law 9.62 (; -$\lhd \rhd$ left dist) and Law 9.1 (; skip unit)}.

Then from Definition 9.12 (Approximate inverses) we have

(RHS ; $\sqcup$ q)= $(\mu X\cdot((p; X)\lhd b \rhd q)); q \sqsupseteq$

$\qquad (p; ((\mu X\cdot((p; X)\lhd b \rhd q)); \sqcup q) \lhd b \rhd \text{skip}$

$\qquad \sqsupseteq b * p$ {Law 9.26 (μ least fixed point) and Definition 9.12

$\qquad\qquad$ (Approximate Inverses)}.

So RHS $\sqsupseteq$ LHS, according to Definition 9.12.

The following law is surprisingly important, mainly in proving the correctness of the normal form reduction of sequential composition.

Law 9.78 (b * p); (b∨c) * p = (b∨c) * p   (* sequence)

Proof   The proof once again is done by two sides RHS $\sqsupseteq$ LHS and LHS $\sqsupseteq$ RHS. At first, RHS $\sqsupseteq$ LHS.

RHS= RHS$\lhd b \rhd$ RHS   {Law 9.50 ($\lhd \rhd$ idemp)}

$\quad = ((p; \text{RHS})\lhd b∨c \rhd \text{skip})\lhd b \rhd ((b∨c) * p)$

$\qquad$ {(Definition 9.10 (Iteration) and Law 9.25 (μ fixed point)}

$\quad = ((p; \text{RHS})\lhd b∨c \rhd (b∨c) * p)\lhd b \rhd((b∨c) * p)$ {Law 9.49

$\qquad (\lhd \rhd$ void $b^\top$) and Law 9.72 (* elim)}

$\quad = (p; \text{RHS}) \lhd b \rhd ((b∨c) * p)$ {Law 9.54 ($\lhd \rhd$ cond conjunction)}

$\quad \sqsupseteq \mu X\cdot(p; X)\lhd b \rhd((b∨c) * p)$ {Law 9.26 (μ least fixed point)}

$\quad \sqsupseteq (b * p); ((b∨c) * p)$ {Law 9.77 (* -μ tail recursion)}

$\quad = \text{LHS},$

LHS= (q; (b * p))$\lhd b \rhd\text{skip}$); (b∨c) * p)   {Definition 9.10 (Iteration) and
Law 9.26 (μ fixed point)}

$= (p; LHS)\lhd b \rhd RHS$ {Law 9.52 (; -$\lhd$ $\rhd$ left dist) and Law 9.1

(; - skip Unit)}

$= (p; LHS)\lhd b \rhd((p; RHS)\lhd b\lor c \rhd skip)$ {Law 9.26 (μ fixed point)}

$\sqsupseteq (p; LHS)\lhd b\lor c \rhd skip$ {Law 9.55 ($\lhd$ $\rhd$ cond disjunction)} and

LHS $\sqsubseteq$ RHS}

$= (b\lor c) * p$.

18. Static Declaration

The notation dec x · p declares the list of the distinct variable x for use in the program p (the scope of the declaration). Local blocks of this form may appear anywhere a program is expected.

It does not matter whether variables are declared in one list or singly.

Law 9.79 If x and y have no variables in common,

dec x · (dec y · p) = dec x, y · p   (dec assoc)

The order in which variables occur does not matter either.

Law 9.80   dec x·(dec y · p)= dec y · (dec x · p)   (dec commu)

If a declared variable is never used, its declaration has no effect.

Law 9.81   If x is not free in p,

dec x · p= p   (dec elim)

One may change the name of a bound variable, provided that the new name is not used for a free variable.

Law 9.82   If y is not free in p, then

dec x · p = dec y · p[x←y]   (dec rename)

The value of a declared variable is totally arbitrary. Therefore, the initialization of a variable may reduce nondeterminism.

Law 9.83

1) dec x · p $\sqsubseteq$ dec x·x := e; p   (dec- := initial value)
2) dec x · p $\sqsubseteq$ dec x·x :$\in$ b; p   (dec- :$\in$ initial value)

An assignment to a variable just before the end of its scope is irrelevant. But a generalized assignment cannot be completely ignored, since it may result in a miracle.

Law 9.84

1) dec x · p = dec x · p; x := e   (dec- x:= final value)
2) dec x · p $\sqsubseteq$ dec x · p; x :$\in$ b   (dec- x :$\in$ final value)

The scope of a variable may be increased without effect, provided that it does not interfere with the other variables with the same name. Thus each of the programming constructs has a distribution law with declaration.

For example, if one of the arguments of the sequential composition operator declares the variable x then the scope of the declaration can be extended with the other component, provided that there is no capture of free variables.

Law 9.85 If x is not free in q,

   1) (dec x·p); q = dec x·p; q   (; -dec left dist)
   2) q; (dec x ·p) = dec x· q; p   (; -dec right dist)

When both arguments declare the same variable, the two declarations can be replaced with a single one.

Law 9.86 (dec x·p); (dec x· q) $\sqsubseteq$ dec x ·p; q   (dec-; dist)

But note that this may reduce nondeterminism. Consider the case that q is y := x. Then the final value of y on the left-hand side of above inequation would be totally arbitrary. On the right-hand side, however, it may be the case that x was assigned a value in p; thus the final value of y would be that of x. In all cases, the right hand-side is at least as deterministic as the left-hand side.

If each component of a guarded command set or conditional declares the variable x then the declaration may be moved outside the constructor, provided that x does not occur in the guard or in the condition.

Law 9.87 If x does not occur in a or b,

   a$\rightarrow$(dec x·p) $\square$ b$\rightarrow$ (dec x· q) = dec x·a$\rightarrow$p $\square$ b$\rightarrow$ q   (dec-$\square$ dist)

Law 9.88 If x does not occur in b,

   (dec x·p)$\triangleleft$ b $\triangleright$(dec x· q) = dec x ·p$\triangleleft$ b $\triangleright$ q   (dec -$\triangleleft$ $\triangleright$ dist)

Note that it is possible to deal with cases where x is only declared in one of the branches (and is not free in the other ones) being used in Law 9.81.

Declaration can also be moved outside an iteration, possibly reducing nondeterminism. As shown below, this law can be derived from more basic ones.

Law 9.89 b * (dec x·p) $\sqsubseteq$ dec x·b * p   (dec- * dist)

Proof Our proof starts with right–hand side.

RHS= dec x· (p; b * p) $\triangleleft$ b $\triangleright$skip   {Definition 9.10 (Iteration) and
            Law 9. 26 (μ fixed point)}

   = (dec x ·p; b * p) $\triangleleft$ b $\triangleright$skip   {Law 9.88 (dec-$\triangleleft$ $\triangleright$ dist) and
            Law 9.81 (dec elim)}

   $\sqsupseteq$ ((dec x·p); dec x· b * p)$\triangleleft$ b $\triangleright$skip {Law 9.86 (dec-; dist)}

   = b * (dec x·p) = LHS   {Definition 9.10 (Iteration) and
            Law 9.26 (μ fixed point)}.

19. Dynamic Declaration

The command var x introduces a dynamic scope of x that extends up to
- the end of the static scope of x,
- the execution of the command end x,

whichever comes first.

An operational argument may help to clarify how the two kinds of declarations relate to each other. The general idea is to associate an unbounded stack with each variable. One can think of a static declaration of x as introducing a new variable (that is assigned an arbitrary value) with its (implicit) unbounded stack that is initially empty. Rather than creating a new variable, commands for the dynamic declaration operate on this stack. The effect of var x is to push the current value of x onto the stack, assigning to x an arbitrary value; end x pops the stack and assigns the popped value to x. If the stack is empty, this value is arbitrary.

As our language does not enforce the variable declaration, we must consider how is the view of an undeclared variable in this scenario. The operational interpretation in this case is that an unbounded (and initially empty) stack is automatically associated with the undeclared variable, when the variable is first used. The effect of var and end concerning this stack is the same as discussed above.

Recall that having separate commands to introduce and end the scope of a variable is an essential feature to define the encoding and decoding programs used in our approach to data refinement: the encoding program introduces the abstract state and ends the scope of the concrete state whereas the decoding program introduces the concrete state and ends the scope of the abstract state.

The commands var and end obey laws similar to those of dec. Nevertheless, one immediate difference is that renaming is not valid in general for dynamic declarations (except when static and dynamic declarations have the same effect as explained later in this section).

Both var and end are associative in the sense described below.

Law 9.90 If x and y have no variables in common,
   1) (var x; var y) = var x, y   (var assoc)
   2) (end x; end y) = end x, y   (end assoc)

The (dynamic) scope of a variable may be increased without effect, provided that this does not interfere with other free variables.

Law 9.91 If x is not free in p,
   1) p; var x = varx ; p   (var change scope)
   2) end x; p = p; end x   (end change scope)

Both var and end distribute rightward through the conditional, as long as no interference occurs with the condition.

Law 9.92 If b does not mention x,

1) (var x; p) ◁ b ▷(var x; q) = var x; (p◁ b ▷ q)   (var- ◁ ▷ right dist)

2) (end x; p)◁ b ▷(end x; q) = end x;   (p◁ b ▷ q) (end- ◁ ▷ right dist)

As explained above var x assigns an arbitrary value to x. The nondeterminism can be reduced by initialization of x.

Law 9.93

1) var x ⊑ (var x; x := e)   (var- := initial value).
2) var x ⊑ (var x; x: ∈ b)   (var- : ∈ initial value).

An assignment to a variable just before the end of its scope is irrelevant. But a generalized assignment cannot be completely ignored, as it may result in miracle.

Law 9.94

1) end x= (x := e ; end x)   (end- ; = final value)
2) end x ⊑   (x : ∈ b; end x) (end- : ∈ final value)

The next two laws are essential for reasoning about data refinement. They are precisely the ones that assign the dynamic declaration semantics to var and end. The first law says that end x followed by var x leaves all variables but x unchanged; var x followed by end x has no effect (even on x). Therefore, the pair (end x, var x) is a simulaton.

Law 9.95   (end x; var x) ⊑ skip ⊑ (var x; end x)   (end-var simulation)

The second law postulates that the sequential composition of end x with var x has no effect whenever it is followed by an assignment to x that does not rely on the previous value of x.

Law 9.96   (end x; var x; x: ∈ b) = x: ∈ b   (end-var skip)

Observe that this law holds even when x occurs in b because an occurrence of x in b does not refer to the previous value of x; rather, it is a requirement for the current value of x. Also note that the syntax of the static declaration (dec) promptly disallows the above two laws, since there is no separate construct to end the scope of a variable.

The following two laws relate the two kinds of declarations. They formalize the intuitive meaning given before.

If the first command in the scope of a static declaration of x is var x or end x, this command has no effect.

Law 9.97

1) dec x·var x; p = dec x·p   (var elim 1)
2) dec x· end x; p = dec x·p   (end elim 1)

First we give a justification of 1). Recall that a static declaration of x creates an implicit stack that is initially empty. Then the effect of var x on the left-hand side of 1) is to push the current value of x (that is arbitrary) onto this stack and to assign the arbitrary value to x. But the value of x was already arbitrary; thus the assignment has no effect. Furthermore, the effect of pushing an arbitrary value onto the empty stack is also immaterial. The only command that may access this value is a subsequent end x that would assign an arbitrary value to x if the stack was empty anyway. The justification of 2) is simpler. As the stack associated with x is initially empty, the effect of end x is to assign an arbitrary value to x; but the value of x was already arbitrary.

As we mentioned before, the dynamic scope of a variable x cannot extend further than its static scope. Therefore, starting or ending a dynamic scope of x just before the end of its static scope is irrelevant.

Law 9.98

    1) dec x·p; var x= dec x·p   (var elim 2)

    2) dec x·p; end x = dec x·p   (end elim 2)

In some cases, there is no need to distinguish between a static and a dynamic scope of a given variable. So we must examine when the two kinds of declarations have the same effect.

As already discussed, having separate constructs to introduce and end the (dynamic) scope of a variable allows more flexibility than with a single construct. This fact has been well illustrated by the simulation concept introduced before; it would not have been possible to express this notion in our language if we had only allowed static declaration.

Therefore, a static declaration cannot, in general, replace a dynamic declaration.

However, under certain conditions this can be achieved. One immediate requirement is that each var x in a program has a corresponding, statically determined, end x, so that replace blocks of the form

    var x; q; end x,

with

    dec c · q.

This requirement is captured by the following definition.

Definition 9.18 (Block-structure) A program p is block-structured with respect to a variable x if it is built according to the following two rules:

    1) all the programs that do not contain the commands var x or end x are block-structured with respect to x.

    2) if p is block-structured with respect to x, so is

    var x; p; end x.

While the above condition is clearly necessary to allow the replacement of a dynamic by a static declaration of x, it is not sufficient. The reason is that a static declaration is governed by static scope rules, whereas a dynamic declaration is governed by dynamic scope rules, as illustrated by the following example.

Suppose that the program identifier x is bound to the program text x := y. Now consider the following program (assuming that x, y, and z are distinct variables)

var y; y:= z; X; end y,

where the above occurrence of X stands for a call of the program bound to it: x := y. Dynamic scope rules determine that the occurrence of y in the program (identified by) X is bound to the above (dynamic) declaration of y. Therefore, one can easily conclude that the effect of the above program is to assign z to x.

Now let us consider what is the effect of the program

dec y · y:= z; X.

In this case, because the declaration of y is static, any call command in the scope of this declaration is governed by static scope rules. That means that the occurrence of y in the program X is bound to the declaration of y whose scope includes the definition of X, and not to the above declaration whose scope includes a call of X. Therefore, the y introduced in the above declaration is a different variable from the occurrence of y in X; they just happen to have the same name. Renaming the local declaration of y above (recall that renaming in general is allowed only for static declaration), say with a fresh variable w, does not change the behavior of the above program. This leads to

dec w · w:= z; X

that can itself be easily transformed (using simple laws of declaration) into

x:= y.

As a result, we observe that static and dynamic declaration of the same variable in this case have distinct effects. This happens only in the presence of call commands since these are governed by different scope rules, depending on whether static or dynamic declaration are introduced.

To capture the precise context where one cannot distinguish between a static and a dynamic declaration of a given variable, we need the following concept:

Definition 9.19 (Contiguous scope)   We state that a variable x has a contiguous scope in a program p if

- p contains no free program identifiers (standing for call commands) or
- if the program identifier X is free in p, then the variable x must not be free in (the program defining) X.

Note that in the situation exemplified above by the program

dec y; y:= z; X

the variable y does not have a contiguous scope, since there is a free program identifier X in which y is free(recall that X is bound to the program x := y). Finally, we present the law that precisely relates the two forms of the variable declaration.

Law 9.99   If p is a block-structured with respect to x, and x has a contiguous scope in p, then dec x · p = var x; p; end x   (dec-(var, end) conversion)

We can ensure that programs will always have contiguous scope (with respect to any local variable) by requiring that nested declarations always use distinct names for variables (that are also distinct from the names used for global variables). When applying the above law we will assume that the condition of contiguous scope is always satisfied.

For example, as explained above, the scope of y in

dec y; y:= z; X

is not contiguous, but renaming allows us to transform this program (assuming that w is a fresh variable) into one that clearly satisfies the contiguous scope condition concerning w, since w does not appear in the program (x := y) bound to X. Now we can deduce that the above is equivalent to

var w; w:= z; X; end w

that is itself equivalent to x, x := y, as expected.

From Law 9.99, we derive the following law about introduction of local declarations.

Law 9.100 If p is block-structured with respect to x, and x has a contiguous scope in p, then

x :∈ b; p; x :∈ c = (dec x · x :∈ x :∈ b; p); x :∈ c   (dec introduction)

Proof

LHS = end x; var x; x: ∈ b; p; end x; var x; x: ∈ c

{Law 9.96 (end-var skip)}

= end x; (dec x · x: ∈ b; p); var x; x: ∈ c

{Law 9.99 (dec- (var-end) conversion)}

= (dec x · x: ∈ b; p); end x; var x; x: ∈ c

{Law 9.91 (end change scope)}

= (dec x · x: ∈ b; p); x: ∈ c   {Law 9.96 (end-var skip)}

= RHS.

The above two laws will be used in the next section to perform transformations on source programs. These are always block-structured, since var and end are not part of our source language. We have explained how to ensure that programs always have contiguous scope (with respect to any local variable). Therefore, these laws will be applied assuming that these conditions are always satisfied.

20. Correctness of Basic Laws

In a purely algebraic view, the laws of a given language are an algebraic semantics for this language. There is no place for the task of verifying the validity of the more basic laws; they are axioms that express the relationship between the operators of the language. However, the method of postulating is questioned by those who follow a model-oriented approach, especially when the set of axioms is relatively large as it is the present one. Postulating an inconsistent set of laws could be a disaster: it would allow one to prove invalid results, like the correctness of an inaccurate compiler.

The way to avoid the danger is to link the algebraic semantics of the language with a (non-trivial) method in which the laws can be proven. There are many references concerning this issue. It is also possible to link the algebraic semantics of the language to a more concrete (operational) model. This allows to check for feasibility (implementability) of language operators. But in our case, this is impossible, as our reasoning language includes non-implementable operators.

Once the laws have been proven, in whichever model, they should serve as tools for carrying our program transformation. The mathematical definitions that allow their verification are normally more complex, and therefore, not appealing to practical use.

But even after the model has served its intended purpose, additional results of practical interest can be achieved. For example, from the experience in the application of basic laws of programming to solve a given task, one discovers more elaborate transformation strategies that allow more concise and elegant proofs. This was illustrated in the section on iteration where all the laws were derived from more basic ones.

The existence of these nontrivial models for the reasoning language shows that its algebraic laws in some sense consistent. In the following, we use the predicate transformer model to illustrate how the basic laws of our language can be verified.

We deal with a few operators only. Their definitions were given in the last section, but will be repeated again for convenience. In the following a ranges the set of predicates, p and q stand for arbitrary programs, and P stands for an arbitrary set of programs.

$$\text{skip} \Leftrightarrow (\text{def as})\lambda a \cdot a$$

$$\bot \Leftrightarrow (\text{def as})\lambda a \cdot \text{false}$$

$$\top \Leftrightarrow (\text{def as})\lambda a \cdot \text{true}$$

$$\sqcup P \Leftrightarrow (\text{def as})\lambda a \cdot (\exists X \mid X \in P \cdot X(a))$$

$$\sqcap P \Leftrightarrow (\text{def as})\lambda a \cdot (\forall X \mid X \in P \cdot X(a))$$

$$p; q \Leftrightarrow (\text{def as})\lambda a \cdot p(q(a)).$$

The binary versions of $\sqcup$ and $\sqcap$ are defined as special cases of the above definitions:

$$p \sqcup q \Leftrightarrow (\text{def as})\lambda a \cdot p(a) \vee q(a),$$

$$p \sqcap q \Leftrightarrow (\text{def as})\lambda a \cdot p(a) \wedge q(a).$$

The definition of the remaining operators can be given similarly. One can also found them from, for example [3]. From the above definition we can prove that the laws of the corresponding operators. For example, from the definition of $\sqsubseteq$ we can derive its characteristics in terms of weakest preconditions:

$p \sqsubseteq q \equiv (p \sqcap q) = p$ {Definition 9.1 (The ordering relation)}

$\equiv (\lambda a \cdot p(a) \wedge q(a))$ {definition of $\sqcap$}

$\equiv \forall a \cdot (p(a) \wedge q(a) \Leftrightarrow p(a))$ {the axiom of extensionality}

$\equiv \forall a \cdot (p(a) \Rightarrow q(a))$ {predicate calculus}.

That corresponds precisely to the definition of refinement adopted in all approaches to the refinement based on weakest preconditions, as discussed in the previous section. As another example, we verify law ($\sqcup$-$\sqcap$ dist) (Law 9.25):

$(\sqcup P) \sqcap p = \lambda a \cdot (\sqcup P)(a) \wedge p(a)$ {definition of $\sqcap$ }

$= \lambda a \cdot (\exists X | X \in P \cdot X(a)) \wedge p(a)$ {definition of $\sqcup$}

$= \lambda a \cdot (\exists X | X \in P \cdot (X(a) \wedge p(a)))$ {Assuming that X is not free in p}

$= \lambda a \cdot (\exists X | X \in P \cdot (X \sqcap p) (a))$ {definition of $\sqcap$ }

$= \lambda a \cdot (\exists X | X \in \{X | X \in P \cdot (X \sqcap p)\}) \cdot X(a)$ {set theory}

$= \sqcup \{X \in P \cdot (X \sqcap p)\}$ {definition of $\sqcup$}.

9.4 A Simple Compiler

In this section, we will exemplify our system to see how it works in producing a compiler. Of course, it is a simple one and not practical as its purpose is only to show that our approach to compiler design works. In this section, we first describe the normal form of a model of an arbitrary executing mechanism. The normal form theorems in the section are concerned with control elimination: the reduction of the nested control structure of the source program to a single flat iteration. These theorems are largely independent of a particular target machine.

Then we design and prove the correctness of a compiler for a subset of our source language, not including procedures or recursion. The constructions considered here are skip, assignment, sequential composition, demonic nondeterminism, conditional, iteration and local declaration.

As mentioned early, the compilation process is split into three main phases: simplification of expressions, control elimination and data refinement (the conversion from the abstract space of the source program to the concrete state of the target machine).

Each of these generic transformations has the status of a theorem. The more specific transformations that illustrate the compilation process for a specific target machine have a status of a rule. Each rule describes a transformation that brings the source program closer to a normal form with the same structure as the specific target machine. Taking collectively, these rules can be used to carry out the compilation task.

It is necessary to emphasize that one should notice the different roles played by the algebraic laws of the last section and these reduction rules: the laws express general properties of the language operators, whereas the rules serve the special purpose of transforming an arbitrary program to a normal form. In one word, the laws are necessary to prove the rules, and these (not the laws) are used to carry out compilation.

9.4.1 The Normal Form

A program of the form
$$\text{decv} \cdot v :\in a; b * p; c_{\perp}$$
can be interpreted as a very general model of a machine executing a stored program in the following way:

1) The list of variables represents the machine components (for example, registers). They are introduced as local variables since they have no counterpart at the source level; therefore their final values are irrelevant.

2) a is an assumption about the initial state. If it is impossible to make a true by assigning to v, the machine behaves like a miracle; this saves the compiler designer from dealing with states not satisfying a. Observe that the use of the nondeterministic assignment v: $\in$ a to initialize the machine allows us to abstract from the way control state is encoded.

3) P is the stored program; it is executed until the condition b becomes false. Usually, P will be a guarded command set of the form
$$b_1 \to p_1 \square \ldots \square b_n \to p_n.$$
Whenever the machine is in the state b_i the action (or instruction) p_i is executed. In this case, the condition b is given by
$$b_1 \vee \ldots \vee b_n.$$

4) c is an assertion about the final state of the machine; if execution of the stored program does not assert c, the machine ends up behaving like abort. Notice that, upon termination of the iteration b * p, b is false and we have
$$b * p; c_{\perp} = b * p; (\neg b)_{\perp}; c_{\perp} = b * p; (\neg b \wedge c)_{\perp}.$$

Thus, there is no loss of generality in assuming that c= ($\neg$ b$\wedge$c), and consequently that (b$\wedge$c)= false. The normal form theorems will rely on the assumption that b and c are disjoint.

A normal form program will be abbreviated as follows:

Definition 9.20 (Normal form)

$$v : [a, b \to p, c] \Leftrightarrow (\text{def as}) \text{ dec } v \cdot v :\in a; b * p; c_{\perp} \text{ where } (b \wedge c) = \text{false}$$

For convenience, we will sometimes use the form

$$v : [a, (b_1 \to p_1 \square \ldots \square b_n \to p_n), c]$$

as an abbreviation of

$$v : [a, (b_1 \vee \ldots b_n) \to (b_1 \to p_1 \square \ldots \square b_n \to p_n), c].$$

9.4.2 Normal Form Reduction

To reduce arbitrary program to normal form, it is sufficient to show how each primitive command can be rewritten in the normal form, and how each operator of the language (when applied to operands in the normal form) yields a result expressible in the normal form. The following reductions involve no change of data representation. Therefore, we can directly compare the source constructs with the associated normal form programs.

Some of the theorems state very simple results (some are just corollaries of algebraic laws or lemmas), but they have this status because each one shows how a given operator of the source language can be reduced to normal form. These theorems can be regarded as expressing generic transformations in that they are independent of the target machine.

If the initial state coincides with the final state, the machine does not perform any action. In the more concrete terms, the empty code is a possible implementation of skip.

Theorem 9.6 (Skip) $\text{skip} \sqsubseteq v : [a, b \to p, a]$

Proof

$$\begin{aligned}
\text{RHS} &= \text{dec } v \cdot v: \in a; a_\perp &&\{\text{Law 9.75 (*elim) (, remember } a \wedge b = \text{false)} \\
&= \text{dec } v \cdot v: \in a; \text{skip} &&\{\text{Law 9.66 (: } \in \text{void } a_\perp \text{) and} \\
&&& \text{Law 9.1 (; -skip unit)}\} \\
&\sqsupseteq \text{skip} = \text{LHS} &&\{\text{Law 9.93 (dec- : } \in \text{initial value) and} \\
&&& \text{Law 9.91 (dec elim)}\}.
\end{aligned}$$

The following lemma shows how a primitive command can be written in normal form. Actually, the lemma is valid for all programs p, but we will not make use of it for non-primitive constructs because we follow an innermost (bottom-up) reduction strategy.

Lemma 9.2 (Primitive commands) If v is not free in p then
$$p \sqsubseteq v: [a \to (p; v: \in c), c]$$

Proof

$$\begin{aligned}
\text{RHS} &= \text{dec } v \cdot v: \in a; p; v: \in c; c_\perp \\
&&&\{\text{Law 9.73 (*unfold) and Law 9.72 (*elim)}\} \\
&\sqsupseteq \text{dec } v^*p; v: \in c \\
&&&\{\text{Law 9 83 (dec -: } \in \text{initial value) and Law 9.66 (: } \in \text{void } c_\perp \text{)}\} \\
&\sqsupseteq p &&\{\text{Law 9.84 (dec- : } \in \text{final value) and Law 9.81 (dec elim)}\}
\end{aligned}$$

= LHS.

The following normal form representations of skip and assignment are initialization of the above lemma. The one of skip is further simplified by the fact that it is an identity of sequential composition. The operational interpretation is that skip can be implemented by a jump.

Theorem 9.7 (Skip)
$$\text{skip} \sqsubseteq v : [a, (a \rightarrow v :\in c), c]$$

Theorem 9.8 (Assignment)
$$x := e \sqsubseteq v : [a, a \rightarrow (x := e; v :\in c), c]$$

The reduction of sequential composition assumes that both arguments are already in the normal form, and that the final state of the left argument coincides with the initial state of the right argument. The guarded command set of the resulting normal form combines the original guarded commands. First we consider the particular case where the guarded command set of the right argument includes that of the left argument.

Lemma 9.3 (Sequential composition)

$$v : [a, b_1 \rightarrow p, c_0]; v : [c_0,, (b_1 \rightarrow p \square b_2 \rightarrow q), c] \sqsubseteq v : [a, (b_1 \rightarrow p \square b_2 \rightarrow q), c]$$

Proof   Let $R = (b_1 \rightarrow p \square b_2 \rightarrow q)$, then

$$
\begin{aligned}
\text{LHS} = \ & \text{dec } v \cdot v : \in a; \ b_1 * p; \ c_{0\perp}; \ v : \in c_0; \ (b_1 \vee b_2) * R; \ c_\perp \\
& \qquad\qquad\qquad\qquad \{\text{Law 9.86(dec-; dist)}\} \\
\sqsubseteq \ & \text{dec } v \cdot v : \in a; \ b_1 * p; \ (b_1 \vee b_2) * R; \ c_\perp \quad \{\text{Law 9.95 (v: } \in c_0 \text{ refined}} \\
& \qquad\qquad \text{by } c_0^\top) \text{ and Law 9.37 } (c_{0\perp}\text{-}c_0^\top \text{ conversation})\} \\
= \ & \text{dec } v \cdot v : \in a; \ b_1 * R; \ (b_1 \vee b_2) * R; \ c_\perp \quad \{\text{Law 9.75 } (*\text{-}\square \text{ elim})\} \\
= \ & v : [a, (b_1 \rightarrow p \square b_2 \rightarrow q), c] = \text{RHS} \quad \{\text{Law 9.78 } (*\text{sequence})\}.
\end{aligned}
$$

Now we show that the guarded command set of a normal form program can be reduced by eliminating arbitrary guarded commands; the program obtained is worse than the original one. Put the other way round, extending the guarded command set by introducing new guarded commands leads to refinement.

Lemma 9.4 (Eliminate guarded command)
$$v : [a, (b_1 \rightarrow p \square b_2 \rightarrow q), c] \sqsupseteq v : [a, b_1 \rightarrow p, c]$$

Proof

$$
\begin{aligned}
& \text{Let } R = (b_1 \rightarrow p \square b_2 \rightarrow q) \\
& \text{LHS} \sqsupseteq v : [a, b_1 \rightarrow p, c]; \ v : [c, r, c] \\
& \qquad\qquad \{\text{Lemma 9.3 (sequential composition)}\} \\
& \qquad \sqsupseteq v : [a, b_1 \rightarrow p, c] \\
& \qquad\qquad \{\text{Theorem 9.7 (skip) and Law 9.1 (; - skip unit)}\} \\
& \qquad = \text{RHS}.
\end{aligned}
$$

The reduction of sequential composition is proven directly from the above two lemmas. These lemmas will be of more general utility.

Theorem 9.9 (Sequential composition)

$$v : [a, b_1 \rightarrow p, c_0]; v : [c_0, b_2 \rightarrow q, c] \sqsubseteq v : [a, (b_1 \rightarrow p \,\square\, b_2 \rightarrow q), c]$$

Proof

RHS $\sqsupseteq$ v: $[a, b_1 \rightarrow p, c_0]$; v: $[c_0, (b_1 \rightarrow p \,\square\, b_2 \rightarrow q), c]$

  {Lemma 9.3 (sequential composition)}

$\sqsupseteq$ v: $[a, b_1 \rightarrow p, c_0]$; v: $[c_0, b_2 \rightarrow q, c]$

  {Lemma 9.4 (eliminate guarded command)}

= LHS.

The following lemma shows how to eliminate a conditional command when its branches are normal form programs with identical components, except for the initial state. The first action to be executed in the resulting normal form program determines which of the original initial states should be activated.

Lemma 9.5 (Conditional)

If v is not free in b then

$\quad$ v : $[a_1, R, c] \lhd b \rhd$ v : $[a_2, R, c] \sqsubseteq$ v : $[a, R, c]$

where R= $(a \rightarrow (v: \in a_1 \lhd b \rhd v: \in a_2) \,\square\, b_1 \rightarrow p)$.

Proof

RHS = dec v·v: $\in a$; (v: $\in a_1 \lhd b \rhd v$: $\in a_2$); $(a \lor b_1)$*R; $c_\perp$

  {Law 9.74 (*- $\square$ unfold)}

= dec v·v: $\in a$; (v: $\in a_1$; $(a \lor b_1)$*R; $c_\perp$) $\lhd b \rhd$

  (v: $\in a_2$; $(a \lor b_2)$*R; $c_\perp$)   {Law 9.52 (; -$\lhd$ $\rhd$ left dist)}

= (dec v·v: $\in a$; v: $\in a_1$; $(a \lor b_1)$*R; $c_\perp \lhd b \rhd$

  (dec v·v: $\in a$; v: $\in a_2$; $(a \lor b_1)$*R; $c_\perp$)   {Law 9.68 (: $\in \lhd$ $\rhd$

  right dist) and Law 9.88 (dec-$\lhd$ $\rhd$ dist)}

= v: $[a_1, R, c] \lhd b \rhd$ v: $[a_2, R, c]$= LHS

  {Law 9.93 (dec-: $\in$ initial value)}.

The above lemma is useful for intermediate calculations. It is used in the proof of the normal form reduction of conditional and iteration commands.

Theorem 9.10 (Conditional)

If v does not occur in b then

$\quad$ v : $[a_1, b_1 \rightarrow p, c_1] \lhd b \rhd$ v : $[a_2, b_2 \rightarrow p, c] \sqsubseteq$ v : $[a, R, c]$

where R = $(a \rightarrow (v: \in a_1 \lhd b \rhd v: \in a_2) \,\square\, b_1 \rightarrow p \,\square\, c_1 \rightarrow v: \in c \,\square\, b_2 \rightarrow q)$

Proof

RHS = v: $[a, R, c]$

$\sqsupseteq$ v: $[a_1, R, c] \lhd b \rhd$v: $[a_2, R, c]$ {Lemma 9.5 (conditional)}

$\sqsupseteq$ (v: $[a_1, b_1 \to p, c_1]$; v: $[c_1, c_1 \to v: \in c, c] \lhd b \rhd$ v:

$[a_2, b_2 \to q, c]$ {Lemma 9.3 (sequential composition)

and Lemma 9.4 (eliminate guarded command)}

$\sqsupseteq$ v: $[a_1, b_1 \to p, c_1] \lhd b \rhd$ v: $[a_2, b_2 \to q, c]$ = LHS

{Theorem 9.7 (skip) and Law 9.1 (; - skip unit)}.

The next lemma establishes a simple fact that if the unique effect of the first guarded command to be executed is to make a certain expression true. We may substitute the expression for the initial state of the normal form program.

Lemma 9.6 (Void initial value)

$$v : [c_0, (c_0 \to v : \in a \,\square\, b \to p), c] \sqsupseteq v : [a, (c_0 \to v : \in a \,\square\, b \to p), c].$$

Proof

LHS = v: $[c_0, (c_0 \to v: \in a \square b \to p), c] \sqsupseteq$ v: $[a, (c_0 \to v: \in a \square b \to p), c]$

= dec v·v: $\in c_0$; v: $\in a$; $(c_0 \vee b)^*(c_0 \to v: \in a \,\square\, b \to p)$; $c_\perp$

{Law 9.73 (*-$\square$ unfold)}

$\sqsupseteq$ v: $[a, (c_0 \to v: \in a \,\square\, b \to p), c]$ = RHS

{Law 9. 83 (dec-: $\in$ initial value)}.

In order to reduce an iteration command, we assume that its body is in the normal form. Let a_0 and c_0 be the initial and final state of this normal form program. The normal form of the whole iteration behaves as follows: The first action to be executed is a conditional command that tests if the condition of the iteration holds, in which case a_0 is activated; otherwise, the program reaches its final state. When c_0 is activated, the guard of the first action is activated so that the conditional command is executed again.

Theorem 9.11 (Iteration)

If v does not occur in b then
$$b * v : [a_0, b_1 \to p, c_0] \sqsubseteq v : [a, R, c]$$
where $R = (a \to (v: \in a_0 \lhd b \rhd v: \in c) \,\square\, c_0 \to v: \in a \,\square\, b_1 \to p)$.

Proof

RHS = v: $[a, R, c]$

$\sqsupseteq$ v: $[a_0, R, c] \lhd b \rhd$ v: $[c, R, c]$ {Lemma 9.5 (Conditional)}

$\sqsupseteq$ v: $[a_0, b_1 \to p, c_0]$; v: $[c_0, R, c] \lhd b \rhd$ skip   {Lemma 9.3 (sequential composition) and Theorem 9.7 (skip)}

$\sqsupseteq$(v: $[a_0, b_1 \to p, c_0]$; RHS) $\lhd b \rhd$ skip {Lemma 9.5 (Void initial state)}

$\sqsupseteq$ b*v: $[a_0, b_1 \to p, c_0]$ = LHS   {Law 9.37 (μ least fixed point)}.

The demonic nondeterministic choice $\sqcap$ of two programs can be implemented by either of them. We can actually eliminate the choice at the source level, and avoid compiling one of the component.

Theorem 9.12   (Nondeterminism)
1) $(p \sqcap q) \sqsubseteq p$
2) $(p \sqcap q) \sqsubseteq q$

Proof   It follows from Law 9. 22 ($\sqsubseteq$-$\sqcap$ glb).

9.4.3   The Target Machine

The compiler which we design produces code for a simple target machine that consists of four components:

A   Accumulator
P   a sequential register (program counter)
M   a store for instructions (ROM)
m   a store for the data or operand

The idea is to regard the machine components as program variables and design the instructions as assignments that update the machine state.

P and A will be represented by single variables. Although we do not deal with types explicitly, P will be assigned integer expressions, standing for locations in ROM. A will be treated as an ordinary source variable; it will play an important role in the decomposition of expressions, that is the subject of next section. M will be modeled as a map (finite function) from addresses of the program counter in P to address where the instruction to be executed is stored, and m as a map from the address variable in expression to the location in RAM.

In order to model M and m, we need to extend our language to allow map variables. We use the following operators on maps:

$\{x{\to}e\}$ singleton map

$m_1 \cup m_2$ union

$m_1 \odot m_2$ overriding

$m[x]$ application

Perhaps the least familiar of these operators is overriding: $m_1 \odot m_2$ contains all the pairs in m_2 plus each pair in m_1 whose domain element is not in the domain of m_2. For example,

$$\{x \to e, y \to f\} \odot \{y \to g, z \to h\} = \{x \to e, y \to g, z \to h\}.$$

Furthermore, we use the following abbreviations:

$$\{x_1, \ldots, x_n \to e_1, \ldots, e_n\} \Leftrightarrow (\text{def as})\{x_1 \to e_1\} \cup \ldots \cup \{x_n \to e_n\}.$$

Problems

Problem 9.1   Using the derivative language of this chapter, express the following computation

$$a \times (1+p)^n - a.$$

Problem 9.2   Using the derivation language of this chapter, express the following computation

$$Area = (s(s-a)\ (s-b)\ (s-c))^{1/2}$$

where $s = (a+b+c)/2$.

Problem 9.3   Using the derivation of this chapter, write a program to compare three numbers a, b, and c, find out the biggest one.

Problem 9.4   Using the derivation language of this chapter, find out the smallest n such that

$$1+2+\ldots+n \geqslant 500$$

and compute the real sum.

Problem 9.5   Using the derivation language of this chapter, write two versions of program of finding the greatest common divisor. The definition of greatest common divisor of two integers x and y is

y,	if y$\leqslant$and x mod y$= 0$
$\gcd(x,\ y) = \gcd(y,\ x),$	if y$>$x
$\gcd(y,\ x \bmod y),$	otherwise.

Problem 9.6   Using the derivation language of this chapter, convert the input decimal integers into the number of any system.

Problem 9.7   Using the derivation language of this chapter, write a program that receives a character from keyboard, then sort these characters according to the increasing order of these characters. Delete the replicated characters (if any).

Problem 9.8   Using the derivation language, write a program to compute the following the proposition formula:

$$(P \to (Q \wedge R)) \wedge (\sim P \to \sim Q) \wedge \sim R).$$

Problem 9.9   Write a program that realizes the function of the accumulator, it accumulates the input of user until the input is zero. Then output the result of the accumulator. Then using the methods provided in the chapter, compile the program.

References

[1]   Dijkstra EW (1976) A discipline of progranmming. Prentice-Hall, Englewood Cliffs, New Jersey.

[2] Sampio A (1997) An algebraic approach to compiled design. World Scientific, Singapore.

[3] Guinan PJ, Cooprider JG, Sawyer S (1997) The effective use of automated application development tools. IBM System Journal 36, (1) 124–139.

[4] Hoare CAR (1969) An axiomatic basis for computer progamming. Communications of the ACM 12, pp 567–583.

[5] Dijkstra EV (1968) A Constructive approcach to the problem of program correctness. BIT 8 (3): 174–186.

[6] Meyer B (1985) On Formalism in Specifications, IEEE Software 2, pp. 6–26.

[7] Hoare CAR (1987) An overview of some formal methods for progran design. IEEE Computre 20, pp 85–91.

[8] Fenton NE, Fleege SLP (1997) Software Metrics: A rigorous and practical approach, 2nd eds. IEEE Society, Los Alamitos (Chapter 5).

[9] Tracz WJ (1979) Computer programming and the human thought process. Software: Practice and Experience 9, pp 127–137.

Chapter 10   Generation of Intermediate Code

*Our task is to cross the river but without the bridge we
have no way to cross it. In order to build the bridge,
we have to prepare all the materials needed for the construction of the bridge.*

Mao Zedong

*We cross the river via touching the stones on the bot-
tom of the river.*

Deng Xiaoping

10.1 Motivation of the Chapter

After finishing the first phase, i.e., the analytical phase of compilation, naturally we may enter the second phase, i.e., the synthetic phase. And the main
task of this phase is to generate the target code. Why don't we directly generate the target code instead of bothering to generate the intermediate code?
The first question should be answered in this chapter.

Theoretically there is no any difficulty for us to generate the target code
after finishing the analysis of the source program and storing all the information (data). It will be beneficial for generating efficient target code by
generating the intermediate code instead of directly generating the target
code.

The so-called intermediate code means the program rewritten from the
source program in the intermediate language. Actually if we compile the
source program in a number of passes, the intermediate language has already
existed.

We use it as the media that transits from one pass to the next pass. That
means that the output of a pass is the input of the next pass. They are the
same thing and it is in the intermediate language. At first after the lexical
analysis, a rewriting source version is yielded. The lexical analysis transformes
the identifiers, variables, constants and reserves words of the language into
the machine version with the fixed-length. Therefore after lexical analysis, the

program text will consist of the text with a series of symbols of fixed-lengths. They are the replacements of the original symbols with variable lengths. The simplest form is integers, some of which correspond to the reserved words, while the others represent the pointers to the identifier table or constant table and so on. We may call this form of the program the intermediate code. The difference between this kind of intermediate form and the source text is that this kind of intermediate code contains no original information which the source text contains. It can only contain all the information when it combines with the various tables which the lexical analyzer generates.

Therefore, the intermediate code which we mentioned here is the kind which the analytical phase generates in the last pass. It is closer to the machine code though it is independent of the machine. In general the analyzer generates the syntax trees or parser trees as the intermediate form that is not yet the intermediate code. The parser trees still remain the tracks of most of the source language and program paradigm to which the parser trees belong to. It is not beneficial to carry out the generation of the target code. Therefore, we hope that by the generation of the intermediate code, the specific set of nodes is reduced to a small set of general purpose concept nodes. Such set is easier implemented on real machines, and thus it is also easier to generate the target code. Therefore, the intention of this chapter is to cover all issues concerning the generation of the intermediate code.

Besides, we want to point out that there is another advantage with the intermediate code, i.e., an optimization program that is independent of the machine may be applied to the intermediate code [1]. Fig. 10.1 shows the positions of the intermediate code generator and code optimizer.

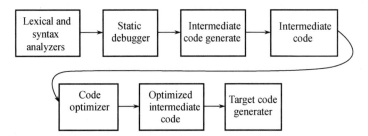

Fig. 10.1 the Position of the intermediate code generator and code optimizer.

10.2 Intermediate Code Languages

Suppose that through an analytical phase we obtain a parser tree. In this tree, the nodes may be divided into three classes: management, expression, and control stream.

Management nodes are those nodes that correspond to the declaration, the indication of module structures, etc. The management nodes may contain the evaluation of expressions, e.g., the evaluation of the address of an array element. In the normal situation, they seldom has the code that corresponds to the target code. However, in other cases, for example, for modules, the compiler must generate the code to execute the initialization of modules. However, the code which management nodes need is very short.

Control stream node [2] describes many characteristics: the branch caused from conditional statement, the multi- selections drawn from switch statement, computational goto statement, function invocation, abnormal handling, method applications, Prolog rule selection and remote procedure invocation. The characteristics of the code which control stream nodes need depend on the category to which the source program belongs. Correspondingly the code needed by control stream nodes is not much either.

Expressions occur in all the categories. Expressions explicitly occur in the codes of almost all languages. Expressions are the main object that the intermediate code needs to handle. Therefore, we need to consider how to select the intermediate language. In principle, the intermediate language should satisfy the following conditions:

1) independent of machine;

2) simple;

3) easy to generate intermediate code, moreover, it is also easy to transfer to the machine code;

4) easy to handle the optimizing code program.

According to these requirements of the intermediate language, through extensive theoretical research and massive practice, people gradually form the intermediate languages that are rather mature and popularly accepted. They are acyclic directed graph (ADG), postfix expression and three address code.

In the following, we will successively introduce the ways of generating the intermediate code by these languages.

10.2.1 Graphic Representation

A parser tree describes the natural layer structure of a source program. An acyclic directed graph presents the same information with more compact mode as it can identify common subexpressions. For example, for assignment statement $a := (b+c) \times (b-c) - (b \times c)/3$, its parser tree and acyclic directed graph representations are shown in Fig. 10.2.

The parser tree of the assignment statement above is generated from the syntax-driven definition. The syntax-driven definition of the assignment statement is defined as follows:

$$S \rightarrow id := E,$$

$$E \rightarrow E_1 + T | E_1 - T,$$

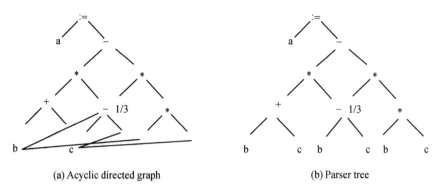

(a) Acyclic directed graph   (b) Parser tree

Fig. 10.2 The graphic representation of a := $(b + c) \times (b - c) - (b \times c)/3$.

$$E \to T,$$
$$T \to T_1 \times F,$$
$$T \to F,$$
$$F \to (E),$$
$$F \to id,$$
$$F \to num.$$

Notice that in these productions, E_1 and T_1 are not new nonterminals, actually they are E and T respectively. It is for convenience that we introduce them. Meanwhile, id and num represent identifiers and numbers respectively, so they are terminals. According to these production rules, we may obtain the semantic rules as shown in Fig. 10.3.

Production	Semantic rule
S→id:=E	S.nptr:=mknode(':=',mkleaf(id,id.place,E.nptr))
E→E₁+T|E₁-T	E.nptr:=mknode('+'|'-',E₁.nptr,T.nptr)
E→T	E.nptr:=T.nptr
T→T₁×F	T.nptr:=mknode('×',T₁.nptr,F.nptr)
T→F	T.nptr:=F.nptr
F→(E)	F.nptr:=E.nptr
F→id	F.nptr:=mkleaf(id,id.place)
F→num	F.nptr:=mkleaf(num,num.val)

Fig. 10.3 Syntax driven definition of parser tree for assignment statement.

According to the syntax driven definition given above, the parser tree in Fig. 10.2 (a) is formed and a series of function calls is carried out:

p_1:=mkleaf(id, entry a);

p_2:=mkleaf(id, entry b);

p_3:=mkleaf(id, entry c);

p_4:=mknode('+', p_2, p_3);

p_5:=mknode('−', p_2, p_3);

p_6:=mknode('×', p_4, p_5);

p_7:=mkleaf(num, 1/3);

p_8:=mknode('×', p_2, p_3);

p_9:=mknode('-', p_7, p_8);

p_{10}:=mknode('-', p_6, p_9);

p_{11}:=mknode(':=', p_1, p_{10});

We now explain function calls and relevant symbols. In the semantic rules, the nptr indicates the node pointer. mknode means the construction of the node. The construction node includes separated components. The first component is the label of the node while the second and third components are the left child and right child. The mkleaf means the construction of leaf. It has two components, the first of which is the identification or type while the second is the identifier. If it is a constant, then the first component represents type, and the second one is the value. There is one left that is id.place. It points to the corresponding pointer or address of this identifier in the symbol table.

The acyclic directed graph is also generated from the same syntax driven definition. If the function mknode(op, left, right) or mkunode(op, child) (represents that it is a node with only one subnode) are encountered, then before the construction of the node, it needs to check whether its left child and right child have already existed. If they exist, then the only thing that needs to do is to establish the pointer that points to the node. And also the node itself has to be created. In this way, the acyclic directed graph in Fig. 10.2 is generated.

There are two ways to represent the parser tree of Fig. 10.2 (a), as shown in Fig. 10.4.

In Fig. 10.4 (a), each node represents a record in which the leftmost field is the operator, and the last two fields are the pointers of the left child and right child of the operator, respectively. They contain two fields. One is its type and another is its name or value (if it is a number). In Fig.10.4(b), the node is distributed from a record array, and the index or position of the node is taken as the pointer of the node. From the root node located on position 15, and following the pointers, all the nodes of the parser tree may be visited.

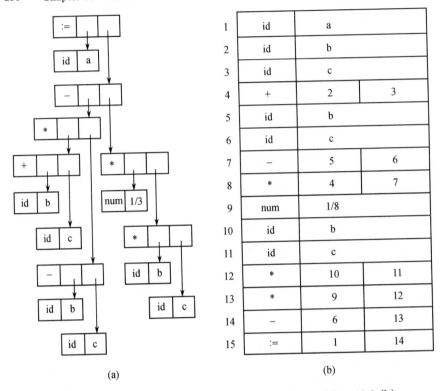

1	id	a
2	id	b
3	id	c
4	+	2	3
5	id	b
6	id	c
7	−	5	6
8	*	4	7
9	num	1/8
10	id	b
11	id	c
12	*	10	11
13	*	9	12
14	−	6	13
15	:=	1	14

(a)   (b)

Fig. 10.4 Two representations of the parser tree of Fig. 10.2 (b).

10.2.2 Postfix Representation

Postfix representation is only the linearization representation of the parser tree. It is the list of the nodes of the tree in such an order that a node directly follows its children. According to the principle, the postfix representation of expression $a := (b + c) \times (b - c) - (b \times c)/3$ is

$$abc \times bc - (1/3)bc \times \times - := .$$

Now we will further introduce postfix representation. At first we present the definitions of trees.

Definition 10.1 A finite set T of one or more nodes is called tree, if in which
   1) there is a special node called the root of the tree;
   2) the rest nodes are divided into m ($\geqslant 0$) disjoint sets $T_1, \ldots, T_m$, and each of them is also tree. Then $T_1, \ldots, T_m$ are called the subtrees of T.
   Especially, if m=2, the tree is called binary tree.

In computer science, one is especially interested in binary trees as they have wide applications in data structures. We may represent any expression with binary tree. The way to do it is to denote the operator with the root, and its two childrens represent two operation numbers as shown in Fig. 10.5.

Fig. 10.5 The representation of a+b with binary tree.

Definition 10.2 Given a binary tree, we call systematically visit each of the nodes of the tree the traversal of the tree.

D.E.Knuth proposed three types of the traversal of a binary tree. They are postorder, inorder and preorder respectively. The three types are recursively defined. When the binary tree is empty, nothing to visit has realized traversal; otherwise the traversal may be proceeded in three steps as follows:

Preorder	Inorder	Postorder
visit root	traverse left subtree	traverse left subtree
traverse left subtree	visit root	traverse right subtree
traverse right subtree	traverse right subtree	visit root

For example, for the parser tree in Fig. 10.2(b) that corresponds to expression

$$(b + c) \times (b - c) - (b \times c)/3.$$

The binary tree that represents the expression is shown in Fig. 10.6. If we traverse it with preorder, we get

$$- \times +bc - bc \times 1/3 \times bc,$$

where each operator occurs before its operands, and so it is called preorder. Preorder is also called Polish notation as the inventor of the notation Lukasiewicz is a Polish. If we traverse it with inorder, what we get is just

$$(b + c)(b - c) - (b \times c)/3,$$

where the parentheses indicate the priority of the operators. It is just the original expression. Since the operators are always located between the operands, it is called inorder.

Finally, if we traverse it with postorder, we have

$$bc + bc - \times 1/3bc \times \times -,$$

where each operator occurs after the operands, so it has the name. It is also called reversed Polish notation.

Postorder is very suitable for the stack machine that also has the postorder form of expressions. The so-called stack machine is the machine that uses stacks to store and operate. It has no register. It has two kinds of instructions: One kind is to copy or move values between the top of the stack and other places. The other kind is to perform operations upon the element on the top of they stack and other stack elements. The other kind of machines that are in contrast to this one is pure register machines that have one memory (values are stored in it) and a set of registers. This kind of machines has also two types of instructions. One kind is to copy value between memory and registers; the other kind is to perform operations upon two values on the registers, and then store the result into one of the registers.

In order to generate code for the stack machine, the only thing that needs to do is to read in the expression in postorder, then perform the following actions:

1) when a variable is met, generate code that pushes the value to the top of the stack;

2) when a binary operator is met, generate code that performs the operation of the operator upon the two top elements of the stack, and replace second top element of the stack (the top of the stack is removed);

3) when a unary operator is met, generate code that performs the operation of the operator upon the top element of the stack, and then replace the top element with the result.

All the operations are based on the assumption that we can discern the unary operators and binary operators. The code that pushes the value of variable on the top of the stack will include the computation that transforms the variable address of the form

    (number of block layer, offset)

on compilation time into the real address on run-time.

10.2.3 The Quadruple Code

The general form of the quadruples is

    y op z = x,

where x, y, and z are names, constants or temporary variables which the compiler generates. Op represents any operator, e.g., fix-point, float-point arithmetic operators, or logical operators that perform operations upon boolean data.

The grammar of quadruples has the following production rules:

$$QUAD \rightarrow operand\ op1\ operand = INT|$$
$$op2\ operand$$
$$operand \rightarrow INT|ID$$

$$\text{INT} \to \text{DIGIT}|\text{DIGIT INT}$$
$$\text{DIGIT} \to 0|1|2|3|4|5|6|7|8|9$$
$$\text{ID} \to a|b|c|d|\ldots|z|(a|b|c|\ldots|z)\text{ID}$$
$$\text{op1} \to +|-|\times|\div|\text{and}|\text{or}$$
$$\text{op2} \to -|\sim.$$

The example of quadruples is as follows:

$$-a = 3,$$
$$a + b = 5,$$
$$b + 1 = 3,$$
$$a \text{ and } b = 2.$$

The expression

$$(b + c) \times (b - c) - (b \times c)/3$$

may be expressed as quadruple form as follows:

$b + c = 1$		$(+b\ c) = 1$
$b - c = 2$		$(-b\ c) = 2$
$1 \times 2 = 3$	or expressed as	$(\times 1\ 2) = 3$
$b \times c = 4$		$(\times b\ c) = 4$
$\#(1/3) \times 4 = 5$		$(\times \#(1/3)4) = 5$
$3 - 5 = 6$		$(-3\ 5) = 6$

where the integers correspond to the identifiers which the compiler assigns to. The constants should be preceded with #. The code is also called three address code in which two addresses are used for operands, and the other address is used for the result. We assume here that the operator is of binary one. As for unary operator, it can be considered as the special case of the binary one that only needs one operand address and one result address. If the operator is unary, then the second operand is empty. Quadruples may be replaced by triples or two address code. Each triple consists of two operand addresses and an operator. Obviously, the operands of two address code are the same as the operands of the quadruples. Apart from being variables and constants, the operands may be the indices of other triples. For example, the triple code of

$$(b + c) \times (b - c) - b \times c/3$$

is

position	triple
1	$b + c$
2	$b - c$
3	$@1 \times @2^*$
4	$b \times c$
5	$(1/3) \times @4$
6	$@3 - @5$

Note*: we have used @ to precede the index to the triple, so for numbers, no need to use # to precede them again. In the following, we present a triple code from which one may easily derive the computation which it performs.

position	triple
1	$a + 1$
2	$@1 \times @1$
3	$b + @2$
4	$@3 + c$
5	$@4 =: x$
6	$@1 + 1$
7	$d \times @6$
8	$@7 =: y$

It presents the computations of x and y as follows:

$$x := b + (a + 1)^2 + c,$$
$$y := d \times (a + 2).$$

Quadruples and triples are widely used as the intermediate code. Therefore, we should transform the parser tree that is generated from analytical phase into quadruple form, then can finally the target code that is equivalent to the source program be formed, or the target code that is expected by the source code.

Now we analyze the quadruple form of intermediate code generated by various statements:

1. Assignment statement

The assignment statement has the following form:

    v := e

where v is a variable, and e is an expression. We have introduced the quadruple form of intermediate code previously in the chapter. Now the problem is about variable that may be a simple variable, it may also be an indexed variable. If it is a simple variable, then the intermediate code of the assignment statement is

    <v:=e>≡ the quadruple code that evaluates e
      := v << e >>

where <e> denotes the address that stores the expression, so <<e>> denotes the value of the expression.

2. The address evaluation for the elements of the arrays

We have mentioned that in the assignment statement, the variable at the left hand side may be an indexed variable. If it is the case, then the assignment statement needs to assign the value f the expression at the right hand side to the address of the indexed variable. Therefore it involves how to evaluate the address of indexed variable from its index. Besides, in the evaluation of the expression of the assignment statement, the indexed variables may also be involved; hence we also need to evaluate their addresses from their indices. Therefore, addressing array elements is an issue which the compiler cannot avoid.

The arrays may be of the one-dimension, two-dimension and even higher dimension. For the simplest one-dimension, the general form is

    array (num) of T,

where num indicates the number of the elements. The count of the number may start from 0, if it is the case, the real number of the elements is num+1; if the count starts from 1, then the number is just num itself. T is the type of elements, it may be the integer or float, etc. The type determines the length or width of elements, and is denoted by w.

In order to make the access of the elements more convenient, in general, the elements of the array are allocated in a contiguous block, sitting one by one. And the first element is put on the start location that is called the base address. In order to make the number more explicit, num is written as low..up, that is

    array (low..up) of T.

Suppose that the ith element is to be visited, then it needs to check whether i satisfies

$$low \leqslant i \leqslant up.$$

If the condition does not hold, it means that the element which we want to access is not within the range, then the compiler reports error. If the condition holds, and the width of each array element is w, then the ith element of the array begins in location

$$base + (i - low) \times w, \tag{10.1}$$

where low is the lower bound on the subscript and base is the relative address of the storage allocated for the array. That is, base is the relative address of A[low], A is the name of the array.

Expression (10.1) can be partially evaluated at compilation time if it is rewritten as

$$i \times w + (\text{base} - \text{low} \times w).$$

The subexpression $\text{base} - \text{low} \times w$ can be evaluated when the declaration of the array is seen, it is fixed after the array is allocated. Hence we assume that $c = \text{base} - \text{low} \times w$ is saved as an entry in the symbol table for the array A, so the relative address of A[i] is obtained by simply adding $i \times w$ to c. Every time when A[i] is accessed, only $i \times w$ needs to be evaluated while c has existed in the symbol table.

For the address evaluation, we have the quadruple form of intermediate code:

$$(\times \text{low w}) = 1,$$
$$(-\text{base 1}) = 2,$$
$$(\times \text{i w}) = 3,$$
$$(+3\ 2) = 4,$$

or simply

$$(\times \text{i w}) = 1,$$
$$(+\text{c 1}) = 2.$$

The last quadruple implies that $\text{base} - \text{low} \times w$ has been saved in c. The practice for c is called the compilation-time precalculation.

This practice can also be applied to address calculations of elements of multi-dimensional arrays. For the two-dimensional array, it has the following form

array $A(i_1..u_1, i_2..u_2)$,

for example, the array $A(1..2, 1..3)$ of integer. This declares that A is an array of integers with 2 rows and 3 columns. There are 6 elements in A. A two-dimension array is normally stored in one of two forms, either row-major, i.e., row-by-row, or column-major, i.e., column-by-column. Fig. 10.6 shows

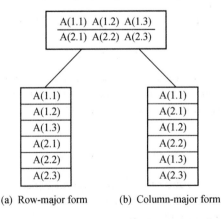

(a) Row-major form   (b) Column-major form

Fig. 10.6 the layout of a 2×3 array A.

the layout of a 2×3 array A in (a) row-major form and (b) column-major form.

The same as in the case of one dimension. If one wants to access the element of the array $A[i, j]$, at first it needs to check whether $[i, j]$ satisfies

$$i_1 \leqslant i \leqslant u_1 \text{ and } i_2 \leqslant j \leqslant u_2.$$

Only if both inequalities hold then can the address of $A[i, j]$ be evaluated. In the case of a two-dimensional array stored in the row-major form, the relative address of $A[i, j]$ can be calculated by the following formula

$$\text{the address of Array } A[i, j] = \text{base} + ((i - i_1) \times (u_2 - i_2 + 1) + j - i_2) \times w. \quad (10.2)$$

Once again, where w is the width of the element. The calculation can also be partially evaluated if it is rewritten as

$$\text{base} - (i_1 \times (u_2 - i_2 + 1) + i_2) \times w + (i \times (u_2 - i_2 + 1) + j) \times w, \quad (10.3)$$

where base=the address of $A[i_1, i_2]$. The first term of Expression (10.3) is a fixed value if the array A is allocated already in the memory, it has no any relation with $[i, j]$, it has relation with the array itself, so can be saved as an entry in the symbol table entry for A, thus the relative address of $A[i, j]$ is obtained by simply adding the second term of Expression (10.3) to that value saved in the symbol table (assuming that it is also denoted c, then we just simply add the term to c).

The quadruple form of the intermediate code for Expression (10.3) is as follows:

$$(-u_2 \ i_2) = 1,$$
$$(+1 \ \#1) = 2,$$
$$(\times 1 \ 2) = 3,$$
$$(+3 \ j) = 4,$$
$$(\times 4 \ \#w) = 5,$$
$$(+5 \ c) = 6.$$

Similarly, if the array is stored in the column-major form, then we have

$$\text{the address of } A[i, j] = \text{base} + (j - i_2) \times (u_1 - i_1 + 1) + i - i_1) \times w. \quad (10.4)$$

The expression can also be partially evaluated at compilation time if it is rewritten into two parts as we did in the raw-major form.

As for a three-dimensional array

array $A[i_1..u_1, i_2..u_2, i_3..u_3]$ of T.

If the array is stored in row-major form again, then for the address of $A[i, j, k]$, the calculation is as follows: The address of

$$A[i, j, k] = \text{base} + ((u_2 - i_2 + 1) \times (u_3 - i_3 + 1) \times (i - i_1) + (u_3 - i_3 + 1) \times$$
$$(j - i_2) + (k - i_3)) \times w. \quad (10.5)$$

Expression (10.5) can also be rewritten into two parts: a fixed part on compilation time and a changing part as i, j, and k change.

We can generalize the row-major or column-major form to multidimensional arrays. The generalization of row-major(column- major) form is to store the elements in such a way that, as we scan down a block of storage, the rightmost (leftmost) subscripts appear to vary fastest. The expression (10.3) generalizes to the following expression for relative address of $A[i_1, i_2, \ldots, i_k]$ is

$$\text{(base} + (i_1 n_2 + i_2) \times n_3 + i_3) \ldots) \times n_k + i_k) \times w +$$
$$((\ldots(i_1 n_2 + i_2) \times n_3 + i_3) \ldots) \times n_k + i_k) \times w, \qquad (10.6)$$

where for all j, $n_j = u_j - i_j + 1$ and they are assumed fixed, the first term of the expression (10.6) can be computed at the compilation time and saved with the symbol table entry for A.

However, the generation code for the computation of array address can also be done at the syntactical analysis. In order to do so, the production rules of the grammar need to be transformed, that is, actions are inserted into production rules so that the corresponding quadruples are generated. We illustrate the procedure with the grammar of the expression. The production rules for the expression are as follows:

S → EXP

EXP → TERM|

       EXP + TERM,

TERM → FACT|

       TERM × FACT,

FACT → −FACT|

       ID|

       (EXP).

In order to describe actions, we need to use a stack that keeps the array consisting of concrete records. Each of its entry contains an integer or character (when quad=true, it stores qno meaning the number of the quadruple; otherwise it stores idop meaning the operator). ptr is the pointer of the stack. quadno is a variable, of which the value is the number of quadruple just allocated last time. Initially both the values of ptr and quadno are 0. Suppose that the character (or symbol) that has just read last time is kept in "in".

The following is the production rules that have attached actions:

1) S → EXP {ptr:=ptr−1 (the stack grows bottom-up)}
2) EXP → TERM |

      EXP+{ptr:=ptr+1:   (notice the interpretation on the text,

         stack[ptr].quad:=false: if quad=true it stores qno;

         stack[ptr].idop:=in}   otherwise it stores operator)

TERM{for (i=ptr−2;i=ptr;i++)

    if stack[i].quad then

       emit (stack[i].qno)

    else emit(stack[i].idop);

    quadno:=quadno+1;

    emit('=', quadno);

    (/* print '=' and the quadruple number */)

    ptr:=ptr−2;

    stack[ptr]:=true;

    stack[ptr]:=quadno;}

3) TERM → FACT|

  TERM ×{ptr:=ptr+1;

    stack[ptr].quad:=false;

    stack[ptr].idop:=in;}

  FACT {for(i=ptr−2:i=ptr;i++)

    if stack[i].quad then

       emit(stack[i].qno)

    else emit(stack[i].idop);

    quadno:=quadno+1;

    emit('=', quadno);

    ptr:=ptr−2;

    stack[ptr]:=true;

    stack[ptr]:=quadno;}

4) FACT → − {ptr:=ptr+1;

    stack[ptr].quad:=false;

    stack[ptr].idop:=in}

  FACT {for (i=ptr−1;i=ptr;i++)

    If stack[i].quad then

       emit(stack[i].qno)

    else emit(stack[i].idop);

    quadno:=quadno+1;

    emit('=', quadno);}

  | ID {ptr:=ptr+1;

    stack[ptr].quad.:=false;

    stack[ptr].idop:=in}

| (EXP)

5) ID → a | b| c | d |...|z

For the places without any action attached in the productions above, it means that no action needs to attach to.

Now in order to do the same for array, that is, when syntactical analysis is performed upon array, the actions are put to the production rules so that the quadruple form can also be generated, we need to set up the production rules for the array. At first, in order for the elements of the array may also be visited at where id appears in the expression grammar, we need to introduce a nonterminal called N to replace id. We then have

$$N → id[Elist]|id,$$
$$Elist → Elist, E|E.$$

However, in order to make use of the bounds of various dimensions when we combine the expressions of subscripts to form Elist, when forming N, we need to attach the array name at the leftmost of the subscript expression, rather than connecting it with Elist. Thus the inserting actions can be done easier. Therefore, the productions above are rewritten as

$$N → Elist]|id,$$
$$Elist → Elist, E|E.$$

In this way, the pointer of symbol table entry of the array may be transmitted as the synthetic attribute of the array of Elist.

After rewriting the production rules above, we may now define the grammar of arrays. And the element of the array may occur either at the left of production rules or the right of production rules. The production rules are as follows:

1) S → N:=E;
2) E → E+E;
3) E → (E);
4) E → N;
5) N → Elist];
6) N → id;
7) Elist → Elist, E;
8) Elist → id[.

In order to attach actions to these production rules, we need to explain the symbols that will be used. At first, we use Elist.dim to record the dimensions in Elist, i.e., the number of subscript expressions. Function limit (array.j) returns the value of n_j, that is in the symbol table entry of the element number of jth-dimension of array pointed by 'array'. Finally, Elist place represents the temporary unit that stores the value computed from subscript expression.

When accessing the array element [3] $A[i_1, i_2, \ldots, i_k]$, the actions generated in the production rules will use the following recurrence relations:

$$
\begin{cases}
e_1 := i_1, \\
\quad \vdots \\
e_m := e_{m-1} \times n_m + i_m
\end{cases}
\tag{10.7}
$$

to compute the first m indices of kth-dimensional array

$$
(\ldots(i_1 n_2 + i_2) \times n_3 + i_3)\ldots) \times n_m + i_m.
\tag{10.8}
$$

Thus, when m=k, a multiplication by the width w is all that will be needed to compute the second term of Expression (10.6). Note that the i_j's here may really be values of expressions. And the first term of Expression (10.6) is fixed and stores as an entry in the symbol table of array A.

By passing, we state that the grammar aforementioned is ambiguous as it contains left recursion. We may transform it to remove the left recursion. After that we get the following grammar:

1) S → N:=E;
2) E → (E);
3) E → N;
4) E → (E)A;
5) E → NA;
6) A → +E;
7) A → +EA;
8) N → Elistid];
9) N → id;
10) Elist → id[;
11) Elist → id[E B;
12) B →, E;
13) B →, E B.

Notice that this is not an LL(1) grammar yet as many productions with the same left part have common derivation symbols. But it is not difficult to transform it into of LL(1). We just do not do it.

Strictly speaking, we should use these production rules to insert the actions that would generate the quadruples. However, since the address computation for array, in general, cannot cause the problem of ambiguity, therefore for simplification, we still attach the actions to the general productions:

1) S → N:=E
       {if N.offset=null then /*N is simple id*/
       emit(N.place':=' E.place);
       else
       emit(N.place'['N.offset']'':='E.place)}
2) E → E_1+E_2
       {E.place:=newtemp:
       emit(E.place':='E_1.place '+' E_2..place)}
3) E →(E_1)
       {E.place:=E_1.place}

We have mentioned before that E_1 and E_2 are not new nonterminal. They are actually E itself. We use them only for discerning them from the E at the left hand side.

4) E → N

    {if N.offset=null then / ∗ N is a simple id ∗/

        E.place:=N.place

    else begin

        E.place:=newtemp;

        emit (E.place ':=' L.place '[' N.offset ']')

        end}

In the case of indexed variable, we want to get the value of some element of the array. N.place[N.offset] is just the value of the element which the index corresponds to.

5) N → Elist]

    {N.place:=newtemp;

    N.offset:=newtemp;

    emit(N.place':='c(Elist.array));

    emit(N.offset':='Elist.place'∗'width(Elist.array))}

Where N.offset is the new temporary variable that represents the second term of Expression (10.6); function width (Elist.array) returns w in Expression (10.6). N.place represents the first term of Expression (10.6), returned by the function c (Elist.array).

6) N → id

    {N.place:=id.place;

    N.offset:=null}

A null offset indicates a simple name, so this corresponds to a simple variable.

7) Elist→$Elist_1$. E

    {t:=newtemp;

    m:=$Elist_1$. ndim+1;

    emit(t':='$Elist_1$. place'∗'limit($Elist_1$. array, m));

    emit(t':='t'+'E.place);

    Elist.array:=$Elist_1$.array;

    Elist.place:=t;

    Elist.ndim:=m}

Here the actions are produced using the recurrence relation above, where $Elist_1$.place corresponds to e_{m-1} of Expression (10.7) while Elist.place corresponds to e_m.

8) Elist → id[E

    {Elist.array:=id.place;

    Elist.place:=E.place;

    Elist.ndim:=1}

Here E.place holds both the value of Expression E, and the value of Expression (10.8) for m=1

Example 10.1 Suppose that A is a 15×25 array with $i_1=i_2=1$. Therefore, $n_1=15$ and $n_2=25$. Take w to be 4. Assignment statement $x := A[y, z]$ corresponds to the following parser tree (Fig. 10.7):

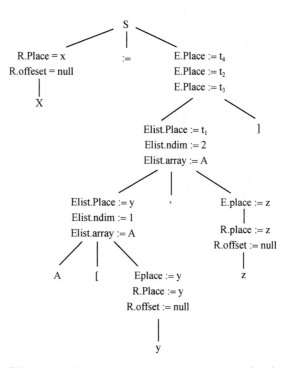

Fig. 10.7 The annotated parser tree of x:=A[y, z].

The assignment statement may be translated into the following sequence of quadruples or three address statements: Notice that as the array takes 0 row and 0 column as the initial address, and now $i_1=i_2=1$, that means that the 0 row is deleted. However, the base address is still taking 0 row and 0 column. Hence the real base address should take the base address of A minus $26 \times 4 = 104$.

Y * 25 =1		$t_1:=y * 25$
1+z=2		$t_2:=t_1+z$
$base_A$-#104=3	or	$t_2:=base_A$-#104
2*#4=4		$t_3:=4*t_1$
3[4]=5		$t_4:=t_2[t_3]$
5:=x		x:=t_4
quadruple code		three-address code

3. Type conversion within assignments

In programming languages, various different types of variables and constants are defined. For some types, the operations between them are not allowed or there is no definition for the operations between them. However, for other types, the operations between them are allowed, provided that some of them is transformed to another type that will operate to the former one. For example, suppose that there are two types — real and integer, with integers converted to reals, these two types may operate together. Therefore, the compiler must be able to determine according to the grammar [4], either prohibit the operation or perform the conversion first, to have the operation between different types.

For the grammar of the assignment statement introduced above, we introduce another attribute, whose value is either real or integer. The semantic rule type associated with the production E $\rightarrow$ E+E is

E $\rightarrow$E+E
    {E.type:=
        if E_1.type=integer and
            E_2.type=integer then integer
        else real}

This rule is not enough to generate the quadruple form of intermediate codes. And we omit the checks for type errors. The entire semantic rule for E $\rightarrow$ E+E and most of the other productions must be modified to generate, when necessary, three-address statements of the form x :=inttoreal y, whose effect is to convert integer y to a real of the equal value, called x. We must also include with the operator code an indication of whether fixed or floating-point arithmetic is intended. The complete semantic actions for a production rule of the form E $\rightarrow$ E_1+E_2 is as follows:

```
E.place:=newtemp;
if E1. type=integer and E2. type=integer then
   begin
      emit(E.place':=' E1.place'int+' E2.place);
      E.type:=integer
   end
   else if E1.type=real and E2.type=real then
     begin
        emit(E.place':=' E1.place':=' E1.place 'real+' E2.place);
        E.typr:=real
     end
   else if E1.type=integer and E2.type=real then
     begin
        u:=newtemp;
        emit(u':=' 'inttoreal' E2..place);
        E.type:=real
     end
     else if E1.type == real and E2.type=integer then
       begin
```

```
        u:=newtemp;
        emit (u':=' 'inttoreal'E₂.place);
        emit(E.place ':=' E₁.place a'real+'u);
        E.type:=real
    end
else
    E.type:=type-error;
```

We just present the conversations between integers and reals for addition within assignments. For subtract, multiplication and division, the cases are similar to this one. The semantic action stated above uses two attributes E.place and E.type for the nonterminal E. As the number of types that are subjects to conversion increases, the number of cases that arise increases quadratically (or worse, if there are operators with more than two arguments). Therefore, with large numbers of types, the careful organization of the semantic actions becomes more critical.

For example,

$$x := y \times z + a \times b,$$

where x, y, and z are reals while a and b are integers. Then the output of the intermediate code is as follows:

$$t_1 := a \text{ int} \times b,$$
$$t_2 := y \text{ real} \times z,$$
$$u := \text{inttoreal } t_1,$$
$$t_2 := t_2 \text{ real} + u,$$
$$x := t_2.$$

4. Conditional statements

Previously, we have encountered the problem regarding the generation of intermediate codes of conditional statements. Now we will discuss it again in more detail.

The form of conditional statements is as follows:

if e then S_1 else S_2

For the execution of the statement, at first, it calculates the value of the expression e. Hence, there will be a series of quadruples for the calculation. For simplicity, we just express it as <e>. Then the truth or false of the value of e needs to be judged. If it is true, then subsequently the statement (or statements) represented by S_1 is (or are) executed. The statement(s) should follow the judgment of e. When the execution finishes it will exit from the sequence. Otherwise if the value of e is false, then the statement (or statements) represented by S_2 is (or are) executed. Therefore, the quadruple code that corresponds to the conditional statement is

      <e>   (a series of quadruple code that evaluates the

                                   expression e)

  (then, <<e>>, 0, 0) (if e is true, then sequentially execute the

```
                              following statement)
<S₁>                          (the code of the statement S₁)
(goto, , , )                  (branch address after S₁ is executed)
(else, , , )                  (if e is false, branch to here)
<S₂ >                         (the code of the statement S₂)
(if end, , , )                (the end if the conditional statement).
```

Example 10.2 Suppose that a nesting conditional statement is

```
if E₁ then S₁ else
      if E₂ then S₂ else S₃
```

Then the quadruple form of its intermediate code is

```
<E₁ >
(then, <<E₁ >>, 0, 0)
< S₁ >
(goto, , , )
(else, , , )
<E₂ >
(then, <<E₂ >>, 0, 0)
<S₂ >
(goto, , , )
(else, , , )
<S₃ >
(ifend, , , )
(ifend, , , )
```

5. Loop statements

Consider the loop statement with while type

```
While B do S
```

The statement is similar to the conditional statement. At first, B has to be evaluated. We need to introduce a label to denote the branch address which we use L:<B> to represent. It represents the first address of the code that evaluates <B>. Hence we have

```
L: <B>
(while, <<B>>, 0, 0)
<S>
(goto, L, 0, 0)
(wfend, 0, 0, 0)      (when B is false, branch to the
                       end of while statement)
```

Another form of the loop statement is

$$\text{for } (i=a; i \leqslant b; i++)$$
$$\text{do S}$$

The quadruple code that corresponds to it is

(:=, i, a, 0)

L:<S>   (the intermediate code sequence where i should be replaced

by its current value and L represents the first quadruple)

(+, I, 1, i)

($\leqslant$, I, b, 0)

(goto, L, 0, 0)   (when i $\leqslant$ b branch back to continue the execution

of S)

(forend, 0, 0, 0) (if the extent has been exceeded the loop ends)

6. Procedural statements [5]

We use the following grammar to represent the procedure calls

S $\rightarrow$ call id(Elist)

Elist $\rightarrow$ E

Elist $\rightarrow$ E, Elist

where there should be other production rules that correspond to the nonterminal E to generate the arithmetic or boolean expression. Since we are only concerned the generation of intermediate code for procedure calls, we omit those productions here.

S $\rightarrow$ call id(Elist)   {execute the evaluation for every E in the

Elist queue

Elist $\rightarrow$ E   then execute assignment E.place:=E;

Elist $\rightarrow$ E, Elist   then execute emit('actpar', E.place);

Emit('call' id.place n)}

For example, if the procedure statement is

G(E_1, E_2, E_3, E_4, E_5)

Then the quadruple code is as follows:

E_1.place:=<E_1>   (<E_1> represents the code for evaluation of

E_1. The assignment here indicates that

value evaluated is stored in E_1.place. The

same for the following)

E_2. place:=<E_2>

E_3. place:=<E_3>

E_4. place:=<E_4>

E_5. place:=<E_5>

(actpar, E_1.place, 0, 0)

(actpar, E_2.place, 0, 0)

(actpar, E_3.place, 0, 0)

(actpar, E_4.place, 0, 0)

(actpar, E_5.place, 0, 0)

(call, G.place, 0, n)

where actpar is specially used for indicating the real parameter, it can also indicate the mode of the transfer of real parameters. The final (call, G.place, 0, n) implements the function call, where n indicates the number of parameters.

Example 10.3 Given a procedure statement $g(x \times 3, y+z)$, the quadruple code that corresponds to the statement is

$(\times, 3, x, T_1)$

$(+, y, z, T_2)$

(actpar, T_1.place, 0, 0)

(actpar, T_2. place, 0, 0)

(call, g.place, 0, 2)

Example 10.4 Suppose that there is a procedure statement

$$G(x \times 3, g(x+2) \times 2)$$

Then the quadruple code that corresponds to the statement is

$(+, x, 2, T_1)$

(actpar, T_1. place, 0, 0)

(call, g. place, 0, 1)

$(\times, 3, x, T_2)$

$(\times, 2, g(x+2), T_3)$

(actpar, T_2. place, 0, 0)

(actpar, T_3. place, 0, 0)

(call G. place, 0, 2)

Example 10.5 Suppose that there is a procedure statement $R(S(T(x)))+3$, we are required to present its intermediate code. According to the principle of the bottom-up, we generate it.

(actpar, x. place, 0, 0)

(call, T. place, 0, 1)

$(:=, T. place, 0, T_1)$

(actpar, T_1. place, 0, 0)

(call, S. place, 0, 1)

$(:=, S. place, 0, T_2)$

(actpar, T_2. place, 0, 1)

(call, R. place, 0, 1)

$(:=, R. place, 0, T_3)$

$(+, T_3, 3, T_4)$

7. Boolean expressions

At the beginning of the chapter when we introduce the grammar of quadruples, we have included the quadruples of boolean expressions. The only form which we did not define is

E → id_1 relop id_2

where relop means relation operator that is regarded as binary operator. Therefore, it will correspond to the code of three-address relop id$_1$ id$_2$ T

where T is used to store the value of the relop operation of the operands id$_1$ and id$_2$. Then we can determine the value of T.

Consider an example

a∧b∨c∧(b∨(x=0))∧d

The quadruple form of the intermediate code of the expression is

$$(\wedge \text{ a b}) = 1$$
$$(= \text{ x } 0) = 2$$
$$(\wedge \text{ 2 d}) = 3$$
$$(\vee \text{ b } 3) = 4$$
$$(\wedge \text{ c } 4) = 5$$
$$(\vee \text{ 1 } 5) = 6$$

8. Switch statements

The "switch" or "case" statement is available in a variety of languages. It provides the possibility of multi choice of a condition. For example, in a competition of four awards are set up: the champion, the runner-up, the third place and the rearguard. These four will be awarded with different levels of bonus. Then this can be processed with a case statement with five cases that correspond to first, second, third, fourth, and the last one that does not get any bonus again. There is a variety of the setting of switch statement. The following is its general form:

```
switch E
    begin
        case V₁:  S₁
        case V₂:  S₂
        ...
        case Vₙ₋₁:  Sₙ₋₁
    default:  Sₙ
    end
```

There is a selector expression which is to be evaluated, followed by n constant values that the expression might take, including a default "value" that always matches the expression if no other value does. The intended translation of a switch statement is as follows [6]:

1) Evaluate the expression.

2) Find which value in the list of cases is the same as the value of the expression. Recall that the default value matches the expression if none of the values explicitly mentioned in cases does.

3) Execute the statement S$_i$ associated with the value found V$_i$.

According to the requirement of the execution, there are two ways to generate the intermediate code for the statement. The first practice is that after the value of e is evaluated, it is stored in, say location t, then branch to the test of value t, and according to the result of test, statement S$_i$ is selected and executed.

```
<the intermediate code of evaluation of e>
    t:= <e>
    goto test
L₁:  intermediate code of S₁
    goto exit
L₂:  intermediate code of S₂
    goto exit
    ...
Lₙ₋₁:  intermediate code of Sₙ₋₁
    goto exit
Lₙ:  intermediate code for default value
    goto exit
test:  if t=V₁ then goto L₁
    if t= V₂ then goto L₂
        ...
    If t=Vₙ₋₁ then goto Lₙ₋₁
        goto Lₙ
exit:
```

The another method is that after the evaluation of E and store it in t, the test is successively done. At first, to check whether t is equal to V_1 or not; if it is equal, then execute the corresponding statement S_1; otherwise check whether it is equal to V_2, ..., and continue doing so until it meets a value, or it is not equal to any value (in this case it is regarded as being equal to V_n). It should be equal to notice that as V_1, V_2, ..., V_{n-1} are arranged, those V_i's that have bigger probabilities that the expression takes should precede the lower ones so that the efficiency is higher. The intermediate code is as follows:

```
<the intermediate code of the evaluation of e>
    t:= <e>
    if t ≠ V₁ goto L₁
    the intermediate code of <S₁ >
    goto exit
L₁:  if t ≠ V₂ goto L₂
    The intermediate code of <S₂ >
    goto exit
L₂:
    ...
Lₙ₋₁:  if t ≠ Vₙ₋₁ goto Lₙ
    the intermediate code of <Sₙ₋₁>
    goto exit
Lₙ:  the intermediate code of default
exit:
```

So far, for almost all the statements of languages we have introduced how to generate the intermediate code that corresponds to them. There is still one more thing that should be noted that we do not consider how to make the code generated more efficient, for example, how to make it shorter, or how to use less amount of storages. We just consider their implementation.

Problems

Problem 10.1 Develop a program to implement the translation from the parser tree to quadruple form of intermediate code.

Problem 10.2 Prove that given a string consisting of operators and operands, if among them all the operators are binary, then the string is a postfix expression if and only if (1) there is exactly one fewer operator than operands, and (2) every nonempty prefix of the expression has fewer operators than operands.

Problem 10.3 Show that infix expressions cannot be translated into prefix form by translation schemes in which all actions are printing actions, and all actions appear at the ends of right sides of productions.

Problem 10.4 Some languages permit a list of names to be given a list of attributes and also permit declaration to be nested within one another. The following productions abstract the problem:

```
D→namelist attrlist|
   (D) attrlist
namelist→id, namelist|
      id
attrlist→A attrlist|
      A
A→decimal|fixed|float|real
```

The meaning of D→(D)attrlist is that all names mentioned in the declaration inside parentheses are given the attributes on attrlist, no matter how many levels of nesting there are. Note that a declaration of n times and m attributes may cause mn pieces of information to be entered into the symbol table. Give a syntax-directed definition for declarations defined by this grammar.

Problem 10.5 Translate the following assignment statement into three-address code:

A[i, j]:=B[i, j]+C[i, j]+D[i, j]

Problem 10.6 Translate the executable statements of the following program into three-address code (where printf and scanf may be retained):

```
void main( ) {
    in n; float m;s:
    printf (`` the amount of copies!'');
    scanf (``%d'', &n);
    m=n×24;
    if (m>20000)
        S=m×0.75;
    else if (m>10000)
        S=m×0.8;
    else if (m>2000)
        S=m×0.85;
    else if (m>100)
        S=m×0.9:
    else S=m;
```

```
                    printf(''the amount of payment¥;%g\n\n'', s);
                }
```

Problem 10.7   Translater the following procedure statements into quadruple form:

       1) g(x(x-1), i+2),
       2) f(g(x+1), x-1),
       3) p(q(r(x)), r(x)).

References

[1] Davidson JW, Fraser CW (1984) Code selection through object code opti-
     mization, TOPLAS 6(4): 505 – 526.

[2] Tanenbaum AS, van Staveren H, Keizer EG, et al (1983) A practical tool for
     making portable compilers. Comm. ACM 26(9): 654 – 660.

[3] Laverett TW, Cattell RGG, Hobbs SO, et al (1980) An overview of the
     production-quality compiler-compiler project. Computer 13(8): 39 – 40.

[4] Fraser CW, Hanson DR (1982) A machine-independent linker. Software —
     Practice and Experience 12, pp 351 – 366.

[5] Nori KV, Ammann U, Jensen K, et al (1981) Pascal implementation notes
     in Barron, pp 125 – 170.

[6] Nawey MC, Waite WM (1985) The robust implementation of equence-
     controlled iteration. Software — Practice and Experience 15(7): 655 – 668.

Chapter 11   Debugging and Optimization

Nothing is perfect. For doing everything, there is always room for improvement.

Chinese maxim (anonymous)

There is no the best, there is only the better.
Chinese advertisement word

11.1   Motivation of the Chapter

Before turning the intermediate code generation to target code generation, we are still facing a number of works that require us to do.

For the target code generated by the compiler, we hope that it will run fast and well. Today no matter whether it is the computer itself or capacity of the storage, no one is regarded as precious and scarce things again. Nevertheless, it does not mean that they can be abused. Excessively using these things definitely are not acceptable. With this principle in mind, when there are two programs that both are competent to do the work, but one of them runs faster and the other slower, or one spends fewer storage, definitely people prefer the former instead of the latter. In this chapter we will discuss the issues on debugging and optimization. We regard them necessary steps towards target code generation.

11.2   Errors Detection and Recovery

The errors that occur in programs mainly have three types: Mistyping misspelling in input, Syntax errors, Semantic errors.

Mistyping and misspelling often happen in input, especially when one who types the program is not the writer of the program, or is not good in English, then the rate of the errors over the whole program must be high.

We can classify the errors into two kinds. One belongs to isolated errors that have limited impact to the whole program, and another belongs to global errors that will affect the whole program.

Isolated errors include the mistyping of the reserved words. For example, one mistyped begin as bigin or begen. When the lexical analyzer starts working the mistakes can be spotted easily. The user-friendly compiler may correct the mistake without causing the stop of the analytical procedure, as long as it informs the programmer/user of the error message.

In addition, isolated mistakes contain the mistyping/misspelling of identifiers, i.e., some of letters in an identifier is wrongly typed. For example, if AI was wrongly typed as A1, then in the program, there would be two identifiers that simultaneously occur. If in the declaration part AI is declared, and A1 would not be declared.

Therefore, in the symbol table there is the record of AI instead of the record of A1. That means that A1 has not been declared yet. However, the compiler does not know that A1 is actually the same as AI. It must deem that the user forgets to declare it. Then it is likely adding a record for A1. But later this will be discovered, as its occurrence was due to the mistyping of AI, the number of accesses to it must be few, either never assigned or never accessed. Therefore, for the following cases that some identifiers are assigned but never referred or only referred but never assigned, it must be caused by mistyping/misspelling. Therefore, with an assignment counter and a reference counter that are set in the built-in symbol, we can check whether an identifier is correct or not. The checking method is just to check in the checking phase which built-in symbol occurs like the cases mentioned above.

According to the statistics of experience, there are mainly the following four kinds that belong to mistyping:

1) A letter is missing in a word or identifier.
2) A letter is excessive in the word or in the identifier.
3) The adjacent two letters are transposed.
4) One letter is wrong in a word or identifier.

The way of correcting them is as follows.

Select those built-in symbols from the symbol table that are most likely to be mistyped or misspelled. And check every occurrence of these objects to see whether there is the case in which some identifier is misspelled or mistyped.

Select a subset instead of the whole set to carry out the checking limit the number of the identifiers that are checked. According to the statistics of experience, if the number of the letters within the identifier to be checked is n, the lengths of the identifiers that need to be checked are only $n-1$, n and $n+1$. When $n \leqslant 2$, the check against mistyping and misspelling may not be necessary.

What we have talked so far is about the analysis of isolated mistakes, and now we analyze the mistakes that affect the global situation, for example, the mismatching of parentheses.

When there are many pairs of parentheses that appear in the expression, the mismatching of pairs of parentheses often happens. In some cases, however, it does not affect much. For example, in the following expression

$$x := a/((b + c) - d * (e + f)),$$

if the last right parenthesis is missing, it becomes

$$x := a/((b + c)\_d * (e + f).$$

Through analysis, the mistake can be found easily, so this sill belongs to the isolated mistake.

However, if in the expression above, the right parenthesis for (b+c) becomes a left parenthesis, then the expression becomes

$$x := a/((b + c(-d * (e + f)).$$

It becomes a mistake that has the global effect. Obviously, we can find out that there is mismatching of parentheses, but it is hard to deal with it properly. Of course, through careful analysis, we can guess that the left parenthesis that follows c should be a right parenthesis. After we spot it and correct it, the problem can be solved. We found the problem that the multiplication of $-d$ and (e+f) has $*$ in between, while the multiplication of c and $(-d*(e+f))$ has no the corresponding $*$. However, since the inconsistency is not always regarded as a problem, it causes the difficulty for checking.

In the current rapid interactive systems, usually when a mistake is found from debugging, the procedure will immediately stop, and it informs the user or programmer of the mistake, letting him/her to make correction. If this is done, the procedure resumes. However, from the stand of the user or programmer, he/she obviously wants to know more about the mistakes. It will be most welcome by them if all the mistakes are found. Therefore, he/she wants that after a problem was found, the debugging procedure continues its work until it really cannot go further or it has found out all the problems. When the mistake really affects the global situation, the procedure cannot do anything again except that the program has been recovered from the previous mistake, even if the recovery is made presumably.

Therefore, there are two strategies towards recovery from mistakes: one is the correction of mistakes. This strategy is to make the continue analysis or debugging possible through the modification of input symbol streams or internal states of the syntactical program. But the strategy is very prone to deviate from the analytical program and yield a lot of pseudo mistake messages.

The other strategy is called non- correction of mistakes. It does not modify the input stream, and delete all the information generated by the analytical program. It uses the "remaining" program to continue the analysis of the remaining part of the program. If the analysis succeeds, there is no mistake again; otherwise, there must be other mistakes and that means that a correct parsing tree cannot be generated.

Actually, when we introduce the parsing trees of LL(1) and LR(1), we have considered the cases in which mistakes occurred, and we have also correspondingly established the mechanism for debugging and recovery. We consider the situations of mistakes that exist, that will make the compiler running more friendly towards users.

11.3 Debugging of Syntax Errors

In LL(1) parsing and LR(1) parsing, we have mentioned the situations in which errors occur. In the following, we analyze them further respectively. We first should consider the type errors — the most common errors taking place in syntax.

In order to check the type error, we must establish the type grammar first, and then insert the semantic actions into the grammar. Based on these grammars and actions we carry out the type check, discover the errors and recover from errors. The following is an example that is the grammar from very common source language where P stands for the program, and consists of a series of declaration D followed by a series of statement S. We will discuss how the type check is added into the statement soon. The following is the list of productions regarding declaration D.

$$P \rightarrow D; S$$
$$D \rightarrow D; D| \text{ id: } T$$
$$T \rightarrow \text{integer}| \text{ real}| \text{ char}| \text{ boolean}| \text{ array[num] of } T| \uparrow T$$

We postulate that when there is no type error taking place, the type error checking program returns void, and void is idempotent, i.e., void void = void. Hence any number of void linking together is equal to single void. But if an error of the type is found, a type-error message is immediately issued. Hence we have the type grammar with the semantic action rules inserted.

$P \rightarrow D; S$ {P.type := if S.type = void then void else

   type-error. Notice that the number of

   S.type more than one}.

$D \rightarrow D; D$

$D \rightarrow$ id: T {addtype (id, entry, T.type)}

$T \rightarrow$ integer {T.type := integer}

$T \rightarrow$ real {T.type := real }

$T \rightarrow$ char {T.type := char}

$T \rightarrow$ boolean {T.type := boolean}

$T \rightarrow$ array[num] of T {T.type := array [1..numval, T_1.type]}

$$T \to \uparrow T \qquad\qquad \{T.type := Pointer(T_1.\ type)\}$$

For T, we may extend it as follows:

$$T \to T \ `\to' \ T$$

that expresses type of functions, that is the transformation from arguments to the function value. Correspondingly we have

$$T \to T_1 \ `\to' \ T_2 \qquad \{T.type \to T_1.type \to T_2.type\}$$

The semantic actions of statements S are as follows:

$S \to id := E$ {S.type := if id.type =E.type then void
else type-error}

$S \to$ if E then S_1 {S.type := if E.type = boolean then S_1.type
else type-error}

$S \to$ while E do S_1 {S.type := if E.type = boolean then
S_1.type else type-error}

$S \to S_1;S_2$ {S.type := if S_1.void and S_2.type = void
then void else type-error}

As for expressions, we have the grammar with semantic action rules

$E \to$ truth   {E.type := boolean}

$E \to$ num   {E.type := integer}

$E \to$ literal   {E.type := char}

$E \to$ id   {E.type := lookup (id, entry)}

$E \to E_1$ mod E_2 {E.type := if E_1.type = integer and E_2.type =
integer then integer else type-error}

$E \to E_1[E_2\ ]$ {E. type := if E_2.type = integer and E_1. type =
array then E.type = array[s,t] else type-
error}

$E \to E_1 \uparrow$ {E.type := if E_1.type = pointer(t) then t else
type-error}

In addition, comparative symbols like $<, \leqslant, >, \geqslant, =$ and $\neq$ and connectors and or may be introduced into the productions of E, yielding the type of E being boolean. We then may similarly carry out the check of types.

11.3.1 Error Handling of LL(1) Parser

We now consider the handling and recovery of errors for LL(1) parser. In the previous chapter, we have discussed which cases are regarded as errors in LL(1) parser. Here what we want to discuss is that if the error happens how should we deal with? We are mainly concerned with two points:

1) How should we avoid infinite loop? As infinite loop will cause the analytical procedure running without termination.

2) How to avoid to generate a parsing tree with error? If the parsing tree generated contains the error, naturally the goal expected by the compilation cannot be achieved.

Therefore, we need a good strategy in order to avoid the infinite loop via removing at least one input symbol: make sure that to avoid the generation of parsing tree with error via not to throwing away the next symbol that is guessed or inserting a symbol. The expected symbol means that using LL(1) parser the sequence of the symbol that will match the input stream. We will put these expected symbols into a stack called guess stack.

Allowable set method is a frame construct that systematically constructs a safety method for recovery from errors. The key to the method is to construct the allowable set and the following three steps are included. When the error is found, the three steps are executed.

1) Making use of some appropriate algorithms to construct the allowable set A according to the state of the parser, where A should contain the symbol of end of file (EOF) and the symbols in Follower Set of nonterminal.

2) Throwing away the symbols from the input stream that is not acceptable for symbols in A until the first symbol t_A that is acceptable by some symbol in A.

3) Making the parser going on via a suitable algorithm so that after t_A is processed, the guess stack and input stream can go ahead simultaneously.

There is an improving method for this method. It also contains three steps:

1) Constructing allowable set.

2) Skipping over the non-acceptable symbol.

In this way, there will be zero or multi symbols that will sequentially be thrown until a symbol in allowable set is met. As the symbol EOF is always in A, it will terminate when the step is skipped over.

3) Once again, making guess stack and input stream going ahead simultaneously.

Let modified parser continuously go to carry out analysis. It first attempts to do the normal guess or matching shift. If it succeeds, the parser once again normally runs. If the shift fails, then for the nonterminal at the top of stack, it guesses the shortest candidate expression. And for terminal, before it is inputted the top symbol of the guess stack is inserted. Then step 3) is repeated until the success of shift. In this way, once again let the parser make a guess stack and input stream go ahead simultaneously.

11.3.2 Error Handling in LR(1) Analysis [1]

In LR(1) analysis the recovery from errors is rather difficult, as most of the information which it collects is with the property of an assumption. When a syntax error is found, the LR(1) parser is in the state of S_x, the current input is t_x, and in the analytical table the entry that corresponds to (s, t_x) is empty. This corresponds to error. In order to recovery from errors, we need to select a nonterminal as the one that recovers from error. We denote it R and add candidate form errorneous to it. Suppose that the original productions are

$$N \rightarrow \alpha . R\beta$$
$$R \rightarrow . GHI$$

Now we add

$$R \rightarrow . erorneous\_R.$$

Pseudo-terminal errorneous_R represents a dumb node that is allowed to be the replacement of R. The process of recovery from errors starts from moving out the elements from top of stack one by one, until a state of recovering from errors is found. Suppose that the state of recovery from errors is s_v, due to that we construct a dumb node errorneous_R for R, hence the entry that corresponds to $(s_v, errorneous\_R)$ cannot be empty, and it is just the symbol that is allowed by s_v.

We denote the state t_z. Once again we move out the elements one by one until a symbol that is in the allowable set of t_z is found. The purpose of the process is to move out the remaining part of production of R from input in order to avoid the repetition of the loop. But this measurement may not be successful in avoiding the generation of parsing tree with errors. The algorithm of recovery from errors for LR(1) is very complicated, we do not talk much here.

11.4 Semantic Error Check [2]

The lexical error check and syntax error check which we discuss previously all are carried out when the source program has not run (actually it is unable to run yet), hence they may be called static check. For semantic check, it is mainly dynamic check as by static check, the following errors cannot be found.

1) Zero is divisor, for example in a/b, b may take zero as value in running time.

2) As the result of operation, an expression may have the value that exceeds the range of numbers that the computer can express. For example, the values of a+b, a ×b, a/b, or a ↑ b, may have the values that exceed the maximum of numbers in the computer.

3) A variable i is taken as the index (i.e., a[i]) to access the element of A[l..u]. But i is not in the range l..u.

4) Others.

If some of the cases aforementioned happen the computer definitely cannot produce correct result of the evaluation, only when the program is modified then it can evaluate correctly.

11.5 Optimization of Programs [3]

The program generated through intermediate code cannot be most efficient one. The so-called efficient includes time efficiency and space efficiency. The former one means it runs the fastest among those that implement the same task; the latter means that it uses the fewest amounts of memories. This is also in terms of the programs that implement the same task. However, there may be a variety of programs that implement the same task. It is almost impossible for us to compare all of them every time when we measure the efficiency of a program. As we have mentioned that there is no the best in the world, there is only the better that might exist.

Therefore, the only thing that is reasonable is that based upon the intermediate code, we see what we can do for improvement, so that after making it, the target code obtained from it will be more compact, the amount of used storage is reduced and saver.

The other functions of the compiler are to optimize the intermediate code generated [4]. The intermediate code after optimization will generate better target code. The optimization done in this way is called peephole optimization or local optimization, and its counterpart is called global optimization. Global optimization entails the optimization of the whole source program, and the program is determined by the algorithm which the program was developed according to. Hence the global optimization requires that in order to optimize the program, and the corresponding algorithm should be modified. For example, if we want to sort a series of numbers, and we have developed a sort program based on the bubble algorithm. We know that the bubble algorithm has worse performance. Therefore, the global optimization would replace the algorithm by one of the other algorithms that has better performance and quick sort or Shellsort can be the choice. Besides, if the the original program is a recursive one as recursive programs are elegant and compact in structure, but its efficiency is not as good as the iterative one, then we may replace the recursive program by iterative program.

Now we list the criteria for local optimization and some optimization techniques [5]:

The criteria of local optimization are:

1) An optimization step must preserve the purpose of the program. That is, an optimization must not change the output produced by a program for a given input. If the so-called optimization causes an error, such as a division by zero, that is not optimization at all, it is simply a deterioration.

2) An optimization should make the program more efficient. That means that it may run faster, and it reduces the space taken. If it cannot make any improvement in these two aspects, of course we cannot say optimization either. At least we should have the improvement of the speed at the price of the space or vice versa.

3) An optimization must be worth doing the effort. The result of the optimization should deserve the effort. That means that what we get from the optimization is more beneficial in comparison with our effort. Otherwise if we made a big effort but what we got is the only little benefit, why should we pay the cost?

The following is the techniques that can be adopted in local optimization.

Pre-processing of expressions

(1) Permanent folding method [6].

For expressions the most widely used pre-processing methods for optimization are permanent folding method and arithmetic simplification method. The first one, permanent folding method is as follows: The name permanent folding is a traditional term in the compilation of evaluation of constant expressions. For example, most of the compilers will translate the following program

```
char lower-case-from --- capital (char ch){
    return ch+('a'-'A');
}
Into
char lower-case-from-capital (char ch) {
    return ch+32
    };
```

as 'a' has integer value 97 and 'A' has integer value 65 in ASCII.

Permanent folding method is a simplest and most efficient optimization, although the programmer rarely writes directly constant expressions they may come from character constants, macros, symbol interpretations and intermediate code generation.

(2) Arithmetic simplification

Arithmetic simplification method uses the lower cost arithmetic operations to replace the higher cost operation. In this way we get the profit. The possible substitutions are listed as follows:

Operation	$\rightarrow$	Substitution
E $*2**$ n	$\rightarrow$	E $<<$ n
$2*$ V	$\rightarrow$	V+V

$3*V$	$\rightarrow$	$(V<<1)+V$
$V**2$	$\rightarrow$	$V*V$
$E+0$	$\rightarrow$	E
$E*1$	$\rightarrow$	E
$E**1$	$\rightarrow$	E
$1**E$	$\rightarrow$	1

In this table, E stands for (sub) expression, V stands for variable, $<<$ stands for left shift operator, $**$ stands for exponential operator. It is assumed that the cost of multiplication is higher than that of addition and shift, but is lower than that of exponentiation. It is true for most of the computers. Using the operations with lower cost replaces that with higher cost, this is called strength reduction. If an operation can be totally removed, it is called nullification transformation.

The following is a program of the 3D text written in Java that shows the optimization of the program.

```
// decide where to place the text...
  If (!Isstyleset(CAPTION)) {
      switch(text placement) {
        case CENTER:
        xx=(bound.width/2)-(fm.stringwidth(text)/2);
        yy=(bound.height/2)-(fm.getheight()/2);
        break;
        case LEFT
        xx=thickness+TEXT-OFFSET;
        yy=(bound.height/2)-(fm.getheight(1/2));
        break;
        case RIGHT:
        xx=bound.width-thickness-EXT-OFFSET-fm
            string.width(text);
      yy=(bound.height/2)-(fm.getheight( )/2);
      break:
          }
      }
  else{
      int space=fm.char width('i');
      xx=thickness+ TEXT-OFFSET + spaces;
      yy=0;
      // fill a rectangle in bounding space of string...
      get.set color (getbackground( ));
      g.setcolor(getbackground( ));
      g.fillrec(xx,yy,
      fm.stringwidth(text)+(spacer*2),
      fm.getheight());
      xx+=spacer;
  }
```

After we transform it into an abstract syntax tree the following intermediate code may be obtained:

1) if CAPTION = StyleSET then goto 30

2) T := textplacement
3) if t <> 1 goto 9
4) xx := bounds.width/2
5) xx := xx − fm.stringwidth(text)/2
6) yy := bound.height/2
7) yy − (fm.getheight())/2
8) goto
9) if t <> 2 goto 15
10) xx := thickness
11) xx := xx + TEXT − OFFSET
12) yy := bound.height( )/2
13) yy := − fm.getheight( )/2
14) goto
15) xx := bounds.width
16) xx := xx − TEXT − OFFSET
17) xx := xx − fm.stringwidth(text)
18) yy := bound.height/2
19) yy := yy − fm.getheight( )/2
20) goto
21) w := fm.char width('i')
22) space := realpoint(w)
23) xx := thickness
24) xx := xx + TEXT − OFFSET
25) xx := spacer
26) yy := 0
27) t_1 := g.set color(getbackground ( ))
28) t_2 := g.fillrec(xx,yy,
            fm.stringwidth(text),(spacer*2),
            fm.getheight( ));
29) xx := xx + spacer
30) (the exit of the program) Notice that in the program above, some goto's have no destinations yet and for each case fm.getheight() should be used, and apart LEFT, other cases also need to use fm.stringwidth(text).

Therefore, we may optimize the program to get:
1) if CAPTION + Styls then goto 23
2) t := fm.getheight( )
3) t_1 := textplacement
4) goto 34
5) xx := thickness
6) xx := xx + TEXT − OFFSET
7) yy := bounds.width/2
8) yy := yy − t/2
9) goto 34
10) xx := bounds.width/2
11) xx := xx − t_2/2

12) yy := bounds.height/2
13) yy := yy − t/2
14) goto 34
15) xx := bounds.width
16) xx := xx - thickness
17) xx := xx −− t_2
18) yy := bounds.height/2
19) yy := yy − t/2
20) goto 34
21) If $t_1 = 2$ goto 5
22) t_2 := fm. String width(text)
23) if $t_1 = 1$ goto 8
24) if $t_3 = 3$ goto 13
25) t_2 := fm.stringwidth(text)
26) t_3 := fm.charwidth('i')
27) space := realpoint(t_3)
28) xx := thickness
29) xx := xx + TEXT − OFFSET
30) xx := xx + spacer
31) yy := 0
32) t_2 := fm.stringwidth(text)
33) t_3 := g.setcolor (getbackground( ))
34) t_4 := g.fill rect(xx, yy, t_2, (spacer*2),t)
35) xx := xx + spacer
36) (the exit of the program)

The length of this program is longer than that of the original one, but it is indeed the improvement of it. The reader may check it oneself.

11.6 Principal Ways of Optimization

The principal ways of optimization are: elimination of common subexpressions, copy propagation, dead-code elimination, loop optimization, elimination of induction variables and reduction in strength, etc. In the following we will explain each of them one by one. But before we start our explanation, we should point out that these optimizations will not change the functions of programs that they intend to implement. As the optimization is performed only at the statements in a basic block, so they are called local optimization.

11.6.1 Elimination of Subexpressions

At first we present the definition of common subexpressions.

Definition   Common subexpression. An expression E is called common subexpression, if it is

1) an expression;

2) its value had been evaluated previously somewhere.

For example, if we have a program shown in Fig. 11.1(a), then by the elimination of common subexpressions, we get the Fig. 11.1(b) that is obtained from 11.1(a).

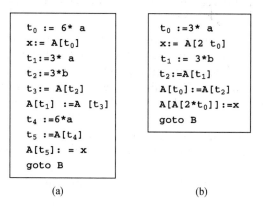

(a)   (b)

Fig. 11.1 Elimination of common subexprssion.

11.6.2 Copy Propagation

The assignment such as a := b is called copy propagation or copy. If we investigate the example of elimination of common subexpression deeper, we can find out that there is also copy propagation in it. Very often, there is also the case in other algorithms. For example, if there are two branches in a program.

```
        if E goto B₁
        x := t₃
        t₁₄ := a[t₁]
        a[t₂] := t₁₄
        a[t₁] := x
        goto B₀
B₁:     x := t₃
        a[t₂] := t₅
        a[t₄] := x
        goto B₂
B₀
```

In the program given above, the assignment x:=t₃ is a copy that occurs twice. Copy propagation applies to it yields

```
x := t₃
a[t₂] := t₅
```

```
a[t₄] := t₃
goto B₂
```

The idea of copy propagation is that after the copy assignment a:=b, using b instead of using a as often as possible.

11.6.3 Dead-Code Elimination

A variable is live at a point in a program if its value can be used subsequently; otherwise, it is dead at that point. A related idea is that a segment of code is dead or useless if the value which it computes has never been put to use. The programmer himself/herself is unlikely to write some segment of code that is never executed, or assign a value to variable but later in the execution of the program the value is never accessed. However, the cases may appear as the result of previous transformations. These situations may also happen due to modifications of the program for many times and unintentionally generating the problem.

For example, in the design of the switch statement, the common practice is as follows:

```
switch E
begin
case    V₁:S₁
case    V₂:S₂
...
case    Vₙ₋₁:Sₙ₋₁
default:Sₙ
end
```

Later it was found that the treatment for some cases is the same, for example, V_2 and V_5, V_3 and V_7 have the same treatments, hence they may be combined together. But if rewrite it as

```
switch E
begin
case V₁:S₁
case V₂,case V₅:S₂
case V₃,case V₇:S₃
case V₄:S₄
case V₅:S₅
case V₆:S₆
case V₇:S₇
...
end
```

then case V_5 : S_5 and case V_7 : case S_7 both are dead-code, as they can never be executed. They should be removed from the program.

Apart from the case, there is another case. That is when a program has been modified, it was found that it should move out from somewhere then a goto statement is added to the original program

```
...
...
goto L
...
```

Then the code following goto L becomes dead-code as it will not be executed. Therefore, when we have a goto statement we have to be careful of the code following it to make sure there is some instruction to access it.

11.6.4 Loop Optimization

Loop programs belong to such a situation that the execution time is not proportional to the length of the program. It can be the case that the length of the program is short, but it repeats for many times. Then the running time can also be very long. We will especially pay attention to the inner loops where programs tend to spend the bulk of their time. The running time of a program may be improved if we decrease the number of instructions in an inner loop, even if we increase the amount of code outside that loop. We regard that the following three techniques are important for loop optimization: code motion that moves code outside a loop; induction-variable elimination which we apply to eliminate variables from the inner loops; and reduction in strength that replaces an expensive operation by a cheaper one, such as a multiplication by an addition. In the following, we explain these techniques one by one.

Code motion

The factors that determine the length of execution time are the length of the loop body and the number of the execution of the loop. Therefore, an important modification that decreases the amount of code in a loop is code motion, especially when the number of the execution of the loop is fixed.

The variable that should remain in the loop is one that really needs to be executed in the loop. If a variable does not change while the loop is executed, then the variable is called loop invariant variable. For loop invariant variable, we do not need to keep it inside the loop to spend time on its computation. For example, if we have

```
u := a
v := b
...
while (i < (u + v)(u - v))
```

If the while loop body does not change the values of u and v, then $(u+v)(u-v)$ is a loop invariant variable and we do not need to repeat the evaluation of it. So we may have the code motion as follows:

```
u := a                    . . .
v := b
t := (u+v)(u-v)
while (i<t)...
```

The induction variable elimination

We have mentioned before that in a loop for the computation that is really needed we should make the computation more efficient. The induction variable elimination and the reduction of strength just belong to the category.

Now we consider the induction variables' elimination. When there are two or more variables in a loop it may be possible to get rid of all but one, by the process of the induction-variable elimination.

For example, we have the following program with loop

```
       i := n-1
       j := m
       t₁ := 5*j
       v := a[t₁]
B₂:
       . . .
    B₃: j := j-1
        t₁ := 4*j
        t₂ := a[t₁]
     if t₂ > v goto B₄ else B₃
    B₄:   if i ⩾ j goto B₆ else B₅
    B₅:   goto B₃
    B₆ :
```

In this program B_3 forms an inner loop and both j and t_1 are induction variables. As t_1 changes along with the change of j, so we cannot get rid of either j or t_1 completely, t_1 is used in B_3 and j in B_4. However, we can make some modification so that partly reduces the strength of the computation. By further analysis, we can even really realize the induction variable elimination.

11.6.5 Reduction of Strength [7]

The following is a program that evaluates $\sum_{k=0}^{n} a_k x^k$.

```
double power-series(int n, double a[],double x){
    double result=0.0;
    int k:
    for (k=0; k⩽n; k++) result+=a[k] * (x ** k);
    return result;
}
```

If we set x as 1.0, the segment of the program above becomes

```
double power-series x-1(int n, double a[]) {
    double result=0.0;
    int k;
```

```
    for (k=0; k≤n;k++)
    result+=a[k] * (1.0 ** k);
    return result;
}
```

Through reduction of strength 1.0 ** k=1, we obtain

```
double power-series x-1 (int n, double a[]) {
    double result=0.0;
    int k;
    for (k=0; k≤n; k++) result +=a[k];
    return result ;
}
```

Optimization of programs involves pre-processing before the generation of intermediate codes, the generation, and pos-processing of correct codes. The pre-processing before the generation of intermediate codes means the improvement of abstract syntax trees. The generation of correct codes means that when codes are to generate one should manage to replace intermediate codes with better codes (more efficient and even optimal); post-processing means that even after the code has been generated, there is a possibility to make some optimization (peephole optimization).

In the whole course, we focus on control stream, data flow and code sequence, where control stream is most critical. But if we want to get the best effect of optimization, then every aspect should be valued.

Problems

Problem 11.1 Explain why does a configuration A of prediction stack always contain the notation EOF in its allowable set.

Problem 11.2 The following is the simple grammar of the top-down parser analysis

input → expression EOF
expression → term rest-expression
term → IDENTIFIER | parenthesized-expression
parenthesized-expression → '(' expression ')'
rest-expression → '+' expression|ε

Using it and the relevant knowledge in this chapter, determine the allowable stack of parenthesized-expression rest-expression EOF for LL(1) parser.

References

[1]   Graham SL, Haley CB, Joy WN (1979) Practical LR error recovery. ACM SIGPLan Notices 14 (8): 168 – 175.

[2]   Alfred V Aho, Ravi Sethi, Jeffrey Ullman D (2003) Compilers, principles, techniques and tools. Prentice-Hall, Englewood cliffs.

[3]   Giegerich R (1983) A formal framework for the derivation of machine-specific optimizers. TOPLAS 5(3): 422 – 448.

[4]   Cocke J, Kennedy K (1977) An algorithm for reduction of operator strength. Comm. ACM 20(11): 850 – 856.

[5]   Graham SL (1984) Code generation and optimization. In B Lorho (ed) Methods and Tools for Compiler Construction: An Advanced course, pp, 251 – 288.

[6]   Cocke J, Markstein J (1980) Measurement of code improvement algorithms. Information Processing 80, 221 – 228.

[7]   Allen Fe, Cocke J, Kennedy K (1981) Reduction of operator strength. In: Muchicks, Jones N (ed) Program Flow an algsis: theory and application. Prentice-Hall, Englewood Cliffs, pp. 79 – 101.

Chapter 12   Storage Management

Management involves the planning, Monitoring, and
control of the people, process, and events that occur . . . .

Roger S. Pressman

The task of compilers is to translate the source programs to the target programs. Therefore, strictly speaking there is nothing to do for a compiler with
the storage management. Storage management is not its task. However, compilers can only work when they stay in the memory and the target code
which they generate is also in memory. During the compilation, the compiler
should consider the layout of the source program, the various tables and the
placements of intermediate code and target code, etc. If the layout is not
appropriate, the compiler will not be able to efficiently access and the work
of compiler cannot be efficient either. Therefore, in this sense, compiler has
intimate relation with the storage management.

12.1   Motivation of the Chapter

Now that we have known that compilers have related to storage in many ways.
It is the task of the chapter to illustrate the storage management that affects
the process of compilation. We will explain what the storage management
means for compilers. In order for compilers to run efficiently how should
one realize the storage management? What strategies should be adopted to
realize the storage management? etc.

Suppose that the compiler obtains a block of storage from the operating
system for the compiled program to run in. Of course, before this the compiler
needs to compile the source program, and build up a number of symbol tables
that are stored in the memory too. From the lexical analysis, the syntax
analysis and the generation of intermediate code, etc., finally we just have
the compiled program that is called the target code. During these phases, how
does the storage management work? This chapter should explicitly explain
the issues in details.

12.2 Global Allocation Strategy

The operating system is in charge of the whole management of storage, as well as other resources of the computer. When a compiler starts its work, executing various tasks of the compilation of the source program. In order to support the compiler, it will allocate the storage to compiler. The operating system at least will allocate the following three segments of storage to compiler:

- Code segment. It contains program code. Code segment is accessed via program counter.
- Stack segment. It contains stack, it can also contain the monitor mechanism for lower bound and upper bound constraint. The stack segment is accessed via one or more pointers, usually it is automatically executed by machine instructions.
- Data segment. This is a continuously extendable unit alone. It may be controlled by program to store data. The start address and the size are available for the program, and the content is addressable for machine instructions. We call data segment as a heap that corresponds to the stack above.

The task of the storage management is to allocate and reclaim subsegments in data segments so that these subsegments may be properly loaded to data segments. In this way, the main memory address is guaranteed not to be in multi subsegments. In addition, the other important goal of storage management is that when the storage space is enough to satisfy the need, it should not reject the applications for storage space. According to the particularities of the called program, the correspondence between real parameters and formal parameters is realized in different ways.

The size of the generated target code is fixed at the compile-time, so the compiler can place it in a statically determined area, perhaps in the low end of memory. Similarly, the size of some data objects may also be known at the compile-time, and these too can be placed in a statical area, as follows.

code	code segment
static data	
stack	stack segment
↓	
↑	
Heap	data segment

The reason for statically allocating as many data objects as possible is that the addresses of these objects can be compiled into target code. All data objects in some programming language can be allocated statically.

Implementations of languages use extensions of the control stack to manage activations of procedures [1]. When a call occurs, execution of an activation is interrupted and information about the status of the machine, such as the value of the program counter and machine register, is saved on the stack, along with other information associated with the activation.

Stack allocation is based on the idea of a control stack; storage is organized as a stack, and activation records are pushed and popped as activations begin and end, respectively. Storage for the locals in each call of a procedure is contained in the activation record for that call. Thus locals are bound to fresh storage in each activation, because a new activation record is pushed onto the stack when a call is made. Furthermore, the values of locals are deleted when the activation ends; that is, the values are lost because the storage for locals disappears when the activation record is popped.

We now describe a form of stack allocation in which sizes of all activation records are known at compile-time. Situations in which incomplete information about the size is available at compile-time are considered below.

Suppose that register top marks the top of the stack. At run-time, an activation record can be allocated and deallocated by incrementing and decrementing top, respectively, by the size of the record. If procedure q has an activation record of size a, then top is incremented by a just before the target code of q is executed. When control returns from q, top is decremented by a.

A separate area of run-time memory, called a heap, holds all other informations. In some languages, they provide facilities for the dynamic allocation of storage for data, under program control. Storage for such data is usually taken from a heap. The stack allocation strategy cannot be used if either of the following is possible:

1) The value of local names must be retained when an activation ends.

2) A called activation outlives the caller. This possibility cannot occur for those languages where activation trees correctly depict the flow of control between procedures.

In each of the above cases, the deallocation of activation records need not occur in a last-in-first-out fashion, so storage cannot be organized as a stack. Heap allocation parcels out pieces of the contiguous storage, as needed for activation records or other objects. Pieces may be deallocated in any order, so over time the heap will consist of alternate areas that are free and in use.

The difference between heap and stack allocations of an activation records is that the record for an activation of procedure, say r, is retained when the activation ends. The record for the new activation, say q(1, 9), therefore, cannot follow that for s physically. Now if the retained activation record for r is deallocated, there will be free space in the heap between the activation records for s and q(1, 9). It is left to the heap manager to make use of this space.

The sizes of the stack and heap can change as the program executes, so we show these at opposite ends of memory where they can grow towards each other if need be. By convention, stacks grow down. That is, the 'top' of the stack is drawn towards the bottom of the page. Since memory addresses increase as we go down a page, "downwards-growing" means towards higher addresses. If top marks the top of the stack, offsets from the top of the stack can be computed by subtracting the offset from top. On many machines, this computation can be done efficiently by keeping the value of top in a register. Stack addresses can then be represented as offsets from top.

12.3 Algorithms for Allocation

12.3.1 Algorithm for Stack Allocation

The stack allocation is run-time allocation. It is used to allocate memory for the need of procedure that calls for other procedures to implement specific tasks. As we have mentioned that, the register top marks the top of the stack. At run-time, suppose top marks the location of the end of a record. The address of a local name x in the target code for the procedure might therefore be written as dx (top), to indicate that the data bound to x can be found at the location obtained by adding dx to the value in register top. Note that addresses can alternatively be taken as offsets from the value in any other register r pointing to a fixed position in the activation record.

Therefore, the algorithm for the stack allocation will start with the initialization of register top [2]. Then it dynamically arranges the calling sequences. A call sequence allocates an activation record and enters information into its fields. A return sequence restores the state of the machine so the calling procedure can continue execution.

Calling sequences and activation records and activation record differ, even for implementations of the same language. The code in a calling sequence is often divided between the calling procedure (the caller) and the procedure it calls (the callee). There is no exact division of run-time tasks between the caller and callee — the source language, the target machine, and the operating system imposes requirements that may favor one solution over another.

A principle that aids the design of calling sequences and activation records is that fields whose sizes are fixed early are placed in the middle. In the general activation record, the control link, access link, and machine-status fields appear in the middle. The decision about whether or not to use control and access link is part of the design of compiler, so these fields can be fixed at compiler-construction time, if exactly the same amount of machine-status information is saved for each activation. Moreover, programs such as debuggers will have an easier time deciphering the stack contents when an error occurs.

Even though the size of the field for temporaries is eventually fixed at compile-time, this size may not be known to the front end. Careful code generation or optimization may reduce the number of temporaries needed by the procedure [3], so as far as the front end is concerned, the size of the field is unknown. In the general activation record, we therefore show this field after that for local data, where change in its size will not affect the offsets of data object relative to the fields in the middle.

Since each call has its own actual parameters, the caller usually evaluates actual parameters and communicates them to the activation record of the callee. Methods for passing parameters will be discussed in the next section.

In the run-time stack, the activation record of the caller is just below that for the callee. There is an advantage to placing the fields for parameters and a potential returned value next to the activation record of the caller. The caller can then access these fields using offsets from the end of its own activation record, without knowing the complete layout of the record for the callee. In particular, there is no reason for the caller to know about the local data or temporaries of the callee. A benefit of this information hiding is that procedures with variable numbers of arguments can be handled. Some programming languages require arrays local to a procedure to have a length that can be determined at the compile-time. More often, the size of a local array may depend on the value of a parameter passed to the procedure. In that case, the size of all the data local to the procedure cannot be determined until the procedure is called.

A common strategy for handling variable-length data is some how different from the handling of fixed-length data. Suppose that procedure p has four local arrays. The storage for these arrays is not part of the activation record for p; only a pointer to the beginning of each array appears in the activation record. The relative addresses of these pointers are known at compile-time, so the target code can access array elements through the pointers.

Suppose that there is a procedure called q that is called by p. The activation record for q begins after the arrays of p, and the variable- length arrays of p, and the variable-length arrays of q begin beyond that.

Access to data on the stack is through two pointers, top and top-sp. The first of these marks the actual top of the stack; it points to the position at which the next activation record will begin. The second is used to find local data.

Suppose that top-sp points to the end of machine-status field. The top-sp points to the end of this field in the activation record for q. Within the field is a control link to the previous value of top-sp when control was in the calling activation of p.

The code to the reposition top and top-sp can be generated at compile-time, using the size of the fields in the activation records. When q returns, the new value of top is top-sp minus the length of the machine-status and parameter fields in q's activation record. After adjusting top, the new value of top-sp can be copied from the control link of q.

Having introduced the details of handling communications of procedure and the procedure it calls, we can now introduce the call sequence and return sequence, or the algorithms for doing so. Once again, we should make it clear that register top-sp points to the end of the machine- status field in an activation record. This position is known to the caller, so it can be made responsible for setting top-sp before control follows to the called procedure.

The code for the callee can access its temporaries and local data using offsets from top-sp.

The call sequence is as follows:

1) The caller evaluates actual.

2) The caller stores a return address and old value of top-sp into the callee's activation record. Then the caller increments top-sp to the position with the new pointer value. That is, top-sp is moved past the caller's local data and temporaries and the callee's parameter and status fields.

3) The callee saves register values and other status information.

4) The callee initializes its local data and begins execution.

As for return sequence, it is likely to be as follows:

- The callee places a return value next to the activation record of the caller.
- Using the information in the status field, the callee restores top-sp and other registers and branches to a return address in the caller's code.
- Although top-sp has been decremented, the caller can copy the returned value into its own activation record and use it to evaluate an expression.

The above calling sequences allow the number of arguments of the called procedure to depend on the call. Note that, at compile-time, the target code of the caller knows the number of arguments it is supporting to the callee. Hence the caller knows the size of the parameter field. However, the target code of the callee must be prepared to handle other calls as well, so it waits until it is called, and then examines the parameter field. Using the organization described above, information describing the parameters must be placed next to status field so the callee can find it.

12.3.2   Algorithm for Heap Allocation

We will be more concerned with that techniques needed to implement dynamic storage allocation depend on how storage is deallocated. Some languages provide the facilities for the dynamic allocation of storage for data under program control [4]. Storage for such data is usually taken from a heap. Allocated data is often retained until it is explicitly deallocated. The allocation itself can be either explicit or implicit. If deallocation is implicit, then the run-time support package is responsible for determining when a storage block is no longer needed. There is less a compiler has to do if deallocation is done explicitly by the programmer. We now consider the explicit allocation strategy first.

For explicit allocation, we need to consider two different situations: one is for fixed-sized blocks and another one is for variable-sized blocks.

The simplest form of dynamic allocation involves blocks of a fixed size.

In this situation, we organize the blocks in a list into a link. Allocation and deallocation can be done quickly with little or no storage overhead.

Suppose that blocks are to be drawn from a contiguous area of storage. Initialization of the area is done by using a portion of each block for a link to the next block. A pointer called available points to the first block.

Allocation consists of taking a block off the list and deallocation consists of putting the block back on the list.

The compiler routines that manage blocks do not need to know the type of object that will be held in the block by the user program. We can treat each block as a variant record, with the compiler routines viewing the block as consisting of a link to the next block and the user program viewing the block as being of some other type. Thus there is no space overhead because the user program can use the entire block for its own purposes.

When the block is returned, the compiler routines use some of the space from the block itself to link it into the list of available blocks.

With the variable-sized blocks, when they are allocated and deallocated, storage can become fragmented; that is, the heap may consist of alternate blocks that are free and in use.

For example, if a program allocates five blocks and then deallocates the second and fourth, then the fragmentation is formed. Fragmentation is of no consequence if blocks are of fixed size, but if they are of variable size, then it will be a problem, because we could not allocate a block larger than any one of the free block, even though the space is available in principle.

One method for allocating variable-sized blocks is called the first-fit method. When a block of size s is allocated, we search for the first free block that is of size $f \geqslant s$. This block is then subdivided into a used block of size s and a free block of size f–s. Note that allocation incurs a time overhead because we must search for a free block that is large enough.

When a block is deallocated, we check to see if it is next to a free block. If possible, the deallocateed block is combined with a free block next to it to create a larger block. Combining adjacent free blocks into a larger free block prevents further fragmentation from occurring. There are a number of subtle details concerning how free blocks are allocated, deallocated, and maintained in an available list or lists. There are also several tradeoffs between time, space, and availability of large blocks. The reader is referred to articles [5] and [6] for a discussion of these issues.

12.4 Reclamation of Used Space

The so-called reclamation of used space means automatically reclaims the storage space which targets program no longer uses in order to continue using it. Dynamically allocated storage can become unreachable. Storage which a program allocates but cannot refer to is called garbage. Therefore, this kind of reclamation usually is called garbage collection, or implicit reclamation because it is not done by programmer using free() function to manually reclaim the storage space unavailable. The purpose of providing such reclamation is for freeing programmer from manually using free() function to reclaim the storage space that is usually fault-prone.

Before we further discuss garbage collection, we introduce a concept called dangling reference. Whenever storage can be deallocated, the problem of dangling references arises. A dangling reference occurs when there is a reference to storage that has been deallocated. It is a logical error to use dangling references, since the value of deallocated storage is undefined according to the semantics of most languages. It is even worse since that storage may later be allocated to another datum, mysterious bug can appear in the program with dangling references. Many programmers had experienced such things that they deallocated the space, and then they referred to it. For example, consider the effect of executing dispose (head↑.next) as follows:

    insert(7, 1); insert(4, 2); insert(73, 3);
    dispose(head↑.next)
    Writeln(head↑.key, head↑.info);

The call to dispose deallocation of the cell is followed by the one pointed to by head. However, head↑.next has not been changed, so it is a dangling pointer. If the deallocation was made long time ago and the reference to it was made indirectly, then the error cannot be found easily. The reasons for this are:

1) dangling pointer possibly has long been released wrongly in storage space before it was referred, hence it is difficult to discover it.

2) After dangling pointer was referred, the program that referred to it probably has run on incorrect data for a while before it found the error of inconsistency.

3) Only when the steps of storage allocation and that of the deallocation are the same, then can the errors be discovered, otherwise this kind of errors is hard to discover.

Therefore, garbage collector is regarded as an important feature of modern compilers, it can remarkably reduce the workload of programming.

12.4.1   Basic Garbage Collection Algorithm

The goal of the garbage collection is to automatically reclaim the storage fragments that are already not in use. Therefore, naturally one may ask when is it carried out as it is automatically done it? If it is carried out frequently, then it must affect the normal operations of the program. It is something like the work of cleaning. If the work of cleaning for offices is carried out frequently, it definitely must affect the work of people who work in the offices. But as another extreme, if the work of cleaning did not carry until the offices are full of wastes. Or in the storage, it has been such full that the garbage collector has no room to be inside the storage, how can it carry out the reclamation work? Therefore the work of the garbage collection should be done regularly or periodically. It cannot be suspended until the garbage has occupied the whole storage space.

The second problem is even more important, in order to correctly carry out the work of collection, we need to make it very clear, what is garbage? For this purpose, people propose two concepts that are approximate but actually are different. One is "the set of storage fragments that have no pointers pointing to" and the next is "not reachable set of fragments from the data of allocator of non heap style." The data in these two sets obviously are not accessible by any program. They incur the techniques which garbage collectors depend upon. The first one incurs the technique called reference counts. And the second one incurs marking scanning and the copies of two spaces.

- Reference counts. This approach directly identifies wasted fragment. It is relatively simple and efficient. But it requires that while a program runs all the activities of pointers be monitored, and it is not unlikely to cover all the wasted fragments.
- Token and scan. This approach defines the reachable fragments, and the rest is regarded as garbage. It is rather efficient and it needn't carry out the pointer detection. But it is rather complicated. It can cover all the available spaces.
- The dual space copy. This approach copies the reachable fragments of the storage area within the so-called source space into the storage area of the so-called target space. The rest of the target space is of free fragments. This approach is also very efficient and needn't carry out pointer detection, but it is also complicated, and it wastes about half of the space.

Once the wasted fragments have been determined through these approaches, they should be transformed into free space available for use. Those that are discovered by reference counts or token and scan should be returned to free space link table via the specific algorithm. Those that are discovered by the dual space copy may automatically create new free space link table that is a single storage fragment that contains all free storage spaces.

Regarding storage allocation, we need to further explain the concept of the fragment. As we mentioned before, if a program in execution requires a storage space with length of s, the allocator found a space with length f from free storage link table, where f > s. Then it allocates a part of the storage with length s to the program. Then there is storage with length f − s left. This is a fragment.

Gradually, these fragments will scatter over the storage space. Though all these fragments may have limited lengths only, the sum of them may be quite big. Therefore, if a program applies for a space that its length is bigger than the size of the current biggest storage fragment in the table, then the allocator must fail to satisfy the requirement. However, if a compressing technique is adopted, that is, to combine these fragments together and move them to one side of the storage, forming an independent and single free space, it will be used to satisfy the requirement of the program. It may be seen from here that this is the best approach that collects the storage space being not in use.

Compressing technique is not perfect either. The main problem with it is that it needs to shift the reachable fragments around and in these fragments it is likely that they contain pointers pointing to other fragments also needing to shift. Therefore, in order to correctly shift them the careful design must be done first.

Garbage collector algorithms may have three kinds:

- Working at once. After the garbage collector is initialized, it will completely control all the storage fragments until it finishes running, then it returns back. After the processing, the situation of storage will be improved that wasted fragments will not scatter over the storage again. Since this kind of the garbage collector completely controls the storage fragments when it runs, the situation is simpler. But if there is unexpected activation happening, there will be some sort of damages. This is possibly a problem in compiler but it is not the case in application programs.
- Dynamic (also called incremental). Some garbage collector starts working when procedure malloc or free is called. These activities will locally modify the structures of the storage fragment in order to enhance the ability of searching free fragments. The dynamic garbage collector is more complex than the kind of working at once in structure, but its execution is more stable, and has smaller damage. When it cannot meet the requirements, it may need the help from the former one.
- Concurrent one. In this kind, the garbage collector concurrently works with the application program. They work on different processors, and each runs in one processor. These two run parallel but each carries out its own task.

Garbage collectors need lots of help from compiler, and it is the aim of this book to explain them.

12.4.2 Supports to Garbage Collector From Compilers

At first, we need to point out that, only when a program has a pointer directly pointing to the storage fragment, then the fragment is reachable for the program, or it has a pointer indirectly pointing to that storage fragment, then it is so. The pointer available to the program depends on its specific implementation, it may be located in different locations such as a global variable, local variable, routine parameter, register, and other. We call those non heap-style storage space which the program code may directly access to the area of program data, and the set of all pointers in the area of program data the root set. Notice that the root set is only an overall concept, rather than a kind of structures. It is the set of all pointers in the area of program data, rather than the list of their values. The root set usually cannot be implemented directly. It only occurs conceptually inside of the program code of garbage collector.

The pointers in the root set may point to storage fragments that are controlled by garbage collector, hence they are reachable. The reachable fragments in a heap also contain pointers of other fragments. These fragments pointed to by pointers are also reachable.

Compilers must provide the root set and the distributive information of each storage fragment to the garbage collector, meanwhile, it must ensure that when the garbage collector is activated, all the reachable pointers in the area of program data and heap are effective. Based on the support from compilers, the garbage collectors resolve the following three problems:

1) To determine the root set via searching all the pointers and their types in the area of program data.

2) To search for all the pointers and their types in some given storage fragment.

3) To find out all the reachable storage fragments using 1) and 2).

From these one may see that, without the supports from compiler, the garbage collectors cannot complete the task of collecting garbage. Compiler completely controls the distribution of pointers of storage fragmentation, hence the problem is how to transmit the information to garbage collector. The following is some methods that garbage collector in compiler provides information of distribution of pointers.

1) Compiler generates a bit image for every fragment type to assign which field in that type segment points to the pointer of other fragments. When this method is used, the fragment must be self-described, because as long as there is pointer the garbage collector is ensured to keep working. Therefore, every storage fragment must contain each own bit image, or the pointer that points to the bit image.

2) Compiler generates a specific routine for each fragment type that calls for garbage collector, and passes each pointer in the fragment as the parameters. This method avoids the explanation of the bit image in running time and the requirement for self-description because the code can transmit the fragment types and pointers to garbage collector.

3) Compiler organizes the fragments to form an array that contains all the internal pointers, followed by other data structure types. Through this organization, the garbage collector can start working as long as it knows the addresses of the pointers in the array and the number of pointers in the fragment.

12.4.3   Reference Counts

Reference counts is an intuitive algorithm for the garbage collection. It records the number of pointers that are pointed to it in each storage block. When the number drops to zero, that means that the block is not used because it cannot be referred to. The block now becomes the garbage that can be collected. Here we regard the pointer pointed to it as the reference to it, maintaining reference counts can be costly in time. The pointer assignment $p := q$ leads to changes in the reference counts of the blocks pointed to by both p and q. The count for the block pointed to by p goes down by one, while that for the block pointed to by q goes up by one. Reference counts are best used when pointers between blocks never appear in cycles.

The two main problems with the implementation of reference counts are tracking all the operations of references and recursive reclamation of blocks with reference counts zero. Compiler plays an essential role, and recursive reclamation is done by the execution of routine procedure.

Compiler adds special code for all the operations of references. When the references to blocks are copied, the reference count is increased 1, while the reference to the block is removed, the reference count is decreased 1. In the source language, reference is copied in the assignment operations. Besides assignment operations, compilers should also supplement the code for increase of references in parameters passing because references taken as parameter passing is an efficient assignment to local variables of calling routines.

The removal of references happens when a procedure call returns. When a procedure returns, all the local variables need to remove. For those local variables that contain block reference, it needs the decrease handling of the references counts. Meanwhile, for those parameters that contain block references the same handling is also needed.

Reference counts technique is a simple one, and it has some serious drawbacks. These problems limit its applications. At first, reference counts method cannot reclaim the cyclic structures. For example, if the reference counts for a includes a reference to it from the root set and now the reference is cut off then even the reference counts have not dropped to zero, but it has become unreachable from the root set, and so it has become garbage. Another block that has reference to it has also become garbage as they become cycle. In order to reclaim a cyclic structure, one needs to reclaim all the nodes in the cyclic structure. But it is impossible if they are unreachable.

The second problem with reference counts is its efficiency. Compilers have to monitor all the reference operations, and each reference operation entails to adjust corresponding reference counts. In comparison with other techniques that do not need to monitor these operations, this is a big overhead.

The third problem with reference counts is that the number of free fragments in the list will increase as the number of reclamation increases, but they still appear in the form of fragments.

Although there exist above problems, reference counts method is still a popular method when it is used to manage dynamic distributed structures with relatively small in sizes.

12.4.4 Tokens and Scans

The tokens and scans garbage collection algorithm may be divided into two processes. The first one is making token process that is used to mark all reachable blocks. The second one is the scanning process that is used to scan distributed storage space and regard those that have not been marked as reachable blocks free blocks so that they may be reused. The tokens and scans garbage collection algorithm sometimes is also called marking and removing garbage collection algorithm. In comparison with the reference counts the garbage collection algorithm that was introduced before and the dual space copy algorithm that will introduce soon, the efficiency of tokens and scans is highest because it can claim all the storage space that can be claimed while by reference counts algorithm the cyclic reference counts structures cannot be claimed. As for dual space copy algorithm it leaves half of the storage space that is not available.

1. Tokens

Token marking is based on two principles, one is that those storage blocks that are reachable from the root set are reachable. The second one is that any storage block that is reachable from a pointer in reachable blocks is reachable. Suppose that the root set resides in program data area or in the highest end of the active record. Its data type specification has been constructed and for compilers it is accessible. Now from the earliest form token program data area is reachable, by its data type description the internal pointer may be found. If the recursive procedure found that a block has no pointer or the block that has been marked, then it backtracks and uses the next pointer to continue the recursive procedure. As the number of reachable blocks is limited, and the processing of each storage block is only for finite times (in general, is only once, occasionally it can be more than twice). Therefore, the depth-first-search scanning algorithm can terminate and the time it spent increases linearly proportional to the increase of the number of reachable fragments.

Besides the free bit, marking process needs another auxiliary bit — marking bit in the head of management field of storage blocks. Initially, the bit is in the state of "removal".

2. Scan and reclamation

The reclamation of unreachable fragments is relatively easy. According to the length of record in the fragment, we traverse storage fragments one by one. With every fragment, we check whether it is marked as reachable. If it has been marked reachable, then remove its marking bit, otherwise open its free bit.

The adjacent free fragments can also be combined together using scanning algorithm from left to right. When the algorithm finished, we reserve a pointer and let it point to the first free fragment and record its size. As long as we meet free fragments, we accumulate their sizes until we meet an occupied block, or we reached the end of the storage. At the time the size in the management field is just the total size of free fragments. In this way, we create a bigger space. Continuing the scanning process whenever a free fragment is met then the process repeats, and so forth.

The outcome of the marking and scanning process is the generation of a heap where all the blocks that are marked occupied reachable. Moreover, occupied block must be between free fragments. This is the best method for the implementation of reclamation of fragments under the situation that the fragments do not need to move. If once again using the contracting process to combine all the free fragments to form a bigger free block, then the efficiency of the execution may be further raised.

12.4.5 Dual Space Copy

The token (marking) process of the tokens and scans the garbage collection algorithm only involves reachable blocks, but the scanning process involves all the storage blocks. When it is working the most part of the heap consists of garbage and the workload of the algorithm is huge. Considering the problem, the dual space copy algorithm avoids the scanning of all the storage blocks, it only scans the reachable blocks. Therefore, it saves time through the requirement for storage increases almost doubly. As the price of storage gradually decreases to save the time at the expense of storage is worthwhile. The idea of the dual space copy algorithm is to divide the available heap into two equal parts: source space and target space.

In daily computation the new storage block can be obtained in the source space simply using the moving ahead of the pointer. When the source space consumes up, all the reachable blocks will be copied to the empty target space through garbage collector.

The operation of the dual space copy starts with the copy of source space storage which is referred to by the pointers in the root set, it puts the copy starting from beginning position to the target space. Then the primitive storage blocks of source space are marked "copied" and in the block a forward pointer is set that points to corresponding copy in the target space. When the copying operation finishes the content may be destroyed. In copying, there is no update of pointers hence the pointers still point to the blocks in source space. Subsequently, a "scanning pointer" is used to scan the storage blocks of the target space from left to right in order to search for the pointers of storage blocks in the target space. Suppose that the one of scanning pointers of storage block R points to a storage block S in the source space, then there are two possibilities: S is marked "copied" or S has not been marked "copied". In the first case, it contains a forward pointer to update the pointer in R, while in the second case it should be immediately copied. When the copying operation finishes, it is marked "copied" and its content is replaced by the copy which the pointer points to. Repeat this process until the target space does not contain the pointers that point to the storage blocks in the source space.

Finally, all the reachable blocks in the source space have been copied to the target space, and all the pointers are updated, pointing to the target space. Now the roles of the two spaces exchange. The computation continues.

By using copying garbage collector the overhead of fragmentation and time complexity which the tokens and scans the garbage collection algorithm incurs may be solved. The key problem is that moving storage blocks makes free space keeping consecutive and this can be done by moving ahead a global pointer. The main drawback of dual space copy is that it may waste half of the heap space, and when the heap is nearly full, the performance of the algorithm will deteriorate. The dual space copy algorithm is a highly efficient algorithm while it entails rigorous requirements. When running efficiency is more important in comparison with space efficiency, then it is a good choice.

12.4.6 Contract

The problem of fragmentations is one of the important problems which the garbage collection algorithms need to resolve. Fragments actually are the available free space. But due to that the size of every fragment is far too small, and it is unable to put them in use, unless they are put together to form an even biggest free space. Therefore, the contract of fragments is significant for their availability. If there are only two types of fragments, either marked "occupied" or free, and the pointers in storage blocks that are marked "occupied" are consistent, then the contract algorithm can be performed. Even when some of the storage blocks marked "occupied" are in fact unreachable, the contract method still can be used because the fragments can be found by scanning. From the point of view, the contract algorithm can almost be put in execution in any time. It is independent from garbage collector to a great extent, and it is a technique that improves the free lists. After the execution of the garbage collector, then the contract program runs, it will get very good effect.

Through adding one more extra pointer to every storage block, and scanning the storage for three times from left to right, the contract of the storage can be done. The three times of scanning are: the first scanning computes the address of new position of the storage block, the second scanning updates the existing pointer to point to the new position, and the third really move the storage block.

1) Address computation. Scanning the storage blocks down-up, computing the new position for ever storage block after contract. The corresponding address of the new position is kept in the management field of the storage block. Since we know the new position of the first occupied storage block (located at the lower end of the storage), we also know the size of the storage block, hence there is not any problem for the computation of address.

2) Update of pointer. Scanning the program data area and storage blocks, to search for the pointers of the heap where every pointer that points to the storage blocks should be updated to the new position in the management field of the storage block.

3) Move of the storage blocks. The storage program scans the storage blocks from low to high. Every occupied block is moved to new position. The new position can be found from the management field of the storage block. The storage blocks can only be moved to left (moved to low end), or kept still, hence the work can be done by single way scanning from left to right. All the pointers in the blocks are repointed to the storage blocks that are pointed at the beginning of the contract.

12.5 Parameter Passing

In programming languages people use procedures to handle the multi uses of the same operations. But in the different uses of these operations there may be different values of the parameters. In order for the procedure to meet the need of using different values of parameters, the formal procedure does not involve the specific values of these parameters, and positions are in place of them. This is what we say of formal parameters. People found that different effects may be produced if one uses different methods to associate the actual parameters and formal parameters, and the association naturally is related to the management of storage.

Several common methods for associating actual and formal parameters are discussed in this section. They are call-by-value, call-by-reference, copy-restore and call-by-name.

One should be aware that, the method used for passing actual parameters is very important for a language (or a compiler), because the outcome of a program may depend on the method.

Why are there so many methods? These different methods come from different explanations of the implication of an expression. For example, for the simple assignment such as

$$a[i] := a[i]$$

where a[i] represents a value. While a[j] represents the address where the value of a[i] is put. Whether the storage address which an expression represents is used or the value of the expression is used, depends on where does the expression appear, either the left hand side or the right hand side of the assignment symbol. Therefore, we use the term l-value to refer to the storage represented by an expression, and r-value to refer to the value contained in the storage. The prefix l- and r- come from "left" and "right" side of an assignment. Differences between parameter passing methods are based primarily on whether an actual parameter represents an l-value, an r-value, or the text of the actual parameter itself.

12.5.1 Call-by-Value

This is, in a sense, the simplest possible method of passing parameters. The actual parameters are evaluated, and their r-values are passed to the called procedure. Call-by-value can be implemented as follows:

1) A formal parameter is treated just like a local name, so the storage for the formal parameters is in the activation record of the called procedure.

2) The caller evaluates the actual parameters and places their r-values in the storage for the formal parameters.

A distinguishing feature of call-by-value is that operations on the formal parameters do not affect values in the activation record of the caller. A procedure called by value can affect its caller through nonlocal names or through pointers that are explicitly passed as values.

12.5.2 Call-by-References

Call-by-references is also called call-by-address or call-by-location. When the method is used for Parameter passing, the caller passes to the called procedure a pointer to the storage address of each actual parameter.

The following is its implementation:

1) If an actual parameter is a name or an expression having an l-value, then that l-value itself is passed.

2) If the actual parameter, however, is an expression, like 5 or a+b that has no l-value, then the expression is evaluated in a new location, and the address of that location is passed.

A reference to a formal parameter in the called procedure becomes, in the target code, an indirect reference through the pointer passed to the called procedure. Arrays are usually passed by reference.

12.5.3 Copy-Restore

A hybrid between call-by-value and call-by-reference is copy-restore, it is also known as copy-in-copy- out or value-result. Its implementation is as follows:

1) The actual parameters are evaluated before control flows to the called procedure. The r-values of the actual parameters are passed to the called procedure as in call-by-value. In addition, however, the l-value of those actual parameters having l-values is determined before the call.

2) When control returns, the current r-values of the formal parameters are copied back into the l-value of the actual parameters, using the l-value computed before the call. Only actual parameters having l-values are copied, of course.

Therefore, the first step "copies in" the values of the actual parameters into the activation record of the called procedure (into the storage for the formal parameters). The second step "copies out" the final values of the formal parameters into the activation record of the caller (into l-values computed from the actual parameters before the call). The difference between copy-restore and call-by-reference shows up if the called procedure has more than one way of accessing a location in the activation record of the caller.

12.5.4 Call-by-Name

Call-by-name is traditionally defined by the copy-rule of early language Algol, that is:

1) The procedure is treated as if it was a macro; that is, its body is substituted for the call in the caller, with the actual parameters literally substituted for the formal parameters. Such a literal substitution is called macro-expansion or in-line expansion.

2) The local names of the called procedure are kept distinct from the names of the calling procedure. We can think of each local of the called procedure being systematically renamed into a distinct new name before the macro-expansion is done.

3) The actual parameters are surrounded by parentheses if to preserve their integrity is needed.

Although call-by-name is primarily of theoretical interest, the conceptually related technique of in-line expansion has been suggested for reducing the running time of a program. There is a certain cost associated with setting up an activation of a procedure — space is allocated for the activation record, the machine-status is saved, links are set up, and then control is transferred. When a procedure body is small, the code devoted to the calling sequences may overweight the code in the procedure body. It may therefore be more efficient to use the in-line expansion of the body [7] into the code for the caller, even if the size of the program grows a little.

The usual implementation of call-by-name is to pass to the called procedure parameterless subroutines, commonly thunks, that can evaluate the l-values or r-value of the actual parameters. Like any procedure passed as a parameter in a language using lexical scope, a thunk carries an access link with it, pointing to the current activation record for the calling procedure.

Problems

Problem 12.1 When a procedure is passed as a parameter in a lexically scoped language, its nonlocal environment can be passed using an access link. Give an algorithm to determine this link.

Problem 12.2 What is printed by the following proram, if the parameter passing is a) call-by-value; b) call-by-reference; c) copy-restore linkage; d) call-by-name:

```
program main (input, output);
    procedure p(x, y, z);
        begin
            y := y+1:
            z := z+x;
        end;
        begin
            a := 2;
            b := 3;
            p(a+b, a, a):
        print a
    end.
```

Problem 12.3 The statement f:=a on line 11 of the following pseudo-program calls function a that passes function addm back as a result.

```
1) Draw the activation tree for an execution of this program.
2) Suppose that lexical scope is used for nonlocal names.
Why will the program fail if stack allocation is used?
3) What is the output of this program with heap allocation?
(1) program ret (input, output);
(2) var f:  function (integer):  integer;
(3) function a:  function (integer):  integer;
(4) var m:  integer;
(5) function addm(n:  integer):  integer;
(6) begin return m+n end;
(7) begin m:=0; return addm end;
(8) procedure b(g:  function (integer):  integer);
(9) begin writeln (g(2)) end;
(10) begin
(11) f := a; b(f)
(12) end
```

Problem 12.4 Certain languages have the ability to return newly created procedures at run time. In the following pseudo- program, all functions, whether defined in the source text or created at run time, take at most one

argument and return one value, either a function or a real. The operator
· stands for composition of functions: that is $(f \cdot g)(x) = f(g(x))'$

1) What value is printed by main?

2) Suppose that whenever a procedure p is created and returned, its activation record becomes a child of the activation record of the function returning p. The passing environment of p can then be maintained by keeping a tree of activation records rather than a stack. What does the tree of activation record when a is computed by main in the program?

3) Alternatively, suppose an activation record for p is created when p is activated, and made a child of the activation record for the procedure calling p. This approach can be used to maintain the activation environment for p. Draw snapshots of the activation records and their parent-child relationships as the statements in main is executed. Is a stack sufficient to hold activation records when this approach is used?

```
function f(x:  function);
   var y:  function;
      y := x · h;           /* creates y when executed */
      return y
end {f};

function h():
    return sin
end {h};
function g(z:  function);
   var w:  function;
      w := arctan · z:       /* creates w when executed */
      returned w
end {g} ;

function main ( );
    var a:  real:
        u, v:  function;
        v:= f(g);
        u:= v( );
        a:= u(π/2);
     print a
   end { main }
```

Problem 12.5 Write a procedure that inserts a new entry to a link list through passing a list head pointer.

Problem 12.6 List the characteristics of the garbage collection that makes the concurrent garbage collection algorithms very hard to work.

Problem 12.7 The possible way to decrease walk and stop of token and scan algorithm is to increasingly use the scan procedure. After token procedure we do not scan all the storage again, instead, we change the code of main() so that when a suitable size free fragment is scanned, the scan procedure stops(the original one continues). Outline the modified increasing module.

References

[1]   Bentley J L, Cleveland W S, Seth R (1985) Empirical analysis of Hush functions, manuscript. AT&T Bell Laboratories, Murray Hill, New York.

[2]   Ableson H, Sussman G J (1985) Structure and interpretation of computer programs. MIT Press, Cambridge, Mass.

[3]   Aho A V, Sethi R, Ullman J D (2003) compilers, principles, techniques and tools. Addison-Wesley, Reading, Mass.

[4]   Grune D, Bal H E, Jacos C, et al (2002) Modern compiler design. Wiley, New York.

[5]   Knuth D E (1998) The art of computer programming. Vol.3 Updated and revision version. Addison-Wesley, Reading, Mass.

[6]   Aho A V, Hopcroft J E, Ullman J D (1974) The design and analysis of computer algorithms. Addison-Wesley, Reading, Mass.

[7]   Steele G L Jr (1984) Common LISP. Digital Press, Burlington, Mass.

Chapter 13 Generation of Object Code

*If one wants to get to one hundred miles away, reaching
ninety miles is only half of the destination.*

Chinese maxim

13.1 Motivation of the Chapter

After we travelled from the lexical analysis, syntactical analysis, semantic
analysis, generation of intermediate code, and debugging and optimization,
etc. till now, we are ready for getting to the last phase — the generation
of target codes. But before we formally discuss the matter some sorts of
preparation is still needed to do.

What we said of the target code, strictly speaking, should be the code of
the target machine that is an immediately executable. As currently, however,
in every machine, there is assembler installed on it. Therefore, even though
what we generated is not the machine code, but the code written in the
assembly language is not a problem at all. The assembler installed on the
machine will translate it into an executable machine code.

Since the code generated in this way may not be the optimal one, the
compilers have a further function that performs the optimization so that the
target code generated is more efficient. This step is critical for productive
programs as this kind of programs will run day after day for a long period.
So even in one running period it saves only a few seconds, the accumulation
will be significant.

In general, there is a rigorous requirement for the generator of target
codes. In one word, the output code should be of correct and high efficient.
It means that it must make best use of the resources of the target machine.
Moreover, the generator itself should execute effectively.

However, in theory, the problem of generating optimal codes is undecide-
able. Hence, in practice, we must manage to generate the code as good as
possible. It may not be the most optimal one, but we have done what we
can. In order to reach the extent, we must resort to the heuristic searching
techniques. The selection for the heuristic search is very important because a

carefully selected algorithm for the design of generators will be much easier to generate a highly efficient code than that was rushed out in a short time.

In this chapter, we shall discuss those issues that are related to the design of target code generators. Though lots of the details about the target code generation are related to the object language and operating systems, the storage management, the selection of instructions and registers, the order of computation, etc. confront almost all the generators of target codes. It will help the reader to better comprehend the essence of problems which we explain in the following.

13.2 Issues of Design of Generators of Target Codes

13.2.1 Input of Code Generators

The input of code generators consists of the intermediate code representation of source programs and the information in symbol tables. The information is arranged by the front end (the analytical phrase). The information in symbol tables is used to determine the running addresses of data objects marked by the names in the intermediate code representation.

We have mentioned that, the intermediate code may be represented in several ways such as reversed Poland form, quadruples or three-address representation, or pseudo machine representation (e.g., stack machines). In addition, there are also the graphical representations of syntax trees and acyclic directed graphs (adg). Even though in this chapter, our algorithms are expressed in three-address code, trees and acyclic directed graphs, there are many techniques that are suitable for the intermediate code representation.

We assume that before the generation of codes, the compiler has finished the scanning and analytical analysis of source program, and also has translated the source program into the intermediate code with bountiful details. Therefore, the values of names that appear in the intermediate code may be represented in quantities (binary bits, integers, real numbers, pointers, etc.) that can directly be operated in the target machines. We have also assumed that the necessary type checks have been established. Therefore, the type transformation operators have been put in case of needs. The obvious syntax errors (e.g., the attempt of taking floating number as the subscript) have been checked out too. Therefore, the code generation phrase may be carried out under the assumption that the input has no error. But in some compilers, this kind of semantic checks is carried along with the code generation.

13.2.2 Target Programs

The output of the code generator is the target program. As the intermediate code, the output may have a variety of forms such as the absolute machine code, float machine code, or assembly language code.

The advantage of generating programs in the absolute machine language as output is that the programs may store in fixed positions of the storage and they can immediately be executed. A small-size program may be compiled and executed quickly. The compilers for a number of "student programs", such as WATFIV and PL/C just generate such absolute machine code.

The advantage of generating programs in the float machine language as output (target modules) is that it allows the independent compilation of subprograms. A group of float target modules may be linked up together by a linker, and then install in storage to execute. If we generate float target modules, we must add the overhead of corresponding linking and loading. But due to independent compilation of subprograms and being able to call for other programs that have been compiled from a target module, the flexibility is significantly raised. If the target machine cannot automatically handle floating, then the compiler must provide specific float information to loader in order to link together the independently compiled program segments.

To generate programs in assembly language as output makes the progress of the code generation a bit easier, as we may generate symbolic instructions and making uses of macro facilities provided by assembler to help the code generation. Of course, the expense that must be paid for the benefit is to make it in the assembly language again after target generation, but the generation of assembly code does not repeat the whole task of assembler. This is a reasonable choice, it is especially true for machine with the smaller size of storage, as on this type of machines the compiler must be of multipasses. In this chapter, for sake of readability, we also choose assembly language as the target language. But we want to emphasize that, as long as addresses can be computed from offsets and other information in symbol tables, then code generator may generate float addresses and absolute addresses of names, as easy as generating symbol addresses.

13.2.3 Storages Management

To map the names in source programs into addresses of data objects in storages is part of the jobs of the front end of the compiler and it is done through cooperation with code generation programs.

We have assumed that a name reference in the three-address statement is the name entry in the symbol table, and the references of entries of the symbol table are done after checking the declaration of the procedure. The type in the declaration determines the width of the type that is the quantity of the storage needed for storing it. The relative address of the name in the data area of the procedure can be determined by the information in symbol tables.

If the machine code is to generate, the labels in the three-address statements need to transform to instruction addresses. This procedure adopts the so-called back-patching technique as we introduced before in the previous chapter, Suppose that the label refers to a quadruple number in a quadruple, when we scan every quadruple in turn, we will eventually derive the position of the quadruple that holds the label. What we need is only to maintain the count that records the number of words which the generated instructions used. The number can be stored in the array of quadruples (in the other field). Therefore, if a reference is met, for example j: goto i, if i is less than j, then we just need to establish a jump instruction of which the target address is the storage location of the first appearance of quadruple i. But if the jump is forward, i exceeds j, then we need to use a table to store the location of the first appearance of i. When we handle quadruples, we can advance to location where the first appearance of i stays, and then by back-patching we replace all the appearances of i's in quadruples by the location.

13.2.4 Selection of Instructions

The essence of the instruction set of target machine determines the difficulty of the selection of instructions. The consistency and completeness are important factors for the determination of an instruction set. If the target machine cannot support each kind of data type with consistent manner, then it will need to have special treatment for every abnormal situation.

The speed and the common usage of the instructions are also important factors. If we do not care of the efficiency of the target program, then the selection of instructions is very simple. For every type of three-address statements, we may design a code frame that describes the target code which the frame generates. For example, for every three-address statement with the form c := a + b, it has static allocations for a, b, and c. So it may be translated into the following sequence of code:

```
MOV a, R1      /* load a into register R1 */
ADD b, R1      /* add b to R1 */
MOV R1, c      /* store R1 to c */
```

But the method that it generates the code one by one often generates very poor code. For example, if we want to translate the following sequence and we adopt the one by one method:

$$x := y + z,$$
$$u := x + z.$$

Then we will have the following code as the result of the translation:

```
MOV y, R1
ADD z, R1
MOV R1, x
MOV x, R1
ADD v, R1
MOV R1,v
```

Instead, if we consider the translation systematically, we might generate more compact codes that saves two instructions:

```
MOV y, R1
ADD z, R1
ADD v, R1
MOV R1, v
```

The quality of the code generated depends on the length of the running time and length of the program. The target machine that possesses bountiful instruction set may realize any given operations in many modes. The overheads of different modes may have dramatic differences.

Some translation of the intermediate code may be correct but may also be very inefficient. For example, if the machine has an INC (increment) instruction, then by one instruction alone the three-address statement x := x + 1 may be efficiently realized. In contrast, if we adopt the following mode:

```
MOV x, R1
ADD #1, R1
MOV R1, x
```

then the speed will naturally be much slower. But in order to determine which implementation is better and which one runs faster, it needs to comprehend the execution of instructions.

13.2.5 Register Allocation

The sequence of instructions that contains registers as operands is shorter than that contains operands in storage, and the speed of execution is usually faster. Therefore, in the course of the generation of codes, it is especially important to efficiently make use of registers [1]. For the uses of registers, it may be divided into two subproblems:

1) During the allocation of registers, we select the variables that will reside in registers in some period of the execution of the program.

2) In the following phrase of the assignments of registers, we select a special register where a variable would reside in.

Even for single register, searching a register for the optimal assignment of variable is also very difficult as it is a NP complete problem. As the hardware and operating system of the target machine maybe have to obey some regulations about the usage of the registers, it makes the problems more complicated.

13.2.6   Selection of Order of Computation

The order of computation may also affect the efficiency of the target code. Probably we have seen that by adopting some order of the computation the need for registers to store intermediate results will decrease. To choose the best order is the other NP complete problem. Therefore, at the beginning, we must take the order by which the intermediate code generator generates three-address statements. Then the problem is avoided.

13.2.7   Method of Generation of Codes

No doubt, the most important principle for the code generation is that it generates correct code. As a code generator may encounter some special cases, the principle of correctness is extremely important. After the priority of the correctness, our important design goals are easy implementation, easy to debug, and easy to maintain.

13.3   Target Machine MMIX

To choose target machine, of course we take practicality as the principle. Where will we install the compiler of some programming language? The machine should be selected as the target machine. Being familiar with the machine and its instruction set is the premise of designing good generator of code. However, in the present general discussion, what specific machine should we choose as the target machine? We think that any current machine in the market is improper as it will make our book to be the advertisement of it, and the users of other machines in market must be not interested in our book. Therefore, we decide to choose a pseudo machine that represents the common characteristics of current machines, and MMIX becomes our choice. MMIX is the new pseudo machine updated from MIX, both are introduced by Professor D. E. Knuth in his classical monumental *The Art of Computer Programming* vol. 1 original version and updated and revision version, respectively [2].

   If MMIX is taken as Roman number notation, it denotes 2009. This number is obtained from taking 14 type numbers of currently available machines (on these machine the simulation of MMIX can be carried out easily), and then make the mean of them with each one having equal weight. The evaluation is as follows:

(Cray I + IBM 801 + RISC II + Clipper C300 + AMD 29 k + Motorola 88k + IBM 601 + Intel I 960 + Alpha 21164 + POWER 2 + MIPSR 4000 + Hitachi Super H4 + Strong ARM 110 + Sparc 64)/14 = 2009

13.3.1 Binary Bits and Bytes

MMIX works on the model of 0 and 1, and usually treats 64 bits once. For convenience, we partition them into groups of four bits each, so each represents a hexadecimal number. The hexadecimal numbers are:

$$
\begin{array}{llll}
0 = 0000 & 4 = 0100 & 8 = 1000 & c = 1100 \\
1 = 0001 & 5 = 0101 & 9 = 1001 & d = 1101 \\
2 = 0010 & 6 = 0110 & a = 1010 & e = 1110 \\
3 = 0011 & 7 = 0111 & b = 1011 & f = 1111
\end{array}
\tag{13.1}
$$

In order to differentiate decimal digits 0~9 and hexadecimal digits 0~9, we will use different form to denote hexadecimal digits. For example, a hexadecimal number

$$1001111000110110110111100110111000000010111111110110010100111110000010110. \tag{13.2}$$

In hexadecimal system, it becomes

$$\#9e3779b97f4a7c16. \tag{13.3}$$

It would be looking better if we write it as #936A47B3197259C, but in terms of the meaning, they are the same. # means hexadecimal.

Eight binary bits or two hexadecimal digits forms a sequence, usually it is called a byte. Now most of the computers take bytes as the basic, indivisible programmable data units. An MMIX program may refer to up to 2^{64} bytes, where each one has its address, ranging from #0000000000000000 to #ffffffffffffffff. Like language such as English, its alphabet, numbers and punctuation usually are represented in ASCII (American Standard Code for Information Interchange), and one byte represents one character. For example, the equivalent of MMIX in ASCII is # 4d4d4958. ASCII actually is a code with 7 bits and contains control characters #00~1f, the printing characters #20~#7e, and a "removal" character #7f. In 1980s, it was extended to international standard with 8 bits and was called Latin−1 or ISO 8859−1. Hence the characters with emphasis such as pâté is encoded #70e274e9.

In 1990s, the 16 bit code that supports almost every contemporary language becomes an international standard. This code is formally called ISO/

IEC 10646 UCS-2 or informally Unicode UTF-16. It not only contains the Greek letters such as Σ and σ (#03a3 and #03c3), Cyrillic letters likes Ш and щ (#0429 and #0449), Armenia letters like Օ and շ (#0547 and # 0577), Hebrew letters like ש (#05e9), Arabic letters like ش (#0634), and Indian letters like श (#0936) or শ (#09b6) or ଶ (#0b36) or ৗ (#0bb7), etc., but also tens of thousands of East Asian ideographs such as the Chinese character for mathematics and computing, 算(#7b97). Even it contains the special encodes for Roman numerals, such as MMIX = # 216f216f21602169. Through simply adding leading 0 byte to each character, the normal ASCII and Lain–1 characters may be represented, such as the Unicode of pâté is #007000e2007400e9.

We will use convenient term to describe characters with width up to 16 bits like Unicode, as the numbers with two bytes are very important in practice. For those words that have 4 bytes or 8 bytes, we will call them double words and four words respectively, hence

$$2 \text{ bytes} = 1 \text{ word}$$
$$2 \text{ words} = 1 \text{ double word}$$
$$2 \text{ double words} = 1 \text{ four word}$$

According to D. E. Knuth, 2 bytes are also called 1 wyde, 2 wydes are called 1 terra, and 2 Tetras are called 1 octa. One octabyte equals four wydes equals eight bytes equal sixty-four bits. Of course, the quantity consisting of one or more bytes may represent alphanumerical characters. Using binary system,

one byte without sign may represent numbers 0..255;

one word without sign may represents numbers 0..65535;

one double word without sign may represent numbers 0..4294967295;

one four word without sign may represent numbers

0..18446744073709551615.

Integer numbers usually may be represented in complementary representation in which the left most bit represents sign. In this representation, if the leading bit is 1, we obtain the n bit integer by decrease the number from 2^n. For example, −1 is a number with sign. It is #ff in bytes in complementary representation, and it is #ffff in words in complementary representation, while in double words it is #ffffffff, and in four words it is #ffffffffffffffff. Thus we have:

one byte with sign may represent numbers – 128.. 127;

one word with sign may represent – 32768.. 32767;

one double word with sign may represent – 2147483648..2147483647;

one four word with symbol may represent numbers

– 9223372036854775808..9223372036854775807.

13.3.2 Memory and Registers

From the point of views of a programmer, a MMIX computer has 2^{64} memory units and 2^8 general registers, in addition to 32 special-purpose registers (see Fig. 13.1) [3]. Data are transferred to registers from memory units, and the operations are performed in the registers, then the numbers are transferred back to the memory, The memory units are called M[0], M[1],..., M[$2^{64}-1$]. Hence, if x is any four word byte, M[x] is a memory byte.

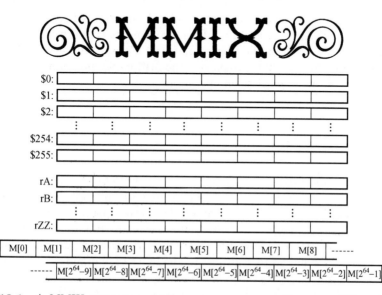

Fig. 13.1 A MMIX computer which a programmer sees there are 256 general-purpose registers and 32 special-purpose registers, along with 2^{64} bytes of 2 pseudo memories, each register has 64 effective bits.

General registers are called $0, $1, ..., $255. If x is an arbitrary byte, $x is a four word byte. The 2^{64} bytes of the memory are grouped into 2^{63} words.

$$M_2[0] = M_2[1] = M[0]M[1], M_2[2] = M_2[3] = M[2]M[3], \dots ..$$

Every word consists of two consecutive bytes

$$M_2[2k]M_2[2k+1] = M[2k] \times 2^8 + M[2k+1],$$

hence it can either be represented as $M_2[2k]$ or $M_2[2k+1]$. Similarly, there are 2^{62} double word bytes.

$$M_4[4k] = M_4[4k+1] = \dots = M_4[4k+3] = M[4k]M[4k+1]M[4k+2]M[4k+3]$$
$$(13.4)$$

and there are 2^{61} four word bytes.

$$M_8[8k] = M_8[8k+1] = \ldots = M_8[8k+7] = M[8k]M[8k+1]\ldots M[8k+7]. \quad (13.5)$$

Generally speaking, if x is four word byte, then the notation $M_2[x]$, $M_4[x]$, and $M_8[x]$ represent word, double words, four words that contain byte $M[x]$.

When referring to $M_t[x]$ we neglect lg t bits of the lowest effective bits of x. For the sake of completeness, we also write $M_1[x] = M[x]$, when x<0 or x$\geq 2^{64}$, we define $M[x] = M[x \bmod 2^{64}]$.

The 32 special-purpose registers of MMIX are denoted rA, rB, ..., rBB, rTT, rWW, rXX, rYY, and rZZ. It is the same as their intimate relatives, each one may store four word bytes. Later their usage will be explained. For example, we will see that rA controls the arithmetic interruptions while rR stores the residue after division operations.

13.3.3   Instructions

The memory of MMIX not only contains data, but also contains instructions. An instruction or "order" is a double word bytes of which four bytes may conveniently be called OP, X, Y, and Z. OP is the operation code, X, Y, and Z are the operand. For example, #20010203 is an instruction with OP = #20, X = #01,Y = #02, and Z = #03. And the meaning is to put the addition of the registers $2 and $3 to register $1. The bytes of operands are regarded as integers without sign.

Since MMIX provides the operators the length of one byte, it has totally 256 operations. Each of the 256 operators has a convenient mnemonic symbol forms. For example, the operator #20 is denoted ADD. Thereafter, we will adopt the symbol forms of operators, we will also provide the complete instruction table. X, Y, and Z have also symbolic representation. They are consistent with the assembly language which we will discuss later. For example, #20010203 may be conveniently written as "ADD $1,$2, $3". Generally, addition instruction is written as "ADD $X, $Y, $Z". Most of the instructions have three operands, but there are some that have two operands, even some have only one operand. When there are two operands, the first one is X, and the second one is number YZ with two bytes. Then the symbolic notation contains one comma only. For example, the instruction "INCL $X,YZ" is an instruction that increases the register X with a quantity YZ. When there is only one operand, it is number XYZ with three bytes and without sign. In its symbol notation, there is no comma at all.

For example, the instruction "JMP @+4*XYZ" will tell MMIX that the next instruction can be obtained by jumping to double word byte XYZ. The instruction "JMP @+1000000" has the form #f003d090 in hexadecimal system, as JMP = #f0, while 1000000 = #03d090.

We will introduce each instruction of MMIX neither formally nor informally. For example, the informal meaning of "ADD \$X, \$Y, \$Z" is to put into \$X the sum of \$Y and \$Z, while the formal meaning is "s(\$X)←s(\$Y) + s(\$Z)", where s(X) represents a signed integer number that corresponds to x mod modulo bit number according to the convention of 2's complement. The assignment like s(X)←N implies that X is to be set to the bit pattern for which s(X) = N mod bit number. (If N is too big or too small to put in X, the assignment causes integer overflow or underflow. For example, if the sum s(\$Y)+ S(\$Z) is less than -2^{63} or greater than 2^{63}, then ADD will overflow or underflow. When we informally explain an instruction, we will point out the possibility of flows but the formal explanation will accurately describe everything. In general, the assignment s(X)←N puts X into the binary representation of N mod 2^n, where n is the bit number in X. If $N < -2^{n-1}$ or $N \geqslant 2^{n-1}$, then it claims that it flows).

13.3.4 Load and Store

We will see that It may be classify 256 instructions of MMIX into a number of groups. We now start with the instructions that transfer information between the register and memory.

In the following every instruction has the address A of the memory that is used for storing the sum of addition of \$Y and \$Z. Formally speaking,

$$A = (u(\$Y) + u(\$Z)) \bmod 2^{64} \qquad (13.6)$$

is the sum of \$Y and \$Z that is an integer without sign. Through neglecting any carry that happens at the left end of the sum when the two numbers are added, the sum will reduce to a binary number with 64 bits. In this formula, u(X) is similar to s(X), but it regards X as a binary number without sign.
- LDB \$X, \$Y, \$Z (Load byte): s(\$X)←s($M_1[A]$)
- LDW \$X, \$Y, \$Z (Load word): s(\$X)←s($M_2[A]$)
- LDT \$X, \$Y,\$Z (Load double word): s(\$X)←s($M_4[A]$)
- LDO \$X, \$Y, \$Z (Load four word): s(\$X)←s($M_8[A]$)

These instructions store data into register \$X from memory, meanwhile, if necessary, these numbers will be transformed from one byte, one word or double word with sign into a four word byte without sign. For example, suppose that the four word byte $M_2[1000] = M_2[1002]$ is

$$M[1000] = M[1001] = M[1002] = \ldots = M[1007] = \#fedcba9876543210. \qquad (13.7)$$

Hence, if \$2 = 1002 and \$3 = 2, then A = 1002. We have:
- LDB \$1, \$2, \$3 sets \$1←#0000 0000 0000 00ba
- LDW \$1, \$2, \$3 sets \$1←#0000 0000 0000 ba98
- LDT \$1, \$2, \$3 sets \$1←#0000 0000 fedc ba98

- LDO $1, $2, $3 sets $1←#fedc ba98 7654 3210

But if $3 = 5, making A = 1005, then we have:

- LDB $1, $2, $3 sets $1←#ffff ffff ffff ff54
- LDW $1, $2, $3 sets $1←#ffff ffff ffff 7654
- LDT $1, $2, $3 sets $1←# ffff ffff 7654 3210
- LDO $1, $2, $3 sets $1←#fedc ba98 7654 3210

When a byte or a word, or a double word byte is transformed into a four word byte with sign, its sign bit is expanded to all the positions at the left:

- LDBU $X, $Y, $Z (load byte without sign): $u(\$X)←u(M_1[A])$
- LDWU $X, $Y, $Z(Load word without sign): $u(\$X)←u(M_{[2}[A]]$
- LDTU $X, $Y, $Z (Load double word without sign) : $u(\$X)←u(M_4[A])$
- LDOU $X, $Y, $Z (Load four word byte without sign): $u(\$X)←u(M_8[A])$

These instructions are similar to LDB, LDW, LDT, and LDO, but they handle the data in memory as ones without symbol. When a short number is lengthened in this way, the binary positions at the left hand side of the register are set to zeros. Therefore, in the example LDBU $1, $2, $3 above, $2 = $3 = 1005, it sets $1← #0000 0000 0000 0054.

Instructions LDU and LDOU actually have the same characteristics, as when a four word byte is put into a register, it need not expand symbol bits or add 0. However when symbol matters, a good programmer will use LDO, while it does not matter, he will use LDOU. In this way, the reader of the program will further understand the meaning of the content loaded.

- LDHT $X, $Y,$Z (Load high part of double word): $u(\$X)←u(M_4[A])×2^{32}$.

Here the double word byte $M_4[A]$ is loaded to the left side of $X while the right side is a set to zeros. For example, LDHT $1, $2, $3, and $2 + $3 = 1005, and with the definition (13.7), then set $1←# 7654 3210 0000 0000.

- LDA $X, $Y, $Z (Load address): $u(\$X)←A$.

This instruction stores an address into a register, it is actually the same as ADDU that is described later. Sometimes the word "load address" better describes the purpose than the word "add number without symbol" does.

- STB $X, $Y, $Z (Store byte): $s(M_1[A])←s(\$X)$
- STW $X, $Y, $Z (Store word): $s(M_2[A])←s(\$X)$
- STT $X,$Y, $Z (Store double word): $s(M_4[A])←s(\$X)$
- STO $X, $Y, $Z (Store four word): $s(M_8[A])←s(\$X)$

These instructions go to the other direction, that is, they put the data from registers to the memory. If the number in register (with sign) is outside the extent of the numbers in memory, then overflow takes place. Suppose that the register $1 contains number −65536 = #ffff ffff ffff 0000, and if $2 = 1000, $3 = 0002, hence, the definition (13.7) holds.

- STB $1, $2, $3 sets $M_8[1000]←$#fedc ba98 7654 3210 (and overflow takes place)
- STW $1, $2, $3 sets $M_8[1000]←$#fedc 0000 7654 3210 (and overflow takes place)
- STT $1, $2, $3 sets $M_8[1000]←$#ffff 0000 7654 3210

- STO $1, $2, $3 sets $M_8[1000] \leftarrow$ #ffff ffff ffff 0000
- STBU $X, $Y, $Z (Store byte without sign): $u(M_1[A]) \leftarrow u(\$X)$ mod 2^8
- STWU $X, $Y, $Z (Store word without sign): $u(M_2[A]) \leftarrow u(\$X)$ mod 2^{16}
- STTU $X, $Y, $Z (Store double word without sign): $u(M_4[A]) \leftarrow u(\$X)$ mod 2^{32}
- STOU $X, $Y, $Z (Store four word without sign): $u(M_8[A]) \leftarrow U(\$X)$

These instructions have the same effects as the corresponding ones STB, STW, STT and STO with sign, but they never overflow.

- STHT $X, $Y, $Z (Store high part of double word): $u(M_4[A]) \leftarrow \lfloor \frac{u(\$X)}{2^{32}} \rfloor$

The left half of register $X is stored in double word unit $M_4[A]$ of the memory.

- STCO X, $Y, $Z (Store constant four word byte): $u(M_8[A]) \leftarrow X$

The constant number between 0 and 255 is stored in four word unit M_8 [A] of the memory.

13.3.5 Arithmetic Operations

Most of the operations of MMIX strictly perform between registers. We may investigate the operations between registers through considering addition, subtract, multiplication and division.

- ADD $X, $Y, $Z (addition) : $s(\$X) \leftarrow s(\$Y) + s(\$Z)$
- SUB $X, $Y, $Z (subtract): $s(\$X) \leftarrow s(\$Y) - s(\$Z)$
- MUL $X, $Y, $Z (multiplication): $s(\$X) \leftarrow s(\$Y) \times s(\$Z)$
- DIV $X, $Y, $Z (division): $s(\$X) \leftarrow [s(\$Y)/s(\$Z)]\{\$Z \neq 0\}$ and $s(rR) \leftarrow s(\$Y)$ mod $s(\$Z)$

Addition, subtract and multiplication need not further discussion. Division instruction DIV form quotient and residue, and the residue enters the special register rR. Through the instruction GET $X that is described later, it may be observed from rR. If the divisor $Z is zero, DIV sets $X←0 and rR←$Y, there also "integer division check" appearing.

- ADDU $X, $Y, $Z (addition of numbers without sign): $u(\$X) \leftarrow (u(\$Y) + u(\$Z))$ mod 2^{64}
- SUBU $X, $Y< $Z (subtract of numbers without sign): $u(\$X) \leftarrow (u(\$Y) - u(\$Z))$ mod 2^{64}
- MULU $X, $Y, $Z(multiplication of numbers without sign): $u(\$X) \leftarrow (u(\$Y) \times u(\$Z))$ mod 2^{64}
- DIVU $X, $Y, $Z (division of numbers without sign): $u(\$X) \leftarrow \lfloor \frac{u(rD\$Y)}{u(\$Z)} \rfloor$, $u(rR) \leftarrow u(rD\$Y)$ mod $u(\$Z)$, if $u(\$Z) > u(rD)$; otherwise $X \leftarrow rD$, $rR \leftarrow \$Y$

The arithmetic operations of numbers without sign never cause overflow. A complete multiplication between two 16 byte numbers is done by MULU in which the upper half enters special purpose high mult register rH. For example, the number without sign #9e3779b97f4a7c16 times itself, we get

$$rH \leftarrow \#61c8864680b583ea, \qquad \$X \leftarrow \#1bb32095ccdd51e4. \qquad (13.8)$$

In this case, the value of rH is just the difference of subtracting the original number #9e3779b97f4a7c16 from 2^{64}. This is not coincidence, the reason is that, if we put the decimal point at the left of the number, it is golden ratio $\phi^{-1} = \phi - 1$. After the exponent we get the approximation $\phi^{-2} = 1 - \phi^{-1}$, and the decimal point is placed at the left of rH.

The quotient of eight bytes and the residue obtained from the division between dividend of 16 bytes and divisor of 8 bytes are obtained through the instruction DIVU. The upper half of dividend appears in the special-purpose register rD that is specially used for storing dividend. At the beginning of the program, its initial value is zero. Through the instruction PUT rD, \$Z that will be described soon, the register can be assigned to any desired value. If the value of rD is greater than that of divisor, then DIVU \$X, \$Y, \$Z will only set $\$X \leftarrow rD$ and $rR \leftarrow \$Y$ (when \$Z is zero, the case always happens) But DIVU never has an integer division check occurring.

According to Definition (13.7), instruction ADDU evaluates an address A of the memory location. Therefore, sometimes we give the other name LDA to it.

The following related instructions are helpful to address evaluation:
- 2ADDU \$X, \$Y, \$Z (times two and addition of numbers without sign): $u(\$X) \leftarrow (u(\$Y) \times 2 + u(\$Z)) \bmod 2^{64}$
- 4ADDU \$X, \$Y, \$Z (times four and addition of numbers without sign): $u(\$X) \leftarrow (u(\$Y) \times 4 + u(\$Z)) \bmod 2^{64}$
- 8ADDU \$X, \$Y, \$Z (times eight and addition of numbers without sign): $u(\$X) \leftarrow (u(SY) \times 8 + u(\$Z)) \bmod 2^{64}$
- 16ADDU \$X, \$Y, \$Z (times sixteen and addition of numbers without sign): $u(\$X) \leftarrow (u(\$Y) \times 16 + U(\$Z)) \bmod 2^{64}$

If overflow is not a problem, then the execution of instruction 2ADDU \$X, \$Y, \$Z is faster than multiplication by 3, this is why we have 2ADDU \$X, \$Y \$Z in place of multiplication by 3. The result of execution of the instruction is

$$\$X \leftarrow (u(\$Y) \times 2 + u(\$Y) \bmod 2^{64} = 3 \times u(\$Y) \bmod 2^{64}.$$

- NEG \$X, \$Y, \$Z (takes negative): $s(\$X) \leftarrow Y - u(\$Z)$
- NEGU \$X, \$Y, \$Z (take negation without sign): $u(\$X) \leftarrow (Y - u(\$Z)) \bmod 2^{62}$

In these instructions, Y is a constant number without sign, rather than a register number (as in the instruction STCO, X is a constant without sign). Usually, Y is a zero. In this case, we may simply write NEG \$X, \$Z, or NEGU \$X, \$Z.

The following four instructions are shift instructions:
- SL \$X, \$Y, \$Z (shift left): $\$X \leftarrow s(\$Y) \times 2^{u(\$Z)}$

- SLU \$X, \$Y, \$Z (shift left of number without sign): $u(\$X) \leftarrow (u(\$Y) \times 2^{u(\$Z)}) \bmod 2^{64}$
- SR \$X, \$Y, \$Z (shift right): $s(\$X) \leftarrow \lfloor s(\$Y)/2^{u(\$Z)} \rfloor$
- SRU \$X, \$Y, \$Z (shift right of number without sign); $u(\$X) \leftarrow \lfloor u(\$Y)/2^{u(\$Z)} \rfloor$

Both SL and SLU yield the same result in \$X, but SL may overflow while SLU never overflow. When shift right operation executes, SR expands the sign bit while SRU moves 0 in from right hand side. Therefore, SR and SRU yield the same result if and only if \$Y is nonnegative and \$Z is zero. SL and SR run much faster than the execution of MUL and DIV to perform the exponent operations with 2. SLU runs faster than using MULU to perform exponent operations with 2, although SLU does not affect rH while MULU affects rH. Instruction SRU runs much faster than using DIVU to perform the exponent operation with 2, although it is not affected by rD. The notation Y$\ll$ Z is used to represent the result of shifting Y to left for Z bits. Y$>>$Z denotes the result of shifting Y to right for Z bits.

The following are two comparison instructions:

- CMP \$X, \$Y, \$Z (comparison): $s(\$X) \leftarrow [s(\$Y) > s(\$Z)] - [s(\$Z) < s(\$Y)]$

Where if $s(\$Y) > s(\$Z)$, then $[s(\$Y) > s(\$Z)]$ equals 1. Correspondingly, $[s(\$Z) - -s(\$y))]$ equals 0. Hence, when \$Y is greater than \$Z, the result is 1. When \$Y $<$ \$Z the result is -1. When they are the same, both two terms equal 0 and the final result is also 0. In summary, depending whether \$Y is less than, or equal or greater than \$Z, \$X is set to -1, 0 or 1. Similarly.

- CMPU \$X, \$Y, \$Z (comparison without sign): $s(\$X) \leftarrow [u(\$Y) > u(\$Z)] - [u(\$Z) < u(\$Y)]$

13.3.6 Conditional Instructions

Many instructions determine their works according to whether the value in a register is positive or negative, or zero.

- CSN \$X, \$Y, \$Z (sets condition if negative): if $s(\$Y) < 0$, then set $\$X \leftarrow \$Z$
- CSZ \$X, \$Y, \$Z (sets condition if zero): If $s(\$Y) = 0$, then set $\$X \leftarrow \$Z$
- CSP \$X, \$Y, \$Z (sets condition if positive): if $s(\$Y) > 0$, then set $\$X \leftarrow \$Z$
- CSOD \$X,\$Y, \$Z (sets condition if odd): if $s(\$Y) \bmod 2 = 1$, then set $\$X \leftarrow \$Z$
- CSNN \$X, \$Y, \$Z (sets condition if nonnegative): if $(\$Y) \geqslant 0$, then set $\$X \leftarrow \$Z$
- CSNZ \$X, \$Y, \$Z (sets condition if nonzero): if $s(\$Y) \neq 0$, then set $\$X \leftarrow \$Z$
- CSNP \$X, \$Y, \$Z (sets condition if not positive): if $s(\$Y) \geqslant 0$, then set $\$X \leftarrow \$Z$
- CSEV \$X, \$Y, \$Z (sets condition if even): if $s(\$Y) \bmod 2 = 0$, then set $\$X \leftarrow \$Z$

If the register $Y meets the conditions above, then the register $Z is copied to register $X, otherwise anything is not done. A register has negative value if and only if its leading bit (its leftmost bit) is 1. A register has odd value if and only if its end most (its right most) bit is 1.

- ZSN $X, $Y, $Z (sets or being zero if negative): $X←$Z [s($Y) < 0].
- ZSZ $X, $Y, $Z (sets or being zero if zero): $X←$Z[s($Y) = 0].
- ZSP $X, $Y, $Z (sets or being zero if positive): $X←$Z[s($Y)>0].
- ZSOD $X, $Y, $Z (sets or being zero if odd): $X←$Z[s($Y) mod 2 = 1].
- ZSNN $X, $Y, $Z (sets or being zero if non-negative): $X←$Z[s($Y)⩾0].
- CSNZ $X, $Y, $Z (sets or being zero if nonzero): $X←$Z[s($Y)≠0].
- ZSNP $X, $Y, $Z (sets or being zero if not positive): $X←$Z [s($Y)⩽0].
- ZSEV $X, $Y, $Z (sets or being zero if even number): $X←$Z [s($Y) mod 2 = 0)].

If the register $Y meets the condition, then the value of $Z is copied to $X, otherwise set $X to zero.

13.3.7 Bit Operations

We often discover that it is very useful to imagine a four word bytes as a vector of 64 bits, and to perform operation on each component of the two vectors.

- AND $X, $Y, $Z (bitwise AND): $\mathbf{v}(\$X)←\mathbf{v}(\$Y)\&\mathbf{v}(\$Z)$
- OR $X, $Y, $Z (bitwise OR): $\mathbf{v}(\$X)←\mathbf{v}(\$Y)|\mathbf{v}(\$Z)$
- XOR $X, $Y, $Z (bitwise XOR): $\mathbf{v}(\$X)←\mathbf{v}(\$Y)⊕\mathbf{v}(\$Z)$
- ANDN $X, $Y, $Z (bitwise and-not): $\mathbf{v}(\$X)←\mathbf{v}(\$Y)\&\bar{\mathbf{v}}(\$Z)$
- ORN $X, $Y, $Z (bitwise or-not): $\mathbf{v}(\$X)←\mathbf{v}(\$Y)|\bar{\mathbf{v}}(\$Z)$
- NAND $X, $Y, $Z (bitwise not-and): $\bar{\mathbf{v}}(\$X)←\mathbf{v}(\$Y)\&\mathbf{v}(\$Z)$
- NOR $X, $Y, $Z (bitwise not-or): $\bar{\mathbf{v}}(\$X)←\mathbf{v}(\$Y)|\mathbf{v}(\$Z)$
- NXOR $X, $Y $Z (bitwise not-xor): $\bar{\mathbf{v}}(\$X)←\mathbf{v}(\$Y)⊕\mathbf{v}(\$Z)$

Where $\bar{\mathbf{v}}$ denotes the inverse of $\mathbf{v}$, it is obtained via changing 0 to 1 and vice versa. The binary operation &, |, and ⊕ are defined as follows. They are independently applied to each bit:

$$
\begin{array}{llll}
0\&0 = 0 & 0|0 = 0 & 0 ⊕ 0 = 0 & \\
0\&1 = 0 & 0|1 = 1 & 0 ⊕ 1 = 1 & \\
1\&0 = 0 & 1|0 = 1 & 1 ⊕ 0 = 1 & (13.9) \\
1\&1 = 1 & 1|1 = 1 & 1 ⊕ 1 = 0 &
\end{array}
$$

AND operation and minimum operation are the same in taking the minimal value, while OR operation and maximum operation are the same in taking maximal value. XOR operation and addition mod 2 are the same in terms of the result.

- MUX $X, $Y, $Z (bitwise multiplex): $\mathbf{v}(\$X)←\mathbf{v}(\$Y)∧\mathbf{v}(rM)|(\mathbf{v}(\$Z)∧\bar{\mathbf{v}}(rM))$

MUX operation selects the those $Y bits that correspond to 1 in rM and selects those $Z bits that correspond to 0 in $Z through observing the special-purpose multiplex mask register rM and then combining the two bit vectors.

- SADD $X, $Y, $Z. $X←s($\Sigma$(v($Y)&v̄($Z)))

The SADD operation counts the number of those $Y bits that are 1 and those $Z bits that are 0.

13.3.8 Byte Operations

Similarly, we may take four word x as vector $\mathbf{b}(x)$ with 8 bytes where each byte is an integer between 0 and 255; or we can take it as a vector $\mathbf{w}(x)$ with 4 words, or we take it as a double word vector t(x). The following operations handle all the components once.

- BDIF $X, $Y, $Z (byte difference): b($X)←b($Y)-·-b($Z)
- WDIF $X, $Y, $Z (word difference) w($X)←w($Y)-·-w($Z)
- TDIF $X, $Y, $Z (double word difference) T ($X)←T($Y)-·-T($Z)
- ODIF $X, $Y, $Z (four word difference): O($X)←O($Y)-·-O($Z)

Where the operation -·- is a saturated subtract (or "dot subtract") operation:

$$y\text{-·-}z = \max(0, y - z).$$

These operations have important applications in computer graphics (when bytes or words represent the values of graph elements) and text processing.

We can also take a four word bytes as an 8×8 boolean matrix, i.e., as a 8×8 array of 0's and 1's. Let $\mathbf{m}(x)$ represent such a matrix of which the rows from top to bottom represent the bytes of x from left to right, and let $\mathbf{m}^T(x)$ be the transposed matrix, whose columns are the bytes of x. For example, if x = #9e3779b97f4a7c16, then

$$
\mathbf{m}(x) = \begin{pmatrix}
1 & 0 & 0 & 1 & 1 & 1 & 1 & 0 \\
0 & 0 & 1 & 1 & 0 & 1 & 1 & 1 \\
0 & 1 & 1 & 1 & 1 & 0 & 0 & 1 \\
1 & 0 & 1 & 1 & 1 & 0 & 0 & 1 \\
0 & 1 & 1 & 1 & 1 & 1 & 1 & 1 \\
0 & 1 & 0 & 0 & 1 & 0 & 1 & 0 \\
0 & 1 & 1 & 1 & 1 & 1 & 0 & 0 \\
0 & 0 & 0 & 1 & 0 & 1 & 1 & 0
\end{pmatrix}, \quad
\mathbf{m}^T(x) = \begin{pmatrix}
1 & 0 & 0 & 1 & 0 & 0 & 0 & 0 \\
0 & 0 & 1 & 0 & 1 & 1 & 1 & 0 \\
0 & 1 & 1 & 1 & 1 & 0 & 1 & 0 \\
1 & 1 & 1 & 1 & 1 & 0 & 1 & 1 \\
1 & 0 & 1 & 1 & 1 & 1 & 1 & 0 \\
1 & 1 & 0 & 0 & 1 & 0 & 1 & 1 \\
1 & 1 & 0 & 0 & 1 & 1 & 0 & 1 \\
0 & 1 & 1 & 1 & 1 & 0 & 0 & 0
\end{pmatrix}.
$$

$$(13.10)$$

The explanation of the four word bytes suggests two operations to be very similar to that of mathematics. But now we define them from very beginning.

If $\mathbf{A}$ is an $m \times n$ matrix, and $\mathbf{B}$ is an $n \times s$ matrix. If $\circ$ and $\cdot$ are binary operations, then the extended matrix multiplication $\mathbf{A} \cdot \circ \mathbf{B}$ is defined as

$$\mathbf{C}_{ij} = (\mathbf{A}_{i1} \cdot \mathbf{B}_{1j}) \circ (\mathbf{A}_{i2} \cdot \mathbf{B}_{2j}) \circ \ldots \circ (\mathbf{A}_{in} \cdot \mathbf{B}_{nj}), \qquad (13.11)$$

where $1 \leqslant i \leqslant m, 1 \leqslant j \leqslant s$ and $\mathbf{C}$ is an $m \times s$ matrix [4]. We assume that $\circ$ is associative. $\mathbf{A}$ common matrix multiplication is just one taking $\circ$ as $\oplus$ while taking $\cdot$ as $\times$.

However, if we let $\circ$ be $|$ or $\oplus$, then we obtain the important operations on Boolean matrices:

$$(\mathbf{A}| \times \mathbf{B})_{ij} = \mathbf{A}_{i1}\mathbf{B}_{1j}|\mathbf{A}_{i2}\mathbf{B}_{2j}|\ldots|\mathbf{A}_{in}\mathbf{B}_{nj}, \qquad (13.12)$$

$$(\mathbf{A} \oplus \times \mathbf{B})_{ij} = \mathbf{A}_{i1}\mathbf{B}_{1j} \oplus \mathbf{A}_{i2}\mathbf{B}_{2j} \oplus \ldots \oplus \mathbf{A}_{in}\mathbf{B}_{nj}. \qquad (13.13)$$

Notice that if each row of $\mathbf{A}$ at most contains one 1, then in the Expressions (13.12) or (13.13) there is at most one non-zero entry. If every column of $\mathbf{B}$ at most contains one 1, the same fact also holds. Therefore, In these situations, the results of $\mathbf{A}|\times\mathbf{B}$ and $\mathbf{A}\oplus\times\mathbf{B}$ are the same as the usual matrix multiplication $\mathbf{A}+\times\mathbf{B}=\mathbf{AB}$.

- MOR \$X, \$Y, \$Z (multiple OR's) : $\mathbf{m}^{T}(\$X)\leftarrow\mathbf{m}^{T}(\$Y)|\times\mathbf{m}^{T}(\$Z)$; equivalently, $\mathbf{m}(\$X)\leftarrow\mathbf{m}(\$Z)|\times\mathbf{m}(\$Y)$
- MXOR \$X, \$Y, \$Z (multiple XOR's): $\mathbf{m}^{T}(\$X)\leftarrow\mathbf{m}^{T}(\$Z)\oplus\times\mathbf{m}(\$Y)$; equivalently, $\mathbf{m}(\$X)\leftarrow\mathbf{m}(\$Y)\oplus\times\mathbf{m}(\$Z)$

These instructions observe the corresponding bytes of \$Z and use their bytes to select the bytes of \$Y. Actually these operations set up the bytes of \$X. Then the bytes selected are combined together by OR or XOR. For example, if we have

$\quad$ \$Z $= \#$ 0102 0408 1020 4080.

It can be written as the following matrix

$$\mathbf{M}(z) = \begin{pmatrix} 0 & 0 & 0 & 0 & 0 & 0 & 0 & 1 \\ 0 & 0 & 0 & 0 & 0 & 0 & 1 & 0 \\ 0 & 0 & 0 & 0 & 0 & 1 & 0 & 0 \\ 0 & 0 & 0 & 0 & 1 & 0 & 0 & 0 \\ 0 & 0 & 0 & 1 & 0 & 0 & 0 & 0 \\ 0 & 0 & 1 & 0 & 0 & 0 & 0 & 0 \\ 0 & 1 & 0 & 0 & 0 & 0 & 0 & 0 \\ 1 & 0 & 0 & 0 & 0 & 0 & 0 & 0 \end{pmatrix}. \qquad (13.14)$$

Therefore, Both MOR and MXOR instructions would reverse the bytes of \$Y: The kth byte of \$X from left is set to kth byte of \$Y from right, $1 \leqslant k \leqslant 8$.

On the other hand, if

$$\$Z = \#00000000000000\text{ff},$$

both MOR and MXOR will set all the bytes of $X to zero's with right most byte as an exception that is the OR or XOR of all eight bytes of $Y.

Float point operations. MMIX contains complete implementations of standard 754 on float arithmetic. It is famous IEEE/ANSI (Institute for Electrical and Electronic Engineers/ American national standard Institute) standard.

Every four word byte x represents a float binary number that determines the floating binary f(x), the leftmost of x is the sign (0 = '+', 1 = '–'), the next 11 bits are the exponent E, the rest 52 bits are fraction (decimal number) F. The value it represents is:

- ± 0.0, if E = F = 0 (zero)
- ± 2^{-1047F}, if E = 0 and F ≠ 0 (abnormal)
- ± $2^{E-1023}(1+F/2^{52})$, if 0<E<2047 (normal)
- ± ∝, if E = 2047, and F = 0 (infinite)
- ± NaN (Non a Number) ($F/2^{52}$), if E = 2047 and F ≠ 0 (it is not a number)

The "short" float number f(t) that is represented by a double word bytes is similar, but its exponential part consists only of 8 bits while its fraction part consists only of 23 bits. The normal case of a float number (0<E<255) represents $+-2^{E-1127}(1+f/2^{23})$.

- FADD $X, $Y, $Z (float add): f($X)←f($Y)+f($Z)
- FSUB $X, $Y, $Z (float subtract) f($X)←f($Y)–f($Z)
- FMUL $X, $Y, $Z (float multiplication): f($X)←f($Y)×f($Z)
- FDIV $X, $Y, $Z (float division): f($X)←f($Y)/f($Z)
- FREM $X, $Y, $Z (float remainder): f($X)←remainder of f($Y)/f($Z)
- FSQRT $X,$Z or FSQRT $X, $Y, $Z (float square root): f($X)←f($Z)$^{1/2}$
- FINT $X, $Z or FINT $X, $Y, $Z (float integer): f($X)←int f($Z)
- FCMP $X, $Y, $Z (float comparison): s($X)←[f($Y)>f($Z)]-[f($Y)< f($Z)]
- FEQL $X, $Y, $Z (float equality): s($X)←[f($Y) = f($Z)]
- FUN $X, $Y, $Z (float disorder): s($X)←[f($Y)||f($Z)]
- FCMPE $X, $Y, $Z (float comparison with respect to ∈): s($X)←[f($Y)> f($Z)f(rE)]–[f($Y)<f($Z)(f(rE))]
- FEQLE $X, $Y, $Z (float equality with respect to ∈): s($X)←[f($Y)≈ f($Z)(f(rE))]
- FUNE $X, $Y, $Z (float disorder with respect to ∈): s($X)←[f($Y)|| f($Z)(f(rE))]
- FIX $X, $Z or FIX $X, $Y, $Z (float number is transformed to fixed point number): s($X)←int f($Z)
- FIXU $X, $Z or FIXU $X, $Y, $Z (float number is transformed to fixed point number without sign): u($X)←(int f($Z)mod2^{64})
- FLOT $X, $Y, $Z or FLOT $X, $Y, $Z (fixed point number is transformed to float number): f($X)←s($Z)

- FLOTU $X, $Z or FLOTU $X, $Y, $Z (fixed point number is transformed to float number without sign): f($X)←u($Z)
- SFLOT $X, $Z or AFLOT $X, $Y, $Z (fixed point number is transformed to short float number): f($X)←f(T)←u($Z)
- SFLOTU $X, $Z or SFLOTU $X, $Y, $Z (fixed point number is transformed to short float number): f($X)←f(T)←u($Z)
- LDSF $X, $Y, $Z or LDSF $X, $Y, A(short float number is loaded): f(X)←f(M_4[A])
- STSF $X, $Y, $Z or STSF $X, A (store short float): f($ X)←f(M_4(A))

When precise assignment cannot be carried out, the assignment of a float quantity may be done with current round methods to determine proper value. We support four modes: (1) ROUND-OFF; (2) ROUND-UP; (3) ROUND-DOWN; (4) ROUND-NEAR. For the Y field of instructions FSQRT, FINT, FIX, FIXU, FLOT, FLOTU, SFLOT, and SFLOTU, a different round method from given method may be used if desired. For example FIX $X, ROUND-UP, $Z sets s($X)←⌈f($Z)⌉. The operations SFLOT and SFLOTU first round the number as if storing an anonymous double word T, and then they transform the number to four word form.

"int" operation rounds up the number to integer. Operation y rem z is defined as y − nz, where n is an integer close to y/z, or an even integer in the case of equality. When the operand is infinite or NAN (not a number), and any special convention that dominates the result of zero, special rules apply. The values +0.0 and − 0.0 may have different float representations, but FEQL takes them as the same.

Instant constants. Programs often need to handle small constants. For example, we may need to increase or decrease a register, or we need to move 32 bits, etc. in these cases, loading a small constant from memories to registers is cumbersome. MMIX provides a general rule by which an instruction itself may obtain such a constant. Each instruction we discuss so far has its version, where $Z is replaced by Z, except that the instruction takes $Z as a float number.

For example, "ADD $X, $Y, $Z" has its corresponding peer "ADD $X, $Y, Z" with meaning that s($X)←s($Y)+Z. The corresponding peer of "SRU $X, $Y, $Z" is "SRU $X, $Y, Z" with the meaning that u($X)← ⌊u($Y)/2^Z⌋. "FLOT $X, $Y, $Z" has the peer "FLOT $X, Z" with the meaning that f($X)←Z. But "FADD $X, $Y, $Z" has no direct corresponding peer.

The operation code of "ADD $X, $Y, $Z" is #20, while the operation code of "ADD $X, $Y, Z" is #21. For simplicity, we use ADD in both cases. Generally, the operation code of the direct version for an instruction with register mode is one bigger than the original version.

There are several instructions that characterize direct constants ranging from #0000 = 0 till #ffff = 65535. The constants that appear on YZ bytes may be moved to the high position, middle-high, middle-low position and low position of four word bytes.

- SETH $X, YZ (sets high position): u($X)←YZ×$2^{48}$

- SETMH $X, YZ (sets mid-high position): $u(\$X) \leftarrow YZ \times 2^{32}$
- SETML $X, YZ (sets mid-low position): $u(\$X) \leftarrow yz \times 2^{16}$
- SETL $X, YZ (sets low position): $u(\$X) \leftarrow YZ$
- INCH $X, YZ (increases the value of high position): $u(\$X) \leftarrow (u(\$X) + YZ \times 2^{48}) \bmod 2^{64}$
- INCMH $X, YZ (increases the value of high-mid part): $u(\$X) \leftarrow (u(\$X) + YZ \times 2^{32}) \bmod^{64}$
- INCML $X, YZ (increases the value of mid-low position): $u(\$X) \leftarrow (u(SX) + YZ \times^{16}) \bmod 2^{64}$
- INCL $X, YZ (increases the value of low byte): $u(\$x) \leftarrow (u(\$X) + YZ \times 2^{16}) \bmod 2^{64}$
- ORH $X, YZ (bit wise OR operation is carried to high position): $v(\$x) \leftarrow (v(\$X)) | (YZ \ll 48)$
- ORMH $X, YZ (bit wise OR operation is carried out to mid-high position): $v(\$X) \leftarrow (v(\$X)) | (YZ \ll 32)$
- ORML $X, YZ (bit wise OR operation is carried out to mid-low position): $v(\$X) \leftarrow (v(\$X)) | YZ \ll 16$
- ORL $X, YZ (bit wise OR operation is carried out to low position): $v(\$X) \leftarrow ((\$X)) | v(YZ)$
- ANDNH $X, YZ (bit wise Not-AND operation is carried to high position): $v(\$X) \leftarrow (v(\$X)) \& \overline{v}(YZ \ll 48)$
- ANDNMH $X, YZ (bit wise Not-AND operation is carried to mid –high position): $v(\$X) \leftarrow (v(\$X)) \& \overline{v}(YZ \ll 32)$
- ANDNML $X, YZ (bit wise Not-AND operation is carried to mid-low position): $v(\$X) \leftarrow (v(\$X)) \& \overline{v}(YZ \ll 16)$
- ANDNH $X, Y Z (bit wise Not-AND operation is carried to low position): $v(\$X) \leftarrow (v(\$X)) \& \overline{v}(YZ)$

We can obtain any desired four word bytes in a register without loading anything from memory, just through using at most four instructions aforementioned. For example, instruction SETH $0, #0123; INCMH $0, #4567: INCML $0, #89ab; INCL $0, #cdef put #123456789abcdef into register $).

MMIX assembly language allows us to use SET to represent the simplification of SEET and we use SET $X, $Y to simplify the common instruction OR $X, $Y, 0.

13.3.9 Jumps and Branches

Usually, instructions are executed sequentially in the order they appear. In other words, the commands that is performed after MMIX obeyed the tetrabyte in memory location @ is normally the tetrabyte found in memory location @+4 (The symbol @ denotes the position where MMIX currently stays). However, jump and branch instructions allow us to break the order.

- JMP RA: @←RA

Here RA represents a relative address with three bytes that may be more specifically written as @+4*XYZ, that is, double word XYZ is added to the current position @. For example, "JMP @+ 4*Z" may be in the symbol form #f00000Z. If this instruction appears in location #1000, the next instruction that will be executed is in location #1008. In fact, we may write "JMP #1008", but the value of XYZ will depend on the position from where the instruction jumps out.

The relative address may have negative value. In this case, the operator increases one, and the XYZ is the offset plus 2^{24}. For example, "JMP @-4*Z" is double word byte #f1ff fffe. The operator #f0 tells the computer to "jump ahead", while the operator #f1 tells the computer to "jump backward". But we may write both as JMP. Actually, when we want to jump to the location Addr, we just need to write "JMP Addr", and MMIX assembler will figure out the proper operator and proper value of XYZ. Such jump or branch is possible unless the offset exceeds current position for more than 67 million bytes.

- GO $X,$Y, $Z : u($X)←@+4, then @←A

The instruction GO allows us to go to absolute address in any location of he memory. From Formula (13.4), the address A is evaluated, it is the same as in load and store instructions. Before go to a special address, usually the next instruction to appear is located in the register $X. Therefore by, say, the instruction "Go $X, $X, 0", that is, taking Z = 0 as the instant constant, we may return to that address later.

- BN $X, RA (branch if negative): If s($X)<0, then set @←RA
- BZ $X, RA (branch if zero): if s($x) = 0, then set @←RA
- BP $X, RA(branch if positive): If S($X)>0, then set @←RA
- BOD $X, RA (branch if odd): if s($X)mod 2 = 1, then set @←RA
- BNN $X, RA (branch if non negative): if s($X)⩾0, then set @←RA
- BNZ $X, RA (branch if non zero): if s($X)≠0, then set @←RA
- BNP $X, RA (branch if non positive): if s($X)⩽0, then set @←RA
- BEV $X, RA (branch if even): if s($X) mod 2 = 0, then set @←RA

A branch instruction is a conditional jump depending on the content of the register $X. The extent of the destination address RA is limited in comparison with that of JMP instruction, because there are only two bytes that may be used to express the relative offset. Nevertheless, we still may jump to any double word bytes between @-2^{18} and @$+2^{18}-4$.

- PBN $X, RA (possibly branch if negative): if s($X) <0, then set @←RA
- PBZ $X, RA (possibly branch if zero): if s($X) = 0 then set @←RA
- PBP $X, RA (possibly branch if positive): if s($X)>0 then set @←RA
- PBOD $X, RA (possibly branch if odd): if s($X) mod 2 = 1, then set @←RA
- PBNN $X, RA (possibly branch if non negative): if s($X)⩾0, then set @←RA

- PBNZ $X, RA (possibly branch if non zero): if s($X)≠0 then set @←RA
- PBNP $X, RA (possibly branch if non positive): if s($X)⩽0 then set @←RA
- PBEV $X,RA (possibly branch if even): if s($X) mod 2 = 0 then set @←RA

If high speed computer can predict when will it handle a branch instruction, then usually it works fastest because the previous knowledge will help it look forward, and prepare well for handling instructions in the future. Therefore, MMIX encourages the programmer to provide the indication whether a branch instruction is possible. Whenever there is more than half of chance that a branch instruction will appear, then the programmer may use the possible branch instructions, rather than the branch instructions.

13.3.10 Subprogram Calls

MMIX also provides many instructions that facilitate effective communications between subprograms through a register stack. But its details are rather technical, we just present an informal description here. For short programs, it need not use these characteristics.

- PUSHJ $X, RA(push to register and jump): PUSH(x),and set rJ←@+4, then set @←RA
- PUSHGO $X, $Y, $Z (push to register and jump):PUSH(x),and set rJ← @+4, then set @←RA

The special-purpose return-jump register rJ is set to the address of double word following instruction PUSH(X). Roughly speaking, the action of PUSH (x) means that the local register $0 and $X are kept and made them unaccessible temporarily. The original $(x+1) now becomes $0, $(x+2) becomes $1, etc. But for all the registers $k where k⩾rG, they remain unchanged. rG is a special-purpose global threshold register, its value is always between 32 and 255 (inclusive).

If k⩾rG, then the register $k is called global; if k⩽rL, then it is called local. Where rL denotes special- purpose threshold register that tells currently how many local registers are there active. Otherwise, if rL⩽k⩽rG, then register $k is called boundary, and whenever it is used in an instruction as an operand, $k is equal to 0. If a boundary register $k is used as source operand in an instruction, then $k is equal to 0; if a boundary register $k is used as target register in an instruction, then before the instruction is executed, rL automatically increases to k+1, so that $k becomes a local one.

- POP X, YZ (pop out from register and return): POP (X),then set @←rJ+ 4*YZ

Roughly speaking, "POP (X)" indicates that apart from X, all the local registers become boundary ones. And then the most recent "PUSH (X)" hides the local register that hasn't been popped and restores its original value.

- SAVE $X,0 (save process state): u($X)←contents
- UNSAVE $X (restore process state) : contents←u($X)

The instruction SAVE stores all the current registers to the top of register stack in memory, and push the top four word's address to stack u($X). The register $X must be global, and X must be greater than or equal to rG. All the current local registers and global registers must be stored, along with rA, rD, rG, rH, rM, rR, and several registers which we have not discussed so far. The instruction UNSAVE takes such a top four word bytes address and restores the relevant contents. Actually, it undoes what a previous SAVE instruction did. The value of rL is set to zero by SAVE instruction, and then UNSAVE restores it.

MMIX has special registers called stack offset register (rO) and stack pointer register (rS), they control the operations of PUSH, POP, and UNSAVE.

So far, we have introduced main instructions of MMIX with target registers. In the target code generated by compiler these instructions will appear. But for completeness, we will also list those instructions which MMIX attempts to use in super speed and parallel operations and the instructions that are used for handling interruptions.

System considerations. Here we list the instructions which high-level users may be interested in using for super speed and parallel operations of MMIX structure. In the sense that these operations provide the machine with how to plan in advance to realize maximal efficiency, the relevant operations are similar to the "possible branch" instructions. Apart from probably using instruction SYNCID, most of the programmers do not need to use these instructions.

- LDUNC $X, $Y, $Z (load four word that are not in adjusted buffer): S($X)←S(M_8[A])
- STUNC $X, $Y, $Z (store four word that are not in adjusted buffer): S(M_8[A])←S($X)

These instructions implement the same operations as LDO and STO did, but they also inform the machine that the loaded and stored four word bytes and their adjacent words will be read or written in the nearest future.

- PRELD X, $Y, $Z (preload data).

It states that many bytes from M[A] till M[A+X] will be loaded or stored in the nearest future.

- PREST X, $Y, $Z (prestore data)

It states that many bytes from M[A] till M[A+X] will definitely be written (stored) before next time they are read (loaded).

- PREGO X, $Y, $Z (pretake to branch)

It states that many bytes from M[A] till M[A+X] will probably be used for instructions in the future.

- SYNCID X, $Y, $Z (synchronized instructions and data)

It states that all of bytes M[A] through M[A+X] must be fetched again before being interpreted as instructions. MMIX is allowed to assume that a program's instructions do not change after the program has begun, unless the instructions have been prepared by SYNCID.

- SYNCD X, $Y, $Z (synchronize data)

It states that all of bytes M[A] through M[A+X] must be brought up to date in the physical memory, so that other computer and input/output devices can read them.

- SYNC XYZ (synchronization)

Different processors can reliably cooperate together through confining the parallel activities.

- CSWAP $X, $Y, $Z (compare and exchange four word bytes)

If $u(M_8[A]) = u(rP)$, where rP is a special prediction register, set $u(M_8)$ ←u($X) and u($X)←1,otherwise set u(rP)←$u(M_8[A])$ and u($X)←0. This is an atomic operation (indivisible) that it is used when a number of computers share a common memory.

- LDVTS $X, $Y, $Z (load a pseudo translation state)

This instruction is only provided for operating system, and the details are omitted.

13.3.11 Interruptions

The usual activities from a double word byte to the next instruction, not only may be changed by jump and branch instructions but also by unpredictable events such as overflow or output signals. The real world computers also need to cope with the matters like violations of the security regulations and hardware failures. MMIX distinguishes two kinds of interruptions: Trips and traps. A trip sends control to the trip handler that is a part of the user program; a trap sends control to trap handler that is a part of the operating system. When MMIX is doing arithmetic operation, there may be eight unexpected conditions, they are: integer division check (D), integer overflow (V), flow to fix-point overflow (W), incorrect float operations (I), float overflow (O), float underflow (U), float division by zero divisor (Z), and float incorrect (X). Special arithmetic state register rA maintains current information of these unexpected situations. Its 8 bits of the right most byte are called its event bits. They are in the order of DVWIOUZX, and is called D_BIT(#80), U_BIT(#40), ..., X_BIT(#01). The left 8 bits of the event binary bits in rA are called enable bits. They also appear in the same order as DVWIOUZX. When some arithmetic operation is executed and some condition occurs, before MMIX proceeds to the next instruction, it searches for the relevant enable bit. If the enable bit is 0, then the corresponding event is set to 1; otherwise machine will go through trip to location #10 and handle unexpected event D, to location #20 to handle unexpected event V, ..., to location #01 to handle unexpected event X, invoking a trip handler. Thus the event binary bits of rA record the unexpected events that have not caused the trips occurring (if there are more than one enable bits occurring, then the left most bit is handled first. For example, if both O and X occur simultaneously, then O is handled first). On the left most enable bits in rA, two binary bits maintain round off mode 4, the other 46 bits of rA should keep 0's. By using the PUT instruction to be discussed below, a program may change the setting of rA at any time.

- TRIP X, Y, Z, or TRIP X, YZ, or TRIP XYZ (trip)

This instruction forces a trip to jump to the trip handler starting at location #00.

Whenever a trip occurs, MMIX uses 5 special-purpose registers to record current states: bootstrapping register rB, where does interrupt occur register rW, execution register rX, Y operand register rY and Z operand register rZ. At first, rB is set to $255. Then rJ is also set to $235, and rW is set to @+4. The left part of rX is set to #80000000, the right half is set to trip instruction. If the interrupted instruction is not a store instruction, then the left part of rY is set to $Y and rZ is set to $Z (or under the situation of instant constant it is set to Z). Otherwise rY is set to A (the store address of a store instruction), and rZ is set $X (the number to be stored). Finally the control is transferred to the handler through setting @ as the handler address (#00 or #10 or... or #80).

- TRAP X, Y,Z or TRAP X, YZ or TRAP XYZ (trap).

This instruction is similar to TRIP, but it forces a trap to jump to the operating system. The special-purpose registers rBB, rWW, rXX, rYY and rZZ replace rB, rW, rX, rY, and rZ. Special trap register rT provides the address of trap handler. To finish a program, the usual method is to have "Trap 0" of which the double word bytes are #00000000. Hence, a program may fall to trap due to mistake.

- RESUME 0(continue after interruption)

If s(rX) is negative, MMIX simply sets @←rW−4 and executes the instruction at left half of rX as if it occurs there (even if there is no interruption happening, the characteristics may also be used, but the instruction that is inserted cannot be RESUME).

The complete instruction set.   Table 13.1 shows all the names of 256 operators that are sorted in the hexadecimal number order. For example, ADD occurs on the upper half of the rows labeled #2x and the top of the columns labeled #0. Therefore, the operator of ADD is #20. ORL occurs on the lower half of the rows labeled #EX and the bottom of the columns labeled #B, so the operator of ORL is #EB.

We have now discussed almost all the operators of MMIX, there are two more as follows:

- GET $X,Z (Flow in from special register): $u(\$X) \leftarrow u(g[Z])$ where $0 \leqslant Z < 32$

Table 13.1 MMIX operators

	#0	#1	#2	#3	#4	#5	#6	#7	
#0x	TRAP 5v	FCMP v	FUN v	FEQL v	FADD 4v	FIX 4v	FSUB 4v	FIXU 4v	
	FLOA[I] 4v		FLOTU[I] 4v		SFLOT[I] 4v		SFLOTU[I] 4v		#0x
#1x	FMUL[I] 4v	FCMPE 4v	FUNE v	FEQLE 4v	FDIV 40v	FSQRT 40v	FREM 4v	FINT 4v	
	MUL[I] 10v		MULU[I] 10v		DIV[I] 60v		DIVU[I] 60v		#1x
#2x	ADD[I] v		ADDU[I] v		SUB[I] v		SUBU[I] v		
	2ADDU[I] v		4ADDU[I] v		8ADDU[I] v		16ADDU[I] v		#2x
#3x	CMP[I] v		CMPU[I] v		NEG[I] v		NEGU[I] v		
	SL[I] v		SLU[I] v		SR[I] v		SRU[I] v		#3x
#4x	BN[B] v+π		BZ[B] π+v		BP[I] v+π		BOD[B] v+π		
	BNN[B] v+π		BNZ[B] v+π		BNP[B] v+π		BEV[B] v+π		#4x
#5x	PBN[B] 3v−π		PBZ[B] 3v−π		PBP[B] 3v−π		PBOD[B] 3v−π		
	PBNN[B] 3v−π		PBNZ[B] 3v−π		PBNP[B] 3v−π		PBEV[B] 3v−π		#5x
#6x	CSN[I] v		CSZ[I] v		CSP[I] v		CSOD[I] v		
	CSNN[I] v		CSNZ[I] v		CSNP[I] v		CSEV[I] v		#6x
#7x	ZSN[I] v		ZSZ[I] v		ZSP[I] v		ZSOD[I] v		
	ZSNN[I] v		ZSNZ[I] v		ZSNP[I] v		ZSEV[I] v		#7x
#8x	LDB[I] μ+v		LDBU[I] μ+v		LDW[I] μ+v		LDWU[I] μ+v		
	LDT[I] μ+v		LDTU[I] μ+v		LDO [I] μ+v		LDOU[I] μ+v		#8x
#9x	LDSF [I] μ+v		LDHT[I] μ+v		CWAP[I] 2μ+2v		LDUNC[I] μ+v		
	LDVTS[I] v		PRELD[I] v		PREGO[I] v		GO[I] 3v		#9x
#Ax	STB[I] μ+v		STBU[I] μ+v		STW[I] μ+v		STWU[I] μ+v		
	STT[I] μ+v		STTU [I] μ+v		STO[I] μ+v		STOU[I] μ+v		#Ax
#Bx	STSF[I] μ+v		STHT[I] μ+v		STCO[I] μ+v		STUNC[I] μ+v		
	SYNCD[I] v		PREST[I] v		SYNCID[I] v		PUSHGO[I] 3v		#Bx
#Cx	OR[I] v		ORN[I] v		NOR[I] v		XOR[I] v		
	AND[I] v		ANDN[I] v		NAND[I] v		NXOR[I] v		#Cx
#Dx	BDIF[I] v		WDIF[I] v		TDIF[I] v		ODIF[I] v		
	MUX[I] v		SADD[I] v		MOR[I] v		MXOR[I] v		#Dx
#Ex	SETH v	SETMH v	SETML v	SETL v	INCH v	INCMH v	INCML v	INCL v	
	ORH v	ORMH v	ORML v	ORL v	ANDNH v	ANDNMH v	ANDML v	ANDNL v	#Ex
#Fx	JMP[B] v		PUSHJ [B] v		GETA[B] v		PUT[I] v		
	POP 3v	RESUME 5v	[UN]SAVE 20μ+v		SYNC v	SWYM v	GET v	TRIP 5v	#Fx
	#8	#9	#A	#B	#C	#D	#E	#F	

Notice: If the branch is executed, then π = 20v; if the branch is not executed, then π = 0.

- PUT X, $Z (Write to special register): u(g[x])←u($Z) where 0⩽X<32

Every special register has a number between 0 and 31. That we say registers rA, rB, ..., is for easier understanding of human being. But from the point of view of computer, actually rA is g[21], and rB is g[0], etc. Table 13.2 shows these numbers.

Get instruction has no constraint, but for PUT instruction there are some things that are not feasible: In rG it is not allowed to put any number greater than 255 or less than 32, it cannot store any number that is less than the current setting value of rL. In rA, it is not allowed to put any number greater than #3ffff. If a program attempts to use PUT instruction to increase the value of rL, the value of rL will keep unchanged. Moreover, a program cannot use PUT instruction to put any value to rC, rN, rO, rS, rI, rT, TT, rK, rQ, rU, or rV. These "extra special" registers have the numbers in the extent of 8–18.

Table 13.2 The special-purpose registers of MMIX

Name	Meaning	Number	Store	Output
rA	arithmetic register	21	√	√
rB	bootstrap register	0	√	√
rC	loop counter	8		
rD	dividend	1	√	√
rE	∈ register	2	√	√
rF	failure location register	22		√
rG	global threshold register	19	√	√
rH	high multiplication register	3	√	√
rI	duration register	12		
rJ	return- jump register	4	√	√
rK	interruption register	15		
rL	local threshold register	20	√	√
rM	multiplex mask register	5	√	√
rN	serial number	9		
rO	register stack offset register	10		
rP	prediction register	23	√	√
rQ	interruption request register	16		
rR	remainder register	6	√	√
rS	register stack pointer	11		
rT	trap location register	13		
rU	usage counter	17		
rV	virtual translation register	18		
rW	where is interruption register (trip)	24	√	√
rX	execution register	25	√	√
rY	Y operand (trip)	26	√	√
rZ	Z operand (trip)	27	√	√
rBB	bootstrap register (trap)	7		√
rTT	dynamic trap location register (trap)	14		
rWW	where is interruption register (trap)	28		√
rXX	execution register (trap)	29		√
rYY	Y operand (trap)	30		√
rZZ	Z operand (trap)	30		√

Relating to some special instructions, we have mentioned most of the special-purpose registers. But MMIX has also a "time register" or loop counter rC that keeps going on; a failure register rF that assists the detection of hardware failures; a duration counter that keeps backward, and when it reaches value 0, it requests an interruption. A serial number register rN that assigns a unique number to every MMIX machine. A usage counter rU that increases one whenever a special operator is executed. There is a virtual translation register rV that defines mapping from "virtual" 64 bit address to the "real physical location that is installed in the memory. These special registers assist MMIX to be a completely feasible machine that can be realistically constructed.

- GETA $X, RA (gets address) u($X)←RA

This instruction uses the same convention as the branch instructions that puts a relative address into register $X. For example, "GETA $0, @" puts $0 to be the address of the instruction itself.

- SWYM X, Y, Z or SWYM x, YZ or SWYM XYZ (SWYM means "sympathize with your machinery")

This is the last of the 256 instructions. Fortunately it is simplest. Actually, it is usually called empty operation, because it does not do anything. However, it makes the machine running smoothly. Here, X, Y, Z are omitted.

Timing

We have mentioned that, in the generation of the target code, we need to compare different generation schemas, to specify which one is better. Apart from the comparison of the memory volumes which they used, the another index is the time they consumed. In other words, we may compare those target programs that all solve the same problem or were generated for the same problem, to see which one runs faster. However, generally speaking, such comparisons are not easy to carry out as the architecture of MMIX can be implemented in many different modes. The running time of a program not only depends on the timing progress, but also depends on the dynamic energetic units that can be synchronously active as well as the degree by which they form the stream line. It depends on the size of randomly access memory that offers the illusion of 2^{64} virtual bytes. It also depends on the adjustment strategy of buffer and other areas, the sizes of these areas, and allocation strategy, etc.

In order to be pragmatic, the measurement of the running time of a MMIX program may often be based on the running time which a high performance machine with large volume of main memory can achieve. For every operation, an overhead is assigned to it. By this way, the satisfactory estimation may be given. Suppose that every operation takes an integer v that represents a unit of the time loop that a streamline uses. Even though as the development of science and technology the value of v is decreasing, we can always keep the newest value instead of using ns to measure. In our estimation, we will also assume that the running time depends on the quantity of memory mems which a program accesses. This is the number of instructions that are loaded and stored. For example, we will assume that, every LDO (load four words) instruction takes $\mu+v$, where μ represents the average overhead of a memory access. The whole running time of a program may be reported $35\mu+1000v$, meaning that it has 35 memory accesses plus 1000 time units loops. For many years, the value μ/v gradually increases no one knows whether the trend will continue or not. But the experience has proved that, the values of μ and v deserve independent consideration.

Table 13.1 has demonstrated the assuming running time of each operation. Notice that, most of the instructions just spent 1v of the running time, while load and store operations spent μ+v. If the prediction is done correctly, a branch or a possible branch take also 1v time. But if the prediction is not done correctly, it will take 3v time. The float operations usually take 4v time, although FDIV and FSQRT spend 40 v time. Integer multiplication takes 10v while integer division takes 60 v.

Though we usually use the assumptions of Table 13.1 to make the estimation of the running time, we must keep in mind that the real running time may be very sensitive to the order of the instructions. For example, if we can discover that between the time we issue our instructions and the time we need, there are 60 pieces of other works that have to handle, the integer division maybe only take one period. Several LDB (load bytes) instruction maybe only needs one access to memory if their accesses are to the same four word bytes. However, the result of one load instruction usually does not provide preparations for uses of the following instructions. The experience has shown that some algorithms are good in adjusting the buffer, but other algorithms are not. Therefore, μ is not a constant. Even the addresses of the instructions in memory would have important effect to performance, because some instructions may be taken along with other instructions.

Therefore, the software package MMIXware provided by MMIX not only contains a simple simulation program, but also contains a meta modulation program. It runs MMIX program under extensive different technical assumptions. The user of meta modulation program may determine the characteristics of memory general bus, as well as other parameters such as adjusted buffer of instruction and data, virtual address translation, stream line and simultaneous issue of instructions, branch prediction, etc. Given a configuration file and a program file, meta modulation program may precisely determine how long will the specific hardware run the program. In fact, only the meta modulation program may be trusted that it may provide reliable information about the real behavior of a program. But this kind of result is hard to interpret because there may be infinite configurations. Hence, we usually present rather simple estimation by means of Table 13.1.

So far, we provide rather complete introduction to target machine. Sequentially, we may consider the issues of the generation of target code directing at the machine.

13.4 Assembly Language of MMIX

When generating target code, of course we may directly generate the instructions of MMIX. But in this way many details introduced above must be involved and it will be easily prone to inevitable errors. Therefore, we have stronger trend in using the symbol language which it provides, i.e., the assembly language called MNIXAL. It is the extension of the mnemonic notation of the instruction. By using it, the MMIX programs can be written and read easier, the programmer does not need to worry about the tedious details that often lead to errors. Its main characteristics are that it selectively uses the mnemonic symbols to represent numbers, uses a label field to associate the name, memory cell, and number of registers.

We may introduce it by giving each convention of MMIXAL. But if we really do so, we would still do not know how to use it. Therefore we would rather use a simple example instead. In this example, various symbols in MMIXAL will occur. The following code is a part of a bigger program that is used to find out the maximum of n elements x[1], ..., x[n]. The idea of the algorithm of the subprogram is that, suppose that the maximal element is the last element. We put this element into a special location. Then we compare it with the elements in its left hand side in turn. If it is greater than any of these elements, it still stays in the location. But if it is less than anyone, the winner of the competitors will take its place over and becomes the new host of the location. When all the n elements have finished the battle, the one now staying in the location is the maximal value.

Program M (find maximal). At the beginning, n is in register \$0, and the address of x[0] is the register x0(a global register that is defined in somewhere else).

Assembly code	Row number	Label number	Operator	Expression	Times	Note
	01	j	IS	\$0		j
	02	m	IS	\$1		m
	03	kk	IS	\$2		8k
	04	xk	IS	\$3		X[k]
	05	t	IS	\$255		temporary storage
	06		LOC	#100		
#100: #39 02 00 03	07	Maximum	SL	kk,\$0, 3	1	M1. Initialization. k←n,j←n
#104: #8c 01 fe 02	08		LDO	m,x0, kk	1	m←X[n]
#108: #f0 00 00 06	09		JMP	DecrK	1	goto M2 with k←n−1
#10c: #8c 03 fe 02	10	Loop	LDO	xk,x0,kk	n-1	M3. Comparison
#110: #30 ff 03 01	11		CMP	t,xk,m	n-1	t←[X[k]>m]- X[k]<m]
#114: #5c ff 00 03	12		PBMP	t, DecrK	n-1	if X[k]⩽m, then goto M5
#118: #c1 01 03 00	13	ChangeM	SET	m,xk	A	M4 Change m. m←X[k]
#11c: #3d 00 02 03	14		SR	j, kk,3	A	j←k
#120: #25 02 02 08	15	DecrK	SUB	kk,kk,8	n	M5. Decrease k, k←k−1
#124: #5502 ff fa	16		PBP	kk, Loop	n	M2. Test all? If k>0, then return to M3
#128: #f802 00 00	17		POP	2,0	1	return to main program

This program also shows the usage of the relevant symbols of MMIXAL.

1) The columns "label", "operator", and "expression" are more interesting as they contain the program written in MMIXAL machine language.

2) The column "assembly code" lists the real numerical machine language that corresponds to MMIXAL program. The translation usually is done by the so-called assembler or another versions of the assembler that is another

computer programs. Therefore, the programmer may use MMIXAL to write all programs and need not take the troubles to write the equivalent numerical program by hand.

3) The column "row number" actually is not a part of MMIXAL program. We add it just for the convenience of references.

4) The column "note" presents the explanation information.

5) The column "time" represents the profile, i.e., in the process of the execution of the program, how many times does the statement on the line execute. Therefore, the instruction on line 10 will be executed n–1 times, etc. From this information, we may determine how long does the program take, it is n−1 times, etc. From this information, we may determine how long does the program take, it is $n\mu + (5n+4A+5)v$, where A is the quantity that was analyzed by D. E. Knuth in his book. Now we may specifically discuss Program M of the MMIXAL part. The line 01 " j IS $0" states that symbol j represents the register $0. The line 02 to 05 are analogous. The effects of lines 01 and 03 can be seen from line 14 where the numerical value of instruction "SR j kk 3" appears as # 3d 00 02 03, that is, "$R $0, $2, 3".

The line 06 states that, from #100, the successive addresses should be sequentially determined. Therefore, the symbol Maximum that appears in the label Field of line 07 becomes equivalent number #100; in line 10, the symbol Loop is the consecutive three double word bytes, hence it is equivalent to #10c.

The operators on lines 07 to 17 contain the symbol names SL, LDO etc. of MMIX instructions. They are different from that appear on lines 01 to 06. IS and LOC are called pseudo operators as they are operators of MMIXAL rather than that of MMIX. Pseudo operators provide special information on symbolic programs but they are not the instructions of the programs. Therefore the line "j IS $0" only involves program M, it does not mean that when the program runs, any variable will be set to equal to the content of the register $0. As they are pseudo operators, there is no instruction in lines 01 to 06 that will be assembled.

The line 07 is a shift left instruction that sets k←n via setting kk←8n. That program works based on the value of 8k, rather than k, as the four word bytes on line 08 and 10 need 8k.

The line 09 makes the control jumping to line 15. As the assembler knows that the jump instruction is in the location #108 while DecrK is equivalent to #120, it computes the relative offset (#120–108)/4 = 6. The relative address is also computed for the jump instructions in lines 12 and 16.

The rest of symbolic code is self-explained. As early pointed that program M is intended to be part of a larger program, elsewhere the sequence

SET $2, 100

PUSHJ $1, Maximum

STO $1, Max

would, for example, jump to program M through setting n to be 100. Program M will search the maximal of elements x[1], ..., x[100]. And by storing the maximal value into $1 and storing its address into $2, it will return to instruction "STO $1, Max".

Now we have a look at the complete program once again, instead of only the subprogram. We call the following program "hello world" because the message it prints is "Hello world", then it stops.

Program (Hello)

Assembly code	Row number	Label number	Operator	Expression	Note
	01	argv	IS	$1	argument vector
	02		LOC	#100	
#100:#8fff0100	03	Main	LDOU	$255, argv, 0	$255←the name of program
#104:#00000701	04		TRAP	0,Fputs, StdOut	print the name
#108:#f4ff0003	05		GETA	$255,String	$255←the address of ''world''
#10c:#00000701	06		TRAP	0, StdOut	print the sstring
#110:#00000000	07		TRAP	0,Halt,0	stop
#114:#2c20776f	08	String	BYTE	'', Hello'', #a,0	The string with line feed and end symbol
#118:#726c6490	09				
1#11c:#00	10				

It needs to explain that in order to execute the program, a concise computer document that contains LABEL, OP, and EXPR should be prepared first, the document is called "Hello.mms". And it is assembled through, say, "mmixal Hello.mms". The assembler will generate a document called "Hello. mmo", the postfix of which .mms indicates that it is "MMIX symbolic", and .mmo implies "MMIX target". Now the simulation program is called via saying "mmix Hello".

The MMIX simulator implemented some simplest characteristics of an assumed operating system called NNIX. If there exists a target called, say, foo.mmo, then when an instruction line is given, for example, it is

        foo.bar xyzzy

then NNIX will initiates. The simulation program is called using instruction line "mmix <option> foo bar xyzzy", where <option> is a sequence of 0 or more special requests from which corresponding feature may be obtained. For example, after NNIX stopped, an option P will print a profile of the print program.

A MMIX program always starts with a symbol unit Main. At the time, the register $0 contains the number of arguments in the instruction line, that is the number of the words in the instruction line. The register $1 contains the address of the storage of the first such argument that is always the name of the program. The operating system has put all arguments into consecutive four word bytes, and starts with the address in $1 and ends with an all zero's four word bytes. Every argument will be represented as a string, meaning that it is the address in memory of a sequence of zero or more nonzero bytes followed by a zero byte. The nonzero bytes are characters of the string.

For example, the instruction line (1) will cause $0 being 3 initially. We may have:

```
              $1=#4000000000000008    the pointer of the first string
M₈ [#4000000000000008] =#4000000000000028    the first argument, string foo''
M₈ [#4000000000000010] =#4000000000000030    the second argument, string "bar"
M₈ [#4000000000000018] =#4000000000000038    the third argument, string "xyzzy"
M₈ [#4000000000000020] =#4000000000000000    the empty pointer after the last
                                             argument
M₈ [#4000000000000028] =#666f6f0000000000    'f''o''o' 0, 0, 0, 0, 0
M₈ [#4000000000000030] =#6261720000000000    'b''a''r', 0, 0, 0, 0, 0
M₈ [#4000000000000038] =#787977a7a79000000    'x''y''z''z''y', 0, 0, 0
```

NNIX establishes the string of every argument so that its character starts at the boundary of four word bytes. However, in general, string may start at any location in the four word bytes.

In line 03, the first instruction of program H puts the string pointer $M_8[\$1]$ into the register $255. The string is the name of the program "Hello". Line 04 is a special instruction Trap that requires that the operating system put the string $255 into the standard output document. Similarly, lines 05 and 06 require that NNIX contribute "world" and a line feed to the standard output. The symbol Fputs is prearranged to be 7 while symbol stdOut is predefined to be1. The line "TRAP 0, Halt, 0" is a usual way to end a program. This belongs to a special trap instruction.

The string output characters of lines 05 and 06 are generated by BYTE instruction in line 08. BYTE is a pseudo operator of MMIXAL, rather than an operator of MMIX. But BYTE is different from the virtual operators like IS and LOC in that it does assemble the data to storage. Generally speaking, BYTE assembles a series of expression to a constant of one byte. The construction of line 08 "world" is the abbreviation of seven single characters

```
    "," "," "w", "o", "r", "l", "d"
```

The constant #a on line 08 is the symbol line feed in ASCII. If it appears in a file in printing, it will cause the action of line feed. The final "0" on line 08 is used to end the string. Therefore line 08 is a table of nine expressions and it causes the showing of nine bytes on the left sides of lines 08–10.

The summary of the language. Now that we have seen three examples that demonstrate what can we do in MMIXAL, it is the time to carefully discuss several rules, especially we have to investigate what cannot be done in the language. The following are few rules that define the language.

1) A symbol is a string that starts with a letter and followed by letters/numbers. As the purpose of the definition, underline "_" is regarded as a letter, and all the Unite codes with value more than 126 are also letters. For example, PRIME1, Data-Segment, Main, __, pâté.

Special constructions dH, dF, and dB, where d is a single number. According to the convention of "local symbols" explained above, it is substituted effectively by unique symbol.

2) A constant is:

(1) A decimal constant. It consists of one or more digits of decimal num-

bers {0, 1, 2, 3, 4, 5, 6, 7, 8, 9} that represent a four word bytes without sign in decimal notation.

(2) A hexadecimal constant. It starts with a # and followed by one or more digits of hexadecimal numbers {01, 2, 3, 3, 4, 5, 6, 7, 8, 9, a, b, c, d, e, f} that represent a four word bytes without sign in the hexadecimal notation.

(3) A symbolic character. It starts with a quotation mark " ' ", followed by any characters that are different from line feed, then followed again by another quotation mark " ' ". This represents a quoted ASCII code or Unite Code value. For example:

'65', '#41', 'a', '39', '#27', '31639', '#7B97', '算'

A string constant starts with a double quote " " ", followed by one or more characters that are different from line feed and double quote mark, followed again by another double quote " " " This construction is equivalent to a series of character constant of individual characters that are separated by commas.

3) We say that in a MMIXAL program, the every appearance of a character is either a "defined symbol" or a "future reference". A defined symbol is a symbol that already occurred in the label field of some line in the previous MMIXAL program. A future reference is a symbol that hasn't been defined in this way.

The symbols such as rR, ROUND_NEAR, and V_BIT, as well as W_Handler and Fputs are predefined as they are the constants that are related to refer to MMIX hardware or its basic operating system. These symbols may also be redefined as MMIX does not assume that every programmer knows their names, but there is no any symbol that can be used for a label for more than once.

Every defined symbol has its equivalent value, it is either pure bytes(an unsigned octabyte) or a register number ($0 or $1 or ... or $255).

4) A main symbol is:

(1) a symbol; or

(2) a constant; or

(3) character @; or

(4) an expression included in a pair of parentheses;

(5) an unary operator followed by a main symbol.

Unary operator is +(determined, and it does not do anything), − (negative, it is reduced from zero), ∼ (negate, it changes all 64 binary bits) and $ (registerization, it transforms a value to be the number of a register.)

5) A term is a series of one or more than one main term divided by a strong binary operator; an expression is a series of one or more terms divided by a weak binary operator. The strong operators are * (multiplication), / (division), // (fractional division), % (remainder), << (shift left), >>(shift right), and & (bitwise and). Weak binary symbols are + (addition), − (subtract), | (bit wise or) and ⊎ (*bit wise* not or). These operations are carried out to octal bytes without sign. If x<y, x//y represents $\lfloor 2^{64}x/y \rfloor$, and if x⩾y then it is not defined. The binary operators with the same strength are

carried out from left to right, hence a/b/c is (a/b)/c while a-b+c is (a-b)+c.

Example [5]: #ab<<32+k&~(k–1) is an expression. It is the addition of term #ab<<32 and term k&~(k–1), and the later term is the bitwise and of main terms k and ~ (k–1).The later main term is the complement of (k–1) that is the complement of an expression included in parentheses that is the difference of term k and term 1. 1 is also main term, actually it is a constant of decimal system. If the symbol k, say, to be equivalent to #cdef00, then the whole expression #ab<<32+k& ~ (k–1) is equivalent to #ab000001000.

The binary operations are only allowed to perform on the pure numbers, except for the exceptional cases like \$1+2 = \$3 and \$3–\$1 = 2. The future reference cannot be combined with anything else, the expression such as 2F+1 is always illegal, because 2F never corresponds to any defined symbol.

6) An instruction consists of three fields:

(1) LABEL field. It is either blank, or is a symbol.

(2) OP field. It is either an MMIX operator or a virtual operator of MMIXAL.

(3) EXPR field. It is a list of one or more expressions, separated by commas in between. The EXPR field may also be blank, in which case it is equivalent to the expression 0.

7) The assemble of an instruction is carried out in the following three steps:

(1) If it is needed, the current location @ can be aligned through adding to it the multiples of

8, if the operator is OCTA;

4, if the operator is TETRA or an operator of MMIX;

2, if the operator is WYDE.

(2) If the symbol in LABEL exists, it is defined as @, unless OP = IS or OP = GREG.

(3) If OP is a virtual operator, please refer to rule 8, otherwise OP is an instruction of MMIX and it is as explained in Section 13.2, OP and EXPR fields define a tetra (double word) bytes, hence @ should be added 4. Some instructions of MMIX have three operands in the EXPR field, while others have two, there are some that have one operand only.

If OP is, say, ADD. MMIXAL may predict that there are three operands, then it will check if the first and the second operands are register numbers. If the third operand is a pure number, MMIXAL will change the operator from #20 (add) to #21 (prompt add) and it will check if the prompt value is less than 256.

If the OP is SETH, then MMIX will expect that there are two operands. The first operand should be a register number, and the second should be a number less than 65536.

An OP like BNZ takes two operands: a register number and a pure number. The pure number should be expressed as a relative address. In other words, its value should be able to express as @+4k where $-65535 \leqslant k \leqslant 65536$.

Accessing memory. The OP like LDB or GO has two forms: either two operands $X, A or three operands $X, $Y, $Z or $X, $Y, Z. When the memory A may be expressed as the sum of a base address and a byte Z: $Y+Z, the option of two operands may be used.

8) MMIXAL contains the following virtual operations:

(1) OP = IS. The EXPR should be a single expression; If there exists a symbol in LABEL, it is regarded to be equivalent to the value of the expression.

(2) OP = GREG. The expression is a single expression with a pure equivalent value x. If the symbol in LABEL exists, it is taken to be equivalent to the maximal register number that has not been allocated. Moreover, when the program starts, this global register will contain x. If x≠0, then x is regarded as the base address, and the program will not change the global register.

(3) OP = LOC. EXPR should be an expression with a pure equivalent value x. The value of@ is set to x. For example, the instruction "T LOC @+ 1000" defines T as the start address of the series of 1000 bytes, the @ is advanced to the byte after the series.

(4) OP = BYTE,WYDE, TETRA, or OCTA. The EXPR field should be a list of pure expressions each of which may load in 1, 2, 4, or 8 bytes.

9) MMIXAL confines the future reference so that the process of assemble may be completed in one pass scanning of the program. The future reference is allowed only when it is the following case:

(1) In a relative address, like the operand of JMP, or the second operand of branch instructions, possible branches, PUSH, or GETA.

(2) In an expression that is assembled by OCTA.

MMIXAL has also some additional characteristics that are related to system programming [6], we do not introduce them here. For a complete description of the details of the language, they appear in the file <MMIX ware>, along with a complete procedure of working assembler.

13.5 Generation of MMIXAL Target Codes

Having the language of target codes, our next task is to discuss how to translate various kinds of intermediate code to target codes [7]. The intermediate codes we have introduced include reversed polish form, triple form, quadruple form and syntax tree form. No matter which one is adopted, what we need to translate are expressions and statements, including sequential statements, conditional statements and loop statements.

No matter which intermediate code is used, the algorithm that is used to translate them into target code is to put the intermediate code that needs to handle into stack, then take them out one by one to translate. In this process of analysis, the corresponding target will come out.

In the following, we take reversed Polish form to express expressions to show the translation procedure and further explain our algorithm. In this way, we do not need to make any explanation regarding the problem later.

13.5.1   Translation of Expressions in Reversed Polish Form

In order to generate the target code of the expressions in the reversed Polish form, we need to use a stack. The stack is called component stack that stores each intermediate syntax tokens that constitute the expressions, each element is denoted s[i]. The rough translation procedure is that, from the reversed Polish form area the tokens of the token string are taken, and put them into the stack. If the one that is scanned is a variable, then at the same time as it is put into the stack, it is also put into register in order to perform the operation. If the one that is scanned is an operator, then it needs to check which type of operator is it? If it is a unary operator, then it only needs to perform the operation on the operand preceding the operator. If it is binary operator, then the corresponding operation should be performed over the two operands before the operator. Similarly, if it is an n-ary operator, then the operation will be performed over the preceding n components. But so far we have not met n-ary operator. Hence for the translation of expressions in the reversed Polish form, the most important thing is to put variables into registers. Thus when operator is met, the corresponding instructions will directly come out.

For example, suppose that the expression is $(x * y + w * z) * x - -y/z$, then its reversed Polish form is

$$xy * wz * +x * yz/ - .$$

According to the algorithm above we may generate the MMIXAL code:

```
LDW $1, $2, $3        set s($1)←x
LDW $2,$4, $5         set S($2)←y
MUL $3, $1, $2        set s($3)←s($1)*s($2)=x*y
LDW $4, $6, $7        set s($4)←w
LDW $5, $8, $9        set s($5)←z
MUL $6, $4, $5        set s($6)←s($4)*s($5)=w*z
ADD $7, $3, $6        set s($7)←s($3)+s($6)=x*y+w*z
MUL $8, $1, $7        set s($8)←s($1)*s($7)=(x*y+w*z)*x
DIV $9, $2, $5        set s($9)←s($2)/s($5)=y/z
SUB $10, $8, $9       set s($10)←s($8)-s($9)=(x*y+w*z)*x-y/z
```

13.5.2   Translation of Triple Expressions

Suppose that there is an expression

$$((x * y + u) - w * y)/x.$$

Its triple expression is as follows:

1) $(*, x, y)$;
2) $(+, ①, u)$;
3) $(*, w, y)$;
4) $(-, ②, ③)$;
5) $(/, ④, x)$.

Therefore, its target code in MMIXAL is as follows:

```
LDW $1, $2, $3      set s($1)←x
LDW $4, $5, $6      set s($4)←y
MUL $7, $1, $4      set s($7)←s($1)×s($4)=x*y
LDW $8, $2, $3      set s($8)←u
ADD $5, $7, $8      set s($5)←s($7)+s($8)=x*y+u
LDW $6, $2, $4      set s($6)←w
MUL $7, $6, $4      set s($7)←w*y
SUB $8, $5, $7      set s($8)←(x*y+u)-w*y
DIV $8, $8, $1      set s($8)←s($8)/s($1)=((x*y+u)-w*y)/x
```

Notice that in the two examples above, we used load instructions, e.g., LDW $1, $2, $3 is used to load variables x, and y into register. The load in addresses are formed by the two registers in the instruction. For example, if we have instruction LDW $X, $Y, $Z, then the load in address is given by

$$A = (u(\$Y) + u(\$Z)) \bmod 2^{64}.$$

Therefore, we assume here that in registers 2 and 3, the numbers that form the addresses are stored. If they were not set in advance, then it is necessary to use some instructions to set up the numbers.

13.5.3 Translation of Expression Quadruples

The instructions of MMIXAL are closest to quadruples. Therefore, it is most convenient to translate quadruple form into MMIXAL target code.

Suppose that there is an expression

$$x * (y + u * v - y/w).$$

Then the corresponding quadruples are:

1) $(*,u,v,T_1)$;
2) $(+, y,T_1,T_2)$;
3) $(/,y,w,T_3)$;
4) $(-,T_2,T_3,T_4)$;
5) $(*,x,T_4,T_5)$.

And its MMIXAL target code is as follows:

```
LDW $1, $2, $3      set s($1)←u
LDW $4,$5, $6       set s($4)←v
MUL $1, $1, $4      set s($1)←s($1)*s($4)=u*v
```

```
LDW $7, $8, $9       set s($7)←y
ADD $2, $7, $1       set s($2)←s($ 7)+s($1)=y+u+v
LDW $10,$5, $6       set s($10)←w
DIV $7,$7,$10        set s($7)←s($7)/s($10)=y/w
SUB $2, $2, $3       set s($2)←s($2)-s($3)=y+u*v-y/w
LDW $5,$11,$12       set s($5)←x
MUL $5,$5, $2        set s($5)←s($5)*s($2)=x*(y+u*v-y/w)
```

13.5.4 Translation of Expressions

Through the introduction given above, we have known how to translate expressions. In simple cases, we can even directly translate them without through intermediate code form.

For example, suppose that there is expression

$$x/(x * y - u * w) - z$$

then it target code in MMIXAL is as follows:

```
LDW $1, $2, $3       set s($1)←x
LDW $4, $5, $6       set s($4)←y
MUL $4, $1, $4       set $($4)←s($1)*s($4)=x*y
LDW $7, $8, $9       set s($7)←u
LDW $10, $11, $12    set s($10)←w
MUL $5,$7, $10       set s($5)←s($7)*s($10)=u*v
SUB $6, $4, $5       set s($6)←s($4)-s($5)=x*y-u*w
DIV $8, $1, $6       set s($8)←s($1)/s($6)=x*(x*y-u*w)
LDW $9, $11, $12     set s($9)←z
SUB $8, $8, $9       set s($8)←s($8)-s($9)=x/(x*y-u*w)-z
```

As for boolean expressions, as it has the same structure of the target code as arithmetic expressions, meanwhile, MMIXAL has the instructions that handle boolean operations, therefore to generate the target code of boolean expressions in MMIXAL is not difficult either.

Suppose that there are following boolean expressions:

1) $x \lor y \land (u \lor w)$;
2) $x[\ ] \lor (B \land y[\ ])$;
3) $x[\ ] \land (y[\ ] \lor z \land x[\ ])$.

In the expressions above, the form x[ ] represents the array. Meanwhile, one should notice that, the boolean operations in MMIXAL are carried out for four word bytes (i.e., sixty-four bits). Therefore, it is different from the arithmetic variables, we have to imagine that the variables here are 64 bits. We get the target code in MMIXAL as follows:

```
1) LDO $1, $2, $3        set s($1)←x

   LDO $4,$5, $6         set s($4)←y

   LDO $7, $8, $9        set s($7)←u

   LDO $10, $11, $12     set s($10)←w
```

OR $7, $7, $10	set v($7)←v($7)|v($10)=u∨w
AND $4,$4,$7	set v($4)←v($4)&v($7)=y∧(u∨w)
OR $1, $1, $4	set v($1)←v($1)|v($4)=x∨y∧(u∨w)
2) LDO $1, $2, $3	set s($1)←x[ ]
LDO $4, $5, $6	set s($4)←B
LDO $7, $8, $9	set s($7)←y[ ]
AND $4,$4,$7	set v($4)←v($4)&v($7)=B∧y[ ]
OR $1, $1, $4	set s($1)←v($1)|v($4)=x∨(B∧y[ ])
3) LDO $1, $2, $3	set s($1)←x[ ]
LDO $4, $5, $6	set s($4)←y[ ]
LDO $4,$5,$6	set s($7)←z
AND $7, $7, $1	set v($7)←v($7)&v($1)=z∧x[ ]
OR $4,$4, $7	set v($4)←v($4)|v($7)=y[ ]∨z∧x[ ]
AND $1,$1,$4	set v($1)←v($1)∧v($4)=x∧y[ ]∨z∧x

13.5.5 Translation of Syntax Tree Form of Expressions

The other form of intermediate code is syntax trees which we have introduced
in preceding sections [8]. Not only expressions can be represented in syntax
trees, but also various statements can be represented in syntax tree form. In
order to translate expressions in syntax trees to the target code in MMIXAL,
either we can transform the syntax trees to the reversed Polish form (actually
it is only the post order visit to the syntax trees), or we transform the syntax
trees into triples or quadruples. Then we use the methods introduced above
to translate the triples and quadruples into the target code in MMIXAL.
Besides, we can also directly translate the syntax trees to the target code
required. Notice that we use the visit rules for post order visit. For example,
given a syntax tree as shown in Fig. 13.2, its target code in MMIXAL is as
follows:

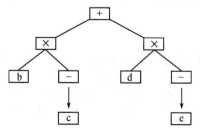

Fig. 13.2 Syntax tree of b ∗ (−c) + d ∗ (−e).

LDW $1, $2, $3   set s($1)←b
LDW $4, $5, $6   set s($4)←c
NEG $4, $4   set s($4)←-s($4)=-c
MUL $1, $1, $4   set s($1)←s($1)×s($4)=b*(-c)
LDW $7, $8, $9   set s($7)←d
LDW $10, $11, $12   set s($10)←e
NEG $10, $10   set s($10)←-s($10)=-e
MUL $7, $7, $10   set s($7)←s($7)×s($10)=d*(-e)
ADD $1, $1, $7   set s($1)←s($1)+s($7)=b*(-c)+d*(-e),

13.5.6 Translation of Various Statements

1) The translation of assignments
Assignment statements may have several forms:
(1) X := E;
(2) a[ ] := E;
(3) f := E.
The first form indicates that the value of the expression on the right hand side is assigned to the variable on the left hand side; The second form indicates that the value of the expression on the right hand side is assigned to an element of array; The third form indicates that the value of the expression on right hand side is assigned to a function. In MMIXAL, for these statement what we need to do is to put the data from registers to memory as al the operations are carried out on registers. If we have put the value of expression E into $X, while all the memory addresses of x, a[ ] or f are in A. A is

$$A = (u(\$y)+u(\$Z)) \bmod 2^{64}$$

then the translation statement is only

STW $X, $Y, $Z

2) Branch statements
In programming languages, the branch statements generally have two forms:
(1) goto L,
(2) goto S(E),
where L is a label. During the compilation, we may determine its specific value. As for the form S(E), at first the value of the expression E is evaluated, then it is added to the address in the name cell <S>, and it determines the final value. Therefore, through the instruction GO of MMIXAL,

GO $X, $Y, $Z

is realized as

U($X)←@+4

and the evaluation of A is realized via

$$A = (u(\$y)+u(\$z)) \bmod 2^{64}$$

3) Loop statements

For the loop statement with the form

for (i = 1; i⩽n: i+1)

we only need to set up constants 1 and n in the target code.

```
01 i₀    IS     1
02 SET     jj, i₀   jj←1
03 SET     ℓℓ n    ℓℓ ←n
04 1H
   Loop body
        INCL jj, 1       jj←jj+1
k      CMP jj, ℓℓ        compare jj and ℓℓ
k+1    BNP jj, 1H        if jj⩽0, i.e., jj⩽n, then goto 1H.
```

Regarding conditional branches, there are more instructions available. The execution procedure is always to perform a comparison operation first, then the result of the comparison will be shown on a Pertinent registers. According to the result shown, the instruction is executed. These instructions contain:

- BN $X, RA Branch if negative, i.e., if $s(\$X) < 0$, then @←RA
- BZ $X, RA Branch if zero, i.e., if $s(\$X) = 0$, then @←RA
- BP $X, RA Branch if positive, i.e., if $s(\$X)>0$, then @←RA
- BOD $X,RA Branch if odd, i.e., if $s(\$X) \bmod 2 = 1$, then @←RA
- BNN $X, RA Branch if not negative, i.e., if $s(\$X0 \geqslant 0$, then @←RA
- BNZ $X, RA Branch if non zero, i.e., if $s(\$X) \neq 0$, then @←RA
- BNP $X, RA Branch if not positive, i.e., if $s(\$X) \leqslant 0$, then @←RA
- BEV $X, RA Branch if even, i.e., if $s(\$Z) \bmod 2 = 0$, then @←RA

Besides, there are some branch instructions that provide even faster branch, the condition is that the situation of future is foreseen.

We have introduced the relevant contents regarding the generation of target code in MMIXAL. Based on these principles, we believe that the reader will be able to solve them via self analytical ability and knowledge when some details are provided.

Problems

Problem 13.1 Translate the following inverse Polish expression into MMIXAL target code:

ab*ed/+ac*-

Problem 13.2 Translate the following intermediate code in triple form into MMIXAL target codes:

1) (/,x,y)
2) (-,x,y)

3) (*,u,(2))
4) (+,(1),(3))
5) (*,(4),x)

Problem 13.3 Translate the following intermediate code in quadruple form into MMIXAL target code:

1) $(+,x,y,T_1)$
2) $(*,x,y,T_2)$
3) $(/,T_2,u,T_3)$
4) $(+,T_1,T_3,T_4)$
5) $(*,T_4,X,T_5)$

Problem 13.4 Write down the corresponding MMIXAL target code of the Following expression:

$$(x*y+w*(x+y)-u*y/x)*y$$

Problem 13.5 Write down the corresponding MMIXAL target code of the following statement:

```
if x<5 the x := x+1 else x := x-8
```

Problem 13.6 Write down the MMIXAL target code that realizes the following function:

$$S = \begin{cases} x + 3x^2 + 5x^3 & x < 0 \\ x + 4x^2 + 6x^3 & x \geqslant 0 \end{cases}$$

Problem 13.7 Write down the MMIXAL target program that realizes the following statement:

```
while i⩽ 100 do s := s+3
```

Problem 13.8 Given the following program

```
void f (x,a,y)
float x[] [4],a[] [4],y[]{
    int i,j;
    float  s;
    for(i=0;i<3;i++){
        s=0;
        For(j=0;j<4:j++)
        {s=s+x[i][j]
            a[i][j]=x[i][j]*x[i][j];}
        y[i]=s;
    }
}
```

Translate it into MMIXAL target code.

Problem 13.9 Write down the corresponding MMIXAL target code of the following relation expression:

$a \leqslant b \lor a > 0 \lor b \geqslant 0 \land (c \geqslant d)$

Problem 13.10   Write down the corresponding MMIXAL target code of the following expression:

$a \land b \lor c \land (b \land y = 3.14 \land a = 2.18)$

References

[1] Chow F, Hennessy J L (1984) Register allocation by priority-based coloring. ACM SIGPLAN Notices 19(6): 222 – 232

[2] Knuth D E (2005) The art of computer Programming, NO.1, volume 1. Addison–Wesley, Reading, Mass

[3] Knuth D E (1984) The T$_E$Xbook. Addison-Wesley, Reading, Mass.

[4] Tjiang S W K (1986) Twig language manual. Computing Science Technical rReport 120, AT&T Bell Laboratories, Murray Hill, New York

[5] Knuth D E (1984) Literate programming. Computer J. 28(2): 97 – 111

[6] Knuth D E (1977) A generalization of Dijkstra's algorithm. Information Processing Letters 6, pages 1 – 6

[7] Henry P R (1984) Graham-Glanville Code Generators. Ph. D. Thesis, University of California, Berkeley

[8] Aho A V, Ganapathi (1985) Efficient tree pattern matching: an aid to code generation. Twelfth Annual ACM Symposium on Principles of Programming Languages, pp 334 – 340

Chapter 14   Compilation of Object-oriented Languages

*In the absence of meaningful standards, a new industry
like software comes to depend instead on folklore.*

Tom DeMarco

14.1 Motivation of the Chapter

In the previous chapters, the grammars, lexical analysis, syntactical analysis, context processing, intermediate code generation, target code generation, debugging, optimization of programs in programming languages are explored. The management of memory for the execution of compiler and the target code is also involved. The contents are directed at a variety of programming languages instead of any specific language. However, we should also admit that they are more suitable to the so-called procedural languages or imperative languages.

From 1980s, due to the software crisis, a new programming paradigm gradually demonstrates itself, and it tends to replace the old programming style at least in the area where it has dominated the status. Besides object – oriented programming, there are function programming, logical programming, etc. The compilation of the programs written in these programming languages must be somehow different from the methods we introduced so far for the traditional languages. The main differences between them are that the structures of the source programs different, causing the difference in handling of the analysis and synthesis. Consequently, the target codes for these paradigms are different too.

The compilers of most (but not all) imperative and object-oriented languages generate assembly programs or even lower-level of target codes. While many (not all either) functional programming, logical programming, parallel, and distributed programming languages generate C or C++ programs as the target codes. In comparison with functional and logical programming languages, the object-oriented programming languages are now becoming more popular. Among those paradigms that take C or C++ as the target code, the parallel and distributed languages are more important than functional and logical programming languages. Therefore, as one of frontiers in the field of principles of compilers, we will discuss the compilation of object-oriented languages first, and sequentially we will discuss what we regard as also frontiers. For example, Chapter 16, we will introduce briefly the newest technique — grid computing and the compilation of the language (if any) that writes programs to implement grid computing.

Object-oriented languages and procedure-oriented (or imperative) languages are similar in many aspects apart from that the target code they generate may have different levels. The former ones tend to generate lower level while the latter ones tend to generate assembly target code. Therefore, in this chapter we will introduce the special characteristics of object-oriented languages and the corresponding special handling techniques in compilers.

14.2 Objects and Compilation

If one enquires the most fundamental difference between object-oriented languages and traditional languages, the prompt answer obviously is objects.

How is an object-oriented language? Why is a method considered to be object-oriented? What is an object? As object-oriented gained widespread adherents during the 1980s and 1990s, there were many different opinions (e.g., [1 – 4]) about the correct answers to these questions. Today, a coherent view of object-oriented has emerged.

Object actually means anything in the nature, including concrete physical things and abstract concepts. Therefore, it is analogous to variables in languages. The variables may have attributes and their corresponding values. The so-called attributes are a collection of data values that describe an object. For example, if we consider a person as an object, then the attributes that may be used to describe the person include name, gender, ages, height, weight, nation, birth-place, occupation, and living address, etc. These attributes can be represented as values.

As a variable, an object will be put in operations in the process of programming, viz., it will play a role in solving problem. Therefore, it should be able to participate operations as the operand.

For example, a number should be able to participate in various operations depending on which number is it. That means that objects need to be grouped. And this is where the concept of class comes from. A class is a generalized description (e.g., a template, pattern, or blueprint) that describes a collection of similar objects.

The intent of object-oriented programming is to solve problems through taking components of problem as objects. Therefore, it has to define all classes concerned (and the relationships and behavior associated with them). To accomplish this, a number of tasks must occur:

Instead of examining a problem using a more conventional input-process-ing-output (information flow) model or model derived exclusively from hier-archical information structures, object-oriented programming builds a class-oriented model that relies on an understanding of object-oriented concepts.

1) Classes must be identified (i.e., attributes and methods are defined), The so-called methods here, as well as services, provide representation of one of the behaviors of a class.

2) A class hierarchy is defined.

3) Object-to-object relationships (object connections) should be repre-sented.

4) Object behavior must be modeled.

5) Tasks 1–4 are reapplied iteratively until the model is complete or the problem is solved.

The distinguished feature of object-oriented programming is that the class encapsulates the data and procedural abstractions required to describe the content and behavior of some real world entity.

In addition, we define some other concepts. At first, inheritance, it means receiving some properties from the ancestors. So, as instances of a specific class, objects inherit a class' attributes and operations (methods and ser-vices). The second concept is subclass, it is a specialization of the superclass. A subclass can inherit both attributes and operations from a superclass. Now superclass is also called a base class, is a generalization of a set of classes that are related to it.

In the languages, objects and abstract data types are similar. The differ-ence is that for object, only its methods (or operations) are externally avail-able, this is because of the encapsulation technique — as we have mentioned that encapsulates the objects that belong to a class and the operations. From outside, the objects can only be access and operated through the methods.

The basic operations on objects are "fields (object attributes) selection", "copy" and "method invoking" or "method calling". Though many object-oriented languages do not allow directly access to the fields of objects, the operations of accessing to the fields of objects through internal methods are essential. The operation of copy is simple, and the compilation of it is only to make copy. Therefore, the important thing is to realize the method calling or method invoking. The first problem regarding the method calling is which method needs to be called. Only after it is correctly identified then can it be called. The method calling, in essence, is the routine calling. Therefore, the object calling methods, and the method calling related to the control stream, as well as the effect of the calling and that of the routine calling are consistent. But there are also differences between method calling and routine calling. One difference is that, routine callings are basically statically determined while method callings can only be determined through deliver table during running time. The second difference is that method can directly access to the fields of objects. This kind of accesses is realized through passing pointer as additional parameter to object. This parameter is called extra hidden parameter.

1) Method identification. Before the translation of the calling of the object methods, it is necessary to identify which one needs to be called. For the routine calls, of course there is also the problem of the identification though it is rather simpler. Moreover, it can be solved through semantics check. But for objects, in many cases it needs to find out the method to be called through looking up the deliver table during running time.

2) Message Passing. Many people depict object-oriented programming as objects plus message passing as the object-oriented programming is based data-centralization. The basic units for activities are objects. All the activities of objects are message-driven. Therefore, message passing is the unique means for object communications.

Methods, as we have said, are the operations upon objects. They are just implemented via message passing. Therefore, so called identification method actually is message identification. Because when some operation needs to implement upon the object, the message is sent to the object. Upon receiving message and deciding the operation required by the message, the corresponding operation is called and it is performed to completion. When the point is reached, it has no difference again with the routine calling.

In most object-oriented languages objects have also constructive functions and structured functions. They are called when objects are created and released, respectively. Their calls and the calls in other methods are not different in principles.

Suppose that our objects are just like what we said. Then the compilation of objects is very simple. Suppose that we have an object A that has method m1 and m2, as well as fields a1 and a2. Then the running table of object class A consists of fields a1 and a2, as shown in Fig. 14.1.

Besides, the compiler maintains the method table on compilation of class A as shown in Fig. 14.2.

Fig. 14.1 The fields of object.   **Fig. 14.2** The method table of object.

In Fig. 14.2, we add a postfix on the method names, representing that they are the operations upon class A. In this simple module, the selection of fields may be realized just like the selection of fields in records. Moreover, the copy of objects is also just like that of in records. The selection of methods is implemented by identification process in the compiler.

By an additional parameter, that is a pointer that points to the object, the method can be realized as the realization of the routines. Therefore, the methods m1_A and m2_A can be translated to be the routines of C language. For example, for method m1_A it may be implemented as follows:

```
Void m1_A (class_A.*this,int i){
    Program body of method m1_A, by this → x visit any object
    field x
}
```

Suppose that m1_A has a parameter with type integer and without return value, and class_A is the language type name of class A in C, then the method calling a.m1(3) may be translated to m1_A(&a.3).

14.3 Characteristics of Objects

There are innumerable objects in the world. Each object has its own characteristics. If we want to investigate them individually, it will not be possible. Fortunately, many objects have common characteristics, apart from peculiarities. Through the common characteristics, we may group those objects with the same common points. Then we concentrate to investigate these classes so that our research can be given great convenience.

We take the division of books as an example. Fig. 14.3 shows the division of books.

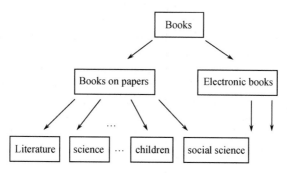

Fig. 14.3 Classification of books.

In the hierarchical structure of classes, the lower nodes all have the characteristics of upper nodes. But in comparison with the upper nodes, the lower nodes have their own new characteristics. The lower nodes hold the characteristics of the upper nodes, this is called inheritance. Inheritance is one of the most important characteristics of objects.

14.3.1 Inheritance

Inheritance exists in all object-oriented languages. It allows programmer to create class B based on class A. Hence class B possesses its own fields and methods, and it also inherits the fields and methods of class A. This feature is also called type extension. Class B can extend the class A through zero or more fields and methods of class A. Class A is called the parent of class B and class B is called the child class of A. Now suppose that class B complements class A with method m3 and field b1, then the representation of class B during running time is shown in Fig. 14.4. In addition, Fig. 14.5 shows the methods of class B on compilation time.

a1
a2
b1

Fig. 14.4 Fields of class B.

m1_A
m2_A
m3_B

Fig. 14.5 Method table of class B.

14.3.2   Method Overload

When class B extends class A, it may redefines one or more methods of class A. This characteristics is called method overload. This implies that if class A has defined a method, then in all the classes that are the direct and indirect inheritances of A may also have the method. But when the method is redefined (overload), the implementation of the method in the sub-class may be different from the original one. More specifically speaking, the method that is defined in the declaration of class A may be redefined in any sub-classes of A. These two definitions may be different. Here we use two statements to depict them: "the declaration in class A" and "definition in A". The former one indicates where the statement exists and the latter one indicates what does it depict.

Now suppose that in the example above class B redefines method m2, while the method has been defined in class A. Therefore the definition of method m2 in class A is its unique declaration, it is also its first definition. The definition in class B is its redefinition. In some languages, e.g., C++ and Java, they allow the existence of declaration of undefined methods. This kind of methods is called virtual methods. At least, there exists a class of virtual methods that is an abstract class. The practical method must be defined in the inheritance class of abstract class.

We will change the mode of naming of methods so that the names of methods not only reflect the class in which it is declared, but also reflect the class that defines it. We use three parts to name methods: method name, name of the class that declares the method, name of the class that defines the method. The underline is used to partition various parts. Therefore the method m2 that is declared in class A, and is defined in class B has the name m2_A_B.

Method overload will affect the compilation time. According to the assumption above, class B redefines method m2, while the method has been declared and defined in class A. Hence the method table of class A is shown in Fig. 14.6, and the method table of class B is shown in Fig. 14.7.

Fig. 14.6 Method table of class A.   **Fig. 14.7** Method table of class B.

Now suppose that a is an object of class A, and b is an object of class B. the method call a.m2(...) will be translated to calling method m2_A_A, and method call b.m2(...) will be translated to calling method m2_A_B. The difference between these two is explicit, as m2_A_A is declared and defined in class A, while m2_A_B is declared in class A, and is defined in class B. The translation form of m2_A_A is

   void m2_A_A (class_A*this,int i);

and the translation form of m2_A_B is:

   void m2_A_B (class_B_*this,int i);

14.3.3 Polymorphic

Polymorphic is an important characteristics that is intimately related to inheritance. In the levels of hierarchical class, the parent class may derive many child classes. It may also say that from parent class a variety of child classes may be derived that they have different behaviors but they possess the methods with the same method names. More specifically, the same method name (possesses the same operation) may operate on different method code on the class chain, and may gain different results. This kind of mechanism is called polymorphic. Fig. 14.8 shows an example of polymorphic.

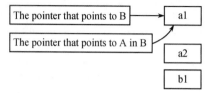

Fig. 14.8 Polymorphic.

The polymorphic also demonstrates that when class B is the sub-class of A, it is allowed that the pointer of pointer type of class B is assigned to a pointer typed variable of class A. The pointer typed variable of class A actually refers to an object of class A or an object of its extended class.

The implementation of this function requires a new operation, that is the superclass of pointers. It will transform the pointer of object of subclass B to the pointer that points to the pointer of object of parent object A. For example, suppose that the operation is used in the assignment statements:

     class B *b= ...;

     class A*a=b

Notice that the second line refers to the first line. Hence it is translated to

     class A a*= convert_ptr_to_B_to_ptr_to_A(b);

Now the routine convert_ptr_to_B_to_ptr_to_A( ) is an operation of types on compilation. Since the object of B also starts with the fields of class A, the value of pointer does not need to change, the only thing that is affected is that the same pointer now points to different object.

14.3.4 Dynamic Constraint

A link of a method call and the corresponding body code of the method is called constraint. As we have just mentioned that the same method name may play role on different objects on the class chain. That means that method calling may correspond to the method body code of different objects.

There are two modes of constraints, viz. static constraints and dynamic constraints. The static constraint indicates that on compilation time it is known already that of which object the method body code should be called. For example, if in the source program the calling method of object is m2, and from the example above we know that there are m2_A_A and m2_A_B.

Since it is static constraint, on the compilation time the calling object has been determined, the calling object is m2_A_A.

As for dynamic constraint, it indicates that the correspondence of the method name and method body code is created on running time. When the program runs, before implementing the calling of the method body, the code is run first. According to the type of object and the position of the object on the object chain it is determined that of which object the method body should be called. For example, in the example above, which one should be called, m2_A_A or m2_A_B? Therefore, dynamic constrain involves the following cases:

1) There are multiple types of A (polymorphic), at that time all the classes on the class chain are regarded to A. For example, for the example above, there are two A's. One is the "true' A; while another one is A "embedded in B". For the true A, it needs to use m2_A_A, and for the A embedded in B, it needs to use m2_A_B. Therefore in the code which the compiler generates for the method calling, needs to discern whether it is A or B based on the dynamic type message.

2) Method B needs a pointer that points to B so that it can visit all the fields in B. If there are several sub-types, then every sub-type needs such pointer. However, m2 may be dynamically pointed to a pointer call that is class A – like pointer in B. Hence we need the other operation called (re) subtyping. That operation reconstructs pointer that points to B from the pointer that points to A, e.g., the method calling p → m2(A), where p is a static pointer that points to object A. It can be translated as follows:

```
switch (Dynamic_type_of(p)) {
    case Dynamic_class_A:m2_A_A(p); break:
    case Dynamic_class_B:
        m2_A_B (convert_ptr_to_A_to_ptr__to_B(p));
        break;
}
```

Here the dynamic type message is enumeration type with two values Dynamic_class_A and Dynamic_class_B. When p is a static pointer, p → m2(A) call may be translated to

m2_A_B

Notice that, this code line is consistent with declaration void m2_A_A(class_A* this, int i) and void m2_A_B (class*this, int i).

Apart from the methods aforementioned, the following method may also be used.

In order to determine the method of which the routine is used, switch statement is one that is a function used in a small range. It may be evaluated in advance. After the evaluation, we transform the pointer that points B from A and merge it to the routine m2_A_B. Now the method may accept the pointer that points to A.

```
void m2_A_B (class_A*this_A, int i){
    class_B*this=convert_ptr_to_A_to_ptr_to_B(this_A);
    The program body of method m2_A_B,
    visits any object field x through this → x
}
```

More generally, for the translation of every method m_x_y, the first parameter points to the pointer that points to class_x. That pointer may be transformed to class_y through application of convert_ptr_to_x_to_ptr_to_y( ). If x and y are the same, then the transformation may be omitted.

The method call p → m2(A) may be translated to the following form through this modification of m2_A_B():

```
dynamic_type_of(p)==Dynamic_class_A?m2_A_A:m2_A_B(p);
```

The formula above is a computation function that makes the calling with p as the parameter, where p is a static pointer that points to the object of class A. Every time when the operation is executed on p, it is not to evaluate the function, rather it is to merge the resultant function address to the dynamic type information based on the dynamic type information of p. The type information of objects of class B is a record with three selection symbols, i.e., m1_A, m2_A and m3_B. They contain the addresses of calling routines for m1, m2, and m3. Their first parameters all are the pointers that point to the objects of class A. This kind of record that possesses the method calling routine addresses is called delivery table, and each type information of object provides a pointer that points to the delivery table. Fig. 14.9 shows the representation of objects of class B.

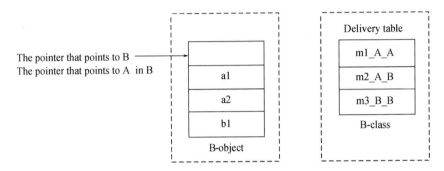

Fig. 14.9 Representation of objects of class B and the delivery table.

The type information of objects of class A is a delivery table with two fields, including the addresses of the routine m1_A_A( ) and m2_A_A( ). These two both have the pointers that point to the object of class A as their first parameter. Therefore, in the two delivery tables, selection symbol m1_A may select the routines with the same types. If m2_A is selected then the selection will come from either m1_A_A or m2_A_B. The dynamic constraint is to make the selection of m2_A_A or m2_A_B on running time.

14.3.5 Multiple Inheritances

In object-oriented programming languages, an object is allowed to have more than one parents. Correspondingly, it is also allow one object to inherit from more than one parents. This characteristics is called multiple inheritance. It is contrast to that an object can inherit from one parent only and this kind of inheritance is called single inheritance. The main object-oriented programming languages al support multiple inheritances.

For example, Suppose that object class C possesses fields c1, c2 and methods m1, m2, and object class D possesses field d1 and methods m3, m4. Object class E comes from the inheritances of class C and D, but it adds one field e1 and one method m5, and redefines methods m2, and m4, as shown in Fig. 14.10.

Different from single inheritance, multiple inheritance is unable to use the pointer of delivery table that points to all object fields to represent one object. Especially, for E, the delivery tables of E, "C in E" and "D in E" can

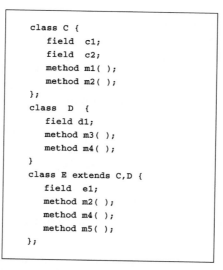

```
class C {
    field  c1;
    field  c2;
    method m1( );
    method m2( );
};
class  D  {
    field d1;
    method m3( );
    method m4( );
}
class E extends C,D {
    field  e1;
    method m2( );
    method m4( );
    method m5( );
};
```

Fig. 14.10 An example of multiple inheritances (E inherits C and D).

be combined together. However, they have to use different pointer indication. Therefore, the delivery table of E now becomes

m1_C_C

m2_C_E

m3_D_D

m4_D_E

m5_E_E

E and "C in E" in the delivery table still have the same address, and the delivery table of "D in E" is just below, as shown in Fig. 14.11.

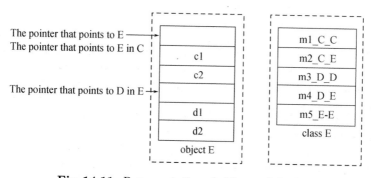

Fig. 14.11 Representation of objects of class E.

Notice the operations of supertyping and subtyping, the former one transforms child classes into parent classes, and the latter one transforms the parent classes into child classes.

supertyping

convert_ptr_to_E_to_ptr_to_C(e)=e

convert_ptr_to_ptr_to_ptr_D(e)=e+sizeof (class C)

subtyping

convert_ptr_to_C_to_ptr_to_E(d)=d-sizeof(class C)

When an object class E inherits from class C and class D, it may generate ambiguities. For example, C and D may contain methods with the same name; and class E inherits these methods. When class E uses the method, it can use only one of them but it cannot determine which one it should use. The rules of the language should make it clear when the ambiguities or conflicts happen how should compiler detect and resolve them.

14.3.6   Multiple Inheritances of Inter-reliance

Regarding multiple inheritance, there is one more situation called repeated inheritance. For example, if in the example above, both class C and class D are the extensions of class A. Then what is the meaning of "A in E"? Different languages will have different rules. But roughly speaking, there are two cases: either one object of E contains only one object of class A. This is called independent inheritance. Or one object of E contains two or more objects of class A. This is called inter-reliance inheritance. Some languages allow these two inheritances even the mixture of these two, viz. some fields may inherit relying each other, while others independently inherit.

Independent multiple inheritances may be realized using the mode specified above. The only complication is the procedure of identification. The rules of the language should be explicitly established. When the fields and/or methods come from different classes with the same name, how should they be handled must have specific regulation.

Now we discuss the issue of inheritances of inter-reliance. For these the complication is not on the choice of methods, rather, it is on the representation of the object data. Because in the example above, A has two data, so the data must be handled properly to make sure that only one data be obtained.

Suppose that both object class C and object class D were obtained from the extension of object class A. The class A has fields a1, a2, and methods m1 and m3. The object class C redefines method m1, while object class D redefines method m3, as shown in Fig. 14.12.

Thus the object data array may be put in the object according the following order. The first entry points to the pointer of delivery table of E (and C in E). Then is the fields of A; subsequently it is those fields in C that have not inherited from A; then it is the pointer that points to delivery table of "D in E" (inside the delivery table of E); then it is those fields in D that have not inherited from A. Finally it is those fields in E that have not inherited from C and D. Fig. 14.13 shows the implementation.

```
class A {
      field a1;
      field a2;
      method m1( );
      method m3( ):
};
class C  extends A {
      field c1;
      field c2;
      method m1( );
      method m2( );
};
class D extends A {
      field d1;
      method m3( );
      method m4( );
      method m5( );
};
class E extends C, D {
      field e1;
      method m2( );
      method m4( );
      method m5( );
};
```

Fig. 14.12 Multiple inheritances of inter-reliance.

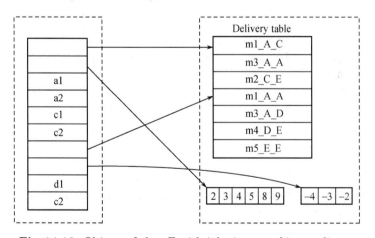

Fig. 14.13 Objects of class E with inheritances of inter-reliance.

This order is correct for the objects of class E and "C in E", but how is it for "D in E"? Whenever the compiler compiles the object class D without being aware of the situation of C and E, the compiler must determine the representation of objects of class D. Suppose that D consists of the pointer that points to its delivery table, followed by the fields of D after the delivery table. D will not be able to work as when D is in the objects of type E, the fields that it inherits from A precede the pointer of the delivery table for a distance. Moreover, the fields of D are behind the pointer of the delivery table. Therefore, when the generated code accesses the fields of objects, the compiler maybe cannot find the fields of the objects. Usually the problem will be solved by the specification symbols on running time. For the pointer that points to object itself, the specification symbol allows the methods of the object to visit the fields of the object. For every field, the specification symbol must contain the offset from the beginning of the object pointer to where the pointer is now. We enumerate the fields of the objects, hence we can use the enumeration indices as the indices of offset table. Apart from the pointer of delivery table, the representation of the object must contain the pointer that points to the offset table. As it is unknown in advance which object class will be contained in multi inheritance, hence all the objects should follow these two schemas of pointers.

Take Fig.14.13 as example, suppose that the size of all pointers and fields is 1, then from the pointer of E, the offset of field a1 is 2,the offset of a2 is 3, and then for c1 and c2, they are 4 and 5, the field e1 is 9. Therefore, we have the indices of class E

$$2 \quad 3 \quad 4 \quad 5 \quad 8 \quad 9$$

and or "D in E", the indices contain

$$-4 \quad -3 \quad -2$$

Notice that for an object of class E, both m1 and m3 have ambiguity. When an object of class E is applied, the rules of the language or the programmer should specify m1 and m3 clearly.

As multiple inheritance may cause complexity and the overhead of the method calling, so some languages (e.g., Java) do not allow to use it.

Problems

Problem 14.1   The following is the representation of class Shape given in java language:

```
abstract class shape {
    boolean lsShape(){return true;}
    boolean lsRectangle() {return false;}
    boolean lsSquare() {return false;}
    boolean double Surface Area();
}
    class Rectangle extend shape {
        double surface Area() {
        ...
        }
```

```
      boolean lsRectangle() {return true;}
}
class Square extend Rectangle {
  boolean ls Square() {return true;}
}
```

Give the method lists of Rectangle and Square.

Problem 14.2 Refer to the polymorphism given in the Fig. 14.10 and Fig. 14.11, give an object of a given class E, present the compilation code of method calls e.m1(), e.m3() and e.m4().

Problem 14.3 Refer to the multi-inheritance of mutual dependency. Suppose that the method m5 in class E is defined as follows:

```
void m5(){
    e1=d1+a1;
}
```

Suppose that all of the fields here are type int. Give the compilation code of m5 in C.

Problem 14.4 When a language supports polymorphism, sometimes it is necessary to test the real type of the current object. The method Square in exercise 1 may realize this function. Some language has built-in operator used for this operation, for example there is instance of operator in Java, the expression "A instance of C" is a Boolean expression. If the object pointed by a is an instance of C, then the value yielded is true. Design an implementation scheme for the operator.

References

[1] Pressman R S (2005) Software engineering: a practitioner's approach. McGraw-Hill International, New York.

[2] Berald E V (1993) Essays on object-oriented software enginering. Addison-Wesley, Reading.

[3] Budd T (1996) An introduction to object-oriented programming. 2nd edn. Addison-Wesley, Reading.

[4] Wirfs-Brock R, Wilkerson B, Weiner L (1990) Designing object-oriented software. Prentice-Hall, Englewood Cliffs.

Chapter 15   Compilation of Parallel Languages

Parallel changes not only happen as social trend, but also happen on science and technology.

15.1 Motivation of the Chapter

This chapter will be totally different from previous chapters as so far there is no really grand new parallel programming language to be used already. What people have are only the parallel facilities parasitically affiliated to the existing languages. The discussions before mainly focus on the issues of compilation of sequential programming languages, and in this chapter and the following chapter we will discuss the issues on the compilation of parallel languages. Is it important? The answer is definitely yes. Because in the new century, no doubt, parallel computers will dominate the whole market of computers. Then developing programs for this kind of computers will be the must if some one wants to be the programmer of the new century. Of course he/she also needs to know how his/her programs are compiled by the corresponding compilers. It is not exaggerating that parallel compilation will become the main theme in compiler field.

15.2 Rising of Parallel Computers and Parallel Computation

The explorations and pursuing of people in science and technology are always continuing without cease. It is also true in computer science and technology. Since 1991 the U.S.A. proposed the plan of developing high performance computing and communication (HPCC). Many countries around the world correspondingly invested huge fund to carry out the development of high performance super computers. So far, the United states has successfully developed the super computer with the speed up to about one thousand trillions per second. China recently has also announced that the scientists and engineers of their country have also successfully developed the super computer with the speed up to one thousand trillions per second. Other countries such as Germany, Japan, Russia, etc. also make their endeavor to develop the computers of this kind.

Since the speeds of the computers with single processor have almost reached the limitation — the information flows inside the computers of this kind cannot exceed 300 thousand kilometers per second. In order to develop high performance super computers, the only approach is depending on parallelism — to develop the cluster of high amount of computers working in parallel. For example, if each unit of the cluster computers has the speed of 10 millions per second, ten thousand units connected together and they are assembled well, then the speed of the cluster definitely will be one trillion per second. It may be said that the high performance computer is parallel in structure. Now the parallel processing modes experienced several phrases, from single instruction stream and multiple data stream (SIMD), parallel vector processors (PVP), storage-sharing symmetric multiprocessors (SSSM), massively parallel processors (MPP) to cluster. These parallel architectures may roughly be divided into five classes [1]:

1) Single instruction multiple data stream array processors: They consist of thousand-thousand processors with very simple functions. Data flow through each processor with certain modes and then are processed. SIMD type parallel computers played an important role in the stimulation development of parallel computers. However, since the development of the micro processing chips, SIMD type parallel computers used in scientific and technological computation have basically retreated from the stage after 1990s.

2) Parallel vector processors: In addition to scalar registers and scalar components, vector processor computers have also special vector registers and vector stream function components that can quickly handle vector computation.

3) Main memory-sharing processors systems: Multi-processors share one centralized memory and also possess special multi-processor synchronous communication component that can support the development of data parallelism and control parallelism. But when there are too many processors, the channels that link each processor with central memory will become bottleneck, so that they constrain the development of the computers of this kind. People then turned to investigate large-scale parallel computers.

4) Distributed memory multi-processor systems: They are computers composed of lots of nodes. Each node has its own processors and memory and Internet is the link among nodes. It mainly supports the parallel development of data, as well as control.

5) Computer cluster systems: They are the sets that consist of all computer nodes physically connected each other by high performance networks and local networks. In usual case, each computer node is a symmetric multiprocessor server, a work station (WS), or a PC. The nodes may be isomorphic, they may also be isomeric. The number of the processors generally is several

or even several tens, or hundreds, supporting the operations of control parallel and data parallel. Each node has an integral operating system. Networks and user interfaces may be taken to be control nodes and operational nodes. As cluster has superior cost/performance, flexibility and well parallel ability, it has been widely applied in various fields, apart from being taken as research topic. In the recent years, it has been much concerned.

Parallel computers provide the platforms which parallel computation relies upon. The requirements to parallel computation come from human's activities in scientific research, also come from production practice. We may classify them from different angles.

The objects which parallel computation handle may be classified. There are following classes:

1) Numerical computation: This means that the computational problems are based on operations of algebraic relations. For example, matrix operations, polynomial evaluation, solution of linear equation systems. Algorithms for solving the problems of numerical computation are called numeration algorithms.

Take the matrix computation as an example. It involves the addition of two matrices, the multiplication of two matrices with the number of columns of the first matrix being the same as the number of raws of the second matrix, the solution of the inverse of a nonsingular matrix, and so on. For matrix operations, They can be performed in parallel, because the computation of each entry is independent of that of other entries. Therefore to perform them in parallel may speed up the computation.

The computation in science and engineering, e.g., computational mechanics, computational physics, and computational chemistry, etc., generally are problems of numerical computation.

2) Non-numerical computation: Non-numerical computation is based on operations of comparison relations. This kind of computation does not aim at getting the value of algebraic relation operations, rather is the result based on comparison relation. For example, the processing of objects (symbols), such as sorting, selection, searching, matching, etc. The corresponding algorithms are called non-numerical algorithms.

Take sorting as an example, given n numbers, it is required to sort them into increasing order. Then the multiplex way sort algorithm may be used. In the intermediate course of multiplex sort (e.g., for five way sort), the sorting on each way is independent, they can be performed in parallel.

From the requirements of applications, they can be classified into three classes:

1) Computation intensive: The large-scale scientific and engineering project and numerical modeling such as the areas of construction and modeling of prediction models, project design and automation, energy exploration, medicine, military research, and fundamental theory research, etc., all propose very high requirements to computation. For example, regarding the computation of celestial body motion, as the giant number of the celestial

bodies and their extreme far distances in between (in general, it is counted with light year as the unit) the computation size is hard to imagine, it can also imagine that the parallel computation can apply upon them. Another example, in order to increase precision of the numerical weather forecast, it is estimated that based on the longitude, latitude and the atmosphere layer, at least $200 \times 100 \times 200 = 4\ 000\ 000$ grid nodes need to take into account, and then the parallel computation is performed upon these grid nodes.

2) Data intensive: numerical library, data warehouse, data mining, and visual computation, etc., all involve massive data. Data intensive processing also entails high-level parallel computation.

3) Network intensive: At first we explain the concept of network parallel computation. The combination of computer science and technology and communication technology makes computer systems developing towards networks. Various technologies make computer networks gradually to be wide areas, international, wide band, low delay, multimedia, synthetic and intelligent. Thereby, the concept of network parallel computation is also proposed. The so-called network parallel computation is based on the computation of individual computer, and plus the message passing between computers to form the computation of high-level. It sufficiently makes use of conditions provided by high speed information networks (or called information high way), implementing resource sharing, inter-communication, message passing service. Hence network intensive is the computation performed in the intensive network environment.

From the implementation of the parallel computation, they can be classified as:

1) Synchronous parallel computation: the so-called synchronous parallel computation means that two or more computation are required to begin at the same time and also finish at the same time.

2) Asynchronous computation: Asynchronous computation does not require the beginning and finish of the computation at the same times, it just require that the parallel computation keep necessary and normal communication and information interconnection.

Again, we can classify parallel computation from the memory it needs:

1) Memory-sharing parallel computation: Under the mode, several processors (each one may have or may not have own memory) share memory. In this case, the access to the shared memory may be constrained in some ways.

2) Distributed memory parallel computation: Under the mode, there is no any constraint to the access of memory. But it is likely that a data may have several copies, hence the whole amount of the memory may be reduced.

In the following, we introduce the practical applications of parallel computation in more details in order for reader to have deeper impression on the concept. Many challenging topics of application fields have proposed parallel computation. For example, in the field of magnetic record technology, the research on the computation and emulation of static magnetic and inter induction with the aim of reducing the high noise of graduated disc;

in new medicine ingredient design application, the research on the computation and emulation of developing medicine for curing cancers and AIDS through restraining the role of virus proteinase that affects human immunity. In aviation manufacture, the research on computation and emulation of hydromechanics to develop the engine of supersonic jet; in liquid faction application field, the research of modeling of bionic catalytic promoters, the research on the computation and emulation of the role of enzyme in the process of analytic-composition. In fuel burning application field, the research of new engine design aiming at the exhibition of the role of fluid mechanics through the computation of chemical dynamics. In ocean science applications, the research on the computation and modeling of the heat exchange of atmospheric flow and ocean activities with the aim at the modeling of the ocean as a whole. In ozone consumption application field, the research on the computation and emulation of chemistry and dynamics mechanism in the course of controlling the consumption of ozone. In mathematical analysis application field, the research on applying computer to form clinical images, analytical technique of computation layers, the computation and emulation of magnetic resonance imaging. In atmosphere pollution application field, the research on the emulation of atmosphere quality model, in order to control the wide spread of pollution, and the exhibition of the physical and chemistry mechanism of pollution. In protein structure design application field, the research on the computation and emulation of the three dimension structure of protein using computer imitation. In computer graphics application field, the research on computation and emulation of real-time image forming and immolation design. In cryptographic applications, the break of the encode with long digit keys, the computation and emulation for finding the two factors of a large number that is used for encoding and decoding.

15.3 Parallel Programming

In Section 15.2, we have attempted to explore the parallel computers and parallel computation from a number of aspects. One may notice from the introduction that the parallel computation can only be realized on the computers. And the computers that realize parallel computation should also be parallel type. Besides, to implement parallel computation, one must also use parallel programming language to develop the programs. This kind of language should use the explicit structure to express the parallelism. Obviously, parallel programming is far more difficult than sequential programming. The difficulty comes from the traditional way of thinking of people. No one gets used to think in parallel. Besides, it is also difficult to determine which part of the program can be explicitly expressed as parallel one. And also the size of granules of the parallelism changes as the program runs. For example, in order to sort 16 numbers, at the beginning, the 16 numbers can be divided in to 8 pairs to compare, then they can be formed into 4 groups with each group containing 4 numbers. Subsequently, the sort is performed in parallel in two groups with each containing 8 numbers. It is seen that the size of granules changes as the program proceeds. Therefore even though there is parallel language that can explicitly express the parallelism, the programmer still needs to give the rein to his/her own professional talents to really find out the parallelism, and correctly express it.

The so-called explicitly express parallelism, usually adopts two forms, viz. cobegin ... coend and parbegin ... parend. the omission between two words means that there may be arbitrary more parallel program segments. In this case, the responsibility of finding and organizing the parallelism falls on to the programmer. As for the compiler, its work is rather simple. What it needs to do is to assign the programs or program segments that need to run in parallel to different processors. It can be done with master/servant fashion. In this fashion, the parallel computer consists of one controller (process) and several subordinators (also processes). The responsibilities of the master process are to maintain the global data structure, partition the tasks and interfaces between users, including receiving tasks, initiate computation and reclaim the results of the computation. As for the responsibilities of each subordinator, they have to carry the computation assigned to them, including local initialization, computation, communications between modules and finally return the results to the master process.

The hidden parallelism of programming languages is more difficult and challenging field. In this field, the determination and partition of the tasks of parallelism fall on the compiler. Directing at the source program, the compiler has to find out which parts can be done in parallel and then organize them in this way so that the program may be run in parallel. The compiler has also to automatically generate the communication code.

In the rest of this section, we introduce five types of parallel programming. Then in Section 15.4 we concentrate on the discussion of hidden parallel programming, mainly exploring the instruction level parallelism (ILP), especially for very long instruction word (VLIW) and superscalar, how do they generate target code.

15.3.1 Shared Variables and Monitors

The simplest model of parallel programming is realized through process set that shares variables and carries communications.

A process is an abstraction of a physical processor. Each process sequentially executes program code. Conceptually, a process is a virtual processor that has processing ability and address space where the address space is used for storing data. Therefore, the address space is the abstraction of the physical storage.

A process may create many processes to get the parallelism. The address spaces of different processes at least partly overlap. Therefore, many processes may access the same variable. This is what we said of shared variable. A shared variable may be read or written by many or even all processes, and it becomes an important mechanism of communications.

In this type of programming, an important issue is to access shared variable synchronously. For synchronization, we have explained it before. But now we need to introduce the concept of exclusive synchronization. Let us observe an example first. In this example, suppose that two processes synchronously execute the following program with an attempt of increasing the value of shared variable X.

```
X: shared integer:
X:=X+2:
```

Suppose that the initial value of X is 6. Obviously, if both processes add 2 to X, the value of X will be 10. But what will really happen? If the two processes initially read 6, then they synchronously add 2 to X and wrote it back to X, then the result is 8, rather than adding 2 again to X. obviously this is not our expectation. The reason for this is that both two processes did the addition operation simultaneously. In order to avoid this situation, we adopt the measurement of mutual exclusive synchronization.

Mutual exclusive synchronization means that in any given time, there is only one process that may access the shared variable. To implement this simple synchronization, the primitive operation may use the lock variable. The lock variable possesses an undivisible operations: gain and release. The so-called undivisible means that the whole operation is an integral process: gain and release. After some process gains the lock variable, other processes cannot gain it until the process releases the lock variable. The situation is like that other processes are locked by the lock variable. When the process completes its task, it releases the lock. Thereby other processes may compete for gaining it. But next time, there will be only one process that can gain the lock and then continues its execution. Therefore, the function of the lock variable is making the constraint : In one time, there is only one process that can access the shared data structure. With the lock variable, the example above may be written as:

```
X: shared integer:
X-lock; lock;
Acquire-lock(X-lock);
X:=X+2:
Release-lock(X-lock);
```

Now, we have ensured that in any given time, there is only one process that executes the operation of adding 2 to X. But the problem with this fashion is that it is inefficient and it is prone to failure. The main problem is that, when there is somewhere the statement is not protected properly, the program will go to failure. The more structured and higher level of the solution to mutual exclusive synchronization is monitor. The monitor is similar to an abstract data type. It contains data and the operations for accessing the data. The data encapsulated by monitor are shared by multi-processes. The most crucial point is that at any time the operations of monitor is carried out in the fashion of mutual exclusion.

Apart from mutual exclusion synchronization, we also need condition synchronization. In condition synchronization, a process is locked until the condition holds. For example, until a process generates the result that meets the need of continuous computation. In the monitor, condition synchronization usually is expressed by condition variable. Condition variable is shared variable of Condition type. For Condition variables, two undivisible operations are defined: wait( ) and signal( ). For condition variable c, its operation wait(c) locks the applying processes while signal(c) wakes up one of the waiting processes. These two primitive operations can only be applied during the operation of the monitor. One of the important functions of operation wait(c) is that the process locked by it temporarily left the monitor. In this way other processes may have chance to be allowed to enter the monitor when signal(c) happens.

15.3.2   Message Passing Model

The parallel programming model with shared variables has a problem, that is, it is based on the machine with physically shared memory. This model is not suitable for multi-computer systems as multi-computer systems have no shared memory that can be used for shared memory variable. Therefore another model of parallel programming is proposed — message passing model. Message passing model is not only suitable for the multi-computer systems without shared memory but also for the computer system with shared memory.

In parallel computer systems using message passing model, the data exchange between processes is realized through message passing. This work can be done by two primitive operations send and receive. They are as follows:

```
process1
    send(process2, message);
process2
    receive(process1,message);
```

This represents that process1 sent to process2 a message. The format of the message depends on the programming system. In the low layer, message usually is a byte array. And in the high-level language, message may be similar to a structural value of a record where may have different fields of types. After process2 calls receive( ), it then stays in the locked state until the message arrives.

There are many basic models of send/receive. The problem that needs to be solved is how to establish the connection with each other between send side and receive side. Obviously, this requires that both sides know the address and communication mode of the counterpart. The more flexible mode is to let the receive side receive the message sent by any process in the program. For example, on internet, one can receive the message sent by anyone. This mode is very useful in the case that the receive side does not know in advance who will send message to it. But the disadvantage is that rubbish message may be received. The method of increasing flexibility is to use indirect process name rather than directly assigning process name. For example, the port names which many languages use may realize the function. The send side just needs to put the message to the port, and the process that issues receive statement on the port may receive the message. The match of send side and receive side is done by the system.

The another problem is when the send side can continue the sending? In asynchronous message passing, the send side and the receive side operate at different places. Hence the send side may continue after it finishes one operation. But in synchronization environment, the requirements of synchronous message passing are strict, it continues passing only when it is determined that the passing message from send side has safely arrives at the destination. This mode has its advantage in this way.

In some languages, the receive side can control the type and the length of message received. For example,

```
    receive print(size, text) such that size<4096;
# it indicates that it can only receive the print message with length
less than 4096.
```

or

```
    receive print (size, text) by size;
// this indicates that the print messages are required to be received
in increasing order.
```

What we introduced above is about receiving message by receive statement with explicit mode. Corresponding to this, there is another mode called hidden receiving mode. It creates a new thread process for every message received.

What is a thread process? Simply speaking, a thread process is a light level sub-process that possesses its own program counter and stack. We explain the concept further now. Talking about process, we know that the most basic process is sequential process, that is, the activities that happen from the execution of the program on a sequential computer. Process consists of program and data, both can reside in the memory. Process also contains program counter and stack. The program counter points to the instruction that is currently executing, while the stack records the calling order of embedded functions. We call those sub-processes that possesses program counter and stack as thread process. Fig. 15.1 shows the relation between process and thread process.

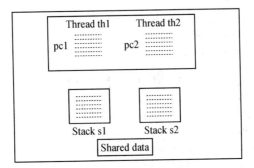

Fig. 15.1 Thread process in process.

In Fig.15.1, there are two thread processes, thread 1 and thread 2. They execute on the same code of process p. Each thread process is identified by its own program counters pc1 and pc2 and calling stacks s1 and s2. The process data area is shared by the two thread processes. Since this type of thread process was used as early as 1980s by Mesa Language. Its form was simple and this is why it is called "light level". We still keep using the name. Thread process executes in the context of process. It has no address space, but it can access to the address space where it resides. The thread process will execute a message handler that is a routine defined by programmer to handle various types of message.

Therefore, we create a thread for every message received. When the message handler is completed, it ends. These thread processes can access global variables of the process.

In hidden reception, a process can activate multi-thread processes.

Thread processes can be used for other purposes. For example, if a process needs a remote process to send requirements, it can create a thread process to send message and wait for the result. At the meantime, the original process (e.g., the main program, it can be regarded as thread too) can continue its work. Thread process has become an important concept in parallel programming system.

We stipulate here that a thread process executes in a pseudo parallel mode. The so-called pseudo parallel means that each thread process sequentially executes on the same processor as the process does. It is also called concurrent execution. Besides, the multi-processors of the multi-processor system with shared memory can be assigned to a process, and in this way, the threads can have the parallel execution in the real sense.

15.4 Object-oriented Languages

Shared variables and message passing are the low layer model of parallelism. They directly reflect the architecture of shared memory and distributed memory. Many other parallel programming languages are designed based on more abstract model. These kinds of languages include parallel functional, logical and object-oriented languages. We just introduce the situation of object-oriented languages here.

The important idea of object-oriented languages is to "encapsulate" data into objects. The data in the objects can only be accessed via the operations (or methods) defined for objects. As we introduced in Chapter 14, other important structures include classes, inheritances, and polymorphism. The biggest superiority of object oriented programming is that it can write programs with well structures. From the technology point of view, it is suitable for writing large-scale programs and may realize re-used software packages. No matter whether it is for parallel programming or for sequential programming, this superiority is extremely important. This is why people are interested in parallel object oriented languages.

Parallelism usually may be introduced from the execution of a number of objects at the same time. It can also be introduced through allowing several processes execute on the same processor at the same time. The communications between objects are expressed via operation requirements. One object may cause the operation of another object on the same processor or different processors. The operation requirements and message passing are similar, but from the semantics of language, operation requirements are more integral. Meanwhile, it may have many substitution methods. Many parallel object oriented languages allow that the internal processes of objects may consist of multiple control threads. One common mode is to use one thread as the main process of an object, and let that thread dynamically create an additional thread to handle each operation.

This manner realizes hidden reception. The synchronization of the thread processes may be represented using monitor, many parallel object oriented languages are based on monitor.

15.5 Linda Meta Array Space

The another method that gets higher abstraction level of programming model is using suitable communication data structure, to design meta space as a part of Linda system [2]. Linda is a small set of simple primitive operations. These primitive operations may be added to existing sequential language, so that the language becomes a parallel language. There are many basic languages of which the idea is applied to generate parallel languages, for example, C/Linda, Fortran/Linda and Lisp/Linda all are parallel languages.

Meta array space is a kind of shared memory that in structure is accessed in combination. Meta array space is regarded as records. No matter on which processor does a process run, the record can be accessed by all the processes in the program. From the sense, meta array space is a shared memory. However, meta array space can also be efficiently realized in distributed memory systems.

There are three operations that are defined in meta array space:

1) out: adding a meta element to the meta array space;

2) read: from the meta array space, a matched meta element is read;

3) in: from the meta array space, a matched meta element is read, meanwhile, remove it from the meta array space.

For example, in C/Linda, calling

```
out("item",5,3.12);
```

generates a meta element with three components (a string, an integer type number, a float number), and adding the meta element to meta array space. read( ) and in( ) operations are used to meta array space to search for a meta element. For each component of meta element, it is either a real parameter (through the expression of value passing) or determines a formal parameter (a variable beginning with a "?", through introduction transmission).

The "real" and "formal" parameter here are different from the "real" and "formal" which we introduce in procedural languages. For example, calling

```
float f;
in ("item",5, ?&f)
```

stipulates, in order to read a matched meta element with three components from meta array space, and the first component is a string with value "item", the second component is integer type number 5, and the third component is a float number. If from the meta array space, the found element is just ("item", 5, 3.12) that is added to meta array space with

```
out("item",5,3.12)
```

it will be read out by in operation. Then it will be removed from the meta array space. If in the meta array space, besides ("item", 5, 3.12), there are ("item", 5, 2.69) and ("item", 5, 4.65), then it indicates that in the meta array space there are many meta elements that match each other, hence from them one may arbitrarily choose one. But if there is no suitable meta element that fits the requirement, then in( ) or read( ) is locked. The calling process is hanged up, until there is another process that adds suitable meta element to the meta array space.

The primitive operation aforementioned is an atomic operation that is undivisible. That means that either it will be executed until it finishes, or it is locked and cannot run. Therefore if there are two processes that attempt to execute an operation on the same element at the same time, then there will be only one process that will succeed, and the another will fail and be locked.

In Linda, there is no the primitive operation that modifies the existing meta element in the meta array space. In this case, if one wants to modify the existing meta element, it must be that the meta element is taken from the meta array space (through read( ) or in( )), then modify it and finally add it to the meta array space. If there are two or three processes that simultaneously execute the segment of code, then there is only one process that successfully executes the in operation, the rest processes are locked until the meta element is put back to the meta array space.

Linda model is similar to shared variable model, their difference is that meta array space is of combination addressing. One meta element has no address, but read( ) and in( ) operations define the specification of meta element, the system will do the matching of meta element and the specification.

15.6 Data Parallel Languages

The another important parallel programming model is data parallelism. In this model, all the processors define the same algorithm (and code), but it executes on different part of the same data set. The data set usually is an array. In contrast with data parallelism, the another one is task parallelism where different processors execute different algorithms.

Some parallel languages realize parallelism through built-in data parallelism. For example, Fortran 90 supports matrix operations under data parallelism. For data parallel programming, the simplest explicit language structure is parallel loop statement. For example the matrix multiplication using data parallelism may be expressed as follows:

```
parfor i:=1 to N do
   parfor j:=1 to N do
      c[i,j]:=0
   for k:=1 to N do
      c[i,j]:=c[i,j]+A[i,j]*B[j,k];
      od;
   od;
od;
```

It is declared in the example that two external steps may be executed in parallel, and let compiler actually assign computation and data to different processors. The main advantage of data parallelism is that for compiler, the simple structure makes the analysis of the parallelism even easier to realize.

So far we have briefly introduce five models of parallel programming. They are shown in Fig. 15.2

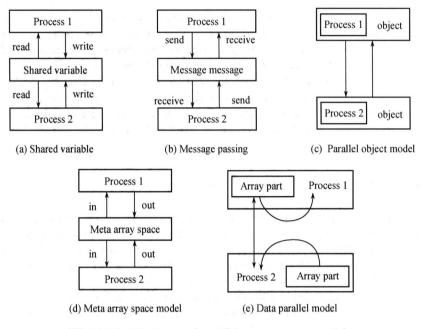

Fig. 15.2   Five types of parallel programming models.

15.7   Code Generation for Hidden Parallel Programs

In this section, we will introduce the compilation of instruction level parallelism, especially of the very long instruction word (VLIW) and super scalar structures with emphasis on the code generation of the post end of compiler. We emphasize the code generation because it is on this aspect that the compilation of instruction level parallelism is different from the usual compilation.

Here we introduce the compilation technique called region schedule technique where "region" means some parts of program that may be compiled simultaneously. The differences between different ILP techniques lie on the extents of the regions in consideration.

At first we briefly introduce the region schedule algorithm:

1) The code to be compiled is expressed in the intermediate code of the compiler. From those codes that are not yet debugged a region is selected. So-called region means a set of operations that come from more than one basic module. Usually (but not must), a region is a set of consecutive basic modules. Sometimes the transformation of the code is done before the selection of the regions. The aim is to enlarge the size of the regions. Fig. 15.3 shows an example of typical region.

2) The operations selected are set-up in the data priority diagram. Sometimes on the edges or for operations additional information that is important

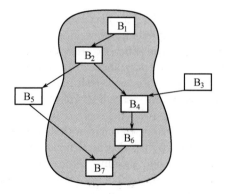

Fig. 15.3 An example of typical region — a multi-entries and multi-exits region.

to the region schedule algorithm are added. Besides, on the diagram, the special edges may be added to show prohibited or illegal or unsuitable code movement. These edges will prevent code from illegal movement, because these movements are likely to violate the flow control, and during the debugging, there is no way to make the compensation.

3) Schedule these operations.

4) Either along the direction, or on the sequential stage, carry out the necessary modifications. These modifications may adopt additional forms of operations, they adjust the illegal transformations caused by the positions of the debugging operations. For example, sometimes an operation that should go along some path of code is moved to somewhere else. In this case, the operation should be moved back to its original position. This kind of additional operations is called patching operation.

5) Return to step 1) to repeat the steps above until there is no unscheduled code.

The steps aforementioned are the kernel algorithm of region schedule. The initial trace schedule technique presented the algorithm. In the last two decades, other region schedule algorithms were also occurring. In any step, they are different from the trace schedule algorithm, i.e., different from the kernel algorithm above. Generally speaking, the main differences are on the step 1), the selection of regions, and also on the step 3), the complexity of the scanning of the schedule structure.

Although region schedule usually involves the region of loopless code, most of the algorithms handle loop in certain manners. For example, many compilers expand important loops in order to enlarge the size of regions. But even in the case, the really scheduled region is still loopless.

In order to schedule loops, a set of techniques called software stream is created. The earliest software stream technique was developed in 1970s that was developed for Fortran compiler of CDC – 6600. It was used by IBM for the compilers of high performance CPV during the same period of time. Under the software stream technology, several loop iteration operations are organized to be a new loop [3]. The new loop combines different iteration operations to form a new single loop. New loop mixs the different iteration operations to fill the "gaps" (on different processors). On the entry and exit of the new loop, similar to the entry and exit of new loop of region schedule, the operations are arranged on the new position that allows the original loop iterations to perform the operations which the single iteration of new loop cannot do.

Interestingly, some ones proposed the idea that combines the region schedule and stream. Conceptually, the idea is to make loop expansion infinitely, then using region schedule to debug until the explicitly reasonable schedule model is formed successfully. The model is used to form a new loop model, establishing software stream. The technique is called perfect stream.

In the following, we discuss three problems concerning region scheduling:

1) The main region types.

2) Once a given region type is selected, how to form the real region from the source program.

3) The construct and issue of schedule.

15.7.1   Types of Regions

Most of the region schedule algorithms differ on the shape definition. Usually, these algorithms are named based on the shapes of the regions. Therefore, we first introduce the most commonly used regions.

1) The basic blocks. The basic block is the degenerate form of the region. It generally consists of a segment of sequential statements with only one entry and one exit.

2) The track. Track is another type of regions. The tracks constitute the basic block. A track is a linear path of the program code.

Suppose that B_0, B_1, ..., B_n are basic blocks of the program, and their order is given. A track is formed from the operations of these basic blocks. And it has the following properties:

(1) Every basic block is the predecessor of the following block in the sequence. That is, for k=0, ... n−1, the descendant of B_k is B_{k+1}, or we say that B_k branches to B_{k+1}.

(2) The code of track does not contain loop, except that the whole region is a part of some extended loop extension. viz. for any i and j, there exists no the path $B_j \rightarrow B_i \rightarrow B_j$. But track does not prohibit the forward branch in the region, or the flow away from the region and then return to the region again later.

In the Fig. 15.3, B_1, B_2, B_3, B_4, B_5, B_6, B_7 are basic blocks, where B_1 $\rightarrow B_2 \rightarrow B_4 \rightarrow B_6 \rightarrow B_7$ is a track that crosses the region (the shade part). Similarly, $B_1 \rightarrow B_2 \rightarrow B_5 \rightarrow B_7$ and $B_3 \rightarrow B_4 \rightarrow B_6 \rightarrow B_7$ are also tracks.

(3) Super blocks. A super block actually is also a track but it contains

some constraints. Apart from the branch that goes to the first block, the braches that go to other blocks are not allowed. Therefore, a super block consists of the operations of the basic block series B_0, B_1, ..., B_n, and it possesses the same properties as the track does. The properties (1) and (2) above hold for super blocks. We have:

- Each basic block is the predecessor of the following block in the basic block series. For each $K=0, 1, ..., n-1$, B_{k+1} follows B_k or B_k branches to B_{k+1}.
- Super block does not have loop, except that the whole region is the part of some of the extended loop activities, viz., for any i and j, there exists no path $B_j \rightarrow B_i \rightarrow B_j$. But for super block, it has one more property:
- In the region, apart from B_0, there is no branch that switches to a block of the region.

In the references on super block regions, the illegal branches are called side doors.

(4) Tree regions: A tree region is a tree shape region in the control stream of the program, and it contains a basic block. A tree shape region consists of the operations of the series of basic blocks B_0, B_1, ..., B_n, and it has the following properties:

- Apart from B_0, each block has just a predecessor. That is, the predecessor of B_j is the basic block B_i, where i<j. B_i is also the parent node of B_j. This implies that a super block will be formed through arbitrary path of the tree region, i.e., a track without side door entry.
- For any j and i, there exits no $B_j \rightarrow B_i \rightarrow B_j$, except for B_0. It contains no loop, except that the whole region is a part of the loop that surrounds it.

As super block, the constraints of not allowing side doors may be removed using tail copy and other expansion techniques. If a region has only one control flow, this case is called linear region. In this sense, track and super block are linear regions while tree region is non-linear region.

(5) Other region. Besides the regions described above, some experts also proposed other regions, e.g., in Fig. 15.3, the track2 is a non-linear region with one entry. It is a bit like the tree region, but there is no constraint of side door. But its implementation is very difficult. The large scale module is also a region module. It is a region of single entry and multiple exits, and it has internal control flow. It is a variant of super block, and contains some prediction operation. It can be scheduled as a module.

15.7.2 Formation of Regions

Once the shape of region is determined, two problems occur. One is how to partition the program to be some regions with specific shapes; and second is how to construct the schedule of them. The first problem is called the formation of the region, and the second is called the construction of the schedule.

We discuss the first one. In order to form the region, the whole control stream of a program must be divided into some blocks that can be provided to schedule construction program to consume and to manage with clear definition. Hence, the formation of regions and the efficiency of schedule construction combination are crucial to the performance. These regions that are wisely selected will cover the context free grammar of the program with such a manner that the execution of the program follows the path that scheduled code predicted. Therefore, the important thing is to make sure that schedule construction combination knows what it needs to do.

The formation of the region aims at finding out the parts of program that can be executed simultaneously, and they are combined to form the same region. If two parts of program can be executed together, but in different regions, it will not be good for instruction schedule. Therefore the designers of the formation of the regions are confronted with three problems: (1) which programs may be executed frequently? (2) how do you know that two programs may be executed together? (3) How are the shape of the region and the two problems above interacted each other?

For the traditional answers to the first two problems, the images are used to measure or use the heuristic search to estimate the execution frequency of each program. Both heuristic search method and profile-based method assign execution frequency to such parts of programs as the nodes and edges of context-free grammar. If the heuristic search method is used, then it should pay more attention on the method of collecting statistic numbers, and how to manage these numbers when the program modified by different parts of the compiler. On the collection of profile types and the techniques of collecting statistic numbers, many creations have been done in the last decade.

Once a set of statistic numbers is available, the rest problem is how to use them to form the regions.

The formation of the regions usually involves the selection of the good regions according to the existing context-free grammars. It also contains the copies of some parts of the context-free grammars to improve the quality of the regions. The results of copies definitely will affect the length of the program. Hence many different algorithms and heuristic search methods are applied to make the tradeoff. The formation of the regions also needs the effective regions which the generation of schedule construction programs may use, this may require additional bookkeeping and program transformation.

The formation of regions is related to the context-free grammar of programs. And only from the height of the context-free grammar, can the concept of region be formalized, so that the formation of regions be clarified.

Reviewing the definition of context-free grammar (CFG) which we discussed before, and the language accepted by a context-free grammar L(G). We have pointed out that most of the parts of all programming languages belong to context-free grammars. Therefore, most of the programs developed from these languages are context-free languages.

For the convenience of the following description, we introduce two concepts:

Definition 15.1 Vertical compilation [4]. Given a program, the procedure of such compilation is called vertical compilation that starts with the program itself, and using reduction method, or bottom-up analysis, finally the program is reduced to the start symbol or statement symbol.

Definition 15.2 Horizontal compilation. Given a program, the procedure of such compilation is called horizontal compilation that the execution of the program is the gradual implementation of the nodes — terminal strings in the derivation diagram of context-free grammars from left to right.

In order to run the programs in parallel, it needs to partition the programs that have been horizontally compiled into regions, then by region schedule algorithm, the parallel execution is realized. The formation of the regions is related to both horizontal compilation and vertical compilation.

Definition 15.3 In the context-free grammar CFG G, for two nonterminals A and B, we say that $A \geqslant B$ if B can occur at the right hand side of the production with A as its left hand side.

Obviously, relation $\geqslant$ is transitive as if $A \geqslant B$ and $B \geqslant C$, then we must have $A \geqslant C$. Because from the derivative relation of productions, we may know that C occurs at the right hand side of the production that has A as the left hand side. Therefore for any nonterminal A in G, we all have $S \geqslant A$ where S is the start symbol of G. Otherwise A is an unreachable nonterminal in G, and it should be deleted as it has no any meaning in G. But in general, the set of nonterminals is of partial order, rather than of total order.

Lemma Every context-free grammar is equivalent to a Greibach normal form of grammar, viz., its all productions have the form
$$A \to a\ \alpha,$$
where a is a terminal and α is a nonterminal string (it may be empty).

Theorem 15.1 In the grammar with Greibach normal form, if in the production $A \to b\ \alpha$, α contains nonterminals A and B but they have no $\geqslant$ relation, then they each constitutes different regions that are disjoint.

Proof Suppose that starting from start symbol S, and the production with S as the left part is $S \to a\alpha$. Then in α, the first nonterminal is B, apart from the first terminal. We continue the derivation. We must get a string with terminals and nonterminals as its elements. Among them there are those nonterminals that they have no relation $\geqslant$. Therefore, there is no conflict happening. They form different regions.

Theorem 15.2 In a context-free grammar, if in some production, there is a nonterminal that occurs twice or more at the right hand side, then each of them form a region.

Example suppose that context-free grammar G has the following set of productions:

$$S \rightarrow dBA | (CBA | aA | CcA | aB | CcB | a\text{---}CC$$
$$T \rightarrow aB | cCB | a | Cc$$
$$A \rightarrow +S$$
$$B \rightarrow *T$$
$$C \rightarrow aBAD | CBAD | aAD | cACD | aBD | cDC | aD$$
$$D \rightarrow)$$

where each production can be numbered and the nonterminals are numbered in the order of their occurrences. According to the relation $\geqslant$, those nonterminals that have no the relation may form different regions, as shown in Fig. 15.4.

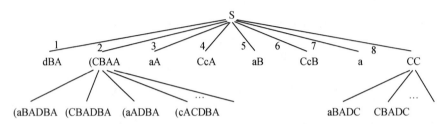

Fig. 15.4   A derivation tree of Greibach normal form.

Theorem 15.3 In a conditional statement, the two branches may form the regions that are able to compile in parallel, then when it runs, it will be decided which branch will be executed according to the condition.

Proof   When the compilation proceeds, both two branches need to be compiled so that the program can decide which branch is executed. While in the phase of compilation the compilation of two (even more) branches do not cause conflict. Even in the phase of running, it is still feasible that let two branches run in parallel first, then the condition is decided to let one run.

For example, for mergesort, we have the program flow stream shown in Fig. 15.5 in which the left and right parts enclosed by dash lines form parallelable compilation regions. After compilation, the execution of the program may be started. It is shown in Figs 15.6 and 15.7.

Theorem 15.4 In Shellsort, the comparisons of different increments can be compiled in parallel as disjoint regions.

Proof   In the shellsort with increments, say 8, 4, 2, and 1, if the number of elements to be sorted is big, then when it starts, 1 and 9, 17 and 25, 33 and 41, ... may be compared. These comparisons obviously may be proceeded in parallel, both in compilation and in execution. Similarly, then the increment

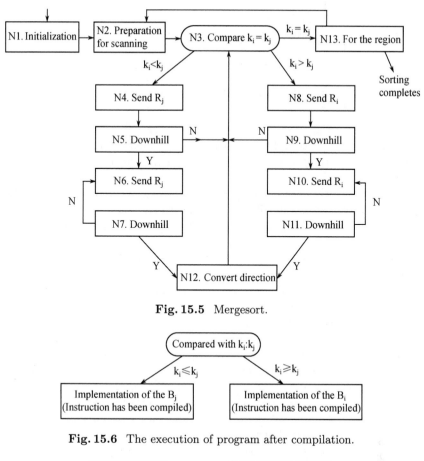

Fig. 15.5 Mergesort.

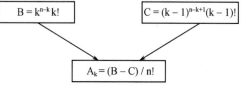

Fig. 15.6 The execution of program after compilation.

$$B = k^{n-k}k!$$

$$C = (k-1)^{n-k+1}(k-1)!$$

$$A_k = (B-C)/n!$$

Fig. 15.7 The execution of program that executes in parallel first then in sequential.

become 4, 1 and 5, 9 and 13, ... may be handled in parallel again. The same holds for increments 2 and 1.

Theorem 15.5 In the evaluation of expressions (either numerical or propositional), if the expression belongs to two disjoint sub-expressions that have no value exchange then they can be regarded as region that can be compiled in parallel.

For example, in $A_k = (k^{n-k}k!) - (k-1)^{n+k-1}(k-1)!/n!$, $k^{n-k}k!$ and

$(k-1)^{n+k-1}(k-!)!$ may be compiled in parallel. Then it executes in such a way that two sub-expressions run in parallel, then it runs sequentially.

15.7.3 Schedule Algorithms for Regions

The research on region schedule algorithms is naturally important after the formation of the regions. The problem is also called schedule construction. The goal of the formation of region is to efficiently implement the compilation and execution.

Instruction level parallel (ILP) computer is the main stream of parallel microprocessors, while explicitly parallel instruction computer (EPIC) is its variant. Therefore we emphatically consider the region schedule algorithms of ILP. According to the schedule system, the region schedule may be divided into loop schedule and operation schedule; according to the style of search, it can be classified to greedy schedule and backtrack schedule; according to flow analysis, it can be classified as linear schedule and graphic schedule.

1) Loop schedule and operational schedule

This kind of schedule aims at minimizing a target function, meanwhile to distribute operations to the loop "sink". Hence, the whole schedule strategy contains loop schedule and operational schedule. Loop schedule repeatedly selects operations from the region to fill the loop. Only when all the operations of current loop have been used up then the next loop is entered.

Operational schedule repeatedly selects the operations of a region and put them into earliest loop that the relevance and target resource allow. Operation schedule techniques differ as the selection methods differ. It may be led by some heuristic search or priority schedule. Operation schedule is more powerful than loop schedule theoretically.But its implementation is more complicated.

2) Linear schedule and graphic schedule

For a region that consists of n operations, the complexity of the linear schedule is $O(n)$. This is the main advantage of the linear schedule. Most of the linear schedule techniques use the quickest possible schedule or suspends the schedule as late as possible. The differences of these two are that operations are put in the earliest (or latest) possible loop that the resource and data constraint allow.

The graphic schedule techniques, i.e., the list schedule, repeatedly selects an operation from the operations ready to be scheduled in the data ready queue. The premise of an operation to be ready is that in the ready queue all its predecessors are scheduled. Once the operation is scheduled, it then is removed from the data ready queue, and inserts its descendant that becomes ready. These iterations continue until all the operations in the region are scheduled.

3) Greedy schedule and backtrack schedule

In the greedy schedule, the candidate of schedule is selected greedily from data ready queue. The backtrack schedule allows to backtrack once the schedule failed, then it searches for suitable candidate again.

As the parallel computers appear massively, the parallel compilation techniques increasingly become the hot topic of the computer technology. Here the issues that involve regions and schedule have important position in parallel compilation technology.

Problems

Problem 15.1 In sequential programming languages, which instructions may be considered to be able to compile parallel or to execute parallel?

Problem 15.2 Determine whether the following program

```
for i:=1 to 1000 do
  for j:=1 to 1000 do
    A[i,j]:=A[i,j] +1
  od;
od;
```

can be compiled and executed in parallel?

Problem 15.3 Among the sorting algorithm which you know, which ones you consider may be compiled in parallel?

Problem 15.4 Linda meta space can be used to simulate message passing and variable sharing. Specify how to use Linda to model sending/receiving of message, and read/write share variables.

References

[1] IEEE Proceedings of the IEEE (2001) Special issue on Microprocessor Architecture & Compiler Technology.

[2] Grune D, Henrie Bal, Ceriel J et al (2001) Modern compiler design. Pearson Prentice Education, Singapore.

[3] Su Y L (2005) The intelligenization of synchronization languages in embedded systems. The Journal of Guangxi Academy of Science 21(4): 236–238.

[4] Su Y L (2004) On the issues about region schedule in parallel compilation. The Journal of Guangxi Academy of Science 20(4): 220–224.

Chapter 16   Compilation of Grid Computing

Grid computing puts every thing done in and between high performance, clusters, peer computers and internet computing sites under a definite big umbrella.

Ian Foster

16.1   Motivation of the Chapter

The rising of the grid computing, no doubt, is a new thing that happened in the end of last century and the beginning of this century. It definitely brought lots of new things with it. If it has become a reality and gradually occupies certain amount of market, everything involved should be taken into account, especially it is not mature yet. For those problems that are still open, we should also make our effort to solve them, to make our contribution to the solutions. This chapter only presents a brief introduction to grid computing. We believe that more knowledge on it will be added as the time goes, and the contents on the topic will be more bountiful in the future.

16.2   Rising of Grid Computing and Intent

In early 1990s, in academic community, there were many research projects. All these projects were on distributed computing. Among them, there was a key research field in which a distributed high performance computer system was developed so that it behaves like a large-scale computer. In 1995, on the IEEE/ACM supercomputing conference held in San Diego, California, 17 sites of high-end resource were linked with 11 high-speed networks, thus demonstrating an attempt of establishing a super "meta computer." This demonstration was called I-Way (represented Internet). It was led by the Alanne laboratory of American Energy Ministry and Ian Foster of Chicago University [1]. Later in this network, 60 different applications were developed. Many scholars from science and engineering community took part in the effort. Due to the teams that created various software so that all computing resources worked together, hence in the device that the demonstration showed covered the exploration of many concepts of early stage of grid computing.

The success of I-Way urged the DARPA (The Administration of American ministry, high-level research project management) to invest fund in the project that creates fundamental tools for distributed computing. This research project was collaboratively led by Ian Foster of Alanne Laboratory and Carl Kesselman of University fo California. It was named Globus. This project team created a set of tools that became the basis of the grid computing research activity for academic research field. On the supercomputing conference held in 1997, the running software from about 80 sites around the world based on Globus tool kit was linked together.

These efforts were called grid computing as it is similar to the electric grid. The functions of the grid computing is like the function of electric grid that it provides the electricity to billions of appliances so that they all have the power. The grid computing makes any one at any time to use the tremendous computing ability with truly transparent manner.

In the academic field, the most concerned problem is still on the establishment of the effective grid frame so that the distributed high performance computing may play role. Since in the same period of time, the Internet developed quickly, the ability of personal computers was increasingly enhanced, scientists made many attempts to establish powerful distributed computing system through the networking of personal computers. In 1997, the Entropia network was established to equip the world wide idle computers to solve the scientific problems interested. Subsequently Entropia accumulated up to 30,000 sets of computers with the trigger speed of 10^{10} per second. A grand new philanthropic computer field occurs, in which users volunteered to provide their computers for use of the analysis of patients reaction to chemistry, also use for the discovery of the medicine for AIDS and other therapeutics.

Although the projects aforementioned have not yet got the investment from any companies and become real product, they have received attention from more multimedia than early stage in any other science research plans. Since the end of 2000, the papers on grid computing were transferred from commercial journals to popular papers and journals. The main news papers around the world all report the development in the field.

Nowadays, the big companies like IBM, SUN Microsystem,Intel, HP, and the smaller companies like Platform Computing, AVaki, Entropia, Datasynapse, United Device, etc., all invest more fund to the research on grid computing. But their focus is rather on the applications to commerce than to scientific research.

Now we may consider the intent of the grid computing. The common definition of grid computing is:

- The flexible, safe and harmonic resource sharing in the individual, research department and resource dynamic set.
- The transparent, safe and harmonic resource sharing, and the cooperation in various sites.

- The organizations that are able to form virtual cooperation. They work together in an open and hyterogeneus server environment to share applications and data, so that they can solve common problems.
- That are able to accumulate great amount of computing resources, these computing resources physically separate in order to solve large-scale problems and workload, just like that all servers and resources may be put together in a site.
- The fundamental structure of hardware and software, it provides reliable, consistent, ubiquitous and cheap accesses to computing resources.
- Network provides us with information, while grid allows us to handle them.
- The definitions listed above each has its unique features, and also grasps some characteristics of the grid computing. But we tend to use the following definition that defines grid wider and so it may better describe grid system.

Definition   Grid computing. In the situation that does not exist central position, central control, and ubiquitous and existing trust relation each virtual organization structure in the procedure of pursuing their common target, the set of resources, including hardware and software that can organize the organization structures to share the resources, is called grid computing.

The virtual organization in the definition involves very wide extent. It ranges from small companies, till the big companies spread around the world, with lots of people coming from different structures. The size of virtual organization may be either big or small, either static or dynamic. Someone can also be temporarily set up for special purpose. When the goal is attained, It is dismissed.

Some of the examples of virtual organizations are:
- The accountant department of a company.
- The competition score statistic department of South Africa Soccer games.
- The urgently organized response team for handling petro leaking in Mexico Bay.

A resource is an entity for share, it may be computing-type, e.g., personal digital assistants, laptop computers, desk computers, workstations, servers, clusters, and supercomputers; it may also be storage-type, e.g., the hard disc drivers, cheap redundant array of magnetic disc, and double word storage device. The sensors are another type of resources, band width is also a kind of resource used for various activities of the virtual organization structures.

That there is no central position and central control implies that there is no need for setting the specific central position for the management of grid resource. Finally, the crucial point that needs to be noted is that in network environment, resources do not need to know the information each other, they do not need to have predefined security relation.

16.3 Grid Computing Model

Grid is a lattice of a × b, on every grid (i, j) ($1 \leqslant i \leqslant a$, $1 \leqslant j \leqslant b$) there is a processor, the edge corresponds to the bidirectional communication link. The processor on the grid is identified by binary array (i, j) (i.e., its position in the grid). Since each processor has a local memory unit RAM, hence it can execute basic operations such as addition, subtract, multiplication, comparison, local storage access, etc. in any time unit. Suppose that the computations are simultaneous, i.e., there exists a global clock, in the time of the clock, every processor may complete each predictable task in the unit time of the clock. For convenience, we only consider square grid, that is, we have a=b. Fig. 16.1 (a) presents a $\sqrt{p} \times \sqrt{p}$ network. Fig. 16.1 (b) presents a linear array.

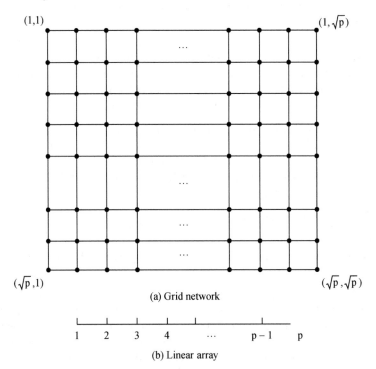

(a) Grid network

(b) Linear array

Fig. 16.1 Grid network and linear array that link computers.

Here we assume that the links between processors are bidirectional. But in linear array, processor 1 has no left adjacent while processor p has no right adjacent. For other processor i, $i - 1$ is its left adjacent while i+1 is its right adjacent. $\sqrt{p} \times \sqrt{p}$ network has several sub graphs, each sub graph contains a linear array with $\sqrt{p}$ processors.

The communication between processors is done under the help of communication links. Any two processors that have links to connect can communicate each other in one unit time. If there is no link between two processors, then their communications need to rely on the path that connects them. The time that the communications between the two processors take would depend on the length of the path (at least it is right for small amount of information.) Suppose that in unit time, one processor may execute a local computation, or at most communicate with four adjacent.

In this grid network, the processors that the first coordinates are equal form a row of the processor grid network, the processors that the second coordinates are equal form a column of the grid network. If each row or each column consists of $\sqrt{p}$ processors, this forms a linear array. Usually, the grid network algorithm consists of the steps on rows or columns.

16.3.1 Group Routing

In a fixed grid connection, the single step communication between processors may be regarded as group routing. Every processor in the network has a group message that needs to send to some processor. All the group messages have to be sent to the correct address at the speed as fast as possible. And on arbitrary link and on some time period at most only one package can pass through. As the band width of any communication channel is limited, hence it is necessary to have the constraint, i.e., at any time period, only one package may pass through channel. If there is two or more packages that arrive at processor V at the same time, and they all need to use the same link to leave V, then in the next unit time, only one package can be sent, other packages have to wait for transmission on the queue of V. In the process of the schedule of these packages, priority scheme may be used. The priority scheme includes furthest destination first (i.e., the package with furthest destination is sent first), furthest source first (the package with furthest source is sent first), and FIFO (first-in-first-out).

Partially Permutation Routing (PRT) is the special case in routing problem. In partially permutation routing, every processor at most contains a group source address, also at most contains a group destination address. In exclusively read and exclusively write parallel random access machine (EREW PRAM), partially permutation routing may execute in a synchronous write step However, in any fixed grid network connection, partially permutation routing may send and receive through communication edges. Usually, it is a sophisticated task. Besides, In any fixed grid network connection, groups enter processor according to some order, and it is hoped that they leave according to some assigned order. However, sorting the rearranged data may involve multiple partially permutation routing. Therefore, in fixed grid network connection any nontrivial algorithm needs partially permutation routing. This is one of the main differences between grid algorithm and parallel random access machine algorithm.

The evaluation of partially permutation routing algorithm usually is done according to the length of running time and the length of the queue. Running time means from begin of running until the time when the last package arrives at the destination. The length of the queue means that during the routing the maximum number of packages that any processor must store. The lower bound of the queue is the largest number of packages to or from any node. Suppose that in the package, it not only contains message (from a processor to another processor), but also contains the source and the destination addresses of the message. Package routing algorithm is determined by the path that every package passes through and the priority scheme. The time that any package takes to arrive the destination depends on the distance from source address to the address of destination, and the waiting time (called delay) of the package in the queue.

Example 16.1   Consider packages a, b, c, and d, as shown in Fig. 16.2(a), their destination is shown in Fig. 16.2(g). Suppose that the FIFO scheme is adopted. When competition takes place, it can be removed with any mode. Besides, the route that every package will pass through is decided by the routing algorithm and it will be the shortest route. When t=1, every package advances one edge towards the destination. Hence packages a and b will arrive at the same node. When t=2, one of a and b will need to line the queue because they arrive at the same position at the same time, so the competition takes place. The competition may be resolved with any mode.

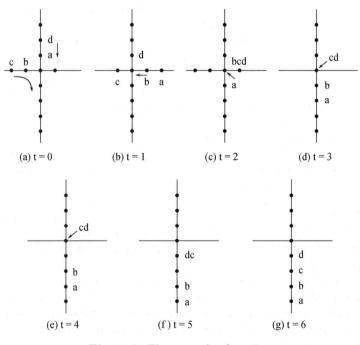

Fig. 16.2   The example of routing.

Suppose that a wins Meanwhile, when t=2, package c and d also advanced one edge towards the destination, they will be together with b (as shown in Fig. 16.3). When t=3, as b has higher priority than c and d, so b goes first. When t=4, packages c and d compete again for advancement. Since they have the same priority, the resolution is arbitrary. Suppose that d is the winner. Then package c will take 2 more steps or delay two more steps to get the destination. Finally each package arrives at the destination.

The moving distance of c is 4, and it lined to queue twice (competed with b and d respectively), so it delayed 2, and the total consuming time is 6. Suppose that the different priority scheme is used, what is the result? If the furthest destination first scheme is adopted, then when t=4, the package c will have highest priority, so it will be handled in advance. In this case, its running time is 5.

16.3.2 Routing in Linear Array

In linear array, as the connection is bidirectional, the processors can send or receive message from each adjacent. This implies that, if there is a package that moves from left to right, and there is another package that moves from right to left, then these two stream will not have competition. We will prove that the partially permutation routing in linear array can complete in $p-1$ or even less steps. It is worth noticing that the worst case needs $p-1$ steps. For example, if a package wanted to pass through from processor 1 to p.

Example 16.2 In Fig. 16.3, the circles represent the packages moving from left to right, the clicks represent the packages moving from right to left. For example, packages a and b move through the same edge in reverse directions at the same time. Since the edge is bidirectional, there is no competition. They can go ahead at any time without any impediment. A package that is from node 1, and destination is p must pass through $p-1$ edges. Hence it takes at least $p-1$ steps.

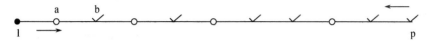

Fig. 16.3 Packages moving to right from left and moving to left from right are independent.

Lemma 16.1 Suppose that in each source address there is only one package. In a linear array with p processors, assume that the destinations are arbitrary. Without losing generality, we now only consider the case of moving from left to right. If package q has the source at processor i and it wants to get to processor j. Then it will need to move $j-i$ to get the destination.

Notice that one package can only passes one edge at a time. Since q does not meet any package on the way, it will not be delayed. For all the packages the routing selection has maximum time $p-1$. Meanwhile, the length of queue for the algorithm is the largest number of packages going to any node.

Lemma 16.2 In the linear array of p processors, any processor i ($i=1$, $2, \ldots, p$) initially has k_i packages and they meet $\sum_{i=1}^{p} k_i = p$. That means that each processor is exactly the destination of a package. If the priority scheme of furthest destination first is adopted, then the time taken by package with source processor i will not exceed the distance that the package moves to the destination. In other words, if the package moves from left to right, the consuming time will not exceed $p-i$; if it moves to left from right, the time is less than $i-1$.

Proof Suppose that package q comes from processor i, and its destination is q. Without losing generality, suppose that the package moves from left to right, and suppose that each package has selected the shortest path from source address to destination address. If package q generates delay, it can only be generated by that the number of destination is greater than j. And it is also caused by that a package has its source at the left of i. Suppose that the numbers of such packages at processors $1, 2, \ldots, j$ are $k_1, k_2, \ldots, k_{j-1}$ (initially), notice that $\sum_{i=1}^{j-1} k_i \leqslant p-j$.

Suppose that m satisfies $m \leqslant m' \leqslant j-1$, k_{m-1} and $k_m \leqslant 1$, the sequence $k_m, k_{m-1}, \ldots, k_{j-1}$ is called free sequence. The package in free sequence cannot generate delay due to other distributions, because according to the priority rule, the package at the left has higher priority than the package at the right to be selected.

Moreover, in every step, at least one package joins the free sequence. Fig. 16.4 shows the example. the numbers represent the number of packages on the nodes. For example, when $t = 0$, on node i there are 3 packages. At the time, 0, 1, 0, 1, 1 is a free sequence. Notice that, as time changes, the number of packages in the sequence will change too. For example, when $t = 1$, a package joins the sequence; when $t = 2$, 4 packages join the sequences again.

Therefore, after $p-j$ steps, all the packages that may cause package q delayed are in the free sequence. Package q needs at most $j-i$ steps to get destination (see Fig. 16.4). The moving of package from right to left is similar.

Fig. 16.4 Demonstration of Lemma 16.2.

Lemma 16.3 In the linear array of p processors, suppose that the packages sent from any processor are more than one, and the number of receiving packages is more than one too. From processors $1, 2, \ldots, j$ the number of sending packages are no more than $j+f(p)$ (for any j, and f is a selected function). Then in the priority scheme of furthest destination first, the routing selection for these packages can be resolved in p+f(p) steps.

Proof   Suppose that q is a package that has source i and destination j (j is located at the right of i). q can be delayed by at most i+f(p) packages because these packages have their source addresses 1, 2, ..., i, and they have higher priority than q. If each package makes q delayed at most once, that means that the package with higher priority cause q delayed. Then the package will not make q delayed again. Then the delay of q will be equal to or less than i+f(p). Since q only needs j−i steps to get to destination, the total time that q takes is less than j = f(p). In summary, for all the packages, the maximum consuming time is p+f(p).

Example 16.3   Fig. 16.5 demonstrates the proof of Lemma 16.3. In this example, there are 8 packages a, b, c, d, e, f, g, h. Suppose that g is the package that is most concerned. Package g can only be delayed by a, b, c, d, e, f, h. When t=9, package g arrives at its destination. It passed the distance of 2, and the dalay is 7. In this graph, the packages that passed node j are not shown.

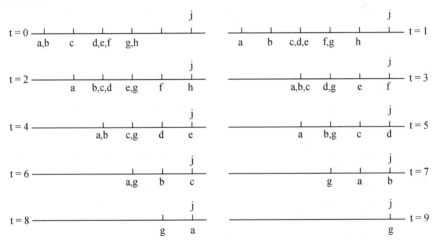

Fig. 16.5   The illustration of Lemma 16.3.

16.4 Compilation of Grid Computing

So far there is no any formal programming language used for grid computing. Therefore we have no way to explore the compilation of this kind of language. However, there are many researches already on the compilations of grid computing programs or compilation between procedures [2]. They have not put into market, especially there is very few works that had been done in the compilation between documents. One of the reasons is that the compilation of the whole programs must make the compilation very complicate, even though there were some researches who stated that it is very beneficial to the correctness and performance of programs. But users usually do not want to have long time compilation.

However, in the future, the tasks of compilation is so heavy and tough. So the compilation between procedures becomes a must rather than a luxurious thing, especially for the compilation of grid computing on distributed heterogeneous computers.

For the compilation of cross procedures, the problems that need to be solved are as follows:

1) The compilation of cross procedures that supports grid application system frame must be able to integrate the whole application performance evaluation program and mapping program. Therefore, in order to construct the execution model of the whole program, a cross compilation of interprocedure is very necessary.

2) The management of binary position (i, j is also the necessary function of the program development time) In order to avoid the expensive phase of partitioning binary components, it is important to connect the parts of programs in shared component based on remote computing resources. These programs have partly stored in the remote computing resources in advance. The optimization of the contingencies is the crucial function of interprocedure cross compilation.

3) In order to avoid the time of compilation being too long, the recompilation of the document in program should be managed. Although there are some researches in the analysis of recompilation, they are not available in market yet.

4) If one wants to put the previous running time analysis into the decision making of the currently running compilation, then the management of recompilation is more complicated. In order to manage this process, the compilation environment should be complicated enough too.

5) Some interprocedure cross compilation analysis needs to be completed in linking time and running time. How to effectively manage the process is still an open problem.

The research on compilers has generated two general techniques for handling the long latency in storage and communications on parallel computers: one is hidden latency, it overlaps the data communication and computing. The another is the reduction of the latency that is used for reorganizing program so that the data in local storage can be more effectively reused. In practice, these two techniques are very effective.

In the compilers used in grid computing, the implementation of these two techniques is very sophisticate, and the hidden latency is especially problematic, because the latency in grid computing is big and changing. Therefore, if we want to be able to determine how to extract the values of the variables, then it will need to spend more time in the estimation of running time and communication delay. This also means that the latency tolerant algorithm is more important.

Running time compilation

The kernel of the compilation of grid computing is its parallel implementation. The important problem that is related to this is the scheme of automatic load balance in the grid. Therefore, there is need for some necessary information, e.g., the upper bound of loops and the sizes of arrays. However for many applications, these messages are unknown before running. The lack of this information is also difficult for the definitions of problems in irregular grid. It makes the implementation of parallelism very difficult even on homogenous parallel computers.

The running time compilation has many forms. After the scalar data have been put into memory, it may be as simple as reconsideration of decision, but it can also be as complicated as planning communication in irregular computation. Because before the crucial data structures are defined, the fundamental grid and position of the computing are unknown.

For the grid, it is necessary to reconfigure the whole program and the implementation of load balance when it is running, this is possibly an extremely time-consuming process. Therefore it needs to have a strategy that may minimize the overhead of these steps. In general, it is necessary to carry out the research on how to minimize the overhead with running time being emphasis and complicated decision factor because more and more the cases in which the requirements will be met in the future.

In order to resolve the problem aforementioned, some designed the method of running time compilation reviewer/executer. In this method, the compilation program partitions the key computing part into two parts: one is the reviewer, and another one is the executer. The former one can only be executed once, after the running time data is allowed to use to establish the plan that will be effectively executed on parallel computer. And the later one executer is called in the execution of every iteration of the computing, and the execution is to implement the plan defined by reviewer.

The idea of the scheme is to amortize the computing cost of running times in many time steps of complicated computing. In the upper costs of loops are unknown, the reviewer may partition the loop into some small loops. Once the upper bounds are known, they may match the power of target machine, meanwhile executer only needs to execute correct computation on the small loops in each machine. The reviewer must follow the rules of making the balance in complicated and irregular problems. The tasks of reviewer and executer are very complicated.

Running time compilation is a powerful tool for tailoring the programs so that they are suitable for execution on any parallel computers. Especially it is structured crucial for distributed heterogeneous structured computers.

For grid computing, the compiler and parallelization tools reside on the middle level of the matrix (grid).

In the current stage, what we know about the compilation of grid computing is limited indeed. But we may predict that, not long after, people will have deeper understanding about it, consequently, there will be more concrete achievements on the research of the field.

Problems

Problem 16.1 Design an algorithm for sorting numbers in the grid with $\sqrt{p} \times \sqrt{p}$ nodes.

Problem 16.2 Suppose that on the $\sqrt{p} \times \sqrt{p}$ grid, it happens that each processor is a source address of a package, and it is also the destination of a package. Design a deterministic routing algorithm to solve the routing problem for the packages. Your algorithm should has the complexity of $O(\sqrt{p})$. The size of queue is $O(1)$. Hint: use the sorting algorithm.

Problem 16.3 On an $\sqrt{p} \times \sqrt{p}$ grid, at first the sorting for the rows is executed, then sorting for the column is performed. Prove that the rows are still in order.

Problem 16.4 Using the ides of problem 2, design a deterministic group permutation routing algorithm. The complexity of your algorithm should be $O(\sqrt{p})$ and the size of the queue is $O(1)$.

References

[1]   Foster I, Keeselman C (2004) The Grid, 2nd edn. Elsevier, Amsterdam.
[2]   Abbas A (2004) Grid Computing: a practical guide to technology and applications. Charles River Media.

Index